The Cathay Story

第廿六屆香港國際電影節
The 26th Hong Kong International Film Festival

舊歡如夢：國泰名作展
Back to Dreamland: Cathay Showcase

2002. 3. 27 – 4. 7

香港電影資料館放映節目
Hong Kong Film Archive Screening Programme

舊歡如夢：國泰回顧展
Back to Dreamland: Cathay Retrospective

2002. 4. 12 – 6. 9

目錄
Contents

前言
Preface

對於喜愛五、六十年代香港電影的人來説，國泰（對更多影迷來説，也許是電懋）代表了一則奇妙、優雅而又帶點哀傷的故事。那段時期，國、粵語電影仍屬於兩個涇渭分明的世界。曾幾何時，長城／鳳凰、電懋和邵氏鼎足三立，主宰了一個時代的國語電影，然後又都成為了歷史。希望此書能為讀者提供一個國泰電影比較全面的輪廓。

一

余慕雲、鍾寶賢、傅葆石等作者的鴻文像一個大舞台，或從家族與工業、或從廣義的文化出發，為讀者呈現一幅國泰全貌，豐富的資料與條理分明的歷史舖陳，提供了一個紮實的研究基礎。羅卡和舒琪從這個基礎出發，分別探討電懋的創作處境，特別是主事人陸運濤的角色以及文人編劇在制度內的位置，後者更嘗試分析個別創作人如張徹在片廠制度內的存適以及片廠風格等問題，

For those who love the Hong Kong films of the 1950s and 1960s, Cathay (for most fans, perhaps it's more appropriate to say: MP & GI) represents a story at once wonderful, elegant and melancholic. It was a time when the Mandarin and Cantonese cinemas were separate worlds. In the Mandarin universe, Great Wall/Feng Huang, MP & GI and Shaws were once the brightest stars. Now, their glories are only part of history. We hope this book will offer readers a more thorough understanding of Cathay's films.

I

The articles by Yu Mo-wan, Stephanie Chung Po-yin and Poshek Fu set a grand stage on which the Cathay story is played out, looking at the organization from the perspectives of family business, the film industry or the cultural background. Rich in information and lucid in historical delineation, they provide a solid foundation on which to conduct research. From that foundation, Law Kar and Shu Kei probe into MP & GI's creative environment, looking at the roles played by studio head Loke Wan Tho and established writers who were involved in the company's scripts. Shu even makes the bold attempt to discuss the issues of house style and how individual filmmakers operate within the studio system. Finally, Stephen Teo focuses on the martial arts films of Cathay's later period, looking at them from a fresh perspective and filling a gap often neglected in Hong Kong cinema.

In the second section, the issue of border crossing is explored. The most direct approach is of course geographic. We are familiar with the glamour of MP & GI, but little did we know that film production at the vertically integrated movie empire started with the Malay films of Cathay Keris; Timothy P. Barnard offers a detailed introduction to that part of history. Another geographic connection is examined by Yeh Yueh-yu, who looks at the complicated ties between Cathay and Taiwan as well as the influence of the company's transnational operation on the film industries of Hong Kong and Taiwan. Crossing another type of border, Yau Ching and Mary Wong dissect the rather modern notions of sexual identity and gender relationships in

大膽精彩；最後，張建德將焦點放在後期國泰的武俠電影上，以一個不尋常的角度豐富了較後期的國泰故事，也為香港電影裡武俠類型的演變，填補了一個鮮為人所注意到的空隙。

在第二部份裡，作者們從不同的角度探討跨界／越界的問題。最直接的當然是地域——我們只知道電懋星光燦爛，卻原來國泰是從馬來亞國泰克里斯製片廠出品的巫語電影開始，才發展成集製作、發行、院線於一身的電影王國的，Timothy P. Barnard 的文章對此作了詳盡的介紹，而葉月瑜則探討了當年國泰電懋與台灣電影千絲萬縷的關係，分析當年國泰的跨國式經營以及其對後來港台電影業的影響。游靜、黃淑嫻剖析電懋作品裡相當具現代意識的性別身份和兩性關係，令人不禁有點慨嘆怎麼我們後來的電影倒開起回頭車來了；李歐梵、容世誠從電懋的經典歌舞片《野玫瑰之戀》（1960）和宮闈粵曲電影《璇宮艷史》（1957）追溯到西方的歌劇和早期的荷里活歌舞片，雅俗、中西文化攪和在一起，卻不失個性；而從來不受國界限制的邁克，原來對天堂裡異鄉人的處境最是觀察入微，腳踏文學與社會學兩條船，倒是名副其實的越界了。

鏡頭推近，作者們將注意力拉回創作人的身上。梁秉鈞、林奕華對電懋的編劇秦羽及張愛玲情有獨鍾，分別探討她們在電懋的成就與處境。秦、張都是都市味濃郁的作家，對現代社會裡的女性處境尤為敏感，她們的創作肯定對所謂的「電懋風格」有不可看輕的貢獻。電懋分國、粵語片組，多產導演王天林橫跨兩組，可說獨一無二，他不但拍了電懋的經典之作《野玫瑰之戀》，也拍了以六十年代初港滬文化衝突為題材的南北喜劇系列，石琪對他的電影軌跡作出了初步的勾劃。粵語片組的基本導演左几，素以製作嚴謹見稱，李焯桃的文章一

MP & GI films, a reminder of the lack of sophistication in this area in the cinema that followed.

MP & GI is also cherished for its musicals and Leo Lee Ou-fan and Yung Sai-shing trace the influence back to, respectively, Western opera and Hollywood musicals, showing how MP & GI films successfully blend together cultures East and West, high and popular. And Michael Lam, who is never trapped by borders, offers an insightful observation on the stranger's predicament in paradise; in so doing, he invokes the disciplines of literature and sociology – that's really crossing borders.

Other authors zoom in on the filmmakers. Leung Ping-kwan and Edward Lam focus on, respectively, Nellie Chin Yu (Qin Yu) and Eileen Chang (Zhang Ailing), both writers with a special sensibility for the modern city woman and whose works play an important role in the establishment of the so-called "MP & GI style". Both Mandarin and Cantonese films are made in MP & GI and prolific director Wang Tianlin worked on both sides of the language divide. He not only directed the classic *The Wild, Wild Rose* (1960) but also the "North vs South" series that find comedy in the conflict between Shanghai and Cantonese cultures. Sek Kei provides a first draft of his cinema.

Tso Kea (Zuo Ji) is a director of Cantonese film known for his dedicated approach. Li Cheuk-to's article continues the preliminary study of the director he began 20 years ago and, in the process, draws a profile of MP & GI's style. Another long-time follower of MP & GI films is Wong Kee-chee, who applies his expertise on Mandarin pop to an essay on the composer Yao Min. And while most MP & GI fans have vivid memories of its gorgeous actresses, Taipei's Tso Kuei-fang makes a case for the men, offering sketches on such stars as Peter Chen Ho (Chen Hou), Kelly Lai Chen (Lei Zhen), Roy Chiao (Qiao Hong) and Chang Yang (Zhang Yang).

The most touching are the remembrances of those who had lived the MP & GI experience. Kei Shang-tong (Qi Xiangtang), who now lives in Canada, gave us more than 10,000 Chinese words of his memories,

方面延續了他二十年前對左几的討論，另一方面也對電懋風格作出了側面的描述。電懋的電影常有輕歌曼舞的場面，其中姚敏的歌曲至今仍為人津津樂道，時代曲迷黃奇智細談其中乾坤；而當人人都只記得林黛、尤敏、葛蘭、葉楓、李湄、林翠等風姿迷人的女明星時，台北的左桂芳倒替男演員叫屈，為雷震、喬宏、張揚、趙雷、唐菁等勾勒了一幅速寫。

最令人感動的自然是當事人說當事話。遠在加拿大的綦湘棠老師洋洋灑灑為我們寫來了萬多字的長文，細說從頭，並不厭其煩地多次校閱及解答我們的疑難雜症；他是電懋電影音樂的大功臣，從原創配樂到作曲編曲，寄托了一個專業音樂人的尊嚴。訪問竇漢勳先生是一次令人難忘的經驗，他是國際及其後電懋粵語片組的製片，一派謙謙君子之風，從言談中看得出他對電懋的長情，我們每次打電話問功課他都盡心幫忙，某週末還親自送來了多本珍藏的電影特刊及劇本。早年影人提起歐德爾先生，誰不豎起大姆指？雖然他只參與過國際開創時期的工作，實則上卻為後來的電懋打下了重要的基礎，功不可沒；訪問時他口操流利的粵語，有時還夾雜着五十年代的俚語，聞之令人莞爾。朱美蓮是現在新加坡國泰機構的主持人，舅父就是電懋的靈魂人物陸運濤，自小在電影的氛圍中長大，聽她憶述其父朱國良與陸運濤的關係以及二人不同的性格，對我們理解國泰後期的發展，有莫大的裨益。而石琪以輕鬆的過來人身份回想七十年代與吳宇森等人在國泰當美工和場記的「窮風流」日子，為原來有點哀傷的國泰故事，添了絲杜魯福式的幽默與浪漫。

二

說是說國泰故事，其實大多數人眼中看到的，還只是電懋的流金歲月，畢竟那段時期的電影最璀燦迷人，而一

afterwards patiently answering our questions and proof-reading our drafts. He was a significant contributor to the music style of MP & GI and had composed many scores and songs for the company's films. In his work is the dignity of a professional musician. Another veteran, Tau Hon-fun (Dou Hanxun) was dearly unforgettable in our interview with him. He was a producer of Cantonese films in both the company's early International Films days and its glorious MP & GI years. A true gentleman, it was obvious that he still harbours deep affection for the company he once worked for. He was extremely helpful every time we asked him for help and one weekend, he showed up at the office with a stack of scripts and artefacts, donating to us what he had kept for years.

Film veterans we talked to always gave a thumb-up whenever the name Albert Odell was mentioned. Although he was only briefly involved in the early days of International Films, he had laid the foundation for the MP & GI to come. Interviewing him was pure delight and listening to the fluent Cantonese with which he spiced his speech, sometimes using slang we had long forgotten or had never even heard of, always brings a smile to our face. We also interviewed Meileen Choo (Zhu Meilian), the head of the Cathay Organisation's modern era. She is the niece of MP & GI founder Loke Wan Tho (Lu Yuntao) and she grew up in the film industry. Her recollections of the relationship between Loke and her father, Choo Kok Leong (Zhu Guoliang), and the men's different approaches to business gave us helpful glimpses into Cathay's development, especially in the later years.

Less dedicated to work was young assistant Sek Kei (Shi Qi), who went on to become one of Hong Kong's top critics. His witty reminiscence of his days at the art department in the 1970s gives the melancholic story of Cathay a humourous and romantic touch of François Truffaut.

2

This is the Cathay Story, but in most minds the real story is the glory days of MP & GI. For its films are simply gorgeous. And it's easy to forget that in

提起電懋，又總是忘記了電懋也曾拍過不少粵語片。國語片和粵語片，彷彿來自兩個截然不同的世界，而電懋合該只能是說國語的世界。《小兒女》（1963）裡王引和他的三名小兒女，住在鑽石山的小樓房裡，小康的生活倒也過得挺舒適，但跟他們毗鄰而居的可憐小女孩和刻薄野蠻的繼母，卻彷彿來自另一個世界——她們身穿唐裝衫褲，與尤敏等人的時髦西服完全格格不入。噢，想起來了，那不是像透了粵語片中陶三姑、高佬泉的世界嗎？《愛的教育》（1961）裡也有相似的兩極世界——王引和女兒林翠是屬於文明的小康世界，窮苦學生洪金寶和酗酒的父親朱牧則屬於另一個世界。電懋的編導，大都是南來的知識份子，而且都挾着點中產的西洋口味，他們拍小康乃至上流社會都是綽綽有餘的，拍低下層卻總有點想當然，不若粵語片的貼近普羅大眾，大抵只能閉門造車，或乾脆從粵語片中直接借用借用好了。

寫到這裡，倒又想起另一部影片《喜相逢》（1960）。片中的丁皓一人分飾窮人家的賣花女和從舊金山回來的千金小姐，賣花女被誤為千金小姐，出席眾多接風飯局，最有趣的是去到某同鄉會，全部都是穿長衫馬褂的老人，吃的是「野蠻」的蛇宴，背景傳來粵曲聲，真是百分百的外省人看廣東佬—— exotic [1]。岳楓導演的《雨過天青》（1959）倒能以較為平等的心態去看待本地的社會。在片中，張揚飾演的小白領本來一家大小樂也融融，卻因失業兼受到勢利姐姐的挑撥，與妻子李湄的關係變壞，繼女陳寶珠離家出走去找小姨蘇鳳；小姨在一家粵式茶樓當收銀員，介紹小姨甥女去做點心妹，看得出岳楓雖然不特別熟悉這個環境，卻也不帶着獵奇的眼光，倒令人對這隔了一層的本地生態長出一份平常自然的好感來。是的，這一幫人南來了香港，確是有點虎落平陽之憾，但他們已將心與身都交托在這個都市的手裡，不作回頭望。

addition to the fabulous Mandarin films, MP & GI had also made lots of Cantonese films. That's because the two kinds of films are exactly that – two kinds and very different kinds. In *Father Takes a Bride* (1963), Wang Yin and his children live in a cottage on Diamond Hill, their middle-class life peaceful and comfortable. Their neighbours are a much-abused little girl and her mean and wretched stepmother. They may live next door, but they seem to belong to a different world. They wear Chinese-style clothes, in sharp contrast to the trendy Western garbs that adorn the beautiful physiques of Lucilla You Min and Kelly Lai Chen (Lei Zhen). Oh yes, isn't theirs exactly the lower depths of the Cantonese film world? Such a polarity of worlds is also found in *Education of Love* (1961). The sheltered bourgeois lifestyle of Wang Yin and Jeanette Lin Cui is the opposite of the dirt-poor harshness of little Sammo Hung (Hung Jinbao) and his drunk of a father, Zhu Mu. MP & GI's directors and scriptwriters were mostly Mainland intellectuals with westernised tastes. They were certainly capable of making films about middle-class or even upper-class life, but their idea of the grass root was rather skewed, unlike Cantonese filmmakers' heart-felt concern for the populace.

I'm mindful of another film, *Dreams Come True* (1960). Kitty Ting Hao (Ding Hao) plays two roles in it, a poor flower girl and a rich repatriate from San Francisco. The flower girl is mistaken for the repatriate and is wined and dined. At one gathering, all the diners are old folks in *cheong sam*, revelling in a barbaric snake banquet, with Cantonese opera playing in the background – unadulterated stereotyping by northerners of their southern brethren as exotic.[1] *For Better, For Worse* (1959), directed by Yue Feng, offers a less biased view of local society. Chang Yang (Zhang Yang) plays a white-collar worker leading a happy life. Hit by sudden unemployment, he succumbs to his sister's lobbying and fights with his wife, causing his stepdaughter Connie Chan Po-chu (Chen Baozhu) to seek employment at a Cantonese restaurant. Such an environment is obviously not familiar to director Yue, yet he manages to avoid looking at it with prejudice,

比較一下電懋的國、粵片，便不難發覺兩個世界的差距。將左几的《琵琶怨》(1957）和陶秦的《龍翔鳳舞》(1959）放在一起來看，是非常有趣的事。影片開始的時候，是民國背景的廣州。芳艷芬飾演的小女伶江小玲，在大新天台遊樂場表演低俗的歌舞，她的第一場戲便是與一班歌舞女孩在舞台上表演三十年代的〈桃花江上〉，唱的是國語流行曲，穿的是西式性感短裙，大家都跳得沒精打采，而她真正喜歡的卻是地道的傳統粵劇。相隔不及兩年拍成的《龍翔鳳舞》也有多場三十年代歌舞，卻表達了編導對三十年代上海通俗文化的懷戀，但畢竟已不是舊時光景，不能老沉溺在落泊焦慮的自傷自憐裡。而且，也只能從新出發，將舊歌從新包裝才可重建信心。對於西方文明對中國文化的衝擊，左几的作品似乎較高警惕，也較保守。

電懋的國語電影，對價值判斷似乎相當寬鬆，譬如《同床異夢》(1960）裡的李湄和《苦命鴛鴦》(1963）裡的李香琴，同是結了婚而仍愛在外面「浦」的太太，但粵語片中李香琴的壞是漂白水也洗刷不了的壞，而李湄則只是一個被寵壞了的女人，充其量受點兒教訓而最終還是要當兩性戰場上的贏家的。即使擺明車馬是朵吃人花，如《春潮》(1960）裡玩弄男性的陸太太（也是李湄飾演），也不會因而受到懲罰，受懲罰的是意志薄弱的男人。「愛情不是每個人都可以有的，你不配。」——說這話的正是經常在天羅地網中佈下迷魂陣的陸太太。相反地，電懋作品裡有不少為了爭取愛情或個人自主而拋家棄子的女性，雖然不能說沒有遺憾，卻始終站穩腳步，維持着體面的尊嚴，如《玉女私情》(1959）和《愛的教育》裡的王萊，甚至《曼波女郎》(1957)裡淪為夜總會洗手間女工的唐若青或《火中蓮》(1962）中為了男人累及女兒尤敏的王萊，編導對她們都是同情多於譴責。

在左几的《琵琶怨》和《黛綠年華》(1957）裡都有一把墮落之匙——七哥（吳楚帆）帶江小玲（芳艷芬）到

giving the alien lifestyle a goodness of the ordinary. Yes, these immigrants with a notable past are stuck in Hong Kong, but they have given their hearts and minds to this city, not taking any looks back.

One can readily see the differences between the worlds comparing the Mandarin films and Cantonese films of MP & GI. Take Tso Kea's *The Sorrowful Lute* (1957) and Tao Qin's *Calendar Girl* (1959), for example. Tso's film takes place in Guangzhou, where a singer works at a rooftop carnival. The film starts with her performing the number "On the Peach Blossom River", backed by a chorus of girls. Singing a Mandarin pop of the 1930s and wearing sexy miniskirts, the performer, a lover of Cantonese opera, is lackluster. Less than two years later in *Calendar Girl*, the same number is staged, but with a nostalgic fondness for the popular culture of 1930s Shanghai. But it's no longer what it was, and instead of indulging in self-pity, a fresh twist is given to the song, not to mention a brand new package. On Western civilisation's impact on Chinese culture, Tso seemed more cautious, and more conservative.

The Mandarin films are less judgemental. Li Mei in *The Bedside Story* (1960) and Lee Hong-kum (Li Xiangqin) in *Bitter Romance* (1963) are both married women who like to go out for fun. But while the Lee in the Cantonese film is a tramp beyond redemption, the Li in the Mandarin film is merely a spoiled woman who needs to learn a little lesson but still ends up a winner in the battle of the sexes. Even an unabashed man-eater like Mrs. Lu (also played by Li) in *Torrents of Spring* (1960) is not punished. "Love is not for everyone; you're not worthy." The speaker is none other than the Mrs. Lu who openly plays with men. By contrast, many women in MP & GI films who give up family for love or personal freedom are treated with sympathy and dignity, though not without regret, like Wang Lai in *Her Tender Heart* (1959) and *Education of Love*. Even the mother who ends up a toilet attendant in *Mambo Girl* (1957) and the mother who harms her daughter because of her man in *Lily of the Valley* (1962) are portrayed with more understanding than reprimand.

一間豪華大宅的門前，遞給她一條屋匙；范太太（黎灼灼）於聖誕夜送了一條獨立房間的鎖匙給寄居她家的韓湘瑩（紫羅蓮），從此單純的少女便陷入了紙醉金迷的生活漩渦裡去。《黛綠年華》裡的夜生活特別惹人暇思，范黛妮招呼同學韓湘瑩回家居住，卻叫她晚上千萬別到樓下去，而她們幾姐妹卻是夜夜笙歌，叫韓湘瑩又如何安坐房間中呢？這隻潘朵拉的盒子，大概沒有誰人抗拒得了，免不了要去打開它。那裡面不但有奢華的物質生活，更有年青人蹦跳着的慾望。對於這一切，編導明顯是帶着強烈的道德判斷的，而在片中引導韓湘瑩重返道德秩序的路軌上去的，當然是吳楚帆飾演的建築師見習生以及他那班同甘共苦的工人朋友——非常「中聯」的世界。片中有一個郊遊的片段，建築師和韓湘瑩及其他友人坐着開篷汽車，眾人齊唱國語歌，是中聯和電懋一個非常有趣的結合。易文編導的《溫柔鄉》（1960）裡也有一間神秘的大廳，打開廳門走進去，只見那裡面黑墨墨的伸手不見五指，待眼睛慢慢適應過來，卻原來都是蠕動着的年青軀體，在那裡燃燒着青春。華語電影裡很少這類描寫現代都市人頹唐生活的場面，而且態度並不道學，倒像一個縱容孩子的慈父，表面上說了他兩句，骨子裡還是護着他的。

三

要是我說，編輯這本書苦樂參半，讀者們定會發笑，這個編者怎麼如此馬虎，搬出這樣老套的門面話來。老套是老套一點，倒是千真萬確的，怪只怪腦筋笨拙，想不出更貼切的話來。

苦，是時間太倉卒，個人修養不夠，題目過於龐大，而自己又貪心。以往對國泰電懋的系統研究並不多[2]，所以最初受命編輯此書，確有老鼠拉龜之惑，幸得多位前輩影人抽出時間接受我們的訪問，余慕雲先生慷慨地提供協助，幫忙整理國泰電懋片目以及撰寫人物小傳，羅

A key of corruption is featured in *The Sorrowful Lute* and *The Tender Age* (aka *The Splendour of Youth,* 1957), both directed by Tso. In the former, the singer is brought to the door of a mansion and offered its key. In the latter, the matriarch of a corrupt family hands to a young woman the key to her room – on Christmas Eve – plunging the innocent girl into the abyss of decadence. The nightlife in *Tender* is full of allure. The young woman is invited by a friend to stay in the latter's home but is told never to go downstairs in the evening. Yet it's party time every night downstairs. No one can resist the urge to open this Pandora's box. Inside are not only the decadence of material life but also the prancing desire of youth. All these are treated with moral high-mindedness by the film and redemption rests with an architect intern – played by none other than Ng Cho-fan (Wu Chufan) – and his worker friends, a very Union film world indeed. Going on a picnic, the girl and the architect are sitting inside a convertible, singing a Mandarin song, a moment in which the worlds of MP & GI and Union film merge. A mysterious sitting room is also featured in Evan Yang (Yi Wen)'s *Bachelors Beware* (1960). It's total darkness when the door is opened; as the eyes adjust, we begin to see the youthful bodies inside, burning off their youth. Seldom are such scenes of degeneration featured in Chinese cinema, even less without judgement. It's like an obliging father who pays his son a lip service of disapproval but indulges him deep down.

3

If I say that putting this book together is a bittersweet experience, readers may laugh at the cliché. It is. But it's also a cliché that's true. I only blame myself for not coming up with a better way to say it.

Bitter because of the lack of time, our own inadequacies, the hugeness of the topic and our greed trying to grab more than we can handle. Systematic studies of MP & GI are rare;[2] that's why when we took up this job, we were a little flabbergasted. Fortunately we received generous help. Film veterans sat down and talked with us, Yu Mo-wan offered his help compiling the filmography and writing biographies,

卡先生出了不少點子，何思穎遠赴新加坡做影人專訪，還有作者們認真地將研究心得寫成文章，始漸漸有了這本書的輪廓。

也有樂。樂，是國泰電懋的作品，於我就像是成長的一部份。說真的，小時候我並沒有看很多他們的電影，倒是長大了每看一部，都有一份回到家裡的親切。看到《雨過天青》裡掛在房間裡的家庭照，就想起了兒時穿着小白裙與父母去影樓拍的全家福——那時哥哥們都還未來港，父母拿了他們的單人照去，師傅們如魔術師般略施小技，一家三口就變成了一家五口，像霧又像花的幻像寄托了千真萬確的希望。看到《小兒女》裡王萊和王引偷得浮生半日閒，在家門前的院子裡喝下午茶，小圓桌上鋪了格仔枱布，就主觀地將黑白菲林上的深灰變成萬里無雲的蔚藍；原來生活可以謙卑而又優雅。看到《青春兒女》(1959)裡的葛蘭粉墨登場演出崑曲的〈春香鬧學〉，腦海裡就浮現了戴家姐姐在舞台上演出上海越劇時的風姿綽約，小小人兒其實早已封了她做偶像。看到《曼波女郎》裡佻皮熱鬧的家庭派對，心裡就不安份起來，要是能坐上時光隧道的直通車，回到五、六十年代去嗅嗅那青春的味道就好了。看到《玉女私情》裡複雜的母女關係，耳畔彷彿響起了母親跟朋友們一邊打麻將，一邊竊竊議論起張家太太本來是陳家太太的故事；「那時候她的孩子才三歲呢！」——不知是誰最後加上這麼一句註腳，大家又若無其事地回到那霹靂叭啦的筒子索子的小小天地裡去……

你的我的他的她的私人故事，拼貼起來就成為了一個時代的底色，現在容許有點褪了色，但以前大抵是斑斕的伊士曼七彩。那是一個轉變中的年代，很多家庭從動蕩的大陸來到這偏安一方的小島，家庭仍是頗為傳統的中國家庭，但畢竟已受到西方文明的沖刷，不再一樣了；

Law Kar gave us many useful ideas, Sam Ho went to Singapore to conduct interviews, and writers contributed their ideas to complete this book.

It's also sweet. Sweet because the films of Cathay and MP & GI are like an integral part of my growing up. Frankly, I seldom watched them as a kid, but every one I watched in adulthood is like a trip back to my childhood home. Seeing the family portrait in *For Better, For Worse*, I remember wearing my little white dress, going to the studio with my parents to have ours taken. My brothers were not yet in Hong Kong and my parents took their photos to the studio; with a little magic, an incomplete family of three became our full family of five, the created illusion carrying the most authentic of hopes. Seeing Wang Lai and Wang Yin stealing away to a quiet corner of her home for a leisurely cup of afternoon tea, sitting by a small table with checkered tablecloth, I coloured in my mind the black-and-white images, turning the dark grey into sky blue – life so humble can actually be so elegant. Seeing Grace Chang (Ge Lan) perform Kun opera in *Spring Song* (1959), memories of our family friend Sister Dai's graceful moves on the Shaoxing opera stage emerge – I had made her my idol early on. When the family party heats up to its fun and clamour in *Mambo Girl*, I was restless, hoping I could fly through the time tunnel to the 1950s and 1960s, to smell once more my youthful boisterousness. Watching the complicated mother-daughter relationship in *Her Tender Heart*, I started to hear the gossips my mother whispered to her mahjong friends, that Mrs. Cheung used to be Mrs. Chen. "Her child was only three!" Someone added this footnote. Then they went back to their game....

Yours, mine, his, hers.... Together, they add up to a backdrop of an era. It may be a little faded now, but back then, it was probably Eastman colour. That was a changing time, when families moved from the turbulent Mainland to this far-off but peaceful island. They were traditional Chinese families, but once exposed to Western civilization, they were not the same again. MP & GI films had learned to be more open-minded a little earlier than the others. Perhaps it

電懋的電影比旁人更早開始學習寬容，也許就是因為懂得接受，那些電影並不呼天搶地，有時候是淡淡的感傷，像熱鬧的小津世界，如陶秦編導的《四千金》(1957)，但更多時候倒是對新的生活方式熱情雀躍的擁抱，如易文編導的《曼波女郎》。

寫着寫着就扯遠了，國泰電懋的電影世界實在太豐富了，而我們在這本書才剛開始沾着邊呢。說真的，書中有不少章節皆可發展成一本獨立的專著。我們希望這個雪球一直滾下去。於此，我要特別感謝為了這本書而夜不成眠的同事及朋友們，祝你們的熊貓眼早日消褪，重返人間。

策劃編輯
黃愛玲
二〇〇二年三月五日

註

1. 有關電懋作品所呈現出來的港滬文化差異問題，本書中邁克的〈天堂的異鄉客〉便有相當細微和有趣的觀察。
2. 翁靈文，〈電懋影業公司粵語片組〉，於《五十年代粵語電影回顧展》，第二屆香港國際電影節回顧特刊，香港：市政局，1978；翁靈文，〈電影懋業有限公司〉，於《戰後香港電影回顧(1946-1968)》，第三屆香港國際電影節回顧特刊，香港：市政局，1979；及杜雲之：《中國電影史》，台北：台灣商務印書館，1972，三者都是簡明清晰的入門介紹。〈電懋國語電影初探——從上海到香港的過渡〉，《電影欣賞》，1997年8月號一輯文章，則分別從制度、類型、意識型態乃至個別作品，初步探討電懋的國語電影。其他如黃卓漢：《電影人生：黃卓漢回憶錄》，台北：萬象，1994；沙榮峰：《繽紛電影四十春：沙榮峰的回憶錄》，台北：國家電影資料館，1994；及李翰祥：《三十年細說從頭》，香港：天地圖書，1983等均以影人的身份記錄了電懋當年種種，是重要的史料。當然，還有 Lim Kay Tong: *Cathay - 55 Years of Cinema*, Singapore: Landmark Books, 1991，是迄今為止對國泰電影事業發展最詳盡的描述。

was because they knew how to receive, they were not as sensational. Their world is only a little sentimental, like a cheered up version of Ozu's, as in Tao Qin's *Our Sister Hedy* (1957). But most of the time, it's an eager embrace of a new lifestyle, like Evan Yang's (Yi Wen) *Mambo Girl*.

I have veered off too far. The world of MP & GI's films is indeed a rich one and this book has only touched upon a fraction of that abundance. Many of the passages in this volume can be expanded into full-length books and we only wish that the snowball would continue to roll. I'd like to thank all the colleagues and friends who had ventured into the deep of night to put this book together. May you get some sleep.

Wong Ain-ling
Editor
5 March, 2002

Translated by Sam Ho

Notes

1. For the differences between Hong Kong and Shanghai cultures, please see Michael Lam, "Strangers in Paradise", in this volume.
2. Weng Lingwen, "The Dian Mou Film Company: Cantonese Film Group" in *Cantonese Cinema Retrospective (1950-1959)*, the 2nd Hong Kong International Film Festival catalogue, Hong Kong: Urban Council, 1978; Weng Lingwen, "Motion Picture & General Investment Company (Dianmou)" in *Hong Kong Cinema Survey (1946-1968)*, the 3rd Hong Kong International Film Festival catalogue, Hong Kong: Urban Council, 1979; as well as Du Yunzhi, "Dian Mou: MP & GI" in *A History of Chinese Cinema* (in Chinese), Taipei: Commercial Press, 1972, are ready introductions to MP & GI. "Preliminary Study of MP & GI films – From Shanghai to Hong Kong" in *Film Criticism* (in Chinese), Taipei: Chinese Taipei Film Archive, August 1997, includes several essays that examine the system, genres and ideology of the company's Mandarin films. Also, Wong Cheuk-hon (Huang Zhuohan) *A Life in Movies: Memoirs of Wong Cheuk-hon* (in Chinese), Taipei: Variety Publishing, 1994; Sha Yung-fong: *Forty Years of Cinema* (in Chinese), Taipei: Chinese Taipei Film Archive, 1994 and Li Hanxiang: *Thirty Years in Retrospect* (in Chinese), Hong Kong: Cosmos Books, 1984, provide glimpses into MP & GI from the perspective of filmmakers. Of course, there is also Lim Kay Tong: *Cathay - 55 Years of Cinema*, Singapore: Landmark Books, 1991, which offers the most comprehensive description of the company's development.

Sun • Moon • Stars

太陽・月亮・星星

四千金

《四千金》（1957）中的蘇鳳、葉楓、林翠和穆虹（左起）

Pretty maidens all in a row. Stars of *Our Sister Hedy* (1957): (From left) Soo Fung, Julie Yeh Feng, Jeanette Lin Cui and Mu Hong.

18

葛蘭

「甚麼叫情，甚麼叫意，還不是大家自己騙自己；甚麼叫癡，甚麼叫迷，簡直是男的女的在做戲。」——《野玫瑰之戀》(1960)

Grace Chang: the Mambo Girl, the Wild Rose… and so much more.

尤敏

「尤敏的出現，將會壓蓋了日本『男明星的時代』熱潮，而掀起『尤敏熱潮』……她的美麗臉型，從任何角度去看，都有不同的情調，有時像八千草薰，有時像三條美妃，有時像水野久美。」
——日本《每日展望報》

Have face, will travel.

Lucilla You Min's delicate beauty made her a big star in Japan, her border-crossing success an emblem of MP & GI's transnational ambitions.

林黛

「我愛熱鬧，越多（男人）越好。」
——《情場如戰場》(1957)

Shoot the piano player:
Linda Lin Dai, her face immortalised on a plate, in a publicity portrait.

Courtesy of Paul Fonoroff

秦羽／陳厚

「剛才我看見一棵梔子花，開得真好。」

「你喜歡梔子花？我去給你摘點來。」

——《情場如戰場》

Peter Chen Ho, "Holy Hand of Comedy", and Nellie Chin Yu, starlet turned scriptwriter, sharing a drink with MP & GI fans.

「憂鬱小生」雷震

「我們一直把電懋當做一個大家庭，下午沒事幹會跑回公司，到編劇部、製片部坐一坐，談一談，再一起到外面喝杯咖啡，相處得很好。」 ——雷震口述歷史訪問，2001 年 12 月

Kelly Lai Chen, "Melancholic Leading Man":

One of the top leading men of his time, Lai is Betty Loh Ti's brother.

「古典美人」
樂蒂

1964 年 2 月 1 日樂蒂加盟電懋，她頭一遭踏進永華片場，拍的電影就是《亂世兒女》(1966)，布衣便服，不減國色。

Betty Loh Ti. One of several MP & GI stars who took their own lives at a young age, there is a touch of sadness to the quiet beauty of the actress nicknamed "Classical Beauty".

24

INTERNATIONAL Screen 國際電影畫報之一

李湄

「夜闌珊為甚麼你還不睡？
花未殘為甚麼色已褪
為甚麼燈紅酒綠夜，
還藏着恨與罪，
人間何處有真愛？」
——〈長夜曲〉，《野火》插曲，
李湄詞

Say cheese.
Li Mei, one of MP & GI's top cheesecakes.

春潮

Torrents of Spring

Courtesy of Paul Fonoroff

「雄師」喬宏

「男人要量八圍尺碼才夠，先從上面量起。我的頸圍是十七吋半，肩寬廿二吋，胸圍四十九吋，上臂十八吋……」

——〈喬宏的八圍多少？〉，《國際電影》，1962 年 12 月

Roy "The Lion" Chiao, the resident beefcake of MP & GI.

「學生情人」林翠

「有女懷春，吉士誘之」

Lin Cui, nicknamed "Student Lover", was frequently given athletic, tomboyish roles. Yet there seems to be a sexuality yearning to burst out.

「銀壇靚女」白露明

「花同燕，雙雙嬉戲互愛憐
人尚幼小心偷羨。」 ——《美人春夢》主題曲

Not on a pedestal – She may be on a swing, all decked out, but there is always a homely charm to Christine Pai Lu-ming, MP & GI's top Cantonese star.

Courtesy of Paul Fonoroff

王萊

是哥羅莉亞史允臣，鍾哥羅福抑或安娜夢茵儀？

不，王萊就是王萊，我們的「千面女星」！

The eternal Wang Lai, in many minds the most important character actress in the history of Hong Kong Mandarin cinema.

張揚

「張揚演年青的智識份子在氣質上最好，最大原因在乎他是在華北受高等教育的，這就不同於在上海受教育的，後者往往顯得『油』了。」 —— 銀冪，《國際電影》

Chang Yang

"Chang Yang is best suited to play an educated man, probably because he went to school in northern China instead of in Shanghai."

– *International Screen*

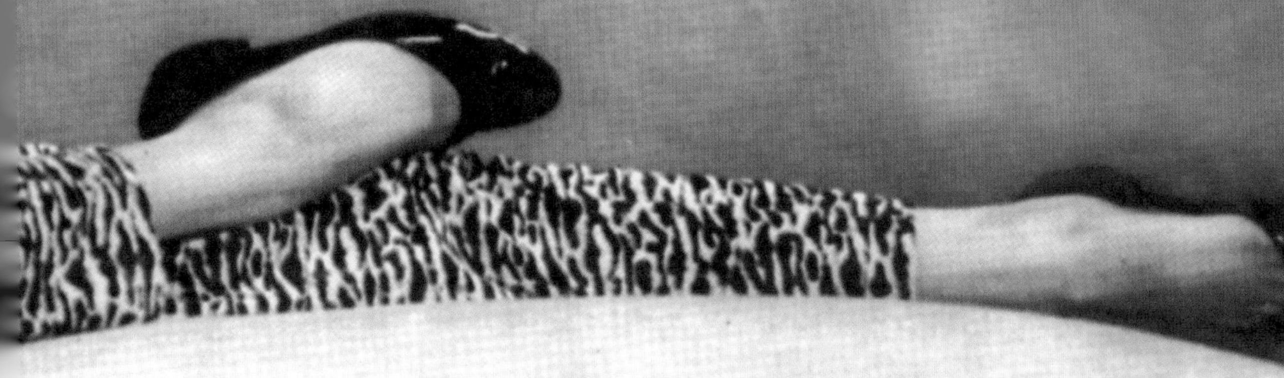

「睡美人」葉楓

「男人，他們好像磁石，具有無限吸引力。一個新的男朋友，我會不惜用盡一切心機去俘擄他，以達到心靈上一霎那的滿足。」

——〈四千金自我介紹〉，《國際電影》，1957 年

Julie "Sleeping Beauty" Yeh Feng.

"I love to sleep."

丁皓／蘇鳳

丁皓和蘇鳳是電懋（前身國際）培養出來的第一代新人，最後在人生路上分道揚鑣，電懋的光芒也隱沒於歷史。

Auld Lang Syne, it's New Year's time.

Kitty Ting Hao and Soo Fung, who eventually met with very different fortunes, celebrate the MP & GI season.

The Grand Cathay Stage

國泰大舞台

星馬實業家和他的電影夢：陸運濤及國際電影懋業公司

- 鍾寶賢 -

引言

電影是一門藝術，也是一種商品；傳統上，電影業最激烈的戰場在於發行（distribution）和放映（exhibition）兩環節，放映窗戶是電影工業的「門市部」，製作精良的影片，若沒有發行和上映渠道提供「門市」，也難逃蝕本命運。回顧歷史，荷里活八大片廠可說是深明此理，它們控制了大量戲院，建立出一套結合製作、發行、院線三環節於一身的制度，這種經營方法被稱為「垂直整合」(vertical integration），是控制市場的最辣手段。[1]

回顧華語電影世界，國際電影懋業公司可說是一個探討「垂直整合」手法移殖亞洲的典型個案，它所帶出的問題反映了十分深刻的時代特色。

背境：香港、上海、新加坡三地的網絡

要了解華語影業的資金循環，便不可忽略香港、上海、新加坡三地的網絡。1841 年後，中國門戶開放，香港與上

陸運濤到澳洲考察時攝
Loke Wan Tho in Australia.

A Southeast Asian Tycoon and His Movie Dream: Loke Wan Tho and MP & GI

- Stephanie Chung Po-yin -

Introduction

Film is at once an art and a commodity. Traditionally, the hardest battles of the film trade are fought at the distribution and exhibition fronts. Exhibition is the trade's "retail department", without which any film, regardless of quality, would fail commercially. The major studios of Hollywood were well aware of this, establishing a system of vertical integration that combined production, distribution and exhibition to maintain total control of the market.[1]

In Chinese cinema, Motion Pictures and General Investment Film Co (MP&GI) Ltd was a typical attempt to adopt vertical integration in Asia. The issues around it are profound indications of its time.

Background: Hong Kong, Shanghai, Singapore

To understand the flow of capital in Chinese film trade, the network between Hong Kong, Shanghai and Singapore cannot be neglected. After the opening of China's door in 1841, Hong Kong and

海成為沿海經濟中樞，電影技術傳入，並出現了南北兩「影院大王」盧根及羅明佑（皆為廣東人），專門發行美國影片到沿海城市或旗下戲院上映。步入1920年代，不少美國片廠自行在遠東成立發行處，華人院商的發行人角色被架空，部份遂轉變策略，投資本土電影製作換取影片發行權，不少華人「院商」與「片商」的合作亦由此建立起來，其中，以「北方戲院大王」羅明佑與來自香港的黎民偉合作在上海成立的「聯華影業公司」最聞名。當時上海為中國電影中心，部份資金更外流至星馬，拓展放映業，勢力蟄伏在華僑社區裡。中日戰爭爆發後，不少上海資金南下，大中華、新華等公司相繼在香港成立，製作國語片，但1945年後，中國政壇風雲變色，中台市場建起重重壁壘，這些公司收支難以平衡，先後倒閉。反觀粵語片業，在星馬戲院商訂金（俗稱「片花」）支持下，卻湧現了眾多小本快拍的小型公司。

原來在戰後，星馬已取代中國大陸，成為港產片最大的出口市場。星馬地區出現三大華語院線：陸運濤家族的國泰、邵逸夫家族的邵氏和何啟榮家族的光藝。邵氏根源在上海，早在1920年代便在星馬辦電影放映；國泰的主事人陸運濤（1915 - 1964）是富甲一方的企業家。光藝投資者何啟榮（1901- 1966）兄弟，為廣東大埔人，幼時往星繼承父親的雜貨業，成星洲富商並經營戲院。自1949年後，中國和台灣的電影進出口也限制重重，華語片來源嚴重收縮。自五十年代，這三大院商便先後北上香港，為穩定片源，在香港建立自己的製片基地，開始流水作業，搖身變成製片商，供片到旗下的院線，其形態恰似荷里活公司，進入了「垂直整合」，一手包辦了生產、發行、上映三環節。

星馬資金登陸後，各有際遇。光藝覓得導演秦劍，捧紅新人謝賢、嘉玲，主力開拍粵語片，成為1950年代四

Shanghai became major economic centres. Film technology was introduced and soon emerged the north and south "kings of theatre", Luo Mingyou and Lu Gen (both Cantonese), who showed American films in major cities along the coast. By the 1920s, American studios had began establishing their own distribution networks, forcing Chinese distributors to switch to investing in local productions to obtain distribution rights. Thus began the cooperation between Chinese exhibitors and producers, like the establishment of United Photoplay by "theatre king of the north" Luo and Li Minwei from Hong Kong. Shanghai was then the centre of Chinese film, but capital had started flowing towards Singapore and Malaya to develop exhibition, establishing roots within overseas Chinese communities. At the advent of the Sino-Japanese War, Shanghai capital flew south to Hong Kong, where Mandarin films were made by companies like Great China Film Company and Hsin Hwa Production Company. But after 1945, political situations gave rise to various barriers in different markets, forcing these companies to close. Yet, on the Cantonese side, the practice of advance payments to cement exhibition deals resulted in a large number of small companies that specialized in low-budget films.

After WWII, Southeast Asia had replaced the Mainland as the biggest export market for Hong Kong films. Theatres there were dominated by three major chains: Cathay, operated by the Loke Wan Tho family of Guangdong origin; Shaw Brothers, of the Run Run Shaw family, which came from Shanghai but had gotten into the Southeast Asian market since the 1920s; and Kong Ngee company, of the He Qirong brothers, who came from Guangdong and got rich running their father's provision business in Singapore. After 1949, heavy restrictions on film were enforced in China and Taiwan, severely shrinking the supply of Chinese films. To ensure supply, the families established production facilities in Hong Kong, thus vertically integrating their exhibition, distribution and production businesses.

大粵片公司之一。國泰與邵氏抵港初期，也曾迎合潮流設立粵語片組，自 1960 年代初，則主力拍攝國語片，掀起連番歌舞片、黃梅調片熱潮，搖身變成香港最大製片商，在人才及市場方面，引起連場激戰，片廠制被推至高峰。值得注意者，儘管邵氏和國泰都標榜片廠制，但兩者都依然是傳統家族式經營，除了與導演、影星簽有合約外，一般運作都沒有穩定的行政制度，主事者的個性往往影響全局。[2] 由是之故，要了解電懋的演變，便得先從陸氏家族的興替說起。

陸氏家族的經營

電懋的董事長陸運濤乃星馬首富陸佑之子。若與邵逸夫家族及何啟榮家族相比，陸家明顯較洋化，與祖家連繫較疏，家族網絡的規模亦較少。這些特色正好模鑄了電懋的興衰歷史。

據現存資料，陸佑（1846 - 1917）本姓黃，名如佑，祖籍廣東鶴山縣雅瑤區黃洞村，由於父母雙亡又沒兄弟姐妹，七歲時便孤身到新會為商人陸顯當工，並改姓陸。少年時以「契約華工」（所謂「豬仔」）身份到馬來亞羅奇生煙酒莊當雜役。數年後在新加坡創立興隆號雜貨店。英人目睹暹羅國力壯大，有南下吞併馬來半島之勢，遂先發制人，把英殖民勢力擴展至當時仍未開發的馬來半島上，控制島上豐富的錫礦。為鼓勵華人遷入馬來半島開荒，英人遂把「餉碼」（tax-farming，如賭餉、煙餉等收稅專利權）連帶開礦權以價高者得方法開投，陸佑正是得此餉碼權起家。除經營十多個礦場外，他也興辦橡膠園、咖啡園、椰子園、胡椒園、椰油廠、洋灰廠及鐵廠等，僱用千多員工，1913年，他還創立吉隆坡廣益銀行。第一次世界大戰期間，因為東興隆分號眾多，英政府更准許它自行印發鈔票流通，兌現政府發鈔。陸

陸佑
Loke Yew

They met different fortunes after landing here. Kong Ngee recruited director Chun Kim (Qin Jian) and discovered stars like Patrick Tse Yin (Xie Xian) and Ka Ling (Jia Ling), becoming one of four major Cantonese film companies of the 1950s. Cathay and Shaws also started with Cantonese films but soon concentrated on Mandarin films, creating popular trends with musicals and regional dialect films. They became the biggest film companies of Hong Kong and a rivalry developed as competition grew intense, pushing the studio system towards new heights. It's worthy to note that although both Shaws and Cathay assumed the studio system, they also retained the structure of family business. There might be contracts for directors and stars, but company operations depended largely on the temperament of the families' patriarchs.[2] To understand MP & GI, we must therefore start with the Loke family.

氏有四位妻子，過繼和親生兒女八名（分別為四子四女），但彼此聯繫卻並不緊密。1917年，陸佑辭世，遺產估計值一千多萬英磅，當時他的第一、第二任妻子及長子已身故，由第四任妻子林淑佳暫掌家業，林氏為陸佑誕下一子二女，其獨子陸運濤當時只有兩歲。[3]

陸佑遺下的基業及人脈網絡，皆有助幼子陸運濤實現其夢想。究竟陸運濤有甚麼夢呢？陸運濤在1915年生於吉隆坡，在維多利亞書院接受歐式教育，十三歲往瑞士留學，1929至1933年間在瑞士齊隆大學修讀文學，1933至1936年間在劍橋大學修讀文學及歷史，取碩士學位，1937年在倫敦經濟學院攻讀經濟。1940年回新加坡，接管家業，除了銀行、橡膠園、錫礦生意外，還發展地產、飲食、酒店和娛樂事業。他是《馬來亞論壇報》的東主、馬來西亞航空公司、華聯銀行、廣利銀行及多間錫礦、橡膠、進出口公司的董事和董事長，亦是旅遊協會、新加坡圖書館名譽主席，並出任新加坡攝影學會主席、新加坡大學藝術博物院董事，屢獲馬來西亞、柬埔寨及日本政府頒授最高勳章。陸氏一生醉心文藝、歷史、電影、攝影，品味與作風也十分洋化。他熱愛騎馬、高爾夫球、攝影及觀鳥等活動，曾多次到庫特奇沙漠和克什米爾探險、到新畿內亞森林拍攝雀鳥生態，並在1958年出版《A Company Of Birds》一書，他亦坦言觀鳥和攝影遠比經營他的商業江山有趣。[4]

陸氏電影王國的演變

1. 戲院及發行商時期

陸運濤自1946年建立的電影王國，絕不單是一項錙銖計算的商業投資，它是一項個人夢想的實踐，隨其人生閱歷改變，這個電影夢的內容和實踐方法也同步演變。陸運濤母親林淑佳在1936年創辦吉隆坡光藝戲院（Pavilion Theatre），1939年，她又在新加坡建成國泰大

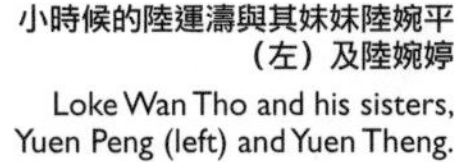

小時候的陸運濤與其妹妹陸婉平（左）及陸婉婷

Loke Wan Tho and his sisters, Yuen Peng (left) and Yuen Theng.

Loke Family Business

Loke Wan Tho is the son of the wealthy businessman Loke Yew (Lu You). Compared to the Shaws and the Hos, the Lokes were certainly more westernized, with weaker connections to the ancestral family and a smaller family network, factors that affected the rise and fall of MP & GI.

Loke Yew (1846-1917) was born to the Wong family of Hesan, Guangdong, but was orphaned young. He left home at age 7 to work for a businessman named Loke and assumed the boss's surname. He went to then Malaya in his teens as "contract labour" but earned enough to open his own provision store within a few years. It was at the time when the British, worried that a strengthening Siam might expand into Malaya, colonised the peninsula to gain control of its rich tin reserve and auctioned off tax-farming and mining rights to the Chinese to help develop the territory. Loke struck it rich after obtaining the

廈，為新加坡當時最高之樓宇，內有酒店、餐廳及戲院。當時這兩所戲院每月觀眾僅11萬8千人次，收益在陸氏王國中可算是無關輕重。1940年，陸運濤學成回星，接掌家族生意，惜當時中日戰爭已在蔓延。1942年，日軍侵略馬來亞，國泰大廈亦被日軍佔用，陸逃往印尼，但其所乘船隻卻遭日軍襲擊，陸氏重傷被送往椰加達就醫，曾短暫失明，痊癒後他在庫特奇沙漠探險四個月，又到克什米爾爬山探險。

1945年，二次大戰結束後，陸運濤重返新加坡，重組名下的地產與銀行業務，其興趣亦延伸至時尚的電影業。1946年，他與英國蘭克公司（J. Arthur Rank Organisation）簽定協議，把蘭克影片發行到星馬上映。為開拓影片的上映場地，自1947年，他向檳榔嶼的Ong Keng Huat購買多間戲院；於1948年4月，成立國際戲院有限公司（International Theatre Ltd.）；自1949年，又以合夥形式在星馬建立多所新式戲院，引進闊銀幕、新式放映機、空調設備和動向新歷聲等，務求達到「每一地區有一家戲院，每一個東南亞人士都能享受到高尚的娛樂」。在短短數年間，旗下院線有戲院四十多間，[5]每月觀影人次超過一百萬（相等於當時新加坡總人口）。除發行英語片到星馬外，陸氏亦在1953年與富商何亞祿成立國泰克里斯製片廠（Cathay Keris），拍攝馬來語影片，供應旗下院線。[6]

星馬華僑對華語片需求龐大，尋找足夠片源、供院線上映正是陸氏首要難題。為穩定片源，陸運濤遂於1951年在新加坡成立國際電影發行公司，專營電影發行。1953年，星洲國泰機構登陸香港，成立子公司國際影片發行公司（簡稱「國際」），由英籍猶太人歐德爾執掌，朱旭華協助，負責在港購買影片往星馬上映。歐氏在1924年生於香港，操流利廣東話，日戰期間曾代表

rights, operating over a dozen mines and running rubber, coffee, coconut and pepper plantations as well as cement and iron factories, hiring over a thousand employees. He opened a bank in Kuala Lumpur in 1913 and, during WWI, was allowed to print currency due to the large number of branches enjoyed by his provision store. He had four wives and eight children, though interactions between households were infrequent. When he died in 1917 with an estimated estate of over £10 million, family business was turned over to his fourth wife, who had one son and two daughters. The son, Wan Tho, was only two.[3]

Loke Yew's business empire and its built-in connections were instrumental in helping his son realise his dream. But what is that dream? Loke Wan Tho was born in Kuala Lumpur in 1915 and received a European education there before attending a Swiss boarding school at 13. He studied at Switzerland's Chillon College, then read Literature and History at Cambridge,

「猩猩」懷中的陸佑太太

Mrs. Loke Yew and a furry friend.

荷里活雷電華公司（RKO）在重慶發行電影，戰後，在香港可口可樂公司任市場經理，陸運濤身在新加坡，正好透過歐氏遙控業務。[7] 歐氏熟悉香港市場，在1953年以試驗性質開拍由吳楚帆及紫羅蓮主演的粵語片《余之妻》，由剛成立的粵語組主持林永泰任監製，由竇漢勳任助理製片及發行。為進一步穩定華語片片源，國際更模仿當時美國聯美公司，以借貸或預繳形式支持一些獨立公司開戲，成品則交國際旗下院線上映，這些公司分別是嚴俊主持的國泰（出品有《金鳳》〔1956〕及《菊子姑娘》〔1956〕）；朱旭華主持的國風（出品有胡蝶、蕭芳芳主演，卜萬蒼導演的《苦兒流浪記》〔1960〕）；白光主持的國光（出品有《鮮牡丹》〔1956〕、《接財神》〔1959〕）；秦劍主持的國藝（出品有《大馬戲團》〔1964〕）。[8]

另歐德爾也積極開拓香港的國語片院線，打破當時西片壟斷首輪映期的局面，聯合起永華、龍鳳、自由等製片公司，與璇宮、仙樂及金城三家戲院組院成線，自1956年農曆年始，長期上映國語片，此舉屬試驗性質，但卻有不俗成績，其中以林黛、嚴俊主演的《菊子姑娘》成績最理想，票房凌駕西片紀錄。[9]

2. 戲院、發行、製作三環節的整合

1955年是陸氏影業王國的轉捩點——從星馬北上的戲院商國際、從上海南下的製片商永華正式接軌，合二為一。事緣中日戰爭結束後，上海商人李祖永南下香港，成立永華公司，1949年後，永華出品頓失龐大的中國市場。1953年李氏便以片場作抵押，向陸運濤借貸港幣100萬元，合約訂明「永華」在一年內需向「國際」供應十二部影片，但1954年永華片倉卻發生大火，電影底片付諸一炬，歐德爾遂向法院申請接管永華片廠。李祖永雖向台灣方面貸款求助，卻

graduating in 1936, followed by a stay at the London School of Economics. Returning to Singapore in 1940, he took over the family business that included banks, rubber plantations, tin mines, real estate, restaurants, hotels, and entertainment. He was on the board of corporations that ranged from airlines to banks to trading companies while also serving honorary duties with tourism bureaus, libraries and photography clubs. He took adventure trips in far off places and had a passion for art, history, riding, golf, films, photography and bird watching, combining the last two into a 1958 book, *A Company of Birds*. He even admitted that he had more interest in ornithology and photography than running business.[4]

Evolution of Loke's Theatre Empire

1. Theatre and Distribution

The movie empire built by Loke in 1946 was not only a calculated business venture but also the realisation of a personal dream. With changes in life experience, that dream also changed. Loke's mother established the Pavilion Theatre in 1936 and in 1939, the Cathay Building, at the time the tallest building in Singapore, with a hotel, restaurants and a theatre. The two theatres had a monthly attendance of about 118,000, generating profit that could only be miniscule by empire standard. Loke returned to Singapore in 1940 to take over the family business, but by then, WWII had started. When Japan invaded Malaya in 1942, Cathay Building was occupied. Loke fled for Indonesia but was seriously injured when his boat was attacked. Upon recovery, he went on expeditions in India and Kashmir.

After the war, he returned to Singapore in 1945 to reorganise business. He signed with the British firm J. Arthur Rank to distribute Rank films in Southeast Asia and, to expand exhibition outlets, bought several theatres in Penang. He established International Theatre Ltd. in 1948 and starting in 1949, went into partnership to

適逢香港政府收回永華片廠界限街地皮，永華在牛池灣重建新廠所需的50萬資金，也只得再由歐德爾代付。打從1955年始，永華片廠及其製片業務便由國際管轄，陸運濤出任董事長。[10]

陸氏接管永華後，即禮賢下士，招攬自己的「食客」和「智囊團」，如廣招文人，成立了由張愛玲、姚克、宋淇及孫晉三所組成的劇本編審委員會，提供和選擇劇本，[11]並邀請易文、陶秦和岳楓擔任導演，製作國語片。1956年，隨歐德爾被調回新加坡（1957年過檔邵氏），陸氏即把永華和國際合併，改組為電影懋業公司（簡稱電懋），以「巨片標誌・榮譽之徵」作口號，總經理一職由鍾啟文擔任、發行總經理為林永泰、製片部經理宋淇。電懋的管理班底主要回流自歐美，熟悉歐美影業，以鍾啟文為例，他在1919年生於北平，曾在天津、上海及香港三地唸中學，後赴美留學並在霍士公司實習，1949至1952年間曾任永華廠長，後轉職香港柯達公司，1956年被陸運濤羅致旗下[12]，並將歐美的製作路線、管理模式帶進電懋。

3. 片廠制流水作業

電懋仿荷里活片廠制，流水作業生產影片，引入全年製作計劃、財政預算及劇本策劃，片廠內同時拍攝多組不同電影，以節省時間和成本，提供大量質素穩定的影片，應付院線的龐大需要。如自五十年代中，電懋已採用攝製彩色電影技術，流水製作有聲有色的歌舞片，1956年的《歡樂年年》、1957年的《曼波女郎》等都是典型的片廠製作。這種企業化的生產流程在電懋的官方刊物中亦有記載。[13]

另外，電懋亦成立多個部門，專責宣傳、發行、製片、音響。如在宣傳方面，電懋即成立國泰電影畫報社，出版《國際電影》雜誌（先後由朱旭華、黃也白、陳立主編），

build a series of state-of-the-art theatres in Southeast Asia, introducing amenities like widescreen, new projectors, air conditioning and stereo sound. His goal was "one theatre in each area, where every Southeast Asian can enjoy high-class entertainment." Within a few years, he had over 40 theatres in his chain,[5] with monthly attendance that exceeded a million (equivalent to Singapore's total population). in 1951, he also joined forces with businessman Ho Ah Loke (He Yalu) to form Keris Productions, making Malay films for his theatres.[6]

Demand in Southeast Asia for Chinese films was great. To ensure supply of films to fill his theatres' bills, Loke formed International Film Distribution Agency in 1951 and appointed Albert Odell to establish a Hong Kong branch (with a slightly different name: International Films Distributing Agency) in 1953. [1]Born in Hong Kong in 1924, Odell speaks fluent Cantonese. He distributed films in Chongqing for RKO during WWII and worked for Coca Cola after the war. With him in Hong Kong, Loke was able to run things in Singapore through remote control.[7] In 1953, Odell made the first step in production, making *My Wife, My Wife* (1955) with the newly established Cantonese film unit, run by Lam Wing-tai (Lin Yongtai) and assisted by Tau Hon-fun (Dou Hanxun). Emulating United Artists, International Flims started supporting independent companies in the form of loans or advances, in exchange for distribution rights of the films. The companies included Guotai, ran by actor Yan Jun (*Golden Phoenix*, 1956, and *Miss Kikuko*, 1956), Guofeng, by Zhu Xuhua (*Nobody's Child*, 1960), Bai Guang's Guoguang (*Fresh Peony*, 1956, and *Welcome, God of Wealth*, 1959) and Chun Kim's Guoyi (*The Big Circus*, 1964).[8]

Odell also aggressively established the Mandarin theatre market in Hong Kong, breaking the monopoly of first-run theatres by Hollywood films. He collaborated with production companies like Yung Hwa, Longfeng and Liberty

在星馬、印度、三藩市等二十七個地方發行，發行量達十萬，用以宣傳影片製作及明星動態。電影上映前，電懋也會出版電影特刊及明星月曆作宣傳，為影片造勢。[14]

片廠制與明星制是一對雙生子。電懋也成立演員訓練班，培訓新人，製造明星。其課程包括片場及舞台實習、化妝技巧、國語進修、演説風格及社交禮儀等，新人薪金雖然低廉，但有潛質者則會被挑選，制訂策略被捧成明星。總經理鍾啟文採取荷里活控制明星的方法，由公司代為接見傳媒，並控制明星的私人生活（包括婚姻），除操控電影內容外，還同時顧及明星的公眾形象。電懋企業化生產影片之餘，度身製造出的明星有林黛、尤敏、葛蘭、林翠、陳厚等，每位也形象鮮明，耀眼生輝。[15]

在五十年代，香港影片十分倚賴星馬、泰國、越南等市場，但隨民族運動及連串排華潮出現，東南亞多國也先後實施入口限制，不利華語片進口。又由於中國大陸市場緊閉，電影人只好轉向台灣，但當時台灣正實行外匯管制，港產片入口除要申請結匯證外，也要加收百分之二十防衛捐，令國語片在台收入減少約三分一。為打破僵局，自五十年代中，不少香港電影人便組織「回國勞軍祝壽團」，到台灣慶祝雙十節；或在港高調慶祝雙十節。[16]自1962年7月，《國際電影》更採用台灣紀年方法，以「民國」標示出版年月。電懋也積極與台灣聯邦合作，在台招聘編劇、演員和組織發行網，甚至直接資助李翰祥在台灣拍片，期能打入台灣市場。日本市場方面，電懋也於1961年起與東寶合作，推出尤敏主演的《香港之夜》（1961）、《香港之星》（1963）、《香港・東京・夏威夷》（1963）等，以期開拓日本的發行網。由1965年7月起，《國際電影》更增添「東寶之頁」專欄，反映電懋十分重視這段合作關係。[17]

Film to form a chain with three theatres, showing Mandarin films beginning with the 1956 Chinese New Year. This experiment proved successful, especially with *Miss Kikuko*, which raked up sales that bettered Hollywood films.[9]

2. Integrating Theatres, Distribution and Production

1955 was a turning point for Loke's movie empire, when International Film (Singapore), which went north from Southeast Asia, merged with the studio Yung Hwa, which traveled south from Shanghai. The deal dates back to the war, when Shanghai businessman Li Zuyong came to Hong Kong to establish Yung Hwa. The loss of the Chinese market after 1949 brought financial troubles and Li borrowed HK$1 million from Loke in 1953, using his studio as collateral and promising to deliver 12 films for Loke's theatre chain within a year. But a warehouse fire destroyed much of the negatives and Odell filed papers to take control. Li looked to Taiwan for funds but was hit by the Hong Kong government's decision to take back the studio land. International Films paid for the $500,000 to build a new studio and took over the studio in 1955, with Loke serving as Chairman.[10]

He immediately went to work, recruiting writers like Eileen Chang (Zhang Ailing), Stephen Soong (Song Qi), Yao Ke and Sun Jinsan to form a script committee[11] as well as directors Evan Yang (Yi Wen), Tao Qin and Yue Feng to join the studio's ranks. In 1956, Odell was moved back to Singapore (and switched over to Shaws in 1957) and Loke combined Yung Hwa with International Films to form Motion Picture and General Investment Ltd. (MP & GI). Robert Chung (Zhong Qiwen) was appointed General Manager, with Lam Wing-tai serving as Distribution Manager and Soong as Production Manager. The management of MP & GI was comprised mostly of repatriates who were familiar with Western ways. Chung, for example, was born in Beijing

4. 電懋與邵氏的競爭

戰後，星馬邵氏院線由邵逸夫主持，其片源多來自邵邨人在港經營的邵氏父子公司。電懋登陸香港後，邵氏出品的影片即處下風，邵逸夫為保證片源質素，在 1957 年從星到港，策劃興建影城，成立邵氏（兄弟）公司，親自製作電影供應旗下院線。他從美國新聞處挖角，找得鄒文懷出任宣傳經理。相比之下，電懋領導層大多接受歐美教育，其出品亦充滿中產品味。而邵氏的班底則與上海淵源較深（如鄒文懷、何冠昌分別肄業於上海聖約翰大學及復旦大學）。雖然邵逸夫是位典型的上海商人，作風與陸運濤迥異，但邵氏與電懋也同是院商出身，搖身變成製片商後，也沿用大片廠制，流水作業——邵氏影城幅員 46 公頃，在高峰期有片廠十五座，外景場地及影棚十六座，三座錄音及配音廠，各片廠行三班制（每班八小時）。另設南國訓練班，簽定長合約

《寶蓮燈》
The Magic Lamp

and studied in Tianjin, Shanghai and Hong Kong, then went to the U.S. to intern at Fox. He served as Yung Hwa's studio manager from 1949 to 1952, later working for Kodak (Hong Kong). Drafted by Loke,[12] he introduced Western production and management practices to MP & GI.

3. Studio System

Modelled after Hollywood, MP & GI operated under the studio system, introducing practices like annual production plans, financial forecasts and script supervision. Several films were shot at the same time to save time and expenses, as well as controlling quality of the products it supplied to its theatre chains. Such a production process was even promoted in the company's official publication.[13]

Departments for promotion, distribution, production and sound were established. For promotion, a publishing arm was formed to produce the magazine *International Screen* to promote its films and stars. Distributed in 27 locations ranging from Southeast Asia to India to San Francisco, it had a circulation of 100,000. With new films, booklets and calendars were also produced as part of the promotion campaign.[14]

Star system is the twin of the studio system and MP & GI instituted an actors training program to create stars. Classes included set and stage exercises, make-up skills, Mandarin instructions, speech making and etiquette. Pay was low but those with potential were singled out and groomed for stardom. Robert Chung adopted the Hollywood star system, orchestrating media contacts while controlling private lives (including marriage) and public images. Stars it made included Linda Lin Dai, Lucilla You Min, Grace Chang (Ge Lan), Jeanette Lin Cui and Peter Chen Ho (Chen Hou).[15]

In the 1950s, Hong Kong depended heavily on

培育明星。[18]邵氏與電懋都仿荷里活制，一手包辦了影片生產、發行、上映三環節，可謂旗鼓相當。

電懋與邵氏之爭起於五十年代末。邵逸夫抵港後即宣佈起用導演李翰祥，以100萬製作費開拍創業作《貂蟬》（1958）（當時國語片一般成本約10萬元而矣），該片上畫時十分轟動，更在亞洲影展中連奪五獎項，先聲奪人。邵逸夫乘勝追擊，任用李翰祥開拍《江山美人》（1959），上映一週，票房已突破四十萬大關，並在亞洲影展中奪得「最佳影片獎」，邵氏名聲一時無兩，林黛也成為兩大公司的爭奪目標。此外，嚴俊和李麗華夫妻亦在邵氏支持下，自組公司效力邵氏，推出古裝片《楊貴妃》（1962）和《武則天》（1963）。陸運濤見邵氏聲勢直逼電懋，便親自來港與林黛見面，洽談合作，最後，電懋和邵氏平分秋色，林黛分別為兩大公司各簽三部片約。陸運濤又與李麗華、陳厚、尤敏會面，透過林翠拉攏其夫秦劍為電懋成立衛星公司；透過雷震使其妹樂蒂投入電懋旗下，嚴俊與李麗華自組的製片公司也分別成為電懋及邵氏的衛星公司。至1963年，邵氏起用凌波反串《梁山伯與祝英台》，票房大旺，黃梅調電影一時風行。邵氏挾此聲勢，以高薪長約挽留凌波，開拍《鳳還巢》（1963）、《花木蘭》（1964）、《血手印》（1964）、《雙鳳奇緣》（1964）等，將她捧成一級女星。另一邊廂，電懋也積極反擊，推出《星星・月亮・太陽》（1961），將尤敏捧成一級女星，邵氏不甘示弱，以林黛主演的《千嬌百媚》（1961）還擊，使林黛在亞洲影展中三度封后。[19]電懋和邵氏激戰，除了令影業暢旺外，亦史無前例地為華語影壇塑造出無數的璀璨明星。

1961年，兩大公司再短兵相接，搶拍《紅樓夢》，電懋起用易文作導演，由美國聘請張愛玲回港編纂劇本，張

《啼笑姻緣》
A Story of Three Loves

markets in Singapore, Malaya, Thailand and Vietnam. But with the rise of nationalism and anti-Chinese sentiments, import quotas were imposed on many Southeast Asian countries. With the China market closed, filmmakers turned towards Taiwan. But Taiwan was enforcing tight currency control and Hong Kong films not only had to apply for a foreign currency permit but also pay a 20% "defense tax", cutting profit by a third. To reverse the situation, filmmakers began in the mid-1950s to either organise trips to celebrate National Day and to perform for troops as well as staged celebrations in Hong Kong.[16] Starting in 1962, *International Screen* also adopted Taiwan's calendar system, using "Republic Years" to identify publication dates. The company also recruited writers and actors in Taiwan, installing distribution networks and backing director Li Hanxiang's filmmaking efforts. MP & GI also explored other markets, collaborating with Japan's Toho in 1961 to make co-productions like *A Night in Hong Kong* (1961) and *Star of Hong Kong* (1963) and added a "Toho Page" section to *International Screen* in July 1965.[17]

4. Rivalry With Shaws

After the war, the Shaws theatre chain was run by Run Run Shaw, with films coming mostly from Runde Shaw's Hong Kong facilities. After MP & GI landed in Hong Kong, Shaws' films paled by comparison. Run Run decided to move to Hong Kong in 1957 to oversee film production, establishing Shaws Brothers (HK) Ltd, building its own studio and recruiting Raymond Chow to run publicity. While MP & GI's leadership was mostly educated in the West, resulting in their films' middle-class sensibilities, Shaws' were from Shanghai. Although Run Run was a typical Shanghai businessman whose practices were different from Loke's, he shared similar backgrounds in exhibition. Once getting into

屢次修改劇本，使用國語對白，棄用黃梅調，以期慢工出細貨；反觀邵氏則利用清水灣片場和九龍城亞洲片場同時拍攝，劇本高度保密，日以繼夜不停趕工，結果影片搶先推出。[20] 1962年《梁山伯與祝英台》一片亦鬧雙胞，電懋公佈計劃後，邵氏則搶先動工開拍，在服飾佈景方面，邵氏標榜富麗堂皇；電懋則強調清淡優雅。打後，電懋與邵氏同時搶拍《武則天》及《楊貴妃》，邵氏搶先推出影片，電懋兩片只好停拍。1963年，在電懋支持下，「邵氏叛將」李翰祥在台灣起用江青和錢容蓉等開拍《七仙女》(1963)，邵氏反擊，起用凌波、方盈也趕拍《七仙女》(1963)，李翰祥只好親自畫景、改景、處理道具，日以繼夜在一個多月內完成拍攝，趕及與邵氏出品同步上映。雙胞事件接踵而來，1964年，電懋用趙雷、林翠主演張恨水名著《啼笑姻緣》，邵氏便立刻發動集體導演，全體影星分組趕拍，剪輯成《新啼笑姻緣》(1964)，較電懋版本早一個月上映，亦迫使電懋將影片在台灣公映時易名為《京華春夢》(1964)。當邵氏宣佈製作《寶蓮燈》(1965)時，電懋亦還以顏色，總動員搶拍趕拍同一電影。雖然邵氏作品較電懋版本遲了一年才推出，但由於邵氏《寶蓮燈》是林黛遺作，該片明顯較受觀眾歡迎。[21]

從上所見，電懋的經營明顯不易。陸氏究竟為自己的電影夢賠上多少呢？電懋是一所私人公司，筆者在現存文件中未找到可靠資料，但陸氏姪女朱美蓮(Meileen Choo)在接受香港電影資料館訪問時，便有以下有趣的憶述：在製造明星方面，電懋十分成功，令明星在觀眾心目中高不可攀；但就商業角度而言，電懋影片的盈利卻並不多，經營得絕不輕鬆。歐德爾接受香港電影資料館訪問時甚至以「災難性」(disastrous)來形容電懋的經營，他指出電懋只製造

production, he also adopted a studio system. During its prime, his studio was situated on 46 acres, with 15 sound stages, 16 location sets, three sound studios and a staff that work in three shifts of eight hours each. An actor training program was also installed to nurture stars. [18] Both Shaws and MP & GI were modeled after Hollywood in their operation, integrating production, distribution and exhibition.

The rivalry between MP & GI and Shaws started in the 1950s. Shaws made epics like *Diau Darling* (1958) and *The Kingdom and the Beauty* (1959) with director Li Hanxiang, winning great box office and Asian Film Festival awards. Contentions battles were waged to sign stars like Linda Lin Dai and Betty Loh Ti (Le Di) and Loke made deals with other stars like Yan Jun, Li Lihua and director Chun Kim to form satellite companies for MP & GI. In 1963, Shaws' *Love Eterne* was a great success, creating a *huangmei diao* (Yellow Plum Opera) dialect opera craze and making Ling Bo a superstar. MP & GI answered with *Sun, Moon and Star* (1961), putting its promotional machinery behind You Min.[19] The fierce competition between MP & GI and Shaws not only stimulated growth in the film business but also created stars of unprecedented proportions.

The companies tussled again in 1961, both announcing plans to make film adaptations of the classic novel *Dream of the Red Chamber*. MP & GI brought Eileen Chang back from the US, who wanted to make a Mandarin version instead of *huangmei diao* and took time refining her script. Shaws, on the other hand, went into production immediately, shooting at two studios and with secrecy, releasing its film long before MP & GI finished its.[20] This "competing versions" situation repeated itself several times, with Shaws coming out ahead most times.[21]

It was obvious that business was tough for Loke. How much did he lose? MP & GI was a private

出好影片，而沒有製造出盈利，陸運濤當時的虧損高達二千五百萬坡幣。[22]

5. 言和與中興？

由於陸運濤長駐新加坡，香港的業務便先後下放給歐德爾及鍾啟文執掌，但決策權最終仍在陸氏手上。反觀邵氏，大權一直集中在長駐香港的邵逸夫手中，定案自然較電懋快速。1962年8月，深受人事糾紛和傳聞困擾的鍾啟文請辭，轉投麗的呼聲旗下。同年，孫晉三逝世、宋淇請辭。陸運濤最初以玩票性質參與影業，但電懋管理階層經歷這次重大變動後，他只好實行中央集權，親自擔任總經理一職，由「搖控」變為「直轄」電懋。[23]

陸氏空降電懋後，決定增加投資，攝製多部彩色闊銀幕電影，並延攬李麗華及嚴俊夫婦重投電懋旗下，又在1963年1月，宣佈台灣國際影業公司成為電懋的海外組織，以新台幣一千萬元支持其大量拍片，開拓台灣市場。為加強製片業務，陸氏在經濟上也支持國聯，與聯邦合共投資美金五百萬元支持李翰祥，使國聯成為電懋在台灣的製片基地。影圈中人聲稱，電懋由陸運濤直接掌帥後，成功登陸台灣，正出現「中興之象」。[24]

電懋和邵氏歷年激戰，為免兩敗俱傷，在親台的港九影劇自由公會主席胡晉康主持下，在1964年3月5日發表「君子協定」，宣稱日後：一、「不拉對方公司編劇、導演、演員或其他重要職員」；二、「不再鬧雙胞案，每一月或兩月，雙方製片部門之負責人以茶敘方式會面交換意見」；三、嚴俊所拍之《梁山伯與祝英台》及《孟麗君》（1963）會交電懋發行；四、李翰祥與邵氏之合約限制宣佈解除、國聯之《七仙女》可在香港及東南亞公映，而電懋亦同意李翰祥可為其他公司服務。[25]電懋「中興之象」似在延續。

（左起）國際、電懋及六十年代新加坡國泰機構標誌

Logos for (from left) International Films, MP & GI and the Cathay Organisation of the 1960s.

company and I haven't been able to find reliable material on this subject. Meileen Choo, Loke's niece has this interesting memory in her Hong Kong Film Archive interview: "... in terms of creating an image for Cathay, he was very successful.... He created many stars. The system was... very much like Hollywood.... In terms of business, it was very difficult... Not many of the films were profitable." In another HKFA interview, Albert Odell described MP & GI's operation as "disastrous," that Loke "made good films, but not good money." He estimated that Loke's losses were as high as SG25 million .[22]

5. Peace Agreement and Resurgence

While Loke was remote-controlling from Singapore, Run Run Shaw was stationed in Hong Kong and decisions were made more quickly. In 1962, when Robert Chung's resignation was followed by Sun Jinsan's death and Stephen Soong's resignation, Loke was forced to take over as General Manager.[23] He decided to step up investment, making several widescreen colour films and persuading stars Yan Jun and Li Lihua to rejoin the company. In 1963, MP & GI annexed Taiwan's International as a satellite by pumping NT$ 10 million into it. Loke also backed Li Hanxiang's Grand and another company, Union, with an investment of US$ 5 million. With Loke on direct control, MP & GI was enjoying a resurgence.[24]

After years of battling, a peace agreement between MP & GI and Shaws was brokered by pro-Taiwan forces in March, 1964. It was declared that there would be no raiding of personnel and the practice of "competing versions" would stop, with production heads of both companies holding regular tea meetings to enhance understanding. Dispute concerning Yan Jun and Li Hanxiang were also resolved.[25] MP & GI's resurgence continued.

6. 突變和轉型

發展至六十年代，電懋和邵氏都實行高度的中央集權，陸運濤和邵逸夫儼如兩公司的化身，大權全繫於個人身上。集權制的優點很多，但弱點亦不少。例如當陸、邵兩人年華正茂，電懋與邵氏自然也風華絕代，不用憂慮繼承問題，這一點邵逸夫比陸運濤稍為幸運，他的長壽成為邵氏一項可貴「資產」，為公司帶來近半世紀的政策穩定。這點「資產」電懋便無法模仿。電懋與邵氏和解短短三個月後，便突變橫生。1964年6月20日，第十一屆亞洲影展於台灣舉行，陸運濤首次踏足台灣。陸、邵兩人應邀出席影展當局安排之觀光活動，陸氏偕新婚妻子同遊；邵逸夫則有事未能成行。不料飛機回程時卻於豐原發生爆炸，陸氏夫婦、行政人員王植波及製片主任周海龍等共五十七人全部罹難。空難過後，電懋內部一片混亂。[26]

有別於邵家六兄弟的邵氏、何家四昆仲的光藝，電懋的陸運濤與異母兄長的連繫並不緊密，其影業全賴其親信智囊維繫，他辭世後，沒有陸家兄弟或子姪接手，最後由其胞妹夫朱國良接掌。朱氏為陸佑下屬，1910年生於吉隆坡，修業於吉隆坡聖約翰學校，後到英國倫敦及牛津大學深造，修讀農科，替陸氏管理橡膠種植業務。空難後，電懋結業的傳聞紛至沓來。1965年6月，朱氏親自到港宣佈把電懋改組為國泰機構(香港)(1965)有限公司（簡稱國泰），由星洲國泰機構直轄管理，宣稱會繼承陸運濤遺願，貫徹原定計劃製作電影。但事與願違，演員樂蒂自殺；尤敏、葛蘭退休，旗下導演及演員多別覓枝棲，過檔邵氏，邵氏年產量遞增同時，國泰之電影產量、市場佔有率卻大跌。[27]朱國良的出生及性格與陸氏迥異，朱氏延長了電懋的壽命，卻沒有延續陸運濤的夢想，這點朱美蓮亦有相似的觀察，她形容陸運

6. Disaster and Reorganisation

By the 1960s, both MP & GI and Shaws were run by centralised leadership, with Loke and Run Run Shaw calling all the shots. Centralising power had its pros and its cons. When Loke and Shaw were both young and energetic, so were their companies. Succession was not an issue. In this regard, Shaw is more fortunate. His long life is indeed his company's asset, providing half a century of stability. MP & GI enjoyed no such asset. Three short months after making peace with Shaws, disaster struck. On June 20, 1964, Loke visited Taiwan for the first time, attending the 11th Asian Film Festival. Loke and Shaw were both invited to a sightseeing trip and while Shaw was unable to go, Loke obliged with his wife. On the return trip, the plane crashed, killing everyone on board, including Loke and a host of MP & GI executives. The company plunged into chaos.[26]

The Lokes did not have the kind of close relationship enjoyed by the Shaw family or the Ho family of Kong Ngee. After Loke Wan Tho died, brother-in-law Choo Kok Leong (Zhu Guoliang) was called on to oversee the family business. Choo was born in Kuala Lumpur in 1910 and his father was Loke Yew's associate. After studying in Britain, he returned to work for Loke, taking care of the family's rubber business. Amid rumours of the company's dissolution, Choo came to Hong Kong in 1965 to announce MP & GI's reorganisation into Cathay (Hong Kong) and its determination to continue Loke's movie legacy. But with the suicide of Loh Ti, the retirement of You Min and Grace Chang as well as the departure of other actors and directors, Cathay suffered drops in output and market share. Shaws, meanwhile, was stepping up productions.[27] Choo was very different from Loke. He might have continued Loke's business, but not his dream. His daughter Meileen observes that while Loke enjoyed publicity, Choo was more subdued and not a "frontline"

濤是一位享受閃光燈和社交的風流人物；而其父朱國良則十分低調、內向，是一個不屬於「前線」的人。[28]朱氏掌帥期間起用俞普慶（1904-1969），俞氏在1969年辭世後，國泰的製片業務再度收縮，並在1971年正式結束其製片部門。時值鄒文懷脱離邵氏，創立嘉禾，朱國良順勢把「永華製片廠」和攝影設備轉交嘉禾，而嘉禾的出品亦透過「國泰」被發行到星馬，至此，陸運濤的電影王國便只餘下發行及戲院業務，正式結束持續了十年的垂直整合式經營。

小結

從上所見，電懋建立起的垂直整合式經營，反映出十分重要的時代特式：星馬與香港影業的結合、影片在集資、發行與製作三環節的「地區分工」、中國與台灣影業市場的政治變化等。而外表西化的電懋，亦反映出華人家族公司在「權力繼承」方面的共同隱憂，電懋是陸運濤個人夢想的體現，造夢的人離去，美夢也未必有承繼人。步入1999年，國泰改組成上市公司，股份在新加坡股市掛牌買賣，自稱是陸氏後人中「唯一和最後一位」國泰股權人的朱美蓮女士解釋道「國泰現在是一所公眾公司……我是最後一位承繼火炬的人……我總覺得國泰是屬於陸運濤的，我常想自己離去後，國泰還是要延續下去，而唯一令這可能的方法就是讓這公司不再屬於陸家任何人。」[29]電懋歷史吊詭之處或許值得很多華人企業深思。

person.[28] He delegated Paul Yui (Yu Puqing) to handle production and when Yu died in 1969, operation was further scaled down, closing down eventually in 1971. It was at this time that Raymond Chow (Zou Wenhuai) left Shaws to form Golden Harvest and Choo handed over to him the Yung Hwa studio and its equipment while also distributing the new company's films in Southeast Asia. Loke Wan Tho's movie empire was left with only its distribution and exhibition arms, putting an end to its ten years of vertical integration.

Conclusion

As we can see, the vertical integration established by MP & GI is a product of its time. It embodied the special situation in which the Hong Kong film industry was connected to Southeast Asia, the effect of political changes in China and Taiwan on the market, and the geographical division of labour involving capital, production and distribution. The issue of power succession in Chinese family business can also be seen, ironically, in the history of the seemingly westernized MP & GI – when Loke the dreamer departed, no successor for his dream was found. In 1999, Cathay became a public company, openly traded on the Singapore exchange. Meileen Choo: "Cathay is now a public company. ... I'm the last person carrying the torch. ...For some strange reasons, I never consider Cathay as mine. It always belongs to my uncle. I always want that after I am gone, Cathay has to go on. I think the only way that it can happen is that the company is not owned by my family members."[29] It is perhaps worthy for Chinese entrepreneurs to contemplate on the history of MP & G I.

Translated by Sam Ho

註

1. Barry R. Litman: The Motion Picture Mega-industry, MA: Allyn & Bacon, 1998, pp. 64-68 及 Harold L. Vogel: Entertainment industry economics, A Guide for Financial Analysis, fourth edition, Cambridge: Cambridge University Press, 1998, pp. 3-141.
2. 鍾寶賢：《香港影視工業百年》，香港：三聯書店，刊印中。
3. 溫故知：《吉隆坡華人史話》，吉隆坡：輝煌出版社，1984，頁60-67；及Butcher, J.C. & Dick, H.W., ed.: The Rise and Fall of Revenue Farming: Business elites and the Emergence of the Modern State in Southeast Asia, London: Macmillan, 1993.
4. Loke Wan Tho Papers, National Archives of Singapore collection.
5. 〈「國泰機構」的偉大建院計劃〉，《國際電影》，第7期，1956年4月，頁10。
6. 〈崇高的理想陸氏為東南亞人士帶來歡樂〉，《國際電影》，第3期，1955年12月，頁11；楊翼，〈邵氏電影王國六十年（一九二五——一九八五）(6)〉，《當代文藝》，第187期，1999年12月，頁147；及〈國泰機構組織龐大〉，《國際電影》，第120期，1965年11月，頁5-10。
7. Report of the 3rd Annual Film Festival of Southeast Asia, Hong Kong: Film Festival of Southeast Asia, 1956；及Interview with Albert Odell, Hong Kong Film Archive Oral History Project, December 11, 2001, Singapore. 歐德爾是一個傳奇人物，其祖父由俄羅斯經天津移居美國，其父則來港從事電影發行，他在1948年從港抵星，替一所美資獨立公司發行影片，認識大戲院商陸運濤，令陸氏對電影發行業興趣大增，1951年遂合作成立國際電影發行公司，公司資金主要由陸氏提供，其股份則是歐德爾、陸運濤、何亞祿各佔 30 %；餘下 10% 屬陸氏劍橋求學時期的好友 John Ede（歷史科教授）。
8. 〈白光加入國際陣營〉，《國際電影》，第2期，1955年11月，頁18及Lim Kay Tong: Cathay - 55 Years of Cinema, Singapore: Landmark Books, 1991, p. 151.
9. 香港大公報社編：《香港經濟年鑑》，香港：香港大公報社，1956年，頁151及〈國語片建立港九聯映陣線〉，《國際電影》，第6期，1956年3月，頁44。
10. 草原，〈雄偉壯觀的永華新廠〉，《國際電影》，第5期，1956年2月，頁19及黃卓漢：《電影人生：黃卓漢回憶錄》，台北：萬象圖書，1994，頁90。
11. 〈國際影片公司劇本編審委員會成立〉，載《國際電影》，1期（1955年10月），頁53。
12. 同註 8。
13. 〈一部電影的完成〉，《國際電影》，第23期，1957年9月，頁39。
14. 〈「電懋」出品電影特刊〉，《香港電影資料館通訊》，第11期，2000年2月，頁9及Lim Kay Tong，同註8，頁146。
15 〈電懋怎樣訓練三新人〉，《國際電影》，第76期，1962年2月，頁27及〈一個優秀的演員是怎樣培養成的？電懋新人訓練班介紹〉，《國際電影》，第111期，1965年2月，頁54。

Notes

1. See Barry R. Litman: *The Motion Picture Mega-industry*, MA: Allyn & Bacon, 1998, pp. 64-68 and Harold L. Vogel: *Entertainment industry economics, A Guide for Financial Analysis*, fourth edition, Cambridge: Cambridge University Press, 1998, pp. 3-141.
2. See Stephanie Chung Po-yin: *One Hundred Years of Hong Kong Film Industry* (in Chinese), Hong Kong: Joint Publishing Co., to be published.
3. See Wen Guzhi: *History of Kuala Lumpur Chinese* (in Chinese), Kuala Lumpur: Huihuang Publishing, 1984, pp. 60-67 and Butcher, J.C. & Dick, H.W., ed.: *The Rise and Fall of Revenue Farming: Business elites and the Emergence of the Modern State in Southeast Asia*, London: Macmillan, 1993.
4. See Loke Wan Tho Papers, National Archives of Singapore collection.
5. See "Cathay's Grand Plan to Build Theatres" in *International Screen* (in Chinese), vol. 7, April 1956, p. 10.
6. See "With Noble Ideals, Loke Brings Joy to Southeast Asians" in *International Screen* (in Chinese), vol. 3, December 1955, p. 11; Yang Yi, "Sixty Years of the Shaws Empire, 1925 - 1985" in *Contemporary Literature* (in Chinese), vol. 187, December 1999, p. 147 and "Cathay's Organisation is Huge" in *International Screen* (in Chinese), vol. 120, November 1965, pp. 5 –10.
7. See *Report of the 3rd Annual Film Festival of Southeast Asia*, Hong Kong: Film Festival of Southeast Asia, 1956 and Interview with Albert Odell, Hong Kong Film Archive Oral History Project, December 11, 2001, Singapore. Odell is an interesting figure. His grandfather immigrated from Russia to America and his father came to Hong Kong, working on film distribution. He went to Singapore from Hong Kong in 1948 to distribute Hollywood films and got to know Loke Wan Tho. They formed International Film Distribution Agency in 1951, with funds provided by Loke. Odell, Loke, Ho Ah Loke each had 30% share and the remaining 10% went to John Ede, Loke's friend from his Cambridge days.
8. See "Bai Guang Joins International" in *International Screen* (in Chinese), vol. 2, November 1955, p. 18 and Lim Kay Tong: *Cathay - 55 Years of Cinema*, Singapore: Landmark Books, 1991, p. 151.
9. See *Hong Kong Economic Annuals* (in Chinese), Hong Kong: Tai Kung Po, 1956, p. 151 and "Mandarin Films Establish Exhibition Chain" in *International Screen* (in Chinese), vol. 6, March 1956, p. 44.
10. See "The Grand and Spectacular New Yung Hwa Studio" in *International Screen* (in Chinese), vol. 5, February 1956, p. 19 and Wong Cheuk-hon (Huang Zhuohan): *A Life in Movies: The Memoirs of* Wong Cheuk-hon (in Chinese), Taipei: Variety Publishing, 1994, p. 90.
11. See "Establishment of the International Film Script Committee" in *International Screen* (in Chinese), vol. 1, October 1955, p. 53.
12. See "Bai Guang Joins International" in *International Screen* (in Chinese), op. cit. and Lim Kay Tong, op. cit.
13. See "Completion of a Film" in *International Screen* (in Chinese), vol. 23, September 1957, p. 39.
14. See "MP and GI Special Publications and Film Brochures" in *Hong Kong Film Archive Newsletter*, vol. 11, February 2000, p. 9 and Lim Kay Tong, op. cit., p. 146.
15. See "How MP & GI Train Three New Actors" in *International Screen* (in Chinese), vol. 76, February 1962, p. 27 and "How is a Good Actor Nurtured? Introduction to the MP & GI Actors Training Program" in *International Screen*, vol. 111, February 1965, p. 54.
16. See "Freedom Sector of Hong Kong Film Celebrates October 10 National Day" in *International Screen* (in Chinese), vol. 144, November 1967, pp. 12-14; "Looking at the Future of Mandarin Film From Another Angle" in *International Screen*, vol. 6, March 1956, p. 37; Jarvie, I. C.: *Window on Hong Kong: a sociological study*

16.〈香港自由影劇界盛大慶祝雙十國慶〉，《國際電影》，第144期，1967年11月，頁12-14；〈從另一角度看國語片前途〉，《國際電影》，第6期，1956年3月，頁37；Jarvie, I. C.: Window on Hong Kong: a sociological study of the Hong Kong film industry and its Audience, Hong Kong: Center of Asian Studies, 1977, p. 28；顧也魯：《藝海滄桑五十年》，北京：學林，1989，頁104-105、114-115；宇業熒：《戲說李麗華》，台北：全年代，1996，頁178-180；及黃卓漢，同註10，頁72-80。

17. 梁麗娟、陳韜文，〈海外市場與香港電影發展關係（1950-1995）〉，《光影繽紛五十年》，第廿一屆香港國際電影節回顧特刊，香港：市政局，1997，頁137，及「東寶之頁」專欄，《國際電影》，由第116期，1965年7月起。

18. 同註3。

19. Lim Kay Tong，同註8，頁113-114、148；Loke Wan Tho papers，陸氏遺下的文件中有不少有關邵氏的剪報，顯示他十分關心邵氏之動向；及黃卓漢，同註10，頁110-111。

20.〈兩部紅樓夢各有千秋〉，《星探》，第1期，1962年4月，頁73-74。

21.〈邵氏國泰搶拍「梁祝」真相〉，《銀河畫報》，第57期，1962年12月，頁5-6及黃卓漢，同註10，頁113-118。

22. Interview with Meileen Choo, Hong Kong Film Archive Oral History Project, December 10, 2001, Singapore 及 Interview with Albert Odell. 前者的訪問原文是 "...in terms of creating an image for Cathay, he was very successful...He created many stars. The system was...very much like Hollywood...In terms of business, it was very difficult....Not many of the films were profitable." 而後者的訪問原文則是 "I believe he [Loke] sunk his fortune....As far as I know, it was quite disastrous. 25 million Singapore dollars was lost. He made good films, but not good money."；另見Lim Kay Tong，同註8，頁85；黃卓漢，同註10，頁112；及沙榮峰：《繽紛電影四十春：沙榮峰回憶錄》，台北：國家電影資料館，1994，頁31-37。

23. 黃卓漢，同註10，頁120-121；〈港產國片對影壇之貢獻〉，《中國電影三十年》，台北：作者自刊，1980，頁17及〈電懋中興之象〉，《電影世界》，第38期，1962年11月，頁12。

24.〈邵電和解後的影壇大勢〉，《銀河畫報》，第72期，1964年3月，頁6。

25. 黃卓漢，同註10，頁118-123及沙榮峰，同註23，頁31-32。

26.〈連福明伉儷香港視察業務〉，《國際電影》，第120期，1965年11月，頁48。

28. Interview with Meileen Choo，見註22。

29. Interview with Meileen Choo，見註22。 訪問原文是 "Cathay is now a public company. I'm the last person carrying the torch. For some strange reasons, I never consider Cathay as mine. It belonged to my uncle. I always want that after I am gone, Cathay has to go on. I think the only way that it can happen is that the company not owned by my family members."

鍾寶賢，浸會大學歷史系副教授，研究興趣是近代中國社會經濟史。著有《香港影視工業百年》（三聯書店，即將出版）。
Stephanie Chung Po-yin, assistant professor of History at Baptist College. Author of *A Hundred Years of Hong Kong Film and Television Industry* (Joint Publishing, to be published).

of the Hong Kong film industry and its Audience, Hong Kong: Center of Asian Studies, 1977, p. 28; Gu Ye Lu: *50 Years in the Arts* (in Chinese), Beijing: Xuelin, 1989, pp. 104-105, 114-115; Yu Yehyan: *Talking About Li Lihua* (in Chinese), Taipei: Chuan Nan Dai, 1996, pp. 178-180 and Wong Cheuk-hon, op. cit., pp. 72-80.

17. See Leung, Grace L. K. and Chan, Joseph Man, "The Hong Kong Cinema and its Overseas Market: A Historical Review, 1950-1995" in *Fifty Years of Electric Shadows*, the 21st Hong Kong International Film Festival catalogue, Hong Kong: Urban Council, 1997, p. 137 and "Toho Page" in *International Screen* (in Chinese), starting with vol. 116, July 1965.

18. See Wen Guzhi, op. cit. and Butcher, J.C. & Dick, H.W., ed., op. cit.

19. See Lim Kay Tong, op. cit., pp. 113-114, 148; Loke Wan Tho papers, in the documents left by Loke are many clippings about Shaws, indicating that he paid lots of attention to Shaws' activities and Wong Cheuk-hon, op. cit., pp. 110-111.

20. See "Each Version of *Dream of the Red Chamber* Has its Merits" in *Spotlight* (in Chinese), vol. 1, April 1962, pp. 73-74.

21. See "The Truth Behind Shaws' Rush into *Love Eterne*" in *The Milky Way Pictorial* (in Chinese), vol. 57, December 1962, pp. 5-6 and Wong Cheuk-hon, op. cit., pp. 113-118.

22. See Interview with Meileen Choo, Hong Kong Film Archive Oral History Project, December 10, 2001, Singapore and Interview with Albert Odell.

23. See ibid.; Lim Kay Tong, op. cit., p. 85; Wong Cheuk-hon, op. cit., p. 112 and Sha Rong-feng: *Forty Springs of Cinema Glory: The Memoirs of Sha Rong-feng* (in Chinese), Taipei: Chinese Taipei Film Archive, 1994, pp. 31-37.

24. See Wong Cheuk-hon, op. cit., pp. 120-121; "The Contributions of Hong Kong-Made Mandarin Films" in *Thirty Years of Chinese Film* (in Chinese), Taipei: Self Published, 1980, p. 17 and "The Resurgence of MP & GI" in *Screenland* (in Chinese), vol. 38, November 1962, p. 12.

25. See "The Film Industry After Shaws and MP & GI Made Peace" in *The Milky Way Pictorial* (in Chinese), vol. 72, March 1964, p. 6.

26. See Wong Cheuk-hon, op. cit., pp. 118-123 and Sha Rongfeng, op. cit., pp. 31-32.

27. See "Heah Hock Meng and Wife Visits Hong Kong to Look After Business" in *International Screen* (in Chinese), vol. 120, November 1965, p. 48.

28. See Interview with Meileen Choo.

29. See Interview with Meileen Choo.

Editor's note

[1] International Film Distribution Agency was established in 1951 in Singapore. The Hong Kong branch, formed in 1953, has a slightly different name, International Films Distributing Agency. Throughout this book they are referred to as respectively "International Film" and "International Films".

國泰機構與香港電影

- 余慕雲 -

前言

國泰機構是星馬巨富陸運濤（有人估計他的財產有廿億美元）主理的眾多機構之一，它和香港電影有千絲萬縷關係，貢獻很大。本文試圖把國泰機構和香港電影的關係，作出比較全面的探討，可是由於我所掌握的有關資料不多，寫作這篇文章的時間又很短，因此它是膚淺的，更難免有錯誤的地方，這些地方請讀者指正。

國泰機構的建立

1936 年，陸運濤母親林淑佳女士在吉隆坡興建了第一間屬於陸氏家族的戲院——光藝。1939 年，其母在新加坡建成了一間命名「國泰」的新型戲院，它可説是國泰機構的開端，也為其獨子陸運濤日後的電影事業奠下了根基。四十年代開始，屬於後來國泰機構的物業先後建成（例如國泰大廈，是當年新加坡最高的建築物，內有國泰大酒店、國泰大飯店等），在此期間，國泰機構

The Cathay Organisation and Hong Kong Cinema

- Yu Mo-wan -

Cathay is one of several organisations masterminded by Singapore businessman Loke Wan Tho. It had made great contributions to Hong Kong cinema, though the relationship between Cathay and Hong Kong film was very complicated.

Establishment

In 1936, Lim Cheng Kim (Lin Shujia), Loke's mother, opened the Pavilion in Kuala Lumpur, thus starting the family's long ties with film. Three years later, Mrs Loke established Cathay Cinema in Singapore in what can be considered the unofficial beginning of the Cathay Organisation. In the 1940s, properties and business ventures that would later become part of Cathay were established, including real estate and deeper involvement in film distribution and exhibition.

Loke started collaborating with theatre owners in Singapore and Malaysia like Ho Ah Loke (He Yalu) in 1948 and formed such companies as International Theatres and Cathay Theatres.

又開始經營地產等多元化業務。它的業務發展得最快，成績最好的是戲院的創建、戲院的聯營、影片的放映和發行。

1948年，陸運濤和星馬個別有名的戲院商（例如何亞祿）合作，先後組成國際戲院有限公司、陸氏戲院有限公司、國泰戲院有限公司，它們當時在星馬各地擁有數十間新型戲院，放映和發行中外電影，業務發展得很好。

1951年，國際電影發行公司在新加坡成立，它是國泰機構比較重要的工作部門，行政上是獨立的。它的主要業務是代理香港（包括永華、大成）、美國、義大利等國家地區的電影公司的出品，在星馬及東南亞國家放映。

1953年，陸運濤和何亞祿在新加坡創辦國泰克里斯電影製片廠，它是一間專門出產馬來語（即巫語）影片的片廠，創業作《真假王子》（*Buluh Perindu / Bamboo of Yearning*，1953）是第一部馬來語彩色片。從此，國泰機構除放映和發行影片外，還開始了製片業務。

國際影片發行公司

1953年，國泰機構派英籍猶太人歐德爾到香港創立和主持國際影片發行公司（簡稱國際），這是國泰機構在香港創辦的第一個電影機構。國際在香港，除如常收購港產片給國泰機構發行外，更積極支持永華拍片。永華出品的《翠翠》（1953）、《金鳳》（1956）等影片，都是國際借錢給永華製作的。永華因為虧蝕過巨，周轉不靈，和片倉大火焚燬絕大部份影片的拷貝等原因，無力歸還向國際借來拍片的近百萬港元，再加上香港政府收回製片廠地皮，亦無力在新地皮上重建新廠，李祖永被迫在1955年把永華餘下的固定資產，用來償還國際的債務，亦即是説，永華被國際收購和接管了。

電懋眾星於1959年第六屆亞展中與國泰克里斯旗下眾星合照

A multi-cultural family: MP & GI stars pose with Cathay Keris stars at the 6th Asian Film Festival.

Together, they operated dozens of theatres, showing Mandarin, Cantonese, American and Japanese films to good business.

In 1951, International Film Distribution Agency, an important affiliate of Cathay, was formed in Singapore. Operating independently, it distributed films – from Hong Kong, US, Italy etc – in Southeast Asia. Later, the company also provided backing to the Hong Kong studio Yung Hwa, thus beginning Cathay's direct link to Hong Kong film.

In 1953, Loke and Ho formed Cathay Keris in Singapore to make Malay films, starting Cathay's involvement in production. Its debut, *Bamboo of Yearning* (*Buluh Perindu*, 1953), is the first Malay film in colour.

International Films

In 1953, Cathay officially landed in Hong Kong by dispatching Albert Odell to establish International Films Distributing Agency, stepping up its support of Yung Hwa's productions by financing films like *Singing under the Moon* (1953) and *Golden Phoenix* (1956). Yung Hwa was already in dire financial shape and was borrowing from International Films when it was hit with a warehouse fire, followed by the government's decision to reclaim the studio land. Unable to

1954年，國際開始在香港製作影片，由林永泰首先成立粵語片組，製作粵語片，創業作是《余之妻》（1955）。從1954到1964年，國際粵語片組共拍了近四十部粵語片，其中有叫好又叫座的《璇宮艷史》／《璇宮艷史續集》（1957，1958）、《苦心蓮》（上、下集，1960），它們的票房收入都創下空前的紀錄。其他出色的作品，還有《愛情三部曲》（1955）、《斷鴻零雁記》（1955）、《火》（1956）、《魂歸離恨天》（1957）、《黛綠年華》（1957）等，《自作多情》（1966）是它出品的最後一部粵語片。

在1955至1956年間，國際又製作過三部國語片，其中《春色惱人》（1956）獲得第六屆亞洲影展金爵獎，被台灣著名影評人黃仁評為中國名片一百部之一。

1955年末，國際支持名演員／導演嚴俊成立國泰電影製片公司，創業作是《菊子姑娘》（1956）。其後出品過《歡樂年年》（1956）等多部優秀影片，其中《亡魂谷》（1957）曾參加柏林影展並獲得好評。翌年，它又支持名演員白光，成立國光，創業作是《鮮牡丹》（1956）。

國泰機構的電影宣傳刊物《國際電影》於1952年在新加坡創刊，1955年10月改在香港出版，主編是朱旭華。它一共出版過321期，是香港有名的、長壽的電影雜誌之一。

電影懋業有限公司

電影懋業有限公司（簡稱電懋）是國泰機構在香港建立的第二個電影機構。它建立於1956年，由國際正式接收永華和新永華片場後擴充改組而成。它的董事長是陸運濤，總經理及主事人是鍾啟文。

國際創業作《余之妻》
My Wife, My Wife, International Films' debut feature.

rebuild a new studio on the land offered by the government and to repay its loans, it was forced in 1955 to hand over its assets to International. Odell would run the studio, which continued to produce films under the Yung Hwa banner.

Meanwhile, International Films had already started its own productions in 1954, under the Cantonese Film Unit run by Lam Wing-tai (Lin Yongtai), releasing in 1955 its first film, *My Wife, My Wife*. The division went on to become an important presence in Cantonese film. Between 1955 and 1964, it turned out 39 films, including the box office record-breaking hits *My Kingdom for a Husband* (aka *The Romance of Jade Hall*, 1957), its 1958 sequel *My Kingdom for a Honeymoon* (aka *The Romance of Jade Hall, Sequel*) and *Bitter Lotus, Parts I & II* (1960). Other works include *Three Stages of Love* (1955), *Fire* (1956), *The Tender Age* (aka *The Splendour of Youth*, 1957) and *I'll Make My Own Choice* (1966)

Between 1955 and 1956, International Films also

電懋的創業作是《金蓮花》（1957），女主角林黛憑此片獲亞洲影展最佳女主角獎，榮封亞洲影后。尤敏亦憑主演電懋出品的《玉女私情》（1959）及《家有喜事》（1959）而兩度封后。

從1956到1965年，電懋一共出產過一百多部國語片，其中包括榮獲第五屆亞洲影展最佳影片獎的《四千金》（1957）和第八屆亞展最佳紀錄片獎的《香港》。其他在亞展中獲獎的，還有得到金爵獎的《情場如戰場》（1957）、金鼎獎的《龍翔鳳舞》（1959）和《空中小姐》（1959）、金鑼獎的《玉女私情》等。

電懋的電影工作者，在亞展中得到最佳導演獎的有王天林（《家有喜事》）、最佳編劇獎的汪榴照（《家有喜事》）、最佳剪接獎的王朝曦（《玉女私情》和《深宮怨》／1964）、最佳美術設計獎的包天鳴（《玉樓春夢》／1970）、最佳音樂獎的姚敏（《龍翔鳳舞》）等。

電懋的出品在台灣金馬獎中得獎的有《星星．月亮．太陽》（1961，第一屆最佳劇情片獎，片中女主角尤敏同時獲得第一屆金馬影后的榮銜）。在金馬獎中獲得優秀劇情片獎的有《小兒女》（1963）、《深宮怨》（1964）和《蘇小妹》（1967）等。電影工作者獲獎的則有最佳編劇獎的秦亦孚（《星星．月亮．太陽》、《蘇小妹》），最佳攝影獎的何鹿影（《荷花》，1963），最佳音樂獎的周藍萍（《水上人家》，1968）等。

電懋其他叫好又叫座的影片還有《曼波女郎》（1957）、《南北和》（1961）、《雲裳艷后》（1959）、《姊妹花》（1959）、《我們的子女》（1959）、《無語問蒼天》（1961）、《西太后與珍妃》（1964）、《啼笑姻緣》（1964）、《聊齋誌異》（1965）等，其中《愛的教育》

made three Mandarin films; among them, *Gloomy Sunday* (1956), which won Best Picture at the 6th Asian Film Festival. Also in 1955, it backed actor-director Yan Jun to form Guotai Film Company, debuting with *Miss Kikuko* (1956), followed by several highly regarded films like *The Valley of the Lost Soul* (1957), which was shown in the Berlin International Film Festival. In 1956, International Films helped actress Bai Guang to form Guoguang, releasing *Fresh Peony* (1956).

Cathay also published a company magazine, *International Screen*, which was launched in Singapore in 1952 and moved to Hong Kong in 1955. With a total of 321 volumes, it's one of Hong Kong's longest running film magazines.

MP & GI

International Films was renamed MP & GI (Motion Picture and General Investment) in 1956. Loke remained Chairman, with Robert Chung (Zhong Qiwen) serving as general manager.

MP & GI concentrated on making Mandarin films, debuting with *Golden Lotus* (1957). Between 1956 and 1965, it released over one hundred films. The company was regarded for quality and many of its films and filmmakers won awards at the Asian Film Festival and Taiwan's Golden Horse Film Festival.

In 1960, it backed Zhu Xuhua to form Guofeng, making *Nobody's Child* (1960), which was shown at the San Francisco Film Festival and was the box office champ of Taiwan. It also supported director Qin Jian to form Guoyi in 1964, releasing *The Big Circus* (1964).

General manager Robert Chung resigned in 1962 after getting enmeshed in personnel problems; he was replaced by Assistant Manager Lam Wing-tai. It must be noted that Chung had made substantial

（1961）更在威尼斯影展中獲得好評。

1960年電懋支持朱旭華組成國風影片公司，出品的《苦兒流浪記》（1960）在舊金山電影節中獲得好評，並成為台灣的年度賣座冠軍。

1962年，電懋主事人鍾啟文因人事糾紛及另有高就等原因辭職，由原來的副總經理林永泰繼任。值得指出的是，鍾啟文是一個非常有才幹的人，電懋取得卓越成績，特別是自行製作彩色片方面，他的貢獻是巨大的。

1963年，名導演李翰祥脫離邵氏，在國泰機構的支持下，在台灣組織了國聯電影公司（有一說國聯是李翰祥和陸運濤二人合組的），國聯在台灣出品過不止一部的傑作（例如《冬暖》〔1969〕和《破曉時分》〔1968〕），也培養了不少傑出的電影工作者（例如甄珍、秦漢等），它對台灣電影事業有很大的貢獻和影響。如果沒有國泰和陸運濤對國聯在財力方面極大的支持，國聯不可能如此大張旗鼓地開展它的電影事業。無可否認，國聯所取得的成績，國泰和陸運濤功不可沒。

1964年，電懋曾支持名導演秦劍組成國藝影片公司，創業作是《大馬戲團》（1964）。

同年6月20日，國泰機構和電懋的董事長陸運濤，在台灣一次空難中喪生。陸的喪生是電懋的一個極大的損失，他熱中電影事業，不惜工本，不怕長期虧蝕（只有他才能有此財力和意志），決意把電懋的製片事業搞好，他的志向有如國泰機構當年的口號：攀登娛樂事業的最高峰！

電懋在香港電影史上，是一個很有成就的國語電影製片機構，在香港電影史上佔有一定的地位。

contributions to the company, especially in the area of colour productions.

In 1963, director Li Hanxiang left Shaw Brothers and, with the support of Cathay, formed Grand Motion Picture Company (Guolian) in Taiwan. (There had been talk that it was formed jointly by Li and Loke.) Grand played an important role in the history of Taiwan cinema, having made many important films - *At Dawn* (1967) and *The Winter* (1969), for example - and nurturing a large number of outstanding talents, such as Chen Chen (Zhen Zhen) and Chun Han (Qin Han).

On June 20, 1964, Loke, together with several company executives, was killed in a plane crash in Taiwan. It was a devastating blow to the company. Loke was dedicated to film and was willing to sink his business empire's funds into the company to reach his goal, which can be summed up by Cathay's slogan: "Climb to the top of entertainment business."

Cathay Organisation Hong Kong Ltd (COHL)

After Loke's death, MP & GI was renamed Cathay Organisation Hong Kong (1965) Ltd (COHL) in July 1965. It's the third company the organisation established in Hong Kong. Loke's brother-in-law Choo Kok Leong (Zhu Guoliang) took over as Chairman, and Paul Yui (Yu Puqing) was sent from Singapore to serve as General Manager, assisted by Yeo Ban Yee (Yang Manyi).

The company continued to produce Mandarin films and, with the departure of key personnel like director Yue Feng, scriptwriter Qin Yu and stars Linda Lin Dai and Lucilla You Min, some of them having left before Loke's death, devoted much effort into developing new talents. An actors workshop was formed and several new stars were discovered, such as Maggie Li Linlin, Charles Chin

國泰機構（香港）有限公司

國泰機構（香港）（1965）有限公司（簡稱國泰）是國泰機構（新加坡）在香港建立的第三間電影機構。它於1965年7月成立，由電懋改組而成，改組的主因是電懋董事長陸運濤的去世。國泰的董事長由陸運濤的妹夫朱國良接任，它的總經理和主事人由新加坡調來的俞普慶擔當，副總經理是楊曼怡。

陸運濤死後，國泰的人事有了很大的變動，不獨最高領導人有變，旗下的名導演、名編劇、名演員等，絕大部份都陸逐離開國泰，因此，網羅和培養人才是國泰新領導的首要工作。經過俞、楊的努力，特別是演員訓練班主任陳銅民等的努力，在短期內便培養出新的人才，尤其是演員（秦祥林、陳曼玲、李琳琳等），在名導演易文、王天林、楚原和國泰全體同人的共同努力下，用新人和低成本，亦製作了不少優秀的影片，在年產量上一度超越電懋時代。

國泰在製作上的第一次嘗試便是支持明星公司拍攝的《鎖麟囊》（1966）。從1965到1970年，國泰出產了接近一百部國語片，總體成績遠遠不如電懋，不過它有佳作，有如被杜雲之和黃仁評為中國名片一百部之一的《家有賢妻》（1970）和《路客與刀客》（1970）。其他名作還有《虎山行》（1969）、《玉樓春夢》（1970）、《我愛莎莎》（1970）、《雪路血路》（1970）等。

國泰的總經理俞普慶不幸在1970年6月病逝香港。俞病逝不久，協助他負責製片工作的楊曼怡亦離開國泰，另起爐灶，自組長江影片公司拍片。俞的逝世，楊的離開，令國泰沒有了製片的領導人而日益低沉。

1970年初，鄒文懷、何冠昌等人聯袂離開邵氏，他們在國泰的支持下，組成嘉禾電影公司。國泰機構的最高領導人，認為國泰既然缺乏領導製片的人才，他們又認

《愛情三部曲》
Three Stages of Love

定鄒文懷等人對製片工作，非常有實力有把握，肯定做得好，於是決定國泰從 1971 年開始完全停止製片工作，全力支持嘉禾製片。國泰不獨在財力上全力支持嘉禾（包括發行它的影片），而且連新永華片場以及它的服裝、道具等物資，都交給嘉禾使用和管理。新永華片場從此變成嘉禾片場。

嘉禾後來日益發展，成為香港最重要的電影公司之一。可以這樣說，如果嘉禾沒有國泰對它如此大力的支持，它很難會有今天的成就。

七十年代後的國泰機構

國泰自從 1971 年停止了在香港的製片業務後，亦宣告結束。不過新加坡國泰機構的電影業務仍繼續經營，它的業務已經退回到國際電影發行公司時代一樣，主要是收購及代理中外影片，發行給國泰機構屬下的戲院放映。

國泰機構是東南亞——特別是星馬——最大的電影發行商之一。它的特點是出價最高，購片最多，它的發行業績一向都很出色，有很高的票房：五十年代有《金鳳》、《龍翔鳳舞》，六十年代有《星星．月亮．太陽》、《西施》（1965，台灣出品），七十年代有《唐山大兄》（1971）、《精武門》（1972），《鬼馬雙星》（1974）和《半斤八兩》（1976），八十年代有《師弟出馬》（1980）、《少林寺》（1982）、《最佳拍攝大顯神通》（1983）和《奇謀妙計五福星》（1983）等，其中尤以李連杰主演的《少林寺》最為轟動，打破了國泰發行影片五十年來的最高票房紀錄。

國泰機構的電影部門，從1964到1984年，一直由朱國良主管。1985 年朱國良退休，國泰便由他的女兒朱美蓮繼承。朱小姐早在六十年代，已協助他的父親參與國泰機構電影發行的工作。

(Qin Xianglin) and Melinda Chen Manling, joined by director Chor Yuen (Chu Yuan). With new blood and a decision to lower budgets, Cathay managed to make some good films, at one point surpassing MP & GI in terms of production figure.

Cathay's first film endeavour was *The Lucky Purse* (1966), produced by Mingxing with the full support of Cathay. Since then, it had produced close to 100 Mandarin films between 1965 and 1970. Although the restructured company's accomplishment as a whole could not measure up to MP & GI, it did release some outstanding films, like *The Homemaker* (1970) and *From the Highway* (1970).

In early 1970, Raymond Chow and Leonard Ho left Shaw Brothers and, with Cathay support, formed Golden Harvest. Meanwhile Yui died in June, 1970 and shortly after his death, Yeo also left to form Changjiang. Thus, the top brass of Cathay decided in 1971 to halt productions and threw its support behind Golden Harvest, in the form of financial backing, distribution agreements and turning over the new Yung Hwa Studio – costumes, props and all – it had been operating since 1955, which was renamed Golden Harvest Studio. Golden Harvest would go on to become one of the most important companies in Hong Kong film history and it can be safe to say that without Cathay, it would likely not enjoy such success.

Cathay in the 1970s and Beyond

After stopping production, Cathay also ended its operation in Hong Kong, running its film business out of its Singapore headquarters, concentrating on distributing films for exhibition in its theatres.

Cathay is one of the biggest distributors in Southeast Asia, counting in its rosters an impressive list of box office hits. They include

1984年，由於馬來西亞規定所有大企業，必須有馬來西亞人擁有股份和在領導權中佔優，為了保持國泰和馬來西亞人的良好合作關係，國泰機構把名下所有馬來西亞戲院都售給馬來政府經營的一個影業機構（BFO公司）；新加坡國泰機構的電影院，則仍由國泰擁有。

從1985年至今，國泰機構的電影部門仍然由朱美蓮主管。二年前，她把它上了市，完成了當年陸運濤希望它能夠上市的願望。亦在此時開始，朱小姐在行政領導上已退居幕後。現在國泰機構的電影部門，已由他人領導。

後記

如此所述，從五十年代開始，國泰機構已經收購港產片在東南亞發行，而且支持永華、國泰（嚴俊創辦的電影公司）、國聯、嘉禾等公司拍片。它又在香港創辦了國際、電懋、國泰機構（香港）（1965）有限公司，共製作了接近三百部影片，而且有不少傑出的作品，得了不少獎，也創造過不少賣座紀錄。國泰機構對香港電影事業，作出過極大的貢獻。

本文對國泰機構和香港電影的關係，它對香港電影的貢獻，敘述得過於簡單，希望我有機會，或者另有高明，把它敘述得更全面，更深入，更有歷史價值和參考價值。

余慕雲，資深香港電影史研究者，前任香港電影資料館研究主任，著有《香港電影史話》（卷一至五，次文化堂，1996-2001）。
Yu Mo-wan, writer and Hong Kong film historian, former research officer at Hong Kong Film Archive. Recently published *Hong Kong Film History* (vol 1-5, Subculture, 1996-2001).

Golden Phoenix and *Calendar Girl* (1958) in the 1950s, *Sun, Moon and Star* (1962) and *Hsi Shih Beauty of Beauties* (1965, made in Taiwan) in the 1960s, *The Big Boss* (1971) and *The Private Eyes* (1976) in the 1970s, and *Young Master* (1980), *The Shaolin Temple* (1982, which established the best box office receipt in Cathay's 50 year history) and *Winners and Sinners* (1983) in the 1980s.

In 1984, upon the passing of laws in Malaysia requiring Malaysians to have majority shares and control power in all major business, Cathay sold its theatres in Malaysia to the state run BFO, putting an end to a long-running era.

Choo Kok Leong ran Cathay until he retired in 1985, handing over the business to his daughter Meileen Choo (Zhu Meilian), who had been learning the ropes by her father's side since her teenage years. In 2000, Cathay became a public company, a dream that Loke had wished to eventually realize, ending the era of family-run Cathay.

The Cathay Organization had been closely related to Hong Kong cinema since the 1950s. Throughout the years, its many ventures had produced an impressive list of almost 300 films, some of them record breakers and many of them award winners. It had contributed greatly to Hong Kong film.

Translated by Sam Ho

港星雙城記：國泰電影試論

- 傅葆石 -

1950年代是香港國語電影業動盪不穩、呈現劇變的時期。國語電影工業本來由組織鬆散的小公司拍攝小成本製作，發行渠道不多，但是在這個年代裡出現了轉捩點，急劇發展至由組織龐大的資本主義企業，作具有全球視野的大量生產。出現這個轉變，與以新加坡為基地的亞洲娛樂業巨子國泰機構進軍香港電影業有莫大關係。同時，國語片的轉型其實反映了戰後香港在經濟上和文化上的重大變遷。另外，要了解香港電影在六十年代至七十年代初，何以會出現了像一位社會學家所謂「國語化」的情況[1]（即市場由國泰在香港電影業中的死對頭邵氏兄弟公司主導），也必須認識國語片在五十年代的轉變。然而，這個重要時期卻一直為評論界忽略。本文旨在補充這方面的不足，探討1950至1960年間，在香港轉變中的社會和文化環境下，國語片如何發展；特別着重勾畫國泰的跨國娛樂網絡（及其在香港的製作分支）在過程中起着甚麼重大影響。

Hong Kong and Singapore: A History of the Cathay Cinema

- Poshek Fu -

The 1950s was a period of turmoil, uncertainty, and tremendous changes in the Mandarin cinema of Hong Kong. It marked a transition point in which the industry developed haphazardly from a loosely organised business of small-budget productions with limited outlets to a highly structured capitalist organisation of mass production and global vision. This development was markedly shaped by the entry of a Singapore-based Asian entertainment giant, the Cathay Organisation, into Hong Kong film business. The transformation of Mandarin cinema therefore reflected the enormous economic changes and cultural shifts in post-war Hong Kong. And to the extent that Hong Kong cinema in the 1960s and early 1970s was marked by what a sociologist has called "Mandarisation"[1] (that is the domination of the Shaw Brothers Studio, Cathay's arch-rival, in Hong Kong film industry), it is imperative to understand the changes of Mandarin cinema in the 1950s. Yet this important period has attracted little critical attention. My essay aims to address this imbalance by exploring the development of Mandarin cinema in the changing social and cultural contexts of Hong Kong between

一

在五十年代，不斷有人從中國內地遷徙來港。這源於四十年代的國共內戰，及中國共產黨 1949 年取得政權後，以至在五十年代推行多次群眾運動—由「土改」、「反右」以至「大躍進」—令全國陷入混亂苦困之中，赤貧和饑荒隨處可見，具有「資產階級」或「反動」背景的人成為「人民公敵」，遭公開批鬥，在社會上備受歧視。這種動盪環境促使不少人逃難來港。香港這位於珠江三角洲的英國殖民地，自二十世紀初已是華南最重要的轉口港，加上有西式司法制度和政治文化，成為了想改變生活的中國人（追求自由或財富，或兩者兼得）的避難所（一如 1945 年前的上海外國租界）。[2]

根據資料顯示，由1945至1949年共有120萬中國人跨越邊界來港。令香港人口從1945年（日治時期結束後）的60萬，到1951年升至200萬以上。[3] 移民在五十年代持續湧入，1960 至 1961 年人口已劇增至超逾 300 萬。大部份當時的新移民都不名一文，但是也有一些是富裕、有學識、具國際視野的，他們帶着金錢（像船王包玉剛和董浩雲、紡織世家唐氏家族等商人）或文化（像作家劉以鬯和哲學家唐君毅等學者、藝術家）南來香港。不過，無論是貧是富，目不識丁還是學富五車，這些移民都對推動香港工業化和現代化，在勞動力、知識技能或資金上作出了貢獻。

為了打擊共產主義勢力在全球擴張，美國於 1949 年後對中國內地實施貿易禁運，令香港經濟蒙受沉重打擊，不能再將經濟活動繫於轉口貿易，必須另謀出路。就在這個歷史轉折時機，新移民帶來的廉價勞動力和企業領導技能在殖民地政府的自由放任政策鼓勵下，推動了香港的經濟結構和商業文化轉型。這個過程快速暢順，到了五十年代中期，殖民地政府已可自詡，香港已從以轉

現代化的漫漫長路？
——《星星・月亮・太陽》
The long, rough road ahead:
Sun, Moon and Star.

1950 and 1960. It is my aim in particular to delineate the shaping role the transnational entertainment network of Cathay (and its production arm in Hong Kong) occupied in this development.

I

Hong Kong in the 1950s saw a continuous influx of migrants from the Chinese mainland. The Civil War in China and the subsequent Communist takeover in 1949, which began a series of mass campaigns in the 1950s from the Land Reform to the Anti-Rightist campaign and Great Leap Forward, brought massive suffering and dislocations to the country. Poverty and starvation prevailed while people with "bourgeois" or "reactionary" backgrounds became "enemies of the people", publicly humiliated and socially stigmatised. The turmoil forced many to find safety in Hong Kong. As a British colony situated across the Pearl River from Guangdong, Hong Kong had since the turn of the century been the premier entreport to South China as well as, with its Western-style legal system and political culture, a major refuge (like that of the foreign concessions in Shanghai before 1945) for Chinese who sought a different life (to be free or rich or both). [2]

According to published figures, between 1945 and 1949 about 1.2 million Chinese moved across the southern border, increasing the population of Hong Kong from 600,000 in 1945 (when the city was liberated from the Japanese occupation) to over two million in 1951. [3] The massive influx of migrants continued throughout the 50s until the total population jumped to over 3 million in 1960-1961. Most of these "newcomers", as they were called at the time, were poor and destitute, but some were from privileged, cosmopolitan backgrounds. The latter fled to the colony with money (businessmen such as shipping magnates Y. K. Pao and C.Y. Tung, the prominent textile family of Tang) or culture (artists and scholars such as writer Liu Yichang and philosopher Tang Junyi). Whether poor or rich, illiterate or well-educated, all of them contributed their labour, talents or capital to push Hong Kong toward industrialisation and modernity.

In fact, in its crusade against international communism, the US imposed an embargo on the mainland after 1949, which caused enormous damage to the Hong Kong economy. The colony could no

口貿易為主的社會，「迅即成為工業城市」。帶動工業化的主要是紡織業，其次是航運業，兩者都由新近從上海移居香港的企業家主導。[4]

除了擁有優良的港口設施和易於接觸世界各地市場外，香港能迅速工業化，主要得力於剝削廉價勞工。五十年代香港工廠的工作環境，即使與其他亞太發展中地區（例如南韓和印度）相比，也顯得十分惡劣。根據一項資料，當時所有亞洲地區之中，只有香港的紡織工人要每周工作七天；而女工更要每更工作二十小時，才賺取到最微薄的工資。這種剝削在政府極少干預的政策推波助瀾之下，令社會變得極不公平，很多人一貧如洗，朝不保夕。雖然有一小撮富人仍可過着近乎紙醉金迷、十里洋場的舊上海那種豪奢生活，大多數人卻要住在沒有電力供應和衛生設施的木屋或寮屋內，隨時會遇上祝融肆虐。事實上，在五十年代初香港出現過多次重大火災，包括令數以萬計居民喪生的石硤尾大火，逼使殖民地政府要推行規模不大的徙置計劃。那種稱為「徙置區」的房屋，套用一位殖民地官員的說法，是一個「平均每人只有 24 平方呎的三合土盒子，七層高，沒有升降機，沒有玻璃窗，只有木蓋板，沒有獨立水喉，只可多戶共用廚房和浴室。這聽來很可怖，事實上也的確如此，不過市民卻拚命爭取入住這種新房屋，因為那是你合法擁有的單位，而且不會燒毀。」到五十年代末期，約有 20 萬人住在徙置區。[5]

五十年代的香港，更是亞洲冷戰三大政治勢力——中國、台灣和美國——進行間諜活動和政治宣傳的中心。基於全球圍堵共產主義的政策，當時華府支持蔣介石的流亡政府。三股勢力在港均有代理機構，籌辦和資助各種蒐集情報、群眾宣傳和政治煽動的活動和組織，目標在於醜化進而摧毀敵方。譬如說，北京及台灣政權均在

longer build its economic activities around entreport trade. To survive, Hong Kong had to change its economic practices. It was at this historical juncture that, encouraged by the colonial government's laissez-faire policy, the cheap labour and entrepreneurial leadership provided by the recent migrants propelled the transformation of the economic structure and business culture of Hong Kong. The transformation was so swift and effective that by the middle of the 1950s the colonial government could boast of: "the rapid emergence of Hong Kong as an industrial producer" from a entrepot economy. Leading the way in this industrialisation were the textile and, to some extent, shipping sectors which were dominated by entrepreneurs who recently arrived from Shanghai. [4]

Aside from Hong Kong's excellent port facilities and easy access to the world market, the rapid industrialisation was fuelled largely by exploitation of cheap labour. The working condition of Hong Kong factories in the 1950s were appalling, even in comparison with those of other developing countries in Asia-Pacific (e.g., South Korea and India). According to one source, among all Asian countries only Hong Kong textile workers had to work seven days a week. And women workers worked twenty hours each shift for minimal wages. This exploitation, exacerbated by the colonial government's policy of limited intervention, bred glaring social inequalities.

Poverty and economic insecurity prevailed in the colony. While a few riches lived a life of luxury and glamour reminiscent of the grand, cosmopolitan lifestyle of old Shanghai, most people lived in wooden huts and "squatters", a euphemism for slums, without electricity or sanitary facilities, and susceptible to fire. In fact, several disastrous fires in the early 1950s, including one in Shek Kip Mei, which had cost tens of thousands of lives, forced the colonial government to launch a limited resettlement programme. The resettlement houses, in the words of a colonial official, provided a "concrete box allowing 24 square feet a head, in a seven-storey structure with no [elevator], no windows but wooden shutters, no water but access to communal kitchens and bathrooms. If this sounds dreadful, it was, but such was the alternative that people fought to get into the new blocks where you

香港開設了大量傳媒機構、百貨公司、娛樂場所，以及成立地區組織，致力爭取群眾認同其政權的正統地位，以及鼓勵敵方陣營的成員叛變投誠（因此，從共產陣營投奔國民黨政府的人，就會獲右派傳媒譽為「反共義士」）；而美國則資助學術機構和文化刊物，以圖操控輿論。[6]處身於政治兩極衝突的夾縫之中，加上社會上充斥隨着工業化而來的不滿情緒，香港在五十年代曾出現多次騷動，大部分由右派分子挑動。正是在各股政治、社會力量糾纏的漩渦中，香港的國語片奮力適應了這個由移民潮、現代化、冷戰政治塑造的歷史新局面。

二

五十年代香港的國語電影業，主要是解放前上海非左翼製作傳統的延續。業內所有主腦都來自上海，其中像邵氏的邵邨人早在三十年代中期已於香港拍片，不過大部分卻是1945年後因內地政局動盪才來港。例如，有「中國影戲大王」之譽的張善琨由於在日本佔領上海時期有「投敵附逆」之嫌，決定流亡南下；而企業家李祖永則在1949年因逃避共產統治而來。兩人於1947年合組「永華影業公司」，用李的雄厚資金建立了一個龐大而設備齊全的製片廠，並簽下數百名從上海來港的導演和演員。永華最早期的出品——卜萬蒼的《國魂》（1948）和朱石麟的《清宮秘史》（1948），都是古裝大製作，叫好又叫座。不過，1949年中國解放後，香港與內地之間的貿易中斷，令香港國語片無法發行至賴以生存的內地市場。事實上，所有遷徙來港的電影工作者，都只視香港為安全而方便的製作基地，他們的電影是拍給內地（尤其是上海）觀眾看的。所有電影公司都因市場變化而面臨困境，永華所受的打擊尤其沉重，因為公司財政管理混亂，營運成本又高。[7]永華財政陷於崩潰，李祖永變得更加獨斷獨行——張善琨和多位紅星

own your place legally, and it would not burn down." By the late 1950s, about 200,000 people lived in these resettlement houses.[5]

Hong Kong in the 1950s was also a center for espionage and propaganda for the three powers - Beijing, Taiwan, and Washington D.C. – involved in the Cold War in Asia. Washington supported Chiang Kai-shek's exiled government as part of its strategy of global containment. All three powers had agencies in Hong Kong to organise and fund activities and groups in relation to intelligence collection, mass propaganda, and political agitation. Their aims were to demonise and ultimately destroy the Other. For example, both Beijing and Taiwan operated chains of mass media, department stores, entertainment venues, and local organisations whose main purposes were to build support for their respective claims of legitimacy and to plot and encourage defection from the enemy. (Thus new converts to the Nationalist cause were hailed in the pro-Taiwan press as "anti-Communist loyalists", or *fangong yishi*, while the US funded academic institution and cultural publications in an effort to shape public opinion.[6] Being thrown into the middle of the Cold War politics of binary conflicts, and feeding on the massive social discontent accompanied with the industrialisation process, the colony went through a series of riots during the 1950s, mostly instigated by pro-Nationalist supporters. And it was in this vortex of intertwining political and social forces that Mandarin cinema in Hong Kong struggled to adapt to a new historical situation marked by displacement, modernisation, and Cold War politics.

2

The Hong Kong Mandarin cinema of the 1950s was mainly a continuation of the non-left-wing filmmaking tradition of Republican Shanghai. All the leaders of the industry were migrants from Shanghai. Some of them, like Runde Shaw (Shao Cunren) of the Shaws Studio, began to make films in Hong Kong during the mid-1930s, but most came as a result of the political turmoil on the mainland after 1945. The "King of Chinese Cinema" Zhang Shankun, for example, was exiled to the colony because of his ambiguous involvement with the Japanese in occupied Shanghai, while Li Zuyong, a successful entrepreneur, left Shanghai to escape from Communism after 1949.

被逼離開。公司在東南亞發行商國泰機構和國民黨政府的財政支持下，再苦苦支撐了好幾年（詳見下文）。

包括永華在內，五十年代初香港共有三十三家國語片製作公司。其中大部分都是小公司，財力薄弱，沒有本身的製作隊伍，要找到投資者撥出資金和發行商對題材感興趣，才可以開拍電影。不過，在惡劣的經營環境中，這種靈活性卻讓這批公司比永華更易於生存。在失去內地市場後，電影業（除了長城等少數左派電影公司）開始將市場重心轉至台灣和東南亞的華僑社群，同時也試圖增加在香港的市場佔有率。

可是這些地區的國語片熱潮只是曇花一現，市道迅即惡化。到1955年，慘淡不安的氣氛瀰漫着國語電影業。在同年一次圓桌會議上，主要的製片家警告，要是沒有新方法阻止「市場進一步收縮」，這個行業將會崩潰。當時片商無法賣片到新加坡和馬來亞（現稱馬來西亞）以外的東南亞地區，因為當地政治動盪，經濟也出現危機。而在新、馬兩地，國語片又要與流行的荷里活電影、各種方言片（粵語、潮語、廈門語），以至配上國語的外語片（例如法國、意大利和日本的）競爭。另一方面，香港的電影檔期又遭粵語片和大受中產階級歡迎的荷里活製作壟斷。事實上，在1950至1955年，有超過一百二十部國語片拍攝完畢卻無法排期上映。[8]

眾多市場中，台灣的情況最令人失望，所有電影人都對當地政府反共理念背後那套使人費解的思維感到氣餒。理論上，台灣的基本政策是協助所有國語電影工作者——除了與受北京資助的左派影片公司有關的。按照當時的說法，他們是「自由影人」，矢志在香港（和海外）推廣國民黨政府的理念。台灣政府會給予津貼，以及准許影片進入膨脹中的台灣市場，以換取影人的政治忠誠和參與政治宣傳——例如到台灣作勞軍表演，以及推動

Zhang and Li teamed up to form in 1947 Yung Hwa Motion Picture Industries Ltd. With Li's capital, the company built a large, well-equipped studio and signed up hundreds of directors and actors who had just moved to Hong Kong from Shanghai. Its debut films, Bu Wancang's *The Soul of the China* (1948) and Zhu Shilin's *Sorrows of the Forbidden City* (1948), both huge-budget costume dramas, won both critical acclaim and box office success. Yet, the Communist victory in 1949 and the consequent US trade embargo between Hong Kong and the Mainland meant the close of the China market which was vital to the survival of the colony's Mandarin cinema industry. In fact, to all the migrant filmmakers Hong Kong was only a safe and convenient production site; their films had been produced for the mainland (particularly Shanghai) audience. While all film companies were dealt a serious blow by the market change, Yung Hwa was particularly hard hit because of its poor finance management and huge operation costs.[7] It tumbled and Li became more authoritarian. "Zhang was forced out and so were many major stars. Yung Hwa survived for a few years thanks to financial backing by the Southeast Asian distributor, the Cathay Organisation and the Nationalist government (more later).

Yung Hwa was one of 33 Mandarin film studios in Hong Kong in the early 1950s. Most of them were small and without their own production crews. Their financing was weak, only starting a project when they acquired funding from investors and found distributors interested in its market potential. Yet this flexibility enabled them to survive better than Yung Hwa in the worsening business condition. After the loss of the China market, the film industry (except "leftist" studios, like Great Wall, that were connected to Beijing) began to shift its focus to Taiwan and to the Chinese diasporic community in Southeast Asia while trying to increase market shares in Hong Kong.

But after an initial boom, market conditions quickly deteriorated. By 1955 the Mandarin film industry was permeated by a sense of gloom. In a roundtable discussion that year leading filmmakers warned that the industry would collapse unless there were new ways to prevent the "increasing contraction of market". Because of political and economic troubles, they could no longer sell to Southeast Asia except

左派影人投向台灣陣營。不過，這個政策卻隨着冷戰政局而轉變。例如，《秋瑾》（1953）和《半下流社會》（1957）等「自由」電影，雖然曾憑藉技巧地宣揚反共和親台的意識，獲得國民黨陣營頒予獎項，但是卻連同其他六十部國語片在1956年遭禁映，原因是影片有「左派」影人參與製作（雖然有影評人指出，其實這些影人在完成遭禁的電影之後很久才告「變節」）。[9]此外，在1955年，台灣又提高國語片的進口稅百分之二十，以懲罰它們對反共運動「缺乏貢獻」。不過，正如一位作者指出：「自由」影人已盡力在不冒犯（香港和東南亞的）電檢尺度下，宣揚支持台灣國民黨的理念，加稅這種懲罰只會摧毀國語電影業，反而令支持者投向共產陣營。[10]

發行渠道少，自然吸引不到多少投資者；投資金額小，又導致產量減少，水準下跌。據製片商胡晉康所說，在1951至1955年間，每部電影的平均利潤減少近半，製作預算也由30萬港元降至12萬元；產量方面，1955年比1953年少了三分一。[11]到1955年，倒閉和失業已成為國語電影業的普遍現象，令整個行業都憂心忡忡，如臨末日。在這個衰落期中，國泰機構計劃將製作業務和發行網絡擴展至香港，着實為國語電影業帶來了前景美好的希望。[12]

三

國泰機構1947年於新加坡創立，在亞洲和歐洲很多人心目中，國泰的歷史差不多等同其創辦人陸運濤的個人魅力。他是獨子，父親是中國出生的馬來亞億萬富翁陸佑，母親是陸佑的四太太，生意頭腦精明。陸運濤中學開始在西方（瑞士和英國）受教育，外表洋派而現代化，在公開場合，他總像英國紳士般，穿着一絲不苟，溫文有禮，不斷跟世界各地的紳商名流打交道。性格

Singapore and Malaya (now Malaysia), where they had to compete with popular Hollywood films, various dialect films (i.e. Cantonese, Chaozhou, and Amoyese), and a host of foreign-language films (e.g., French, Italian, and Japanese) dubbed in Mandarin. At the same time, screen times in Hong Kong were dominated by Cantonese productions and Hollywood imports, which were immensely popular with the middle class. In fact, over 120 Mandarin films produced between 1950 and 1955 were still in backlog, waiting to be distributed.[8]

Taiwan was however the most disappointing; its intricate politics of anti-communism frustrated everyone in the industry. In theory, it was Taiwan's policy to help and support Mandarin filmmakers not affiliated with "leftist" studios. In the parlance of the time, they were "Freedom filmmakers" (*ziyou yingren*), dedicating to promote the Nationalist cause in Hong Kong and overseas. The supports included subsidies and access to the growing Taiwan market in exchange for the filmmakers' political loyalty and propaganda efforts such as organising troupes to entertain troops in Taiwan and inciting defection of filmmakers from the leftist circle. But the policy was subjected to the contingencies of Cold War politics. For example, while a few "Freedom" films such as *Qiu Jin, the Revolutionary Heroine* (1953) and *Half Way Down* (*1957*) won awards from the Nationalist regime for skilfully projecting anti-communism and pro-Taiwan nationalism, they were later banned along with 60 other Mandarin pictures in 1956 because "leftist" filmmakers were involved in their production (although critics claimed that many of them "defected" to the left long after completing the films).[9] Similarly, in 1955 Taiwan raised import duties for Mandarin films by twenty percent as a punishment for their "lack of contributions" to the anti-communist crusade. But as one writer remarked: "Freedom filmmakers" had done their best to help "promoting pro-Taiwan nationalism" without offending censorship (in both Hong Kong and Southeast Asia), these punishments would only "destroy the Mandarin cinema ," thereby pushing more sympathizers to "defect to the Communist cause."[10]

Limited outlets attracted few investors; and small investments resulted in a decrease in productions and lower standards of production. According to producer

上，他卻像學者多於像生意人，喜歡探索意念，追求真理，不會經常將利潤、交易放在心上。事實上，陸運濤選擇事業也經過細心思量。雖然他知道自己「註定」要繼承業務繁多的家族生意，卻還是選擇在劍橋攻讀本身真正喜愛的歷史和文學。他回到新加坡後，決定將事業集中於電影生意。我相信，這決定的部分原因是協調個人興趣與家庭責任的衝突，另外也是為了避開父親成就帶來的陰影。陸運濤沒有簡單的接管家族生意，也同時在這基礎上選擇獨創新事業——作為現代娛樂的電影。他深信這門事業既可證明自己的「企業精神」，也可令東南亞的生活文化更趨現代化。[13]

創新和現代正是陸運濤發展電影業的兩個主要理念。他在家族經營了兩家電影院的基礎上，創立了國泰機構，使命是在新加坡和馬來亞建立電影放映王國。他這樣解釋自己的夢想：「我對影業的如此費盡心力，原不過是個人對於這種事業具有濃厚的興趣，而在我本人的理想中，最終的目的，是要為東南亞的每一個角落的每一個人，帶來歡樂。」[14] 但是要實現將東南亞的生活文化現代化的夢想，卻絕不容易，因為在五十年代，非殖民化運動席捲整個地區，政治、經濟動盪隨之而來。而且，要在東南亞建立電影放映王國，不啻是直接跟邵氏兄弟競爭。邵仁枚、邵逸夫兩人眼光、魄力、人脈關係和營商技巧均極出色，自三十年代起已雄霸東南亞電影放映業。邵氏在區內有超過一百家戲院，要挑戰他們的領導地位，財力、毅力、創造力缺一不可。而陸運濤擴展其放映網絡時，不單部署精心，步伐也迅速。由1948至1955年，國泰機構的戲院數目增至逾四十間；兩年後，再增加十一家。1957年，陸運濤宣佈會在三年內，投資1,000萬元叻幣再興建六家電影院，令國泰旗下的影院總數超越六十。這急劇擴張的步伐在六十年代初仍持續。

Hu Jinkang, while profits from each film dropped almost half between 1951 and 1955, production budget per film decreased from HK$300,000 in 1951 to $120,000 in 1955. Similarly, there were one third fewer films produced in 1955 than in 1953.[11] By 1955, a sense of doom and anxiety prevailed in the Mandarin cinema industry, which was experiencing widespread business failures and massive unemployment. In the midst of this "depression", the plan of the Cathay Organisation to expand its film production and distribution circuit in Hong Kong brought hope for a "better future" for Mandarin filmmaking.[12]

3

The Cathay Organisation was founded in 1947 in Singapore, and its history was synonymous in the minds of many in Asia and Europe with the charm and charisma of its founder, Dato Loke Wan Tho (1915-1964). The only son of the fourth (and most business-minded) wife of the Chinese-born Malayan billionaire Loke Yew, Loke received his post-primary education in the West (Switzerland and England), affecting a Westernised, highly cosmopolitan outlook. In public at least, he always appeared a British gentleman, immaculately dressed and graciously mannered in his constant socialising with the rich and famous. Loke was by temperament more a scholar in love with the world of ideas and truth than a businessman obsessed with deals and profits. In fact, choosing his career had been an agonizing decision. Despite his awareness that he was "destined" to be a businessman taking charge of the sprawling family business, he chose to pursue his true passions, history and literature, at Cambridge. When he later returned to Singapore, he decided to focus his career on the film business. This decision, I believe, was sparked in part by his effort to harmonize the conflicts between his personal interests and family obligation and in part by his desire to escape from his famous father's tall shadow. Rather than taking over the family business, Loke sought also to build a *new* venture around the *modern* entertainment of motion pictures which he believed would both prove his "entrepreneurial spirit" and modernise the everyday culture of Southeast Asia.[13]

Indeed new and modern were the major themes of Loke's approach. On the basis of two movie houses

陸運濤不單迅速果敢地在新加坡、馬來亞、汶萊和北婆羅洲拓展放映網絡，新建成的影院更是東南亞(以至東亞)最為現代化和堂皇的。為了與「全球的現代化電影院」看齊，讓觀眾可以在「最好的氣氛下徹底鬆弛享受」，陸運濤旗下的戲院全都建築設計優美，技術和設施新穎，有空調設備，裝置最先進的音響和放映系統（例如Cinemascope闊銀幕），佈置同樣豪華，有從歐美進口的座椅和地氈。他最喜歡的其中一家戲院——有1,557個座位的新加坡奧迪安，正好顯示了他何等欣賞西方的新生事物：地下一層有兩個大型停車場；「全球最佳」的約克牌空調機；東南亞第一部GB-Kele放映機；以及設置了「最新穎先進」設備的豪華觀眾席。戲院更設有專供有聽力障礙的觀眾使用的特製耳筒，以及一家由陸運濤親自設計、有「最時尚裝修」的荷里活式咖啡座。[15]

據《國泰：電影五十五年》的作者林繼堂說，為了供應電影予旗下急劇膨脹的網絡放映，國泰除了增強其發行分支國際電影發行公司（供應十四種語言的電影予國泰所有戲院，以及東南亞其他二百家獨立戲院）的實力外，在1955至1956年開始考慮自行製作。[16] 1955年，香港最大的「自由電影」製片公司永華雖獲得國泰和台灣貸出大量款項，仍面臨破產的危機，結果陸運濤接管永華，並且投入資金改進公司設備，又簽下更多影人。1956年3月，永華正式為電影懋業(電懋)取代，成為國泰的華語電影製作分支，由曾在永華當行政人員、到過荷里活學習拍攝彩色電影的鍾啟文出任公司主管。電懋宣佈在1956至1957年會拍攝四十至五十部電影。以當時國語電影業正面對危機，製作技術又差劣看來，這無疑是極具野心（較悲觀的人更會視為不智）的計劃。[17]

1959年的國泰戲院
The Cathay Cinema in 1959.

operated by his family, Loke founded the Cathay Organisation whose mission was to build a film exhibition empire in Singapore and Malaya. As he explained his dream: "I dedicate myself entirely to the film business not only because I have a strong personal interest in it, but because, ultimately, I want to bring pleasures (that is, modern, sophisticated entertainment) to every person in Southeast Asia..."[14] To pursue his dream of modernising the everyday life of Southeast Asia was however a formidable challenge because of the decolonialisation movement and the accompanying political and economic turmoil that swept through the region in the 1950s. Also, to build a film exhibition empire in Southeast Asia was to compete directly with the Shaw brothers, Runme and Run Run, whose vision, energy, personal network, and entrepreneurial skills had enabled them to reign over the Southeast Asian exhibition industry since the 1930s. The Shaws owned a chain of over one hundred cinemas across the region, so to challenge their dominance required money, determination, and creativeness. In fact, Loke set out to expand his exhibition circuit both quickly and strategically.

Between 1948 and 1955, Cathay expanded its cinema chain to over 40 theatres, and two years later, eleven more were added. In 1957, Loke announced he would invest Strait currency $10 million in building six more new venues in three years, increasing the Organisation's cinemas to a total of over 1960. And the rapid expansion continued in the early 1960s.

Loke not only expanded his exhibition circuit in Singapore, Malaya, Brunei and N. Borneo quickly and determinedly, he also made his new cinemas the most modern and opulent in Southeast Asia (and East Asia as well). In order to be on par with all "modern cinemas of the world" and to enable the audience to "have the best atmosphere in which to relax completely", all his movie palaces were sleek in architectural design and modern in technology and amenities. They were fully air-conditioned, generously equipped with the most advanced Western-made acoustic and visual technology (e.g., Cinemascope), and lushly decorated with chairs and carpets imported from USA or Europe. The 1557-seat Singapore Odeon, one of Loke's favourite cinemas, demonstrated his aspiration for Western-style modernity: It boasted two

不過，在1957年電懋卻成為了首家在亞洲影展贏得大獎的香港電影公司（林黛憑《金蓮花》獲得「最佳女主角」獎）。翌年，電懋在第五屆亞洲影展更差不多囊括所有大獎，其中包括「最佳電影」（陶秦的《四千金》，1957）。公司其後拍了很多大受歡迎的作品，例如唐煌的愛情喜劇《長腿姐姐》（1960）、易文的史詩式作品《星星・月亮・太陽》（1961）和王天林的喜劇《南北和》（1961）。這些成就獲得業內一致好評，有些評論者甚至稱譽陸運濤的製作大計是令國語電影復興的催化劑。不過，國泰成功進軍製作業務，也令它與邵氏的競爭更形激烈。1957年，邵逸夫來港，宣佈會投資數百萬元，建立一個設施齊全的電影城，邁進「彩色電影紀元」（跟電懋的黑白製作、簡陋的片廠形成強烈對比），務求將華語電影現代化和全球化。因此可以說，國泰在香港擴展製作業務的計劃，以及因擴展而引發的電懋、邵氏敵對競爭的白熱化，為國語電影業帶來了資金、活力和魅力，結果，國語片得以在接着的二十年主導香港的娛樂事業。

學者和評論家往往將電懋早期的成就歸功於鍾啟文的眼光和才能；而在他1962年辭職後，國泰在香港便直走下坡。這看法未免流於表面化。鍾啟文無疑是能幹的製片家，對國語電影業運作有實際認識，又能與陸運濤維持和諧的關係。比方說，他說服了陸運濤將每年拍片數量由四五十部減至十二至十四部。[18]他又能招攬到業內最具創意的人才，包括編劇家孫晉三和製片家／編劇宋淇等，他們都為電懋作品帶來優雅風格和現代氣味。不過，鍾啟文似乎欠缺財政管理技巧。據國泰的總會計師連福明說，電懋雖有一些賣座作品，但是在經營上卻從未能站得住腳，公司能維持全賴陸運濤以家族生意賺到的金錢注資。到1963年，電懋已虧損了共達600萬港

（右起）歐德爾、陸運濤、朱旭華及嚴俊等在擴建中的永華片場
The new Yung Hwa Studio under construction. (From right) Albert Odell, Loke Wan Tho, Zhu Xuhua and Yan Jun.

huge parking lots on the ground floor, the "world's best" York air-conditioners, GB-Kele projectors that were the first available in Southeast Asia, and a luxurious auditorium decorated with the "newest and most advanced" furnitures. It also provided special earphones for audience with hearing problems and featured a Hollywood Cafe with the "most modern" decor, designed by Loke himself. [15]

To supply film for his rapidly expanding exhibition network, besides strengthening its distribution arm International Film Distribution Agency (which supplied films of 14 languages to all Cathay venues plus 200 other independently owned cinemas across Southeast Asia), Cathay began in 1955-1956 to pay attention to film production. [16] When Yung Hwa, the leading studio of the "Freedom cinema" in Hong Kong, approached insolvency in 1955 despite massive loans from Cathay and Taiwan, Loke took over its management and took steps to update its studio facilities and sign up new recruits. In March 1956 Yung Hwa was officially replaced by Motion Picture & General Investment (MP & GI) which served as the Chinese-language film production arm of Cathay. Robert Chung (Zhong Qiwen), a former Yung Hwa executive who had studied colour filmmaking in Hollywood, became the company head. MP & GI announced plans to make 40 to 50 films in 1956-1957. This was a very ambitious (and to some skeptics, seemingly imprudent) plan in view of the crisis facing the Mandarin cinema industry and its inferior production technology. [17]

Yet, MP & GI became the first Hong Kong studio to win a major prize at the Asian Film Festival in 1957 (Best Actress Award for Linda Lin Dai's role in *Golden Lotus*). The following year, at the 5th Asian Film Festival, MP & GI took away almost all the major awards, including Best Picture (Tang Huang's *Our Sister Hedy*, 1957). And it went on to produce a series of well-received films such as romantic comedy *Sister Long Legs* (1960), Evan Yang's (Yi Wen) historical epic *Sun, Moon, and Star* (1961), and Wang Tianlin's comedy *The Greatest Civil War on Earth* (1961). These successes drew wide praise from the film industry and some critics went so far as to laud Loke's ambitious plan as a catalyst for the "renaissance of

元。[19]在那段時期，國泰在新加坡的辦事處也忙於應付本身在東南亞急速擴展的放映和發行業務，無暇緊盯香港的財務運作。Yiu Tiong Chai 認為，陸運濤試圖嚴謹監管電懋的製片業務。但他未必有時間長期這樣做，因為他生意大和公務活動繁多，更有廣泛的個人興趣（特別是鳥類學）。而且，他不像邵逸夫，對製作電影沒有甚麼實際經驗，除卻他的個人魅力、友善態度和洋派外表對吸引著名影人（例如女明星尤敏和林翠）加盟大有幫助外，在創作路向上，陸運濤不能給予電懋多大指引。1960 年以後，有眾多原因促使國泰的新加坡總部逐步收緊對電懋在財政和行政上的監管：包括電懋長期出現財政困難，亟需擴大影片生產（由於美國和歐洲產量下降）；邵氏圓滑的公關技巧，加上嚴謹控制製作預算和質素，吸引了大量影人（包括女明星林黛和導演岳楓）從國泰轉投。由於電懋仍主要拍攝黑白片（反觀邵氏所有國語片都是彩色製作），加上鍾啟文與新加坡總部的關係日益緊張（如與多個女明星傳出緋聞），於1962年宣告辭職。[20]其實自 1960 年起，在陸運濤的笑臉和樂觀態度背後，國泰機構已因業務發展過速（由在香港製作到在東南亞放映和集資）以及邵氏圍攻引發的問題，而疲於奔命。

四

電懋的運作模式仿效荷里活的片廠制度，而且正如不少影評人指出，電懋大部分作品從故事結構、剪接技巧以至鏡頭運用都深受荷里活影響。[21]這不足為奇，五十年代一如過往，美國流行文化主導了全球市場；而荷里活雖受到世界各地電影工作者非議，指為文化帝國主義入侵，而且摧毀了本土電影業，但卻仍被普遍視為電影製作的「唯一」標準。不單陸運濤跟荷里活有廣泛的業務和私人聯繫、鍾啟文曾在美國學藝，大部份電懋主要的

Chinese [i.e. Mandarin] cinema". But Cathay's successful extension into production also intensified its rivalries with the Shaw Brothers. In 1957, Run Run Shaw came to Hong Kong and declared to modernise and globalise Chinese cinema by building a multi-million dollar, well-equipped Movietown and launching an "age of colour films" (comparing to the MP & GI's black and white productions and small, poorly equipped studio). Thus, Cathay's plan to expand production in the colony (even after the MP & GI's collapse soon after Loke's untimely death) and the rivalries with Shaws, brought capital, energy, and prestige to the Mandarin cinema which dominated the Hong Kong entertainment business for the next two decades.

Scholars and critics tend to credit the initial success of MP & GI to the skills and vision of Robert Chung, whose resignation in 1962 marked the downfall of Cathay in Hong Kong. This is an over-simplistic view. It is true that Chung was a capable studio executive with an understanding of Mandarin film industry and an amicable relationship with Loke. For example, he was able to persuade Loke to scale back production from 40 to 50 films each year to the more practical 12 to 14 films.[18] He also surrounded himself with some of the most creative minds in the industry, including scriptwriter Sun Jinsan and producer/writer Stephen Soong (Song Qi), all of whom succeeding in bringing a sleek, sophisticated style and modern sentiment to MP & GI products. Yet Chung seemed to lack skills in financial management. According to Cathay's Chief Accountant Heah Hock Meng, even with a few hits, MP & GI never made itself a financially viable studio. Its survival depended entirely on the money Loke took out of his family business. By 1963, MP & GI had lost a total of over HK$ 6 million.[19] At the same time, the Singapore office struggled to keep up with the rapid expansion of its exhibition and distribution business in Southeast Asia, leaving little time to keep track of the financial operation of Hong Kong. In the opinion of Yiu Tiong Chai, Loke tried to keep a vigilant eye on the production end, but it was doubtful he could do it consistently because of the heavy demands on his schedule, not to mention personal interests (especially ornithology). Moreover, unlike Run Run Shaw, Loke had little actual experience with filmmaking. He could provide little creative guidance to MP & GI, except that his charisma, grace and cosmopolitan outlook played a critical part in attracting major talents to the

導演如易文、岳楓和陶秦，於三、四十年代在上海都曾透過觀看、翻譯或評論荷里活電影，琢磨導演技巧。他們欣賞荷里活電影的另一原因，是在群眾意識中，荷里活代表了現代化在民間的體現，而這批導演的志願，跟國泰的目標一樣，正是在華人社會營造一個現代世界——有着嶄新的生活方式和思想模式。同時，國泰和電懋也無意之中牽涉入冷戰政治的反共運動。說是無意之中，因為陸運濤雖然外表西化，卻一直視自己為「炎黃子孫」(他將國泰的英文名稱定為「Cathay」，那正是「中國」的舊式叫法）。[22] 正如歷史學者王賡武所說，四、五十年代在東南亞認同中國，其實就等於認同台灣。[23] 據跟政府關係密切的台灣電影行政人員沙榮峰說，陸運濤非常親近國民黨政府。[24] 因此，他會在五十年代初出資拯救永華，而其後他創立電懋，所有僱員都是屬於「自由影業」的。現代化和反共這些主題，在電懋的豪華製作《空中小姐》中強烈地顯現出來，不過這部電影既不叫好，也不叫座。

《空》片由易文執導，他在上海出生，抗戰時期寫過影評。這是高成本製作，演員陣容強大——有葛蘭、喬宏、葉楓和雷震，在香港、台灣、新加坡和泰國等地作實景拍攝，更是電懋少數彩色作品之一。製作如此大手筆，一方面固然可作為賣點，同時也突出了《空》片的主題：亞洲要現代化所需的文化意識。「現代」這特色由新行業空中小姐體現，當時一篇宣傳稿這樣解釋：「航空事業是人類文化進展的標誌……照料旅客的『空中小姐』，成了名副其實的『天使』，在空中工作，為人服務。這是一種新興的職業，也是一種最現代化的職業……『縮短人間距離，促進國際往來』。」[25]

《空》片的主線是空中小姐林可蘋（葛蘭）與機師雷大英（喬宏）的愛情故事。他們敬業樂業，力求在工作中找

studio (e.g., actresses Lucilla You Min and Jeanette Lin Cui). The financial failures and the desperate need to increase productions after 1960 (as a result of production declines in USA and Europe) – combined with the Shaws' public relations savvy and tough control of budget and production quality that brought massive defection from Cathay (including actress Lin Dai and director Yue Feng) – probably compelled headquarters to impose strict budgetary and administrative supervision on Hong Kong. Hence the prevalence of black and white productions (while all the Shaw Brothers Mandarin films were in Eastman colour) and the increasing tension between Singapore and Chung (with his many romantic entanglements with starlets), leading to Chung's resignation in 1962.[20] The Cathay Organisation – a transnational empire that stretched from production in Hong Kong to exhibition and financing in Southeast Asia – was actually constantly struggling after 1960 to sustain and maintain itself against problems arising from its rapid expansion and the Shaw offensive, despite the public image of Loke's smiling face and sanguine optimism.

4

MP & GI was modelled after the studio system of Hollywood, and as many critics pointed out, most of its products exhibited strong Hollywood influence from plot construction to editing techniques and camera movements.[21] This was no surprise. In the 1950s, as in earlier decades, American popular culture dominated the global market; and Hollywood, despite dissent from filmmakers around the world for its cultural imperialism and destruction of local cinemas, became *the* "universal" standard of filmmaking. In fact, not only did Loke enjoy extensive business and personal connections with Hollywood and Robert Chung receive his training in the US, most of MP & GI leading directors like Evan Yang, Yue Feng, and Tao Qin honed their skills by watching, translating or reviewing Hollywood films in Shanghai in the 1930s and 1940s. And Hollywood's identification with vernacular modernity in the public consciousness also explained the fascination it held on MP & GI filmmakers, whose aspiration, echoing Cathay's mission, was to project the creation of a modern world marked by a new way of life and a new habit of mind in Chinese societies. At

到意義，表現卓越。這是典型的港產國語片，片中所有角色都來自中產家庭，住在寬敞、裝修豪華的大宅中（配備現代化設施，如鋼琴和大沙發等），生活舒適；上文提及當時香港社會常見的經濟困境，跟他們全無關係。[26]開首的一場，會令人想起 1957 年將葛蘭捧成紅星的電懋作品《曼波女郎》，同樣以歌舞開始，可蘋在舞會中，對着大群流露欣賞眼光的觀眾，唱出她要「飛上青天」的夢想，訴說乘搭飛機周遊列國的刺激和吸引力。正如可蘋自己形容，她是思想獨立的「摩登女性」，因此不顧母親的意願，拒絕下嫁想她做家庭主婦的富翁；她想做的，當然是空中小姐。

在五十年代，華人甚少離開香港（或新加坡或馬來亞）外遊，乘搭飛機的更少，大多數觀眾對飛行這種現代經驗都感到陌生。選擇空姐作為現代生活象徵的念頭，或許來自以推動亞洲日常生活現代化為己任的陸運濤，他是馬來亞航空和國泰航空公司的董事，亦經常乘搭飛機周遊世界。像是為了作公眾教育，《空》片有多個冗長的片段，描繪可蘋要接受各式各樣的訓練和實習（例如身體檢查、姿勢糾正、機艙介紹、遞上咖啡的正確方式——這令人聯想起美國文化，以及如何應付乘客），才可成為空姐，藉此詳細介紹了飛行服務的運作和程序。這些場面仿似直接取自航空公司的宣傳短片，充滿資訊，卻全無戲劇味道。

基於工作需要，可蘋和其他空姐（由葉楓和其他女星飾演）就像現代的吉卜賽人，在亞洲各大城市短暫停留。這讓影片在與故事推展無關之下，展示各地風貌：現代化的新加坡（穿插着拍攝摩天大樓和國泰電影院的鏡頭）；以及充滿異國風情的泰國。這讓觀眾感覺像在看吸引他們到東南亞旅遊的風光片。不過，片中最惹人爭議的，還是一個很長的片段，介紹「自由中國的進

《空中小姐》— 現代化的職業

"A most modern profession": *Air Hostess.*

the same time, Cathay and MP & GI were inadvertently involved in the Cold War politics of anti-communism. Inadvertently because Loke saw himself as a "son of the Yellow Emperor",along with his highly Westernised outlook. (Thus his company was named Cathay, an old English name for China.)[22] To identify with China in Southeast Asia in the 1940s and 1950s, as historian Wang Gengwu argues, meant identifying with Taiwan.[23] In fact, according to Sha Rongfeng, a Taiwan movie executive closely associated with the government, Loke was very close to the Nationalist government.[24] It was therefore natural that he helped finance Yung Hwa in the early 1950s and that when he established MP & GI, all its employees came from the "Freedom film industry". All these themes of modernity and anti-communism come out powerfully in MP & GI's prestigious picture, *Air Hostess* (1959), which was poorly received by the critics and the audience alike.

Directed by Evan Yang (Yi Wen), who wrote film reviews during the war, *Air Hostess* was a big budget film with a strong cast – Grace Chang (Ge Lan), Roy Chiao (Qiao Hong), Julie Yeh Feng (Ye Feng), and Kelly Lai Chen (Lei Zhen) – and involved location shootings in Hong Kong, Taiwan, Singapore, and Thailand. It was also one of the few MP & GI films shot in Eastman colour. These high-cost production strategies became the films's selling points, while also serving to highlight its main theme: the cultural politics of being modern in Asia. This modernity is represented by the new profession of flight attendants. As a publicity article puts it: "Airline business marks the progress of human civilisation…. Air hostesses, whose job is to take care of the passengers, are virtually 'angels'. Working up on the sky, serving the people [travelling the world], air hostess is a new profession, a *most modern* profession.... They help shorten the distance between people and facilitate movement between nations."(my italics)[25]

Air Hostess revolves around a love story between aspiring flight attendant Lin Kepin (Grace Chang) and airline pilot Lei Daiying (Roy Chiao) who try to excel and find meaning in their careers. Typical of Hong Kong Mandarin cinema, all characters in the film come from a middle-class background, live in large, well-decorated apartments (filled with such modern amenities as pianos and big sofas) and enjoy a

展」，展示台北的豪華酒店和其他台灣旅遊名勝（例如烏來瀑布）。葛蘭的角色甚至在一個派對中唱出台灣小調〈大家心一條〉：「我愛台灣同胞，呀，唱個台灣調……白糖茶葉買賣好，家家戶戶吃得飽……大家心一條。」香港的左翼影評人立即指出，這部電影是親台的群眾宣傳，為冷戰的反共運動張目。[27] 從陸運濤和電懋不少人員認同台灣，以及影片有明顯的説教意味看來，這種批評有其道理。

事實上，《空》片中最具娛樂性的部分，卻有着最濃厚的説教意味。影評人何觀（導演張徹的筆名）批評，影片無法為可蘋塑造統一而具説服力的性格。她思想獨立，意志堅強，不肯接受想對她作家長式管束的富裕求婚者，但是面對航空公司諸多不公平、不合理的規條（例如：「乘客永遠是對的，因為他們付了錢」，又或「穿上制服就沒有私人生活」），她卻在沒有太多心理矛盾下輕易接受；同時，她又愛上大男人主義、置她尊嚴和意願於不顧的機師雷大英。[28] 例如有一場，可蘋在駕駛艙向幾名機師（全是男性）遞上咖啡，雷大英似乎全神貫注於工作之上，完全沒有理會她。在另一個機艙中的場面，可蘋跟一名乘客調笑，雷大英立即跑出來，在大庭廣眾之下罵她「不檢點」。角色性格塑造如此失敗，源於《空》片背後的文化意識。在片中，雷大英和航空公司都代表了現代福特——泰特式資本主義的意識形態，要求個人全身投入於講求自覺和紀律的大量生產系統。不論是辦公室或工廠的員工，都要全無異議地接受自己的工作任務，這是必須的道德操守。這套意識形態的支持者深信，雖然制度有時看來嚴苛而沒有人情味，但卻永遠是公平、合理而人道的——它會以金錢和愛來獎賞最勤力工作的人。在片中的高潮戲，航空公司經理（唐真）告訴可蘋，其實公司和雷大英都十分關心

「乘客永遠是對的。」
"Passengers are always right."

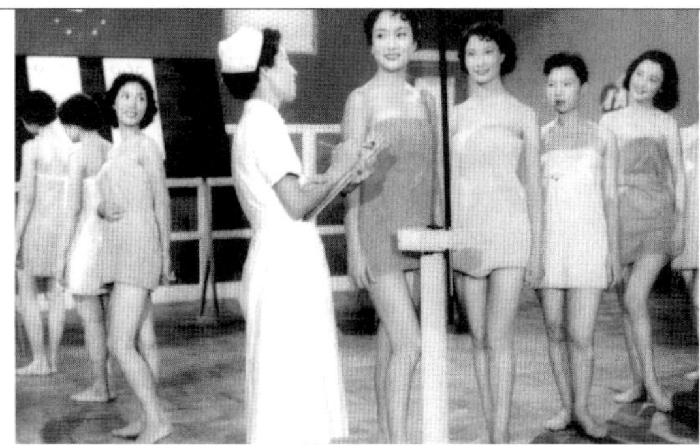

comfortable life devoid of the financial problems that were prevalent in the colony.[26] And reminiscent of MP & GI's 1957 hit *Mambo Girl* (1957), which launched Chang into a superstar, the film opens with a party scene in which Kepin sings of her dream of "flying to the sky", of the thrill and glamour of jet-setting around the world to an admiring crowd. An independent-minded "modern woman", as she describes herself, Kepin defies her mother's wish to marry a rich man whose desire is to make her a housewife. Rather she wants to become, of course, an air hostess.

In the 1950s, few people travelled outside of Hong Kong (or Singapore or Malaya) and even fewer travelled by aeroplane. The airborne experience of modernity was totally alien to most of the audience. The choice of air hostess as a symbol of modern life probably came from Loke, a tireless jet-setter who hopped from city to city who was on the board of the Malayan Airways and Cathay Pacific Airlines, as part of his aspiration to modernise the everyday of Asia. As if for public education, the film contains several long, tedious sequences describing the training Kepin has to go through (medical check-up, posture corrections and proper ways of serving "coffee" – which conjures a sense of American culture). These scenes seem to be taken directly from airline publicity shorts, full of information but lacking drama.

As part of their work, Kepin and other air stewardesses (played by Yeh Feng and other starlets) live like modern-day gypsies, stopping over at cities around Asia. This allows the film to show case, without narrative relevance, the modernity of Singapore, with montages of sky scrapers and Cathay-owned movie palaces, and the exotic beauty of Bangkok – like watching a "travelogue" enticing audiences to visit Southeast Asia. But most controversial at the time was a long scene featuring the "progress of Free China" – luxurious hotels in Taipei and other Taiwan tourist attractions. The Chang character is also made to sing "We Share the Same Heart", with such lines as: "I love my fellow countrymen of Taiwan/Let me sing a song of Taiwan.... Trading in sugar and sugar canes goes so well/ every household has so much to eat.... All our hearts are linked together as a line." Leftist critics were quick to point out that the film was pro-Taiwan propaganda,

她；當雷大英為自己的無禮行徑向可蘋道歉時，她表示諒解，說：「我知道你全部心思都放在工作上，我很尊重你這種態度，我也應該這樣。」《空》片似乎表達了，現代生活不單包含豪華而多姿多采的享受，同樣重要的是勤懇工作、緊守紀律和專業精神等操守。只有這些現代的價值觀才可讓亞洲趕上西方（航空公司本身就是西方事物），然後可成為有多個富強國家的地區。濃厚的說教意味，加上易文失色的劇本、累贅的敘事風格（例如重複使用某些場景來換場）、沉悶的鏡頭運用，令《空》片的票房教人失望。

五

這個關於國泰機構的歷史討論確實只是初步的一我的資料有限，在很多重要層面均需要依賴電懋發放的宣傳資料；我的分析需要更深入探討背景因素的具體情況，以及與更多國語片以至粵語片作更透徹的比較。不過我試圖將國泰的歷史地位，放在更大的背景下討論，因素包括香港的社會狀況、陸運濤的個性、亞洲區冷戰的政治思維，以及五十年代的國語片危機。這個取向為研究香港國語片的複雜發展和與東南亞的跨國聯繫，提供了新的視點。這些都是進一步探討香港電影業的歷史和政治聯繫有用的課題。

馬山翻譯

lending itself to anti-communism crusade.[27] This critique makes sense in view of the identification of Loke and MP & GI filmmakers with Taiwan and the evidently pedagogical appeal of the film itself.

In fact, the most entertaining part of the film carries the heaviest weight of its pedagogical appeal. Critic He Guan (Pen name of Chang Cheh / Zhang Che) observes that the film fails to create a coherent, convincing character in Lin Kepin. She is independent-minded and strong-willed, unwilling to subject herself to the patriarchal control of her rich suitor, yet she allows herself to accept with little show of inner tension all the unfair and unreasonable rules of the airline (e.g., "passengers are always right because they pay" or "no personal life is allowed in uniform"), and to fall in love with pilot Daiying, who is a male chauvinist totally ignoring her dignity and desires.[28] When Kepin serves coffee to the pilots (all male) in the cockpit, Daiying seems to be so engrossed in his work that he does not even care to acknowledge her. And in a long sequence inside the cabin, when Kepin makes small talk with a passenger, Daiying comes out and scolds her for her "misbehavior" in front of everyone. This points to the cultural politics of *Air Hostess*. Daiying and the airline function alike as metaphors for Fordist-Taylorist capitalism, demanding total dedication of the individual to the mass production regime of vigilance and discipline. It was a code of ethical imperative for all workers, in offices or factories, to accept their work with total compliance. According to its proponents, the system may at times seemed harsh and impersonal, it's always fair, reasonable, and humane – it would reward the hardest working with wealth and love. Indeed, the airline manager eventually tells Kepin that both the company and Daiying care the most for her, and when Daiying apologies for his rudeness, she understandably replies: "I know you are only devoted to the work and I respect you for that. I should do the same." Thus modern life, *Air Hostess* seems to suggest, entails not just glamour and luxury, but most importantly, also the ethics of hard work, discipline, and professionalism. Only these modern values could enable Asia to catch up with the West (which invented the airline business in the first place), thereby transforming itself into a region of modern nations. This pedagogical tendency, in addition to Evan Yang's

註

1. I. C. Jarvie: *Window on Hong Kong: A Sociological Study of the Hong Kong Film Industry and Its Audience*, Hong Kong: Centre of Asian Studies, 1977.
2. Elizabeth Sinn, Hong Kong's Role in The Relationship Between China and The Overseas Chinese in Lynn Pan, ed.: *The Encyclopedia of The Chinese Overseas*, Cambridge: Harvard University Press, 1999, pp. 105-107.
3. Wong Siu-lun: *Emigrant Entrepreneurs: Shanghai Industrialists in Hong Kong*, Hong Kong: Oxford University Press, 1988, pp. 3, 23.
4. Frank Welsh: *A History of Hong Kong*, London: HarperColins, 1997, pp. 445-453 及 Wong Siu-lun，同註 3。
5. Frank Welsh，同註 4，頁 455-459。
6. 香港在冷戰中的重要角色是過去甚少人觸及的研究課題，有待更為系統化的研究。作為導論，可參看羅卡，〈傳統陰影下的左右分家〉，於李焯桃編：《香港電影的中國脈絡》，第十四屆香港國際電影節回顧特刊，香港：市政局，1990，頁 10-20。
7. 黃愛玲編：《理想年代：長城、鳳凰的日子》，香港：香港電影資料館，2001，頁 8-10。
8. 〈國語電影面臨的困難〉，《國際電影》，第 1 期，1955 年 10 月，頁 41-42、50-51。
9. 《國際電影》，第 8 期，1956 年 8 月，頁 40-41。

weak script, tedious narrative style and dull camera movements, made *Air Hostess* a box office disappointment.

5

This historical discussion of Cathay Organisation is preliminary in the true sense – my sources are limited, and in many important aspects dependent on MP & GI publicity materials and my analysis requires deeper contextual grounding and a better comparison with more Mandarin films and Cantonese cinema of the time. But my approach to contextualise the historical role of Cathay in the larger context of the social situation of Hong Kong, the personality of Loke Wan Tho, Cold War politics in Asia, and the crisis of Mandarin Cinema in the 1950s offers a new perspective to the complex development of Hong Kong Mandarin cinema and its transnational connection with Southeast Asia. These would be helpful themes for further research on the history and politics of Hong Kong filmmaking.

Notes

1. See I. C. Jarvie: *Window on Hong Kong: A Sociological Study of the Hong Kong Film Industry and Its Audience*, Hong Kong: Centre of Asian Studies, 1977.
2. See Elizabeth Sinn, "Hong Kong's Role in The Relationship Between China and The Overseas Chinese" in Lynn Pan, ed.: *The Encyclopedia of The Chinese Overseas*, Cambridge: Harvard University Press, 1999, pp. 105-107.
3. See Wong Siu-lun: *Emigrant Entrepreneurs: Shanghai Industrialists in Hong Kong*, Hong Kong: Oxford University Press, 1988, pp. 3, 23.
4. See Frank Welsh: *A History of Hong Kong*, London: HarperColins, 1997, pp. 445-453 and Wong Siu-lun, ibid.
5. See Frank Welsh, ibid., pp. 455-459.
6. The important role of Hong Kong in the Cold War has been a significantly understudied subject that cries for more systematic research. For an introductory study, see Law Kar, "The Shadow of Tradition and the Left-Right Struggle" in Li Cheuk-to, ed.: *The China Factor in Hong Kong Cinema*, the 14th Hong Kong International Film Festival catalogue, Hong Kong: Urban Council, 1990, pp. 10-20.
7. See Wong Ainling, ed.: *An Age of Idealism: Great Wall & Feng Huang Days*, Hong Kong: Hong Kong Film Archive, 2001, pp. 8-10.
8. See "Difficulties Facing Mandarin Cinema" in *International Screen* (in Chinese), no. 1, October 1955, pp. 41-42, 50-51.
9. See *International Screen* (in Chinese), no. 8, August 1956, pp. 40-41.

10. 郎如鐵，〈誰說香港自由影人沒有工作表現〉，《國際電影》，第2期，1955年11月，頁42、52及《國際電影》，同註8，頁46-47。

11.《國際電影》，同註8，頁50-51及《國際電影》，第6期，1956年1月，頁56。

12. 同註11。

13. Lim Kay Tong: *Cathay - 55 Years of Cinema,* Singapore: Landmark Books, 1991, pp. 1-20 ，及Lynn Pan: *Sons of the Yellow Emperor: A History of the Chinese Diaspora*, Boston: Little, Brown and Company, 1990, pp. 185-190.

14. 陸海天，〈崇尚的理想〉，《國際電影》，第3期，1955年12月，頁10。

15.《國際電影》，第25期，1957年11月，頁56-57；第16期，1957年2月，頁2-3；第2期，1955年11月，頁6-7；第3期，1955年12月，頁10-11。

16. Lim Kay Tong，同註13，頁27。

17. 易文，〈在日本拍攝伊士曼彩色片〉，《國際電影》，第3期，1955年12月，頁50。

18. Yiu Tiong Chai, "Dian Mou: MP & GI" in Lim Kay Tong: *Cathay - 55 Years of Cinema,* Singapore: Landmark Books, 1991, p.150.

19. Lim Kay Tong，同註13，頁56-65。

20. Lim Kay Tong，同註13；杜雲之：《中國電影史》，台北：商務印書館，第3卷，1986，頁123-135及沙榮峰：《繽紛電影四十春：沙榮峰回憶錄》，台北：國家電影資料館，1994，頁35-52。

21. 例子見Lim Kay Tong，同註13，頁150-153。

22. Lim Kay Tong，同註13。

23. Wang Gungwu: *China and The Chinese Overseas*, Singapore: Times Academic Press, 1991, pp. 160-180, 190-221.

24. 沙榮峰，同註20，頁30-33。

25.《國際電影》，第20期，1957年6月，頁37。

26. 來自內地的電影工作者對「現代」的想像，可追溯至當年上海的現代大都會文化。關於這課題的研究，見Leo Ou-fan Lee: *Shanghai Modern: The Flowering of A New Urban Culture in Urban China, 1930-1945*, Cambridge: Harvard University Press, 1999. 同期的粵語片卻有較強的本土意識，風格迥然不同，更貼近現實生活。關於這課題一系列出色的論文見李焯桃編：《香港喜劇電影的傳統》，第九屆香港國際電影節回顧特刊，香港：市政局，1985。

27. 例子見高山月，〈空中小姐別有用心〉，《大公報》，1959年6月10日。

28. 何觀，〈空中小姐〉，《新生晚報》，1959年6月14日。

傅葆石，美國伊利諾大學Urbana-Champaign分校歷史及電影研究副教授。近年專注研究1930至1950年代中國及香港電影文化史，現正在編寫成書。

Poshek Fu, associate professor of history and cinema studies at the University of Illinois at Urbana-Champaign. Co-editor of *The Cinema of Hong Kong: History, Arts, Identity* (Cambridge University Press, 2001). Currently completing a book on the politics of Chinese and Hong Kong cinemas between the 1930s and 1950s.

10. See Lan Rutie, "It's Wrong to Accuse Hong Kong Freedom Filmmakers Not Making Contribution" in *International Screen* (in Chinese), no.2, November 1955, pp.42, 52 and *International Screen*, no. 1, October 1955, pp. 46-47.

11. See *International Screen* (in Chinese), no. 1, October 1955, pp. 50-51 and no. 6, January 1956, p. 56.

12. Ibid.

13. See Lim Kay Tong: *Cathay - 55 Years of Cinema,* Singapore: Landmark Books, 1991, pp. 1-20 and Lynn Pan: *Sons of the Yellow Emperor: A History of the Chinese Diaspora*, Boston: Little, Brown and Company, 1990, pp. 185-190.

14. Quoted from Lu Haitian, "Lofty Ideal" in *International Screen* (in Chinese) no.3, December 1955, p.10.

15. See *International Screen* (in Chinese), no. 25, November 1957, pp. 56-57; no. 16, February 1957, pp. 2-3; no. 2, November 1955, pp. 6-7 and no. 3, December 1955, pp. 10-11.

16. See Lim Kay Tong, op. cit., p. 27.

17. See Evan Yang, "Making Eastman Color Films in Japan" in *International Screen* (in Chinese), no. 3, December 1955, p. 50.

18. See Yiu Tiong Chai, "Dian Mou: MP & GI" in Lim Kay Tong, op. cit., p. 150.

19. See Lim Kay Tong, op. cit., pp. 56-65.

20. See Yiu Tiong Chai, op. cit.; Du Yunzhi: *A History of Chinese Cinema* (in Chinese), Taipei: Commercial Press, vol. 3, 1986, pp. 123-135 and Sha Yung-fong, *Forty Springs of Cinema Glory: The Memoirs of Sha* Yung-fong (in Chinese), Taipei: Chinese Taipei Film Archive, 1994, pp. 35-52.

21. See, for example, Yiu Tiong Chai, op. cit., pp. 150-153.

22. See Lim Kay Tong, op. cit.

23. See Wang Gungwu: *China and The Chinese Overseas*, Singapore: Times Academic Press, 1991, pp. 160-180, 190-221.

24. See Sha Yung-fong, op. cit., pp. 30-33.

25. See International Screen, no. 20, June 1957, p. 37.

26. The imagination of modern among the diaspora filmmakers should be traced to the modern cosmopolitan culture of Shanghai. For a study of this subject, see Leo Ou-fan Lee: *Shanghai Modern: The Flowering of a New Urban Culture in Urban China, 1930-1945*, Cambridge: Harvard University Press, 1999. Cantonese Cinema of the time had a more distinct local consciousness and a different, more engaged style. For a fine collection of essays on this topic, see Li Cheuk-to, ed.: *The Traditions of Hong Kong Comedy*, the 9th Hong Kong International Film Festival catalogue, Hong Kong: Urban Council, 1985.

27. See, for example, Gao Shanyue, "The Real Intention of Air Hostess" in *Ta Kung Pao* (in Chinese), June 10, 1959.

28. See He Guan, "Air Hostess" in *New Life Evening Post* (in Chinese), June 14, 1959.

管窺電懋的創作／製作局面：一些推測、一些疑問

- 羅卡 -

一

1955年中，新加坡國泰機構香港分公司國際影片發行公司負責人歐德爾正忙於籌建牛池灣斧山道永華新廠；永華影業公司卻處於日暮途窮，大部份員工已經遣散，製片廠則轉手給國泰接管經營。李祖永在1947年建立、也曾顯赫一時的永華，至此已名存實亡。

那邊廂，歐德爾的國際卻招兵買馬，等待新廠建成即大展拳腳，大量開拍國、粵語片，以供應港、台、南洋市場。這一年，國際拉攏了陶秦、岳楓兩名編導好手加盟，又邀得姚克、宋淇、張愛玲、孫晉三組成劇本編審委員會，為影片增產作好準備。與此同時，繼續投資獨立公司拍製多部粵語片。

1956年，易文加盟，執導徐訏小說改編的《春色惱人》，岳楓則執導了林黛主演的《歡樂年年》，並由日本松竹歌舞團和日本技師協助拍攝歌舞場面，成績理

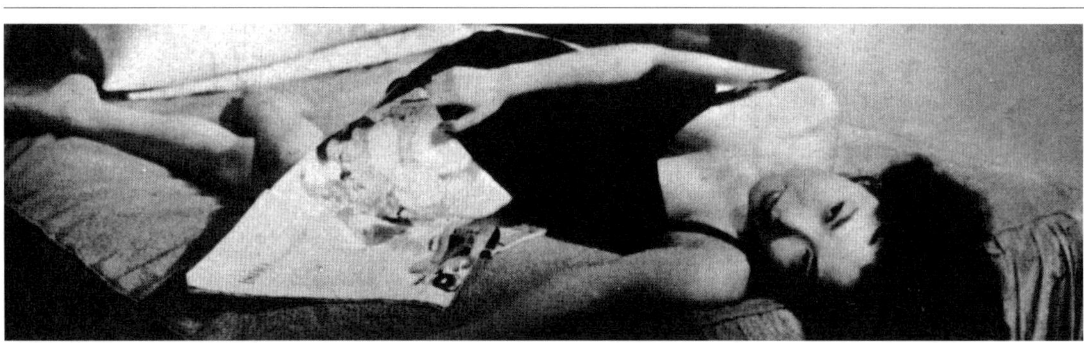

A Glimpse of MP & GI's Creative/ Production Situation: Some Speculations, Some Doubts

- Law Kar -

I

In mid-1955, Albert Odell, the man in charge of International Films Distributing Agency, a subsidiary of Singapore's Cathay Organisation, was busy planning for the building of a new Yung Hwa Studios on Hammer Hill Road. Yung Hwa Motion Picture Industries Ltd itself was on the decline. Many of its staff members had been sacked, with Cathay taking over the operation of its production studios. The movie empire established by the magnate Li Zuyong in 1947 existed in name only.

In the mean time, Odell was actively recruiting filmmakers to join the International Films rank, awaiting for the new studios to go into production to supply markets in Hong Kong, Taiwan, and Southeast Asia with Cantonese and Mandarin features. Within that same year, International Films had lined up the director-writer duo Tao Qin and Yue Feng, and extended invitation to Yao Ke, Stephen Soong (Song Qi), Eileen Chang (Zhang Ailing), and Sun Jinsan to become members of a script committee, gearing up to

想。翌年，國際正式改組為電影懋業有限公司，在新廠拍攝的影片，在這一年增至五部，其中易文的《曼波女郎》(葛蘭、陳厚主演)公映反應熱烈，奠定了葛蘭能歌善舞的地位。

也是1957這一年，永華公司已完全停產，親中的「左派」長城公司，業務已上軌道，但因沒法進入台灣，而南洋並無自己的院線，發展有限。獨立公司中最活躍的新華，因張善琨在日本心臟病發去世而大受打擊。在港、台與南洋市場一直與國泰直接競爭的邵氏，此時意識到不能讓電懋坐大。邵逸夫乃御駕親征，來港成立邵氏兄弟（香港）有限公司，在清水灣加快興建規模更大的邵氏製片廠，實行與電懋展開長期抗爭。

香港的電影製片由此進入長達十數年的大片廠爭霸期。自戰後1946年起，大中華公司、永華公司、舊長城公司已嘗試實行片廠制度，卻由於政治、經濟種種變動，一波三折，未能落實。直至1957年電懋、邵氏相繼建廠，與新長城鼎足而三，香港才真正出現大片廠競爭的局面。

二

本文要談的倒不是1950至1960年代片廠的競爭，而是在這樣背景下電懋的劇本創作情況。

誠如題目所示，本文只是一次「管窺」——猶如站在遠處用望遠鏡窺探，加上我對電懋中人的一點認識，而作出的一些主觀推斷——自問不無臆測成份，只望能提供一些初步的，即使是粗淺的線索。

首先理解一下所謂劇本編審委員會的作用。自三十年代上海的明星、藝華、聯華公司起，較有規模的影片公司、片廠都有編劇委員會或編審委員會之設，延請有文名的文學、戲劇界人士為顧問或成員撰寫劇本，亦藉他們的關係，拉攏其他文藝家、劇作家為公司提供劇本，

《春色惱人》中的李湄——星期天總是在寂寞中渡過

Li Mei in *Gloomy Sunday*: If Sundays can always be so gloomy ...

step up production. Meanwhile, it continued to finance Cantonese features produced by independent companies.

In 1956, Evan Yang (Yi Wen) joined the group, directing a script adapted from Xu Xu's novel *Gloomy Sunday* (1956); Yue Feng directed Linda Lin Dai's highly successful *Merry-Go-Round* (1956), with filming of its dance scenes assisted by a Japanese dance troupe and a crew of Japanese technicians. Yang went on to direct the hit *Mambo Girl* (1957, starring Grace Chang and Peter Chen Ho [Chen Ho]) which established Chang as a musical diva. In 1957, International Films was renamed Motion Picture & General Investment Co Ltd (MP & GI), and shifted its production to the new studios.

It was in the same year that production of Yung Hwa came to a complete halt. Though the operation of the 'left-wing' Great Wall was getting established, its development was hindered by its lack of market niche in Taiwan and a proper distribution circuit in Southeast Asia. Hsin Hwa Motion Picture Company, once most active among all independent companies, was struck a terrible blow following the untimely death of Zhang Shankun in Japan. Shaws, Cathay's rival in Asia, felt MP & GI's threat gathering strength and Run Run Shaw decided to interfere. He landed in the colony to oversee the establishment of Shaws Bros (Hong Kong) and the construction of a scaled-up studio in Clearwater Bay to prepare for a long-term battle with MP & GI.

And there, Hong Kong films entered a "warring states" period between studios that lasted over a decade. Since after the war in 1946, Great China Film Company, Yung Hwa, and the Great Wall have been attempting to introduce the studio system, but its full launch was obstructed by political and economic upheavals. It was not until 1957, when MP & GI and Shaws emerged to compete with the reorganised Great Wall that a triangular balance of forces was established.

以及為公司的製作／創作路向提供意見。三十年代初，明星公司就延聘了阿英、鄭伯奇為劇本委員，再引入夏衍、田漢、陽翰笙等人寫劇本，這就首開「左翼文人」（以「左聯」、「劇聯」兩個全國性文藝協會為陣地的進步文人的統稱）進入商業電影圈從事創作之風。同期或稍後，左翼文化人又大量滲入藝華、聯華等大公司從事編、導工作。三、四十年代「進步電影」運動由此形成。這是另話。

戰後，大量上海電影人南來香港工作，亦把這個文藝界人士或以客卿身份或全身投入商業電影創作之風帶入香港電影界。大中華、永華，戰後最具規模的兩大公司都延聘有頭有面的文化人組成「智囊團」，為公司大量撰寫劇本，並有所謂編劇委員會或編導委員會之設。大中華延請了上海的名家柯靈、師陀等作客卿編劇，據說「每月除有車馬費致送外，編劇時還奉以劇本費」。[1] 此外，亦招攬了編導皆能的朱石麟、但杜宇、胡心靈、陳煥文、洪叔雲、方沛霖，和抗戰時期在大後方名噪一時的劇作家吳祖光加盟編而優則導。

永華公司在李祖永的主持下，更大手筆請得劇戲大家歐陽予倩主持編導委員會，專任編劇有柯靈、周貽白、顧仲彝、沈寂、姚克等。編導如卜萬蒼、朱石麟、張駿祥、吳祖光、程步高、李萍倩等皆國內影界前輩，或文壇名家、飽學之士，可以說是文藝氣氛非常濃厚。李祖永本人亦是飽學之士，曾在上海大學任教，亦是腰纏萬貫的上海大亨。難得他興致勃勃重金投資電影業，羅致國內大批文化人／藝術家共襄是舉，有意在香港把中國電影辦成一項為國爭光的事業。單是創業作《國魂》（1948）據說已投資一百萬港元。

但問題也出在這裡。電影事業畢竟不同於搞文藝，那需要健全的工商管理、創作、製作與發行的高度配合。永

2

This essay is not to discuss the power struggle among film studios in the 1950s and 1960s, instead its focus is on the screenwriting activities at MP & GI against such a background. As set out in the title, the essay serves to offer a glimpse of the MP & GI world and some subjective deductions based on personal contacts with MP & GI personnel. There are admittedly speculative elements but the sole intention is to provide clues to the many links, however crude they are.

First, let's try to understand the functions of the script committee. Ever since the days of Mingxing, Yihua, and Lianhua in Shanghai in the 1930s, well established film companies all had script committees. Noted literary and stage figures were invited to either serve as advisers or join the committees, and, with their connections, lined up other figures to write scripts or offer advise. In the early 1930s, Mingxing recruited A Ying and Zheng Boqi to their script committees, and further introduced Xia Yan, Tian Han, and Yang Hansheng into its pool of screenwriters. This sets the trend for the 'left-wing intelligentsia' (a collective name for progressive figures from two national arts associations, Zuolian and Julian) to venture into commercial filmmaking. This led to a surge of left-wing figures into film companies like Yihua and Lianhua as writers and directors and marks the birth of the Progressive Film Movement in the 1930s and 1940s. But this is another story.

After the war, Hong Kong played host to a massive number of southbound filmmakers from Shanghai, bringing with them the practice of literary figures' involvement in commercial filmmaking, either as guest writers or staff. Great China and Yung Hwa, the biggest film companies in the post-war era, extended invitation to famed culturati to form their own think tank, and produced large numbers of scripts for the companies while also establishing script or screenwriting/directing committees. Great China played host to famed writers like Ke Ling and Shi Tuo. It was said that "apart from transportation allowance, a writing fee was paid for screenwriting effort."[1]

華旗下的一群文化人／藝術家都各有主見，處於 1947 至 1950 年中國政局大轉變期，更有各自的政治取向。這些執着，對藝術創作來說可以是原動力，對公司的營運來說卻是重大障礙。永華中後期就因左派意識的擾動，加上管理不善、經濟困難而引致一再罷工、停產，終致四分五裂。

三

電懋承接了永華的製作廠房、設備和部份製作班子，總經理鍾啟文正是永華後期的廠長，卻也汲取了永華失敗的教訓，在管理製作、創作上避免重蹈覆轍，因此電懋的運道與整體業務的發展遠比永華為佳。

首先是時代已不同了。 1957 年，中國大局已定，香港影界左右陣營形勢分明，電懋和邵氏由於影片要進口台灣，歸入「右派」（長城、鳳凰則歸於「左派」），電懋內部不存在意識形態之爭。其次，電懋的大老闆是在星馬經營工商業的陸運濤，接受英國貴族教育，亦喜愛藝術，而又長於現代管理；他任用的香港總經理鍾啟文接受的是美式教育，專攻管理與電影技術；製片部的宋淇（筆名林以亮）亦是飽學之士，在上海時已從事戲劇、文學創作。他們之間有個共通點，乃是心儀荷里活電影和荷里活式片廠管理，講求分工合作，以現代管理協調藝術創作。一開始，已不像永華那般愛唱高調，不作史詩式鉅製，往後的出品亦盡量擺脫中國文化人／知識份子慣於表現的憂患、沉重意識，而以荷里活的輕歌曼舞、浪漫溫馨出品掛帥，走迎合中產趣味的夢幻路線，即講求格調與質素的娛樂。

電懋雖在正式成立之前的 1955 年已有劇本編審委員會之設，考其往後的運作，劇本審訂與素質控制不似是由這四人決定，而更像是集權於宋淇手上，編委會起不了作用。 1955 年秋，成員之一張愛玲已移居美國，此後

Besides, fine directors-writers such as Zhu Shilin, Dan Duyu, Wu Xinling, Chen Huanwen, Hung Suk-wan and the famous playwright Wu Zuguang were also recruited.

Yung Hwa, under the leadership of Li Zuyong, lavished on eminent playwright Ouyang Yuqian to chair its script and directing committee. Members specialised in screenwriting included Ke Ling, Zhou Yibai, Gu Zhongyi. Shen Ji and Yao Ke, all drawn from a pool of literary giants and intellectuals. Directors-cum-screenwriters included Bu Wancang, Zhu Shilin, Zhang Junxiang, Wu Zuguang, Cheng Bugao and Li Pingqian. The place was filled with a literary air. Li Zuyong, a rich Shanghai tycoon, was an educated man, once teaching at the University of Shanghai. So it was a rare chance for someone of his stature to enthusiastically invest in the film industry and head-hunt the host of mainland literati and artists to join his squad for a common cause – to turn Chinese cinema into a national pride using Hong Kong as their base. An astronomical figure of $1million was invested in its debut *Soul of China* (1948) alone.

But this is exactly where the problem lies. The movie industry is unlike cultural endeavours. The former requires a robust business administration and demands that the creative, production and distribution faculties be highly accommodating to each other. These opinioned literati and artists, facing great political upheavals between 1947 and 1950, followed their own respective political inclinations. While these beliefs could be driving forces for creativity, they created obstacles to the company's operation. Yung Hwa soon found itself besieged by political arguments, poor management and financial troubles, leading to strikes, production stoppage and irreparable divisions.

3

MP & GI inherited Yung Hwa's production studios, equipment and some of its crew. General manager Robert Chung was the production manager of the late Yung Hwa dynasty. Learning from past experience, he managed to produce results that far outshone the Yung Hwa era.

多年有應宋淇之邀編寫了多個劇本，但人在美國，很難直接參與編審其他人的劇本，或制訂劇本創作路線。另一成員孫晉三於 1962 年英年早逝。至於名望最高、資格最老的姚克，他在永華、長城都曾受重用，寫過多個博得盛譽的劇本，如為永華寫的《清宮秘史》(1948)，是創業的第二炮；長城代表作之一，白光、嚴俊主演的《一代妖姬》(1950) 亦出自他手筆。據説他曾用化名「許炎」寫出《阿Q正傳》(徐遲合編，1958)，[2]關山憑此片在瑞士盧卡諾影展奪得男主角獎。但進入電懋後，未見他具名寫過甚麼劇本，他最擅長的歷史劇亦未見有所發揮——至 1963 年為止，電懋幾乎沒拍過古裝歷史片。他不可能影響電懋的創作路線。

從電懋／國泰的官方喉舌《國際電影》經常見到劇本討論會是由宋淇主持的。當年在電懋執導不少影片的王天林在訪問中亦透露，當年操劇本大權的是宋淇，不少編劇、導演亦是經由宋淇引薦延攬。可能因此物以類聚，電懋結集編劇如秦羽、汪榴照、張愛玲、張徹、蕭銅；導演如易文、陶秦，皆寫作人、文化人出身。王天林有這樣的説法：「程序是這樣的：劇本是先交製片部，製片部從中選幾部最優秀的給鍾啟文，再由鍾決定分派給哪個導演。」但導演也有權修改劇本。王天林就説過，曾把汪榴照的《家有喜事》劇本大加修改，由鬧劇改成重人情味的輕喜劇。此片在 1959 年的亞洲影展奪得最佳導演、編劇、女主角三個獎項。[3]

王拍攝《南北一家親》(1962)、《小兒女》(1963)、《南北喜相逢》(1964) 時，即使宋淇囑咐不要改動編劇張愛玲寫的情節、對白，他還是作了一些改動：如《南北一家親》的兩間食店劇本上寫明是面對面的，拍攝時改成是相隔幾個舖位，以方便搭景；他又為《南北喜相逢》加進了地道的笑料；或改動了《小兒女》開場尤敏

名作家張愛玲與電懋董事周海龍夫婦合照於紐約

Novelist Eileen Chang poses in New York with MP & GI director Harry Chow and his wife.

First, the times were different. In 1957, the political situation had settled in China. There were also clearly segregated left and right camps in the film industry. Because the films of MP & GI and Shaws needed to be distributed in Taiwan, they were broadly categorised as 'right-wing' companies (Great Wall, Feng Huang were 'left-wing'). Ideological struggles were non-existing at MP & GI. Second, MP & GI boss Loke Wan Tho (Lu Yuntao) had a business background, himself an art lover who had received elite education in England. Loke excelled in modern management. His general manager, Robert Chung, was educated in America and specialises in management and cinematic techniques. His production supervisor/manager Stephen Soong was no less educated, having been involved in drama and literature back in Shanghai. They shared a common goal – a desire to produce films modelled after Hollywood, in a studio system using modern management to cooperate with artistic creation. From the beginning, they refrained from the high-brow, big-budgeted epics of Yung Hwa. Its productions were free of the burdened morality typical of the Chinese intelligentsia, opting instead for light-hearted romances and musicals that catered to middle-class interests. They were shooting for quality, classy entertainment.

MP & GI had a script committee set up in 1955, but judging from its subsequent operation, script decisions were apparently not made by the committee, but more likely by Stephen Soong. In 1955, one of the members, Eileen Chang, migrated to America. Though she would go on to produce several scripts upon Soong's invitation, distance would bar her from direct involvement in the drafting of scripts or issues of creative directions. Sun Junsan passed away in 1962. Yao Ke was the most respected among the four. His contributions were valued at both Yung Hwa and Great Wall, having written the scripts for such prestigious projects as Yung Hwa's *Sorrows of the Forbidden City* (1948) and Great Wall's *A Strange Woman* (1950). He was reputed to have scripted *The True Story of Ah Q* (1958) under the pseudonym Xu Yan, with which actor Guan Shan won Best Actor in the Locarno Film Festival.[2] Yao had yielded no scripts

被雷震手持的一串大閘蟹纏住的場面（變成是竹籠中的蟹伸出爪夾着尤敏的衫裙）之類。王天林認為改動是為了合乎情理之餘增加多點噱頭、趣味。「至於選角方面，多是宋淇提議，我再加一兩個人選，大家一起參考一下。也不是完全由一個人決定，總之是大家都可以提意見，再一起考慮。」[4]

四

看來在宋淇主持創作／製作時期（1955至1964年），是採取比較合理、有彈性的領導，以編、導協商方式處理創作的，既不放任亦不專制。宋淇在此起的應是協調人才，讓品質有所保證的作用。

事實上，電懋這段時期的出品，從製作路線、製作質素到業務營運，都相當穩定，可以說是穩步上揚地發展。製作上已形成特色，就是偏重喜劇、歌唱／歌舞片和軟性文藝片三個類型。

喜劇和文藝片走的是中乘路線，近似宋淇一再提及的文學上的middle-brow：「泛指夠不上經典小說水準，而比迎合讀者低級趣味的小說高雅的那種說部。」[5]就是說，通俗而不粗俗，不追求嚴謹高深但也要求高雅格調。

喜劇片是輕鬆而不流於胡鬧：《情場如戰場》（張愛玲編，岳楓導，1957）、《桃花運》（張愛玲編，易文導，1958）、《青春兒女》（易文編導，1959）、《香車美人》（易文編導，1959）、《家有喜事》（汪榴照編，王天林導，1959）、《温柔鄉》（易文編導，1960）、《長腿姐姐》（汪榴照編，唐煌導，1960）、《快樂天使》（汪榴照編，易文導，1960）、《南北和》（宋淇編，王天林導，1961）、《南北一家親》（張愛玲編，王天林導）、《南北喜相逢》（張愛玲編，王天林導）等，較能體現這種特色。

under his real name at MP & GI, not even for his signature historical epics. Until 1963, MP & GI had not once made a historical drama. Yao could not have influenced MP & GI creative direction.

In *International Screen*, official publication and mouthpiece of MP & GI/Cathay, Soong was most frequently seen as the chairperson leading its script seminar. Wang Tianlin, a prolific director at MP & GI, revealed in his interview that it was Soong who had a firm hold over scripts, and many of the writers and directors were introduced by Soong. Birds of a feather flock together, as the saying goes. The pool includes Nellie Chin Yu (Qin Yu), Wang Liuzhao, Eileen Chang, Chang Cheh (Zhang Che), Xiao Tong, and directors like Evan Yang (Yi Wen) and Tao Qin also unsurprisingly hailed from a literary or culture background. On the flow of screenplay production, Wang says: "such was the process: scripts were first submitted to the production department and the best works were handed to Robert Chung, who assigned them to directors." But directors retained the right to revise the scripts. Wang had talked about giving a face-lift to Wang Liuzhao's *All in the Family* (1959), transforming a farce into a warm, light-hearted comedy which went on to win Best Director, Best Screenplay and Best Actress awards in the Asian Film Festival in 1959.[3]

While shooting *The Greatest Wedding on Earth* (1962), *Father Takes a Bride* (1963) and *The Greatest Love Affair on Earth* (1964), Wang would make a few changes to the scripts, despite Soong's reminder that no revisions were to be made. For instance, the two food stalls in *The Greatest Wedding on Earth* opposite each other in the scripts were rearranged on the same side of the street to facilitate set construction. Vernacularised gags and in-jokes were introduced into *The Greatest Love Affair on Earth.* The opening scene of *Father Takes a Bride,* in which Lucilla You Min is caught in Kelly Lai Chen (Lei Zhen) strand of crabs, is turned into You's dress being pinched by crabs in a basket. Wang believes that these revisions would make the story appear plausible while adding a little spice. "As for casting, the names were mostly suggested by Soong. We would add in a name or two for others to consider. It was more or less a joint decision."[4]

文藝片是趨温馨、哀艷、傷感而避大悲、嚴肅、沉重：《金蓮花》（岳楓編導，1957）、《曼波女郎》（易文編導，1957）、《四千金》（陶秦編導）、《玉女私情》（秦羽編，唐煌導，1959）、《蘭閨風雲》（陶秦編導，1959）、《春潮》（陶秦編導，1959）、《無語問蒼天》（張徹編，羅維導，1961）、《星星・月亮・太陽》（秦羽編，易文導，1961）、《珍珠淚》（張徹編，王天林導，1962）、《啼笑姻緣》（秦羽編，王天林導，1964）、《亂世兒女》（易凡編，袁秋楓導，1966）皆如是。

至於歌唱／歌舞片，其實是以唱為主，舞只是聊備一格，比較算得上歌舞並重的只有《歡樂年年》（岳楓編導，1957）、《龍翔鳳舞》（陶秦編導，1959）、《三星伴月》（秦羽編，陶秦導，1959）、《教我如何不想她》（易文編，王天林、易文導，1963）、《鶯歌燕舞》（易文編導，1963）和《雲裳艷后》（王月汀編，唐煌導，1960）。而《空中小姐》（易文編導，1959）、《野玫瑰之戀》（秦羽編，王天林導，1960）、《桃李爭春》（張徹編，易文導，1962）只能說是加插了大量歌唱的影片。即使《曼波女郎》有數場熱舞，不少歌唱，其實只是以劇情為主要吸引力的文藝片。

事實上，電懋的喜劇片、文藝片也跟隨當時的潮流，加插一些歌曲，或是青年人時興的流行舞，作為加強趣味與賣點。1962 年以後古裝黃梅調大興，電懋亦未能免俗，嘗試和邵氏競爭，趕拍、搶拍一些黃梅調歌唱片，如《梁山伯與祝英台》（1964）、《寶蓮燈》（1964），但都不是邵氏敵手。

五

至此不妨與邵氏作一比較，大致可以看到電懋創作／製作上的強項和弱點。1957 年邵氏仍未摸索到創作／製

4

It appears that the era under Stephen Soong's leadership (1955 – 1964) was a fairly reasonable and flexible leadership period that enabled communication between screenwriting and directing. Neither indulgent nor dictatorial, Soong coordinated between talents to ensure quality.

In fact, films made during this period benefited from MP & GI's stable creative direction, production quality and business operation. Quality was gradually improving with productions sharing a common inclination toward the genres of comedy, musicals and melodrama.

Comedies and melodramas were all heading toward the same middle brow direction Soong had repeatedly mentioned: "The kind of fiction not quite the standard of classical literature but more tasteful than lowbrow fictions catering to popular interests."[5] In short, popular but not vulgar, classy but not profound.

Comedies are light-hearted but not farcical, as in *The Battle of Love* (1957), *Spring Song* (1959), *Our Dream Car* (1959), *All in the Family*, *Bachelors Beware* (1960), *Sister Long Legs* (1960), *Happily Ever After* (1960), *The Greatest Civil War on Earth* (1961), *The Greatest Wedding on Earth*, and *The Greatest Love Affair on Earth*. Melodramas tended to be tender, mournful and sentimental but not overly tragic or serious: *Golden Lotus* (1957), *Mambo Girl* (1957), *Our Sister Hedy* (1957), *Her Tender Heart* (1959), *Wedding Bells for Hedy* (1959), *Torrents of Spring* (1959), *Songs without Words* (1961), *Her Pearly Tears* (1962), *Sun, Moon and Star* (1961), *A Story of Three Lovers* (1964), *A Debt of Blood* (1966). As for musicals, singing is more important than dancing. *Merry-Go-Round*, *Calendar Girl* (1959), *The More the Merrier* (1959), *Because of Her* (1963), *Mad about Music* (1963), and *Cinderella and Her Little Angels* (1960) are the only films that give equal weight to singing and dancing, while *Air Hostess* (1959), *The Wild, Wild Rose* (1960), and *Miss Secretary* (1962) includes mostly singing. Though *Mambo*

作的主要路向：一方面以古裝歷史宮闈大製作（由李翰祥帶領）作前導打響招牌，另方面嘗試不同的類型，以求找出某種可以開創潮流的片種作為主流。此時，電懋專注於喜劇、文藝、歌唱／歌舞片，特別是前兩類型，製作已走上軌道，產量和品質都穩步上揚，到 1962 年可說是進入高峰。

一個顯著的差別是，電懋擅於製作時裝片，其技術部門如劇本、美工、音樂、攝影在這方面都配合得純熟。邵氏從建廠開始就預設了古裝街道，顯然是有計劃要發展古色古香與中國氣派作為其製作特色與賣點。相反，國際／電懋在前七年都集中於拍當代或現代背景的影片。這一方面與其主事人傾向西化趣味，喜愛荷里活式的溫馨妙曼風格有關，歐德爾主持建廠，也沒有想到要興建古裝街道。這樣的輕騎出擊，當然有其成本輕、產量多而又易於管理、控制的優點，但太專注於幾個現代、當

陸運濤夫婦與
柯德莉夏萍及友人合影
Loke Wan Tho and his wife with Audrey Hepburn and friends.

鍾啟文與陸運濤攝於東京，背後是
《東京之夜》的大型廣告
Robert Chung (left) and Loke Wan Tho in Tokyo, in front of a billboard for *Night in Tokyo*.

Girl features a few feverish dance scenes and provides no shortage of singing, it is essentially a melodrama drawing strength from its story.

In fact, most MP & GI comedies and melodramas are decorated with songs or trendy dance steps to enhance their appeal. When *huangmei diao (*Yellow Plum Opera*)* period musicals became popular in 1962, MP & GI jumped onto the bandwagon to compete with Shaws, releasing such films as *Liang San Bo and Zhu Ying Tai* (1964) and *The Magic Lamp* (1964), though they didn't measure up to Shaws products.

5

Perhaps a comparison between MP & GI and Shaws can offer insight into the strength and weakness of the former. In 1957, Shaws had not quite found its direction. While making historical epics (led by Li Hanxiang) to establish the company's prestige, they ventured into different genres, trying to identify trends that could be developed. MP & GI, on the other hand, had already settled on light comedies, melodramas, song-and-dance films and sing-song musicals. With a well developed system and a steady output, MP & GI reached its peak in 1962.

MP & GI was distinguished by its contemporary films, its various departments such as scripts, arts direction, music and photography coordinated towards this direction. By comparison, Shaws set out to build a studio with historical sets, indicating its goal to make films that highlight Chinese cultures and history. For its first seven years, MP & GI focused solely on contemporary films. It was largely due to a management that preferred Hollywood-style entertainment. When its studio was built, it never occurred to overseer Albert Odell to build period sets. This low-budget approach undoubtedly had the merits of easy management and control, but it proved vulnerable to Shaws' period *huangmei diao* offensive, which enjoyed unexpected success.

In 1963, Shaws' *The Love Eterne* swept into Southeast Asia and raised the curtain on the *huangmei diao* trend and 'mountain song' features that triggered an onslaught of similar films. Lacking in period film

代類型，一遇到邵氏以古裝黃梅調突擊成功，就有點不知所措。

1963年，邵氏以黃梅調歌唱片《梁山伯與祝英台》創出風靡東南亞的紀錄，掀起黃梅調熱潮之後即大拍類似的黃梅調、山歌片，電懋由於缺乏拍古裝片的經驗，至此才急追趕拍，未免落後於形勢。與此同時，邵氏亦在嘗試發展其他類型：青春片、大型歌舞片、占士邦片驚險片，以及武俠片，皆以動作趣味為主要吸引，而非依靠劇情、對白，卒之在1966至1967年間繼黃梅調之後，再發展出「武俠新世紀」主潮。

強調實戰血腥的武俠片最能充份發揮利用邵氏的古裝廠房設備，亦切合1967年香港大暴動以後，港人備受困擾、壓抑而追求逃避發洩的心態，以及年輕一代不滿現實、反抗建制的反叛心理。與此相對，多年以來慣於搞溫馨、浪漫輕快的怡情小品或哀艷、奇情文藝格局的電懋，經此一役似乎難以適應，無法在短期內在創作／製作上順利轉型以抵禦強敵，重新緊抓住觀眾。這是否與電懋一向以來有太濃重的文人氣質，和注重中產趣味的寬鬆氣氛有關呢？

當然，1963年前後，電懋的人事變動亦大大影響了電懋的行政效率與業務運作。比如，1962、63年間宋淇因病請假了多個月，病癒後即被邵氏拉攏，主持編劇部門。同年，總經理鍾啟文掛冠而去，不久改投麗的電視。此後要勞煩陸運濤自任總經理，在星、港、台之間走動，行兵調將，和邵氏硬拼。但作為企業家也好，電影人也好，陸運濤和邵逸夫畢竟有很不相同的性格。陸在星馬一向經營的主要是電影製作以外的實業，到五十年代才逐漸對電影事業產生興趣；邵則從二十年代開始

experience, MP & GI was clearly disadvantaged in this battle. At the same time, Shaws was trying other genres: youth films, grand musical, James Bond style thriller and martial arts films. Its appeals were action and thrills, not plots or dialogues. From that developed the new trend of "New Style Martial Arts" that came out around 1966, taking over the popularity of *huang mei* musicals. The violence and combat action that characterise marital arts films made full use of the Shaws studios' period facilities. They echoed the sentiments of a troubled and repressed Hong Kong people seeking channels to vent their anger after the 1967 riots, and the younger generation's discontent and rebelliousness. By contrast, MP & GI was too accustomed to making light, romantic entertainment to deal with these drastic changes, unable to withstand its arch-enemy's market offensives to recapture the hearts of its audience. Perhaps it had something to do with the relaxed atmosphere of its bourgeois literati tradition.

Of course, the personnel changes at MP & GI around 1963 also greatly affected its operation. For instance, Stephen Soong was on sick leave for several months in 1962 and Shaws, upon his recovery, seized the chance to recruit him to chair its script department. Robert Chung also handed in his resignation in 1963. Since then, Loke Wan Tho had to jet between Singapore, Hong Kong, and Taiwan to personally marshal his army to battle Shaws. Entrepreneurs or filmmakers, Loke and Run Run Shaw had radically different personalities. Loke's business in Singapore was non-film related, and his interests in film only began in the 1950s. By contrast, Shaw's involvement with the films business dated back to the 1920s. Loke entrusted his Hong Kong staff to execute productions, and maintained a role of a strategic planner and financier. Shaw, typical of family business patriarchs, attended to affairs personally, never allowing long-term deficits. MP & GI reportedly suffered great loss over the years, though, in exchange, it had earned a great reputation

就全身投入電影作為娛樂事業。陸在電懋前期一向放手讓香港這邊的人員替他執行製作，而國泰那邊只製訂策略和不斷注資。邵則事事親力親為，企業上奉行家族／家長制，亦不容許公司長期虧蝕。據説電懋最終還是虧了不少，雖然賺得的是歷史上的美譽，和不少名作、明星的流傳。而1964年的台灣墜機事件，更令電懋損失了首腦人物陸運濤，令電懋陣腳大亂。此後邵氏乘勝追擊，佔盡上風，電懋也就由高峰不斷滑向下坡了。

六

以往，一般都說電懋是國泰機構屬下的影業公司，然而，電懋中人如王天林[6]、綦湘棠[7]都說過，電懋只是陸運濤個人的投資，並非全資隸屬於國泰機構。此點，曾在國泰機構當權的朱美蓮亦加以證實[8]。至於這其間的從屬與權力關係如何，實在值得研究者繼續追尋下去。

註

1. 見沈西城編著、翁靈文校訂，〈香港電影史初稿（1946-1976）之二〉，《觀察家月刊》，第3期，1978年1月1日。
2. 見黃愛玲編：《理想年代——長城、鳳凰的日子》，香港：香港電影資料館，2001年，頁269。
3. 見王天林訪問（一訪），香港電影資料館口述歷史計劃，1997年4月11日；及王天林訪問（二訪），香港電影資料館口述歷史計劃，2001年10月23日。上述資料現藏香港電影資料館內。
4. 見羅卡訪問、顧豪君整理，〈三個訪問〉(其中訪王天林一節），於羅卡編：《超前與跨越：胡金銓與張愛玲》，第廿二屆香港國際電影節回顧特刊，1998年，頁160-161。
5. 見林以亮：〈《海上花》英譯者〉，《更上一層樓》，台北：九歌出版社，1987年。
6. 見王天林訪問（二訪），同註3。
7. 見本書綦湘棠，〈我在電懋工作的回顧〉一文。
8. 見本書〈朱美蓮：國泰與我〉一文。

羅卡，電影學者。1990至2001香港國際電影節香港電影回顧節目策劃。現任香港電影資料館節目策劃。
Law Kar, film scholar. Programme coordinator of Hong Kong Cinema Retrospective at Hong Kong International Film Festival from 1990 to 2001. Now programmer at Hong Kong Film Archive.

for its glorious films and immortal stars. Loke's death in 1964 left a power vacuum at MP & GI never to be filled. Shaws didn't allow it any breathing room, seizing the opportunity to deal its rival a fatal blow. MP & GI went on an irreversible decline.

6

In the past, MP & GI was often regarded as a company under the umbrella of the Cathay Organisation. But company veterans like Wang Tianlin [6] and Shang-Tong Kei [7] had said that MP & GI was Loke's personal investment and was not solely financed by Cathay. We have verified this point with Meileen Choo, former head of the Organization.[8] As for the power relationships and details of the affiliation, these are issues that require further pursuit.

Translated by Herring Lamb

Notes

1. See Sheng Xicheng, "Development of Hong Kong Cinema Part 2:1946-1976 (the First Draft)" in *The Observers Monthly* (in Chinese), no. 3, 1 January 1978.
2. See Wong Ainling, ed.: *An Age of Idealism: Great Wall and Feng Huang Days*, Hong Kong: Hong Kong Film Archive, 2001, p. 269.
3. See 1st Interview with Wang Tianlin (in Chinese), Hong Kong Film Archive Oral History Project, April 11, 1997; and 2nd Interview with Wang Tianlin (in Chinese), Hong Kong Film Archive Oral History Project, October 23, 2001. Hong Kong Film Archive collection.
4. See "Three Recollections of Eileen Chang" in Law Kar, ed., *Transcending the Times: King Hu and Eileen Chang*, the 22nd Hong Kong International Film Festival catalogue, 1998, pp. 160-161.
5. See Lin Yiliang, "English translator of *Flower of Shanghai*" in *One Floor Up* (in Chinese), Taipei: Jiuge Press, 1987.
6. See 2nd Interview with Wang Tianlin, op. cit.
7. See Kei Shang-tong, "My MP & GI Days" in this volume.
8. See "Last Person Carrying the Torch: Meileen Choo on Cathy's Family Legacy" in this volume.

對電懋公司的某些觀察與筆記

- 舒琪 -

因着時間、資料和能力的局限，本文只能視作為對「國際電影懋業有限公司」（1956 - 65，以下簡稱「電懋」）」的初步觀察和報告，其中提出的部份觀點，也有待進一步的資料搜集來佐證。

一

為完成本文，筆者共參看了二十五部電影。[1]這二十五部作品予筆者的最深刻印象，不是有那幾部特別出色，而是在整體上，它們很可能標誌着香港電影史上最優秀的一家「片廠」（studio）的誕生、成長以至沒落。

「片廠」此一名詞，來自1930至1949年間美國荷里活「黃金時代」（Golden Era），「五大」（the Big Five）製片公司，[2]怎樣把製作、發行與放映（production, distribution and exhibition）集於一身，成為最終的「片廠制度」（studio system）的演變過程。這種以「垂直

Notes on MP & GI

- Shu Kei -

整合」方式（vertical integration，現代的説法是「一條龍」）建立而成的制度，最高峰時是四十年代中葉：當時「五大片廠控制了美國25個大城市中163家首輪戲院中的126家」，[3]八大公司加起來，「控制了超過全美92個最大城市的首輪戲院座位總和的百分之七十」；單是1943 - 44年度，八大的出品便佔了全美票房總收入的百分之九十五！[4]

跟荷里活片廠的發展模式一樣，電懋的電影王國最初也是從放映／戲院開始的（於1948年在新加坡成立國際戲院有限公司），繼而是發行（先於1951年在新加坡成立國際電影發行公司，兩年後登陸香港，成立子公司國際影片發行公司），最後才伸延至製作（首部出品是1955年的粵語片《余之妻》，左几導演，用的名義仍是國際，1956年才正式改組成電懋）。[5]我們手上沒有資料可以證明陸運濤成立電懋之初，確實是有意識地以荷里活的片廠制度為藍本，但我們卻有理由相信後者的模式應該是它努力效法的對象。

首先，陸運濤童年時已接受歐式教育，13歲便往瑞士留學，學士（1929 - 33）和碩士（1933 - 36）學位唸的都是文學，對攝影和觀鳥興趣特濃。[6]他返回新加坡接管及發展家族生意時（包括娛樂事業）是1940年，亦正是荷里活片廠制度的高峰期。根據傅葆石提供的資料，五十年代陸氏在星、馬一帶廣建戲院，引進的都是西方的最新設備，包括霍士公司在1953年起用的「新藝瑪闊銀幕」（Cinemascope）；擁有1,557個座位的新加坡奧迪安戲院裡，甚至有一家「荷里活咖啡廳」（Hollywood Café）。[7]這些均反映出陸氏對荷里活電影及其發展趨勢的熟悉。同年，被陸氏派遣到香港成立國際子公司的，是一名叫歐德爾的英籍猶太人。[8]歐氏在日戰期間曾代表五大之一的雷電華公司在重慶發行過電

《長腿姐姐》
Sister Long Legs

Due to limitation in time, availability of information and this writer's own capacity, the following essay would hopefully serve to provide some preliminary observations on the history of Motion Picture and General Investment Company Ltd. (MP & GI, 1956 – 65). Further research need to be conducted for the verification of some of the viewpoints put forward.

I

25 films were viewed for the purpose of this essay.[1] The most impressive thing this writer finds of these films is not that quite a number are indeed fine works, but that as a body of works, they most probably marked the birth, bloom and decline of the most classical – and best – studio in the history of Hong Kong cinema.

The word 'studio' is taken after the "studio system" during Hollywood's Golden Era (1930 – 1949), under which the Big Five corporations [2] fully integrated production, distribution and exhibition to guarantee enormous profits. The peak of the studio system was the mid-1940s, during which the Big Five controlled 126 first-run cinemas out of 163 in 25 major cities in America, [3] over 70% of all first-run theatres in the 92 largest cities in the US. During the 1943-1944 movie season alone, the Eight Majors collected about 95% of all film rentals in the US. [4]

Similar to the development of the Hollywood studio system, MP & GI mapped out its movie kingdom from exhibition, first setting up International Theatres in Singapore in 1948, extended to include distribution in 1951 with the setting up of International Film Distribution Agency in Singapore and a subsidiary with a similar name (International Films Distributing Agency) in Hong Kong two years later, and eventually ventured into production in 1955 with the Cantonese film, *My Wife, My Wife* (1955), directed by Tso Kea (Zuo Ji) (under International Films, which was renamed MP & GI the following year).[5] There is no available evidence to prove that Loke Wan Tho (Lu Yuntao) indeed modelled MP & GI after the Hollywood studio system, but we do have reasons to believe that the latter had likely been a big influence. First, Loke was educated in the European school system. He studied in Switzerland at 13, and his major in

影，[9] 製片人黃卓漢說他「會說國語、粵語，甚至於閩南語和潮州話。中文字他認識不到幾個，但劇本之好壞，由他太太唸給他一個概要，他就知道有沒有戲劇效果。反應之快，取捨之精，令香港同業為之咋舌。」[10] 而國際後來以「借貸或預繳形式支援一些獨立／衛星公司開戲，成品交『國際』旗下院線上映」的方法，則是「模仿當時美國『聯美公司』」的。[11] 1956年，電懋正式成立，擔任總經理的鍾啟文，也曾在霍士公司實習過。從這種種跡象推測陸氏在設計其電影王國的藍圖時，可能已存在着建立一個東方荷里活的野心，相信不至於太過武斷。

二

「在荷里活『片廠制度』下，每家片廠就好像一個『微型城市』（miniature city），有着它的（合約制）導演、演員、設計師、攝影師等。大片廠簡直就像個自給自足的社區：有醫務所、理髮店、牙醫診所、託兒所、幼稚園，甚至消防局。美高梅的一名宣傳人員便曾說：『如果不幸打仗被關在片廠裡，我們應可支持一段很長的時間』。」[12]

電懋在香港成立初期，基於主觀（總公司遠在新加坡，需要遙控）和客觀（港、英政府尚未輕易賣地）的因素，規模並不如荷里活片廠。[13] 它的總部設在尖沙咀樂宮大廈的二樓和三樓。樓上是辦公室（包括陸氏的私人辦公室、製作部、導演室和宣傳部），樓下是錄音室（主要用來收錄影片的插曲，而非電影配音間或混音室）、排演室和會議室。[14] 攝影棚則接收了上海製片家李祖永在九龍鑽石山搭建的永華片場。放映方面，歐德爾與璇宮、仙樂和金城三家戲院簽訂了長期合約，正式組成了香港有史以來的第一條國語片院線，在1956年2月11日開始生效，每部影片映期最少五天。[15]

university (1929 – 1933) and post-graduate school (1933 – 1936) was literature. He was known for his interests in photography and bird watching. [6] He returned to Singapore to take over family business (including entertainment) in 1940, a time when the Hollywood's studio system had grown into maturity. According to information provided by Poshek Fu, Loke built a large number of cinemas in both Singapore and Malaysia in the 50s, all of which equipped with the most advanced Western facilities, including the Cinemascope screen Fox introduced in 1953. The 1,557-seat Odeon Cinema in Singapore even had a Hollywood Café. [7] All these indicated that Loke was no stranger to Hollywood and its trends. Furthermore, Albert Odell, who represented Loke to set up International Films in Hong Kong in 1953, [8] had served in RKO, one of the Big Five, to distribute films in Chongqing during WWII before he worked for Loke. [9] At least a couple of sources pointed out that when International Films initiated the method of advancing production money to independent companies to produce films in exchange for their distribution rights, Odell was in fact taking his cue from United Artists. [10] Last but not least, Robert Chung (Zhong Qiwen), general manager at MP & GI when it was founded in 1956, had served an internship at Fox. From all these traces, it would not be too arbitrary to conclude that when Loke was designing the blueprint of his movie kingdom, he was most probably imbued with the ambition of building a 'Hollywood of the East'.

2

Under the Hollywood studio system, every studio was a miniature city. It had its own contracted directors, actors, designers, cinematographers, etc. A large studio was similar to a self-sufficient community: it had clinics, hair saloons, dental clinics, day care centres, kindergartens, and even a fire station. An MGM promotion staff once said, 'If there was a war, and unfortunately we're trapped in the studio, we should be able to live in it for a very long time.[11]

When MP & GI was founded, its size paled in comparison to Hollywood studios. [12] Its headquarters

電懋並非香港影壇的第一家片廠：在它之前而又投資相當的，起碼便有也是來自上海的蔣伯英創辦的大中華影業公司（1946 - 49）、上述李祖永創辦的永華影業公司（1947 - 54）、和邵邨人的邵氏父子公司（1950 - 57，邵逸夫從星洲來港後，另設邵氏兄弟公司）三家。但使電懋有別於這些在戰後成立的大小片廠的最大關鍵，是陸氏本人的出身、思想和理念。和蔣、李、邵諸氏（還有長城的張善琨、袁仰安、泰山的卜萬蒼、鳳凰的朱石麟等）不一樣，陸氏出生已是首富（陸佑）之子，註定要承繼父親家族遍佈東南亞的龐大企業——包括銀行、橡膠園、錫礦、地產、飲食、酒店、航空、保險等生意，電影不過是其中一個項目（雖則後來卻佔據了陸氏頗大部份時間和心思）。這樣的家庭背景，加上自幼即放洋海外的經歷，還有是他在考取碩士學位後仍繼續（在倫敦經濟學院）攻讀經濟的學歷，使人不難推想得到，陸氏與他在電影事業上的其他對手競爭時，會佔了起碼如下的優勢：

1. 除了自小即被培養出一份宏觀的企業概念外，陸氏還對西方的現代商管理念有着一手的接觸與認識。片廠制度的垂直整合的模式被吸納成為電懋業務的政策指引（guiding policy），遂十分的順理成章。相反的，他的對手們卻幾乎毫不例外地都來自電影界（大都從拍片／小本製作開始，只小部份是經營戲院起家的），而且又都僅限於上海一地，遂因此而無法不經常受到客觀環境的牽制（時局和政治氣候的變化），鮮具主動地去開拓主觀條件的遠見和氣魄（發展發行與放映業務，套用今天的說法，就是不懂得怎樣去開發「硬體」，為「軟體」裝備配套）。他們兩次南來香港（1945 年抗日戰爭後和1949年共黨「解放」中國後），便完全是因為上海／國內政治形勢的突變；其後在香港的沒落，也基於同一因

was on the second and third floors of an office building in Tsim Sha Tsui. The main office was on the third floor (which included Loke's private office, the production department, directors' room and promotion department). The recording studio (not a dubbing or mixing studio but used mainly for recording film songs), rehearsal room and conference room were on the second floor. [13] The shooting studio was the Yung Hwa Studio in Diamond Hill, obtained by MP & GI from Li Zuyong, a producer from Shanghai. In terms of exhibition, Albert Odell signed a long-term contract with three local theatres, and thus formed the first Mandarin film circuit in Hong Kong. The contract went into effect on February 11, 1956, stipulating that a film's minimum run is five days. [14]

Strictly speaking, MP & GI was not the first 'studio' in Hong Kong: before it, companies with substantial investment had included: Great China (Dazhonghua) Film Development Company (1946–1949), founded by Jiang Boying from Shanghai; Yung Hwa Film Company (1947–1954), founded by Li Zuyong; and Shaw and Sons Company Ltd. (1950 -1957) founded by Runde Shaw (Run Run, Runde's brother, founded Shaw Brothers after he came to Hong Kong from Singapore). But it was Loke's background, ideals and believes that distinguished MP & GI from the other companies founded after the war.

Loke came from a background that was totally different from his above peers. Son of business tycoon Loke Yew, the young Loke was destined to inherit his father's business empire which, spreading all over Southeast Asia, included banks, rubber plantations, mines, real-estate, food, hotels, airlines and insurance. The movie business was just one specialty among many (though this would later occupy most of Loke's time and energy). Such background, plus the fact that Loke actually read economics at the London School of Economics after receiving his Master's degree, at least gave him the following advantages over his competitors:

素（先是 1949 年後國內縮小了港片的發行網，連帶匯款來源也受到影響；繼而是 1956 年後台灣市場也對國語片入口定下限制）。[16] 雄厚的家族實力使陸氏沒有任何類似的後顧之憂，進攻退守，完全控制在自己手上，這是其對手所難望其項背的。

2. 就文化背景方面來說，陸氏比起他們又明顯地少了一份民族使命感。雖然我們找不到很多有關陸氏對電影的個人看法的闡述，但從一鱗半爪的官方報導來看，起碼可以肯定的，是電影對他來說，並不似其對手般有着「憂國憂民」、以至「救國救民」的沉重責任，而是一種很實際的興趣與享受的結合。[17] 是以當南來的上海影人們仍迷醉在懷緬昔日時光、和視發揚及承繼民族精神為己任的時候，陸氏的目光卻早已投射到二次大戰後逐步擺脫貧窮，欣欣向榮的香港都會身上。只要比較一下他們的製作類型，便不難找到端倪：蔣伯英成立大中華後拍攝的第一部國語片《蘆花翻白燕子飛》（何非光，1946），即以抗戰前後的上海為背景。故事描寫一對男女徘徊在民族道德與物質誘惑之間，最後以男主角「重返建國隊伍」作結。[18] 永華的首二作，是改編自吳祖光舞台劇《正氣歌》的《國魂》（卜萬蒼，1948）、和姚克《清宮怨》的《清宮秘史》（朱石麟，1948），都是別有寄託的大型歷史劇。1957 年，邵逸夫接手邵氏父子組成邵氏兄弟後，立即開拍中國的「四大美人」系列（《貂蟬》／1958、《楊貴妃》／1962、《武則天》／1962、《西施》[19]）。相對之下，打響電懋招牌的三部頭炮作品中，除了《金蓮花》（岳楓，1957）是以舊中國（二十年代）做背景外，其他兩部都是時裝片：《情場如戰場》（張愛玲編劇、岳楓導演，1957）是一部典型的兩性喜劇，寫一段一女周旋於三男之間的愛情爭奪戰，《四千金》（陶秦，1957）雖以親情為主，但主要

1. He was able to develop a macroscopic view on corporate enterprises as well as acquire first-hand experiences and knowledge in Western business management. Probably because of this, the model of 'vertical integration' easily and logically became the guiding policy of MP & GI's strategy. By contrast, almost all his competitors were from the industry (most started with productions, with only a small fraction in exhibition), with their business based and limited in Shanghai, as a result of which, their development would almost inevitably be affected by the political situation. They also rarely had the vision and determination to explore and open up new possibilities – to branch into distribution and exhibition (in modern terms, it can be said that they didn't know how to set up a 'hardware' system to market their 'software'). Indeed, the two occasions they took refuge in Hong Kong, once in 1945 after WWII and later after the 1949 Communist takeover of China, stand as proof of how they were affected by the political situation of Shanghai/China. Similar causes also led to their later decline: distribution of Hong Kong films in China shrank drastically after 1949 and capital was not allowed out of the country, followed by the imposition of import quota of Mandarin films by the Taiwanese government in 1956. [15] Supported by his family, Loke was almost always in full control and did not have to worry about political influences, an advantage his competitors obviously lacked.

2. Unlike his competitors who went through foreign invasion and political turmoils, Loke did not have a strong sense of nationalism, let alone a sense of responsibility to educate or promote patriotism through films. For Loke, the cinema is both a personal interest and a form of leisure. [16] While his peers from Shanghai were still indulging in nostalgia for the past and considered themselves crusaders of Chinese heritage, Loke had already set his eyes upon the blooming metropolis of Hong Kong after WWII. The genres in which they made their first productions offer ready hints. *Gone are the Swallows When the Willow Flowers Wilt* (1946), the first Mandarin film made by Great China, is about a young couple's struggle between nationalism and materialism set in wartime

的戲劇性卻建築在性、愛情與婚姻的衝突身上。事實上，在電懋的二百多部片目裡，時裝片的比例遠超於古裝片（包括歷史宮闈片、武俠片和黃梅調歌唱片），幾次與邵氏搶拍同一題材的古裝片和民初片——《梁山伯與祝英台》（1964）、《寶蓮燈》（1964）、《啼笑姻緣》（1964）——也都落敗。我們沒有資料顯示陸氏本人對電懋的製作／創作路線有着很嚴密的監管或控制，但若干作品乃受其個人品味影響而開拍者，卻有跡可尋。根據葛蘭小姐的說法，《曼波女郎》的拍攝意念，便是來自一次她與陸氏及電懋中人往夜總會，陸氏親睹她大跳曼波熱舞時靈機一觸啟發出來的。[20] 1959年的《空中小姐》上映時被左派報章大肆抨擊為替台灣塗脂抹粉的宣傳片（皆因影片佔了相當篇幅介紹台灣風光，並唱了一首叫〈大家心一條〉的插曲），[21] 但不要忘記的，是作為這部在更大程度上其實是替新興航空事業打廣告的影片老闆的陸氏，本身也同時是馬來亞航空公司的董事之一。1961 年的《香車美人》的靈感來源，是一個配合了名車展覽的「香車美人」的年度選舉玩意，舉辦和參加者都是上流社會人物（從片中的實錄片段中所見，評審和佳麗大部份是洋人）。可以想像，這也應是陸氏十分熟悉的活動之一。

三

片廠制度是在二十年代開始逐漸成型，至三十年代達臻成熟。其中一項最大的優點，是使跟它簽訂了合約的員工（不論幕前抑或幕後）都有一種安全感，可以在可見的未來日子裡，安（專）心地發展自己的技藝以至事業。對演員來說（特別是新演員），片廠不啻是一個資源充沛的訓練場，還會按照其個性和氣質來塑造合適的角色讓她們演出，為她們建立鮮明的形象，並制訂出一套完整的計劃來行銷（market）這個形象，務求令她們

《啼笑姻緣》
A Story of Three Loves

《聊齋誌異》
Fairy, Ghost, Vixen

得到大眾的歡迎。對其他技術人員來説，穩定的工作量可使他們熟能生巧，應付不同的挑戰。創作者也然：長期被指派執行某種類型電影的結果，雖則很容易會變得陳規化，但換轉另一角度看，視之為風格的磨練卻也未嘗不可；如在這基礎上加上個人的歷練與洞察力，最終成為一名電影作者，也是常見的事情。

把上述的荷里活經驗比照電懋的九年歷史，會發現很多相類的地方。兩者最接近的是對培植演員／製造明星的不遺餘力。在未正式改組前，即還屬國際時期，電懋已設有演員訓練班，培訓了新人雷震、丁皓、蘇鳳、田青等，[22]改組後，則先後羅致了林黛（原屬「永華」）、葛蘭（自由身）、尤敏（原屬邵氏）、林翠、陳厚、李湄（均原屬自由公司）、白露明（原粵語片演員）、葉楓（新人）等，當中又以女演員為主。泰半以上作品，都是專門為這些女星「度身」訂造的（此語包括字義上和比喻上的意思）。舉例説，葛蘭能歌擅舞，遂有《曼波女郎》的產生；《長腿姐姐》（1960）的指涉對象自是身材高挑的葉楓；《四千金》和《玉樓三鳳》（1960）雖然都改編自鄭慧的小説，但角色的分配，卻彷彿完全按照着幾個女演員的特質來編寫似的，前者的穆虹（温順賢良）、葉楓（性感誘人）、林翠（活潑好動）、蘇鳳（小鳥依人）和後者的王萊（幽怨鬱結）、李湄（曾經滄海）和丁皓（任性妄為），全都貼切得不作他人想；[23]《桃李爭春》（葉楓、李湄）和《鶯歌燕舞》（葉楓、夷光）則把兩名戲路相近的女星放在一起爭妍鬥麗一番，來製造鬥氣冤家（the odd couple）的戲劇效果；但最「肆無忌憚」的，卻莫過於《青春兒女》（1959）了：影片號稱以大學生活為題，但稀薄的劇情，卻不過是為了湊合兩名女星（葛蘭和林翠）的同場演出，好讓她們有機會展覽其多面性的才華（於是前者除載歌載舞外，還演出了

《青春兒女》中的葛蘭與林翠，一個唱崑曲，一個滑水

Grace Chang (left) and Jeanette Lin Cui in *Spring Song*, Chang performing on stage and Lin water skiing.

Shanghai, which ends with the man's eventual decision to 'return to the nation-building team'. [17] The first two films of Yung Hwa, *The Soul of China* (1948) and *Sorrows of the Forbidden City* (1948), are both historical epics with subtle political implications. Having taken over Shaw and Sons and restructured the company into Shaw Brothers in 1957, Run Run Shaw immediately started filming the 'Four Great Beauties of China' series (*Diau Darling*, 1958; *Yang Kwei-fei, the Magnificent Concubine*, 1962; *Empress Wu Tse-tien*, 1962; *Hsi Shih The Beauty of Beauties*, 1965).[18] By contrast, among the first three films MP & GI made, only *Golden Lotus* (1957) is a period drama, set in 1920s China. The other two were both set in contemporary Hong Kong, of which *The Battle of Love* (1957) is a classic screwball comedy, while *Our Sister Hedy* (1957) is a comedy-drama about sex, love and marriage. One only needs to browse through the filmography of MP & GI, with about 200 titles, to see that there are much more contemporary films than period films (inclusive of historical epics, martial arts films and opera films).

Although no information is available to indicate Loke had a tight control of creative strategy, incidents did show that some of the films were influenced by his personal tastes. [19] An example would be *Mambo Girl* (1957), whose concept, according to Grace Chang (Ge Lan), was born out of an evening at a nightclub with Loke and company personnel, during which Loke was so impressed by her hot Mambo dancing that he jokingly suggested that a film be made out of it. When *Air Hostess* (1959) was released in 1959, the film was heavily criticised by leftist papers as Taiwan propaganda (at one point the film was like a Taiwan travelogue, and a song entitled "We Share the Same Heart" was performed). [20] It should be noted that Loke was also on the Board of Malayan Airways, and that the film can be said to be an extended commercial of the up-and-coming airline industry. The concept of *Our Dream Car* (1959) came from an annual beauty pageant organised as a side-bar event of a car exhibition. From the documentary footage of the exhibition, one can see that both the organisers and participants were mostly members of the upper class

一場崑曲；後者則表演了游泳、滑水、騎馬和跳牛仔舞等技能）。類似這樣的star vehicles在當時的國、粵語影壇雖然並不罕見，但卻無疑以電懋最具規模、進取性和策略性，在同期幾家片廠中，也是最成功的。事實上，不獨上述的女星各個個性特出、形象立體，就連男演員（陳厚的靈活矯健、雷震的斯文內向、張揚的風流倜儻、田青的雞手鴨腳、喬宏的魯鈍戇直）也各具特色。不過就整體而言，主力仍是放在女星們身上。[24]

但這項政策影響所及，卻使電懋的電影幾乎都以陰柔的風格為主。以類型言，則以都市喜劇、文藝言情片（通俗劇）和歌舞片佔了大多數。有趣的是電懋解體後，取其位而代之的「邵氏」公司卻發展出一條與之完全相反的純陽剛路線（主要類型是以動作取勝的新派武俠片）。這是一個十分值得研究的課題，不過已非本文範圍所能涵蓋。筆者想特別提出來一談的，是這份純陽剛風格的始作俑者張徹。在成為邵氏的當家導演前，張氏本是電懋的編劇，[25]其中《遊戲人間》[26]和《桃李爭春》[27]，若把前者流露出來的那份對性身份與性傾向的迷惘和曖昧寄託、與充斥着後者每格膠卷的camp品味，拿來跟他後來在邵氏拍攝的一系列武俠片裡其實相當昭然若揭的homo-eroticism意識比較，將會是件很revealing的事情。Revealing，是因為它說明了下列兩件事情：

1. 張氏是一名結結實實的電影作者，其真情真性並不輕易為客觀的因素而轉移（風格好壞與境界高低則是另一問題）；

2. 但面對着片廠的強大權力架構（hierarchy of authority）時，即使有着強烈創作意欲和表達力的作者如張氏，也無法不服膺在其底下。

這兩項事實又引伸到一項爭論：即在風格與權力互相抗

(the jurors and most of the pageant candidates were, in fact, expatriates). One could easily imagine this was an activity Loke was familiar with.

3

One of the advantages of the studio system is that it offers a sense of security to all the contracted staff (whether they are stars or crew), allowing them to focus on developing their craft and even a career in a foreseeable future. For actors, especially newcomers, the studio not only provides them a resourceful training arena but also creates tailor-made roles for them based on their personalities, and help them build up unique images. The studio would also design strategies to market these images to ensure popularity among the public. For technical members of the crew, a steady amount of work provides them the necessary drill to improve their craft and enable them to better handle difficulties and challenges. This also applies to directors. One may suspect that their films easily become clichés if they have been making films of the same genre for a long time. But looking at it from another angle, one can consider it as a style-polishing process. With the gradual development of a personal vision and accumulation of experiences, it is not unusual for a filmmaker to eventually emerge as an auteur.

Compare this mode of the Hollywood studio system with the nine-year history of MP & GI, one would find many similarities, the first of which is the effort to train and produce stars. Before it was restructured into MP & GI, the company had organised an actors' workshop, training such talents as Kelly Lai Chen (Lei Zhen), Kitty Ting Hao (Ding Hao), Dolly Soo Fung (Su Feng), Tian Qing *et al.* [21] After it was formally set up, it signed Linda Lin Dai (from Yung Hwa), Lucilla You Min (from Shaw Brothers), Grace Chang, and Jeanette Lin Cui, Peter Chen Ho (Chen Hou) and Helen Li Mei (all from Liberty Film), Chistine Bai Luming (originally a Cantonese film actress), and Julie Yeh Feng (Ye Feng) (a newcomer). Most of these were actresses, for whom more than half of the films were tailored (both in the literal and allegorical sense) to showcase their

衡（style vs authority）、創作自由與創作監管互相對峙（creative expression vs creative control）時，二者之間究竟由何者去決定一家片廠的標記與特色？這其實是研究片廠制度與主張作者理論（auteur theory）的兩派學說一直爭議不休的一項議題。這裡，張徹的例子也許可以為此提供一個解答：個人（作者）沒可能凌駕制度（片廠）——這所以作者的風格要被迫隱藏在片廠的風格下（熟悉張氏武俠片風格的觀眾，不可能想像他會寫出像《遊》片和《桃》片似的「軟性」劇本）；但有着強烈個性和vision（視野、世界觀）的作者，卻必然可透過「隱藏」的風格來表達自我——即所謂「暗渡陳倉」。最理想的情形，自是個人（不論是編劇、導演、演員、抑或攝影、美術以至配樂）的風格，能夠與片廠的製作流程、管理架構、資源以至敘事傳統、行銷策略等互相融合。但即使這樣，個人的風格最終仍不免是整個片廠風格的屈折變化（inflection）。[28]此亦正是張氏在邵氏時期的情形：其作品中的同性愛嚮往和因罪疚感而產生的自殘傾向，與當年邵氏積極地在電懋底陰柔、都市的現代風格以外尋找並建立另一品牌標記的意圖，無獨有偶地在「武俠片」這個類型和「陽剛氣息」此一風格身上，找到了微妙的結合；張氏過去一直被屈折和壓抑着的性情，終於得以被釋放出來，被發揮得淋漓盡致。但這卻並不表示張的風格即界定了邵氏的風格，因為同時期邵氏不獨也有其他的導演拍攝同類型的武俠片（雖然未必優勝得過張氏），而且還生產其他以男性觀眾為主要對象的、同屬陽剛路線的電影（如仿《鐵金剛》片集的動作片、功夫片、古裝豔情片、血腥恐怖片、「軟心」色情片等）。正確的說法，其實應該是邵氏的風格容納了（contain）張氏的風格。

talents. Thus, Chang's singing and dancing talent gave birth to *Mambo Girl*, and *Sister Long Legs* (1960) refers, of course, to the tall and slim Yeh Feng. Although *Our Sister Hedy* (1957) and *Between Tears and Laughter* (1960) were both adapted from the novels by Zheng Hui, the female lead roles in each film seemed to have been specially written according to the temperaments of the actresses. The gentle and virtuous Mu Hong, the sexy and seductive Yeh Feng, the boyish and outgoing Lin Cui, and the affectionate and fragile Soo Fung of the former; the depressed and bitter Wang Lai, the sophisticated and love-lorn Li Mei and the eccentric and headstrong Ting Hao of the latter, all match perfectly with their roles. [22] *It's Always Spring* (1962, starring Yeh Feng, Li Mei) and *Mad About Music* (1963, starring Yeh Feng, Ye Kwong) put together two actresses with similar style and appeal to create the comic effect of an odd couple. But the most 'unbridled' was undoubtedly *Spring Song* (1959). The film claims to be an account of university life, but the thin narrative is no more than an excuse for the two female leads (Grace Chang and Lin Cui) to perform in the same film and showcase their versatility (with Chang displaying her song-and-dance skills, plus an excerpt of *kun opera* as a bonus; and with Lin showing off her talent in swimming, water skiing, horseback riding and cowboy dancing). Such star vehicles were not rare in both the Mandarin and Cantonese cinema in those days, but the practice of MP & GI was definitely the largest in scale, the best in strategy and the most aggressive. It was also the most successful among its contemporaries. In fact, not only every actress had her established star image, even the male stars had each developed a personal style (the agile and smart Peter Chen Ho, the gentle and intellectual Lai Chen, the womanising Chang Yang, the clumsy Tian Qing, and the awkward but straightforward Roy Chiao [Qiao Hong]). The main focus, however, was still on the women.

The result of such a policy was that almost all MP & GI films were affected with a style that can be termed feminine. This was reflected in its choice of genres, which were mostly limited to urban comedies, melodramas and musicals. As such, it's a point of

四

或曰：作為「只是」它的編劇，張徹是無從左右一部電影的風格的——這正是筆者提出張氏來做例子的第二個原因：想藉着他説明電懋的另一項特色，即是它對劇本／編劇的重視。

上面説過，我們沒資料證明陸氏個人對電懋的製作路線到底有多大程度的監管（他大部份時間都在新加坡），但電懋從開始已把劇本／編劇的地位凌駕於導演之上，卻是很清楚的事情。早在歐德爾掌管的國際時期，在朱旭華的協助下，它已成立了一個劇本編審會員會，由宋淇擔任主任， 委員成員有姚克、秦亦孚（即秦羽）、張愛玲、汪榴照、易文、陶秦等，顧問是孫晉三，所有劇本都要經他修改。[29]這個制度的成立，可能與朱旭華本身也出身自編劇有關，[30]但環顧當時的眾多國、粵語片公司，這樣的做法卻應屬破天荒（這之前，片場被國際接管的永華設有一個「編導部」、大觀和長城也在1950年成立了編導委員會，[31]但成員大都是編導集於一身的writer-director；電懋的劇本編審會員會中，則只易文和陶秦又編又導，但二人有的時候也會只編不導）。

構成這份對劇本／編劇的重視的另一可能，是荷里活的影響。在後者的片廠制度架構裡，大都設有一個「故事部門」（Story Department），聘備若干合約制編劇（最高紀錄是美高梅公司，在三十年代早期同時僱用了四十名編劇）；有的片廠甚至在這部門下，再細分一個「閱覽部門」（Reading Department），聘有若干「閱稿人」（readers），負責閱讀大量的小説、舞台劇本和短篇故事，寫成故事大綱（差不多每天要讀完一本書），適合改編成電影的，則詳列原因和意見，交給部門總管再呈上級。三、四十年代時，大部份片廠還制定了一個編劇訓練計劃，由一名資深編劇帶領着十到二十名年輕編

interest to note that Shaw Brothers, which replaced MP & GI and became the top studio in Hong Kong, in contrary actually developed an almost purely masculine style in its films (most of which belonged to the action-packed martial-arts, or *wuxia*, genre). This is an area which deserves further research and study, but is beyond the scope of this essay. What I intend to do here is to have a brief discussion on Chang Cheh, the creator of this pure masculine style. Before he became one of the major directors in Shaw Brothers, Chang worked briefly as a screenwriter in MP & GI from 1960 to 1962, [23] during which he wrote the scripts for *You were Meant for Me* (1961) and *It's always Spring.* The former, which involves the sporty and boyish Ting Hao in a gender-bending plot that requires her to play both sexes, displays a sense of perplexity and ambiguity on gender identity. The latter, with its plot playing out like a prolonged competition between two sexy popular song divas, has the word "camp" stamped on almost every single frame. Compare these films with the more-than-obvious homo-eroticism in Chang's series of *wuxia* films for Shaw Brothers and one will find it particularly revealing. What it reveals are:

a. That Chang was a true auteur in that he would not allow his personality and style to be distorted by the environment or other objective elements, although the achievements of his works might be subject to further discussion;

b. That faced with the hierarchy of authority of the studio system, even such auteur as Chang had to subjugate himself under such power structure.

This leads us to an oft argued controversy: in cases of style vs authority and creative expression vs creative control, what determine the signature and style of a studio? Here, Chang and his films might be able to provide an answer: it is almost impossible for an individual (auteur) to override the system (studio), as such, the style of the auteur has to hide itself under the style of the studio (audience who are familiar with Chang's *wuxia* style would simply find it impossible to imagine that he is capable of writing such 'soft' scripts as the two mentioned above); on the other hand, an

劇，讓他們隨便發問和參與編寫。不過荷里活真正重視的，其實是劇本多於編劇。曾替荷里活寫過劇本的文學家和戲劇家可說是不計其數（順手拈來的便有費茲傑羅／Scott Fitzgerald、赫胥黎／Aldous Huxley、福克納／William Faulkner、咸密／Dashiell Hammett、陳德勒／Raymond Chandler、布萊希特／Bertolt Brecht等），但卻鮮有愉快的經驗和結局。從德國去到荷里活發展的費立茲・朗（Fritz Lang）便曾說：「在歐洲，編劇十分重要，但在這裡卻淪為技工。在任何一家片廠，一個劇本起碼會有超過十名編劇寫過。」[32] 監製過《星海浮沉錄》（A Star is Born, 1937）、《亂世佳人》（Gone with the Wind, 1939）和《蝴蝶夢》（Rebecca, 1940）等名片的製片人大衛・塞茨尼克（David O. Selznick）在一次哥倫比亞大學的講演上說：「劇本是決定一部電影的品質最基本和最重要的東西。」但不到五分鐘卻續說：「有時候你要把（劇本）修改過六、九、十以至十五次才會滿意。這個過程可能已打砸了起碼半打甚至更多的編劇。」[33]

電懋雖受荷里活影響，但在這方面卻與它相反，由始至終都沒出現過類似塞茨尼克形容的情形。就創作的角度而言，可說是一種進步。[34] 我們不知道黃仁所指「所有劇本都要經孫晉三修改」一語，具體上究竟如何執行，但下列三個例子，卻可以進一步證明電懋對編劇的尊重與器重：

1. 1957 年的《四千金》改編自鄭慧的同名短篇小說，編劇是陶秦。但「編審會」的主任宋淇卻在影片推出時，發表了一篇洋洋四千字、題為〈小說與電影〉的文章，語重深長地闡述了電影在改動原著時作出的詳細考慮。[35] 文章引用了很多荷里活電影的例子，包括《紅粉忠魂未了情》（*From Here to Eternity*, 1953）、《蓬門淑女》（*The Country Girl*, 1954）、《叛艦喋血記》（*The Caine*

《四千金》
Our Sister Hedy

auteur with a strong personality and clear vision should be able to express himself/herself through a 'hidden' style, the so called 'undercover' style. The ideal case, of course, is when the style of the individual (screenwriter, director, actor, cinematographer, art director or composer) "fused with the studio's production operations and management structure, its resources and talent pool, its narrative tradition and marketing strategy." But even in such an ideal case, the personal style must inevitably become an inflection of the general style of the studio.[24] This is exactly the case with Chang when he was with Shaw Brothers: the homo-erotic style and the self-destructive tendency generated from his sense of guilt manifested in his violent and masochistic *wuxia* films had found a subtle fusion with Shaw Brothers' intention to establish itself as a brand name which would be an alternative to MP & GI's modern, urban and feminine style. Chang's personality, inflected and suppressed by MP & GI's style, was thus finally released and expressed in full. Yet this does not mean that Chang's personal style had defined Shaw Brothers', not only because the company also had other directors making *wuxia* films (though they might be inferior to Chang's), but the company was also developing other 'masculine' genres for its mostly male audience, such as James bond-style action films, kung fu films, erotic period dramas, exploitative slashers and 'soft core' erotica. To put it correctly, it is Shaw Brothers' style that contains Chang's personal style.

4

Some may point out that Chang Cheh was *only* the screenwriter, and not in a position to determine the style of a film. This is exactly the other reason for my citing Chang as a case study. Through him I want to discuss a second characteristic of MP & GI – the way the company treated scripts and scriptwriters.

As mentioned before, no information is available to indicate Loke had great control over MP & GI's production strategy. However, there is evidence to show that MP & GI had allowed the scriptwriter to override the director from the very beginning. It could be traced back to the days when Albert Odell was

Mutiny, 1954）、《巨人》（*Giant*, 1956）、《巫山春色》（*Tea and Sympathy*, 1956）、《苦雨戀春風》（*Written on the Wind*, 1957）和《碼頭風雲》（*On the Waterfront*, 1954）等，[36]「目的就是想説明：所有一枝一節都經過審慎的考慮，並不是貿貿然隨便處理的。」文中提到陶秦在處理希棣（林翠）與何炎（雷震）的結局時，曾作過三度修改，但由頭到尾都未有其他人插手過。這篇文章充份反映出電懋對不論是原著作者抑編劇都愛護有加、亦恭亦敬。難怪後來鄭慧也寫了一篇《魔術的手杖》，盛讚陶秦「真是一個神奇的織補匠……來為我這故事安排得更美滿、完整」。[37]

2. 1960年的《六月新娘》的編劇是張愛玲，也是她最不成功的一個劇本（故事説到葛蘭與張揚見面後，即還不到影片的一半，劇情便完全無法發展下去，要不斷加插夢境、香港風光的旅遊片段來充塞時間。香港國際電影節在幾年前舉辦的「超前與跨越：胡金銓與張愛玲」回顧專題的特刊中，指《六》片「故事吸引人的地方是張愛玲創造了這種內容豐富、人物性格特出的內在戲劇世界」、是「張替香港國語片編寫的劇本中最完熟的其中一個」，[38]明顯是溢美之辭）。根據葛蘭的憶述，影片的劇本是張從美國郵寄回港的，本身就寫得不完整，導演唐煌幾乎是完全按照着原著拍攝的。[39]眾所周知，宋淇與張愛玲的關係十分密切，對導演改動她的劇本都處理得格外小心，[40]唐煌拍來有所制肘是可以想像的。因為出於對編劇的尊重，卻連劇本有欠妥善也不作出修改，未免有點矯枉過正，但這個例子卻足以證明編劇在電懋裡的崇高地位（宋對張可能會有偏袒的成份，但從他處理《四千金》的手法來看，原則還是一致的）。

3. 也是根據葛蘭的憶述：同年的《野玫瑰之戀》，創作意念最先乃來自編劇秦羽。後者一早事先張揚，要為她

《蘭閨風雲》
Wedding Bells for Hedy

度身編寫一個全新形象的劇本。她讀過完成劇本後，立刻致電宋淇，表示片中綽號「野玫瑰」的女歌星鄧思嘉一角，由葉楓演出會比自己更適合。但宋淇卻告訴她這角色秦羽心目中非她莫屬。結果是葛蘭一路下來都演得心驚肉跳，王天林也導的戰戰兢兢，卻就此成就了這部不獨是電懋二百多部出品中最傑出的電影、甚至是（arguably）六十年代香港最優秀的國語片。在明星制度掛帥下，動用龐大的資源去力捧某個演員是每家片廠都有的事情；但容許、而且還近乎義無反顧地支援一名編劇的個人構思，去改變已成名演員的形象[41]——更甚者是這個野性、潑辣和充滿動物本能的奔放形象本身並不容易討好（從傳統角度來看，甚至十分「危險」），卻是連荷里活也不敢輕易為之的事，但「電懋」和《野》片卻都做了。

五

接下來想談的是「電懋」的導演。

一個很奇特的現象：就是在電懋的歷史裡，雖然其出品一直維持在一個穩定的水平上，而且佳作不少，但卻可説從未出現過一個「作者派」的導演，甚或權傾一時的所謂「大導演」。

在片廠制度的架構下，導演一職一般僅次於監製（和某幾個大明星）之下。在荷里活的黃金時代裡，不同的片廠都先後出現過為數不少的「大導演」。這些導演不單擁有幾乎可以與監製看齊的權力，還發揮出獨特的電影風格。尊・福（John Ford）、侯活・鶴斯（Howard Hawks）、尊・侯斯頓（John Huston）、魯賓・孟穆里安（Rouben Mamoulian）、喬治・寇克（George Cukor）、希治閣（Alfred Hitchcock）等都是箇中表表者。無可置疑地，他們都是才氣橫溢的創作者，但真正能確保他們地

manager of International Films, during which a "Script Committee" was set up by Stephen Soong (Song Qi). Members of the committee included famous playwright Yao Ke, writers Nellie Chin Yu (Qin Yu), Wang Liuzhao, novelist Eileen Chang (Zhang Ailing), Evan Yang (Yi Wen) and Tao Qin. Consulting the committee was Sun Jinsan, who was supposed to read all scripts and polish them.[25] Such serious attitude toward script / scriptwriter might have been influenced by the Hollywood system, under which most studios had a Story Department composed of as many as forty contracted writers. Some studios even had a Reading Department to read and make summaries of all available fictions, stage plays and short stories to submit to senior management (each reader finishing on average one book a day). There is a difference: it was the script that Hollywood considered important, not the scriptwriter. Numerous novelists and playwrights had written scripts for Hollywood studios (ready examples included Scott Fitzgerald, Aldous Huxley, William Faulkner, Raymond Chandler and Bertolt Brecht), but the experience was far from happy and the result less than satisfactory. Fritz Lang, who went to Hollywood from Germany, once said, "The writer is very important in Europe, but here he is transformed into a mechanic. In any major studio there are ten writers working on a single script." Contrary to Hollywood, MP & GI treated its writers with great respect. We have at least the following examples to prove this.

a. *Our Sister Hedy:* this was adapted from a short story by female novelist Zheng Hui. The script was written by Tao Qin, the director. On the eve of the film's release, Soong published a 4,000-word article, *Fiction and Film*, in *Internaitonal Screen*, explaining in great length the reasons for the changes on the story.[26] He cites Hollywood examples for his argument, including *From Here to Eternity* (1953), *The Country Girl*, *The Caine Mutiny*, *On the Waterfront* (both 1954), *Giant*, *Tea and Sympathy* (both 1956), and *Written on the Wind* (1957).[27] "The purpose (of the article) is to assure the readers of the short story that every change has been considered thoroughly and that the script is not written hastily."

位的，仍得賴商業上（票房）的成功。一個最好的例子，是環球片廠的合約導演占士・威爾（James Whale）。他在三十年代拍攝的四部奇幻電影，《科學怪人》（*Frankenstein*, 1931）、《The Old Dark House》（1932）、《隱形人》（*The Invisible Man*, 1933）和《科學怪人的新娘》（*The Bride of Frankenstein*, 1935）均叫好叫座，把他的事業推上了巔峰：「環球」的總指揮小卡爾・拉姆耳（Carl Laemmle, Jr.）開綠燈讓他拍攝有史以來最昂貴的歌舞片《畫舫璇宮》（*Show Boat*, 1936）。影片共花了120多萬美元，但收入卻只佔當年票房榜的第25位。[42] 威爾在翌年開拍的《The Road Back》（《西線無戰事》續集）隨即遭到被大幅削減製作費的命運。拍完該片後，威爾也就離開了環球，事業從此迅速滑坡，不到四年即黯然退出荷里活。

前述的張徹是另一例子。他正式獲邵氏重用的，是在《獨臂刀》（1967）的票房紀錄創出超過港幣100萬元之後的事情（他也因而被冠以「百萬大導」的稱號）。這之後他幾乎每部作品都保持在票房榜首，在邵氏的地位簡直可說是已到了呼風喚雨的地步，除不斷增加自己的導演數量外，還用與別人合導的名義，藉以生產更多同類型的作品，但七五年後，他的權力也隨着市場的飽和、潮流的衰退和影片的票房下滑而慢慢萎縮，不再受到重視。很有趣地，這種兩極的情形卻好像從沒有在電懋怎樣出現過。在某程度上，上述劇本／編劇先行的政策會解釋了部份原因。除此之外，最直接的原因，恐怕便是有關創作者本身的能力問題了。

電懋的正式合約導演（即只能獨家替電懋拍片）本就不多，大概只岳楓、陶秦、易文、王天林、嚴俊、唐煌、鍾啟文、汪榴照、吳家驤等幾個。從他們現存的作品成績來看，岳楓和陶秦應眾人中創作才華最高的二人，但

Soong also revealed that the ending of the film had been altered thrice, but another writer was never involved and Tao himself did all the rewrites. The article amply showed that MP & GI regarded its writers with revere and esteem.

b. *June Bride:* written by Eileen Chang, this comedy was also undeniably her worst script. The story stops developing soon after Grace Chang, a young woman from Singapore, meets her fiancé, Chang Yang, in Hong Kong. And the film hasn't even reached its halfway point. As a result, the remaining screen time is filled with dream sequences and travelogue shots of Hong Kong. The film was over-praised, probably due to Eileen Chang's fame. According to Grace Chang, the writer mailed in the script from America. Though it was not fully realised, director Tang Huang followed almost every single detail. [28] It was well known Soong and Eileen Chang were close friends, and Soong was extremely careful making changes to her script. One can easily imagine the limitations Tang faced. It was certainly excessive that when a script was problematic but no efforts were made to improve it simply out of deference to the writer. Yet this again serves to illustrate MP & GI's respect for its scriptwriters.

c. *The Wild, Wild Rose:* also according to Grace Chang, the film's concept also came from the writer, Chin Yu, whose sole purpose, she told Chang, was to write a completely different role for the latter. Upon reading the script, Chang called Soong and offered to give the role to Yeh Feng, genuinely thinking that Yeh was more appropriate. Soong told her that Chin insisted she played the character. Chang admitted that both she and director Wang Tianlin were overcome with anxiety during the shoot. Despite such uncertainties, the film not only became the most distinguished film among the 200-odd library of MP & GI films, it is arguably the most extraordinary Mandarin film of the 1960s. Under the 'star system' it is not unusual for a studio to use a great amount of resources to promote just one particular actor; but not even Hollywood would have given full support to a screenwriter to change the established image of an already famous star, [29] let alone a "dangerous" image of a "broad" who is crude, bitchy and filled with animal instincts. Yet MP & GI did it.

可惜很早便已蟬過別枝，轉投邵氏。（這裡指的「才華」，除了基本技藝外，還指較強烈的個性和風格。）餘者之中，依筆者暫時的結論，會是以王天林的技藝修養最純熟，整體表現也最平均和穩定，但卻病在無法貫徹任何主題上的統一性，更遑論個人風格了。也就是說，當交到他手上的是個本身已屬不錯的劇本時，他總會交出一部不錯的電影（例：《小兒女》（1963）、《遊戲人間》），如果各種因素能夠因緣際會配合無間的話，例如是《野玫瑰之戀》，他甚至會拍出教人刮目相看的傑作。一個未必完全恰當的比喻：王就好比是從匈牙利移民到荷里活的米高・寇蒂斯（Michael Curtiz），一生多產、作品類型豐富多端、技巧閑熟（當然，後者的影像感要比王氏優勝得多），但卻始終是一流（或接近一流）的工匠多於殿堂裡的大師（其實已經一樣難得）；1945年的《Mildred Pierce》（或許還可以加上1942年的《北非諜影》／Casablanca）之於寇蒂斯，便像《野玫瑰之戀》之於王。與陶秦同是writer-director的易文，優於王氏的是掌握劇本的能力，但缺點卻是水準時高（《曼波女郎》、《香車美人》、《桃李爭春》）時低（《青春兒女》、《鶯歌燕舞》、《星星・月亮・太陽》），更經常有虎頭蛇尾的情況出現（《溫柔鄉》（1960）、《空中小姐》、《好事成雙》（1962））。至於其他人，除個別作品不乏趣味性外（例：唐煌的《玉樓三鳳》），也就不足論矣。

結論：以下的說法可能有點吊詭，但正因為電懋沒有出現過真正標青的作者導演，大多數的時候只有佳作而無傑作（《野》片是獨一無二的了），所以才益突顯出它作為一家「片廠典範」（classic studio）的重要性。

在電懋之前，與導演簽署獨家合約的做法在香港電影界其實並不普遍（在粵語影圈裡更為少有），一般只有「基

5

Another interesting and unique phenomenon about MP & GI concerns its directors. Despite the stable high-quality of its productions, none of its directors can be termed an 'auteur', nor was there a dominant 'maestro' to be found in its pool of filmmakers.

Within the structure of the studio system, the power of a director is usually next to that of the producer (and stars). In Hollywood's Golden Era, there were many 'maestros' from different studios. They not only had power almost equal to producers, they also developed unique film styles. John Ford, Howard Hawks, John Huston, Rouben Mamoulian, George Cukor and Alfred Hitchcock were several distinguished examples. Undoubtedly, they were talented directors, yet their status rested largely on their pictures' commercial success. A good illustration was James Whale. Contracted to Universal, he directed four horror films in the 1930s: *Frankenstein* (1931), *The Old Dark House* (1932), *The Invisible Man* (1933) and *The Bride of Frankenstein* (1935). All were critical and commercial successes, bringing him to the summit of his career. They also earned him the green light from Carl Laemmle, Jr., head of Universal at the time, to make *Show Boat* (1936), the most expensive musical ever made until then. The total production cost was over $120 million, but the film ranked twenty-fifth on the year's box office chart.[30] When Whale started shooting *The Road Back* the next year, the budget was severely cut. Humiliated, he left Universal after the film, only to witness his own continuing downfall.

Interestingly, such polarity seemed never to have occurred at MP & GI. The emphasis on script / scriptwriter partly explain this. The rest has to do with the capability of the directors. MP & GI only had several contracted directors who worked exclusively for the company. They included Yue Feng, Tao Qin, Evan Yang (Yi Wen), Wang Tianlin, Yan Jun, Tang Huang, Robert Chung, Wang Liuzhao and Wu Jiaxiang. Looking at their works, one may say that Yue Feng and Tao Qin were probably the most talented; but unfortunately both left the company and joined Shaw

本導演」(即規定每年為某片廠拍攝若干部電影)和「特約導演」(部頭計算)兩種。早期電懋的粵語片組，執行的固然是這個制度，[43]及大量生產國語片後，即使對待獨家合約的導演也好像彈性頗大：例如王天林便曾在合約期間替新華和萬象拍過好幾部電影。把「合約」行使為一種嚴格的商業約束此一做法，編劇和演員似乎才是電懋主要針對的對象。不過儘管嚴格，當出現人情的因素時，其高層管理人員表現出來的，卻會是一種泱泱大度的風範。例子：葛蘭在 1961 年決定息影結婚時，與電懋的合約其實還未屆滿。前此，邵氏已拉攏過她，企圖挖角。但當葛蘭向宋淇提出解約的要求時，後者卻毫無條件地便一口答應了她，還半開玩笑地跟她說了一句直到今日還教她清清楚楚地記得的話："You know, we're really not afraid of the Shaw brothers. It's the Ko brothers that we fear!" [44](「你知道嗎，我們其實並不害怕邵氏兄弟，我們最害怕的是高氏兄弟才對呢！」那是因為當時高氏兄弟正同時追求電懋的兩名當家花旦，葛蘭和尤敏，而在葛蘭結婚息影後不久，尤敏也步其後塵！)

如果說，這個生動的例子反映出來的，正是電懋領導層(在陸運濤的英式紳士作風影響下所表現出)的一種氣度，未知筆者會否被人明病流於過度浮想？但如果這個論點可以成立的話，則電懋大部份影片裡的那份和諧的調子和氣息，還有是整個機構予其成員的那種——容許我再次引述葛蘭的話——「大家庭」氛圍，便不是偶然或沒有原因的了。沿着這個方向追溯下去，電懋／國泰結束後，[45]邵氏以殺氣騰騰、標榜個人英雄色彩、男性中心、消費和感官主義為主的路線，幾近壟斷性地執香港電影的牛耳(從 1970 年開始，每年生產佔超過全年總電影產量的三分一)，未知可否視作香港從一個質樸的手工業社會、過渡到朝氣蓬勃的新興現代都市、再

易文的兩部作品：《香車美人》和《情深似海》
Two films by Evan Yang: *Our Dream Car* (left) and *Forever Yours*.

「成長」成為你死我活、投機掛帥的資本主義社會的縮影呢（當中自也反映出主事者的某種個性）？

六

在電懋的脈絡分明、各有所司的架構下，還有下面幾個部門是特別值得一提的，那是攝影董紹詠、剪接王朝曦、美術包天鳴、費伯夷和音樂綦湘棠、姚敏。其中尤以包（代表作：《曼波女郎》、《野玫瑰之戀》）、費（代表作：《桃李爭春》）二人的立體派裝飾（art deco）風格的場景設計，[46]和綦、姚二人的現代音樂風格最為突出。綦、姚的配樂又全屬原作音樂，每個音節都按照着劇情的起伏來編寫和演奏，在同期的國、粵影壇中幾乎找不到別的例子。二人的對結他和 percussion 的偏好，似乎很受日本電影的影響。筆者在看《四千金》（綦）、《曼波女郎》（綦）和《空中小姐》（姚）的時候，腦海中便一直想起齋藤一郎（Saito Ichiro）在成瀨巳喜男的電影裡的音樂。我猜在這方面服部良一對二人的熏陶應起了關鍵性的作用。[47]另一個可能性，則與當時在新加坡兼營發行業務的總公司國際戲院有限公司有關，那是因為它一直有進口日本電影，所以不少拷貝都會途經香港，遂很多時都會因利成便放映給電懋的工作人員觀賞。葛蘭便説廠裡常會有人通知他們去看這類試片。[48]類似的情形後來在邵氏其實也十分普遍。香港電影（甚至中國電影）在過去一直透過種種迂迴曲折的途徑受到日本電影的影響，是另一個有待日後有心人去開拓研究的課題，這裡便不再贅了。

七

本文原本最想談論的，是佔電懋出品數量中最多的都市喜劇片，但時間和篇幅都已不再容許我繼續下去（編輯候稿已到了燃眉之急的地步了）。下列是我最初擬定的綱領，希望可以作為對其他研究者的刺激：

Brothers. (The word 'talent' here means basic craft as well as a strong personal style.) Among the remaining ones, my provisional conclusion is that Wang Tianlin was probably the most crafted, with the most stable quality. However, it was his inability to develop a vision of an artist, not to mention the lack of personal style, that prevents him from further achievements. In other words, he would make a good film with a good script (examples: *Father Takes a Bride*, 1963; *You were Meant For Me*); if everything was just right, he would even make an extraordinary film, such as *The Wild, Wild Rose*. Here is a comparison that may not be all that appropriate: one may liken Wang to Michael Curtiz, the Hungarian filmmaker who migrated to Hollywood. A prolific director who had made films of different genres with extraordinary skills, Curtiz, however, was more a first class (or close to first class) craftsman than a real *auteur*. Wang might not even have Curtiz's visual sense, but it may not be inappropriate to say that *The Wild, Wild Rose* is to Wang what *Mildred Pierce* (1945) (one may also add *Casablanca*) is to Curtiz.

Evan Yang, a writer-director like Tao Qin, has a better way with scripts, but his works are uneven, with as many highs (*Mambo Girl*, *Our Dream Car, It's Always Spring*) as there are lows (*Spring Song, Mad About Music, Sun, Moon and Star*). Others would start off well but suffer poor finishes (*Bachelors Beware, Air Hostess, Ladies First*). Other directors might produce interesting pieces occasionally (such as *Between Tears and Laughter*, by Tang Huang), but none had a strong style. My conclusion may be a paradoxical one: it is precisely because there was never a talented *auteur* from MP & GI, resulting in many fine films but almost no masterpieces (*The Wild, Wild Rose* the only exception), that highlights the importance of MP & GI as a 'classic studio'.

6

I have intended to discuss the urban comedy, a genre which MP & GI popularised and which occupies a large section of its outputs, in this essay, but with a pressing deadline and limited space, I have to stop here. Following is the original outline draft; I hope they will serve as the starting points for further studies:

- 過去研究香港電影的論者，差不多毫不例外的，都一律把電懋的作品視作四十年代南來上海影人的某種延續，這顯然是不確的（這方面上文已有部份觸及）；

- 論者又習慣把電懋作品裡的片廠風格歸納為純粹荷里活式的舶來品、受眾對象都是小數來自上海的移民，或社會的中、上層階級；提供的是普羅大眾一個可望而不可即的夢，是典型的「逃避主義」娛樂。這些論點都忽略了一個很重要的事實：電懋的電影很多都很是賣座，訴諸的觀眾群，更大部份其實是戰後的新生代，和他們對新興事物底好奇心。他們在這些電影裡找到的，與其說是一個夢，倒不如說是一份對一個轉動和蛻變中的時代與城市的感性（sensibility）的認同；

- 把電懋電影有系統的並置，不難勾勒出一幅現代都市的圖像；這裡面除有着各種新興工業（航空業、酒店業、時裝業、經紀業、汽車業、旅運業、唱片業）外，還有不同的流行玩意（健身比賽、模特兒比賽、各式的運動、社交舞、電視），以至生活方式（分期付款購物、女性獨居或女性群居、社交酬酢、男性續弦）；

- 女性身份的自覺：不少作品的戲劇性都建築在女主角徘徊在兩種身份之間的抉擇身上：public virtues vs private vices的衝突（家庭主婦／職業女性、妻子／後母、蕩婦／聖母、男性化／淑女）；

- 女性性慾的自我認識與測試：葉楓在《四千金》裡的nymphomaniac形象與林翠的tomboy聯想；丁皓在《遊戲人間》裡的性別倒亂；喬宏作為女性慾望投射對象的肌肉形象；《好事成雙》作為一場女性主動出擊的「求偶遊戲」（mating game）的閱讀；

- 夜總會：高思雅提出過的一個意念：夜總會作為一個具有引伸意義的單位（connotative unit）和「他處」（the other place）的發展與再探討。[49]

- Most scholars of Hong Kong cinema have treated the works of MP & GI as a certain extension of the filmmakers from Shanghai in the 1940s, but obviously this is incorrect (this issue has been partially discussed above).

- Scholars also used to define the 'studio style' within MP & GI works as purely an import from Hollywood, and its target audience a minority group of immigrants from Shanghai, or the upper middle class. Those films provide a dream to the general public; it is classic 'escapism' entertainment. This view overlooks a very important fact: most of the MP & GI films were great box office successes, and a large section of their audience was the generation born after the war. These people had a curiosity for the new and the trendy. What they had found in these films was not a dream, but an identity with the sensibility of an evolving time and city.

- A chronological viewing of the MP & GI films may help to map out the process of such an evolution: one can find in them the birth and growth of all the new industries (airlines, hotels, fashion, brokers, automobiles, travel agents, record industry) and social activities (fitness contests, model contests, a variety of sports, social dancing, television broadcast), as well as a new life style (payment by installments, women who live alone or together, social meetings, men remarrying after their wives died).

- The acknowledgement of the female identity: many films were built upon the female protagonist's struggle between two different identities: the conflict of public virtues vs private vices (housewife/career woman; wife/stepmother; vamp/holy mother; boyish/lady-like).

- The self-realisation and experiment with female sexual desire: the nymphomaniac image of Yeh Feng in *Our Sister Hedy* and Lin Cui's tomboy imagination; the gender-crossing of Ting Hao in *You were Meant for Me*; Roy Chiao's masculine (and muscular) image as women's object of desire; *Ladies First* as a reading of a mating game driven by women.

- The nightclub: further development and study of Roger Garcia's concept of nightclub as a connotative unit and the Other place. [31]

Translated by Grace Ng

註

1. 參看之25部電影包括(除特別注明外，餘皆為國語片)：1.《黛綠年華》(左几，1957，粵語)、2.《四千金》(陶秦，1957)、3.《情場如戰場》(岳楓，1957)、4.《曼波女郎》(易文，1957)、5.《青春兒女》(易文，1959)、6.《空中小姐》(易文，1959)、7.《香車美人》(陶秦，1959)、8.《樑上佳人》(王天林，1959)、9.《長腿姐姐》(唐煌，1960)、10.《溫柔鄉》(易文，1960)、11.《六月新娘》(唐煌，1960)、12.《野玫瑰之戀》(王天林，1960)、13.《玉樓三鳳》(唐煌，1960)、14.《愛的教育》(鍾啟文，1961)、15.《遊戲人間》(王天林，1961)、16.《桃李爭春》(易文，1962)、17.《好事成雙》(易文，1962)、18.《錦繡年華》(莫康時，1963，粵語)、19.《小兒女》(王天林，1963)、20.《鶯歌燕舞》(易文，1963)，與及「電懋」在其創辦者陸運濤先生逝世後重新改組及易名「國泰機構」時期的作品：21.《都市狂想曲》(吳家驤，1964)、22.《太太萬歲》(王天林，1968)、23.《試情記》(王天林，1969)、24.《嫁不嫁》(唐煌，1970)、25.《家有賢妻》(1970，劉芳剛導演)。
2. 即派拉蒙(Paramount)、美高梅(Metro-Goldwyn-Mayer)、二十世紀霍士(20th Century Fox)、華納兄弟(Warner Brothers)、雷電華(Radio-Keith-Orphem)；後來再加入「三小」(the Little Three)，即環球(Universal)、哥倫比亞(Columbia)和聯美(United Artists)，合稱「八大」(the Eight Majors)。
3. Thomas Schatz 著，李亞梅譯：《好萊塢類型電影》，台灣：遠流，1999，頁21。
4. Douglas Gomery: *The Hollywood Studio System*, London: Macmillan, 1986, pp. 12-13.
5. 有關電懋的成立與發展歷史，詳見本書鍾寶賢，〈星馬實業家和他的電影夢：陸運濤及國際電影懋業公司〉。該文資料豐富，極具參考價值。
6. 同註5。
7. 見本書傅葆石，<港星雙城記：國泰電影試論>。
8. 大部份的荷里活電影大亨(moguls)都是猶太人，而且都出身自歐洲中部的貧民區。」見 Ronald L. Davis: *The Glamour Factory: Inside Hollywood's Big Studio System*, Texas: Southern Methodist University Press, 1993, p. 16.
9. 同註5。
10. 黃卓漢：《電影人生：黃卓漢回憶錄》，台灣：萬象圖書，1994，頁92。
11. 同註5；另見黃仁編著：《聯邦電影時代》，台灣：國家電影資料館，2001，頁32。
12. 見 Ronald L. Davis，同註8，頁13。
13. 僅就規模和格局而言，先於電懋的大中華影業公司(1946)和後來的邵氏兄弟(香港)有限公司，其實都比電懋更接近荷里活。前者開辦時即接收了南洋片廠，全部職工高達107名，月薪總支出達四萬餘元，片場內除影棚外，還置有職員宿舍、飯堂、小商店與理髮室，見沈西城，《香港電影發展史初稿》，節錄於林年同編：《戰後香港電影回顧：一九四六－一九六八》，第三屆香港國際電影節回顧特刊，香港：市政局，1979，頁

Notes

1. The films are (all films are in Mandarin dialogues, unless stated otherwise): 1. *The Tender Age* (aka *The Splendor of Youth*) (Zuo Ji, 1957, in Cantonese)2. *Our Sister Hedy* (Tao Qin, 1957) 3. *The Battle of Love* (Yue Feng, 1957) 4. *Mambo Girl* (Yi Wen, 1957) 5. *Spring Song* (Yi Wen, 1959) 6. *Air Hostess* (Yi Wen, 1959) 7. *Our Dream Car* (Yi Wen, 1959) 8. *Lady on the Roof* (Wang Tianlin, 1959) 9. *Sister Long Legs* (Tang Huang, 1960) 10. *Bachelors Beware* (Yi Wen, 1960) 11. *June Bride* (Tang Huang, 1960) 12. *The Wild, Wild Rose* (Wang Tianlin, 1960) 13. *Between Tears and Laughter* (Tang Huang, 1960) 14. *Education of Love* (Zhong Qiwen, 1961) 15. *You were Meant For Me* (Wang Tianlin, 1961) 16. *It's Always Spring* (Yi Wen, 1962) 17. *Ladies First* (Yi Wen, 1962) 18. *Make it Mine* (Mo Kangshi, 1963, in Cantonese) 19. *Father Takes a Bride* (Wang Tianlin, 1963) 20. *Mad About Music* (Yi Wen, 1963) (The following titles were produced under the banner of Cathay Organisation, the company restructured from MP & GI.) 21. *Cosmopolitan Fantasy* (Wu Jiaxiang, 1964) 22. *Darling Stay At Home*(Wang Tianlin, 1968) 23. *How Love is Tested* (Wang Tianlin, 1969) 24. *The Homemaker* (Liu Fanggang, 1970) 25. *My Suitors* (Tang Huang, 1970).
2. The Big Five corporations were Paramount, Metro-Goldwyn-Mayer, 20th Century Fox, Warner Brothers and Radio-Keith-Orphem. They were later joined by the Little Three, Universal, Columbia and United Artists, to be termed as the Eight Majors.
3. See Thomas Schatz, translated by Li Yamei: *Hollywood Genres: Formulas, Filmmaking, and the Studio System* (in Chinese), Taiwan: Yuan Liu, 1999, p. 21.
4. See Dogulas Gomery: *The Hollywood Studio System*, London: Macmillan, 1986, pp. 12-13.
5. For details of the development of MP & GI, please refer to Stephanie Po-yin Chung, "A Southeast Asian Tycoon and His Movie Dream: Loke Wah Tho and MP & GI" in this volume.
6. Ibid.
7. See Poshek Fu, "Hong Kong and Singapore: A History of the Cathay Cinema" in this volume.
8. 'Most of the Hollywood moguls are Jewish, and almost all of them came from the ghettos of Central Europe.' See Ronald L. Davis: *The Glamour Factory: Inside Hollywood's Big Studio System*, Texas: Southern Methodist University Press, 1993, p. 16.
9. See Stephanie Po-yin Chung, op. cit.
10. See Stephanie Po-yin Chung, op. cit. and Huang Ren, ed.: *The Union Film Era* (in Chinese), Taipei: Chinese Taipei Film Archive, 2001, p. 32.
11. See Ronald L. Davis, op. cit., p. 13.
12. In terms of scope and structure, both Great China (Dazhonghua) Film Development Company (1946), which was founded before MP & GI, and Shaw Brothers (HK) Co. Ltd., which came after it, were closer to their Hollywood counterparts. The former took over the Nanyang Studio when it was established, and had a total of 107 staff, with a total monthly salary expense of over $40,000. The company had studios, staff dormitories, a canteen, grocery shop and barber

124。後者在1961年於九龍清水灣落成的邵氏影城，則共有11個攝影棚、15個外搭置景場地、配音間、沖印廠、道具房、服裝室、倉庫、木工廠、試片間、辦公室，一應俱全。此外還有貴賓招待所、餐廳、編導美術等高級宿舍、男女演員宿舍、員工宿舍等，共分38部門，員工超過1,200人，簡直傲視全亞洲，見黃卓漢，同註10，頁109。

14. 筆者在2002年1月27日跟葛蘭小姐作的訪問，未發表。

15. 余慕雲：《香港電影史話（卷五）——五十年代（下）》，香港：次文化堂，2001，頁62；及引自《國際電影》，第2期，1955年11月。

16. 在談到荷里活的片廠制度時，不少研究者都很容易錯誤地偏重了製作（影片）的重要性和主導地位。Douglas Gomery便指出：構成「片廠制度」的三環裡，真正處於主導位置的，其實是發行和放映。那是因為後兩者才是實際收取利潤的環節，並反過來決定製作的投資額、方向與路線。它們絕不會輕易容許創作上的任意出軌或實驗（遂有類型電影、潮流、明星制度的產生，見Douglas Gomery，同註4，頁193）。這也解釋了為什麼電懋在陸氏不幸逝世六年後，其新加坡總部（國泰機構）即果斷地結束了製作部門，但直到目前為止，卻仍從未間斷地一直從事著其他兩環的業務。事實上，電懋成立之初（1956年），正是國語片「在本港市場有減無增」、處於「生死存亡掙扎中」的時刻（見余慕雲，同註15，頁48及〈電影業的回顧與前瞻〉，《新生晚報》，1956年12月22日），但這個不利因素卻彷彿沒能打擊到陸氏的半點雄心，原因相信正在於電懋在發行與放映方面早已建立了穩固的網絡。1959年，國語片在香港市場的處境似乎仍沒有很大的改善，很多拍攝完成的作品都被積壓著未能排映，但電懋的製作量仍高達19部，其中重點作《龍翔鳳舞》更在新加坡早於香港上映，在締造了叻幣13萬元的破紀錄成績後，始在香港推出（結果票房也高逾港幣20萬元，位列同年十大最賣座國語片第二位）。這種前未有過的「經外銷進口」的發行和行銷方法，只有邵氏才具與之匹敵的實力。（見《國際電影》，第42期，1959年4月及余慕雲，同註15，頁199；後者見老翁編，〈一九五九年上半年度國語影片香港公映記錄〉，《幸福家庭》，第22期，1970年11月）。

17. 盧海天，〈崇尚的理想〉，《國際電影》，第3期，1955年12月。

18. 傅慧儀編：《香港影片大全第二卷1942 – 1949》，香港：香港電影資料館，1998，頁17。

19. 「四大美人」系列頭三部均由李翰祥導演，但最後一部《西施》卻因成本過高而不獲開拍，成為李氏離開邵氏、遠赴台灣創立國聯的原因之一（國聯的創業作就是上、下兩集的《西施》，見黃卓漢，同註10，頁114-115）。「四大美人」最後一集則被改為《妲己》，由岳楓導演。

20. 同註14。另根據余慕雲的說法（見余慕雲，同註15，頁118），《曼》片是因為葛蘭到台灣勞軍時大跳曼波舞，引得台灣三軍歡呼，稱她做「曼波女郎」，因而引發了易文用這稱號編成劇本的。不過余氏在書中並未引述這個說法的出處。

21. 蔣夏，〈《空中小姐》之「空」〉，《新晚報》，1959年6月8日及高山月，〈《空中小姐》別有用心〉，《大公報》，1959年6月10日。

22. 這類訓練班教授的課程頗有系統，除國語班、聲樂班和演技班外

shop. See Shen Xicheng, "A Preliminary Draft of the History of Hong Kong Cinema" (unpublished), excerpted in Lin Niantong, ed.: *Hong Kong Cinema Survey 1946-1968*, the 3rd Hong Kong International Film Festival catalogue, Hong Kong: Urban Council, 1976, p. 124. The Shaw Brothers studio was built in Clear Water Bay, Kowloon in 1961. It had 11 shooting studios, 15 outdoor studios, a dubbing studio, a laboratory, props rooms, costume and wardrobe departments, warehouses, a carpenters' workshop, screening rooms and other offices. It also had guest houses, a restaurant, dormitories for directors, screenwriters, art directors, actors and staff. The company had 38 departments, with a total of 1,200 staff and was, without doubt, the top studio in Asia at that period. See Wong Cheuk-hon (Huang Zhuohan): *A Life in Movies: The Memoirs of Wong Cheuk-hon* (in Chinese), Taipei: Variety Publishing, 1994, p. 109.

13. An unpublished interview with Grace Chang (Ge Lan) by the author on January 27, 2002.

14. See Yu Mowan (Yu Muyun): *History of Hong Kong Cinema (Vol. 5) – The Fifties (Part II)* (in Chinese), Hong Kong: Sub-Culture Publishing Co., 2001, p. 62 and extracted from *International Screen* (in Chinese), no. 2, November 1995.

15. As Douglas Gomery has pointed out, when discussing the Hollywood studio system, it's common for most scholars to emphasis the importance of film production at the expense of distribution and exhibition. According to him, "Historians' interest in competition for maximum box-office revenues has only served to ignore the total and necessary corporate cooperation which existed on the levels of distribution and exhibition. The inordinate interest in production has also focused too much attention on Hollywood as the center for movies, when in reality throughout the studio era officials in New York 'called the shots'...Each year the New York office decided how much money would be allocated for production...New York officers hoped to regularize returns from the corporation's theatres and so discouraged producers from experimentation." (See Douglas Gomery, op. cit., p. 193) This explains why six years after Loke died, MP & GI's headquarters in Singapore (Cathay Organisation) decisively closed down its production department in Hong Kong, but continued to engage actively in distribution and exhibition up to this date.

When MP & GI was founded in 1956, it was a time when the number of Mandarin films 'was on the rise' and competition fierce, when the Mandarin cinema was 'struggling between life and death' (see Yu Mowan, op. cit., p. 48, quoted from an article "A Retrospect of and Forecast on the Motion Picture Industry" in *New Life Evening Post* on December 22, 1956). Yet Loke did not seem to be deterred by such negative conditions. One reason for that was probably because MP & GI had already established a network in distribution and exhibition. Still, the market of Mandarin films did not have much improvement and in 1959, many finished films could not even get released. However, the number of productions by MP & GI in that year was a 19 high, of which *Calendar Girl* was first premiered in Singapore, reaped an all-time record-breaking taking at the box-office with S$130,000 before it was released in Hong Kong, where it also took in more than HK$200,000, ranking second of the top 10 best-selling Mandarins film of the

（教的都是史坦尼夫拉夫斯基的表演理論），還有電影欣賞班，教授基本的電影知識如鏡頭、蒙太奇理論等，負責教授的都是資深的演員和導演，以至著名聲樂家如林聲翕，同註 14。

23. 相對之下，仿似粵語版《四千金》的《錦繡年華》便弊在選角：演大女兒二女兒的白露明和林鳳還算勉強稱職，但演妹妹的兩名新人黃錦娟和李紅，便拙劣的教人慘不忍睹。

24. 一句題外話：這時期的女星們的藝名，無不體現出一份深厚的文化修涵，各個不獨匠心獨運，還貼切得觀其名簡直如見其人，如葛蘭之高雅大方、尤敏（卻非尤物）之嬌柔婉約、葉楓之耀目逼人、李湄（卻非李媚）之暗裡挑逗、夷（之於蠻夷？）光（之於豔光？）之野性奔放、丁皓之小巧跳脫……歎今追昔，只能說一句：俱往矣！

25. 張徹初期在邵氏當的也是編劇，那是 1962 至 1967 年之間的事情，職銜是編劇主任，寫了超過二十個劇本，期間與袁秋楓合導過古裝黃梅調片《蝴蝶盃》（1963），翌年獨立導演了第一部武俠片《虎俠殲仇》，真正掀起熱潮的，則是1967年的《獨臂刀》（倪匡編劇）。值得一提的是張徹自此之後幾乎未再為自己導演的電影編劇過（只 1968 年的《金燕子》與倪匡合編）。見劉成漢編：《香港功夫電影研究》，第四屆香港國際電影節回顧特刊，香港：市政局，1980，頁 153-154。

26.《遊戲人間》故事大綱：熱愛運動、個性豪爽的羅亞男（丁皓飾）與溫文儒雅的梁愛倫（雷震飾）打賭，由羅假扮男裝，同時追求在梁的醫院中當護士的高式文（白露明飾），看誰較具男子氣慨。高對羅果然一見鍾情，但羅卻發現自己鍾情於高的「肌肉型」哥哥卓然（喬宏飾），遂不惜忽男忽女，周旋於高氏兄妹之間，結果弄出連串誤會。

27.《桃李爭春》故事大綱：新加坡知名女歌星李愛蓮（葉楓飾）來港發展，獲唱片公司老闆許兆豐（喬宏飾）介紹，駐唱夜總會。許之女友陶海音（李湄飾）則為香港紅歌星，一直是夜總會積極拉攏的對象，獲悉李進駐為台柱歌手後，醋意大起，亦毛遂自薦，遂激起兩大女星施盡渾身解數，連場鬥法，是為「桃李爭春」。

28. Thomas Schatz: *The Genius of the System*, London: Faber & Faber, 1998, pp. 4-9.

29. 翁靈文，〈電影懋業公司〉，收錄於林年同編，同註 13，頁 148；及黃仁，同註 11，頁 30；「劇本編審會員會」的這些成員裡，宋淇是燕京大學畢業生，秦羽是香港大學文學系畢業生、張愛玲曾就讀香港大學及上海聖約翰大學（均未畢業）、易文、陶秦畢業於上海聖約翰大學、孫晉三則是北京清華大學生。這幾家大學在當時都十分洋化，又提倡「中學為體，西學為用」的主張。這幾人除國文出色外，英語的能力一樣了得。其中秦羽在大學時便用英文演出話劇，並在《第十二夜》演出時，負責朗誦序幕（見舒琪編：《戰後國、粵語片比較研究：朱石麟、秦劍等作品回顧》，第七屆香港國際電影節回顧特刊，香港：市政局，1983，頁 187）；張愛玲在五三年已用英文撰寫她的《秧歌》和《赤地之戀》；易文在上海時翻譯過《好萊塢工作臨場錄》（見舒琪，同上，頁186）；陶秦也曾替上海的戲院翻譯過很多荷里活電影的「戲橋」（說明書）。電懋在這樣的一個班底領導下，風格遠古近今，這也應是一個原因。

year). Such an "import via export" pattern of distribution was not only unprecedented, but also proved highly successful. Please see *International Screen* (in Chinese), no. 42, April 1959 and Yu Mowan, op. cit., p. 199; the later was quoted from Lao Weng, "A Record of Mandarin Films Released in Hong Kong in the First Half of 1959" in *Sweet Home* (in Chinese), no. 22, November 1970.

16. See Lu Haitian, "A Lofty Ideal" in *International Screen* (in Chinese), no. 3, December 1955.

17. See Winnie Fu, ed., *Hong Kong Filmography Vol. II 1942 – 1949*, Hong Kong: Hong Kong Film Archive, 1998, p. 17.

18. The first three films of 'The Four Beauties' series were directed by Li Hanxiang, but the last one, *Hsih Shi, The Beauty of Beauties*, was turned down by Run Run because of its huge budget. This partly resulted in Li's departure from Shaw Brothers for Taiwan, where he founded his own studio, Grand, debuting it with the two-parts *Hsih Shi, The Beauty of Beauties*. See Wong Cheuk-hon (Huang Zhuohan), op. cit., pp. 114-115. The last film in 'The Four Beauties' series was subsequently changed to *The Last Woman of Shang* (1964) directed by Yue Feng.

19. See note 13. But according to Yu Mo-wan (see Yu Mo-wan, op. cit., p. 118), the idea of *Mambo Girl* actually came from an occasion when Ge Lan went to Taiwan and performed mambo for the military services. The army so loved her performance that they nicknamed her 'mambo girl' afterwards and the title inspired Yi Wen to write the screenplay. But Yu did not provide any source of this piece of information.

20. Jiang Xia, "The 'Air' in *Air Hostess*", *New Evening News*, 8 June, 1959; and Gao Shanyue, "The Hidden Agenda of Air Hosters", *Tai Kung Po*, 10 June, 1959.

21. These workshops were very well designed and organised. Besides Mandarin speech classes, vocal training and acting techniques (the acting theory of Stanilavski was taught), there was also a film appreciation course in which such essential film knowledge as the montage theory was taught. Almost all teachers and lecturers were veteran actors and directors. See note 13.

22. In comparison, one can easily see that the major weakness of *Make it Mine*, which looked like the Cantonese version of *Our Sister Hedy*, is its cast of the four young daughters: Bai Luming and Lin Feng, who played the eldest and second daughter, were at best, adequate for the roles, but the two new comers, Huang Jinjuan and Li Hong, who played the younger siblings, were simply awful.

23. Chang Cheh was Head of the Script Department between 1962-1967 at Shaw Brothers. His first *wuxia* screenplay was *Tiger Boy* (Xu Zenghong) in 1966. But the trend of *wuxia pian* did not materialise until 1967, when Chang himself directed *One-armed Swordsman* (screenplayed by Ni Kuang). The film broke the box-office record with a figure of over HK$1 million at the time and earned Chang the title of "The Million Dollar Director". It maybe worth mentioning that Chang Cheh has since then almost never written any screenplay for the films he directed (the only exception was *The Golden Swallow* in 1968, which he co-wrote with Ni Kuang). See Lau Shing-hon, ed.: *A Study of the Hong Kong Martial Arts Film*, the 4th Hong Kong International Film Festival catalogue, Hong Kong: Urban Council, 1980, pp. 153-154.

24. See Thomas Schatz: *The Genius of the System*, London: Faber & Faber, 1998, pp. 4-9.

25. Weng Lingwen, "Motion Picture & General Investment Company (Dianmao)" in Lin Niantong, ed., op. cit., p. 148 and

30. 朱旭華早在1927年即加入電影界任編劇，筆名朱血花，抗日戰爭時在上海認識了蔣伯英，此人邀請他在其經營的中國戲院任經理。戰後，朱到了香港，代表蔣與邵邨人洽談合作，成立了大中華影業公司。1948年，大中華隨蔣伯英回上海而結束，朱則加入了永華任宣傳部主任。永華在1954年解散，朱便協助歐德爾成立國際。朱其後又在邵氏主理過宣傳部和負責演員訓練中心。見林年同，同註 13 ，頁 124 。
31. 林年同、楊裕平合編：《五十年代粵語電影回顧展》，第二屆香港國際電影節回顧特刊，香港：市政局， 1978 ，頁 47 。
32. Ronald L. Davis ，同註 8 ，頁 160-179 。
33. Rudy Behlmer, ed.: *Memo from David O. Selznick*, California: Samuel French Trade, 1989, pp. 476-477.
34. 諷刺的是這種輕個人風格、重「集體創作」的習慣，反而在「新浪潮」時期（七十年代末期）的香港影業界中流行起來，實行得最「徹底」的是余允抗主理的世紀公司：每部出品都起碼有三名（掛名）編劇，譚家明的《烈火青春》（1982）更高達六人。
35.《國際電影》，第 21 期， 1957 年 6 月，頁 12-13 。
36. 這些例子可窺見到電懋管理層對荷里活電影的熟悉與愛好。
37. 見《四千金》公映特刊，香港：國際電影畫報社， 1957 ，頁 7-8 。
38. 見羅卡編：《超前與跨越：胡金銓與張愛玲》，第廿二屆香港國際電影節回顧特刊，香港：臨時市政局， 1998 ，頁 164 、 188 。
39. 同註 14 。
40. 王天林在回憶他拍攝張愛玲編劇的《小兒女》時對此有很詳細的描述，見羅卡編，同註 38 ，頁 160-161 。
41.《野》片除了製作費較其他出品為高外，更專誠從日本邀請了著名的作曲家服部良一來香港包辦了影片的六首歌曲，在當時來說也是一項開先河的創舉。
42. Schatz ，同註 28 ，頁 228-235 。
43. 林年同、楊裕平合編，同註 31 ，頁 50 。
44. 同註 14 。
45. 後陸運濤時期的國泰，確實只能用一蹶不振四個字來形容。就筆者這次看過的五部作品裡，除了王天林的《太太萬歲》較像樣外（依然保留了電懋時期環繞著女性身份來大做文章的路線），其餘四部都潰不成軍，但最教人難過的，卻是新一代演員底素質之低落（男的有陳浩、鹿瑜、劉丹；女的則有張淇、萬儀、李芝安、李琳琳等）。
46. 得指出的是二人的部門只負責佈景與陳設，主角的造型與服裝概由演員自己包辦。葛蘭告訴筆者她最常參考的，都是當時流行的西方時裝雜誌，如 *Vogue* 、 *Seventeen* 等。
47. 除《野玫瑰之戀》外，服部還在港參與過《小兒女》和《教我如何不想她》的作曲與配樂工作。
48. 同註 14 。
49. 見Roger Garcia, *"The Illicit Place"*，收錄於舒琪編，同註29，頁 145-149 。

舒琪，香港電影導演及影評人，近年執導作品有《虎度門》（1996）、《基佬四十》（1997）、《愛情 Amoeba》（1997）等，現任香港演藝學院電影電視系導演科高級講師。

Shu Kei, film director and critic. Recent films include: *Hu-du-men* (1996), *A Queer Story* (1997), *Love Amoeba Style* (1997). Now teaching at Hong Kong Academy of Performing Arts.

Huang Ren, ed., op. cit., p. 30. Among the members of the Editorial Committee, Stephen Soong was a graduate of Yanjing University, Beijing; Qin Yu was a graduate of Hong Kong University; Eileen Chang had studied in both Hong Kong University and St. John's University in Shanghai (both without graduation), Yi Wen and Tao Qin were graduates of St. John's; and Sun Jinsan was graduated from Qinghua University, Beijing. All of these universities were heavily westernized at the time. As a result, all members of the Committee were well-versed not only in Chinese, but also English. Qin Yu used to act in Shakespeare in English during her university years (See Shu Kei, ed.: *A Comparative Study of Post-War Mandarin and Cantonese Cinema*, the 7th Hong Kong International Film Festival catalogue, Hong Kong: Urban Council, 1983, p. 187); Eileen Chang had published two books, *Rice Sprout Song* and *The Naked Earth* in English in 1953 and 1956; Yi Wen had translated a book on Hollywood in Shanghai (See Shu Kei, ed., op. cit., p. 186); and Tao Qin had also translated numerous film synopses for cinemas in Shanghai. Under the leadership of such a creative team, it is not difficult to account for the modern and "westernized" style of MP & GI.

26. See *International Screen* (in Chinese), no. 21, June 1957, pp. 12-13.
27. These examples illustrated the senior management of MP & GI was very familiar with Hollywood films.
28. See note 13.
29. Wang Tianlin had a detail description of this in his memoir on shooting *Father Takes A Bride*, screenplay by Eileen Chang. See Law Kar, ed.: *Transcending the Times: King Hu & Eileen Chang*, the 22nd Hong Kong International Film Festival catalogue, Hong Kong: Provisional Urban Council, pp. 160-161.
30. Other a budget higher than most other productions, *The Wild, Wild Rose* was also the first Hong Kong film to invite famous Japanese composer Hattori Ryoichi to come to Hong Kong for its music, included the six songs performed by Ge Lan in the film.
31. See Roger Garcia, "The Illicit Place" in Shu Kei, ed., op. cit., p. 145-149.

國泰與武俠電影

- 張建德 -

國泰的沒落

1960年代前半期，國語片的世界是兩大片廠邵氏和電懋之爭，競爭令電影的水準和製作得以進步和提高。東南亞、港、台的國語片觀眾亦因而在影片、片種、明星方面有更多的選擇。到了六十年代中，電懋形勢有變。1964年6月，電懋的母公司，以新加坡為基地的國泰機構主席陸運濤死於台灣空難，陸的死令國泰元氣大傷。[1]

主理電懋片場的陸運濤，是比邵逸夫強的對手。陸既是受高等教育的華人，亦是西方紳士，他的行為修養、善感都對國泰的屬下有所啟發，特別是女星。國語電影長期以來都是女星的天下，最紅的女星片約不斷，身價比與她們做對手戲的男星高得多。電懋旗下的女星顆顆耀目：林黛、葛蘭、林翠、葉楓、尤敏。五十年代末、六十年代初是她們的全盛時期，這期間亦是陸運濤個人性格對片場風格的最大影響，優雅、中產、有教養、現

《虎山行》劇照

Escort over Tiger Hills

Cathay and the *Wuxia* Movie

- *Stephen Teo* -

The Decline of Cathay

Throughout the first half of the 1960s, the Mandarin film world was a sphere of contention between two major studios: Shaw Brothers and MP & GI (Motion Picture and General Investment Co Ltd). Their competition ensured better standards and production values in the Mandarin cinema. Mandarin film lovers all over the Southeast Asian region, Hong Kong and Taiwan, were treated to greater choices in film products, genres and stars. By the mid-1960s, circumstances changed for MP & GI. In June 1964, Loke Wan Tho, the chairman of the Singapore-based Cathay Organisation, the parent company of the MP & GI studio, was killed when his plane crashed in Taiwan. Loke's death was an immense setback to the studio.[1]

Under Loke's stewardship, the studio had a helmsman who was more than a match for Run Run Shaw. Loke was both a cultured mandarin and a cosmopolitan Westernised gentleman, whose bearing and sensibility was an inspiration to the studio staff, particularly the female stars. The Mandarin film world was long the domain of female stars; the top ones were in great

代、西方價值觀等特質，在在體現在歌舞片、通俗劇和喜劇裡。[2] 不知是巧合還是命運的安排，女星的輝煌時期亦隨着陸運濤的去世而黯淡下來。

1965 年，陸運濤離世後一年，邵氏兄弟公司宣佈揭開一個武俠片的新「動作片紀元」。新片種將是「進步運動」，與「傳統的舞台式拍攝」方法分別出來，並引入「新技法以達至更高度的實感，尤其在武打場面」，[3] 這就是「新派」武俠片的本質。「新派」一詞取自金庸、梁羽生等所寫的武俠小說，他們在五十年代在報刊連載的作品，刷新了傳統的類型，而被稱為「新派」作家。其實左派的長城片場是第一家拍攝取材自新派武俠文學作品電影的華語片廠，改編自梁羽生的《雲海玉弓緣》的電影於 1966 年上映，所開闢新的武打路線，幾乎就是邵氏兄弟的所提倡，要呈現更高度的實感，有別於早期粵語武俠片傳統的舞台式拍攝方法。該片的武術設計劉家良和唐佳，迅即被邵氏兄弟羅致，成為武術指導。他們主要與導演張徹合作，後來亦成為導演。

推動武俠潮是邵氏為調整市場的周期性動作的一部份。[4] 差不多每兩年，邵氏便會調校產品，改變戲路，調節觀眾的口味。這樣做可確保有不同的片種，以及不會讓某類型的影片長時間壟斷市場。用「新派」包裝，把武俠電影「循環再用」推出市場之前，邵氏最為受落的戲種是黃梅調戲曲古裝歷史劇，自1963年《梁山伯與祝英台》票房大收後便流行起來。1965 年，邵氏開始以新派武俠電影《醉俠》「調節」市場。[5] 該片後來易名為《大醉俠》，在 1966 年 4 月公映，比《雲海玉弓緣》遲約四個月。《醉》片比《雲》片更成功，並奠定了新派武俠片作為香港電影主流的地位，亦令導演胡金銓和影星鄭佩佩成為這類型電影中的表表者。張徹是邵氏另一位重要的武俠片導演，他

《虎山行》劇照
Escort over Tiger Hills

demand and were much higher paid than their male counterparts. MP & GI had a succession of great female stars: Linda Lin Dai, Grace Chang (Ge Lan), Jeanette Lin Cui, Julie Yeh Feng (Ye Feng), and Lucilla You Min. Their heyday was the late 1950s, early 1960s – the period when Loke Wan Tho's personality exerted its greatest influence over the studio's home style, which was marked by an urbane middle-class gentility and modern, Westernised norms, expressed in such genres as musicals, melodramas and comedies.[2] Whether by coincidence or fate, Loke's death marked the end of the era of the female stars.

In 1965, one year after the death of Loke, the Shaw Brothers studio announced the launching of a new "action era" of *wuxia* movies. These new films would be a "progressive movement", breaking with "conventional 'stagy' shooting methods" and introducing "new techniques to attain a higher level of realism, particularly in the fighting scenes."[3] This was the essence of the "new school" (*xinpai*) *wuxia* movie. The label "new school" was taken from martial arts fiction where writers such as Jin Yong and Liang Yusheng had rejuvenated the genre in the 1950s through the practice of serialised publication in newspapers, and became known as the "new school" writers of a genre with a long tradition in Chinese literature. The left-wing Great Wall Studio was actually the first Mandarin studio to introduce a *wuxia* picture derived from a new school literary source; it produced *The Jade Bow* (1966), based on Liang Yusheng's novel, *The Destiny of the Jade Bow*. The movie, released in 1966, featured a new line in swordplay, which was lifted almost directly from Shaw Brothers' own maxim of introducing a higher level of realism, breaking with the conventional stage-like effects and influences that had hampered the early martial arts films in Cantonese cinema. The choreography was the work of Lau Kar-leung (Liu Jialiang) and Tang Chia (Tang Jia), who were quickly signed up by Shaw Brothers to become martial arts directors (they worked mainly with director Chang Cheh / Zhang Che); both would later become directors in their own right.

是最直接以武俠電影作為反傳統的導演，即自五十年代以來以女星主導的港產片傳統。為了表明與女星主導電影有別，張徹強調「陽剛」——只有男性才有的特質，並憑《獨臂刀》(1967)一片大獲成功，影片大收港幣一百萬，締造了當時的一個票房紀錄，令如印鈔機器般的武俠類型片決定了邵氏作為國語電影大阿哥的地位。

國泰——邵氏的對手——很遲才對這股武俠潮流作出回應。當武俠片愈來愈受歡迎的時候，國泰卻慢下步來，並經歷了因陸運濤逝世而作出的重組。陸死後，國泰機構(新加坡)及電懋由陸的妹夫朱國良接掌，國泰的管理高層原打算關閉電懋片場，但陸運濤的母親，陸佑太太堅持片場要繼續，以延續其子的事業。[6] 1965年，電懋跟隨新加坡母公司的名字，易名國泰。[7] 易名是縮小公司規模的一個藉口。為了「保持水準」，管理層有以下的做法：一、不再製作粵語片，「因為粵語片在星馬市場漸漸式微」；二、所有影片改為七彩大銀幕製作，淘汰黑白片；三、片場每年限量生產十二部電影，如情況許可，最多可生產十五部。[8]

就算改了名，亦改不了其衰落的事實。與邵氏比較，國泰的產量顯得遜色。1964年邵氏破紀錄製片二十七部，[9] 據說，在全盛時期，邵氏在同一天內拍攝的電影達二十一部之多。[10] 回看1959年，電懋拍片二十二部；重組成為國泰之後，片場在1965年只生產了四部電影，1966年更只有三部。[11] 為了爭取至年產十二部(或每月一部)，國泰仍然存在問題。1968年，行內雜誌充斥着邵氏、國泰合併的報導：指一間新公司會成立，邵氏和國泰會投資新公司換取股份。[12] 可是，邵氏要求擁有新公司百分之五十一的股權，並由邵逸夫出任新公司的總經理，邵仁枚任總裁，以使邵氏得到直接控

Shaws' *wuxia* campaign was part of the studio's periodic drive to "adjust" the market.[4] Every two years or so, the studio would change its product line to regulate the tastes of audiences. This way, a greater variety of its products was ensured, and no one genre would dominate the market for too long. Before recycling the *wuxia* movie in its "new school" format, the studio's most popular genre was the historical costume melodrama, with lots of singing in the style of *huangmei diao* (Yellow Plum Opera) – popular since 1963, following the enormous box office success of *The Love Eterne* (1963). In 1965, Shaws began to "adjust" the market by starting production on a new school *wuxia* movie, which they initially called *The Hero with a Bottle*.[5] The title was later changed to *Come Drink with Me* (1966), and released in April 1966, some four months after the release of *The Jade Bow*. The picture was an even bigger success than *The Jade Bow*, establishing the new school *wuxia* picture as a dominant genre in the Hong Kong film industry. It also established the reputations of director King Hu (Hu Jinquan) and star Cheng Pei-pei (Zheng Peipei) as leading practitioners of the genre. Shaws' other leading director in the genre was Chang Cheh, the most forthright of all the directors in representing *wuxia* as a counter-tradition to Hong Kong cinema's well-worn obsession with female stars from at least the 1950s onwards. To delineate the break with the female domination, Chang emphasised *yang gang* (male attributes) – qualities and characteristics that only men could put across, and scored the first big success of the genre, when his *One-armed Swordsman* (1967) grossed over HK$1 million. This was a new record in the box office at the time, and the film's success firmly established the *wuxia* genre as the money-spinning instrument that would seal Shaw Brothers' reputation as the undisputed leader of Mandarin filmmaking.

The Cathay studio, Shaws' rival, was slow to respond to the *wuxia* craze. As the genre was rising to popularity, the studio was undergoing a period of slowdown and restructuring following the death of Loke. Upon Loke's demise, the MP & GI studio came

制權，令談判陷於僵局。[13] 國泰管理層發表聲明，指兩間片場在可見的將來的任何時間，都「絕對不可能」合併。[14] 國泰繼續獨力經營，直至 1971 年的一天，新加坡總部突然下決定，通知香港結束當地的電影製作。[15]

國泰對武俠電影復甦的回應

根據影片製作的資料，在武俠片再次興起的最初數年，國泰的反應似乎是集中嘗試以一系列女星掛帥的電影，來鞏固其市場定位，包括尤敏主演的歷史宮闈片《深宮怨》（1964）、樂蒂主演的兩部黃梅調戲曲電影《金玉奴》（1965）和《紅梅閣》（1968），及林翠主演的一齣由王天林導演的古裝歌舞片《蘇小妹》（1967）。國泰亦成功製作了改編自蒲松齡的《聊齋誌異》（1965）和繼後兩部續集《聊齋誌異續集》（1967）及《聊齋誌異三集》（1969）。這時期的電影，暴露了國泰的基本弱點：過份倚賴女星。

與邵氏不同，國泰很難找到可靠好用的武打演員。邵氏通過其設立的南國電影訓練班，培養了一班年輕的男女演員，帶領片廠的新派武俠電影潮。僅是一兩年內，這些包括王羽、羅烈、岳華、鄭佩佩等演員，通通成為當時得令的紅星。相反，國泰只能依靠與其有合約的舊一輩明星，要他們學習武術，好拍動作片。[16] 國泰以女星掛帥的時代已成過去，1965 年前，最紅的明星如尤敏、林翠和葛蘭的電影事業慢慢走向低調，陸續在婚後引退。有名氣的男演員如張揚、雷震，國泰也由於再不能負擔他們的薪酬，只好讓他們自立門戶，組織獨立製作公司，鼓勵他們離開。[17]

和邵氏一樣，國泰有一個栽培明星的制度，培養新人，以減輕對紅星的倚賴。[18] 可惜國泰缺乏有魅力、能擔演武打片的新人。1966 年，國泰終於決定打開武打片的局面，卻找不到可靠的年輕演員當主角擔大旗，只得靠

under the guardianship of Choo Kok Leong (Zhu Guoliang), Loke's brother-in-law, who assumed command of Cathay Organisation in Singapore. Cathay's high management had contemplated closing down MP & GI, but Loke's mother, Mrs Loke Yew (Lu You), insisted that the studio should carry on, so that her son's legacy would continue.[6] In 1965, MP & GI was renamed Cathay, after its parent company in Singapore.[7] The name change was a pretext for downsizing the company. The management sought to "maintain standards" by doing the following: 1. The company would no longer produce Cantonese pictures "because of their decline in popularity in the Singapore-Malaysia market"; 2. The company would produce all films in colour and in the scope format, phasing out black and white pictures; 3. The company would produce up to twelve films a year, or at most fifteen films where circumstances allow.[8]

Even with a name change, it was clear that the studio was in decline. Its output paled in comparison to Shaw Brothers', which, in 1964 produced a record 27 features.[9] It was said that at its prime, Shaws had 21 pictures in active production on a single day.[10] Back in 1959, MP & GI released 22 films. After being restructured as Cathay, the studio produced only four new films in 1965 and three in 1966.[11] As it strove to increase its output to 12 a year (or one film every month), Cathay remained troubled. In 1968, trade magazines were rife with reports of a Shaws-Cathay merger. A separate company would be formed; both parties would invest in the company by acquiring shares.[12] However, negotiations bogged down over Shaws' demand that it own 51% of the new company, and that Run Run Shaw would be appointed general manager while his older brother Runme (Shao Renmei) would be president of the company, thus giving Shaws direct control.[13] Cathay executives issued statements that it was "absolutely impossible" for the two studios to merge at any time in the foreseeable future.[14] The company carried on alone until 1971, when the Singapore headquarters abruptly decided to call it a day and put an end to its film production activities in Hong Kong.[15]

合約演員趙雷。趙雷於 1964 年離開邵氏，到武打熱潮來到的時候，已近中年。趙自 1964 年起，便幾乎在所有國泰的古裝片內出現，扮演文弱書生或者皇帝。但在屠光啟根據其小說自編自導的電影《第一劍》(1967)中，趙雷卻又成功搖身變成國泰銀幕上的大俠。電影的成功，卻更多歸功於戲內的年輕女演員陳曼玲，她充滿活力的演出無疑巧經計算，是兩部邵氏賣個滿堂紅的胡金銓作品《大醉俠》(1966)裡的鄭佩佩和《龍門客棧》(1967)裡的上官靈鳳的翻版。[19] 在陳曼玲身上，國泰起碼找到了一個武俠女星(國泰很快便用她拍了一系列武打片，通常都是夥拍趙雷)，卻沒有一個如王羽般年輕、能擔大旗的男打星。

趙雷在《決鬥惡虎嶺》(1968)和《七大盜》(1968)等影片中的表現完全沒有王羽那富詩意而又充滿不安的反叛氣質。趙雷的武俠角色是接近原型的：忠心耿耿、胸懷大義、永不犯錯、有情有義。他的角色性格雖然傳統，卻帶有複雜的心理灰色地帶。例如，在王天林導演的《決鬥惡虎嶺》裡，趙雷飾演的賞金獵捕，專門捉拿被懸紅通緝的罪犯，將他們正法，拿取賞金，然後分給窮人。但是骨子裡，卻是因為父親惡貫滿盈，惟有以這種行為來洗刷良心上的不安。他從盜賊手中救了一名俠女(樂蒂)，可是他正是她殺父仇人的兒子，復仇的對象。同是王天林執導的《七大盜》裡，趙雷飾演一名鏢頭，負責護鏢到京城，不擇手段對付七人土匪幫，電影對土匪賦予同情，襯托出趙雷堅定又固執的性格。

「國泰式」大俠

到了六十年代後期，趙雷的中生樣貌和傳統的外型已不合時宜，武俠類型電影愈來愈趨向要求年輕貌美的俠女、年輕健碩的男星。邵氏那邊，張徹發掘了兩名新星：姜大衛和狄龍。張徹的「陽剛」強調男性間的感情

Cathay's Response to the *Wuxia* Resurgence

Based on the evidence of the films produced, Cathay's priorities during the first few years of the *wuxia* resurgence appeared to be focused on consolidating its market position with a series of period films headlining female stars. You Min starred in the historical chamber drama *Romance of the Forbidden City* (1964), Betty Loh Ti (Le Di) starred in two *huangmei diao* melodramas *The Beggar's Daughter* (1965) and *Red Plum Pavilion* (1968), and Lin Cui was in another costume musical *Wife of a Romantic Scholar* (1967), all directed by Wang Tianlin. Cathay also produced a successful version of Pu Songling's *Liaozhai* ghost stories: *Fairy, Ghost, Vixen* (1965), which led to two sequels *The Haunted*, released in 1967 and *The Spirits* , released in 1969. These period movies showed up a fundamental weakness in Cathay's armoury, which was a reliance on female stars.

Unlike Shaws, Cathay was hard put to find credible *wuxia* actors. Shaws had cultivated, through its "Southern Drama School", a group of young actors and actresses who would lead the studio's campaign to launch the new school *wuxia* movie. Within a year or so, these actors, including Jimmy Wang Yu, Lo Lieh (Luo Lie), Elliot Yueh Hua (Yue Hua) and Cheng Pei-pei, became big stars. In contrast, Cathay could only rely on older established stars kept on contract, who were now required to train in the martial arts to prepare themselves for action movies.[16] The studio's era of female domination was in any case coming to an end. The most popular stars such as You Min, Lin Cui and Grace Chang were all winding down their careers by 1965, and going into voluntary retirement after getting married. But even for the established male stars, such as Chang Yang (Zhang Yang) and Kelly Lai Chen (Lei Zhen), Cathay could not afford to keep them on salary, and encouraged their departure by letting them form independent production companies.[17]

Along with Shaws, Cathay cultivated a star system, but trained new talent in order to cut their reliance on established stars.[18] However, Cathay lacked the charismatic young talent for *wuxia* pictures. When

和極度暴力的表現，只有年輕俊朗的演員才勝任。國泰方面，因為仍找不到有明星氣質的年輕男演員來詮釋這種新的英雄典型，便嘗試以加入喜劇元素，重塑傳統武俠英雄。及1968年，武打類型電影發展至一個程度，已露疲態，可作一些不同的嘗試。

國泰想出一條必勝方程式，在兩齣電影中結合武打與諧趣喜劇，分別是姜南導演的《笑面俠》(1968)和王天林導演的《神經刀》(1969)。兩部電影都是輕鬆惹笑諷刺的類型，後者更大膽地醜化及挖苦張徹的《獨臂刀》、胡金銓的《龍門客棧》，甚至影響中國武俠電影的日本盲俠電影。更重要的是，電影改變了武俠類型裡的主角形象，如劍客行俠仗義的精神。

《神經刀》的主角是練武的弟子，拜師學「童子功」的絕技。他師傅臨死前要將武藝秘笈傳授給他，並要他答應娶他的女兒（會破了練童子功的獨身戒條）。成婚當日，新娘要求男主角證明他是一個遊俠，他以惹笑的手法顛覆了所謂「大俠」的觀念。電影的結尾，大獲全勝的主角大方地承認是用詭詐的手段贏了對手，而一名老人更說詭詐是遊戲的一部份，英雄要用這種手段才能成為英雄，這種嬉笑怒罵的態度，正正反映了當時觀眾已不大接受固有的英雄形象了。

同樣地，《笑面俠》的主角由盜賊變為大夫（得到同一監倉裡的老醫師的真傳），雖然他師傅曾教他不要多管閒事，他卻裝成遊俠般行俠仗義。後來他被誤認為殺死恩人的兇手，幾經調查終於水落石出，在恩人的女兒（陳曼玲）面前還自已清白。他的角色說明善良的品德比武功重要，更能贏取人心。《笑面俠》加入了輕鬆的元素，輔以傳統公案小說類型。雖然諷刺的效果並不特別成功，卻把武俠電影糅合了傳統的公案類型、復仇劇、喜劇等，並帶出遊俠的概念。

Cathay finally took up the cudgel to make *wuxia* pictures in 1966, it could not field a reliable young actor for lead parts and had to rely on a contract player, Zhao Lei, who had defected from Shaws in 1964 and was reaching middle age when the *wuxia* craze occurred. Zhao had appeared in practically every costume picture Cathay produced from 1964 onwards, playing effete scholars or emperors, and he was Cathay's *wuxia* front man on the screen. Success was achieved with *The First Sword* (1967), written and directed by Tu Guangqi after his own novel. However, the success of that film was due more to the presence of the young leading lady, Melinda Chen Manling, whose energetic performance was no doubt calculated to follow the examples of Cheng Pei-pei in King Hu's *Come Drink with Me* and Shangguan Lingfeng in the same director's *Dragon Inn* (1967), both of which made a lot of money for Shaws.[19] In Chen Manling, Cathay had at least found a viable female *wuxia* star (and the studio quickly featured her in a succession of *wuxia* movies, often pairing her with Zhao). But it did not have a male star of the calibre of Wang Yu.

Zhao's performances in such *wuxia* films as *Travel with a Sword* (1968) and *The Desperate Seven* (1968) were not a patch on Wang's more poetic and anguished persona. Zhao's *wuxia* characters were more akin to genre archetypes: steadfast loyal men who never deviated from their responsibility or doing the right thing by the chivalric code binding all members of the *wuxia* fraternity. Though traditional, Zhao's characterisations contained grey areas of psychological complexity. For example, in *Travel with a Sword*, directed by Wang Tianlin, Zhao's character is a bounty hunter who hunts down criminals, kills them, and claims the money, which he then gives away to the deserving poor. But his motives are driven by a desire to cleanse his own conscience blemished by the evil deeds his father had perpetrated. His nemesis turns out to be a swordswoman (played by Loh Ti) whose life he had saved when she was abducted by a bandit. She is really an avenger seeking to kill Zhao, whose father killed her father. In *The Desperate Seven*, also directed by Wang Tianlin, Zhao plays the commander of a security service protecting valuables being

《虎山行》中不復見的場面：喬宏和江青
A vanished moment in *Escort over Tiger Hills*, with Roy Chiao and Chiang Ching.

transported to the capital, using ruthless means to fend off a group of seven bandits. The bandits are sympathetically portrayed to highlight the stalwart but rigid qualities of Zhao's character.

Remolding the *Wuxia* Hero on Cathay's Terms

By the end of the 1960s, Zhao's middle-aged look and his traditional posture were a liability as the genre increasingly featured young, pretty, and fighting-tough maidens, or young, fighting-fit muscular men. Over at Shaws, director Chang Cheh had discovered two new stars: David Chiang (Jiang Dawei) and Ti Lung (Di Long). Chang Cheh's theory of *yang gang* underscored the themes of male bonding and the display of extreme violence, which only young good-looking actors could portray. Still lacking the charismatic young actors to portray this new heroic stereotype, Cathay instead tried to remold the traditional *wuxia* stereotype by injecting ingredients of comedy. By 1968, the *wuxia* genre had developed to the point where the genre, having run down its own conventions, could accommodate some experimentation.

To Cathay's credit, it came up with a winning formula of mixing comedy with *wuxia* in two films: *The Smiling Swordsman* (1968), directed by Jiang Nan, and *A Mad, Mad, Mad Sword* (1969), directed by Wang Tianlin. Both films were light-hearted parodies of the genre, but the latter is particularly broad, spoofing the genre through knowing allusions to Chang Cheh's *One-armed Swordsman* and King Hu's *Dragon Inn*, as well as the Japanese "Blind Swordsman" series (which were instrumental in influencing the rise of the Chinese *wuxia* movie). More significantly, the movie revises the popular image of the hero that the genre holds dear, such as the notion of "the chivalric swordsman doing good deeds" (*xingxia zhangyi*).

The chief character of *A Mad, Mad, Mad Sword* is a disciple of a martial arts school that teaches a "celibate technique" based on the training of pre-pubescent boys. On his deathbed, the master bequeaths his legacy to the hero on condition that he marries his daughter (thus breaking the rule of celibacy). On the

喬宏和周萱
Roy Chiao and
Hilda Chou Hsuan.

《笑面俠》另一個重要之處是它勾起北派武術和京劇的傳統，其中一個原因是這段期間，國泰用了北派的韓英傑作為其大部份武打電影的武術指導。韓曾在兩部影響至深的武打片《大醉俠》(1966)和《龍門客棧》(1967)中與胡金銓合作。另一個原因是國泰在業務上，與台灣電影業關係密切，[20] 六十年代後期，國泰更加強與台灣的合作與聯繫，聘請台灣導演和演員執導、演出在台灣拍攝的武俠片。其中兩部是1969年上映的《虎山行》和1970年上映的《路客與刀客》，這兩部是國泰製作的武俠片中最重要的，也是投資最多的。

忠奸分明

王星磊導演的《虎山行》，製作費用高達港幣一百二十萬，是國泰重組後第一部企圖要成為武俠類型的票房大片，片中明顯可見胡金銓《龍門客棧》的影響：仔細的道具和服裝、堅忍的男主角、及他的仇人，白髮白眉毛

day of the wedding, the bride demands that the hero prove himself to be a knight-errant – and this he does, with humourous effect designed to question the whole concept of chivalry. At the end of the movie, the triumphant hero, appearing to be magnanimous, confesses to using "trickery" to overcome his opponents. An elder explains that "trickery" is part of the game a hero must play to become a hero – a cynical remark that appears to reflect the growing mood among the audience that the image of the *wuxia* hero had had its day.

Similarly, the title character of *The Smiling Swordsman* is a thief who becomes a healer (having inherited the skills from an old doctor with whom he shared a prison cell). In his new guise, he conducts himself as an exemplary knight-errant seeking to right wrongs, despite his mentor's advice not to mind other people's business. He is later falsely accused of murdering his benefactor but goes on to solve the crime and redeem himself in the eyes of the benefactor's daughter (played by Chen Manling), a character who emphasises that virtue, rather than the martial arts, is the best means to win peoples' affections. While it injects light comedy into the genre, *The Smiling Swordsman* rekindles the convention of the detective thriller that was also a part of the genre in martial arts fiction (the so-called *gong'an* novels). The movie is much less successful as a parody, but it does present the *wuxia* movie as a conglomeration of traditional genres – the detective thriller, the revenge melodrama, and some light comedy, in addition to its premise of chivalry in the phenomenon of the wandering knight (*youxia*).

Another point of interest in *The Smiling Swordsman* is the evocation of northern styles and Peking opera conventions. One reason for this emphasis arose from the fact that it had employed Han Yingjie, a specialist in northern styles and Peking opera, to choreograph martial arts action in almost all its *wuxia* movies in this period. Han had worked with King Hu on *Come Drink with Me* and *Dragon Inn*, two of the most influential *wuxia* movies of their day. The other

的太監（令人聯想到《龍門客棧》內的白鷹）、女俠、以及韓英傑的武術指導，都令人想起《龍》片。故事的背景是宋朝（1127年），故事是講一班忠於朝廷的官兵押送着一批撻子犯人，在崇山峻嶺的山東省，越過易河，到邊界的軍營，交換犯人。撻子方面的兵馬早在路上埋伏，企圖劫走囚犯（其中包括王子），和殺死荊無忌（喬宏）。荊無忌以前是起義戰士，但已經退隱為僧，卻因為這次押送任務被舊時將領召回。他的對頭撻子司令完顏慶是特務組職的首領，而其養女完顏婉兒（周萱）其實是荊無忌出家為僧之前曾拋棄的妻子。為了報仇，婉兒成了撻子的線眼，監視着荊無忌，等待着他掉落天羅地網的一刻。

《虎山行》攝製時間超過一年，以港產片來說可謂前所未有。電影於1968年在台灣開鏡，拍攝了八個月。國泰很捨得花錢，例如付給主角喬宏七萬港元的片酬，是有史以來香港國語電影男演員最高的片酬，[21] 超越了女星。從國泰對女主角江青的待遇，也看到了因武俠片發展而令女星的地位下降。江青拍了李翰祥的古裝片《西施》（1965）後，是其時台灣最紅的女星。在原來的劇本裡，只有荊無忌的離婚妻子黑如意一個女主角，[22] 但是江青因不滿拍攝時間太長，與國泰發生合約糾紛，[23] 國泰索性在她出場不久便腰斬她的角色，將合約演員周萱飾演的完顏婉兒變成女主角，而江青卻成了大配角，亦令劇本出現前後矛盾。改劇本之後，荊無忌便有兩位妻子，都因荊出家而被拋棄，在電影開始的時候兩人都穿上孝服秘密跟蹤押送隊伍，又為監視荊無忌而大打出手。

雖然劇本前後犯駁，《虎山行》仍不失為國泰的一部好電影。[24] 再一次，對男主角荊無忌的角色處理，使它成為與別不同的大片（例如邵氏的武俠電影，甚至對它有很大影響的《龍門客棧》）。荊無忌已經出家為僧，再被召去為

reason was Cathay's close business links with Taiwan's Mandarin film industry.[20] In the late 1960s, Cathay would strengthen its links with Taiwan, by hiring Taiwanese directors and actors to direct and appear in *wuxia* movies, which were also shot in Taiwan. Two of these productions were *Escort over Tiger Hills*, released in 1969, and *From the Highway*, released in 1970. These two movies are among the key *wuxia* films Cathay ever produced. They were also two of the most expensive movies Cathay ever invested in.

Of Heroes and Villains

Escort over Tiger Hills, directed by Wang Xinglei on a massive budget of HK$1.2 million, was Cathay's first attempt to come up with a *wuxia* blockbuster since its restructuring. The influence of King Hu's *Dragon Inn* was evident, in the meticulous design and costumes, the portrayals of a stoic male hero (played in this instance by Roy Chiao (Qiao Hong)) and his powerful nemesis in the person of an eunuch with grey hair and eyebrows (recalling the eunuch portrayed by Bai Ying in *Dragon Inn*), a female swordfighter (portrayed by Hilda Chou Hsuan [Zhou Xuan]), and finally, the swordfighting choreography by Han Yingjie, that unmistakably evokes the style of *Dragon Inn*. The story, set in 1127, concerns a military unit loyal to the Song emperor, escorting a group of Tartar prisoners to a border command across the Si River in mountainous Shandong province for an exchange of prisoners. Tartar soldiers lie in wait along the route to ambush the unit; their objective is to free the prisoners (among them a Tartar prince) and to kill Jing Wuji (Chiao), an ex-guerrilla fighter recalled by his old general to serve as backup to the military escort. Having retired as a guerrilla fighter, Jing had gone into the monkhood. He assumes command of the military escort after its commanding officer is killed. The Tartar commander opposing Jing is Wanyan Qing, the head of the secret service. One of Wanyan's subordinates is his adopted daughter, Wanyan Wan'er (Zhou Xuan), in reality, Jing's wife whom he had abandoned in order to enter the monastery. In revenge, Wan'er now works as a spy for the Tartars, keeping one step ahead of Jing before springing the final trap.

皇帝和國家出力，但過程中，他個人的誠信備受質疑。在護送官兵的過程中，荊被迫開殺戒，違背了他的宗教。結尾一場，在一輪血腥廝殺之後，荊自覺背叛了自己的靈魂，感到很痛苦，他發了狂，縱然所有敵人已經被殺，他仍揮劍亂斬。最後他手刃敵人，卻犧牲了已重回他的陣營的妻子。她的死令他極度痛苦，他亦再不是電影開場時那個大俠。所以，雖然《虎》仍沉醉於典型英雄的描寫，但整部電影對英雄大俠的典型卻提出質疑。

國泰跟着的一部大製作《路客與刀客》，由張曾澤導演，與《虎山行》不遑多讓，該片耗資一百二十萬港元拍攝，是一般港產片的三倍；[25] 反映出雖然國泰的聲勢已大不如前，但仍有一定的財務資源可用。這兩部電影其實都是在1968至1969年間拍攝，其時國泰拒絕了與邵氏合併，這時期的製作很大程度上由當時的製作總經理楊曼怡個人拍板及監督，以證明國泰的基礎仍健全。

在整整一年的製作中，超過三分之一的預算用在搭建一個民國初期中國北方平原的「城寨」的主景上。整個場景在台灣中部的台中郊區搭建，據報足足有一條飛機跑道那麼大。

這個住了幾百戶人家的城寨，受到土匪的垂涎。城寨的守衛森嚴，土匪首領先派了一班人扮成江湖賣藝人、郎中等混入城寨，這幫人由渾號「辮子張」（台灣演員孫越），因他擅長以辮子作武器而得名。寨主賞識辮子張的武藝，並招攬他為自衛隊的教頭，令他有機會混入城寨之中。一個過路的陌生人（楊群）卻把張的真正身份告知寨主，指他是受土匪首領「鐵葫蘆」之命（崔福生）行事。原來鐵葫蘆是陌生人的殺師仇人；他自告奮勇，保護城寨和住在裡頭的人，救了寨主被綁的兒子，又從鐵葫蘆手中救了寨主，但城寨最後卻被鐵葫蘆攻破，一把火燒毀。[26]

《路客與刀客》
From the Highway

Production on *Escort* took over a year, quite unprecedented for a Hong Kong movie. Shooting began in 1968 on Taiwan locations, and went on for eight months. Cathay appeared to have spared no expenses, for example, paying the leading man Chiao over HK$70,000 in salary and expenses – the largest salary ever paid to an actor in Hong Kong's Mandarin cinema up to that point.[21] If proof was needed that men had taken the lead over women in Hong Kong's film industry, it was that salary. Another sign of how women's status had been downgraded with the rise of the *wuxia* movie may be seen in Cathay's treatment of the star Chiang Ching (Jiang Qing), who was signed to play the female lead. Chiang was by this time the biggest female star in Taiwan's Mandarin cinema after playing the lead in Li Hanxiang's costume epic *Hsi Shih Beauty of Beauties* (1965). In the original completed script, there was only one female lead – the character of Hei Ruyi, Jing Wuji's estranged wife.[22] However, because of a contract dispute with Chiang, who also took exception to the long shooting period,[23] Cathay killed off her character after an initial appearance in the movie, and introduced another female lead, the character of Wan'er, giving the part to Zhou Xuan, a player under contract. Chiang's part was thus relegated to a cameo role, causing inconsistencies in the final film. Jing now has two wives whom he has apparently abandoned to join the monkhood. The two women are given a scene early in the film where they put on mourning clothes in order to shadow the escort platoon, both fighting each other for the right to spy on Jing.

Despite this inconsistency in the script, *Escort over Tiger Hills* remains an impressive achievement for Cathay.[24] Once again, it is the treatment of the central hero (Jing Wuji) that makes the movie stand apart from the usual blockbusters (for example, Shaws' *wuxia* pictures, and even King Hu's *Dragon Inn*, which was a source of influence and inspiration). Jing, having retired into the monkhood, is recalled to serve king and country once more, but in the process of this service, his personal integrity comes into question. In

《路客與刀客》中的楊群
Yang Qun in
From the Highway.

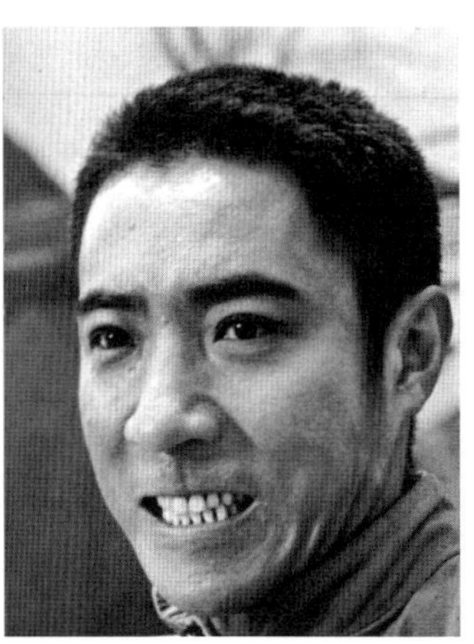

當這個沈默寡言的陌生人騎着馬進入城寨，救眾人於危難的時候，他代表了武俠類型裡的遊俠形象。雖然他作出這樣的行為是出於私人恩怨，但在緊急關頭，他沒有袖手旁觀讓土匪奸計得逞。然而，楊群不是典型的武俠演員，他擅演時裝文藝片，常能帶出一份悲劇色彩，但是片中陌生路客的角色並不是十分討好，雖身為主角，卻往往被饒有特色的反派鐵葫蘆、辮子張蓋掉光芒。他的角色之所以仍有突出之處，是他的武打。在你死我活的打鬥中，他只是赤手空拳，力敵鐵葫蘆和辮子張，是以能一般的比槍弄劍的武俠片中，帶來新鮮感。當然，兩名反派以身體作為武器，又是另一種綽頭。

事實上，《路》片作出的一些變化，令其有別於一般的類型片。影片的背景不在古代，取而代之的是二十世紀民初時期，電影最吸引之處是重構這個時代，展示了傳統中國北方社會，在現代文明的衝激之下，充滿對西方

defending the military escort, Jing is forced to kill, violating a principle of his religion. In one of the final scenes, following a particularly bloody battle, Jing is tormented by the realisation that he has betrayed his soul; he cries out like a mad animal and continues to slash his sword at imaginary enemies after his real enemies have been killed. In the finale, Jing kills his chief opponent Wanyan Qing, but at the cost of his wife's life, who had come over to his side. Her sacrifice leads Jing into another bout of anguish. He is no longer the heroic figure that he is in the beginning. Thus, the whole movie poses a question mark over the heroic stereotype, even though it indulges in the attributes of that stereotype.

Cathay's next blockbuster was *From the Highway*, directed by Zhang Zengze on the same massive HK$1.2 million budget that was allocated to *Escort over Tiger Hills* – a budget three times greater than the normal Hong Kong movie,[25] thus indicating the kind of financial resources that Cathay could still draw on despite its decline (in fact, the two films were produced over the period 1968-1969 after Cathay had rejected a proposed merger with Shaws; these productions being undertaken on a large scale personally overseen by the production chief Yeo Ban-Yee [Yang Manyi], most likely so that Cathay could show that its fundamentals were sound). Taking over a year in production, more than a third of the budget was expended on a huge set of an early Republican-period stockade in the middle of the northern Chinese plains. The set, constructed in the outskirts of Taichung, in central Taiwan, was reported to have covered the expanse of an airport runway.

The stockade, home to hundreds of families, is besieged by a group of marauding bandits. Strongly defended, the bandit chief sends an advance party to enter the stockade disguised as travelling martial arts acrobats-cum-medicine peddlers. The infiltrators are headed by "Pigtail" Zhang (played by Taiwanese actor Sun Yue), so named because his forte lies in using his pigtail as a deadly whip. Zhang's martial arts abilities impress Master An, the lord of the stockade, who hires him as chief coach to his militia, thus giving him access

事物的好奇。因此，電影就如一齣「現代武俠」片，角色既用槍用炮，亦用傳統的武器。功夫打鬥／武打也可視為電影的「現代」特徵——喻示新事物的來臨。當影片在1970年2月首映的時候，《路》片實際上是第一部標示了國語武俠的轉型——由武俠片到功夫片。[27] 不消幾個月，邵氏兄弟便有樣學樣，拍了張徹的《報仇》（1970）和王羽的《龍虎鬥》（1970），這兩部均以民初為背景的電影，加上《路客與刀客》，構成前李小龍的國語功夫片潮，即以北方背景，北派武打動作為特色。直到1971年，李小龍的《唐山大兄》帶出了一種截然不同的南方背景。李小龍源自南方詠春的創新武打風格，加上他在香港長大，最終予以功夫電影南方／廣東的身份。

直至1971年關閉片場以前，國泰還拍了幾部武俠電影。片場所作的最後一件事之一，是停止一部攝製中、由陳曼玲主演的武俠電影《觀音客棧》，[28] 影片最終沒有完成。前邵氏的製作主管鄒文懷自立門戶，創立的新公司嘉禾購入國泰片廠的原址，為國泰發行餘下的電影。嘉禾起用了邵氏的滄海遺珠李小龍，李小龍的崛起，亦帶領了現代功夫電影的熱潮，為1965年至1971年的武俠片時代畫上句號。彷彿是冥冥中自有主宰，武俠類型電影的興衰，正見證了國泰的起落。

（按：本文摘錄自一篇以武打電影為題的博士論文。蒙威斯康辛大學麥迪遜分校大衛．博維爾教授協助，得以觀看以上討論的部份電影，作者謹此致謝。此外，亦感謝香港電影資料館的職員，安排參考其餘電影的機會。）

周淑賢翻譯

to the stockade. A passing stranger, He Yilang (played by Yang Chuen/Yang Qun), informs Master An that Zhang is a bandit doing the bidding of bandit chief Xu Kun (Cui Fusheng). Xu, nicknamed "Iron Gourd" (because his chief weapon is his bald head which he uses as a battering ram), is the man that He wants to kill to avenge the death of his master. The stranger volunteers his services to protect the stockade and its inhabitants, rescuing the master's son after he has been abducted, and finally saving the master himself from Iron Gourd, who, by using his head as a battering ram, had successfully breached the stockade and put it to the torch.[26]

As the taciturn stranger who rides into town on a horse and saves the community from disaster, He Yilang represents the knight-errant figure in *wuxia* fiction. Though motivated by a selfish desire for revenge, the stranger saves the community because he cannot sit by and watch as the bandits carry out their evil plan. However, as played by Yang, not a typical *wuxia* actor (he specialised in contemporary melodramas and could usually be depended upon to bring out the tragic dimensions of heroes, though not here). He is an unrewarding character, a hero who is ultimately overshadowed by the villains – the colourful "Iron Gourd" and "Pigtail" Zhang. Nevertheless, he remains a significant character because of his fighting style. In his fight-to-the-death scenes with "Pigtail" and "Iron Gourd", He uses only his bare hands, a refreshing change from the swordplay in standard *wuxia* pictures (there is of course the additional novelty of watching the two villains employing unusual parts of the body for combat).

From the Highway, in fact, is distinguished by its variations on the genre. Instead of an ancient dynastic setting, the film locates the genre in the early Republican period in the 20th century. One of the film's most attractive features is the recreation of this period, showing its traditional northern Chinese community on the threshold of modernity, indulging in western curiosities such as the peepshow. Hence, the film functions like a "modern *wuxia*" movie where the protagonists use guns and cannons as well as traditional weaponry. The kung fu fighting style may

註

1. 雖然電影史學者普遍認為陸運濤1964年不幸去世是導致國泰衰落的原因，但很多行內人相信早於1962年，片廠總經理鍾啟文請辭後，國泰已開始走下坡。參見沙榮峰：《繽紛電影四十春：沙榮峰回憶錄》，台北：國家電影資料館，1994，頁39。根據沙氏所指，鍾於1956至1962年擔任片廠總經理及製作主管的時候，正是電懋的黃金時期。但自六十年代早期，鍾氏已未能應付與邵氏兄弟公司的競爭，更被邵氏挖去多名紅星及導演。
2. 根據沙氏，這「電懋風格」是由鍾啟文及其下兩名得力助手，製作總監宋淇、劇本總監孫晉三所構思，見沙榮峰，同註1，頁35。這個說法不是沒有道理，但筆者認為陸運濤本身是啟發電懋風格的角色典範。
3. 見《南國電影》，第92期，1965年10月，頁30。
4. 見沈彬，〈從邵氏公司近其製片計劃，展望香港影業趨勢〉，《香港影畫》，第24期，1967年12月，頁61。
5. 見《南國電影》，第91期，1965年9月，頁10 - 11。
6. 見蔣杰，〈我為國泰公司而辛酸落淚〉，《銀色世界》，1971年7月，頁29。
7. 見《國際電影》，第117期，1965年8月，頁5 - 6。國泰新加坡的發行經理俞普慶被派到香港國泰出任經理，楊曼怡則為副經理。
8. 同註7，頁5。
9. 見《南國電影》，第83期，1965年1月。
10. 見《南國電影》，第87期，1965年5月，頁2 - 5。
11. 資料參見黃卓漢：《電影人生：黃卓漢回憶錄》，台北：萬象圖書，1994，頁123 - 124。
12. 見劉亞佛，〈邵氏國泰合併幕後消息〉，《銀河畫報》，第120期，1968年3月，頁27。
13. 見〈邵氏國泰合併之謎〉，《娛樂畫報》，第82期，1968年4月，頁29。
14. 同註13。
15. 見蔣杰，同註6，頁28 - 29。
16. 這段期間，需要武術打鬥訓練的流行動作類型電影不只武俠電影，在亞洲的占士邦熱潮下，也拍攝了一系列需武術技巧的動作片。見李清庭，〈銀幕上的打鬥〉，《國際電影》，第131期，1966年10月，頁2 - 6。
17. 如雷震與其妹樂蒂，及導演袁秋楓在1967年組成金鷹公司，當時仍有國泰合約在身的演員張揚與金鷹簽約，在其兩部電影中擔演主角。見劉亞佛，〈1967香港影壇回顧與前瞻〉，《香港影畫》，第24期，1967年12月，頁41。另見沙榮峰，同註1。

張建德，電影學者。著有《Hong Kong Cinema: The Extra Dimensions》(BFI, 1997)。現正在澳洲RMIT大學寫武術電影的博士論文。
Stephen Teo is a critic and author of *Hong Kong Cinema: The Extra Dimensions* (BFI, 1997). He previously served as English Editor of the Hong Kong International Film Festival and is now finishing his Ph. D at RMIT University (Melbourne).

also be seen as a "modern" feature of the film – a sign of things to come. When it was released in February 1970, *From the Highway* was effectively the first Mandarin movie to signal a shift in the martial arts genre – from *wuxia* to kung fu.[27] Within a few months, Shaw Brothers took up the cue, producing Chang Cheh's *Vengeance* (1970) and Wang Yu's *The Chinese Boxer* (1970), both also set in the early Republican period. Together with *From the Highway*, all these films constituted the pre-Bruce Lee (Li Xiaolong) kung fu boom in Mandarin cinema, featuring northern settings and northern styles of martial arts that were identified with the Mandarin cinema. In 1971, Bruce Lee's *The Big Boss* introduced a distinctively southern setting. Lee's innovative style of kung fu, based on the southern form of *Wing Chun*, as well as Lee's Hong Kong Cantonese upbringing, finally conferred a southern and Cantonese identity on the kung fu genre.

Cathay continued to make several more *wuxia* pictures until its closure in 1971. One of the last acts of the studio was to cancel the production of a *wuxia* movie then in progress, entitled *The Inn of the Goddess*, starring Chen Manling.[28] The movie was never finished. Golden Harvest, the new company set up by Raymond Chow (Zou Wenhuai), Shaws' ex-production chief, bought Cathay's studio premises and agreed to distribute the remaining Cathay productions. It was Golden Harvest who secured the services of Bruce Lee when Cathay's arch-rival, Shaw Brothers, passed on him. The rise of Bruce Lee brought on the rise of the modern kung fu genre, thus ending the *wuxia* resurgence of the period 1965 - 1971. As if bound by destiny, Cathay's existence coincided with the genre's rise and decline.

This article is adapted from a chapter in a Ph. D thesis on the martial arts cinema. The author wishes to acknowledge the assistance of Professor David Bordwell of the University of Wisconsin, Madison, in arranging screenings of some of the films discussed above. Thanks also to the staff of the Hong Kong Film Archive for arranging viewing of the rest of the films.

18. 見劉亞佛，同註17。製片人黃卓漢在其回憶錄中指出，行內普遍認為武俠電影不需要大明星，只要有好的劇本和武術動作，新人亦能擔正，不會影響票房。見黃卓漢，同註11，頁125。
19.《龍門客棧》是台灣聯邦電影公司的製作，但版權卻給予邵氏，以平息胡金銓的合約糾紛。胡在拍完《大醉俠》後，在沒有完成合約的情況下離開邵氏，到台灣拍攝《龍門客棧》。引自張建德的沙榮峰訪問，2001年3月24日於三藩市。
20. 沙榮峰是國泰在台灣的主要商業夥伴，通過其台灣的聯邦電影公司，及子公司國際電影公司將國泰的影片發行到台灣。沙氏與國泰的合作可追溯至1965年的電懋時期，及1963年李翰祥的國聯時代。國聯由新加坡國泰集團及發行網絡聯邦公司出資合組，國聯的名字取自兩間公司的中文名稱第一個字。
21. 見《銀河畫報》，第132期，1969年3月，頁44。
22. 原劇本，英文題名《The Escorts》（中文名字沒有改動），現藏香港電影資料館內。
23. 見《銀河畫報》，第132期，1969年3月，頁45。
24. 影片賣埠海外，配成英語、法語、葡萄牙語。另見《香港武俠電影研究（1945 - 1980）》，第5屆香港國際電影節回顧特刊，香港：市政局，1981，頁250。
25. 見《路客與刀客》特刊，現藏香港電影資料館內，頁8。
26. 耗資超過30萬港元搭建的佈景亦因而報銷。見蔣杰，同註6，頁28。
27.《路客與刀客》是國泰最成功的電影，數收入將近100萬。見蔣杰，同註6，頁28。
28. 同註24，頁237。電影終止製作反映出國泰在不愉快的情況下關閉。陳曼玲曾強烈批評國泰管理層管理不善，錢不用在製作上，而胡亂花費在無謂的事上。關於國泰不光彩的結束的報道，見蔣杰，同註6，頁28 - 29。

Notes

1. Though historians generally attribute Cathay's decline to Loke Wan Tho's tragic demise in 1964, many insiders believed that the decline began as early as 1962, with the resignation of Robert Chung (Zhong Qiwen), the studio's general manager. See Sha Yung-fong (Sha Rongfeng): *Forty Springs of Cinema Glory: The Memoirs of Sha Yung-fong* (in Chinese), Taipei: Chinese Taipei Film Archive, 1994, p. 39. According to Sha, Chung's reign as general manager and production chief from 1956–1962 marked MP & GI's golden period, but in the early 1960s, Chung was unable to withstand the competition from Shaw Brothers, which successfully enticed some of the biggest stars and directors away from the studio.
2. This "MP & GI home style" was, according to Sha Yung-fong, the creation of Robert Chung and two of his ablest lieutenants, Stephen Soong (Song Qi), chief of production, and Sun Jinsan, chief of the scriptwriting committee. See Sha Yung-fong, ibid., p. 35. There is of course a lot of credence to this claim, but to my mind, Loke Wan Tho was himself the ultimate role model for and inspiration behind the MP & GI home-style.
3. See *Southern Screen* (in Chinese), no. 92, October 1965, p. 30.
4. See Shen Bin, "The Prospects of Hong Kong's Film Industry From the Vantage Point of Shaw Brothers' Recent Projects" in *Hong Kong Movie News* (in Chinese), no. 24, December 1967, p. 61.
5. See *Southern Screen* (in Chinese), no. 91, September 1965, pp. 10-11.
6. See Jiang Jie, "The Fall of Cathay Organisation" in *Cinemart* (in Chinese), July 1971, p. 29.
7. See *International Screen* (in Chinese), no. 117, August 1965, pp. 5-6. Paul Yui (Yu Puqing), Cathay's distribution manager in Singapore was appointed manager of Cathay (Hong Kong), with Yeo Ban-Yee (Yang Manyi) as the deputy manager.
8. Ibid., p. 5.
9. See *Southern Screen* (in Chinese), no. 83, January 1965.
10. See *Southern Screen* (in Chinese), no. 87, May 1965, pp. 2-5.
11. These figures are from Wong Cheuk-hon (Huang Zhuohan): *A Life in Movies: The Memoirs of Wong Cheuk-hon* (in Chinese), Taipei: Variety Publishing, 1994, pp. 123-124.
12. See Liu Yafo, "Shaws-Cathay Merger" in *The Milky Way Pictorial* (in Chinese), no. 120, March 1968, p. 27.
13. See "The Puzzle of the Shaws-Cathay Merger" in *Screen and Stage Pictorial* (in Chinese), no. 82, April 1968, p. 29.
14. Ibid.
15. See Jiang Jie, op. cit., pp. 28-29.
16. The *wuxia* movie was not the only popular action genre at this time that required martial arts training; there was also the Asian James Bond fad which featured action sequences requiring all kinds of martial arts expertise. See Li Qingting, "The Action on the Screen" in *International Screen* (in Chinese), no. 131, October 1966, pp. 2-6.
17. For example, Kelly Lai Chen (Lei Zhen) and his sister, Betty Loh Ti (Le Di), formed the Jinying Film Company in 1967, with director Yuan Qiufeng. Actor Chang Yang (Zhang Yang), then still under contract with Cathay, signed up with the company to play the lead in two of its movies. Actor Chao Lei (Zhao Lei) also established his own production company when under contract with Cathay. See Liu Yafo, "1967, A Review and Preview of Hong Kong's Film Circles" in *Hong Kong Movie News* (in Chinese), no. 24, December 1967, p. 41. See also Sha Yung-fong, op. cit.
18. Liu Yafo, ibid. Within the industry, it was widely believed that *wuxia* pictures did not need big-name stars, a point made by producer Wong Cheuk-hon in his memoirs. So long as the story and the action choreography were good, new players could be used as leads without affecting the movies' box office potential. See Wong Cheuk-hon, op. cit., p. 125.
19. *Dragon Inn* (1967) was actually a production of Taiwan's Union Film Company but its overseas distribution rights were given to Shaw Brothers as a settlement of a dispute arising from King Hu's contract. Hu had left Shaws after *Come Drink with Me* (1966), without completing his contract, to make *Dragon Inn* in Taiwan. From an interview with Sha Yung-fong, March 24, 2001, San Francisco.
20. Cathay's chief business partner in Taiwan was Sha Yung-fong, who distributed Cathay's films in Taiwan through his company, Union (Lianbang), and its subsidiary, the International Film Company. Sha's association with Cathay dated back to the MP & GI period beginning from 1956, and to the saga of Li Hanxiang's Grand Motion Picture Company in 1963. Grand (Guolian) was a company that combined the financial resources of Singapore's Cathay Organisation (Guotai), and the distribution network of the Union Film Company (Lianbang); hence the name Grand was made up of the first two Chinese words of the respective film companies.
21. See *The Milky Way Pictorial* (in Chinese), no. 132, March 1969, p.44.
22. Original script (in Chinese), entitled *The Escorts* in English (no change in the Chinese title), Hong Kong Film Archive collection.
23. See *The Milky Way Pictorial* (in Chinese), no. 132, March 1969, p.45.
24. The movie was exported overseas, dubbed into English, French and Portuguese. See *A Study of the Hong Kong Swordplay Film (1945-1980)*, the 5th Hong Kong International Film Festival catalogue, Hong Kong: Urban Council, 1981, p.250.
25. See *From the Highway Special Issue* (in Chinese), Hong Kong Film Archive collection, p.8.
26. The expensive set, costing over HK$300,000 to build, was thus destroyed. See Jiang Jie, op. cit., p. 28.
27. *From the Highway* (1970) was Cathay's most successful movie, its gross takings just falling short of HK$1 million. See Jiang Jie, op. cit., p. 28.
28. See *A Study of the Hong Kong Swordplay Film (1945-1980)*, p. 237. The cancellation of the movie reflected the unhappy circumstances of Cathay's termination. Melinda Chen Manling was highly critical of the management's maladministration, complaining of how money was wasted on frivolous items instead of being spent on the production itself. For a report on Cathay's ignominious end, see Jiang Jie, op. cit., pp. 28-29.

Crossing Borders

越界／跨界

人妖、英雄與弄臣：國泰克里斯滄桑史

- Timothy P. Barnard -

馬來人有一種稱為「克里斯」(keris)的武器，基本上是一柄短劍，劍刃呈波浪形，最好用隕鐵打造。在傳統宮庭中，所有武士都會佩戴克里斯，通常以帶子綁着，繫於腰間。克里斯更具有象徵意義，馬來人相信持着它，可獲庇佑，免受外來政治或文化力量威脅。時至今日，不少馬來人在穿着傳統服飾時，仍會配戴一柄克里斯。當一個精明華人企業家帶領國泰機構開始製作馬來片時，就在公司名稱加上克里斯一字，這不單代表公司希望在文化上取悅觀眾，更意味着他們祈求克里斯的神奇力量，可以將顧客帶入旗下在馬來半島和新加坡的戲院網。

國泰克里斯（Cathay Keris）電影公司的歷史，跟公司名稱那兩個字有很密切的關係。Cathay一字來自早於二次大戰之前已經成立的國泰機構。在馬來亞（現稱馬來西亞），國泰以經營電影院馳名，總部設在新加坡 Dhoby Ghaut 的國泰綜合大樓內。戰後，陸運濤成為國泰在意

編按：當年馬來（巫語）片中的Pontianak，英譯為Vampires，中譯則為「人妖」，與今天的「人妖」一詞意思不同。

Vampires, Heroes and Jesters: A History of Cathay Keris

- Timothy P. Barnard -

The "keris" is both a real and symbolic Malay weapon. Basically a short sword, it is ideally made of meteoric iron and has a wavy blade. All warriors in traditional courts carried a *keris*, usually tucked into a sash tied around the waist. It was believed that the owner of the *keris* possessed talismanic protection against anyone threatening the political or cultural sphere of the Malays. Even today, many Malay men still wear one when traditionally dressed. When the Cathay Organisation began Malay film production with a maverick Chinese entrepreneur, the "keris" in the title symbolized not only their hope to appeal to the audience culturally, but also that the magical power of the *keris* would draw customers into the organisation's chain of theatres throughout the Malay Peninsula and Singapore.

The history of the Cathay Keris film studio thus is bound up in the two words that make up its title. The first word in the title is derived from the Cathay Organisation, which was formed before World War II. In Malaya(now Malaysia) it was known for its various theatres, with the centre of operations being the

念上和業務上的首腦。他來自十九世紀中期移民至新加坡的富裕華僑世家，曾放洋留學，在瑞士、劍橋和倫敦唸書。陸運濤深受這段歐洲經驗影響，成為東南亞最西化的華人之一。從歐洲回來後，他接手國泰機構，在馬來半島和新加坡購買、興建更多電影院。雖然拓展院線甚為成功，但是陸運濤對於沒有甚麼國泰發行的電影能在馬來亞鄉郊賣座，甚感不滿。反觀他的對手邵氏兄弟公司，卻解決了這問題，他們在二次大戰前已開始製作馬來片，更在 1947 年成立 Malay Film Production Studios（下稱 Malay Film）。為了取得馬來電影的片源，陸運濤曾鼓勵馬來半島很多戲院東主自行拍製電影。

國泰克里斯公司的名稱用上「克里斯」一字，是企業家何亞祿的念頭。他 1901 年出生於英屬幾內亞，曾在愛丁堡的 George Watson College 唸書。後來他跟隨家人遷徙到檳城，入讀 St. Xavier's 書院，後來再到香港大學深造。性格上，何亞祿比陸運濤來得粗獷不羈，他返回馬

葛利斯南與何亞祿（右）1956 年攝於古晉
Dato L. Krishnan and Ho Ah Loke (right) in Kuching, 1956.

Cathay complex at Dhoby Ghaut in Singapore. Loke Wan Tho (Lu Yuntao) was the intellectual and business leader of the Cathay Organisation following the war. He was a member of a prestigious Chinese family in Singapore, who studied in Switzerland, Cambridge and London. This period in Europe deeply influenced Loke, and he was one of the most Westernised Chinese in Southeast Asia. Upon his return from Europe Loke took control of the Cathay Organisation and continued its installation of theatres throughout Singapore and the Malay Peninsula. Despite his success at acquiring theatres, Loke was frustrated by the absence of films that would appeal to the predominately Malay rural areas, a problem the rival Shaw Brothers had solved with their production of a few Malay films prior to World War II and the subsequent creation of their Malay Film Production Studios in 1947. Searching for a Malay film source, Loke encouraged several other theatre owners in the peninsula to produce their own films.

The "keris" in the title of the film studio came from an entrepreneur, who was more rough and tumble than Loke Wan Tho, named Ho Ah Loke (He Yalu). Born in 1901 in British Guinea, Ho was educated at George Watson College in Edinburgh. His family eventually moved to Penang, where he continued his education at St. Xavier's before moving on to Hong Kong University. Upon his return to the Malay Peninsula, Ho bought a cinema in Ipoh and also began travelling from village to village showing films off the back of his bicycle. From these beginnings, he expanded his cinema holdings to include theatres in Taiping, Teluk Intan, Kampar and Klang, as well as Ipoh's elaborate The Oriental in 1930. By 1934, however, he decided to sell these theatres to the Shaw Brothers. Following a series of gambling losses and debts, Ho returned to theatre ownership in the late 1930s.

Following World War II, Ho began to contemplate ways to improve attendance at his cinemas. The only company making Malay language films at the time was the Shaw Brothers' Malay Film Productions, which would not allow their films to be shown in rival theatres. Ho was limited to importing Indonesian and Indian films. To counter this problem, Ho founded

來亞後，在怡保買下了一家電影院，並且周遊各個村落，在自己的自行車後面放映電影。在這個基礎上，他將影院業務擴展至太平、直落英丹、金寶、巴生等地，在 1930 年更購入怡保豪華的東方戲院。不過，到了 1934 年，他決定將所有戲院賣給邵氏。在連番賭博輸錢、債台高築後，何亞祿到三十年代末重操故業，經營戲院。

二次大戰後，他設法改善旗下電影院的上座率。當時唯一製作馬來語電影的公司，就是邵氏的 Malay Film，他們不會准許本身的出品在對手的影院上映。何亞祿只有進口印尼和印度電影，試圖吸引觀眾。到 1947 年，為解決片源問題，他與陸運濤達成協議：他成立 Rimau Film Productions，自行製作馬來片，所有作品均可在國泰旗下的影院放映。為國泰發行印度電影的公司 Syarikat Gian Singh 也入股 Rimau，以作支持。Rimau 首兩部作品為《一把米》（*Untuk Sesuap Nasi*）和《戀之花》（*Bunga Percintaan*）。雖然公司與國泰早有協議，但發行和集資仍有困難，主因是 Gian Singh 不願意繼續投資拍攝無甚盈利機會的電影。因此，Rimau 未幾即告倒閉。[1]

1951 年，何亞祿成立完全自資的電影公司，名為克里斯。為了打響頭炮，他決定以一部前所未見的電影打入市場——彩色的馬來片。這部《靜海武士》（*Perwira Lautan Teduh*）拍攝過程頗多波折。由於新加坡沒有沖印彩色底片的設施，底片要送往倫敦沖印，這自然令成本增加。更不幸的是，底片在運送途中遺失了，令這部電影從沒機會放映。這些事故對剛成立不久的克里斯，自然在財政上造成重大打擊。除了製作困難外，發行對何亞祿來說，依然是難題。根據一項資料，當時邵氏會買下電影的拷貝，但卻不在戲院放映，以確保那些電影無法賺錢。[2] 在這個情況下，何亞祿再次找昔日的合作夥伴陸運濤，兩人同仇敵愾，都想跟邵氏的發行網一較高下，於是在 1953 年合作成立國泰克里斯。

Rimau Film Productions in 1947 to produce Malay films, following an agreement with Loke Wan Tho that Cathay theatres would screen any films that the fledging company produced. Rimau was formed with the partnership and support of Syarikat Gian Singh, a company that distributed Indian films for Cathay. The first two films Rimau produced were *For a Handful of Rice* (*Untuk Sesuap Nasi*) and *Flowers of Love* (*Bunga Percintaan*). Despite the agreement with Cathay Keris, film distribution and funding remained a problem, and the company folded quickly, mainly due to Gian Singh's unwillingness to continue producing films that had little possibility of making a profit.[1]

Ho proceeded to establish his own studio, Keris, in 1951. To enter the market with a product that had not been seen before, he decided to make the first Malay film in colour. The film, *Warrior of the Peaceful Sea* (*Perwira Lautan Teduh*) was complicated to make. Since facilities to process the film were unavailable in Singapore, it had to be processed in London, which added to the costs. Tragically, the negative was lost somewhere in its travels and the film was never shown. Such setbacks were financially draining on the fledgling studio. Ho was not only having difficulty making the film, the problem of distributorship remained. According to one source, the Shaw Brothers would buy prints and then fail to show them in their theatres, thus ensuring that the films would not make a profit.[2] Under such circumstances, Ho turned to his former partner, who had shared his desire to compete with the Shaw Brothers' distribution system, Loke Wan Tho and his Cathay Organisation, thus forming Cathay Keris Film Productions in 1953.

1953-59: Vampires

In 1953 Cathay Keris faced numerous obstacles. Its greatest competitor, Shaw Brothers' Malay Film Productions, had a monopoly on Malay filmmaking, and with it numerous actors and directors under contract, as well as the loyalty of a public who knew they were getting a proven product. To break this stranglehold, Ho and Loke wanted to make a grand entrance into the market. They decided to try once again to make a Malay language film in colour. The film, *Bamboo of Yearning* (*Buloh Perindu*, 1953),

1953至1959年：人妖

在1953年，國泰克里斯面對重重障礙。公司最大的競爭對手——邵氏屬下的Malay Film 壟斷了馬來片製作，旗下有很多合約演員和導演，又有大群忠實觀眾，深信Malay Film的作品有一定水準。為了打破對手的獨攬局面，何亞祿和陸運濤想以一部不同凡響的製作殺進市場，於是決定再拍一部彩色馬來片。這齣《真假王子》（*Buloh Perindu*, 1953）攝製時間達六個月，因為要在馬來亞的玻璃市州實景拍攝，並需要有野生動物在背景中。但是彩色拍攝未能補救影片在故事和演出上失色之處，結果票房反應相當冷清。雖然《真》片並沒有為新公司帶來好開始，卻已表現了國泰克里斯各部早期作品的特色——從使用移動鏡頭、外景拍攝，以至原創配樂，均可見該公司在技術層面較為突出。[3]不過，這些作品的票房卻始終不及邵氏Malay Film的熱門電影。因此，國泰克里斯仍要在強大對手的陰影下經營，繼續找尋觀眾。

國泰克里斯的片廠最初設於新加坡東部的Tampines，但未幾公司遷往East Coast Road，在那裡建立一家大型片廠，並購置了一些當時最新的器材。[4]何亞祿除了將不少Rimau和克里斯的員工帶到國泰克里斯外，還吸引了不少在邵氏工作得不愉快的員工加盟。早期其中一項重大成就，是邀得魯邁拿（S. Roomai Noor）和瑪麗亞曼多（Maria Menado）於1954年加入國泰克里斯。來自印尼的瑪麗亞曼多和出生於馬來半島彭亨州的魯邁拿，都是Malay Film旗下的紅星，在五十年代初厭倦了要為邵氏負責多項任務，於是轉投國泰克里斯，除主演電影外，也協助培育新人。不過，當時兩人跟邵氏仍有合約，要等待一段時間才能過檔。為了避免拖延過久，何亞祿約見邵逸夫，兩人達成協議，讓瑪麗亞曼多和魯邁拿提早解

took over six months to film since much of it was shot on location in the Malay state of Perlis and required the presence of wild animals in the background of shots. While the film was in colour, the actual story and acting were considered less than stellar and the film showed to mainly empty theatres. Although it was not an auspicious beginning for the new studio, *Bamboo of Yearning* reflected characteristics of early Cathay Keris films, which were known for their technical expertise, such as the use of moving cameras, outdoor shooting, and original background music.[3] However, the films still trailed the popular releases of Malay Film Productions. In this respect, Cathay Keris continued to operate in the shadows of its larger rival, searching for an audience.

The studio where Cathay Keris employees worked was initially located in Tampines, in eastern Singapore, but soon moved to East Coast Road where a large film studio was created with some of the most modern equipment of the time.[4] In addition to the personnel he brought over from Rimau and Keris studios, Ho Ah Loke was able to entice disgruntled Shaw employees to these new facilities. One of the earliest successes in these endeavours occurred when S. Roomai Noor and Maria Menado moved to Cathay Keris in 1954. Both Menado, originally from Indonesia, and Roomai, from Pahang on the Malay Peninsula, had been very popular stars at Malay Film Productions. By the early 1950s they grown tired of the numerous duties for the Shaw Brothers, and moved to Cathay Keris with the dual responsibilities of starring in films and developing young talent. However, both Menado and Roomai were still under contract with the Shaw Brothers, and faced a period of waiting until their previous obligations had passed. To avoid a long delay, Ho had a meeting with Run Run Shaw and worked out an agreement that released the two stars from their former contracts. Roomai and Menado would go on to star, often together, in 20 of the 27 films that were made at Cathay Keris between 1953 and 1958.[5]

The movement of stars between the two studios was common during the 50s, with the draw usually being richer contracts. Most stars made between $100 and $300 a month, with bonuses provided if

除合約。在1953至1958年間，這兩個明星為國泰克里斯主演了20部電影（同期公司製作總數為27部），其中不少是兩人合演的。[5]

五十年代間，明星為待遇更豐厚的合約吸引，在兩家公司之間跳槽是常見現象。當時大部份明星月薪為一百至三百元，到真的有電影拍攝再加花紅。若明星懂得唱歌或作曲，又可以獲得補貼，因此，很多明星都會在電影配樂中擔任和唱歌手。一個邵氏早期影片的女演員Mariam表示，她轉投國泰克里斯是因為月薪可以倍增至三百元，若有電影開拍，更增至八百元。以往合約通常為期五年，而且電影公司可隨意更改，而Mariam跟國泰克里斯簽的是三年合約。於是，國泰克里斯用條件較佳的合約，加上其他吸引力，得以打破邵氏壟斷藝人的局面。國泰克里斯其中一個吸引之處，是讓演員在製作上參與更多，例如有「馬來片皇后」美譽的 Siput Sarawak，到六十年代初仍留在國泰克里斯，因為公司答允讓她執導演筒，拍攝劇情片《邪惡的眼睛》（*Mata Syaitan*, 1962）。[6]

這些馬來影星工作的天地，就是新加坡社會的縮影：銀幕上擔演的是馬來人；背後輔助的是印度人；管理和出資金的則是華人——何亞祿和陸運濤正好反映了這個特點。馬來演員，特別是在電影業發展初期，多數出身自一種稱為bangsawan的本土傳統戲劇。到電影成為普及的娛樂形式後，就有較多演員來自音樂界，或是選美出身。早期馬來片的幕後工作人員，大多是印度人。印度電影業早已發展蓬勃，當地不少具有技術經驗的人才，經由印度片在東南亞的發行商引介，來到新加坡。結果，在五十年代，差不多所有馬來片的導演都是印度人。例如在國泰克里斯，這段時期內唯一的馬來人導演，就是魯邁拿。這批印度幕後人員對馬來片的影響，

魯邁拿迎接陸運濤
S. Roomai Noor greets Loke Wan Tho.

Courtesy of the National Archives of Singapore

they were actually filming a movie. This salary could be supplemented if the star was able to sing or compose music; thus, many stars also worked as backing singers on the soundtracks of various films. According to one participant, Mariam, an actress for early Shaw Brothers' films, she moved to Cathay Keris because her salary doubled to $300 per month and up to $800 if she was actually making a film. The contracts were usually for five years, and could be renewed at the discretion of the studios. Mariam's contract with Cathay Keris was for three years. Under these circumstances, Cathay Keris helped break some of the stranglehold over the talent by offering an alternative, as well as other inducements, such as greater participation in the production of the films. For example, Siput Sarawak, often proclaimed as the Queen of Malay cinema, remained at Cathay Keris in the early 60s after she was promised the right to direct a feature film, *The Devil's Eye* (*Mata Syaitan*, 1962).[6]

The world these Malay film stars worked in was a microcosm of larger Singapore society, with Malay talent on the screen, supported by Indian labour while being managed and financed by Chinese funding, as characterised by the participation of Ho Ah Loke and Loke Wan Tho. The actors were usually from a local tradition of theatre, known as *bangsawan*, particularly in the early period of filmmaking. Once film was established as a form of entertainment, stars increasingly came from musical backgrounds or beauty pageants. Many of those behind the camera in early Malay films were Indian. Their talents had been developed in the vibrant Indian film industry, and they had been brought to Singapore through connections to the distribution system for Indian films in Southeast Asia. This resulted in almost all of the directors of Malay language films in the 1950s being Indian. At Cathay Keris, for example, the only Malay director was S. Roomai Noor during the period. The influence of these Indian personnel could be seen in the stories and musical sequences in these films, which were often copied directly from their south Asian counterparts. As Malaya and Singapore grew increasingly closer to independence, however, there was a growing

從故事情節和音樂場面顯而易見——這些元素往往直接抄襲自印度片。不過，當馬來亞和新加坡逐步趨向獨立，就有更多馬來人開始做導演和寫劇本，印度人的參與程度因而減退。[7]

國泰克里斯早期的動力主要源自何亞祿，作為領導人，他擅於激勵士氣，但卻離經叛道。他很容易動怒，往往會立即解僱站在身邊的員工，以宣泄怒火；他曾辭退一個演員至少十次，每次都只是因為對方的一些小過錯。不過當他冷靜下來，為了安撫員工，就往往會大派鈔票——據說他會將現金塞滿在一個紙袋中，隨身帶到辦公室。此外，員工又會以各種藉口，例如親戚病了，向何亞祿借錢，但卻永遠不會歸還。他跟幾個影星過從甚密，也借給他們不少錢，其中包括在六十年代成為國泰克里斯紅人的諧星華希得沙爹（Wahid Satay）和密山多（Mat Sentol）。他要跟邵氏一較高下的心態，也擴展至關懷員工的層面：1957年Malay Film員工罷工，何亞祿立即送出十包米和一萬元，以支持罷工者，並希望將他們吸引到國泰克里斯。雖然他跟員工的關係反覆無常，但是大多數人日後回顧他在任的時期，仍充滿緬懷之情。[8]

相對於紅星雲集的邵氏，早期的國泰克里斯一直被人視為次一級的公司。為了改變這個形象，加上獲得陸運濤的慫恿、支持，何亞祿在作品中作大量前所未有的嘗試，力圖在區內的電影製作和發行業打響國泰克里斯的名堂。除了第一部彩色馬來片外，國泰克里斯還拍了首部配上華語的馬來片《吸血人妖》（*Pontianak*, 1957），以及首部闊銀幕拍攝的《人妖之誓》（*Sumpah Pontianak*, 1958）。兩片的故事都取自當地民間傳說——女性臨盆時難產而死，就會變成女妖，然後化身為美女，引誘男人，到吸血的一刻才變回猙獰惡魔，享受獵物。兩部電

movement to have Malays direct their films and write the scripts, thus lowering the participation of Indians.[7]

Ho Ah Loke, an inspiring but eccentric leader, was the focus of the studio's energy in these early years. Ho was easily angered, and would retaliate by firing the employee standing nearest to him. He fired one actor at least ten times over minor offences. When he calmed down, and to placate employees, Ho would distribute wads of cash, reportedly from a paper bag filled with money that he brought to the office with him. Employees would also frequently approach Ho to request a loan, which was never to be repaid, for a variety of reasons, such as a sick relative. Among the few stars that Ho enjoyed interacting with, and giving loans to, were the comedians Wahid Satay and Mat Sentol, who went on to be important stars for Cathay Keris in the 60s. His concern for the employees extended to his desire to compete with the Shaw Brothers. When a strike hit the Malay Film Production Studios in 1957, Ho sent ten sacks of rice and $10,000 to support the strikers, and also hopefully draw them over to Cathay Keris. Despite the volatile nature of his relationship with his staff, the majority look back upon his tenure with affection.[8]

In its early years, Cathay Keris was perceived as secondary to Shaw Brothers, who had many of the most popular stars. To counter this, and with the urging of Loke, Ho tried desperately to make Cathay Keris' mark on filmmaking and distribution in the region by being the first to bring various innovations to the screen. In addition to making the first colour film in Malay, Cathay Keris made the first Malay film to be dubbed into Chinese, *The Vampire* (*Pontianak*, 1957), as well as the first Malay film in Cinemascope, *Curse of the Vampire* (*Sumpah Pontianak*, 1958). These latter two films were based on local folklore that a vampire originates from women who died during childbirth. The spirit of the deceased becomes a beautiful woman who seduces her victims and at the last second becomes a hideous creature who devours her prey. The star of these films was Maria Menado, the early female mainstay of the Cathay Keris studio.

The *Pontianak* series was the turning point for Cathay Keris. Prior to 1957 the studio was having

影都由國泰克里斯早期的當家花旦瑪麗亞曼多主演。

《吸血人妖》系列成為國泰克里斯的轉捩點。在1957年前，該公司難有製作吸引到觀眾入場。[9]《吸》片沿用當時傳統的發行方式，安排於回教最重要的節日（Eid ul-Fitr）在新加坡國泰的龍頭戲院上映兩天，然後再在馬來人聚居地區的小戲院放映。不過，影片獲得熱烈反應，觀眾大排長龍，票房數字驚人，結果在龍頭戲院上映達兩個月，以馬來片來說史無前例。《吸》片更曾配上粵語，在香港上映，以及成為一個「亞洲電影節」的節目，在一家美國電視台播映。《吸》片如此受歡迎，有賴它能吸引到各類觀眾。根據一項估計，購票入場的，六成是馬來人，華人也有三成。[10]

除了賣座以外，《吸》片在很多其他層面也是重要的。該片鞏固了國泰克里斯在馬來電影業的地位，在此之前，公司面對實力強橫的 Malay Film 只能負隅頑抗。1957年，國泰克里斯因恐怕虧損，只發行了三部作品；其後，公司對本身在本土電影業的角色較具信心，每年的製作數量往往較邵氏為多。此外，《吸》片賣座令馬來市場中恐怖片的數目大增，其中不少都相當成功，並吸引到星、馬的馬來語社群以外的觀眾。隨之而來的恐怖片製作有《吸血人妖》系列另外四部作品（除最後一部外，全由瑪麗亞曼多主演），以及《神秘之屋》（*Orang Lichin*, 1958）和《油鬼子》（*Orang Minyak*，1958）。恐怖片大行其道，令邵氏都跟風拍了《油人的詛咒》（*Sumpah Orang Minyak*, 1958）。由此可見，兩公司的競爭導致了大家爭拍同樣題材的電影，甚至片名也相近，這種現象在兩者的歷史中一直存在。

我們可以婉轉地說，相對於 Malay Film 的「商業片」，國泰克里斯在五十年代拍攝的是「藝術片」，但實際上兩者在這段時期的分別不過是盈利能力而已。[11] 不過，

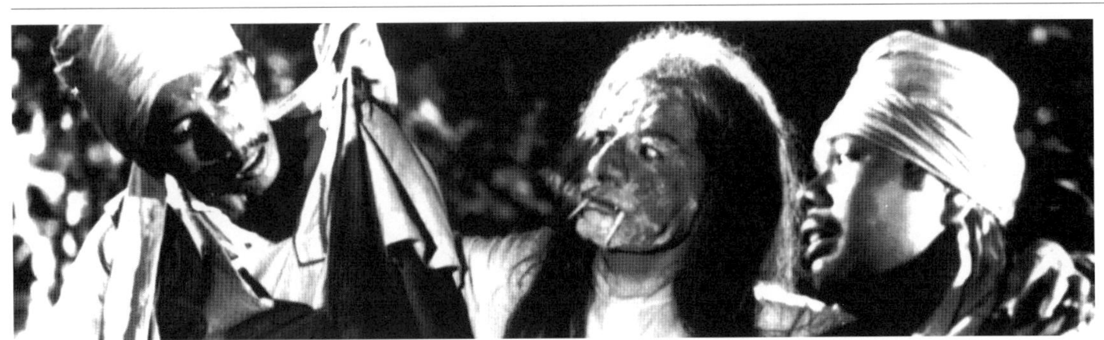

difficulty producing films that would draw audiences.[9] Following traditional release patterns, *Pontianak* was to be shown for two days during Eid ul-Fitr (the most important Muslim holiday) at the main Cathay cinema in Singapore before being sent to smaller cinemas in traditionally Malay areas. But, the long lines and huge box office allowed it to be shown at the main cinema for two months, an unprecedented run for a Malay film. *Pontianak* was so popular with audiences it was dubbed into Cantonese, shown in Hong Kong, and appeared on American television as an entry for an Asian Film Festival. The success of *Pontianak* was due to its ability to attract a diverse audience. By one estimate only 60 per cent of the ticket buyers were Malay, while 30 per cent were Chinese.[10]

Beyond box office, *Pontianak* was also important for other reasons. The film solidified Cathay Keris' presence in the Malay film industry. Prior to the release of *Pontianak*, Cathay Keris had struggled to compete against the mighty Shaw Brothers' Malay Film Productions. In 1957 the studio only released three films, fearing that they would all lose money. After 1957, Cathay Keris was more confident about its role and would often produce more films than Shaws in any given year. In addition, *Pontianak* led to an increase of horror films for the Malay market, many of which were successful and also appealed beyond Malay language communities in Singapore and the Peninsula. Among the films subsequently released were four more *Pontianak* films, all but the last starring Maria Menado, as well as *Slimy Man* (*Orang Lichin*, 1958) and *Oily Man* (*Orang Minyak*, 1958). Horror films became so popular that Shaw Brothers' attempted to cash in on the trend through their release of *Curse of the Oily Man* (*Sumpah Orang Minyak*, 1958), which characterises the competition between the two studios that often resulted in films about the same subject or with similar titles, which was common throughout their history.

During the 1950s it was polite to state that Malay Film Productions made "commercial" films, while Cathay Keris made "cultural" films. The actual difference in the productions during this period was profitability.[11]

國泰克里斯確對期間的馬來文化貢獻良多。公司不單拍攝了多齣在馬來電影史上有「首部」紀錄的電影，更嘗試開創新片種和敘事方法，這對於正在急劇現代化、找尋途徑用新媒介表達本身故事的社會，特別顯得重要。在何亞祿奠下的基礎之上，國泰克里斯在六十年代初雖然財政上仍時有虧損，但卻邁進了公司歷史中最重要的年代。它從屈居於 Malay Film 之後的小公司，搖身一變成為跟邵氏平起平坐的競爭對手，有時甚至更受歡迎，也顯得更有趣。

晉身為重要的馬來片製作商後，國泰克里斯活在邵氏陰影下的草創時期告終，但卻結束得令人傷感——何亞祿於 1958 年辭去在國泰克里斯的職務。當時陸運濤委任了 Percy McNiece 爵士出任國泰機構的行政要員，這正是何亞祿一直渴望得到的職位。特別是在區內殖民地勢力逐漸消退的時刻，這項委任更令這位一直帶領國泰克里斯的精神領袖難以接受。他離開新加坡，前往吉隆坡創立 Merdeka Studios 。何、陸兩人拆夥時的關係，從一個流傳甚廣的故事可窺端倪：他們將國泰克里斯每部作品的名稱分別寫在紙片上，放進一頂帽子中抽籤，以決定影片的擁有權誰屬。何亞祿取得了《吸血人妖》的版權。可惜在六十年代初，因瑪麗亞曼多下嫁彭亨州蘇丹，由她演嗜血妖魔的《吸》片遭馬來西亞禁映。失望之下，何亞祿將拷貝拋進了岡巴克（Gombak）河，結果這部重要的早期電影，在我們已知的範圍內，並沒有拷貝留存下來。[12]

1958 至 1964 年：英雄

何亞祿前赴吉隆坡後，由作風截然不同的Tom Hodge出任國泰克里斯的經理。他以前當過校長，也曾在英國殖民地電影辦事處工作，一年前才加入國泰機構，出任紀錄片和廣告部主管。在公開宣佈國泰克里斯自創立後已

《吸血人妖》系列其中一幕
Scene from the *Pontianak* series.
Courtesy of the National Archives of Singapore

Despite financial difficulties, Cathay made substantial contributions to Malay culture. It had not only produced a number of "firsts" in Malay cinema, but had been at the forefront of developing new genres and ways of storytelling, particularly important in a rapidly modernizing society searching for ways to express its tales in new mediums. While it had not always been financially successful, Cathay Keris would enter its most important era in the early 1960s by building on the foundation Ho Ah Loke had laid. Cathay Keris would move from being a marginal player in Malay film production to being an equal, and often a more popular and more interesting competitor, to the Shaw Brothers' empire.

While Cathay Keris had emerged as a serious producer of Malay films, this early period of operating in the shadow of its larger rival does end in a note of ironic tragedy; Ho Ah Loke resigned from Cathay Keris in 1958. The guiding spirit of the studio could no longer work with Loke Wan Tho following the appointment of Sir Percy McNiece to a high administrative position that Ho had desired in the Cathay Organisation, especially during a period when colonial involvement in the region was diminishing. Ho left Singapore for Kuala Lumpur, where he founded Merdeka Studios. An often told story about the end of the Loke-Ho partnership is how they divided their assets. They placed the titles of the Cathay Keris film catalogue in a hat and pulled out pieces of paper to determine ownership of the prints. Ho Ah Loke gained the rights to *Pontianak*. By the early 1960s, however, Maria Menado had married the Sultan of Pahang. Since the film depicted Menado as a bloodthirsty vampire, it could not be shown in Malaysia. In frustration, Ho threw the print into the Gombak River and there are no known existing copies of this important early film.[12]

1958-1964: Heroes

When Ho moved to Kuala Lumpur, Tom Hodge became the manager of Cathay Keris. Hodge was very different from his predecessor. A former school headmaster and official in the British Colonial Film Office, he had joined Cathay Organisation a year earlier as the head of its documentary and advertising division. Hodge's main goal was to cut costs, which he made clear after

虧損150萬元後，Hodge清楚表明自己的首要任務是削減成本。公司不少藝人習慣了何亞祿那種離經叛道但卻作家長式照顧的管理風格，自然對Hodge的做法興起對抗情緒。事隔多年，一位國泰克里斯員工仍形容Hodge「過份英式作風」和「鐵石心腸」。[13]

Hodge對片廠過去多次創新大感憤怒，特別是因為這些嘗試未能帶來任何利潤。當時一部普通馬來片的製作成本約三萬元，票房有五萬元就大致可以收回成本。Hodge想拍一些較低成本的製作，不同意製作「文化」電影（通常取材自古代傳説或歷史故事），因為這類電影對觀眾吸引力不大。為了鼓勵節省成本，Hodge在1960年創立了分紅計劃，員工在回教齋戒月可以分到國泰克里斯影片利潤的百分之十。這項花紅每人均分，在其後數年，視乎當年表現，每個員工一年可以分到二百至五百元不等。[14]

為了令作品多元化，以及找尋開源新途徑，Hodge試圖發掘新市場來發行國泰克里斯的影片。其中一項嘗試是拍攝一部關於新加坡的華語片，名為《獅子城》（*Lion City*, 1960），故事講述一個橡膠包裝廠的年輕女工愛上廠中的經理。《獅子城》的製作預算較馬來片為高，所持理據是這部電影有較大的市場，不過這卻惹來公司內馬來裔員工不滿。結果影片虧了本，在新加坡拍攝華語片的嘗試也就此中斷。[15]

在多元化這大原則下的另一發展方向是推動獨立電影製作。國泰克里斯會借出片廠及代作發行，再與獨立製作者分享影片上映後的利潤，但卻不會負責拍攝的開支。獨立製作最成功的例子，是《吸血人妖》系列女主角在六十年代初創立的瑪麗亞曼多製作（Maria Menado Production）。她進軍製作事業的第一擊，是試圖打入印尼市場。由於兩地基本上説同樣的語言，這個嘗試是理

「人妖」系列中的瑪麗亞曼多
Maria Menado, the beauty in *Kembali*, the sequel to *Sumpah Pontianak*.

publicly announcing that Cathay Keris had lost $1.5 million since its founding. This attitude created a sense of confrontation with many of the artists that were used to Ho's eccentric but nurturing style of management. Many years after the events, one Cathay Keris employee continued to describe Hodge as being "too English" and having a "hati batu" (heart of stone).[13]

Hodge was appalled by the studio's previous attempts at innovation, particularly since they had not resulted profits. The average Malay film was produced on a budget of $30,000, and the breakeven point was considered to be approximately $50,000. Hodge thus wanted to make films for less money. He frowned upon the making of "cultural" films (usually based on traditional tales and histories), because they often had less box office draw. To further encourage savings, Hodge instituted a plan in 1960 in which 10 per cent of the studio's profits would be given to the employees during Ramadan (the Islamic fasting month). The bonus would be shared evenly, and over the next few years, each employee received between $200-$500 depending on the year.[14]

To diversify the production studios and to search for new ways to produce revenue, Hodge also searched for new markets for Cathay Keris films. One of the first

所當然的。不過，印尼設下大量關卡阻礙外來電影在當地發行。為了解決這問題，國泰克里斯聘請了一些印尼影星，包括 Rendra Sukarno 和 Sukarno M. Noor 等，拍攝一部兩國合作的電影，名為《啞子吃黃蓮》(*Korban Fitnah*, 1959)，瑪麗亞曼多也有參演。就像瑪麗亞曼多公司的其他製作，這部電影用國泰克里斯的設施拍攝，但是結果她要將影片版權賣給國泰克里斯，因為那些印尼影星在新加坡獲招待住在價錢高昂的 Rendezvous 酒店，導致影片超支。瑪麗亞曼多其後再製作了另外四部電影，也得以保留其版權，不過她在下嫁彭亨州蘇丹後，就完全退出影壇，不再演戲和製作。

獨立電影製作是馬來亞本土電影史的里程碑，但對國泰克里斯來說，能令公司發展至藝術上和財政上的高峰的，卻是歷史上的另一里程碑——馬來人開始出任導演。在六十年代初以前，絕大部份電影由印度人執導，他們其中一個惹人批評的地方，是直接抄襲印度的傳統故事，沒有考慮兩地的文化差距。[16]當魯邁拿打破種族障礙，在公司出任導演後，其他馬來人迅即獲得機會，在銀幕上展示自己的視野，以馬來文化和傳統故事為拍攝題材。雖然印度導演拍過不少重要的作品，馬來片在馬來導演手中才步入頂峰。

在六十年代國泰克里斯眾多馬來導演中，最為重要的是哈申漢尼夫（Hussain Haniff）。他原本在公司出任剪接師，因此深諳節奏和攝影對電影何等重要，到他有機會執導時，就特別在這兩方面下工夫。他的首作《古城英傑》(*Hang Jebat*, 1961) 獲譽為國泰克里斯歷來的最佳電影。題材取自傳統民間故事，主人翁為遠古 Melaka時代的一名馬來武士，要在效忠君主和維持朋友之義當中作出取捨。這個故事過去曾由Malay Film於1956年拍成電影，名為《Hang Tuah》，沿用傳統以朋友的角度作

國泰克里斯當家花旦瑪麗亞曼多主演的《啞子吃黃蓮》

Korban Fitnah starred Maria Menado, a mainstay of many Cathay Keris films.

Courtesy of the National Archives of Singapore

attempts was the production of a Chinese language film about Singapore, *Lion City* (1960). The film told the story of a young woman working at a rubber packing plant who falls in love with her manager. The film received a higher budget than Malay films, justified due to the larger distribution market, but this created resentment among Malay employees of the studio. When the film lost money, attempts at developing Chinese language productions in Singapore were abandoned.[15]

Another aspect of this larger policy of diversification was the promotion of independent production. The company would offer access to its studio and distribution, but forgo some of the profits by not paying for the production. The most prominent example was Maria Menado Productions, which the star of the *Pontianak* films founded in the early 1960s. Her first foray into producing was an attempt to enter the Indonesian market. Since Malay and Indonesian are fundamentally the same language, the move seemed natural. However, Indonesia had numerous barriers to the distribution of foreign films. In an attempt to surmount these barriers, Cathay Keris imported a number of Indonesian stars, such as Rendra Sukarno and Sukarno M. Noor, to work on a joint production. The film was *Victim of Slander* (*Korban Fitnah*, 1959), which also starred Menado. The film used Cathay Keris facilities, as was true with all Maria Menado Productions films, but eventually she had to sell the rights to Cathay Keris due to debts incurred from putting the Indonesian stars up at the Rendezvous Hotel in Singapore. Menado would go on to produce four other films, all of which she was able to retain the rights to, but retired from producing and acting once she married the Sultan of Pahang.

While the independent production of films was an important milestone in local film history, it was the prominent role played by Malay directors that led to the greatest years, artistically and financially, at Cathay Keris. One of the common complaints against the Indian directors prior to the early 1960s was that they were simply copying Indian tales, without taking local cultural differences into consideration.[16] While S. Roomai Noor had broken the ethnic barrier to

敘事觀點。但是國泰克里斯和哈申漢尼夫的版本卻對這個歷史傳奇作革命性演繹，將敘事重點放在被君主視為不忠不義的武士身上。影片結果大受歡迎，成為公司歷來最賺錢的作品之一。[17]

哈申漢尼夫不單對民間傳奇故事的演繹是革命性的，在電影業中的地位亦然。他具有藝術家脾氣，要求創作自由，只與自己挑選的演員和助手合作。他會在拍攝前畫下分鏡圖，親自視察外景場地，到現場拍攝時，又會花長時間等待適當的陽光或海浪來捕捉他心目中的場面。對於一向急就章拍攝、製作成本不高的馬來片業來說，這是重大的改革。他的作品常見跟隨動作移動的鏡頭、不尋常的拍攝角度，能充份配合故事的推進，影象異常刺激。哈申漢尼夫其後導演了另外十二部電影，卻在1966年三十二歲英年早逝。

雖然哈申漢尼夫對質素如此執着，國泰克里斯的主要目標還是擴闊觀眾群和增加利潤。公司的製作水準和盈利一直提升，信心也因而不斷增加，這由在1961年公司推出電影的數目（九部）首次多於Malay Film（八部），可見一斑。大收旺場的除了《古城英傑》（讓哈申漢尼夫得以繼續其創新探索）外，還有由露絲葉蒂瑪（Rose Yatimah）和華希得沙爹主演的電影。

兩人都不是在國泰克里斯一炮而紅的；露絲葉蒂瑪從Malay Film轉投，而華希得沙爹則是國泰克里斯的幕後工作人員。不過他們獲看中，就立即成為公司在六十年代的支柱。華希得沙爹一直充滿喜劇細胞，早年在片廠中負責搭佈景時，已不時娛樂眾人。他獲挑選在《吸血人妖》第一集中演一個諧角，然後自己擔正主演一系列滑稽鬧劇。這些影片製作成本低，因此能為公司賺錢。與華希得沙爹在國泰克里斯內逐步爬升比較，露絲葉蒂瑪剛好代表了公司人才另一條常見的出身途徑。她十六歲

directing at the studio, other Malays soon brought their vision to the screen, one that was centred in Malay culture and traditional tales. While many significant films were made under Indian direction, Malay films reached their zenith under Malay directors.

Of particular importance in the 1960s was Hussain Haniff. He originally worked as an editor at Cathay Keris, a job that allowed him to understand the importance of rhythm and cinematography, which he put to use when he was given an opportunity to direct. Haniff's first film was *Hang Jebat* (1961), often considered to be the best film of Cathay Keris. The film tells the traditional story of a Malay warrior in ancient Melaka who must choose between his loyalty to the ruler and his loyalty to a friend. An earlier version of the tale, told from the traditional viewpoint of the friend, was made at Malay Film Productions in 1956 as *Hang Tuah*. The subject matter was important. By focusing on the traditional antagonist, who was treasonous to the ruler in the name of justice and friendship, Cathay Keris and Hussain were presenting a revolutionary interpretation of a Malay historical legend. The film found an eager audience, and was one of the studio's most profitable product.[17]

Not only was Hussain's interpretation of traditional tales revolutionary and profitable for the studio, so was role in film production. He was a temperamental director, demanding creative freedom and working only with artists and assistants he had chosen. He would scout locations, wait for the right amount of sunlight or tide before a shot was made, and would storyboard his shots before going into production. This approach to filmmaking was a distinct change for an industry that had often shot on the run and was known for marginal production values. The result was films in which the camera moves with the action, and is often found at unusual angles, capturing the flow of the story and leading to visually exciting cinema. Hussain would go on to direct 12 more films before dying at the age of 32 in 1966.

Despite the revolutionary role of Hussain Haniff, the main focus at Cathay Keris continued to be the search for wider audiences and higher profits. The confidence

已主演邵氏影片《墮落單身武士》(*Pendekar Bujang Lapok*, 1959)，獲國泰克里斯看中，邀她簽約加盟。她其後在多部熱門電影中擔演年輕漂亮的女角，並曾代表國泰克里斯出席多個國際電影節。

六十年代初是國泰克里斯的光輝歲月。馬來人的參與增加，加上影片能賣錢，令公司得以出產水準較邵氏Malay Film當時作品為佳的電影。三股力量攜手：瑪麗亞曼多等獨立製作人、華希得沙爹等紅星、哈申漢尼夫等目光遠大的導演，拍出了創新而又娛樂性豐富，同時植根於馬來文化的作品。這項動力繼續令馬來片改進質素，擴闊內容，到1963年可説達到高峰——國泰克里斯首次在海外開拍電影，名為《東京之夜》(*Malam di Tokyo*)，講述一個馬來女性在那個城市的不幸遭遇。到1964年，哈申漢尼夫創作力驚人，竟為公司拍了五部電影。其中四部都取材自家傳戶曉的馬來傳奇故事，探討

華希得沙爹和丁皓出席一項宣傳活動。
Wahid Satay and Kitty Ting Hao at a promotional event.

Courtesy of the National Archives of Singapore

that the studio had reached its stride in both production standards and profit is reflected in the fact that in 1961, for the first time, Cathay Keris released more films (nine) than Shaw Brothers' Malay Film Productions (eight). In addition to the financial success of *Hang Jebat*, which allowed Haniff to continue with his innovations, there were also popular films starring Rose Yatimah and Wahid Satay.

Both Rose Yatimah and Wahid Satay became stars at Cathay Keris after following well-worn paths to the studio; Rose came from Shaw Brothers' Malay Film Productions, while Wahid was a crewmember at Cathay Keris studios. Once spotted however, they both became important figures at the studio in the early 60s. Wahid had always been a comedian, entertaining everyone while constructing sets. He was cast in the original *Pontianak* film as comic relief, and went on to star in his own series of slapstick comedies, which made profits for the studio due to their low cost. While Wahid had risen up through Cathay Keris, Rose Yatimah represented the other common route to Cathay Keris. Rose had starred in *Rotten Bachelor Warriors* (*Pendekar Bujang Lapok*, 1959) for Shaw as a sixteen-year old. Spotted by Cathay Keris, she was quickly signed to a contract. She went on to play the beautiful young star in a series of popular films, as well as represent Cathay Keris at several international film festivals.

The early 1960s were the glory years for Cathay Keris. With the rise in Malay participation, and films actually making profits, the studio could continue to provide a product that was in many ways superior to the Shaw Brothers' Malay Film Productions efforts of the time. Independent Malay producers, such as Maria Menado, and popular stars, such as Wahid Satay, combined with visionary directors such as Hussain Haniff to produce a product that was not only entertaining but also grounded in Malay culture while also being revolutionary. This drive to continually improve the quality and scope of Malay film culminated in 1963 when Cathay Keris made its first overseas film, *Night in Tokyo* (*Malam di Tokyo*), about the misadventures of a Malay woman in the Japanese capital, and in 1964

英勇武士如何應付肉體和精神上的考驗。這些故事之中，《亂世奸雄》（*Istana Berdarah*，1964）一如著名日本導演黑澤明的《蜘蛛巢城》（1957），試圖拍一個本土版本的莎劇《麥克白》。至於《兩武士》（*Dua Pendekar*，1964）則有連場打鬥，兩個武士在決鬥之中不斷質疑傳統規條。這些電影都虧了本，令公司有藉口縮減創新的製作。為國泰克里斯創造了黃金年代的英雄人物，經歷了多產但卻短暫的時期，即告淡出。

1964 至 1973 年：弄臣

在 1964 年於台北舉行的第十一屆亞洲影展中，六十年代初擔演多部國泰克里斯影片的露絲葉蒂瑪獲得「最佳新人獎」。這次影展是整個國泰機構發展的轉捩點，不是因為公司旗下一個影星贏了獎項，而因那是公司主腦陸運濤最後一個出席的公眾場合。他在影展期間，從台中飛回台北途中，遇上空難身亡。本來應該一同上機，但因飛機滿座而逃過大難的有魯邁拿，他其後與國泰克里斯的關係，正好反映公司未幾即要面對的難題。自公司創立開始，魯邁拿一直舉足輕重，既是紅星，又出任導演。此外，他的妻子烏美嘉東（Ummi Kalthoum）也是國泰克里斯的主要演員。不過，他們兩人對Hodge的領導甚感不滿。即使在陸運濤委任魯邁拿為公司副監製後，Hodge也不肯接納魯邁拿在電影中呈現馬來文化和生活獨特面貌的建議。沒有了陸運濤的調停，魯邁拿夫婦於 1964 年離開國泰克里斯，轉投給予他們更大創作自由的吉隆坡公司 Merdeka。

到了六十年代中期，國泰克里斯不知在馬來片市場中該何去何從。陸運濤逝世，加上電視出現，令公司要面對新的競爭；管理層也意興闌珊，既不滿製作成本日增，又對本土文化無甚興趣。這段時期內，管理層與員工之間的衝突一直持續。六十年代初，公司間中會出現罷

when Haniff directed an amazing five films for the studio. Of these films that Hussain directed, four focused on the popular Malay tales of heroic warriors facing challenges both physical and mental. One of these tales, *Palace of Blood* (*Istana Berdarah*, 1964) was an attempt to make a Malay version of *Macbeth*, just as famed Japanese director Akira Kurosawa had done with *Throne of Blood* in 1957, while *Two Warriors* (*Dua Pendekar*, 1964) was a series of action sequences in which two Malay warriors fought each other while critiquing traditional rule. When these films lost money, it provided the excuse to scale back on innovative filmmaking. The heroes that had produced this period of greatness for Cathay Keris were coming to pass after a short but fertile period.

1964-73: Jesters

Rose Yatimah, the beautiful young star of a series of Cathay Keris pictures in the early 60s, won the Golden Accolade Award for promising newcomer at the 11th Asian Film Festival in Taipei in 1964. This festival was a turning point for the entire Cathay Organisation, but not because one of its stars won an award. It is remembered as the venue of the last public appearance of the heart of the organisation, Loke Wan Tho, who died in a plane crash on his way back to Taipei from Taichung during the festival. Among those scheduled to be on the ill-fated plane, but who missed it when there were no more seats available, was S. Roomai Noor, whose subsequent relationship with the studio reflects the problems that Cathay Keris would soon face. One of the key figures since the beginning, Roomai had been both star and director for the studio. In addition, his wife, Ummi Kalthoum, was one of Cathay Keris' major stars. She and Roomai, however, chaffed under the leadership of Tom Hodge, who would not listen to Roomai's attempts to present particular aspects of Malay culture and life on the screen, even after Loke had appointed Roomai as an Associate Producer at the studio. Without the mediating presence of Loke, both Ummi and Roomai left Cathay Keris in 1964 for Merdeka Studios in Kuala Lumpur, where they were given more artistic freedom.

By the mid-1960s Cathay Keris was having difficulty determining the direction it should take in Malay

工；到1962年，雙方在談判中顯示的敵意令不少員工決定離開，包括自五十年代中期起效力國泰克里斯的重要印度導演K. M. Basker。[18]削減成本成為了公司在六十年代中期的首要任務。雖然過去數年業務有利可圖，但到那時候國泰克里斯已開始衰落。

為了挽救公司，Hodge繼續向其他電影公司，特別是西方製片商，推銷租賃國泰克里斯片廠的業務。這個新的業務重點令很多員工擔心自己的前途，不少決定轉投吉隆坡的Merdeka，在1965和1966年兩次裁員以減省開支後，更多員工選擇離開。電影製作方面，拍攝像《古城英傑》和《亂世奸雄》等代表馬來文化的史詩式大製作的計劃全遭擱置。不是小成本製作，公司就不會開拍。這方針特別適合Hodge的口味，因為他似乎鄙視描繪古代馬來英雄的「文化」電影。公司最後一部這類型的出品是《靈魂之詩》(*Gurindam Jiwa*, 1966)。當這部電影不能賺錢，公司據説發出了一張通告，宣佈：「本公司以後不再開拍文化電影。」[19]於是，其後國泰克里斯出品的，全都是小成本製作的胡鬧喜劇和差劣的恐怖片。

這段時期國泰克里斯最具代表性的人物是密山多。他參與馬來電影業多年，後來有機會擔正主演一系列喜劇。這系列以笨拙、在新加坡四處做散工的馬特為主人翁，影片通常由很多馬特碰釘、為人誤會的片段組成，最終都是大團圓結局。系列的首作《福至心靈》(*Mat Tiga Suku*, 1964)由哈申漢尼夫執導。最初的版本只長五十五分鐘，製作費僅一萬元，原本是為新加坡電視台試拍的劇集。從不同層面來説，這都是Hodge心目中理想的製作：成本低廉，又可幫助國泰克里斯進軍新的媒介。不過，新加坡電視台只願意每集支付三千元給國泰克里斯。由於不想虧本賣給電視台，密山多決定自行組織工作人員，多拍一些片段，將影片延長至九十分鐘。這部

cinema. The death of Loke Wan Tho, plus the advent of television, left the studio facing new forms of competition while being led by administrators who were increasingly tired of rising production costs and showed little interest in local culture. Continuing tension between the management and workers characterises this period. While there had been occasional strikes against the studio in the early 1960s, and in 1962 negotiations were so vicious that many personnel decided to leave, including K. M. Basker, one of the studio's important Indian directors since the mid-1950s,[18] cost cutting became the order of the day in the mid-1960s. Despite the financial success over the past few years, Cathay Keris was beginning its decline.

In an attempt to save the studio, Tom Hodge continued to promote the Cathay Keris facilities to other film companies, particularly from the West. This new focus made many of the personnel wonder about their role in its future, and many left for Kuala Lumpur's Merdeka Studios, particularly following layoffs at the studio in 1965 and 1966 in attempts to save money. In the world of film production, all attempts at making Malay cultural epics, such as *Hang Jebat* and *Istana Berdarah*, were abandoned. If a film could not be made at a low cost, it would not be made. This was particularly appealing to Hodge, who seemed to despise the "cultural" films depicting Malay heroes in epic circumstances. The last film in this genre was *Sonnet of the Soul* (*Gurindam Jiwa*, 1965). When it did not make a profit, a memo supposedly was issued proclaiming, "no more cultural films will be made at this studio".[19] This resulted in Cathay Keris becoming the home of a series of slapstick comedies and shoddy horror films that were made at limited cost.

Characterising this period was Mat Sentol. While he had been involved in Malay film production for years, he came into his own in a series of comedies that revolved around a bumbling character holding various jobs in Singapore. The films usually involved a series of skits as the Mat character falls down, is misunderstood, and eventually backs into a successful conclusion. The first of these films was *Crazy Mat* (*Mat Tiga Suku*, 1964), directed by Haniff, and was

電影其實並沒有劇本，製作成本又極低，《馬特》系列其他作品也一樣。[20]

拍攝小本簡陋製作的《馬特》系列，正好反映了國泰克里斯已再無意創新。沒有了何亞祿和陸運濤的帶領，加上哈申漢尼夫的逝世，令公司逐步衰亡。雖然公司直至1973年仍一直開拍電影，起用居住於新加坡的馬來明星擔演——當時有不少新加坡演員不願到吉隆坡工作，因為新加坡在1965年脱離馬來西亞獨立後，前往吉隆坡已變得敏感。但是，國泰克里斯對電影業已再無重要影響，位於 East Coast Road 的片廠不再拍攝具創意的劇情片，而是租給外國電影公司和廣告製作公司。公司理論上至今仍然存在，但是自1973年起已再沒有拍攝過馬來片。

在新加坡的電影業中，國泰克里斯一直給人屈居次席的感覺，不單在馬來片製作中不及邵氏，在國泰機構中也只是次要角色。雖然如此，公司在新加坡電影史中也有多個重要意義。國泰克里斯為馬來電影業，以至東南亞電影業作了多項技術上的創新。何亞祿、魯邁拿和哈申漢尼夫等要員堅持，他們的電影不單提供娛樂，更要讓觀眾更深入地了解和質疑本身的文化。在那個推行非殖民運動的時期，國泰克里斯的員工要處理勞資糾紛、外來勢力介入、將傳統故事移植到新媒介，以及民族國家的融合和解體等問題。他們能夠出色地應付這個困難局面，是難能可貴的。國泰克里斯也許是新加坡電影史中為人忽略的一頁。他是家族中的小兄弟，往往扮演弄臣角色，配襯馬來文化之中的英雄、傳奇人物和丑生，以及為當時新加坡和馬來西亞社會面對的問題提供了一面透視鏡。

馬山翻譯

made for only $10,000. The original film was only 55 minutes long because it was made as a pilot for Singapore television. In many respects this was Tom Hodge's dream, a cheaply made film that could be used to help Cathay Keris expand into a new medium. However, Singapore television offered Cathay Keris only $3,000 per episode for the proposed series. Facing such a dilemma, Mat Sentol took a crew out by himself and shot additional footage to expand the film to 90 minutes. As was true with all of the other "Mat" films, it had no script and was shot very cheaply.[20]

The shoddy production values of the "Mat" series represented a distancing of Cathay Keris from innovative filmmaking. Without the guidance of figures such as Ho Ah Loke and Loke Wan Tho, combined with the death of Hussain Haniff, the company would slowly slide into oblivion. While it continued to make films until 1973, often using Malay stars originating from Singapore and who had refused to move to Kuala Lumpur, a very sensitive issue following the independence of Singapore from Malaysia in 1965, Cathay Keris was simply going through the motions. Instead of producing original films for entertainment, the facilities on East Coast Road were now made available to foreign film companies as well as the makers of documentaries and advertisements. The film studio technically still exists, but no Malay language film has been produced since that time.

Cathay Keris was always the younger brother of cinema production in Singapore. It has always been considered secondary to not only the Shaw Brothers' efforts at Malay film production but also larger concerns in the Cathay Organisation. Despite this status, it did fulfil many important functions in the history of Singapore cinema. Cathy Keris was the home to a number of technical innovations in Malay as well as Southeast Asian cinema. Important participants, such as Ho Ah Loke, S. Roomai Noor and Hussain Haniff insisted that their films not only provide entertainment, but also make their audiences question and understand their own culture with greater insight. In a period of decolonisation Cathay

華希得沙爹的摩登廚房故事
Wahid Satay in *Pak Pandir Modern*, 1960.

Keris employees had to deal with issues such as labour disputes, foreign participation, translating traditional tales to a new medium, and nation-states merging and disintegrating. That they were able to negotiate this dangerous terrain with such panache is remarkable. Cathay Keris may be the overlooked story in Singaporean cinema. It was the younger brother, often the jester in the family, who honoured the heroes, legends and clowns of Malay culture and provided a lens into many of the issues facing Singaporean and Malayan society at the time.

註

1. 另一家曾曇花一現的電影公司，是 Hsu Chio Meng 投資的 Nusantara。該公司所用的演員、編劇和配樂人員，不少其後在國泰克里斯變得更為著名。公司的出品同樣面對發行問題，導致 Hsu Chio Meng 在 1953 年將公司結束。見 Hamzah Hussin: *Memoir Hamzah Hussin: Dari Cathay Keris ke Merdeka Studio*, Bangi: University Kebangsaan Malaysia, 1998, p. 19.
2. 見ABI (Ahmad Idris): *Filem Melayu Dahulu dan Sekarang*, Shah Alam: Marwilis, 1988, p. 8.
3. 在國泰克里斯創立後，新加坡著名作曲家 Zubir Said 立即從邵氏轉投，因為新公司讓他可以創作背景音樂，而不單是插曲。以往邵氏的電影只會用現成錄好的音樂。見Zubir bin Said's Oral History Recording, National Archives of Singapore collection, 293, Reel 13 及 Lim Kay Tong: *Cathay - 55 Years of Cinema*, Singapore: Landmark Books, 1991, p. 119.
4. 其後在國泰克里斯執導過多部電影的葛利斯南（Dato L. Krishnan），將公司擁有先進器材歸功於何亞祿是工程師出身，以及他明白要有這種器材方可以成功。見Lim Kay Tong，同註 3，頁 119、132。
5. 見 M. Amin and Wahba: *Layar Perak dan Sejarahnya*, Shah Alam: Fajar Bakti, 1998, pp. 41-42.
6. Siput Sarawak確曾簽了導演合約，不過卻有人反對影片由沒有甚麼導演經驗的她執導，而她是女性也可能有關係。結果，該片由哈申漢尼夫執導。至於薪酬問題，邵氏的管理人員認為，公司為演員在片廠附近提供宿舍，足以彌補薪酬的差距。見 Marian bte Baharom's Oral History Recording, National Archives of Singapore collection, 001898, Reel 3；Hamzah Hussin，同註1，頁27、85、87及Jamil Sulong: *Kaca Permata: Memoir Seorang Pengarah*, Kuala Lumpur: Dewan Bahasa dan Pustaka, 1990, pp. 167, 170, 222-223, 226.
7. 見 M. Amin and Wahba，同註 5，頁 17-28。
8. 見Hamzah Hussin，同註 1，頁51、63-65及Jamil Sulong，同註 6，頁 223、226。
9. 在《吸血人妖》之前，國泰克里斯沒有任何作品可以賺錢。見 Lim Kay Tong，同註3，頁126及Hamzah Hussin，同註 1，頁46。
10. 在五十年代的馬來亞市場，印度裔人和華人分別會看來自本身祖國的電影；而馬來人和部份華人則會看馬來片。見Letter Lionel Gate, Rank Screen Services, September 1, 1958, Loke Wan Tho Private Records (Letter written by Lim Keng Hor), National Archives of Singapore collection, NA 216 及 Hamzah Hussin，同註 1，頁 41。
11. 何亞祿將電影分為兩類：「空洞的電影」，即有藝術價值但不能賺錢的；以及「充實的電影」，指雖遭影評人劣評但卻能賺錢的。見 Hamzah Hussin，同註 1，頁 28、96。
12. 見Hamzah Hussin，同註1，頁96-97；Jan Uhde and Yvonne Ng Uhde: *Latent Images: Film in Singapore*, Singapore: Oxford University Press, 2000, p. 25；Lim Kay Tong，同註3，頁126及Jamil Sulong，同註6，頁84。雖然細節稍有不同，上述各

Notes

1. Another short-lived studio was Nusantara. Owned by Hsu Chio Meng, Nusantara made several films that used the services of actors, writers and musicians who would later move onto greater fame at Cathay Keris. The films, however, also faced distribution difficulties, eventually forcing Hsu to shut its doors in 1953. See Hamzah Hussin: *Memoir Hamzah Hussin: Dari Cathay Keris ke Merdeka Studio*, Bangi: University Kebangsaan Malaysia, 1998, p. 19.
2. See ABI (Ahmad Idris): *Filem Melayu Dahulu dan Sekarang*, Shah Alam: Marwilis, 1988, p. 8.
3. Zubir Said, a prominent Singaporean composer, moved from the Shaw Brothers' studios to Cathay Keris immediately upon its founding because he was allowed to compose background music, not just songs. Previously the Shaw Brothers' would only use pre-recorded music for their films. From Zubir bin Said's Oral History Recording, National Archives of Singapore collection, 293, Reel 13. See also Lim Kay Tong: *Cathay - 55 Years of Cinema*, Singapore: Landmark Books, 1991, p. 119.
4. Dato L. Krishnan, who went on to direct several films at Cathay Keris, attributed the sophistication of the equipment to Ho Ah Loke (He Yalu)'s background as an engineer, and his understanding of the need to have such materials in order to succeed. See Lim Kay Tong, ibid., pp. 119, 132.
5. See M. Amin and Wahba: *Layar Perak dan Sejarahnya*, Shah Alam: Fajar Bakti, 1998, pp. 41-42.
6. Siput Sarawak did sign the contract, but there were protests against someone with little directing experience, and also possibly because she was a woman, being given the right. Eventually Hussain Haniff directed the film. As for the difference in salaries, the Shaw Brothers' studio managers argued that the housing they provided the artists next to the studio compensated for the lower salaries. From Marian bte Baharom's Oral History Recording, National Archives of Singapore collection, 001898, Reel 3; see also Hamzah Hussin, op. cit., pp. 27, 85, 87 and Jamil Sulong: *Kaca Permata: Memoir Seorang Pengarah*, Kuala Lumpur: Dewan Bahasa dan Pustaka, 1990, pp. 167, 170, 222-223, 226.
7. See M. Amin and Wahba, op. cit., pp. 17-28.
8. See Hamzah Hussin, op. cit., pp. 51, 63-65 and Jamil Sulong, op. cit., pp. 223, 226.
9. Until the release of *The Vampire (Pontianak)*, no Cathay Keris film had made a profit. See Lim Kay Tong, op. cit., p. 126 and Hamzah Hussin, op. cit., p. 46.
10. In the Malayan market of the 50s, Indians and Chinese exclusively viewed films from their cultural homelands, while "Malays and Chinese" attended Malay language pictures. From letter Lionel Gate, Rank Screen Services, September 1, 1958, Loke Wan Tho Private Records (Letter written by Lim Keng Hor), National Archives of Singapore collection, NA 216 and Hamzah Hussin, op. cit., p. 41.
11. Ho Ah Loke classified films as "filem kosong" (empty films) – films that were artistic but made no profit; or "filem berisi" (substantial films) – films that made a profit despite negative reviews of critics. See Hamzah Hussin, op. cit., p. 28, 96.
12. See Hamzah Hussin, op. cit., p. 96-97; Jan Uhde and Yvonne Ng Uhde: *Latent Images: Film in Singapore*, Singapore: Oxford University Press, 2000, p. 25; Lim Kay Tong, op. cit., p. 126 and Jamil Sulong, op. cit., p. 84. Despite the story having variations, it is mentioned in all of these works, and culminates in the print being lost, or unavailable to the general public.
13. See Hamzah Hussin, op. cit., p. 96; Despite his bad reputation among many of the employees, Hodge would fight to have their films distributed in theatres where they would find a larger audience. See also Lim Kay Tong, op. cit., p. 64-65, 124, 126.

本著作均有講述這個故事，並且均以拷貝遺失或現在觀眾無緣目睹作結。

13. 見 Hamzah Hussin ，同註 1 ，頁 96；雖然員工對 Hodge 的評價甚差，他至少曾爭取將公司的電影發行至較大的戲院放映，以吸引更多觀眾。另見Lim Kay Tong，同註3，頁64-65、124、126 。
14. 見 Hamzah Hussin ，同註 1 ，頁 31 、 35-36 。
15. 這部電影有否賺錢，是具爭議的問題。策劃現代「新加坡國際電影節」的 Philip Cheah 指影片有微利。不過，國泰克里斯從沒有再開拍華語片。那段時期，國泰也嘗試跟法國製作公司合作拍片，又讓片廠供美國製片商使用。見Jan Uhde and Yvonne Ng Uhde ，同註 12 ，頁 23 及 Hamzah Hussin ，同註 1 ，頁 79 。
16. 見 Hamzah Hussin ，同註 1 ，頁 82-83 。
17. Hodge 公佈影片賺了 145,377 元，以當時來說相當驚人。見 Jamil Sulong ，同註 6 ，頁 229 及 Lim Kay Tong ，同註 3 ，頁 65 、 130-131 。
18. Basker 離開國泰克里斯後，自組 Telefilm 公司，在新加坡一家細小的攝影廠內拍製廣告和紀錄片。見 Hamzah Hussin，同註 1 ，頁 52-53 。
19. 見 Hamzah Hussin ，同註 1 ，頁 31 、 35-36 。
20. 系列中多部作品甚至有「特技效果」，那竟是密山多直接手繪於菲林上的。見 Jamil Sulong ，同註 6 ，頁 235 及 Hamzah Hussin ，同註 1 ，頁 58-59 。

Timothy P. Barnard, 新加坡國立大學馬來亞歷史助理教授。
Timothy P. Barnard, assistant professor of Malay History at the National University of Singapore.

14. See Hamzah Hussin, op. cit., pp. 31, 35-36.
15. Whether the film made a profit can be debated. According to Philip Cheah, who runs the modern Singapore International Film Festival, it made a "small profit". But, Cathay Keris never made another Chinese language film. During this period Cathay also tried to make films with French production companies, as well as allowed their studios to be used by American filmmakers. See Jan Uhde and Yvonne Ng Uhde, op. cit., p. 23 and Hamzah Hussin, op. cit., p. 79.
16. See Hamzah Hussin, op. cit., pp. 82-83.
17. Tom Hodge reported that the film made $145,377, an amazing amount for that time. See Jamil Sulong, op. cit., p. 229 and Lim Kay Tong, op. cit., pp. 65, 130-131.
18. Basker left Cathay Keris to form Telefilm, which made documentaries and commercials at a small studio in Singapore. See Hamzah Hussin, op. cit., pp. 52-53.
19. See Hamzah Hussin, op. cit., p. 31, 35-36.
20. Many of the films even featured "special effects", which Mat Sentol apparently drew by hand onto the film. See Jamil Sulong, op. cit., p. 235 and Hamzah Hussin, op. cit., pp. 58-59.

台灣：國泰與邵氏影業的跨國戰場

- 葉月瑜 -

六十年代的香港影業一般咸認為是片廠制的黃金時期。這時期片廠制的實施以國泰與邵氏為龍頭，對戰後香港影業的發展起了關鍵的作用。但值得注意的是，這個片廠制的高峰期除了以垂直整合的特徵著名之外，也是國泰與邵氏實踐跨國擴張，乃至於「惡性」競爭的一個重要時期。[1]

國泰與邵氏兩家影業均為華僑經營的家族式企業。兩者均以獨資的型態，在南洋發展成熟後，戰後轉往香港，利用香港優厚的政治和「自由」的資本主義經濟條件，生產國語片，搶奪上海影業在戰後放棄的廣大境外國語片市場。這個市場在戰前主要以東南亞幾個華人散居的區域為主，分佈於新加坡、馬來西亞、印尼、泰國、越南、緬甸、柬埔寨、寮國等。但是這個以華僑為主的版圖在戰後卻有了變化。隨着台灣的解殖民，和官方語言的轉換，加上國民黨政權南移至台灣，台灣從一個日片

王植波（左）、張美瑤與林永泰攝於台灣

(From left) Wang Zhibo, actress Zhang Meiyao and Lam Wing-tai in Taiwan.

Taiwan: The Transnational Battlefield of Cathay and Shaws

- *Yeh Yueh-yu* -

The 1960s is generally considered the golden period of the Hong Kong studio system. Cathay and Shaws were the leaders of the studio system and their operations had a profound influence on the post-war Hong Kong film industry. It is worthy to note that the period was characterised not only by the studios' vertical integration but also by their transnational expansion and fierce competition.[1]

Both Cathay and Shaws are overseas Chinese family businesses that reached maturity in Southeast Asia. They landed in Hong Kong after WWII, taking advantage of its political and market freedom to produce films in attempts to corner the vast overseas Mandarin film market vacated by the Shanghai film industry. Comprised mainly of Southeast Asia's Chinese communities before WWII, this market was drastically changed after the war. The de-colonised Taiwan, with the subsequent change in official language and the Nationalist Government's arrival, became an important part of the market.[2] This is the historical factor that contributed to Cathay's transnational expansion.

的殖民市場，變為國語電影的主要消費國度。[2] 國語片市場的版圖因此增加了一大塊，這個轉換提供了國泰影業跨國擴展的歷史條件。

1963 年，港台兩地的電影大事是李翰祥離開邵氏公司，到台灣成立國聯電影。國聯成立的緣由，根據眾多的回憶錄透露，是由國泰公司在台灣的發行片商，聯邦公司所策劃成功的。[3] 聯邦在港的負責人張陶然知悉李翰祥受掣肘於邵氏家長型的管理，無法發揮其才，加上此時國泰與邵氏正為黃梅調歌唱片，上演「雙胞」案，遂向國泰在新加坡的總公司建議，挖走這場類型片爭奪戰的始作俑者李翰祥。國泰提供主要資金，聯邦負責發行，使李翰祥能在上游集資和下游賣片無後顧之憂的條件下，將精力投注於拍攝，做個自由的創作和製片人。1963年底，李將香港的人力搬到台灣，成立一個以片廠制為主，但又容許獨立模式的垂直整合型製片公司。由於國聯在體質上是由國泰與聯邦催生的，因此新公司的名稱便取自兩家公司的第一個字「國」與「聯」。

表面上看來，國泰與聯邦的挖角，是兩家龍頭影業公司的競爭所致，但從工業的操作來看，國泰支持李翰祥到台灣拍片，正是跨國企業運作的特徵。一般來說，跨國企業的運作可透過資金、人力的轉換或以投資的方式，直接在他國生產產品。國泰的角色從星馬的片商轉而成為李祖永的永華片廠在香港的主要債主，並於永華債台高築之時，收購永華，這一連串的商業行徑，表現其跨國運作的端倪。根據聯邦負責人沙榮峰的回憶，當國泰在 1955 年收購永華時，接收人歐德爾的構想是：

仿效美國的聯美公司，本身少拍片，儘量支持大牌演員、導演，組織多家獨立製片公司合作拍片；也與其它非組織內的獨立製片公司合作拍片。當時與國際簽約的

《寶蓮燈》中的國泰三朵小花：李芝安(左)、張慧嫻和劉小慧
The Magic Lamp

In 1963, Li Hanxiang's departure from Shaws to establish Grand Motion Picture in Taiwan was big news. According to the memoirs of those involved, the deal was orchestrated by Union, Cathay's Taiwan distributor.[3] Zhang Taoran, Union's head man in Hong Kong, found out that Li was unhappy with Shaws' monarchial ways. At the time, the competition between Cathay and Shaws was so fierce that they were producing separate versions of the same *huangmei diao* (Yellow Plum Opera). Chang suggested that Cathay could raid Li, who started the genre's craze, by investing capital on Grand while Union would handle distribution, leaving Li free to make films. At the end of 1963, Li moved his operation to Taiwan, forming a vertically integrated studio that also allowed for the mode of independent production.

On the surface, the raiding of Li was caused by the competition of two leading film companies. But from an industry perspective, Cathay's support of Li was a typical move by a multi-national transnational corporation. Generally, multi-national transnational corporations can directly produce in other countries through investment or the transfer of capital or personnel. Starting as a Southeast Asian distributor, Cathay first became a debtor of Hong Kong's Yung Hwa Studios, then buying out the latter after it got into financial trouble. This series of moves was the start of a transnational operation. According to Union's head Sha Yung-fong (Sha Rongfeng) , when Cathay bought out Yung Hwa, its operative Albert Odell's plan was:

Modelling after United Artist, the plan was not to make many films, instead supporting big-name stars and directors to form independent companies and embark on co-productions as well as cooperating with independent companies not in the alliance. Companies that signed with International Films included Yan Jun's Guotai, Zhu Xuhua's Guofeng, Bai Guang's Guoguang and Zhang Shankun's Hsin Hwa...[4]

This is an example of a multi-national corporation's operation when it expands into another country: cooperating with local producers to solve the problem of unfamiliarity and diversifying investment to reduce risk. This is also consistent with Li's recollections that

有嚴俊的國泰公司、朱旭華的國風公司、白光的國光公司、張善琨的新華公司⋯⋯。[4]

沙氏的說法印證了跨國公司在他地初期營運的方式，即一方面和當地的製片商合作，以解決對當地情況不熟悉的問題，二方面以分散投資的方式，減低風險。這兩點和李翰祥在《三十年細說從頭（二）》中，對被國泰接收時的回憶不謀而合。根據李的描述，當國泰接手永華時，當家導演嚴俊和會計主任朱旭華都是歐德爾在進入永華時的內應，交換的條件便是由國泰對其擁有的獨立公司注資，並對拍片不予干預。[5] 但這樣的情形在前永華的製片經理鍾啟文自美習影回港後，有了轉變。首先，國泰將歐德爾調回新加坡總公司，而國泰在接收永華的一年後，即 1956 年，將製片公司改名為電懋公司，由鍾啟文任總經理，聘請宋淇當製片主任，孫晉三擔任劇本評審委員，並請了張愛玲當編劇，展開了電懋的黃金製片，也就是所謂的「電懋風格」。國泰也就在鍾主政的六年期間（1956 - 1962）由跨國的片商變為香港的製片翹楚。

但是國泰的風光在李翰祥投效邵氏，[6] 大力拓展古裝片之後，有了轉變。加上鍾啟文因醜聞離任，使得邵氏有後來居上的態勢。1963 年李翰祥在知悉國泰籌拍《梁祝》（嚴俊，1964），以半個月的時間完成《梁山伯與祝英台》，並在台灣破了所有西片、日片與國片的記錄，[7] 使得李翰祥成了炙手可熱的導演，也使得國泰與邵氏的競爭到了白熱化的階段。為了瓦解邵氏如日中天的盛況，國泰與在台的發行商聯邦遂以相當「變通」的方式，將李翰祥自邵氏挖走，但並非挖入國泰，而是將其外放於第三地台灣，容許他在這個第三地實施片廠型的獨立製作。

先前提到，跨國企業可透過資金、人力的轉換或以投資

國泰、國聯與台製簽訂合作拍片合約，
國聯負責人李翰祥與台製廠長龍芳簽約時合照
Li Hanxiang (left) and Loong Foong, manager of Taiwan Motion Picture Studio, shake hands after reaching a co-production agreement.

when Cathay took over Yung Hwa, Odell had already brokered agreements with top director Yan Jun and head of accounting Zhu Xuhua in exchange for investing in their independent companies without interfering in productions.[5] The situation changed after Odell was moved back to Singpaore. In 1956, MP & GI was established, with Robert Chung (Zhong Qiwen) serving as general manager. Stephen Soong (Song Qi) was hired as production manager, Sun Jinsan as script supervisor and Eileen Chang (Zhang Ailing) as scriptwriter, ushering in the studio's golden period and establishing what's considered the "MP & GI style". In the six years of Chung's reign (1956-1962), Cathay evolved from a multi-national (former transnational distributor) to a top Hong Kong production company.

But Cathay's glory was tarnished after Shaws recruited Li and started exploring the costumes picture front,[6] especially after Chung was forced to resign due to personnel scandals. In 1963, after Cathay announced plans to make *Liang San Bo and Zhu Ying Tai* (1964), Li rushed to finish his version, *The Love Eterne* (1963), in two weeks, which broke all records in Taiwan.[7] With competition becoming fierce, Cathay and Union raided Li, but not to join Cathay. Instead, Li was installed in Taiwan – a third location – where he could produce independent films with a studio system.

Transnational expansion into foreign countries – through investment or exchange of capital and personnel – depends greatly on global and regional political-economical situations. In global political terms, the 1950s and 1960s saw the conflict between capitalism and communism dividing Chinese culture into two areas. Taiwan, Hong Kong and Southeast Asia belonged to the realm where transnational capitalism expanded, while China was capitalism's forbidden zone. In transnational investment terms, Taiwan, the former Japanese colony, was a territory undeveloped by overseas Chinese. The transnational power struggle between Communist and Nationalist also made overseas Chinese more important. The Cold War, capitalism's expansion made Taiwan an appealing place for investment and film production.

《梁山伯與祝英台》中的尤敏（左）與李麗華
You Min (Left) and Li Lihua in *Liang San Bo and Zhu Ying Tai.*

Taiwan was already a major market for Mandarin films in the mid-1960s. Taiwanese language (Min-nan, a branch of Fukienese) films were on the wane as audiences for Mandarin films were on the rise. While the phenomenal success of *The Love Eterne* was an indication of this virgin market's potentials, local Mandarin films were unable to meet the demand – it wasn't until two years later (1965) when Central Motion Pictures Corporation, Taiwan's largest studio, launched into its "healthy realism" phase. Introducing the Hong Kong-style Mandarin films into the Taiwan industry allowed for the benefits of vertical integration and product expansion that provided a steady supply of films. Also, Taiwan was enforcing currency control and a high exchange rate, limiting profit for foreign films. Setting up shop to make co-productions could thus reduce tax burden.[8] Also, cheap labour and land as well as the wide variety of locations made Taiwan an attractive place for an off-shore studio. Under these circumstances, Union, with its extensive social and political connections, brought in Li and Cathay's capital to form Grand, supposedly a local company but in fact part of a transnational operation.

Another factor was the Nationalist Government's policy to court Hong Kong filmmakers. Since the early 1950s, it had been aggressively supporting "right-wing" filmmakers to oppose the "left-wingers" backed by the Mainland government, like sinking HK$500,000 to help Yung Hwa and later persuading Cathay to invest in the studio.[9] In 1953, Zhang Shankun and Wang Yuanlong organised a group of "freedom filmmakers" (those sympathetic to the Nationalist cause) to celebrate the birthday of President Chiang Kaishek in Taiwan. Zhang and Wang were granted an audience with Chiang, who asked them to establish a pro-Nationalist group in Hong Kong, later leading to the formation of the Hong Kong and Kowloon Cinema and Theatrical Enterprise Free General Association (aka Freedom Association). And the next year, Hsin Hwa made *Blood Stained Flowers* (1954), answering the call for political promotion.[10] In 1956, the Taiwan government formed the Motion Pictures Advice Committee, including in its

的方式，直接在他國生產產品，而跨國投資還必須仰賴全球與區域政治經濟的生態，方能跨進他國延伸產業網絡。以五六十年代全球政治而言，資本主義與共產主義的對峙將華人的文化政治經濟版圖分成兩大塊，台灣、香港和整個東南亞屬於跨國資本主義擴張的版圖，而中國大陸則是資本主義禁制區。所以就跨國投資而言，台灣這個日本的前殖民地，是一個華僑尚未開發的新國度，而國民黨和共產黨的跨國（從大陸到香港、台灣乃至所有的華人區域）鬥爭，加重了華僑的重要性。冷戰、資本主義企業的跨國擴張與右派政權的拉攏，都使得台灣成為當時具有相當魅力的投資與製片場所。

從電影市場來看，台灣在六十年代中期開始，已成為國語片的主要市場。此時，台灣的台語片已顯疲態，製片量開始下滑，國片的觀眾日增，《梁山伯與祝英台》的盛況說明了這個處女市場的雄厚潛力。再者，台灣本地的國語製片方興未艾，最大片廠中影的健康寫實主義要到兩年之後（即 1965 年）才大量出爐。此時從香港引進成熟的國語片製作，並將製成品直接在當地販售，一可盡收垂直整合之益，二可擴大生產線，確保片源。第三，以台灣當時對外匯的管制，外國資金難以直接進入，台灣政府另一方面又提高結匯匯率，使外片在台灣的獲利大大降低；因此以合作的方式，在台灣設廠，可免除賦稅之累。[8] 台灣代理港片的龍頭聯邦公司以其廣闊的黨政人脈關係，引進李翰祥與國泰的資金，成立名為在地，實為跨國的國聯公司。而台灣的便宜人力、土地，和實景亦都是成立離岸片廠的有利條件。最後，台灣國民黨政府於冷戰時期對香港影界所實施的籠絡政策，有如虎添翼的效用。打從五十年代初期開始，國民黨政府便積極在香港支持右派影人與製片公司，與中國支持的左派影界抗衡。這在國民黨以港幣五十萬元支助李祖永的永華渡過財政難關，後又遊說國泰增資永華的事例中都可見一斑。[9] 而當初幫助李翰祥製作第一部影

duties the supervision of overseas productions.[11] The spectacular scenes in Grand's epic *Hsi Shih The Beauty of Beauties* (1965), for example, was made with the assistance of the Taiwan military.

Actually, long before the establishment of Grand, Cathay had already wanted to branch into Taiwan. Sha Yung-fong remembers:

In January 1963, Loke Wan Tho (Lu Yuntao) declared his support of Taiwan's International but as MP & GI's overseas outfit, making films in Taiwan with an investment of NT$ 10 million. The new company's plan was to rent facilities from Central Motion Pictures Corporation and Taiwan Motion Picture Studio and to make co-productions with these organisations. It would also go into ventures with MP & GI's satellite companies in Taiwan.[12]

Hong Kong film producer Wong Cheuk-hon (Huang Zhuohan) also remembers in his memoirs that Cathay needed to expand into Taiwan to compete with Shaws:

Shaws and MP & GI had reached the fierce state of filming different versions of the same film. Shaws had its own "film city", an actors training program and a staff of over 1,200. During rush productions, it could easily build and dismantle sets. MP & GI had only two sound stages at Yung Hwa plus one at Asia but not enough land to built location sets, making it difficult to do rush productions... In Taiwan, there was land available.[13]

Tong Yuejuan, Zhang Shankun's widow, also talked about MP & GI's support of Xinhua in a newly published memoir:

Mr. Loke formed MP & GI, producing high-quality films with corporate style management... He supported Xinhua for a long time and we had a good working relationship. For example, he

片《雪裡紅》（1956）的一班人，就是國民黨派駐香港的工作人員。[10] 1953年10月29日，由王元龍、張善琨組織「留港自由人士」的「祝壽勞軍團」抵達台灣，為前領導人蔣介石祝壽。張與王獲蔣介石接見，並囑返港成立自由影劇公會，就是後來的港九影劇自由總會。次年，新華便以《碧血黃花》（1954）一片響應政宣號召。[11] 1956年，台灣國民黨政府更成立「電影事業輔導委員會」，由教育部負責辦理，其中也包括對海外製片的輔導。[12] 執掌電影政策的台灣製片廠廠長龍芳就是當時支持海外合作計畫的主要人物。國聯的大片《西施》（1965），也是承台灣製片廠協助，方能拍出千軍萬馬的大場面。

除開國民黨的積極運作，其實早在國聯成立之前，國泰已經打算在台灣設廠，拓展跨國的製片業務。根據沙榮峰回憶：

1963年1月，香港電懋董事長陸運濤宣佈支持台灣「國際影業公司」為電懋的國外組織，在台灣大量製片，製片資金新台幣一千萬元。新公司的製片計畫是一部份租借中影或台製的攝影廠拍片，另一部份是與中影或台製在互助的原則下合作拍片。新公司並將與香港電懋的外圍公司在台灣合作拍片。[13]

香港影人黃卓漢的回憶錄也印證了國泰必需將業務跨海到台灣，才能與邵氏一較長短：

邵氏、電懋雙方已到了你拍我也拍、大鬧雙胞，尖銳而激烈的時候，邵氏有影城、有基地、又有訓練班和員工一千兩百餘人，搶拍搭景拆景，隨時任意可辦。電懋則雖有永華新廠的兩個棚，再加亞洲的一棚，亦不過三棚而已，片廠無大幅空地可以搭外景，無法趕戲搶拍，陸運濤除在港與邱德根商好合作，邱亦有一大幅土地，位於清水灣到去邵氏影城不及一半的地

葛蘭、白光、林黛、李湄等女星赴台為蔣介石祝壽
Grace Chang, Bai Quang, Lin Dai and Li Mei celebrate President Chiang Kai-shek's birthday.

朱國良（左）夫婦與俞普慶於1965年在台灣與蔣介石合照
Mr. and Mrs. Choo Kok Leung and Paul Yui with Chiang in 1965.

方，提供蓋廠。台灣方面，更多土地提供。[14]

資深影人童月娟（張善琨遺孀）在晚近的回憶錄中也提到電懋對新華在台拍片的支持：

陸先生是星馬國泰機構的負責人，投資成立香港電懋影業公司，以企業化經營方式，出產高素質的影片，與邵氏並稱香港二大製片公司。他也長期支持新華拍片，我們的合作關係一直非常密切，像《鳳凰》，就是由他出資三分之一、邱德根先生和我各出三分之一的資金來拍攝的，影片拍成後再交由「國泰」發行。[15]

童女士這裡提到的《鳳凰》（1965），是新華與電懋於 1964 年在台灣合作的第一部影片。但由於陸運濤於同年在台空難去世，《鳳凰》便成了唯一一部新華與電懋的跨國合資電影。1964 年 6 月陸運濤抵台參加亞太影展，帶領了重要幕僚到台灣與台製廠長龍芳商討在台大舉投資製片（這中間也包含國泰、台製與國聯的合作計畫），並擬在台灣全省各地興建大型影院。就在台灣黨政界熱烈歡迎之際（多次與蔣介石見面），陸運濤夫婦的飛機在台灣豐原發生空難爆炸，同行的台製廠長龍芳、聯邦負責人夏維堂、和國泰高層人員周海龍、王植波等均罹難。國聯失掉了三個主要的支持者，國泰失掉了當家舵手，台灣失掉了富可敵國的華僑投資商。自此國語片的生態由兩雄爭霸變為邵氏獨霸，國聯衰敗，台灣影業也由國、民營雙軌的結構轉為國（民黨）營獨大的局面。隨後聯邦與李翰祥交惡，於 1967 年解約。失掉國聯這個生產線後，聯邦再從邵氏挖來另一個不快樂的導演胡金銓，拍了另一部破票房紀錄的《龍門客棧》(1967)。與此同時，黃卓漢的第一影業將製片移轉至台灣，拍攝武俠片。再過數年，邵氏允許張徹到台灣成立長弓公司，拍攝當紅的武打電影。雖然國泰這個大資本企業自此缺席，但境外製作，已然成為小型公司最為變通的製片模式，為港台兩地日後的跨國影業，奠下建制。

invested a third of the budget for the film Phoenix... with Cathay handling distribution for the film.[14]

Phoenix, made in 1964, was the first MP & GI and Hsin Hwa transnational co-production and it became the only one after Loke died later that year. Loke had gone to Taiwan to attend the Asian Film Festival. He also wanted to meet top leaders in Taiwan to discuss plans to increase his Taiwan investment (including collaborations between Cathay, Taiwan Motion Picture Studio and Grand), including building theatres all over the island state. But his flight crashed, killing him and his wife, together with several top Cathay executives and the heads of Union and Taiwan Motion Picture Studio. In the accident, Grand lost three of its main supporters, Cathay lost its figurehead and Taiwan lost a capital-rich overseas investor. After the accident, Shaws began to dominate the Mandarin film industry. Grand later collapsed and the Taiwan film industry went from both private and government run to only government (in the form of the Nationalists) operated. Union later had a fallout with Li and their agreement was dissolved in 1967. It raided another Shaws alumni, King Hu, and made another record breaking film, *Dragon Inn* (1967). At the same time, independent producer Wong Cheuk-hon moved his company to Taiwan to cash in on the martial arts fever. A few years later, Shaws agreed to let Chang Cheh (Zhang Zhe) to establish an off-shore company Changgong in Taiwan, also to make martial arts films. Although Cathay had since disappeared from the scene, the transnational way of operation had become a way with which small companies could adjust to the circumstances, establishing the foundation for the future transnational film industries of Hong Kong and Taiwan.

Translated by Sam Ho

註

1. 見焦雄屏：《國聯電影：改變歷史的五年》，台北：萬象圖書，1994，頁4。
2. 台灣光復之初，由於禁演日片，再加上回歸祖國，空缺的電影市場除了放映美國片外，也放映許多的國語影片，但由於片源短缺，片商除了進口以永華等香港公司製作的國語片外，還大量放映許多庫存的舊片。見沙榮峰：《繽紛電影四十春：沙榮峰回憶錄》，台北：國家電影資料館，1994，頁10，及葉龍彥：《光復初期台灣電影史》，台北：國家電影資料館，1995，頁91。
3. 這些回憶錄包括沙榮峰，同註2；黃卓漢：《電影人生：黃卓漢回憶錄》，台北：萬象圖書，1994；李翰祥：《三十年細說從頭（二）》，香港：天地圖書，1987，及左桂芳、姚立群編：《童月娟》，台北：國家電影資料館，2002。
4. 見沙榮峰，同註2，頁12。
5. 見李翰祥，同註3，頁45。
6. 據李翰祥的說法，當初因為歐德爾和嚴俊對李所寫的劇本《雪裡紅》的打壓，使得李轉投邵氏。見李翰祥，同註3，頁75-77。
7. 見焦雄屏，同註1，頁17。
8. 見盧非易：《台灣電影：政治、經濟、美學1949-1994》，台北：遠流，1998，頁57-58。
9. 見沙榮峰，同註2，頁12；劉現成：《台灣電影、社會與國家》，台北：揚智文化，1997，頁152，及黃卓漢，同註3，頁91。
10. 見李翰祥，同註3，頁75-77。
11. 這部影片出動了卜萬蒼、屠光啟、張善琨、易文、王天林、馬徐維邦、羅維等各導演一段，並網羅周曼華、李湄、葛蘭、黃河、于素秋、陳厚、鍾情等大牌明星義演。見左桂芳、姚立群編，同註3，頁103-105，及沙榮峰，同註2，頁28。
12. 見劉現成，同註9，頁70。
13. 見沙榮峰，同註2，頁31。
14. 見黃卓漢，同註3，頁120。
15. 見左桂芳、姚立群編，同註3，頁135。

葉月瑜，浸會大學電影電視系助理教授。著有《歌聲魅影：歌曲敘事與中文電影》（台北：遠流，2000）。

Yeh Yueh-yu, assistant professor of Cinema and Television at Baptist University. Author of *Phantom of Music: Song Narration and Chinese-language Cinemas* (Taipei: Yuanliu, 2000).

Notes

1. See Peggy Chiao Hsiung-ping (Jiao Xiongping): *Grand Motion Picture: Five Years that Changed History* (in Chinese), Taipei: Variety Publishing, 1994, p.4.
2. After Taiwan's return to China, Japanese films were banned and the void was filled by Hollywood films and Mandarin films. Because of the film shortage, in addition to importing Hong Kong Mandarin films, many old movies were also shown. See Sha Yung-fong, *Forty Glorious Years in Film: Memories of Sha Yung-fong* (in Chinese), Taipei: Chinese Taipei Film Archive, 1994, p.10 and Yeh Longyen (Ye Longyan): *Taiwan Film History of the Early Liberation Period* (in Chinese), Taipei: Chinese Taipei Film Archive, 1995, p. 91.
3. The memoirs include: Sha Yung-fong, ibid.; Wong Cheuk-hon: *A Life in Film: Memoirs of Wong Cheuk-hon* (in Chinese), Taipei: Variety Publishing, 1994; Li Hanxiang: *Thirty-Year Recollections, Vol.2* (in Chinese), Hong Kong: Cosmos Books, 1987; Tso Kuei-fang and Yao Liqun, ed., *Tong Yuejuan* (in Chinese), Taipei: Chinese Taipei Film Archive, 2002.
4. See Sha Yung-fong, op. cit., p. 12.
5. See Li Hanxiang, op. cit., p.45.
6. According to Li, he went over to Shaws because of dissatisfaction with International's head Albert Odell and Yan Jun's treatment of his script for the film *Red Bloom in the Snow* (1956). See Li Hanxiang, op. cit., pp.75-77.
7. See Peggy Chiao Hsiung-ping, op. cit., p. 17.
8. See Lu Feiyi: *Taiwan Cinema, Society and Nation* (in Chinese), Taipei: Yuanliu, 1997, p. 152 and Wong Cheuk-hon, op. cit., p. 91.
9. See Sha Yung-fong, op. cit., p. 12; Liu Xiancheng: *Taiwan Cinema: Politics, Economics, Aesthetics 1949 – 1994* (in Chinese), Taipei: Yangzhi, 1997, p. 152 and *Wong Cheuk-hon*, op. cit., p. 91.
10. This film features several top directors, such as Bu Wancang, Ma Xu Weibang, Wang Tianlin and Yi Wen, each directing one episdoe, and starred several top stars such as Grace Chang (Ge Lan), Chung Ching (Zhong Qing), Li Mei and Peter Chen Ho (Chen Hou). See Tso Knei-fang and Yao Liqun, ed., op. cit., pp. 103-105 and Sha Yung-fong, op. cit., p. 28.
11. See Liu Xiancheng, op. cit., p. 70.
12. See Sha Yung-fong, op. cit., p. 31.
13. See Wong Cheuk-hon, op. cit., p. 120.
14. See Tso Kuei-fang and Yao Liqun, ed., op. cit., p. 135.

「男子氣，你知道什麼叫男子氣？……肌肉不等於男子氣！」從《遊戲人間》看電懋電影的男性情結

- 游靜 -

起步點

本文企圖借《遊戲人間》(王天林, 1961) 的電影文本分析來探討1950年代末1960年代初電懋浪漫肥皂劇中的性別身份，尤其是男性／陽性的身份，並從而探討這複雜的性別身份情結與流徙中的文化身份之間的關係。我特別選擇了《遊戲人間》中丁皓演的羅亞男為出發點，正是為這角色身份的多重曖昧性，及其所揭示的男創作者透過女演員的表演／喬裝「陽性」，對「理想男性」的一些共同幻想及呈現。丁皓所演的男性及陽性，我以為與電懋當時其他男明星如雷震、喬宏、張揚等在本片及其他電影中再現出來的「男性特質」，有可供對比以及相互參照的地方。所以本文的重點是性別身份（陽性）在電影中作為一種論述的呈現，而不是在（男／女）生理身份上。

"Masculinity… What Do You Know About Masculinity? Muscle Does Not Equal Masculinity!" A Study of Genderisation and the Representation of Masculinity in *You were Meant for Me*

- *Yau Ching* -

This article is an attempt to use a textual study of *You were Meant for Me* (1961) to examine the representation of gender construction, masculinity in particular, produced by the MP & GI Studio in its films of the late 1950s and early 1960s. It contextualizes the film within its specific studio culture, which specializes in romantic melodramas and musicals supported by a star system and the production of media trivia, magazines, handbills and other publicity materials. The possibilities and limitations of gender and sexual identities offered by this "temporary transvestite film", according to Straayer's definition of the genre, [1] foregrounds, among other things, a certain "crisis" in an evolving notion of masculinity. I shall examine the ways this film, as a Hong Kong variation of this primarily Hollywood-defined genre, departs from the characteristics as generalized by Straayer, and the ways it also departs from traditional Chinese narratives of female cross-dressing. In the final part of this essay, I ask how this "crisis" of masculinity could be read as an integral part of a cultural identity in flux and in formation related to a specific experience of

《遊戲人間》的羅亞男，與電懋電影中的其他男性形象呈現了對性別，尤其是對陽性的一些共同期望及憂慮。這些憂慮與冀盼，我以為，與南來影人的文化背景，及其面對新鮮及多元的文化身份上的衝擊不無關係。從性別身份到文化身份，需要更多的篇幅及更廣泛細緻的研讀，本文只是一個起步點。

喬裝男女

梁愛倫：「你以為你穿了一身男人衣服，就是男人？女人是女人，男人是男人，天生不一樣的。你知不知道，你這樣的做法，損害了別人？」

羅亞男：「損害了你是不是？你爭不過我是你自己沒用。」

《遊戲人間》中丁皓飾的富家小姐羅亞男喬裝男生，對白露明飾的護士高式文展開追求。她們首次約會時，式文取笑亞男的名字，說這真像女生。亞男連忙更正說，其實她叫「亞南」才對，父親在「亞洲南面」做生意，她是在那裡出生的。式文笑「亞男」這名字，因為它具體呈現了在重男輕女的家庭體制中女性的弱勢位置，與眼前這斯文有禮的小男生毫不相襯。式文不知道的是，正正是這種體制，孕育了電影中「亞男」這角色，亞男扮演的亞南愈是否認「亞男」的存在，「亞男」便愈是無處不在。

誰是亞男呢？亞男似乎是中國嚴父慈母、中央專權、物質富裕的封建家庭制度的產品。是在這樣的一種制度下，性別不一定是求生的策略，而可（暫時）變成一種遊戲，提供超越自身及環境限制的快感。「亞男」這符號在電影中凸現了制度的無處不在，又揭示了顛覆制度的可能。亞男在生理本質上雖為女性，但這角色最誘人處，是她陽化自身的諸種方式，及其於陽化與陰化之間拉扯，時男性時女性的一種夾雜與不定。亞男這「角

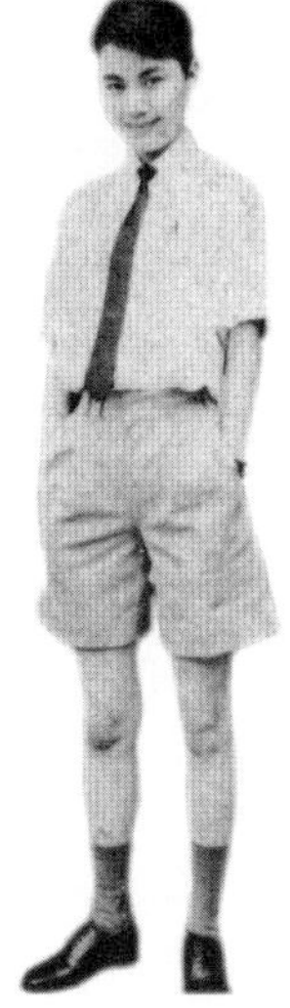

《遊戲人間》中的小男生丁皓
"What do you know about masculinity?" Kitty Ting Hao in *You were Meant for Me*.

migration among the Studio's production staff. Due to the limited scope of this article, the development of the argument from gender and sexual identity to cultural identity is inevitably simplified. An examination of more films and stars is called for in the future in order to provide a more comprehensive study on this issue.

Performativity of Gender

Liang Ai-lun: "You see yourself as a man now that you have men's clothes on? Women are women, men are men, they're not born the same. Do you know what you've done will hurt people?"

Lo Ya-nan: "It hurt you, right? It's your fault you can't beat me."

Tomboy Lo Ya-nan (Kitty Ting Hao / Ding Hao) cross-dresses as a young man in *You were Meant for Me* to court the nurse Kao Shih-wen (Christine Pai Lu-ming/ Bai Luming). During their first date, Shih-wen laughs at the stigmatic girlishness of Ya-nan's name as "girlish". Ya-nan (a not uncommon name for women that translates as "second to male") thus changes "his" name on the spot to Ya-nan – South of Asia, where "his" father had business and where "he" was born. (Note: In Chinese, the "nan" that means "male" uses a different character from the "nan" that means "south", although they are pronounced the same. In the rest of this essay, Ya-nan in male attire is referred to as "the male Ya-nan" while Ya-nan in female attire is either "the female Ya-nan" or simply "Ya-nan".) Cross-dressing gives Ya-nan the opportunity not only to date the same sex, but to reinvent herself, her history and her position within the patriarchal Chinese family system, in which she is now suddenly directly related to her father's "business", and no longer the inferior daughter stuck with a name which only expresses the parents' wish for a son.

Now that Ya-nan has changed her gender through changing her name and her outfit, she is never the same again, even when she *plays* a girl. The male Ya-nan, according to the female Ya-nan's invention, has a twin sister called Ya-lan ("Orchid"). In the film Ya-nan

色」在電影中出現的時間其實不多，因為她一開始跟雷震演的醫生愛倫打賭，説要跟他公平競爭來追求高式文，以顯示她的男子氣後，她便變成男版的亞男，可以換一種聲線，跟式文約會。首次在餐廳約會，她／他更突然把自己的名字也改了，變成「亞南」，而且引出「做生意」的父親這父子的承傳脈絡及地域淵源來把她／他的名字正名化。亞男自此在電影中消失，她的身體一分為二，成為追求式文的「亞南」與被高卓然（式文兄，喬宏飾）追求的「亞蘭」。直至電影結尾時，亞南錯穿了女裝鞋趕去醫院被式文識破，亞南與亞蘭才再次結合，回到「亞男」這夾雜男女的身體／身份內。

亞男雖然被亞南及亞蘭暫時遮蓋，她卻無處不在。觀眾由始至終都知道亞南與亞蘭都是亞男，皆由丁皓這女生來扮演的小姐來扮演，不論這些暫時性的角色是小姐是先生抑或是（在化裝舞會上）先生扮的小姐。焦雄屏認為這種「女扮男裝的愛情遊戲」，襲自三十年代造成評論「軟硬電影」之爭的《化身姑娘》（方沛霖，1936），也承襲中國戲曲投合觀眾逃避現實的心理，由電懋開發，再被邵氏發揚光大。[1] Chris Straayer 論這「暫時易服」的電影類型時，卻以為這種電影的歷久不衰與流行，叫我們必須正視它對普羅大眾帶來的觀賞樂趣。她相信，這種樂趣正正來自大眾共有的顛覆性別構成的幻想，但這類型並沒有真正挑戰到性別差異，所以觀眾一面投射幻想，一面也安心於性別構成的基本矛盾，並沒有被激化。[2]

故此，與其説這類型電影逃避現實，不如説它向我們本來便可笑及可塑的性別現實，再現及凸顯它可笑及可塑的本質。亞男變成亞南後，她穿着深色的西裝，結着領帶，開一輛敞篷跑車，替女友拉椅子開車門付賬，等女友時架着手屁股挨在跑車上。亞男演亞南時有一系列的

switches between *playing* the male Ya-nan and Ya-lan in order to court both Shih-wen and her mucho macho brother Cho-jan (Roy Chiao / Qiao Hong). Through Ya-nan's determination, playfulness and skill, the two genders are translated into a clear set of codes to be performed consistently and repetitively, both in terms of costumes and behaviour. When Ya-nan as a young man is being played out, he has a dark suit on, drives a convertible, opens doors for Shih-wen, orders and pays for their meals. He leans on the front of his car with arms and legs crossed while waiting for Shih-wen. All of this body language constructs Ya-nan's identity as a well-mannered, independent (thus dependable) and educated young man, in contrast to the body language of Ya-lan, which also constructs her femininity. While women need to *appear* to depend on men, men need to *appear* dependable, not to make physical moves unless signalled. In a scene when Ya-nan has to suddenly brake the car in front of a careless pedestrian, Ya-nan shys away when Shih-wen's body bumps into his. Shih-wen is immediately impressed with Ya-nan's manners. From Ya-nan to Ya-lan, s/he moves from a suit to a dress and also puts on a long-haired wig, emphasizing how her womanhood *also* needs to be performed. In a contrasting scene, when the desirable man (in this case Cho-jan) is speeding a vehicle (in this case a jetboat), the female Ya-lan leans her body on the man to complement his dependability.

But in the film, the fact that the male Ya-nan expresses embarrassment when Shih-wen's body leans on his is not so much a result of "his wanting to be gentlemanly" but more of "remembering herself", that fact that she is the same sex as Shih-wen. Ironically, that is what catches Shih-wen's eye the most and becomes most important to her, the sign of "a good man". So, is the best man in a woman's eyes one played by a woman after all? How do I read a film as such which seems to be addressing and foregrounding the crisis of genderization, and one of masculinity in particular?

The more Ya-nan (the girlish boy) refuses to be Ya-nan (the boyish girl), the more Ya-nan asserts her (hybridized) presence. Like other films with cross-

身體語言，表現他是一名斯文有禮不輕佻的男性，跟亞蘭的整個身子像貓咪一樣挨在駕着遊艇的卓然身上那樣子迥然不同。譬如，亞南與式文首次約會後，亞南開車送式文回家，車子突然煞掣，式文撞在亞南身上，亞南趕快避開；亞男不懂得跳舞，老是踩到式文的腳上……這些都大大增強了式文對亞南的好感。觀眾當然知道，這些身體表現，正因亞南始終是亞男，但在式文眼中，這些卻成了「好男人」的符徵。難道女人眼中最理想的男人原來是扮男人的女人？

「暫時易服」電影類型

Straayer界定「暫時易服」這電影類型的特色包括：劇情需要喬裝；角色摘取象徵異性的服裝及言行舉止；喬裝足以使電影中其他人物信以為「真」，但觀眾卻一直知道「底蘊」；電影不時提供指向角色「真」性別的符號；喬裝者對自己「假扮」的性別的苦與樂日益敏感；電影

女人眼中的好男人 — 白露明和丁皓
Too close for comfort?
Kitty Ting Hao and Christine Pai Lu-ming in *You were Meant for Me*.

dressing as theme, the majority of the drama and the comedy in *You were Meant for Me* comes from the awareness of the audience that both "South of Asia" and "The Orchid" are manifestations of the games of the boyish girl. Peggy Chiao Hsiung-ping has criticized this kind of "love games of women cross-dressing" in MP & GI films, which appropriates similar plots from traditional operas and from *The Transforming Lady* (1936) in the 30s, as catering to "the escapist psyche" in the audience.[2] Chris Straayer, however, reminds us to take seriously the temporary transvestite film as a genre exactly due to its continuing popularity and its capacity to sustain mass-audience pleasure,[3] and I would add, cross-culturally. This pleasure, argues Straayer, is "grounded in the appeasement of basic contradictions through a common fantasy of overthrowing gender constructions without challenging sexual difference."[4]

The Temporary Transvestite Film

Such genre foregrounds the mutability and laughability of sexual realities but would not propose to change them. Straayer further examines several generic conventions, including the narrative necessity for disguise, adoption by a character of the opposite sex's gender-specific costumes, the believability of this character's disguise to the film's other characters together with its unbelievability to the film's audience, the character's increasing awareness of pleasures and plight of the opposite sex, references to biological sex differences, accusations and "misinterpretations" of homosexuality, the disguise becoming an obstacle in realizing heterosexual desire, and last but not least, the unmasking of the disguise resulting in heterosexual coupling.

You were Meant for Me conforms largely to these characteristics, but departs in several significant ways. First, there is no necessity for disguise in the narrative. Unlike plots in *Some Like it Hot* (1959), *Victor/Victoria* (1982), *The Ballad of Little Jo* (1993) and so on, and also unlike Chinese legends like *Liang Zhu* (sometimes translated as *The Butterfly Lovers)* or *Hua Mulan*, Ya-nan in *You Were Meant for Me* cross-dresses purely out of whim or a competitive drive to show off to her buddy, or simply

需不時援引生理上的性差異；喜劇成份隨着身體接觸增多而強化；角色的「假扮」使異性戀的慾望觸礁；角色假扮被指為同性戀；喬裝卸下，最後異性戀人結合。

觀乎國際的主流電影歷史，這類型電影實在歷久不衰。由嘉寶演得風靡一時的《克莉絲汀女王》（*Queen Christina*, Rouben Mamoulian, 1933），至嘉芙蓮協賓英姿颯颯的《Sylvia Scarlett》（George Cukor, 1935），加利格蘭在《I Was A Male Bride》（Howard Hawks, 1949）中男扮女裝成過埠新娘，東尼寇蒂斯與積林蒙為求生計扮成樂師的《熱情如火》（*Some Like it Hot*, Billy Wilder, 1959），當然還有無數八九十年代的例子，如茱莉安德絲同時是Victor，又是Victoria的《雌雄莫辨》（*Victor/Victoria*, Blake Edwards, 1982），芭芭拉史翠珊自導自演矢志作男生來向上爬的《恩桃》（*Yentl*, 1983），及香港觀眾熟悉的《杜絲先生》（*Tootsie*, Sydney Pollack, 1982）及《肥媽先生》（*Mrs. Doubtfire*, Chris Columbus, 1993）。

這些例子大致上都符合Straayer概括的類型特色，最大的偏離可能是恩桃最終並沒有與異性戀人結合，史翠珊始終堅持她的獨立。這也是此類型電影中罕有的女導演作品。《遊戲人間》或多或少引證了Straayer分析的論述。但最不同的卻有幾點。首先，跟《梁山伯與祝英台》或《花木蘭》這些傳統敘事不一樣，亞男於劇情上並沒有「必要」喬裝，她扮男裝完全是個人選擇與喜好，出於一種可能是嫉妒（焦雄屏）也可能是淘氣或逞英雄的複雜心理情結。丁皓（飾亞男）演來也很自然，除了與舉重選手喬宏握手時被握痛了以外，他／她甚至很快便掌握了作為式文男舞伴的技巧。電影中完全沒有提示亞男扮男裝的「苦」，她／他看來興奮極了，即使周旋在式文與卓然之間忽男忽女忙得不可開交，又被父

喬宏眼中的「亞南」到底是男是女？
Ya-nan, Ya-nan or Ya-lan? Kitty Ting Hao playing the gender game.

out of personal preference. It is also unexplained in the film why Ya-nan has to keep such disguise for so long, while she is seen rather hectically switching between genders and differently genderized situations, despite her parents' complaints and later orders of grounding. This is further accentuated by the fact that s/he does not show an awareness of the "plight" of the opposite sex; in fact, she seems rather pleased with her (changeable) outfits, and her/his increasing desirability to *both* Shih-wen and Cho-jan. I would argue that most of the visual pleasure in watching this film comes from the enjoyment of watching Ya-nan enjoying her/himself as *both* genders and the satisfaction s/he gets from her mutable genderized appearance, than from the awareness of Ya-nan's biological sex. In contrast, it is the biological male, Ai-lun, who shows the most discomfort of his being male, which in this case also means having the responsibility (and burden) to *seem* always mature, reliable and considerate but also cowardly.

The other major difference is the suppression of homosexuality as a discourse. The Hollywood transvestite films as discussed by Straayer often produce an opportunity to be read as queer subtexts, especially when images which suggest same-sex desire contradict with heterosexual plots and the tension between the images and the diegesis often produces extra room for imagination and identification in the audience, however otherized. These contradictions are most foregrounded when the disguise causes the characters' desires to be "misread" in the narratives as homosexual. In *You were Meant for Me,* however, heterosexual coupling is never problematized by any implications of homosexuality. The emotional and erotic possibilities which might have motivated Ya-nan to continue playing the young man as desired by Shih-wen are never questioned within the diegesis, not even by the I-know-it-all Ai-lun who would have done anything to spoil the arrangement. The compulsory heterosexual paradigm in the film is so hegemonic that Ya-nan's biological sex is enough to completely rule out the possibility of any erotic authenticity she could have shared with Shih-wen. It is only in the spectatorship that such desires become possible; I, for

母責罵甚至下禁令，她／他也毫無悔意。由於劇情上沒有提供他／她「必須」扮下去的動機，作為觀眾，我們在觀賞他／她易服的姿勢而得到樂趣以外，也可分享這角色在易服時自己得到的樂趣。這易服的樂趣顧名思義來自更換衣服；性別於此名副其實是一套衣飾，可以穿上脫下。不論男裝需要「易」，女裝也要，亞男變亞蘭時要戴上長而鬈的假髮。明顯地（即使在外表上），亞南與亞蘭都不是亞男的樣子，但重要的是兩者皆為亞男所設計及享受的角色。

《遊戲人間》與 Straayer 所論的「暫時易服」電影類型另一最大的歧異，是易服與同性／異性戀之間的關係。Straayer剖析的荷里活電影中，角色的易服經常與他／她的異性戀情慾相矛盾，也提供了被「誤」讀為同性情慾的可能。亞男扮亞南追求式文，卻似乎與亞蘭接受及享受卓然的追求並無矛盾，反而是正正因為與式文的關係，亞蘭得以接觸卓然，而且形成佻皮又和諧、互相扶持的兩對兄妹之間的愛情關係（其中「四」個愛人互通求婚消息一場最見兩對兄妹之間的團結互助）。最後亞男決定放棄亞南的身份，回復女兒身，並不是為了她個人的異性戀情，而是不忍傷害善良的式文。式文發現了亞男的「真正」身份後把感情迅即轉移到病榻中的愛倫，也不過是亞南消失後的副作用，在電影中這兩人的結合最為牽強，有點吃不到好橙爛橙也撿一個的況味。

這樣看來，電影中並沒有任何關於同性戀的提示，因為它根本不構成一個問題，即使對整件事由頭到尾都清楚卻有苦難言的愛倫也沒有片刻懷疑過式文與亞南在搞甚麼。對於愛倫，式文與亞男的性別身份完全主宰了她們可享有的性身份。因為亞男是女子，她便一定是在玩弄式文。只有甚麼都看在眼裡的觀眾，會對瀟灑俊俏、

one, have no problem believing that Shih-wen is truly falling for Ya-nan the baby butch, thus could not care less about the "truth" of her/his biological sex. After all, as revealed in the scene of the dance party, it is as clear as day that Shih-wen is more than ready to also temporarily change her own gender identity to comply with Ya-nan's always changing roles. It takes more than one to pull a drag.

Androgyny, Hybridity and Mutability

Stella Bruzzi particularly distinguishes cinematic representations of androgyny from generic cross-dressing comedies through interrogating the expression of desire in the androgynous image.[5] The androgyne, Marlene Dietrich in *Morocco* (1930) for example, is of blurred sex as well as of blurred sexuality, Bruzzi argues, and could be located at the intersection of multiple (at times contradictory) erotic identifications. Through coalescing the real and the imaginary, the figure of the androgyne generates an eroticism which suggests danger and slipperiness. Through *You were Meant for Me* and its publicity materials, Kitty Ting Hao the teenage idol is being manufactured and marketed as an androgynous image marked by its mutability. As seen in the various issues of *International Screen* published during the film's release, Ya-nan's multiple images and seemingly self-determined and switchable genders also become the selling point of the movie.[6] It is worthnoting that the flexibility and hybridity of Ting Hao's identity does not begin with her gender but in fact begins with the exact moment she joined International Film Distribution Agency (which later became MP & GI) at the age of 16. An understanding of her cultural background might help to shed new lights on the (re)construction of gender identity in her star persona.

Born in Macau, studied for two years in Shanghai and moved to Hong Kong at the age of 10, Ting Hao became a Mandarin-speaking actress only because she was too late for the interviews at the Cantonese Production Unit. While she took crash courses in Mandarin from a private tutor after she had joined, she managed to "pass" as a "Northerner" – a non-Cantonese – in more than 20 Mandarin movies. Ironically, these include the North vs. South series, baby butch 一樣的亞南動心，懷疑式文即使早知道亞南是男是女，也寧願不知道；懷疑如果沒有愛倫的恐嚇，亞南是否會繼續維持與享受她與式文的愛戀，直至永遠。尤其化裝舞會一場揭示，式文享受的，不單是亞南的易服，她也享受用自己的易服來配合對方。喬裝從來便不是單方面的遊戲。

電懋出品：丁皓的中性及身份喬裝

Stella Bruzzi 特別把電影視象構築中的中性策略（androgyny），與一般的易服喜劇類型片分開來。[3] 瑪蓮德烈治的女裝襯衣上加男裝踢死兔兼抽煙明顯地並不是要扮男人，而是把一種要變成「其他」的慾望穿在身上。她象徵危險與越界，因為她表示她不滿足於一般女性所得到的。而在電影中，這種危險加強了她的性感，加強了她對男主角及（男女）觀眾的吸引。亞男形象的多樣及自主也加強了觀眾對她的好感，也是電影的賣點，更是丁皓在她事業的高峰期被電懋捧出來作為新派青春偶像的個人風格。1955 年，十六歲的丁皓欲考國際影片公司（電懋前身）的粵語組，但名額已滿，改考國語組被取錄，同期考入的還有蘇鳳、雷震、田青、楊群等。[4] 丁皓生於澳門，七歲到十歲在上海唸書，十歲到香港。所以她雖懂幾句上海話，母語卻是粵語，國語則是考進電懋後才聘請陳又新老師專門教授。換句話說，丁皓這澳門廣東人，在她主演的廿多部國語電影中一直喬裝「外省人」，其中還包括在《南北和》系列中，演京菜館老闆劉恩甲的女兒，教分不清「舌頭」與「石頭」的張清講國語，來討好地域分明的父親。

丁皓的「語言天才」、[5] 年輕活潑（丁皓出道數年一直被稱為「小丁皓」，其吮食奶瓶盛載的牛奶方能入睡的習慣也被廣泛報導）[6] 使她的女扮男裝也成了她的多變身份、佻皮不定的多種變數之一，減低了她這形象對性別

such as *The Greatest Civil War on Earth* (1961), in which she plays a Northerner who teaches her Cantonese boyfriend to speak Mandarin to please her ethnocentric father.

The subtext of the production of Ting Hao the star speaks to a specific history of Hong Kong culture in the 1950s based on migration, hybridity and in many ways, self-transformation and disguise. The film industry of the 1950s was dominated by Mandarin cinema, much of it produced by personnel from Shanghai. Ting Hao's hybrid background of speaking three dialects boosted her survival skills tremendously in such a society of migrants. And in order to have any significance in the Mandarin and Shanghai-dominated MP & GI, Ting Hao needed her Shanghaiese to socialize and her Mandarin to act, thus upholding a relative cultural homogeneity for the image of the Studio. The irony of Ting Hao playing the Northerner's daughter in the North vs. South series speaks further to the demand for binary oppositions (North versus South; Cantonese versus all others lumped into one) in the popular imaginary of this temporarily stable society. While Ting Hao's cultural hybridity needed to be suppressed, her readiness and skills for self-transformation and disguise translated into her star image in terms of gender. Her cultural mutability provided a pretext for her gender mutability and I would argue, rendered it more convenient and less dangerous. The (necessary and always ready) mutability of her ethnic identity, her widely marketed youth bordering on babyishness[7] created an image of a more predictable instability, all of which help to tone down the potential subversiveness and multiple eroticism of her androgyny. The immaturity and adolescence emphasised in both the star image of Ting Hao and the character image of Ya-nan contrasts significantly, for example, with the maturity and self-consciousness embodied by Dietrich.

This is not to say that *You were Meant for Me* does not provide opportunities for problematizing conventions of gender construction. In fact, as seen in MP & GI productions, the room the Studio allowed to experiment with gender, specifically with masculinity, was definitely more flexible than that it gave to

意識的挑戰。在《遊戲人間》的宣傳刊物上，丁皓被兜售的形象主要是一名乖巧的小男生，並沒有瑪蓮德烈治的形象強調的自覺與夾雜一般危險。[7]這不是說《遊戲人間》的電影文本沒有提供顛覆的可能，而是說，把文本放回電影片場制度及市場策略的脈絡中看，可以更明白文本互涉所構成的張力，電懋作為一種工業模式，如何成功地同時造就、裝載也壓抑着顛覆性別構築，或異性戀模式的論述。而且這種對身份危機的探索、思考與重新肯定，不單是在（男性）性別上，更是在文化身份上。（男性）性別身份危機，可看成是文化身份危機的一種呈現，亦是在市場機制中較為隱晦，輕省又無關痛癢的一種。

焦雄屏認為電懋創作班底從上海逃難到香港，「原是小資產階級的文人嚐盡了求生的尷尬及挫折，對自己的處境充滿了自憐與委屈」，而把這種心理投射在女性角色上。[8]這點出性別身份的再現可以是集體文化身份的一種想象與構成，在父權至上的電影片場制度中，女性角色與女明星的製造自然經常是男創作者的慾望反映。但如果只建立電懋的電影中「女星多是尤物，男星多是失敗者」這種二元對立，又實在簡化了電影中呈現出來的更複雜的男性情結。丁皓在《母與女》（唐煌，1960）中身心受創，絕望地等待出了國的富家少爺張揚回來救她，在《喜相逢》（卜萬蒼，1960）中又演無父無母，被後父母刻薄、被黑社會流氓逼迫，又怕被警察追趕的賣花女，似乎都可看成是劫難中男性自憐心理的投射。同時，這些女性苦難的唯一解藥，則是等待敢於向封建家庭反抗的少爺，帶她們逃出生天。這大概也是電懋的才子們對自身及對社會的冀望。表面上看來，電懋的電影好像都是陰盛陽衰，女明星的風采大大超越男演員。但細心看，

《母與女》：女兒變成了媽媽，洋娃娃卻永遠是囡囡。
Ting Hao with mother and doll (on facing page) and with friend and doll (above) in *Devotion*.

電懋營造出來的男性都是一些極其有趣的形象，而且各具特色。

理想男性

舊的價值觀念跟封建的父權一樣不合理，理應被推翻，新的兩性關係五花八門，如何在多元的文化衝擊下，成為一名「新男人」？如果女性可以暫時成為「新男人」，那男人自己也不得不自我翻新一下。翻新一下則還有希望可爭回天下，只是也許不能再依附舊日的標準。《遊戲人間》揭示了在這瞬息萬變的性別萬花筒中，男性拋棄了固有的部份父權模式，又未找到可以倚傍的新標準來重新鞏固自己的特權之前的徬徨與無奈。電影企圖透過女性的陽性對比男性的缺點來尋找男性自我更新的方向。《遊戲人間》中的雷震（愛倫）是一名大輸家，「你爭不過我是你自己沒用」，最後他雖然贏得白露明（式文），但也不過是丁皓（亞男）讓給他的，他對劇情的進展一些主宰權也沒有，並不是 Laura Mulvey 指的那種推展及掌握故事發展的男主角。[9]但雷震的「憂鬱小生」型與喬宏的「雄獅」型，[10]正正形成強烈對比，成為男性的兩極，一個溫文儒雅，一個強健穩重。式文有這樣的哥哥便應該找愛倫這樣的情人，兩個合起來剛好是一名「理想男性」。這樣看來，亞南這名也會打籃球但依然孱弱（一開始便佯病）的小男生畢竟是多餘的。更有趣的，電影選擇了把這些特性放在兩名男性身上，也揭示了文武的不全。[11]電懋的男性角色雖然有自憐，但未嘗沒有自省。實際上，很多電影中的男性也千瘡百孔，雖然犯錯的是男人，受苦的確實是女人居多，但男性的錯仍然是電影所鞭撻的。《母與女》中的林家和（張揚飾）基於無知與懦弱害死了玲玲（丁皓飾），一生負疚。志堂（喬宏飾）從家和的錯中汲取教訓，選擇愛情而放棄名利，在觀眾心理上補贖了家和的罪。這也是懦弱男人經過反省自責後在堅強男人身上得到重生的例證。

喬宏 + 雷震 = 理想男性？
Roy Chiao + Kelly Lai Chen = Ideal Male?

discussions of cultural ethnicity. Using *You were Meant for Me* as a case in point, while intertextual tension and contradiction among various textual elements carve out many discursive spaces around the issue of "what a man could be", it is also quite spectacular to witness the powerful operations of MP & GI during its golden age, being able to simultaneously contain, employ, manipulate and suppress any discourse that might potentially challenge the heterosexually-biased genderization. In comparison, the class and ethnic specificity of the text remain much more stable; all the characters in *You were Meant for Me* are affluent, educated, Mandarin-speaking upper middle class professionals or their dependents.

Male Psyche in Flux

Peggy Chiao Hsiung-ping has argued that the MP & GI creative personnel, many of whom petty bourgeoisie intellectuals, were full of self-pity and frustrations when they fled to Hong Kong from Shanghai, and therefore needed to project their conflicted psyche

舊社會新世界

如果修身是治國平天下的必經階段，那麼懦弱男人也大概可以透過成為新男人而建立新世界。如果性別不是非男則女的二元，而是可變可塑，隨着角色脈絡、個人樂趣與消費規律而調整更易的話，那樣文化身份也不是非南則北，非南來則本地這樣可以明確劃分。這轉變中的新世界是否可容納到更開放多元的性別，更開放多元的中國文化？電懋高峰期的一群編導演員集合了上海、廣州、香港、澳門的人才，雖然一方面流露了南來的流亡情結，但他們對流氓地痞橫行、貧富懸殊、多文化並存的香港未嘗沒審視。電影中也再現及構築了各種各樣的香港文化符號，不能單單以「過渡」一言蔽之（香港幾時不是在過渡？）。這些夾雜的文化符號，夾雜不定的性別身份，可能便是香港文化身份必然的一部份，從而見證了一個永遠都有危機，又永遠都有可能的香港。大家來到新鮮的香港，協助其經濟起飛的同時，企圖尋找一種共同的關注及跨越文化隔膜、鼓勵消費的創作語言，於是深思熟慮地製作了大量愛情通俗劇及歌舞片。透過這種語言，一個理想世界逐漸成形，在這世界裡，女生可以暫時試享男性的特權，男子可以透過反省及努力，自力更新，成為更好的男人。但一如所有理想世界，這黃金時間並不持久，很快，香港電影便被單向的陽剛及更迎合草根的搞笑所壟斷。

onto the female characters in their productions.[8] This points to an argument that representation and construction of sexual and gender identities are inevitably part of a collective cultural imaginary. In the male-dominated film studio system, the manufacturing of female characters and stars are of course, in many ways, the representation of desire and fantasy of their male producers. While I agree with Chiao that the stardom of the MP & GI culture is one dominated by female sexuality, it is also important to note that the male characters and stars in these films are often representations of a masculinity in crisis, one in flux but yet to be "reformed" and refined.

In *You were Meant for Me,* for example, although much of the focus of the diegesis is on Ya-nan the mischievous young woman and the focus of the image is on Ting Hao the young female star, the desirability of such a focus is however, on her adoption, embodiment and reform of masculinity. Leaving the old society behind, the feudalistic father who did not have a sense of humour and failed to communicate with the youth was outdated and too needed to be left behind. In this new refugee society called Hong Kong, Westernized, temporarily stable and intrinsically hybrid, a new kind of male authority was called for. Ai-lun, with much baggage of traditional Chinese intellectuals, is weak and indecisive, therefore does not seem to fit the bill. What makes a "good man" in this new world? Using her class privileges, Ya-nan is able to transform herself into a gentle, sensitive, strong and decisive young man. Cho-jan seems like a role model as well, but his kind of muscular masculinity is relegated in the film to the realm of the spectacle, into a position of an object to be assessed and gazed on. When Ai-lun protests against Ya-nan's notion of masculinity ("Muscle does not equal masculinity!"), he seems to be protesting more against the popularity of types like Cho-jan, betraying possibly the MP & GI bourgeois intellectuals' attitudes towards the muscleman. The characterization of Ai-lun and Cho-jan could be read as a critique of conventional and traditional stereotypes of masculinity, the inadequacies of both *wen* (the

註

1. 見焦雄屏，〈故國北望：中產階級的出埃及記——談電懋片廠家庭通俗劇及歌舞喜劇反映的矛盾與幻想〉，《電影欣賞》，第88期，1997年8月。
2. 見Chris Straayer, "Redressing the 'Natural': The Temporary Transvestite Film" in *Deviant Eyes, Deviant Bodies: Sexual Re-orientation in Film and Video,* New York: Columbia University Press, 1996.
3. 見 Stella Bruzzi: *Undressing Cinema: Clothing and Identity in the Movies,* London and New York: Routledge, 1977, pp. 173-199.
4. 見〈丁皓之頁〉，《國際電影》，第69期，1961年7月。但《娛樂畫報》，第73期，1967年7月報道丁皓死訊時則記載丁皓十四歲考進電懋。
5. 見《國際電影》，第80期，1962年6月，頁26。
6. 見《國際電影》，第69期，1961年7月，頁36及《國際電影》，第38期，1958年12月，頁8。
7. 見〈丁皓變作男兒身〉，《遊戲人間》特刊，國際電影畫報電影小說叢書。
8. 見焦雄屏，同註1，頁11。
9. 見Laura Mulvey, "Visual Pleasure and Narrative Cinema" in *Screen*, vol. 16, no. 3, 1975.
10. 「憂鬱小生」及「雄獅」都是二人被廣泛報導的稱號，尤見於《國際電影》，也見於〈柔馴的雄獅〉，《香港電影》，第5期，1962年12月。
11. 卓然在《遊戲人間》中的「武」，也不過是參加舉重比賽，是一種純粹裝飾性的，供人觀賞與物化的遊戲。這可看成是文人電影對體力的一種不屑，或小資產階級把男性身體也物化，變成可供消費與觀賞的產品。也可看成是電懋黃金時期的通俗愛情劇中對陽剛的一種呈現及理解。

編按

有趣的是，《遊戲人間》的編劇正正是後來在邵氏揭起「陽剛」之風的張徹，他在電懋還編寫了《無語問蒼天》(1961)、《賊美人》(1961)、《桃李爭春》(1962)等多個出色的劇本。

intellectual) and *wu* (the physical) in themselves. The "ideal" form of masculinity seems to lie somewhere between Ai-lun and Cho-jan, an amalgamation who could very well look like the well-off gentleman-athlete Ya-nan. The film points to the reformability of masculinity, a new form of manhood, ironically through the body of a (class-specific) woman. It is in such irony that marks the instability of identity in these formations, culturally and sexually.

Amidst a generation of artists and intellectuals undergoing voluntary and involuntary exile, the ability and will to reform and transform oneself became key. While other ways of transformation, including socially and/or politically, seemed less feasible and definitely less marketable in a refugee society, forms of self-renewal through unconventional genderization could be seen as simultaneously a desirable and irrelevant outlet. *You were Meant for Me* reveals a sense of loss of traditional standards, a will to challenge conventions and a yearning for the new, in order to reinstate and perpetuate the privileges under threat among the male elites in migration. In this imaginary new world this collective yearning temporarily creates and sustains, women can get a taste of some of the male privileges, men can become better men through constant self-reflection, suffering and will (Ai-lun has to go through surgery and the threat of losing Shih-wen). But like any other golden age or new world, the spirit of experimentation and self-reflexiveness did not last long. Hong Kong cinema would soon be dominated by a more homogeneous and self-assured type of masculinity once it entered the 1970s.

其他參考資料

（1）左桂芳，〈我看雷震〉，《電影欣賞》，第88期，1997年8月，頁87-90。
（2）于毅，〈電懋公司的崛起變革及沒落〉，同參考資料（1），頁7-9。
（3）張建德，〈類型、作者與連結：從五十年代電懋公司的喜劇看香港電影的作者問題〉，同參考資料（1），頁18-25。

游靜，電影及錄像工作者，作家。新作有《我餓》（1999），《好郁》（2002）。現任教於香港理工大學設計學院。

Yau Ching, film/videomaker and writer. Recent film/video works include: *I'm Starving* (1999), *The Impossible Home* (2000) and *Let's Love Hong Kong* (2002). Currently teaching at the School of Design of the Hong Kong Polytechnic University.

Notes

1. See Chris Straayer, "Redressing the 'Natural': The Temporary Transvestite Film" in *Deviant Eyes, Deviant Bodies: Sexual Re-orientations in Film and Video,* New York: Columbia University Press, 1996, pp. 42-78.
2. See Peggy Chiao Hsiung-ping (Jiao Xiongping), "Looking North to the Old Country: The Middle Class Exodus" in *Film Appreciation* (in Chinese), no. 88, August 1997.
3. See Chris Straayer, op. cit., p. 42.
4. See Chris Straayer, op. cit., p. 42.
5. See Stella Bruzzi: *Undressing Cinema: Clothing and Identity in the Movies*, London and New York: Routledge, 1977, pp. 173-199.
6. See "Ting Hao Becomes a Man" in *You were Meant for Me* Booklet (in Chinese), International Screen Film Novel Series.
7. Ting Hao (Ding Hao) was often reported as having the habit of carrying a milk bottle with her and drinking milk before she could sleep. For example, see *International Screen* (in Chinese), no. 69, July 1961, p. 36 and *International Screen,* no. 38, December 1958, p. 8.
8. See Peggy Chiao Hsiung-ping, op. cit.

Editor's note

It's worth noting that *You were Meant for Me* was written by none other than Chang Cheh (Zhang Che), who later launched the very masculine martial arts tradition in Shaws. His other scripts for MP & GI include *Song without Words* (1961), *The Girl with the Golden Arm* (1961) and *It's Always Spring* (1962).

跨越地域的女性：電懋的現代方案

- 黃淑嫻 -

前言：現代的處境

1956年正式成立的電懋[1]（電影懋業有限公司的簡稱）是屬於新加坡國泰機構的一部份。電懋是一間跨國公司，主事人陸運濤在管理業務時，亦是採取一種跨國遙控的方式。據記載，雖然電懋當時由前永華片廠經理鍾啟文管理，但身在新加坡的陸運濤，每週星期四都會批閱電懋的財政及合約等，[2]我們可以推測，對於連起電懋在香港和新加坡兩地的辦公室，現代的通訊科技是不可缺少的。另一方面，電懋的班底是一群受過高等教育、對中西文化有所了解的人。從老闆陸運濤，到監製鍾啟文、製片主任宋淇、導演易文，編劇組的姚克、秦亦孚，當然還有張愛玲等等，他們都是懂得中外文化、眼界廣闊的人。[3]可能因為跨國公司在製作上的方便、東南亞市場的要求，再加上製作班底對現代文化的認識，電懋電影有一個特色，就是劇中人（尤其是女性）

Women who Cross Borders: MP & GI's Modernity Programme

- Mary Wong -

Foreword: The Modern Situation

MP & GI was a multi-national company and boss Loke Wan Tho (Lu Yuntao) employed a multi-national style of management to remote-control the company. According to records, MP & GI was managed by Robert Chung (Zhong Qiwen) but Loke would go through all the contracts and financial reports every Thursday.[1] Thus we can say that modern technology is indispensable to link up the offices in Hong Kong and Singapore. Also, MP & GI staffs were well-educated and well versed in both Chinese and western cultures. From Loke to Chung to production manager Stephen Soong (Song Qi) to director Evan Yang (Yi Wen) and screenwriters like Yao Ke, Qin Yifu (Nellie Chin Yu, Qin Yu), and of course Eileen Chang (Zhang Ailing); they shared a broad world view.[2] Perhaps due to the company's border-crossing nature, market demands in Southeast Asia and a creative team familiar with modern culture, MP & GI films often feature characters (especially women) who

經常可以坐飛機或遊船跨越地域、接受現代教育、吸收外國文化，能操多國語言，這是五六十年代的香港電影中比較罕有的現代處境，大概只有好像電懋這樣的組合，才能夠產生這樣的現代處境。

這裡我所指出的現代不限於一種物質的處境，現代亦是一種內心矛盾的處境。[4] 有評論家在分析張愛玲的電懋劇作的時候，指出《六月新娘》(1960) 中的葛蘭不想為父母或者滿堂的親客走入結婚禮堂，她需要先解決內心對婚姻的疑慮，結婚儀式於她才產生意義，評論家認為這是劇本的現代性所在。[5] 評論家指出的現代性是那種要求自己不斷反省，雖然矛盾的處境最終未必一定能夠解決。《六月新娘》及其他張愛玲編的劇本，外表看來好像是無甚特色的男女追逐鬧劇，這個分析卻指出電影的前衛性。「女性不願意無條件接受既來的命運」是電懋電影的現代之處，然而，在精神的層面以外，我們亦不能忽視電影中所呈現的一個現代的物質世界，這一點是構成電懋電影現代性的一個很重要部份。

有影評家指出電懋的電影脱離現實，例如《香港之星》(1962) 等是寄情於一個幻想的國際之上；再者，雖然女性是電懋電影的焦點，但女性只淪為男性的慾望客體。[6] 大概作為商業電影公司的電懋不能忽視票房收益吧，鞏固明星體製及在電影類型中反覆創作是慣用的商業手段。電懋的現代性並不是清教徒式的，正如影評家指出，電影的背景或其物質的世界、女性的歌舞等，可能是用作招徠，但在這以外還有其他嗎？我認為電懋電影中的女性並不全是現代進程中的犧牲者，[7] 她們會在或明或陰的地方駐足考慮身處的處境。我認為與其批評電懋的電影脱離現實，或許我們可以嘗試把電影視作香港電影歷史上一次早來的、對現代的追求，來討論其得失。這樣的考慮或許可以對電懋的評價公平一點。

《香港之夜》中的尤敏

You Min in *A Night in Hong Kong*.

travel abroad, speak many languages, are educated in modern ways and are open to foreign cultures. Rare for 1950s and 1960s Hong Kong films, these are situations that probably only MP & GI could produce.

This modernity is not limited to a materialistic situation, but is also one of inner conflicts.[3] When analysing Eileen Chang's MP & GI scripts, critics have noted that Grace Chang (Ge Lan) in *June Bride* (1960), won't commit to marriage until after she resolves her inner doubts and this is exactly where modernity exists.[4] Modernity, critics explain, is constantly reflecting upon one's self, though at the end there might be no solution to the conflicting situation. *June Bride* and other Eileen Chang scripts might seem like mundane love farces, but this analysis accurately locates the film's progressiveness. The modernity of MP & GI films lies in the women's refusal to accept their destiny. However, besides the spiritual angle, we should not neglect the material world shown in the films. This is an important component in the formation of modernity in MP & GI films.

本文分析電懋的電影如何呈現一段女性與現代的關係，所選取的電影全以女性跨越國界來展現一種現代處境為主，這個選擇是要凸顯電懋作為跨國公司的特質，又帶出現代的物質世界在電懋電影的重要性。本文的討論只能算是一個初步的見解，因為電懋的黃金年代，即 1956 年到 1964 年陸運濤在位管理期間，電懋拍攝了約九十五部國語片，[8] 但我們今天能夠看到的是非常少，希望日後能夠有機會看到更多電懋電影，補充本文的淺見。

《玉女私情》：跨國與曖昧的道德

首先，我們從母親一代的跨國問題開始。由唐煌導演、秦亦孚改編的《玉女私情》(1959)，跨國的並不是玉女尤敏，而是有私情的王萊。《玉女私情》的第一幕是飛機抵達啟德機場，十六年前拋棄親生女兒尤敏及丈夫王引、跟情人私奔到意大利羅馬的王萊，現在要回來跟女兒會面。開始的時候，尤敏雖然並不知道她稱呼為姨媽的王萊其實就是她的生母，但觀眾在王萊的傷感和王引對她的冷淡中已經可以猜出一二。

王萊及飾演她第二任丈夫的藍天虹帶出一個現代的環境、一個物質的世界。他們從羅馬回港住在高級的半島酒店，相對於王引的鑽石山房子；王萊在電影中不斷為尤敏購買很多東西，包括三腳鋼琴、華麗的衣服，甚至連生日蛋糕也要比王引買的大出數倍。但尤敏最後沒有隨王萊到羅馬學音樂，表明了電影對王引所代表的樸實和刻苦的世界有所肯定。最後我們還知道王引患了病不能生育，他其實一早已經懷疑尤敏不是他的親生女兒，但他仍然把她當作自己的女兒撫養，他被描寫為一個值得尊敬的父親和男性。相對於他，勢利自私的藍天虹是電影的諷刺對象。

跨國在《玉女私情》中雖然隱隱帶着負面意義，代表女性對物質的追求及對家庭的不負責任，但王萊這個角

Some critics find MP & GI films divorced from reality, that films like *Star of Hong Kong* (1962) are built upon an imagined internationality. Although women are the focus of MP & GI films, they're always degraded as the object of male desire.[5] A commercial studio, MP & GI couldn't ignore box office and it's a commercial practice to reinforce the star system and make genre films. The modernity in its films is not puritanical. As critics have noted, the background or the material world in the films, and scenes with women singing and dancing are probably commercially motivated. But is there more to it? I think women are not all victims of the modernisation programme.[6] They will slow down and contemplate their situation, in open or subtle ways. Instead of criticising MP & GI films for being divorced from reality, a more objective way maybe to consider their merits as an early search for modernity.

This essay analyses the relationship between women and modernity in MP & GI films. The theme of the selected films is mainly about women who travel to different regions and therefore display a modern situation. This choice is made to emphasise MP & GI 's characteristic as a multi-national company, and to bring out the importance of modern material world in the films of MP & GI. The discussion in this essay is a preliminary one. During the golden age of MP & GI from 1956 to 1964, when Loke Wan Tho was in charge, about 95 Mandarin films were made.[7] Only a fraction them can be seen today. I hope I can have the opportunity to see more of MP & GI films and expand the views in this essay.

Her Tender Heart: Crossing Borders and Moral Ambiguity

We start with border crossing by the mother generation. In *Her Tender Heart* (1959), directed by Tang Huang and written by Qin Yifu, it's not the young Lucilla You Min who goes abroad but the other, Wang Lai. The first scene is a plane arriving. Wang Lai, who abandoned her daughter and husband Wang Yin and eloped to Rome 16 years ago, is coming back for a reunion with her daughter. Though You Min doesn't

色，又帶出另一種比較曖昧的道德。電影中唯一的兩段回憶，都是來自王萊的，她憶起十六年前臨別的矛盾，她又記起十六年後她在羅馬憶念女兒的情形。王萊在這兩場中都表現得不由自主，電影帶着同情呈現她捨棄女兒的矛盾。但對於捨棄一段沒有愛情的婚姻，王萊雖然感到抱歉，但從來沒有表現後悔。她在十六年後面對女兒的質問，她仍然勇於以愛情來解釋她離家出走的原因，電影對婚後的女性追求愛情是肯定的，這樣的道德觀在當年可算相當大膽。在五十年代末的香港電影中，大概我們不可能看到尤敏拋下養育多年的、已成殘廢的父親，遠赴外國尋找理想，但電影為我們寫下另一個女性的命運：王萊最後再一次離開香港，踏上她的跨國旅程。

《空中小姐》：青天上的解放與約束

易文編導的《空中小姐》（1959）為我們提供了一個更貼近現代的跨國故事。這次再不牽涉家庭恩怨，電影是關於年青的女兒葛蘭，她要飛上青天，當一個跟她母親那一代不一樣的女性。空中小姐是當時香港及亞洲非常時髦的行業，這個職業代表了新的科技、新的生活體驗、現代教育和現代的禮儀談吐。女主角葛蘭在投考空姐時以國語、廣東話、英語、法語、泰語等多種語言説出「您要一杯咖啡嗎？」來表示她具有跨國的能力，同時把電影的空間（及吸引力）推到國際的層面上。電影不忘以空姐的訓練來製造娛樂笑料，例如圍着毛巾量度身高體重、頭頂着書手拿着咖啡走路等等。這些訓練場面多用遠鏡頭來拍攝，把一群空姐全攝在鏡頭內，她們整齊的步伐、熨貼的制服，又何嘗不是一個景觀呢？

然而，電影一方面以訓練的場面作招徠，另一方面又通過葛蘭對訓練起懷疑。訓練背後要求的是無條件服從，《空中小姐》的焦點其實是葛蘭逐漸發覺這項工作未必

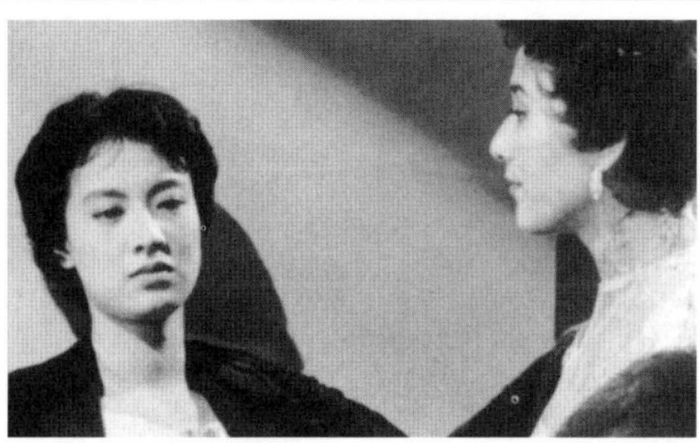

《玉女私情》中的母（王萊）與女（尤敏）

Mother (Wang Lai) and daughter (You Min) in *Her Tender Heart*.

know this "auntie" is her mother, Wang's sadness and Wang Yin's coldness give the audience some ideas.

Wang and her husband bring forward a modern environment, a material world. In contrast with Wang Yin's home in Diamond Hill, the couple returns from Rome and stays in the luxurious Peninsula. In the film Wang Lai keeps buying gifts for You, including a grand piano and fashionable clothes, even the birthday cake she bought is several times bigger than the one Wang Yin bought. However, You Min eventually decides not to go to Rome with her to study music. This implies her affirmation of the simple and frugal world Wang Yin represents. At the end of the film we also know that Wang Yin is infertile and has been suspecting that You is not his blood-tied daughter; yet he brings her up as his own daughter. He is described as a respectable father and man. By contrast, Wang's snobbish and selfish husband is ridiculed by the film.

Going abroad subtly carries a negative meaning. It represents woman's desire for the materialistic world and her irresponsibility towards family. But Wang Lai's role also brings forward a moral ambiguity. The only two flashbacks belong to her. She remembers the conflict when she was about to leave and how she misses her daughter while in Rome. In both sequences Wang's performance suggests she has no choice, and the film portrays her conflict with sympathy. Wang is sorry about ending a loveless marriage but never shows any regret. Confronted by her daughter 16 years later, she bravely explains that love is the reason she left home. The film affirms a married woman's right to pursue love, and considering the time, this is audacious. In the late 1950s Hong Kong films, You Min may not leave her disabled father to pursue her ideals abroad, but the film established another woman's destiny: Wang Lai leaves Hong Kong once again, crossing borders.

Air Hostess: Limitations and Liberation in the Sky

Written and directed by Evan Yang, *Air Hostess* (1959) offers another border-crossing story that is even closer to modernity. Family affairs are not involved this time,

適合她。在第一場化粧舞會中，葛蘭高唱着「我要飛上青天」，保守的男朋友勸她不要當空中小姐，因為這個職業是不能結婚的，但葛蘭要脱離這種以婚姻為終點的女性命運，空中小姐這個越洋的職業，讓葛蘭可以從傳統女性的處境解放出去。

《空中小姐》要説的是葛蘭在解放與約束之間徘徊的故事。葛蘭兩次打算辭退工作，第一次是在訓練期間，她無法服從「客人永遠是對的」的教導，第二次是她在飛機上受到喬宏所飾演的飛機師的無理呼喝，從而感受到工作壓力。葛蘭逐漸發覺這項工作並不如她所想這樣簡單，其實當中有很多約束、有很多因職位帶來不平等的地方。從這方面看，《空中小姐》並沒有把女性的現代處境理想化，反而是實際地指出了問題。

葛蘭在這個跨國的過程中，她究竟要尋找甚麼呢？在第一場的舞會中，保守的男朋友指出空姐是不能結婚這個規條，觀眾大概會預示這將會為葛蘭帶來矛盾，然而《空中小姐》並不是這樣。葛蘭要追求的是在服務性的工作中，保持自己的尊嚴，她希望她和她的客人是平等的，她希望她和她的男性飛機師同事是平等的，這是一個相當現代的考慮。所以我們看到電影中葛蘭瞪着她的大眼睛，配合大特寫，駁斥喬宏傷害了她的自尊心，然後教訓他應該好好檢討一下自已的態度。

雖然喬宏最後「英雄救美」，把女性從跨國的危機（跨國走私）中拯救出來，但電影並沒有特別肯定這個男性角色。相對於細心的機師助手雷震，喬宏處處顯得小家氣及守舊，令人懷疑這樣的結果只是為了當年保守觀眾的大多數不會太難受。葛蘭比喬宏更能享受及溶入外國文化中，葛蘭以她的歌聲為觀眾介紹台灣、曼谷等地，觀眾又隨着她走到新加坡的夜總會中，看她在異地表演歌舞。無疑這些外遊的場面有點

but the film is about the young Grace Chang, who wants to fly up to the sky, to be a woman different from her mother's generation. Air hostess was then a trendy occupation, representing new technology, new experiences, modern education, modern etiquette and manners. When taking the entrance exam, Chang asks "do you want a cup of coffee?" in Mandarin, Cantonese, English, French and Thai to show her ability to go abroad, expanding the scope (and attractiveness) of the film to an international level. The film does not forget to use the training process of the air hostesses to create entertainment, such as going through physicals while wrapped in towels or walking with books on the heads and holding cups of coffee. Shot from a distance to include all the trainees with their uniformed steps and fitted uniforms, these scenes are spectacles in themselves.

The film at once uses the training to entertain and question it, through Chang. Training requires obedience. In fact the focus of the film is that Chang gradually realises that this is not a job for her. In the first scene, she sings *I Want to Fly High to the Sky* in a costume party; but her conservative boyfriend tries to convince her not to be an air hostess because the job is not compatible with marriage. Yet she wants to escape the destiny that marriage is the ultimate goal for women. The border-crossing job of air-hostessing liberates her from the traditional women's situation.

Air Hostess is a story about Chang's struggle between limitations and liberation. She tries twice to quit. The first during training, when she can't obey the teaching of "customers are always right". The second is when the pilot, played by Roy Chiao (Qiao Hong), yells at her, making her feel the pressure of work. Gradually she realises this job is far from easy; that in fact there are limitations and inequality to the job. From this perspective, the film never idealises women's modern situation; in fact it reveals its problems.

What is Chang looking for in her border-crossing journey? In the dance party, when her boyfriend

像旅遊廣告，而葛蘭的歌舞亦收了商業效果，但葛蘭比起保守的喬宏，更能善用這項跨國工作所帶給她的好處。電影完結於一個婚禮中，外表好像一切都很完美，亦可能預示了葛蘭將來的命運。葛蘭這個現代女性並不是要為工作而放棄愛情，但她在完場之前向客人解釋飛機的好處，讓我們感到她還是要繼續當空中小姐，以歌聲跨越文化。

《香港之星》：跨國與性別政治

葛蘭在不少電影中都呈現一種直率但帶點魯莽的性格，在《空中小姐》或者更出名的《曼波女郎》(1957)中如是，就算在《星星．月亮．太陽》(1961)的結局中，她萬念俱灰，退入修院，但她還是在葉楓和尤敏三人之中，最敢於表達自己感情的一個。葛蘭的形象，大概比較符合現代女性的定義，與此相比的另一個跨國女性尤敏，她在不少電影中性格內向柔順，好像接近傳統女性的形象。然而，在電影圈發展下來，尤敏比葛蘭有更多跨國的機會，更能走進現代的亞洲城市裡，這一點是很有趣的。

戰後電懋和日本電影公司東寶曾經有八回的合作，[9]而最具代表性的可算是由尤敏和寶田明合作的三部電影：《香港之夜》(1961)、《香港之星》(1962)、《香港．東京．夏威夷》(1963)。尤敏是第一個在戰後成功打進日本市場的女星，當時她在日本有「李香蘭第二」之稱，[10]在近年出版的《日本映画人名事典女優篇》中，我們仍然可以找到她的介紹。[11]無論在電影的內容上、行銷發行上或觀眾的接受上，尤敏無疑是戰後跨國女性的代表了。然而，她的現代路途要比葛蘭的迂迴得多[12]。

由千葉泰樹執導、笠原良三編劇的《香港之星》是講由尤敏飾演的香港女子，她在日本女子醫科大學讀書，放

mentions the rule against marriage, the audience might expect this will bring conflict, but *Air Hostess* takes another direction. Chang's pursuit is to preserve one's dignity in a service industry. She wants to be treated equally with her customers and the male pilots, a very modern consideration. So we see a close-up of Chang, eyes wide open, scolding Roy Chiao for hurting her self-esteem and asking him to re-examine his attitude.

Though Chiao plays the eventual 'hero' who saves the damsel from a border-crossing crisis (trafficking), the film never shows approval for him. Compared to the considerate assistant pilot, Kelly Lai Chen (Lei Zhen), Chiao is petty and conservative and the ending was probably an effort to please the conservative majority. More so then Chiao , Chang is able to accept and enjoy foreign cultures. Her songs take the audience to places like Taiwan, Bangkok and a nightclub in Singapore. These scenes might seem like travelogue and Chang's musical performances fulfil the commercial requirement, yet next to the conservative Chiao , Chang is more able to take advantage of her border-crossing job. The film ends with a wedding and everything seems perfect again. Chang is a modern woman who won't relinquish love for career, but near the end, she explains the advantages of flying to her customers, making us think that she will continue her job as air hostess, crossing cultures with her songs.

Star of Hong Kong: Border-Crossing and Sexual Politics

Chang often plays a straight, sometimes even blunt, person, as in *Air Hostess* or the renowned *Mambo Girl* (1957). Even in *Sun, Moon and Star* (1961), after losing all hope and retreating to a convent, she is more willing than Julie Yeh Feng (Ye Feng) and You Min to express her feelings. Her image is probably closer to the definition of a modern woman. By contrast, You Min, another woman who crosses borders, is more gentle, an image closer to the traditional woman. Interestingly, it is You who has

假回港的時候遇上由寶田明飾演、在香港工作的日本男子，兩人其後發展出一段愛情。在六十年代的香港電影來説，《香港之星》呈現了一個非常現代的處境。首先，飛機所代表的現代科技，在《香港之星》扮演一個舉足輕重的角色，劇中人可以迅速的在亞洲多個城市之間穿梭，包括香港、東京、北海道、吉隆坡及新加坡，電影呈現了一個現代亞洲的版圖。電影中的語言亦很國際化，尤敏經常在談話中突然改變語言，從日語跳到英語，又從英語跳到國語，在不同的情況下，主動選擇一個能表達自己的語言。這個設計可能是因為尤敏本身的日語水平不高，不能背上一整段日語對白，但這個「缺陷」為尤敏營造了一個有主動力的女性形象。這是當年電懋和東寶合作的電影的一個特色。

現代的處境亦沖淡了一般文藝片既有的離愁別緒。《香港之星》的最後一幕是剛從父親的喪禮走出來的尤敏，正乘坐計程車前往啟德機場跟寶田明見面，但可惜趕不上。尤敏只好站在山頭望着剛上升的飛機緩緩離開這個城市，電影就在這裡完結，沒有交代這段跨國感情的結果。但尤敏在遙望飛機時沒有表現得很傷心；大概現代的觀眾，亦沒有流下同情的眼淚，因為電影的現代處境告訴觀眾，尤敏可以選擇乘坐飛機到東京去找寶田明，他們只是錯失了一次機會，在亞洲城市的現代網絡中，還有很多機會等着他們呢，因此離愁也變為淡淡的、收斂的。

這些都是跨國帶來的現代處境，但《香港之星》的跨國愛情本身有很多陳俗的地方，性別的角力比前述的電影更見複雜。香港女子尤敏追求與日本男子寶田明的愛情，但需要得到林沖飾演的香港男子的准許才能夠達成夢想，尤敏的跨國令她陷入兩個父權社會之中。寶田明是六十年代日本商行的受薪人員，代表了當時經濟發達

more opportunities to go abroad, traveling deeper into modern Asian cities.

After WWII, MP & GI had eight co-productions with Toho of Japan,[8] and the most representative are the three films starring You Min and Takarada Akira: *A Night in Hong Kong* (1961), *Star of Hong Kong* (1962) and *Hong Kong, Tokyo, Honolulu* (1963). You was the first female star who successfully entered the Japanese market after the war. The Japanese audience regarded her 'Yamaguchi Yoshiko the second'[9] and is included in the recently published book *Illustrated Who's Who of Japanese Cinema: Actresses*.[10] Judging from her films, sales and distribution figures or popularity among audience, You is a representative of a border-crossing women. But, compared to Grace Chang, her road to modernity is longer and rougher.[11]

Directed by Chiba Yasuki and written by Kasahara Ryozo, *Star of Hong Kong* is about a Hong Kong woman (You) studying in the Nippon Joshi Ika Daigaku, who comes back home on vacation and falls in love with a Japanese man (Takarada) working in Hong Kong. The situation in *Star of Hong Kong* is very modern for a 1960s film. The airplane, symbol of modern technology, plays an important role. Characters shuttle between Asian cities, drawing a map of modern Asia in the film. The use of languages is also international, with You frequently jumping between Japanese, English and Mandarin during conversations, choosing the language that best fits the occasion. Perhaps her Japanese was not fluent and she found it difficult to memorise long paragraphs of dialogue, but this 'flaw' constructs an image of a woman with active initiatives. This is one characteristic of the MP & GI-Toho co-productions.

The modern situation also dilutes the sentimental mood typical of melodramas. The last scene shows You taking a taxi from her father's funeral to say goodbye to Takarada at the airport. She doesn't make it and the film ends with her standing on a hill, watching the plane as it leaves the city. We don't know what becomes of the lovers, except that You is not particularly sad. The modern audience likely didn't

的日本；林冲是東京大學醫院的醫生，是中國社會受尊重的人物。寶田明被描寫為一個慾望的對象、一個港日女性爭奪的理想情人，電影中不同國籍、階層的女性都不約而同愛上他。林冲則是一個正派、但刻板的香港男子。對於尤敏，林冲扮演一個長者的角色，他代表她的父親、老師，提醒尤敏要專心讀書，不應沉迷於愛情。如此，林冲不但有別於寶田明，這兩個男性更是處於對立的位置。林冲最後回到香港繼承尤敏父親的醫務工作，這是延續一個父傳子的故事。而正因為這樣，尤敏可以離開香港，無牽掛地追尋她在海外的愛情。電影這樣的處理是把香港男性放回一個父權的位置上，讓他在自己的地方發展，同時間亦巧妙地排除了他對這段港日愛情的威脅。

在這個跨國族的愛情故事中，港日男性之間的對立並沒有出現在港日女性之間。儘管尤敏和飾演她的好友的團令子，明顯地同時愛着寶田明，她們卻仍然是一對要好的金蘭姊妹。她們可以互相穿對方的民族服裝、她們經常在房間中互訴心聲，她們是被描寫為很大方的女性，甚至連愛人也可以割愛相讓。這種處理是把港日女性和男性放置在一個典型的性別位置上：女性是平和的，男性是好勇的，而《香港之星》只會讓沒有威脅性的女性跨越港日國界。

儘管王星璉本身有一個專業，但電影要肯定的不是她事業成功的一面，而是她所散發出的一些女性傳統的素質：高雅、温柔、服從，尤敏以這樣的氣質，擊敗性格爽直、富有現代感的團令子，成為日本男性的夢中情人。通過這段跨國的愛情、通過對香港女性的理想化，日本男性好像要告訴當時新一代的日本女性（觀眾），如果她們要叛離傳統女性身份的話，他們將會在另一個文化中尋找他們理想的情人呢！[13]

跨國族愛情故事中的尤敏與寶田明

You Min crosses the Hong Kong - Japan border with Takarada Akira in *Hong Kong, Tokyo, Honolulu.*

shed any tears too, for the modern situation in the film tells the audience that You can always fly to see Takadara. They may have missed an opportunity, but within the modern network of Asian cities, other opportunities await them. The sadness of separation is therefore subdued.

These modern situations are results of border crossings. However, the film's romance is not without clichés and the gender struggle is much complicated then the films mentioned above. You has to gain approval from a Hong Kong man (Lin Chong) before she can pursue her relationship with a Japanese man. Crossing borders traps her in two patriarchal societies. Takarada is a salary man of a Japanese company, a symbol of the prosperous Japan. Lin is a doctor of the Tokyo University Hospital, a respected person in the Chinese community. Takarada is described as an object of desire, chased by both Hong Kong and Japanese women. Lin is a decent but boring man, a father figure to You who keeps reminding her to focus on her studies and not love. In fact, the two men represent opposites. Later, in a situation unlike the passing of family from father to son, Lin goes back to Hong Kong to inherit the practice of You's father. You is thus free to leave Hong Kong to pursue her love. The film puts the Hong Kong man back to a patriarchal position, letting him develop his career in his own place, cleverly dissolving his threat to the border-crossing romance.

In this international love story, the opposition between Hong Kong and Japanese men does not appear between women. Although You's best friend (Dan Reiko) is obviously in love with Takarada, they treat each other as sisters. They exchange ethnic costumes and share secrets in their room. They are portrayed as open-minded women, even willing to let the other have the lover. This representation puts Hong Kong and Japanese men and women in a typical gender position: women are peace-makers, men are fighters. And in *Star of Hong Kong*, only non-threatening women can cross over the Hong Kong-Japan border.

《香港・東京・夏威夷》：一記娛樂性兼歷史性的耳光

電懋和東寶合作，由千葉泰樹執導、松山善三編劇的《香港・東京・夏威夷》繼續把跨國版圖擴大，故事的場地橫跨太平洋，人物穿梭於亞洲和美洲；日本人、中國人、海外日僑和華僑之間所說的語言更變化多端。《香港・東京・夏威夷》要比《香港之星》來得更具國際化。電影有一個娛樂性豐富的跨國愛情故事，尤敏飾演一個有主張、性格開朗的居夏威夷第二代華僑，她獲選為「夏威夷小姐」冠軍，獎品就是往香港及東京的飛機票，她帶着她那洋化的性格走到亞洲，處處碰壁，為電影帶來笑料。寶田明飾演尤敏的大學同學（加山雄三）的哥哥，在夏威夷探望弟弟之時，認識了尤敏，兩人成為一對歡喜冤家，一同到東京及香港，最後結為夫婦。然而，在通行無阻的國際邊界背後，電影沒有呈現一段理想化的國際關係。電影的現代性是帶出不同文化之間既想溝通但又存在着隔膜，每個人物背後有自己的歷史，不能夠一下子向對方說清楚。

電影以一主一副的女性跨國故事為中心，主線是尤敏的故事，站在背後的是草笛光子飾演的戰時新娘的故事。草笛光子原是寶田明中學時代的戀人，其後嫁給美軍，移居夏威夷。寶田明在夏威夷與她重遇，一天，當他們散步的時候，碰上尤敏和加山雄三，草笛光子馬上低下頭，顯得非常尷尬的離去。尤敏遂跟兄弟二人說出草笛光子的故事：她的丈夫曾在尤敏父母的餐館裡工作，是一個吊兒郎當的男人，又對太太使用暴力，草笛光子只好在菠蘿園工作維持生計。這段辛酸的跨國歷史，是由前程光明的尤敏，以熱心提供資料的態度、滔滔的說出來。尤敏對草笛光子雖有同情，但只是一種概括的關懷，草笛光子的故事只是尤敏所知的眾多戰時新娘的故

Although You plays a professional woman, the film doesn't emphasise her career, but her traditional female qualities: elegant, gentle and submissive. With these qualities, she defeats the straightforward, modern Dan to become the dream girl of Japanese men. It is as if through this border-crossing romance and the idealisation of Hong Kong women, Japanese men are telling the new Japanese women that if they give up their traditional role, the men will find their perfect lovers in another culture![12]

Hong Kong, Tokyo, Honolulu: An Entertainment and Historical Slap in the Face

Directed by Chiba and written by Matsuyama Renzo, *Hong Kong, Tokyo, Honolulu* is more international than *Star of Hong Kong*, expanding the border-crossing map across the Pacific into the US, as languages used by Japanese, Chinese and immigrants become complicated. The film has an entertaining story, with You Min playing an assertive, spirited Chinese American. Elected Miss Hawaii, her prize includes a ticket to Hong Kong and Tokyo. Her Americanized personality gets her into trouble in Asia, creating comedic situations. Takarada is the brother of her college friend (Kayama Yuzo) who meets You while visiting Hawaii. A feuding romance develops as they travel to Hong Kong and Tokyo, and they eventually get married. But the international relationship behind the crossing of borders is far from perfect, as the film's modernity reveals the obstacles between cultures despite efforts to overcome them.

Two border-crossing stories are featured, the main one with You and a secondary one involving the war bride played by Kusabue Mitsuko. The latter was Takarada's high school sweetheart and later married an American soldier. They meet again in Hawaii, but running into You and Kayama, she leaves, embarrassed. You tells the brothers that Kusabue's husband once worked at You's family restaurant and is an irresponsible man who beats his wife, who is forced to work at a farm.

事之一。然而，電影為觀眾展現了草笛光子的獨特性格，尤其在第二場草笛光子和尤敏在東京的夜總會再相遇時，我們看到草笛光子是一個自力更生、及勇於面對過去的女性。但因為語言問題，尤敏未能夠完全理解到。草笛光子首先用日語告訴寶田明，她回到日本後，發覺夏威夷才是她想念的地方，她在自己表演的夏威夷歌舞中感受到這點；然後她改用英語向尤敏說她要回夏威夷尋找她的丈夫重新開始。因為不懂日語，尤敏對於草笛光子的感受只能夠明白一半，兩人總是隔了一重，而電影為我們呈現了這個有心無力的隔膜。

另一方面，尤敏和寶田明兩人雖然完滿收場，但他們的所謂結婚，其實只是一則寫在照片後的消息，可以看出電影有意拒絕以傳統的婚禮場面來作結，拒絕一種肯定性。再者，電影最後的一場是尤敏正準備乘坐飛機回夏威夷，好像暗示了她並不打算做一個過埠新娘，不想像草笛光子一樣離鄉別井到另一個文化去。這段現代的跨國愛情留下一點沒有解決：寶田明始終不知道尤敏的身世。外表開朗的尤敏，其實有一段比草笛光子更複雜的歷史。她是一個孤兒，親生父母分別死於北京及香港，另有一妹被香港一個家庭收養；尤敏童年時，曾許配給一名稱鄭浩的男子，訂下了婚約。尤敏的身世連結起中國傳統禮教及一段坎坷的中國歷史，包括戰爭、走難及華人的流徙。成為第二代華僑的尤敏，大可以把這段歷史拋諸腦後，對於所謂的婚約亦可以一笑置之，但尤敏並不能夠這樣。尤敏表現出對倫理有一個開放的觀念，與傳統講求血緣關係的觀念不同，她沒有因為自己不是養父母的親生女兒而耿耿於懷，反而欣賞養父母的偉大。但現代的尤敏雖然口裡說不記掛自己是孤兒，但到了東京，她還是要走到孤兒院，照顧跟她同樣身世的兒童。尤敏對傳統的婚約只當作笑話來處理，但當妹妹在

You, the young woman with a bright future, tells this tragic border-crossing story with a readiness to provide information and a general kind of sympathy for Kasabue, in the sense that this is only one of the many war bride stories. But the film goes on to show Kusabue as a self-reliant woman, courageous in facing her past. Because of language barrier, You fails to see this side of her. Kusabue tells Takarada in Japanese that she missed Hawaii after coming back to Japan and she realises that while performing Hawaiian song and dance. Then, she tells You in English that she's going back to Hawaii to have a new start with her husband. Not understand Japanese, You can only understand half of Kusabue's feelings.

Although You and Takarada's romance has a happy ending, the wedding is announced on the back of a photograph. The film refuses to end with a wedding scene, rejecting a concrete conclusion. Also, the last scene shows You getting ready to fly back to Hawaii, implying that she doesn't want to be married off to a foreign country. This modern, border-crossing love story leaves something unresolved: Takarada is not aware of You's past. In fact, the seemingly cheerful You has a history even much complicated then Kusabue. She was orphaned young when her parents died, one in Beijing and the other in Hong Kong. In her childhood, she was engaged to a man named Zheng Hao. Her background links traditional Chinese ethics with a sad history of China, including war, the fleeing of war and the dispersion of Chinese population. A second generation overseas Chinese, You can ignore this history and the engagement, but You Min doesn't. Her attitude towards family ethics is different from the traditional belief in blood ties. She's not upset for being an adopted child and admires her parents. Though she says she doesn't mind being an orphan, she goes to an orphanage to take care of children with similar backgrounds. She laughs at arranged marriage but when her sister tells her about plans to marry Zheng Hao, You is saddened. Just when she is about to mock

生母的墳前，把鄭浩和自己的婚訊告訴她的時候，開朗的尤敏還是感觸得獨自離去。彷彿當她正想嘲笑歷史的時候，恍然發覺歷史已經在她遠赴他鄉的期間改變了。值得注意的是，寶田明認識的是另一面的尤敏，是一個在夏威夷陽光下長大的快樂人，是一個處處跟他作對的倔強小姐，以上討論的場面寶田明並沒有在場，他沒有機會知道尤敏複雜的一面。

《香港・東京・夏威夷》還包涵了另一段更沉重的歷史。表面是一齣愛情鬧劇，內裡卻牽連着中日歷史關係。寶田明在電影中因為找了半天也找不到走失了的尤敏，其後摑了她一巴掌，尤敏帶點嘲諷的明白到這原本就是日本男性表達愛情的方法。電影到了最後一幕，尤敏在臨上飛機前回報了寶田明一巴掌以代替「Goodbye Kiss」。心水清的觀眾應該記起這一記耳光可以追溯到同是東寶拍攝的《支那的夜》(《支那の夜》，1940)，電影中李香蘭扮演一個中國女郎，她被一個正直的日籍男子（長谷川一夫）掌了一巴掌，然後愛上了他。這一巴掌被中國觀眾視之為一種辱華的行為，其後李香蘭被判為漢奸，她在自傳中寫到這是文化不同的原因。[14]事隔二十多年，戰後東寶和電懋的合拍片中，借尤敏回報寶田明的那一巴掌，似乎要表示日本有意回應歷史，向中國表示歉意呢。但問題大概並不能夠在互相掌摑上解決，《香港・東京・夏威夷》以同一個方法來回應《支那的夜》，這表現出電影未有真正觸到中日文化不同之處。

結論

可能尤敏跨得愈遠，要面對的問題更多，但《香港之星》的背後還有一些故事。據説尤敏不想拍接吻鏡頭，不想做自己不願意的事，因此劇本要大幅度修改。[15]另外，尤敏在她的文章〈日本拍片經驗談〉[16]中，寫下一

history, she realizes that history has changed while she was away from home. Takarada knows only one side of You – the cheerful, strong-willed girl who grew up under the Hawaiian sun and stands sup to him – and not her more complicated side.

Hong Kong, Tokyo, Honolulu also includes an heavier piece of history. In this light comedy, a relationship between the histories of China and Japan is involved. In the film, after spending half a day looking for You, Takarada slaps her on the face when he finds her. You now understands this is the way Japanese men express their love. In the last scene, before You gets on the plane, she returns the slap as a "Goodbye Kiss". In another Toho production *China Night* (1940), Yamaguchi Yoshiko plays a Chinese woman. She is slapped by a righteous Japanese man (Hasegawa Kazuo) and falls in love with him. Chinese audience at the time considered this insulting and Yamguchi was considered a traitor. In her autobiography, Yamaguchi explains this is only a cultural difference.[13] Over two decades later, after the war, in this Toho-MP & GI co-production, with the slap You returns to Takarada, is Japan trying to respond to history, to apologise to China? Yet a problem like this probably cannot be resolved by slapping each other. Using the same method to reply to *China Night* and *Hong Kong, Tokyo, Honolulu* fails to deal with the real difference between Chinese and Japanese cultures.

Conclusion

Maybe the farther You Min goes, the more challenges she encounters, but there are more stories behind *Star of Hong Kong*. It was said that the script was revised because You didn't want to do kiss scenes.[14] She insisted on not doing what she didn't want to do. She wrote about the language problems and cultural differences of the

些兩地合拍時，因語言和習慣上的分別而帶來的困難。尤敏似乎在銀幕以外另有保存自己個性的方法。在美國遊歷五個月後的她，寫下〈在美國看到些甚麼？〉[17]長文一篇，文中處處表現出她作為香港人的身份，從細節去了解海外華人的文化。尤敏另一面的跨國經驗，在她真切與熱情的文字中表現出來。

在五六十年代的香港，電懋電影中的跨國故事和現代處境，可能未必得到大多數觀眾的認同，或者只把電影當作一場幻夢。但在二十一世紀回看，當香港人因為教育普及化、移民、或旅遊種種，開始在不同文化中穿梭往返，我們或可以逐漸認識到這些拍於四十年前的香港電影所有的局限及其現代性。

co-production in an article.[15] She even had her own ways preserving her personality beyond the silver screen. After a five-month trip in the US, she wrote a long article about her attempts to understand oversea Chinese culture through details of life.[16] In her sincere and compassionate writing, You expresses the other side of her border-crossing experience.

The Hong Kong audiences of the 1950s and 1960s might not identify with the border-crossing stories and modern situations in MP & GI films, or they simply considered them fantasies. Looking back from the 21st century, when the people of Hong Kong – with better education, frequent travels and immigration – have more experience negotiating different cultures, perhaps we can also have a better understanding of the limitations and modernity of these Hong Kong films.

Translated by Grace Ng

註

1. 見 Lim Kay Tong: *Cathay - 55 Years of Cinema*, Singapore: Landmark Books, 1991, p. 145.
2. 見 Lim Kay Tong，同註 1，頁 146。
3. 他們各人的生平、留學背景及著作都可以在別的地方找到，這裏從略了。
4. 見 Marshall Berman: *All that is Solid Melts into Air,* London: Versa, 1985, p. 345.
5. 見也斯，〈張愛玲與香港都市電影〉，收錄於羅卡編：《超前與跨越：胡金銓與張愛玲》，第廿二屆香港國際電影節回顧特刊，香港：臨時市政局，1998，頁 147。
6. 見焦雄屏：〈故國北望：中產階級的出埃及記〉，《電影欣賞》，第 88 期，1997 年 8 月，頁 17。
7. 女性作為現代進程的犧牲者，或者是他者（Other of modernity），這個意見在電懋同時期的一些歐洲電影中可以見到，例如意大利導演安東尼奧尼（M. Antonioni）的《赤色沙漠》（*Red Desert*, 1964）等一系列電影。
8. 這個數字，我是參考 Lim Kay Tong，同註 1，頁 213-220 的片目。電懋亦有粵語片製作組（1953-1964），著名的影片如《花都綺夢》及《璇宮艷史》。見翁靈文，〈電懋影業公司粵語片組〉，收錄於林年同編：《五十年代粵語電影回顧展》，第二屆香港國際電影節回顧特刊，香港：市政局，1978 年，頁 50-51。
9. 這裏「合拍」的意思是打正招牌共同製作那種。詳細片目見林佩華整理、羅卡校訂，〈跨界的香港電影片目選輯（1946-1984）〉，於羅卡編：《跨界的香港電影》，第廿四屆香港國際電影節回顧特刊，香港：康樂及文化事務署，2000年，頁180-181。
10. 見門間貴志，〈中華偶像の变遷〉（中華偶像的變遷），於四方田犬彥編：《李香蘭與東アジア》（李香蘭與東亞），東京：東京大學出版會，2001 年，頁 234。
11. 見《日本映画人名事典・女優篇──下卷》，東京：電影旬報社，1995 年，頁 870-871。
12. 對另外一些港日合作電影如《蝴蝶夫人》（1956）、《香港白薔薇》（1967）等的性別分析，我在另一篇文章曾討論到。見〈五、六十年代香港電影中的跨國身份初探〉，《國際東方學者會議紀要》，第46冊，東京：東方學會，2001年，頁36-51。
13. 此論點我是從珍娜・馬卓蒂（Gina Marchetti）的有關《生死戀》（*Love is a Many-Splendored Thing*, 1955）和《蘇絲黃世界》（*The World of Suzie Wong*, 1960）的文章啟發出來的。見Gina Marchetti, "White Knights in Hong Kong: Love is a Many-Splendored Thing and The World of Suzie Wong" in *Romance and the "Yellow Peril" : Race, Sex, and Discursive Strategies in Hollywood Fiction,* Berkeley: University of California Press, 1993, p. 116.

Notes

1. See Lim Kay Tong: *Cathay - 55 Years of Cinema*, Singapore: Landmark Books, 1991, pp. 145-146.
2. Their biographies, academic backgrounds and writings are not listed here because they are available elsewhere.
3. See Marshall Berman: *All that is Solid Melts into Air*, London: Versa, 1985, p. 345.
4. See P.K. Leung, "Eileen Chang and Hong Kong Urban Cinema" in Law Kar, ed.: *Transcending the Times: King Hu & Eileen Chang*, the 22nd Hong Kong International Film Festival catalogue, Hong Kong: Provisional Urban Council, 1998, p. 147.
5. See Peggy Chiao Hsiung-ping, "Looking Back to the Old Country: The Middle Class Exodus" in *Film Criticism* (in Chinese), no. 88, August 1997, p. 17.
6. The idea of women as a sacrifice for modernity or the Other of modernity can also be found in some European films of the same time, such as Antonioni's *Red Desert* (1964) and his other works.
7. This figure is from the filmography of Lim Kay Tong, op. cit., pp. 213-220. MP & GI also has a Cantonese film group (1943-1964). Distinguished works by this team including *Sweet Dreams* and *My Kingdom for a Husband.* (aka *The Romance of Jade Hall)* See Weng Ling-wen, "MP & GI: Cantonese Film Group" in Lin Nien-tung, ed.: *Cantonese Cinema Retrospective (1950 - 1959)*, the 2nd Hong Kong International Film Festival catalogue, Hong Kong: Urban Council, 1978, pp. 58-59.
8. By "co-production" I mean the films produced between Hong Kong and foreign companies. Please refer to a detailed filmography, June Lam compiled, Law Kar, ed., "Border-Crossing Films in Hong Kong (1946-1984)" in Law Kar, ed.: *Border Crossings in Hong Kong Cinema*, the 24th Hong Kong International Film Festival, Hong Kong: Leisure and Cultural Services Department, 2000, pp. 180-181.
9. See Momma Takashi, "Evolution of Chinese Idols" in Yomota Gorky Inuhiko, ed., *Yamaguchi Yoshiko and East Asia* (in Japanese), Tokyo: Tokyo University Press, 2001, p. 234.
10. See *Illustrated Who's Who of Japanese Cinema: Actresses* (in Japanese), vol. 2, Tokyo: Kinema Junposha, 1995, pp. 870-871.
11. I have discussed the issue of gender analysis of other Hong Kong-Japanese co-productions such as *Madame Butterfly* (1956) and *The White Rose of Hong Kong* (1967) in another essay: "Border Crossing Identity in 50s and 60s Hong Kong Film" in *Transactions of the International Conference of Eastern Studies*, Vol. 46, Tokyo: The Institute of Eastern Culture, 2001, pp. 36-51.
12. This point is inspired by Gina Marchetti's essays on *Love is a Many-Splendored Thing* (1955) and *The World of Suzie Wong* (1960). See Gina Marchetti, "White Knights in Hong Kong: Love is a Many-Splendored Thing and The World of Suzie Wong" in *Romance and the "Yellow Peril": Race, Sex, and Discursive Strategies in Hollywood Fiction,* Berkeley: University of California Press, 1993, p. 116.
13. See Yamaguchi Yoshiko, Fujiwara Sakuya: *Li Xianglan: The First Half of My Life* (in Japanese), Tokyo: Shinchosha, 1987, p. 138 and Wong Ainling, ed.: *Li Xianglan/ Yoshiko Yamaguchi Special*, the 16th Hong Kong International Film Festival catalogue, Hong Kong: Urban Council, 1992.
14. See Song Jiacong, "The Legend of You Min" in *City Magazine* (in Chinese), March 1981. The essay is later included in John Chan Koon-chung: *Half Chinese and Half Western City Notes* (in Chinese), Hong Kong: Youth Literary Book Store, 2000, pp.78-82.

14. 見山口淑子、藤原作彌：《李香蘭我の半生》（《李香蘭：我的半生》），東京：新潮社，1987年，頁138及黃愛玲編：《李香蘭（山口淑子）專題》，第十六屆香港國際電影節特刊，香港：市政局，1992年。
15. 見宋家聰，〈尤敏傳奇〉，《號外》，1981年3月；該文後收錄於陳冠中：《半唐番城市筆記》，香港：青文書局，2000年，頁78-82。
16. 見尤敏，〈日本拍片經驗談〉，《國際電影》，第86期，1962年12月，頁34-35。
17. 見尤敏，〈在美國看到些甚麼？〉，《國際電影》，第36期，1958年10月，頁10-33。

黃淑嫻，東京大學中文系訪問研究員，專注研究電影工業中的港日關係。
Mary Wong, visiting researcher at Tokyo University. Now specialising in Hong Kong / Japan relationship within the film industry.

15. See You Min, "My Filming Experience in Japan" in *International Screen* (in Chinese), no. 86, December 1962, pp. 34-35.
16. See You Min, "What I Saw in the US?" in *International Screen* (in Chinese), no. 35, October 1958, pp. 10-33.

通俗的古典：《野玫瑰之戀》的懷思

- 李歐梵 -

香港學者余少華在一次學術會議[1]中提到：1950至1960年代的香港電影的歌舞片有兩大類型——黃梅調（如《梁山伯與祝英台》〔李翰祥，1963〕）和模仿百老匯和荷里活影片的西式歌舞片；前者是中國傳統文化的翻版，而後者則是一種西化的表徵——它代表了海外華人觀眾對西方通俗文化的嚮往。余少華教授並在會議當場播放了一段葛蘭演唱的西式流行歌曲，出自影片《野玫瑰之戀》（1960）。令我倍感吃驚的是：這首歌曲不是百老匯歌舞片的翻版，而是出自西洋古典音樂——比才的歌劇《卡門》，而且唱法與我所聽過的各個西洋歌劇女高音不同，甚至也和荷里活同時期的影片《卡門瓊絲》（*Carmen Jones*, Otto Preminger, 1954）大相逕庭。乍聽之下，我覺得葛蘭的聲音沒有原來角色的野氣和性感（這當然是主觀印象式的看法，不足為憑），但在曲子的抑揚頓挫中大展其「花腔」，雖與歌劇唱法不同，但也自有其風味，遂引起我進一步「追蹤」的興趣。

The Popular and the Classical: Reminiscences on *The Wild, Wild Rose*

- Leo Lee Ou-fan -

In an academic conference entitled "Contemporary Asian Popular Culture ", organised by the Lingnan University's Department of Cultural Studies, 11 October 2001, Hong Kong scholar Yu Siu-wah mentioned there were two types of musicals in the Hong Kong cinema. The first type is the *huangmei diao* (Yellow Plum Opera), of which the most representative example is Li Hanxiang's *The Love Eterne* (1963); the second is the Hollywood-Broadway musical imitation. The former duplicates traditional Chinese culture, while the latter symbolizes Westernization, representing the longing for Western popular culture among the overseas Chinese audience. Professor Yu went on to play a tape of Grace Chang (Ge Lan) performing a Western-style popular song from the soundtrack of *The Wild, Wild Rose* (1960), a film produced by the MP & GI studio. What startled me about the song was that it isn't an imitation of a Broadway musical number but rather that it was derived from an opera, namely Bizet's *Carmen*. Grace Chang's rendition of the number is different from other renditions by the various Western sopranos that I have

承蒙香港電影資料館的黃愛玲女士的安排，我得以觀賞《野玫瑰之戀》的錄影帶，得以窺其全貌，才發現此片中的歌曲除了一首是原作外，其他四首皆出自西洋歌劇選曲，計有：威爾第歌劇《弄臣》(*Rigoletto*) 中的〈女人善變〉(La donna e mobile)，普契尼歌劇《蝴蝶夫人》中的〈一個好日子〉(Un bel di)。萊哈 (Franz Lehár) 的輕歌劇《風流寡婦》的一首選曲，以及《卡門》中的〈哈巴尼拉舞曲〉(Habanera)。

黑色電影的影響

我的記憶或許有差錯（只看了一遍，未能核對），但全片從故事到人物——甚至葛蘭在片中跳的西班牙舞——皆模仿《卡門》，則毫無疑問。此片曾在第七屆香港國際電影節回顧展放映，電影學者李焯桃在節目簡介中說：「本片的故事情節，很容易叫人想起馮・史登堡的名作《藍天使》(*The Blue Angel*, Josef von Sternberg, 1930)：音樂教師漢華（張揚）失去了教職，來到麗池夜總會當洋琴師，卻迷上了綽號『野玫瑰』的女歌星鄧思嘉（葛蘭），甚至為了她而傷人入獄；出獄後與她同居，生活潦倒之餘，又誤會她水性楊花，竟將她扼死。……影片幾乎完全不花篇幅去刻劃兩人熱戀的甜蜜，反而不斷強調它的破壞性（傷害了所有人，最後毀滅了一切）；佔去影片不少時間的六首插曲的曲詞，也無不貫徹這種嘲弄愛情的負面態度。」[2]

另外三位影評人——羅卡、張建德和何思穎都不約而同地把《卡門》的原曲和當代香港的「陰暗」面連起來，有人說這個歌女是香港的「北角卡門」（羅卡），也有人說她在灣仔（張建德），但三人都點出此片之氣氛與荷里活「黑色電影」(film noir) 的關係，從中又演變成另一種「歌舞黑色電影」(musical noir)（何思穎），可謂極有見地。[3] 然而荷里活的黑色電影，往往以男性偵

heard. On first hearing it, I felt that Grace Chang's voice did not possess the wild, untamed nature of the character (naturally, this is a very subjective impression). However, in her modulations of the song and her coloratura passages, Chang conveys her own very special flavour. It aroused my interest to pursue the film further.

Noir Influence

An opportunity came for me to see a tape of the film, by arrangement of Wong Ain-ling of the Hong Kong Film Archive. I discovered that apart from one original number, four other numbers were adapted from well-known operas: "La donna e mobile" from Verdi's *Rigoletto*, "Un bel di" from Puccini's *Madame Butterfly*, a number from Lehár's *The Merry Widow*, and "Habanera" from *Carmen*. My memory of the film may be flawed (I have only seen it once), but from the story and characters – indeed from Grace Chang's Spanish dance number – the film appears to have been wholly derived from *Carmen*. In the programme notes of the 7th Hong Kong International Film Festival, critic Li Cheuk-to wrote: "The plot easily recalls Josef von Sternberg's *The Blue Angel* (1930): music teacher Hanhua (Chang Yang / Zhang Yang) loses his job and works as a piano player in the New Ritz nightclub. He is infatuated with female singer Deng Sijia (Grace Chang) nicknamed 'Wild Rose', and because of her, he goes to jail convicted of inflicting injury upon another person. On his release, he lives with her, but their life together is marked by frustration and deprivation. Misunderstanding her to be unfaithful, he finally strangles her to death.... The film does not attempt to describe the couple as a pair of happy lovers; instead there is an unrelenting thrust to emphasise destruction (everyone is harmed, and everything falls apart in the end): the six songs which occupy much of the film's running time are entirely devoted to mocking love."[1]

Three other critics – Law Kar, Stephen Teo and Sam Ho – coincidentally reached the same conclusion that the film associated *Carmen* with Hong Kong's dark and seedy side. Law Kar stated that the song girl was a "North Point Carmen", while Stephen Teo said the film alluded to Wanchai's nightlife. However, all three noted

探為主要英雄，女性大多是禍水，當然禍水中自有尤物（femme fatale），但「尤物」的命運本身卻並非其「幽暗」的主旨。換言之，從女性理論角度而言，這類影片中的禍水或尤物型女人還是處於被動的「被窺視」地位，而男性仍然處於視野的中心。此片難能可貴之處，我認為是在仍然以男性為本位的價值系統中卻把女性放到主位，也許這就是李焯桃將之與《藍天使》相提並論的原因。（然而我認為此片沒有《藍天使》的頹廢氣氛，而張揚扮演的角色更與《藍天使》中的老教授相差甚遠。）本片主角雖嘲弄愛情，但她仍然是愛情的奴隸，也因愛而死，所以李焯桃説得對：「『愛情』無疑是影片的主題」。我認為王天林的導演手法，也處處在這個「愛情」觀的主題上大動手腳，但也沒有黑色電影所慣有的懸疑性，卻在「鏡頭調度、情調、氣氛、節奏與葛蘭的聲線形體表情高度配合，精彩得簡直是扣人心弦」（羅卡）。換言之，全片的主題就是這位野玫瑰歌星，而歌星的靈魂當然表現在她的演唱，所以此片的六首歌曲（我只記得五首）雖佔去影片不少時間，仍然是全片情緒的關鍵。這就令我回到本文探討的主題——葛蘭所唱的歌曲和西洋歌劇——特別是《卡門》的關係。

中國流行曲與西洋歌劇

為甚麼《野玫瑰之戀》捨中國的流行曲而就西洋歌劇？雖然後者的選曲被改成西洋流行曲的甚多，但是在曲式結構上仍大異其趣。我認為歌劇——特別是義大利歌劇——的作曲及唱法與流行歌基本的不同是它出自詠唱（aria）而不出自節奏（beat），所以聽歌劇很難隨歌起舞，而流行曲必須堅持一種舞步的beat，即使唱法變化再大，這個「步調」不能改變得太多，所以伴奏的樂器中往往用鼓打出音節，就是這個道理。記憶中，我差一點把《野玫瑰之戀》和《曼波女郎》（1957）混在一起，原因除了葛蘭外，就是兩片皆用曼波（Mambo）步。

the film's atmosphere was akin to Hollywood's film noir and that the film's achievement was to have concocted a "musical noir" (Sam Ho)– a very insightful observation.[2] However, the heroes of Hollywood's films noir are often male detectives, and the women are mostly destructive creatures or *femmes fatale*. The substance of noir is not necessarily the fate of the femme fatale. In other words, from the perspective of feminist theory, the femmes fatale are passive objects of the gaze and men remain at the centre of the field of vision. In my opinion, the rare achievement of *The Wild, Wild Rose* is in shifting the traditional male position to the female who becomes the centre of focus. This may be the reason why Li compares the film to *The Blue Angel*. (However, I feel *The Wild, Wild Rose* does not have the decadent atmosphere of *The Blue Angel* and Chang Yang's character is far from being the old professor played by Emil Jannings.)

Though the film's female lead mocks love, she remains a slave to love, and dies because of love. Hence, Li's statement that love is "undoubtedly the main theme of the film" is correct. I do think that director Wang Tianlin has in all respects focused on this theme but without the usual suspense of film noir. Wang's genius is displayed in his "brilliant integration of scene arrangements, the tone and mood, the atmosphere and the rhythm, and the musical form and structure of Chang's voice as well as her performance" (Law Kar). In other words, the film revolves around the songstress Wild Rose, and the spirit of the songstress is expressed in her musical numbers. Hence, the six songs (I can only remember five) are crucial to the plot. I return to the premise that I began with – Grace Chang's songs and their relation to the opera *Carmen*.

Chinese Pop and Western Opera

Why does *The Wild, Wild Rose* eschew popular Chinese songs and turns instead to Western opera? Though many popular songs have been derived from opera, the form and structure of opera retains its own distinctive flavour. The basic difference between opera, particularly Italian opera, and popular song is that in opera, the presentation of song is in the form of aria and is not driven by beat. That's why it is difficult to dance to opera, while popular songs flow to the beat

《野》片中的新作主題曲〈Jajambo〉用的就是曼波步，葛蘭因而使出渾身解數，大跳曼波。但六十年代除了流行曼波外也跳「恰恰」(cha-cha)；前者需要扭動屁股，後者特重走跳步，有時還要手拉手套頭轉圈，充滿青春氣息。《野》片中採用的《卡門》選曲〈哈巴尼拉舞曲〉也是一種舞步，原曲出自歌劇第一幕，卡門從香煙工廠放工，和士兵調情，然後帶跳帶唱地唱出這首著名的「詠唱調」。曲詞大意是：愛情像一隻不馴的小鳥，又像一個吉普賽小孩，目無法紀；你不要我，我偏愛你；如果我愛上你，你可要小心；你以為小鳥是你的，它可要展翅飛翔，你不要它，卻會陷入情網。在我看過的此齣歌劇影片（*Carmen*, Francesco Rosi, 1984）中，這場戲是卡門和諸吉普賽女工合唱，略有載歌載舞，跳的當然是西班牙舞步，但表演並不太成功，因為人物性格尚不明顯。其他歌劇院演出此劇時，還加上卡門與眾女工爭風吃醋的場面，以突出其桀驁不馴的個性。

妙的是在《野玫瑰之戀》中也有葛蘭和另一個女歌星沈雲大打出手的場面，而片頭葛蘭咬着一朵野玫瑰，以此代表愛情的「野性」，也甚切題。這首出自《卡門》的曲子，在片中也以愛情為主題，歌詞（由李雋青填寫）前兩句是：「愛情不過是一種普通的玩意，男人不過是一件消遣的東西……」下面接着是：「甚麼叫情，甚麼叫意，還不是大家自己騙自己；甚麼叫癡，甚麼叫迷，簡直是男的女的在做戲。」這場戲，是葛蘭在夜總會舞台上唱出來的，在形式上和原作頗為接近，所以令人（至少像我這樣的觀眾）憶起原歌劇的唱詞和唱法。

葛蘭受過聲樂訓練，在當時港台影界絕非等閒之輩。1960年10月18日香港《新生晚報》何觀（編按：即張徹）的一篇影評就提到：葛蘭的唱歌「在時下國片女演員中是不作第二人想的，因為她唱爵士，有其『古典』根基」。[4] 我認為正因為她有古典根基，所以才敢向古

《野玫瑰之戀》中的葛蘭與張揚
Grace Chang and Chang Yang in *The Wild, Wild Rose*.

of dance steps even though the style of singing may vary, which explains why the most common accompanying instrument in popular song is the drum. In my subconscious mind, I am prone to associate *The Wild, Wild Rose* with another Grace Chang movie, *Mambo Girl (1957)*, and the reason for this is because I recall that both movies use the Mambo beat. In *The Wild, Wild Rose*, the original song "Jajambo" is performed in the Mambo beat, and Grace Chang utilizes all her skills at her disposal to perform the dance. In the 1960s, apart from the Mambo, the other popular dance beat was cha-cha. The former emphasises movement in the hip area, while the latter emphasises feet movement and occasionally the hands to overlap the head – a dance beat brimming with the spirit of youth.

"Habanera" from *Carmen* was named after a dance. In the opera, it is sung in the first act as Carmen comes out of the cigarette factory and flirts with the soldiers, dancing and singing at the same time. The lyrics stress the theme of love in almost paradoxical terms: "Love is a rebellious bird that no one can tame…Love is a gypsy child, he has never heard of the law. If you don't love me, I must love you; if I love you, look out for yourself! The bird you thought was yours beat its wings and away it flew – you wait for it no longer – and there it is!" In Francesco Rosi's *Carmen* (1984), Carmen and a chorus of gypsy girls perform the aria, in singing and dancing mode. But the performance doesn't strike me as successful because it doesn't bring out the nature of her character. When performed on the stage, some productions add touches to this aria, such as Carmen inciting jealousy among the factory girls, in order to stress Carmen's libertarian, untamed nature. One of the most intriguing scenes in *The Wild, Wild Rose* shows the same effect: Grace Chang fighting with a rival song girl. The film's opening presents a shot of Grace Chang with a rose clenched between her teeth, the rose symbolizing her wild untamed nature.

In the film's adaptation of "Habanera", the lyrics (written by Li Junqing) similarly underline the paradoxical nature of love: "Love is nothing more than a common play thing. Man is only an amusement to kill

典歌劇挑戰，雖然在日本配樂家服部良一的改編後，節奏略有改變，但旋律依舊，所以在曲中「耍花腔」(譬如在詠唱「愛—情」和「男—人」，甚至用法文唱「l'amour」)的時候，就必須施展她自己的招數了。我認為她唱得較不少西洋歌劇名星更有韻味，雖然沒有Julia Migenes-Johnson（上述1984年《卡門》影片的女主角）那麼野，當然也沒有卡拉絲那種獨一無二的戲劇性歌喉。但改編以後，她可以更自由些，不必像受過傳統歌劇訓練的女高音（其實卡門此角是女次高音）那樣受到原曲譜的限制。（如果此文可以附帶錄音的話，我就可以指出葛蘭故意「滑腔」的地方，也是她演唱最精彩的片段，我在嶺南大學的學術會議上第一次聽到，就為之着迷！）

《野》和歌劇《卡門》的互文性

一般關於研究電影的學術文章，很少談到音樂。浸會大學的葉月瑜教授是一個例外，她曾出版過一本專著：《歌聲魅影：歌曲敍事與中文電影》，廣徵博引，但未講到這部電影，也沒有談到五六十年代的香港電影，但書中附有一篇關於電影流行音樂的譯文，卻恰好為本文提供一個理論上的依據，援引於下（原作者是戴樂為〔Darrell William Davis〕)：

假如說最隱諱、最稀有的古典音樂都避免不了互文的運作，那麼流行音樂則是徹頭徹尾處於仲介居中的狀態。流行歌曲除了是互文外，也是富含種類各有不同的多文本。流行歌曲喚起我們對某種歷史時期的聯想、對某表演者的記憶與印象，和對我們自身歷史的各種回想。因此流行歌曲被放到電影中或許會使敍事變為複雜，或者還可能會截斷、破壞敍事。但這正是流行歌曲令電影和媒介研究充滿上下起伏樂趣之處。[5]

所言極是。《野玫瑰之戀》中引用西洋歌劇選曲，當然是一種「互文性」，但它非但使「敍事變得複雜」，而

time. What is love? What is sentiment? A massive fraud perpetrated by all and sundry! What is passion? What is infatuation? A game men and women play!" The whole sequence is Chang's introductory number in the nightclub. The number is similar in style to the original "Habanera", which immediately evokes (at least to me) the original's lyrics and method of delivery. Grace Chang had received vocal and musical training, which made her something of a rare bird in the Hong Kong film industry. In a film review published by the *New Life Evening News*, October 18, 1960, the critic He Guan (a pseudonym of Chang Cheh / Zhang Zhe) wrote: "Among the female stars of current Mandarin cinema, Grace Chang's singing is inimitable, because in singing jazz she brings along a base of classical training."

In my opinion, it is precisely because Chang had received classical training that she dared to take up the challenge of tackling classical opera. Though the Japanese composer Hattori Ryoichi rearranged the song and the rhythm was modified, the melody remained basically intact. Chang seized the opportunity to strut her stuff, particularly in the coloratura passages (where she stretches out the syllables "love" and "men"). In my opinion, her rendition is as good as any of the renditions by Western opera stars, although she doesn't approach the sensuality of Julia Migenes-Johnson (the star of Rosi's film), and of course doesn't attain the dramatic voice of Maria Callas. However, the song is adapted to her special talents, and her rendition is much freer for all that, since there is no need to prove herself as a trained classical singer that traditional sopranos would have been required to do (in fact, the role of Carmen requires a mezzo-soprano). (If it were possible for me to attach a recording of the song to this text, I would be able to demonstrate Grace Chang's coloratura passages – the most outstanding segments of her performance. When I first heard the song in the Lingnan conference, I was immediately hooked.)

Intertextuality

In the writings of film scholars, there have been very few that discuss music in films. An exception is Professor Yeh Yueh-yu's *The Sound of Singing in the*

且更為「跨媒體」的研究理論提供另一種「跨文化」和「跨語文」的複雜性(更遑論「跨歷史」的情境問題)。一般西方學者至此就裹足不前,只為了「政治正確」而提出尊重不同文化的自主性,但很少進入另一種非西方文化作進一步研究;而作中國通俗文化的研究者又太重當代性,沒有歷史感,除了緊跟西方理論外,對西方文化傳統(更遑論西方古典音樂)茫然無知。《野玫瑰之戀》對研究者的挑戰恰在於此,特別是在廿一世紀初重新回顧這部1960年出品的影片,其敍事性已經顯得不重要,幾乎成了一種模式(formula)——我們甚至可以說:所有流行的電影和音樂都脱離不了某種模式——值得回想的反而是某個表演者(如阮玲玉或葛蘭)在某部作品中曾給我們的印象。而這些印象是片段的,而且早已脱離了原作中的敍事結構;而對我們自身歷史的各種回想,也是和這些片段密切相關,我們所作的詮釋其實就是福柯所説的「考古」工作,但福柯兄作知識考古,對流行歌曲沒有興趣。(即使是羅蘭巴特筆下的「神話」研究,也和視覺媒體的關係較密切,和聽覺或音樂的關係不大。)且舉兩個粗淺的例子:一般懷舊者談到三四十年代的上海電影或通俗文化的時候,往往提到周璇和白光,似乎一曲〈四季歌〉或〈夜上海〉就可以勾起無盡的歷史回憶。王家衛在拍攝《阿飛正傳》(1990)和《花樣年華》(2000)時,也談到聆聽當年的流行曲(但他的《旺角卡門》〔1988〕似乎只在片名上與《卡門》偶合)。問題是:那些流行曲經過特殊的演唱者在某種媒體——或跨媒體,如影片和唱片——中展現後,如何勾起我們的回憶?回憶的形式和內容是甚麼?如何找到歷史上的「定位」(contexualization)?這一連串的問題,我認為只靠理論的衍伸或衍義是不夠的,需要作實質性的個案研究。

Cinema: Song Narration and Chinese Cinema (Taipei: Yuan-liou Publishing Co., Ltd. 2000). The book is comprehensive and it quotes copiously from many sources, but it does not mention *The Wild, Wild Rose*, nor does it mention the Hong Kong musicals of the 1950s and 1960s. It does include a text by Darrell William Davis, quoted from the article *In the Event of Sound*, from the Taiwan journal *Film Appreciation*, discussing popular songs in the movies. This text provides a theoretical basis for my own discussions in this essay. I quote below (from page 237 of the book):

If classical music, even the most rarefied and hermetic of serial compositions, is intertextual, then popular music is intermedial. Popular songs are intertextual but also extra-textual, calling up associations from specific historical periods, performers, and all manner of personal memories from one's past. Their inclusion in a film score may complicate or disrupt themes designed into the narrative, but this is exactly what makes them fascinating to film and media studies.

The words are well put. The adaptations of Western opera in *The Wild, Wild Rose* are a case of "intertextuality", but it hasn't complicated the narrative. Rather it has added a cross-cultural and cross-linguistic complexity to the research of cross-media theory (not to mention questions of cross-historical situations). Western scholars generally go no further than mouthing platitudes about the virtues of different cultures for the sake of political correctness; very few venture into a non-Western culture to carry out further research. As to the students of Chinese popular culture, the focus is usually on contemporary developments, lacking a sense of history. At the same time, apart from keeping in step with Western theory, there is ignorance about the traditions of Western culture (not to mention knowledge of Western music). Here lies the challenge of *The Wild, Wild Rose*. Looking back at this 1960 production in the 21st century, the narrative is apparently no longer important, indeed it has been reduced into a pattern, such that we can say that all popular films and music stick to a formula. What usually arouses our attention is the individual performer (Ruan Lingyu or Grace

在追溯《野玫瑰之戀》的「歷史情境」的時候，我感受到很多困難，幸得香港電影資料館（特別是黃愛玲女士）的大力協助，提供了當時的部份印刷媒體資料（如港版雜誌《國際電影》）。我只能從這些資料中找尋一些蛛絲馬跡。

如果談《野》片和歌劇《卡門》的互文性，第一個（也無法完全解答的）問題是：為甚麼選上卡門的故事？當時的資料並沒有提到卡門，只提到葛蘭學西班牙舞，說她「對西班牙舞原來已具根基，為了精益求精，特地延聘這兩位名師來指點，每天下午練足三小時，一連三週，從未間斷」等等。這兩位「名師」卻原是拍片半年前，剛好有一對西班牙的男女名舞師，「遠道來港表演於各夜總會」。也許這個插曲只是偶合，但是中國電影史上——特別是三四十年代的電影——以夜總會作為都市文化的關鍵場景的電影比比皆是，現在視為經典的《新女性》(1934)中，就有一場西洋舞，由一對白俄男女表演；《一江春水向東流》(1947)上集，就有西班牙舞的演出，是片中的壞女人表演的，把它作為異國情調和崇洋媚外的代表。(但在該片中，這場西班牙舞是在紗廠職工慶祝活動上表演的，不是在夜總會)。到了六十年代的香港，西班牙舞的意義又跟以前不同：三十年代的上海和六十年代的香港同是中西文化薈萃的都市，但三十年代的西化尚有「異味」(exoticism)，但到了六十年代也就司空見慣了。在電影中跳西方舞——特別是曼波和恰恰——此片不是首次，而葛蘭的西班牙舞步並不像宣傳資料上所云：「極盡挑逗之能事」，甚至舞蹈的場面也不多，不足以令「葛蘭施展了渾身解數」。而更重要的——也是此種六十年代的歌舞片更吸引觀眾的地方——還是片中的插曲和葛蘭的歌唱。資料中說：「這些歌舞不僅是不同於普通國片所見者，而

「我一旦愛上你，你就要死在我手裏。」
"When I fall in love with you someday, you will be forever in my hands."

Chang) whose performance in a specific film leaves the greatest impression on us. These impressions are nothing more than clips, which have been long disassociated from their original narrative structures.

The odd reminiscences flowing from our own personal histories are invariably related to these impressionistic clips playing in our minds. In interpreting these clips of memory, we are indulging in "archaeology" in the Foucauldian meaning of the term, which is archaeology of the systems of thought. As far as I can deduce, Foucault had no interest in popular song (even if we adopted the Barthesian model of research into "mythology", this model is more pertinent to visual media, not so pertinent to our aural senses or to music). I would just like to raise two rough examples: when nostalgia buffs talk of the cinema of Shanghai or popular culture in the 1930s and 1940s, they will usually refer to Zhou Xuan and Bai Guang, and particularly to the songs they made famous, respectively "The Four Seasons " and "Shanghai by Night". By raising these names and songs, they provoke historical memories. In making *Days of Being Wild* (1990) and *In the Mood for Love* (2000), director Wong Kar-wai (Wang Jiawei) has spoken of listening to old popular standards. The question arises: how do these popular songs awaken our memories, after having been filtered through various media (or cross-media) such as the movies and records? What is the shape and content of these memories? How do we search for the historical contextualizations? It is not enough just to rely on theoretical discourses to answer these questions, it is necessary to conduct substantial case studies.

I encountered much difficulties in tracing the historical circumstances of the production of *The Wild, Wild Rose*. But thanks to the Hong Kong Film Archive (and particularly to Ms. Wong), I have been able to pull a historical thread out of the materials that have been made available to me (such as articles from publications like *International Screen*). If we were to acknowledge that there is "intertextuality" between *The Wild, Wild Rose* and *Carmen*, the first question that should be asked is, why was the Carmen story chosen? The materials did not mention

且，與歐美影片中的歌舞，亦大不相同，原因在何處呢？原來這些歌是出自日本當代音樂大師服部良一之手，據服部稱：『由於香港兼有東方西方的色彩，所以在《野》片中所表演的歌舞，亦具備東西雙方之特色。』」[6]

這正是葉月瑜教授書中所論的「仲介居中的狀態」。

問題是：如何居中仲介？《野》片又如何「具備東西雙方之特色」？更確切地說：《野》片如何把西方的東西「中國化」？這個問題其實也是中國文化中「現代性」的基本問題，從晚清翻譯到香港電影，這一直是我最關心的題目。就香港電影史而言，如果邵氏公司的黃梅調和武打電影當時為中國傳統和地方文化建立一種通俗性基礎的話，電懋公司的部份出品，卻為香港電影奠定了一種都市文化的現代的風格，而且勿論在內容或形式上都較邵氏通俗影片「高調」。陶秦導演的文藝片、張愛玲編劇的喜劇片，以及王天林或其他導演的歌唱片皆可為例。這當然和宋淇在電懋公司擔任要職有關。荷里活電影史上也有某一個時期、某家電影公司以出產某種風格或類型的影片為主的例子，譬如四五十年代華納公司就以黑色電影和文藝片見稱，而五六十年代的美高梅公司則以大堆頭的歌舞片見長。然而在六十年代的香港，無論邵氏或電懋都沒有足夠的資本拍美高梅式的大型歌舞片，所以香港的歌舞片其實歌多於舞，這是中國電影史自周璇以來的傳統。研究當時香港的歌舞片，就必須研究當時的流行曲。

東方與西方

走筆至此，我反而把自己置於困境，因為我對於流行歌毫無研究，僅能從《野》片個案中揣測一點當時的境況。我認為葛蘭的歌唱自有其獨特之處，和當時其他的歌星不同。其實葛蘭和當時走紅的顧媚、靜婷等人都不

Carmen, only that Grace Chang "had had a foundation in Spanish dancing and that for the sake of improving her skill, two experts were specially employed to coach her. Chang would spend three hours every afternoon for three weeks, without break, learning the dance." The experts were themselves Spanish dancers who, six months before the film went into production, "had come from afar to Hong Kong to perform in the territory's nightclubs". It may be a coincidence, but this little anecdote serves to underline the tendency of Chinese films to use nightclubs as cultural settings, particularly in the films of the 1930s and 1940s. A Spanish dance, performed by a White Russian couple, was seen in the classic *New Women* (1934). A Spanish dance was also featured in *The Spring River Flows East, Part 1* (1947), representing the element of exoticism and foreigner-worship in the narrative (however, in this film, the dance was performed not in a nightclub but in a textile worker's entertainment meeting).

By the 1960s in Hong Kong, the significance of the Spanish dance had changed. Shanghai in the 1930s and Hong Kong in the 1960s were both cities that blended cultures of East and West, but in the 1930s, Western culture still carried a touch of exoticism, while in the 1960s, Western culture was a common phenomenon. *The Wild, Wild Rose* was not the first film to feature Western dance forms, but Chang's Spanish dance was not what the studio's publicity machine made it out to be: "tantalizing to the utmost." Indeed, there were not a lot of dance sequences that required Chang "to show off all the skills at her disposal" (the quotes are taken from *International Screen*, August 1960). What was more important were the song interludes and Grace Chang's delivery of them. To quote the materials: "Not only are the songs different from the normal run of Mandarin movies, they are also different from those featured in European and American films. What accounts for this difference? The songs in fact come from the hands of contemporary Japanese composer Hattori Ryoichi. According to Hattori, Hong Kong is a meeting ground for East and West; therefore, the songs and dances presented in *The Wild, Wild Rose* possess attributes

一樣，並非歌星，而是具有相當音樂訓練的明星，但同享盛名的林翠、尤敏等女星，都不會唱歌。我認為她的演技和造型更是此片當時賣座的主要因素。所謂「東西雙方之特色」，毋寧是葛蘭把卡門演成一個「野性妖媚的外表底下有一顆熱情善良的心」的中國女性，「野性妖媚」是西、「熱情善良」才是東。在法國作家梅里美的筆下，小說中的卡門更野，比才改編後的歌劇已經把卡門的吉普賽性格減削了不少，但仍妖媚，而秦亦孚為《野》片所寫的劇本，塑造出來的卻是一個「北角卡門」：「形象可信，以卡門的人物、情節套入當年貧富懸殊的香港社會；上海南來商賈不可一世，文化人和藝人備受歧視，發展出本地化的浪漫癡戀悲劇」（羅卡語）。[7] 換言之，劇本為浪漫的原劇增加了一個現實的層次，如此才可以對當時的觀眾具可信性。葛蘭所演的歌星鄧思嘉（《亂世佳人》的女主角在傅東華的譯本《飄》中也名叫「思嘉」——郝思嘉）造型，其實出自茶花女的成份更大於卡門，野性不足、高貴有餘，所以角色的高貴善良的一面，被葛蘭演活了，跳西班牙舞反而顯得不足，舞步不中不西，既不像歌劇中的卡門，也不像在夜總會獻技的西班牙舞師。好在還有她的歌喉支撐，以及她對這首膾炙人口的古典樂曲的詮釋。

葛蘭在排練此角時有沒有聽過〈卡門〉，資料上沒有提。但《卡門》的流行，卻是有目共睹。自從1872年比才把它譜成歌劇後，雖在1875年首演時備受樂評人譏諷，但此後卻成為西方最受觀眾歡迎、演出次數最多的歌劇。電影史上自1896年開始就有改編卡門的故事的電影，直到五十年代的全以黑人演出的《卡門瓊絲》（演唱卡門的是 Dorothy Dandridge）。在各次電影的改編過程中，卡門的現代形象愈來愈強，而兩個男主角——士兵唐荷西和那個鬥牛士——僅成了陪襯角色。《野》片亦然，鬥牛士一角已經刪除，當然也沒

of both East and West." This is the significance of the "state of the intermediary" quoted from Professor Yeh Yueh-yu's book.

The question is, how does one arrive at this state? In what way does *The Wild, Wild Rose* possess "attributes of both East and West"? More precisely, how does the film Sinicize all things Western? This question relates fundamentally to the modernization of Chinese culture. From the translations of Western texts in the late Qing period to the Hong Kong cinema, this is the subject that has long concerned me. In the history of Hong Kong cinema, if we were to say Shaw Brothers was the studio that established traditional Chinese and local culture (through its genre of *huangmei diao* and *wuxia* pictures) as the basis of a popular cinema, then MP & GI's films were responsible for establishing a city culture and a modern sensibility in Hong Kong cinema. In style and content, MP & GI's films were more "highbrow", as evidenced in the sophisticated melodramas of director Tao Qin, the comedies written by novelist Eileen Chang, and the musicals directed by Wang Tianlin and others. This was no doubt the result of the management of Stephen Soong (Song Qi) as head of production in the studio.

Attributes of Both East and West

In Hollywood, examples of studios being associated with styles and genres are legion: in the 1930s, Warner Brothers was associated with the genres of gangster movies and melodramas; in the 1940s and 1950s, MGM was associated with the musical. In 1960s Hong Kong, neither Shaw Brothers nor MP & GI were capable of making MGM-style musicals, which explains why Hong Kong's song and dance musicals contained more songs than dances – a legacy of the tradition that began with Zhou Xuan. To study the musicals of Hong Kong cinema at the time, one must study the popular songs of the period. Having said that, I find myself in a predicament because I am not a student of popular songs. I can only conjecture about the circumstances of the period from the examples in *The Wild, Wild Rose*. I do think Chang's singing was in a class of its own. She was quite different from singing stars such as Carrie Ku (Gu Mei) or Jing Ting. Chang was not really a singing star but a well-trained professional

有鬥牛的場面，因此西班牙風味全失，僅剩半場西班牙舞聊以充數而已，其實毫不重要。張揚演的是一個落難藝人的角色，在香港流離失所，也失去了唐荷西的浪漫性，原歌劇情節中的浪漫氣氛，至此也蕩然無存，所以李焯桃説：全片雖以愛情為主題，卻處處在嘲諷愛情，「反而不斷強調它的破壞性」。其實原歌劇也強調愛情的破壞性，但它的來源是西方的尤物所代表的強烈慾望熱情（passion）的傳統（類似卡門的《曼儂萊絲葛》的故事，先後也由馬斯耐和普契尼譜成歌劇），恰和東方式的「一顆熱情善良的心」成對比：心地善良、流露的是一種道德熱情，而慾望熱情卻出自身體和性慾。

然而，即使善良的熱情也可以表現得很浪漫。我認為《野》片的幾首插曲，不但沒有佔去影片不少時間，而且不可或缺，構成片中的「浪漫」基調。換言之，沒有這幾首歌，此片會大為遜色，因為它的故事本屬俗套，即使具有當年香港社會的現實面，時過境遷以後，也不見得會引起太多的歷史回憶；也就是説，沒有葛蘭唱的這幾首歌，我們今日也不見得會再看這部電影（當然研究此道的學者例外）。我認為這部電影不能算是佳作，卻可視為「浪漫歌唱片」的經典。曾提及羅卡的論點，我基本上還是同意的，但可惜的是這幾位知名的電影學者都沒有談到此片的歌曲。

《野》片與其他古典音樂

前文提過，除了《卡門》選曲之外，至少還有三首其他古典音樂選曲，而這四首歌曲反而可以把該片的愛情主題連成一線，自成一種敍述：如果「愛情不過是一種普通的玩意，男人不過是一件消遣的東西」（改自《卡門》），那麼男人「愛這種女人最無聊」（改編自《弄臣》

「愛情不過是一種普通的玩意，
男人不過是一件消遣的東西。」
"Love is nothing more than a common plaything..."

entertainer who could sing. Other popular stars in the period, such as Lucilla You Min and Jeanette Lin Cui, could not sing. I think Chang's acting abilities and her performance were the crucial factors contributing to the success of *The Wild, Wild Rose*.

The "attributes of both East and West" were brought out in Chang's interpretation of Carmen as both a seductive, wild creature (the Western side of the character) and a woman with a benevolent heart (the Chinese side of her character). The original Carmen in Prosper Mérimée's novel was a much more uninhibited creature. Bizet toned down the gypsy characteristics of Carmen in the opera but she remained seductive. Scriptwriter Qin Yifu (Qin Yu) transformed the character into a "North Point Carmen": "The image is credible; both the character and the plot of *Carmen* are overlaid into the Hong Kong society of the time, with its huge gap between rich and poor, the snobbery of the Shanghai businessmen who came south, the discrimination against cultural intellectuals and artists, all of this developed into a local tragic-romantic drama." (Law Kar, 21st HKIFF, 1997, p. 189). In other words, the script added a realistic level to the original romance so as to make itself more credible to a local audience. Chang's songstress Deng Sijia (incidentally, the same name given to the Scarlett O'Hara character in the Chinese translation of *Gone With the Wind* by Fu Donghua and others) is in fact more inspired by Camille than Carmen. Deng Sijia isn't as wild as Carmen ought to be, and she retains her self-respect. Chang brings out the self-respect of the character. Her performance of the Spanish dance isn't really up to scratch, belonging neither to the West nor to the East, nowhere like the Carmen of the opera and certainly not like a Spanish dancer showing off her skills in a nightclub. However, Chang's singing and her interpretation of a famous classical melody save the sequence.

It is not known whether Chang herself had seen the opera *Carmen* when rehearsing for the role. However, the fame of *Carmen* was obvious to all. Bizet completed the opera in 1872, and since its premiere in 1875, though a few critics put it down, the opera has become the most popular and most performed in the

野玫瑰原來是蝴蝶夫人
Madame Butterfly: "I blame no one but myself."

Western world. On film, versions of *Carmen* have appeared since the dawn of cinema. One of the most notable versions was Otto Preminger's *Carmen Jones* (1954), acted by a wholly African-American cast (the part of Carmen was played by Dorothy Dandridge). In the various film versions, the modern image of Carmen becomes stronger each time, while the two male parts – Don Jose and Escamillo the bullfighter – are nothing more than foils to Carmen's image. *The Wild, Wild Rose* is no exception in this regard. In the film, the bullfighter has been cut out, and naturally there is no longer a bullring scene. Consequently, the Spanish flavour has all but disappeared; only the Spanish dance sequence serves to remind us of the original setting – but this is no longer important. Chang Yang plays a piano player in the image of the poor, destitute artist. Gone is the romantic nature of the original Don Jose; in fact, the romantic atmosphere of the opera is totally discarded, which is why critic Li Cheuk-to could write that although the theme is love, the film mocks love by "its unrelenting thrust to emphasise destruction". Actually, such an emphasis is already present in the opera, but its source of destruction stems from the Western tradition of desire and passion as represented by the figure of the *femme fatale*. This is in contrast to the Eastern tradition of the woman "with a passionate and benevolent heart". A benevolent heart can only give vent to a passion that is commonplace, while a passion marked by desire stems from the body and sex.

Other Classical Music Influence

However, even a benevolent passion can be treated in a highly romantic fashion. The songs in the movie are indispensable because they form the romantic core of the narrative. The film is much the poorer without the songs because the story itself is conventional. Even if one were to include the realistic background of Hong Kong, I don't think this is enough to arouse very many historical memories. In other words, without the songs performed by Grace Chang, I don't think we would be watching this movie today. In my opinion, the movie is not a masterpiece but it is definitely a classic of the romantic musical genre. I generally agree with what Law Kar has written (the quote cited above). However,

的大意）；如果「我一旦愛上你，你就要死在我手裡」（改編自《風流寡婦》，但與原歌詞完全不同，唱詞是出自女人的立場，但最後死的也是女人）；最後，心地善良的野玫瑰穿上和服，藉着《蝴蝶夫人》的一曲唱出她的自怨自艾：「還是怪自己」，至此影射悲劇的結局。據説葛蘭穿的和服，是曾經主演過《蝴蝶夫人》的日本女星八千草薰送給她的，[8]來頭不小，但在片中的「互文」關係，卻使她變成了一個很軟弱的角色：蝴蝶夫人自殺，野玫瑰卻死在情人之手，劇情還是貫徹了《卡門》的原來故事。卡門加上蝴蝶夫人，使此片的歌劇性更強，反而是新作的主題曲〈Jajambo〉與全片故事無關，也許是為了湊合當時觀眾的跳舞趣味，節奏是曼波和恰恰。

可能畢竟是古典音樂的愛好者，所以在此煞有介事地為古典音樂説項。然而，從音樂的立場而言，《卡門》並不被視為一部嚴肅的作品，比才的歌劇本來是為專演較通俗作品的巴黎「喜歌劇院」(Opéra-Comique)而寫的，本無意永垂不朽，卻反而成了不朽之作。這種「喜歌劇」較易迎合觀眾，內中對話也不少；奧芬巴哈的《赫夫曼的故事》是另一個喜歌劇的例子，而且真的是載歌載舞，為後來美國百老匯的歌舞劇奠定一個基礎。兩者之間的中介和過渡人物是寫過《沙漠之歌》(*The Desert Song*)、《學生王子》(*The Student Prince of Heidelberg*)等歌劇的西蒙隆伯(Sigmund Romberg)，至六十年代的美高梅歌舞片，不少是出自隆伯和其他類似的作曲家(如柯恩〔Jerome Kern〕，作過《畫舫璇宮》〔*Show Boat*〕)的輕歌劇。他們的風格雖然很通俗，但音樂較富古典味，和出自爵士傳統的葛許文(George Gershwin)和愛文柏林(Irving Berlin)不盡相同。當時唱慣歌劇的演唱家，如想「過界」到流行音樂，往往會唱這種輕歌劇，

it is a pity that none of the noted critics I have cited have discussed the songs.

As I have pointed out in the beginning of this essay, apart from the *Carmen* number, there are at least three other classical numbers. The lyrics of all four numbers bespeak the theme of love, forming a common narrative thread. "Love is nothing more than a common plaything, and men are only an amusement to kill time" (adapted from *Carmen*), "men who love such women are the most stupid" (adapted from *Rigoletto*), "when I fall in love with you some day, you will be forever in my hands" (adapted from *The Merry Widow*). Finally, the Wild Rose with a benevolent heart dons a kimono to sing a number from *Madame Butterfly*, "I blame no one but myself", reflecting the tragedy that will finally befall her. It was said that the kimono worn by Grace Chang was given to her by the famous Japanese actress Yachigusa Kaoru, who had played Madame Butterfly. The "intertextuality" has the effect of transforming Grace Chang into a weak and soft character. Madame Butterfly kills herself, but Carmen dies at the hands of her lover. In this way, the plot follows the story of Carmen. Adding *Madame Butterfly* and *Carmen* together strengthens the operatic qualities of the film. In contrast, the original number "Jajambo" has nothing to do with the narrative and I can only surmise that its inclusion was to appease the audience's interest in the popular dance forms of the time (the song's rhythm being keyed to Mambo and cha-cha).

Perhaps it's because I am a classical music enthusiast that has led me to put in a good word for the classical numbers. However, from the viewpoint of music, *Carmen* was not seen as a serious work. Bizet wrote the opera for the more popular *opéra-comique* in Paris, but the work has lasted. The *opéra-comique* was meant to be more accessible to the masses and there were usually a lot of dialogue (Offenbach's *Tales of Hoffmann* is a representative example). The form combined song and dance, prefiguring the Broadway musical that would develop in the United States. The key transitional figure between the *opéra-comique* and Broadway was Sigmund Romberg, whose light operas included *The Desert Song* and *The Student*

當然也會包括隆伯和柯恩的曲子。五十年代末到六十年代初最有名的歌劇通俗歌手是馬里奧蘭沙（Mario Lanza），曾主演過《歌王卡羅素》（*The Great Caruso*, Richard Thorpe, 1951），也是《學生王子》（*The Student Prince*, 1954）的幕後主唱者，他的演唱技巧雖然來自古典歌劇訓練，但唱流行歌時音調特別浪漫，咬字吐詞極為清晰，我在中學和大學時代為之傾倒。

以上所舉的這些音樂例子，為的是為《野》片的當時情境提供另一個小小的例證。何觀評論《野》片的文章中，就提到這個典故。原文如下：

有位朋友在閒談中，提及有家午報的影評，說到本片在不恰當的情形下用『進行曲』。那位朋友並說這歌曲很熟悉，似乎在小孩子讀書時代就唱過的甚麼渡過海洋之類，是在《一百零一首最佳歌曲》中的——那是我們這輩人做小孩時代，學校裡常用的英文歌教材；因他這一說，倒引起了我看本片的興趣。……這首歌是極普通的歌劇選曲，近代最有名的男高音卡魯索的唱片中，本曲是最流行的一章，馬里奧蘭沙在他演的《偉大的卡魯索》那張影片裡，也唱過這支歌，也灌過唱片，怎麼會是『進行曲』？我看了本片之後，覺得場合和改編的歌詞很恰當，因為《一百零一首最佳歌曲》已是改編的英文曲，原歌名為〈女人是水性楊花〉也！[9]

這位影評人頗懂音樂，值得補充的是：這首「進行曲」我在中學時代也唱過，歌詞早已「華化」，叫作〈夏天裡過海洋〉，時隔多年後才知道它出自歌劇《弄臣》。《野》片的幕後功臣都是高手，他們好像早已知道有些歌曲是註定可以膾炙人口的，並非所有古典音樂都是票房毒藥。《卡門》中的〈哈巴尼拉舞曲〉可以經過多次改頭換面仍然受人歡迎，變成經典（而被學院派視為祭酒的法蘭克福學派的掌門人阿多諾〔Adorno〕，所揭櫫

Prince. Many MGM musicals of the 50s were derived from Romberg and other composers (such as Jerome Kern, the creator of *Show Boat*). The style of these composers was popular, but retained the flavour of classical music. Later composers such as George Gershwin and Irving Berlin added jazz. Opera singers at the time who wanted to cross over into the world of popular music would add to their repertoire songs from the light operas, such as those of Romberg and Kern. The most popular singer of this school of popular opera was Mario Lanza, who starred in *The Great Caruso* (1951) and was the voice behind *The Student Prince* (1954). Lanza's skills in singing and performance were derived from his training in opera, but he adopted a romantic tone for popular songs, vocalizing extravagantly and clearly enunciating the lyrics. Mario Lanza floored me in my student days in secondary school and university.

I have mentioned all the examples above in order to provide a small historical background to *The Wild, Wild Rose*. A review of the film at the time of its release by He Guan (pseudonym of Chang Cheh) also alluded to this history. It reads:

During a conversation with a friend, he brought up a film review printed in an afternoon newspaper whereby the reviewer stated that the film had inappropriately used a March tune. My friend said he knew the song from somewhere, most likely from his primary school days when he had sung a song with the lyric, "passing through the ocean", or something to that effect. The song was included in the One Hundred and One Best Songs, a standard textbook that we used to sing English songs in primary school. As a result of this conversation, I went to see the movie. …The song was a very popular song from opera. It was the most popular item in a Caruso album, and it was featured in the film The Great Caruso, starring Mario Lanza, which was also included in an album. How could this be a March? After seeing the movie, I felt that the adaptation and the new lyrics were appropriate. Because the English song in One Hundred and One Best Songs was itself adapted

的現代經典——如荀貝克——的音樂卻真的叫好不叫座，成了音樂會上的票房毒藥），我想最基本的因素是通俗的曲調必須可以琅琅上口，然而有些調子卻更能上口，而且可以古今咸宜、中外相通。我認為「古典」的意義就在於此，是和「通俗」相通的。流行音樂的流行，很受時間的限制，和時裝一樣，但真正流行而歷久不衰的，卻反而接得上傳統，或自創一格後，經過流傳而成為傳統。這其實是一個很粗淺的道理，音樂如此，文學也如此。值得進一步研究的不是「原典」的價值，反而是如何「複製」和複製改編後所製造出來的另一種藝術「魅力」(aura) 的問題。這種新的魅力，就是可以「喚起我們對某種歷史時期的聯想」的主要來源。當然，就流行音樂而言，除了歌曲之外還有唱者；有時候，更是「唱者而不是歌曲」。葛蘭在這個程序中所扮演的更是一個「仲介」的角色，卻因此而永垂不朽。

註

1. 「當代亞洲通俗文化」會議，嶺南大學文化研究系主辦，2001年10月11日。
2. 見舒琪編：《戰後國、粵語片比較研究——朱石麟、秦劍等作品回顧》，第七屆香港國際電影節回顧特刊，香港：市政局，1983年，頁208-209。
3. 羅卡及張建德所寫影片簡介，見羅卡編：《光影繽紛五十年》，第廿一屆香港國際電影節特刊，香港：市政局，1997年，頁189；另何思穎(未署名)以英文寫的影片簡介，見羅卡編：《國語片與時代曲（四十至六十年代）》，第十七屆香港國際電影節回顧特刊，香港：市政局，1993年，頁114。
4. 見何觀，〈野玫瑰之戀〉，「影話」專欄，《新生晚報》，1960年10月18日，頁6。
5. 見葉月瑜：《歌聲魅影：歌曲敘事與中文電影》，台北：遠流，2000年，頁237。原文見戴樂為著，葉月瑜譯，〈聲音的事件〉，《電影欣賞》，第98期，1999年3-4月號，頁21-25。
6. 此處數句引文見《國際電影》(香港版)，第58期，1960年8月，頁26-27；第59期，1960年9月，頁28-29；及第60期，1960年10月，頁26-27。
7. 見《光影繽紛五十年》，同註3。
8. 見《國際電影》(香港版)，第57期，1960年7月，頁18。
9. 見何觀，同註4。

李歐梵，哈佛大學中國文學教授，現為香港大學客座教授。最新著作為《上海摩登》(牛津大學出版社，2000)。
Leo Lee Ou-fan, Professor of Chinese Literature at Harvard University. Currently Visiting Distinguished Professor at HKU. Recently published: *Shanghai Modern* (Harvard University Press, 1999; OUP [translation], 2000); another translation just came out from Peking University Press.

from the original song "Woman is Wayward".

This film critic knew his music, but I might just add this: when I was in school, I had also sung this March. The lyrics were long Sinicized, its title now called "In Summer, We Cross the Ocean". It wasn't until many years later that I finally discovered the song came from *Rigoletto*. The people who worked behind the scenes in *The Wild, Wild Rose* were top hands who knew very early on that some songs were destined to be popular, and that not all classical music was box office poison. "Habanera" from *Carmen* would remain popular no matter how often it is adapted and readapted. I think the chief factor is that in popular music, the melody should be easy to sing. Some tunes are so easy to sing that they transcend period and all age groups. I believe the meaning of "classical" is interlinked with "popular". The popularity of popular song is restricted by time, in the same way that fashion is. But the truly popular and everlasting can come into contact with tradition, or become a tradition from being established as its own creative entity. This is a very simple truth that applies to music as to literature. What is worthy of further study is not so much the value of originality but the question of the artistic aura implicit in a copy. This new aura is the chief source evoking "our associations of various historical periods".

With regard to popular music, we should be concerned not only with the song but also with the singer. In some instances, it is the singer and not the song that preoccupies our attention. In this process, Grace Chang plays the role of the "intermediary" and because of this, she will remain immortal.

Translated by Stephen Teo

Notes

1. See Shu Kei, ed., *A Comparative Study of Post-War Mandarin and Cantonese Cinema: the Films of Zhu Shilin, Qin Jian and Other Directors*, the 7th Hong Kong International Film Festival catalogue, Hong Kong: Urban Council, 1983, pp.208-209.
2. See Law Kar, ed., *Fifty Years of Electric Shadows*, the 21st Hong Kong International Film Festival catalogue, Hong Kong: Urban Council, 1997, p.189 and Sam Ho (uncredited), in Law Kar, ed., *Mandarin Films and Popular Songs: 40's – 60's*, the 17th Hong Kong International Film Festival catalogue, Hong Kong: Urban Council, 1993, p.114.

從《璇宮艷史》到《璇宮艷史》：荷里活電影與五十年代粵語戲曲片

- 容世誠 -

緒言

「璇宮艷史」是一個有趣的文化現象。這個現象，啟端自有聲電影出現不久的 1929 年。這一年，派拉蒙公司推出名片《璇宮艷史》（*The Love Parade*, 1930 年 1 月公映），由劉別謙（Ernst Lubitsch）執導，名角梅禮士司花利亞（Maurice Chevalier）和珍妮麥當奴（Jeanette MacDonald）主演。當時有聲電影剛剛面世，派拉蒙當然盡量利用新科技的優勢，在電影裡面加插多首唱曲作為賣點，其中以〈夢中情人〉、〈御林軍進行曲〉兩首插曲最受矚目。[1] 這部有聲歌唱片在中國各大城市放映後廣受歡迎。承接《璇宮艷史》的熱潮，旅居上海的粵劇名伶薛覺先，率先將這部西片改編成時裝劇搬上粵劇舞台。粵劇《璇宮艷史》由梁金堂編劇，薛覺先飾演阿露佛伯爵，謝醒儂演女皇魯懿絲，丑角葉弗弱演僕人傑克。覺先聲劇團在 1930 年的下半年推出這部新劇，立

From *The Love Parade* to *My Kingdom for a Husband*: Hollywood Musicals and Cantonese Opera Films of the 1950s

- Yung Sai-shing -

Introduction

"Romance of the Jade Hall" (Xuangong Yanshi) is an interesting cultural phenomenon. It actually started in 1929, when Paramount made *The Love Parade* (1930), directed by Ernst Lubitsch and starring Maurice Chevalier and Jeanette MacDonald. Sound was just introduced to film and Paramount included several songs in the film to cash in on the new technology. Among them, "Dream Lover" and "March of the Grenadiers" were the most popular.[1] The film was also very popular in China, and Cantonese opera star Sit Kok-sin (Xue Juexian) quickly adapted it to the Cantonese opera stage as *Xuangong Yanshi*, using the same Chinese title of the Hollywood film, which translates as "Romance of the Jade Hall". Staged in late 1930 by Sit's Kok Sin Sing Opera Troupe, it rocked the opera scene. In around 1931, Sit recorded the "Night Feast at the Jade Hall" number for Pathè Records and it became a quick hit. At about the same time, Ma Si-tsang (Ma Shizeng), the other party in the famous "Sit-Ma Rivalry", came up with his adaptation of *The Love Parade*, pairing himself with Tam Lan-

即轟動劇壇。1931 年左右，薛覺先應法資百代唱片公司之邀，將劇中〈夜宴璇宮〉唱段灌錄成唱片，成為一支街知巷聞的經典名曲。大約在同一時候，「薛馬爭雄」中的馬師曾又改編《璇宮艷史》演出，這次和馬師曾合作飾演女皇的，是下面會再提到的譚蘭卿。劇中〈覲君之風流辯〉和〈夜宴〉兩曲由馬師曾自撰，並由華資的新月唱片公司灌成唱片，1931 年推出市場。[2]

1934年，上海的天一電影公司首先將粵劇《璇宮艷史》拍成電影，由薛覺先自編、自導、自演，女主角是薛覺先的夫人唐雪卿。也是薛覺先離開上海前的最後一部電影。[3]事隔二十多年，電懋公司粵語組於 1957年第二次將《璇宮艷史》搬上銀幕，在香港拍攝。由左几導演，張瑛演皇夫雅里，羅艷卿演女皇羅依，梁醒波演僕人傑克，譚蘭卿演宮女露露。翌年，電懋再接再厲，開拍伊士曼七彩製作《璇宮艷史續集》。在原有演員陣容上，加上新人方華演歌女珍妮一角。《璇宮艷史》的影響一直維持到六七十年代。大約七十年代初，香港風行唱片公司請來了譚炳文、李香琴再次灌錄《璇宮艷史》唱片，由羅寶生等負責填詞製作。現在在市面上仍可購到錄音卡式帶。

《璇宮艷史》對廣東戲曲文化產生過深遠的影響。在時間上從二十年代末伸延到七十年代，地域空間則包括上海、廣州、香港、東南亞和北美地區，媒體方面則牽涉電影、舞台劇、廣播和唱片。更具體地說，從《璇宮艷史》可以看到三十年代粵劇和荷里活電影的關係，當時粵劇圈、電影公司和唱片公司的商業網絡，戰後五十年代香港粵曲電影和電影公司的文化角色，以及廣州、香港、上海、新加坡等城市的普及文化互動。

My Kingdom for a Husband and *My Kingdom for a Honeymoon.*

Courtesy of Paul Fonoroff

hing (Tan Lanqing) and writing the songs “His Romantic Debate” and “Night Feast” himself, releasing them on record through the Chinese label New Moon Gramophone.[2]

In 1934, the Shanghai film company Tianyi made the opera into film, with Sit writing, directing and acting in it. Over 20 years later, MP & GI remade the film in 1957, with Tso Kea (Zuo Ji) directing a cast that includes Cheung Ying (Zhang Ying), Law Yim-hing (Luo Yanqing), Leung Sing-po (Liang Xingbo) and Tam Lan-hing. This was followed the next year by an Eastmancolor sequel, with Fong Wah (Fang Hua) added to the original cast. The play’s influence lasted through the early 1970s, when Fung Heng Company released an album of the film’s songs, sung by Tam Bing-man (Tan Bingwen) and Lee Hong-kum (Li Xiangqin), the cassette of which can still be found today.

The influence of *The Love Parade* on Cantonese opera culture is profound. It extended from the 1920s to the 1970s and from Shanghai to Hong Kong to Southeast Asia to North America, involving media as diverse as film, theatre, broadcast and music. In the phenomenon can be seen the relationship between Hollywood and Cantonese opera in the 1930s; the commercial network comprising the Cantonese opera, film and recording industries; the cultural role played by opera films and film companies in 1950s Hong Kong; and the interactions among the popular cultures of Guangzhou, Hong Kong, Shanghai and Singapore.

Challenge and Response: Cantonese Opera and Hollywood in the 1930s

In the history of Chinese opera, interactions, competitions and mutual influences among different genres of opera are common. The same can be said of

挑戰與回應：三十年代粵劇和荷里活電影

在中國戲曲史上，劇種聲腔之間從互相接觸、競爭，繼而吸納對方的優點、消化後溶入自己的系統，本來就是一個常見的現象。同樣的規律，也適用於三十年代粵劇和荷里活電影。從一篇刊登在覺先聲劇團《璇宮艷史專刊》（1930年序）的文章，可以一窺當時粵劇界面對荷里活有聲電影競爭，所作出的反響和應對。這篇文章，題名〈有聲片和舞台劇：薛覺先之《璇宮艷史》與梅禮士司花利亞之《璇宮艷史》〉。作者署名嘯霞，應該就是覺先聲劇團宣傳部主任麥嘯霞，也是專刊的編輯。[4]他說：

自從有聲電影片異軍突起，風靡一時，啞片已如反舌無聲地被擠於淘汰之列。因此便有許多人懷疑，以為影片有影無聲之缺憾已填，便可消滅舞台劇。此言初聞之似是，若深思之則實大謬不然也。

所謂「舞台劇」實指粵劇。作者隨之羅列有聲電影比不上舞台粵劇的五個方面，這裡不一一細表。文中再三強調粵劇將被電影淘汰之説「大謬不然」，其實正反映了三十年代粵劇業界，面對新興娛樂媒體——有聲電影——的競爭衝擊，所產生的焦慮和不安。文章的結尾説：

薛覺先主演《璇宮艷史》，其表情藝術，均有特殊成績。其佳點迥非有聲片所能冀及。佈置設備雖格於舞台環境之困難而弗能盡稱美善。然所用服裝配景音樂已冠絕一時。舞台劇未有之大觀。且劇中情節較聲片原劇尤曲折有味。最難能可貴者，是盡避舞台劇之所短，而盡取有聲片之所長……斯劇一出，吾知平日讚美有聲片者必不更忽視舞台劇，平日崇拜梅禮士司花利亞者必更崇拜薛覺先。稱道派拉蒙《璇宮艷史》者必更稱道覺先聲之《璇宮艷史》也。

Cantonese opera and Hollywood in the 1930s. Cantonese opera's response to Hollywood's challenge was reflected in the preface of the booklet for the 1930 Cantonese opera version of *The Love Parade*, titled "Sound Film and Theatre: Sit's *Xuangong Yanshi* and Maurice Chevalier's *The Love Parade*", written by Xiao Xia, who should be Mai Xiaoxia (Mak Siu-ha), publicity head of Sit's troupe and editor of the booklet:[3]

Since talkies came out of nowhere and became very popular, silent films were summarily displaced. Hence there were worries that with the silence handicap removed, film will destroy theatre. Such talks may sound reasonable, but are actually erroneous.

By "theatre" the author means Cantonese opera. The article repeatedly emphasizes the "erroneous" notion that talkies will replace theatre, in fact expressing the anxiety felt by the theatre sector over the challenge of talking movies. It goes on to conclude:

Sit Kok-sin's performance in Xuangong Yanshi *can't be equalled by talkies… The story of the opera is also more complicated and dramatic than the film, assimilating all talkies' strengths while avoiding theatre's weaknesses… With this opera, those who praise talkies at the expense of theatre and those who admire Chevalier will admire Sit even more.*

Facing the challenge of Hollywood talkies, Cantonese opera's strategy was to beat it at its own game. "Assimilating talkies' strengths while avoiding theatre's weaknesses" was in fact Cantonese opera's 1930s response to films from the West. Famous operas like *Xuangong Yanshi*, *Platinum Dragon* and *The Vagabond Prince* were all products of this strategy.

Such plays are known as "western costume operas". Although extents of imitation differed, there were four major areas of incorporating Western influence: adapting plots, transplanting characters, borrowing songs and dances and copying costumes and sets. The last area is especially noteworthy. Promotion materials of *Xuangong Yanshi* highlighted the show's sets and costumes. Reading the script today, one can easily

面對荷里活有聲電影的挑戰，粵劇界的對策是「師夷之長技以制夷」，從競爭對手處攝取養份而自我完善。所謂「盡避舞台劇之所短而盡取有聲片之所長」，基本上就是三十年代粵劇對西方電影的回應。當時的名劇《璇宮艷史》、《白金龍》和《賊王子》等，都是這種策略下的產物。

這種模仿荷里活電影的新型劇目，稱為「西裝劇」。模仿的程度和方式，因劇而異；但總離不開故事情節的改編、角色造型的移植、音樂舞蹈的借用和服裝場景的仿效。四者之中，以最後一項最值得留意。覺先聲班宣傳《璇宮艷史》時，特別提到他們的「佈置設備」和「服裝配景」。從現有《璇宮艷史》的文字劇本，可以想像當時舞台設景的堂皇豪華、變化多端，人物服飾的精巧華麗、奪目耀眼。從第一場伯爵在巴黎的「西廳景」，到第二場回返母國之前的「酒店景」，到三、四場覲見女皇的「皇宮」和「御園」，場景和佈景不斷變換，層出不窮。到了第五場的「夜宴璇宮」高潮，佈置更是悉心安排：「舖設華麗輝煌燈飾。中設餐桌、花插、刀叉皿器等具。衣角靚梳化床」。[5] 導演左几替電懋公司在五十年代替重拍這場戲時，還是沿用相似的場景佈置。

總的來說，覺先聲的《璇宮艷史》，是通過各樣精巧道具（巧克力製假手槍、呂宋煙、煙斗、洋酒、酒杯）、奢華歐化的陳設（皇室油畫、藝術家具、名貴古董、長餐桌、西餐餐具、沙發床）、異國情調的裝扮（西式背心、鑽石鏈、襟頭花、禮服帽、手杖、女皇艷裝）等，在舞台上塑造一個充滿異域色彩的視覺世界，建構多樣化的想像西方場景。目的是調動和陳列舞台上的不同符號，從而營造一種新鮮奇特、甚至是奇異的視覺景觀效果。《璇宮艷史》出現在三十年代初，在粵劇舞台上製造視覺景觀效果，主要還是通過靜態的佈景和道具。稍

imagine the extravagance. From the first scene's grand hall in Paris to the second scene's hotel to the third and fourth scenes' palace and imperial garden, the show never stopped presenting new sets and decorations, reaching the climax with "Night Feast at the Jade Hall" in the fifth scene. "Elegant decorations and glorious chandeliers; dinner table in the middle, with flowers and tableware like knives and forks. At the corner is a fancy sofa bed."[4] When Tso Kea adapted the play to screen for MP & GI in the 1950s, he dressed the scene in similar lavishness.

Sit's adaptation was marked by fancy props (chocolate guns, cigars, pipes), luxurious European furnishings (royal paintings, antiques, long dinning table) and foreign costumes (vests, diamond necklaces, lapel flowers, top hats). This created on stage an exotic visual world, a richly diversified imaginary West. The goal was to employ the codified signs on stage to present a spectacle at once new and different, even strange. When *Xuangong Yanshi* appeared in the early 1930s, Cantonese opera created the spectacle mainly through sets and props. Later, it graduated to using "mechanical sets", "fantasy effects" (adopted from Shanghai Peking opera) and "electric costumes", making use of technological advances like electricity, electrical lighting and mechanical contraptions (in the pursuit of modernisation, technology itself was an attraction). This offered the audience a spectacular world that's novel, dazzling and entertaining, leaving a lasting impression.

Continuation of Visual Spectacles in Hong Kong Cantonese Opera Films

Sit's three "western costume operas" – *The Platinum Dragon*, *Xuangong Yanshi* and *The Deadly Rose* – were made into film in, respectively, 1933, 1934 and 1935. All were made by Tianyi, the predecessor of Shaw Brothers. It's interesting to note that when MP & GI made *My Kingdom for a Husband* (aka *The Romance of Jade Hall*)in 1957, Shaw was already its major rival. After WWII, Sit returned to China in 1954. Under the Cold War atmosphere and the Korean War in the 1950s, Hollywood imitations were greatly

後在粵劇舞台上更流行「機關佈景」、「幻術配景」(取法自上海京劇)、「電燈服裝」。借助現代科技,例如電力、電光、機械(在整個追尋現代化過程中,科技本身就是賣點),在舞台上展陳一個巧奇悦目,或具震撼性、令觀眾嘆為「觀」止的視覺景觀世界。

視覺景觀在香港粵語戲曲片的延續

薛覺先的三部西裝戲戲寶《白金龍》、《璇宮艷史》和《毒玫瑰》先後在1933、1934、1935年被搬上銀幕。投資、拍攝這三部電影的是天一電影公司,也就是邵氏公司的前身。有趣的是,當電懋在1957年翻拍《璇宮艷史》時,邵氏公司早已成為它的主要競爭對手。二戰後,薛覺先在1954年回返中國內地定居。歷史是充滿吊詭的。在五十年代韓戰和冷戰的政治環境下,以前改編和模仿美國荷里活電影的粵劇,和當時中國主流的社會主義文藝路線格格不入,因而成為文藝界的批評對象,遭到嚴厲的批判、否定。另一方面,1949年以後,以《璇宮艷史》為代表,追求新奇景觀、崇尚西洋趣味的表達手法,卻得以保留在華南文化孤島——殖民地香港——的粵劇電影裡面。[6] 1957年電懋粵語組拍攝《璇宮艷史》,正是上述荷里活化,標榜娛樂至上,重視視覺景觀的三十年代粵劇文化在香港的延續和發展。(另一部五十年代粵語片經典《無頭東宮生太子》〔1957〕要展示的,是另一類型的神話怪奇景觀。)我們可以從這個粵劇文化史的角度,去了解電懋《璇宮艷史》的位置所在。

《璇宮艷史》是電懋粵語片組的重頭戲。左几在處理這部宮闈歌唱片時,極之注重全片的佈景、場景、畫面結構等景觀效果。就是宣傳時,也特別強調「全片故事、場面、服飾、儀仗,甚至於畫面結構、樂曲撰製,一律以浪漫而誇張的筆觸去加以處理,重現了當年「薛氏戲

《璇宮豔史》
My Kingdom for a Husband

寶」的諸般特色。」[7]電影開始的第一個場景，已經是一個經過特別設計的現代西式酒吧歌廳。張瑛身穿時尚西服，風度翩翩的獻唱悠揚歌曲，拉奏一把白色的小提琴（曲目叫〈鸞鳳和鳴〉，極為傳統。）。穿著時髦的女性觀眾，在歌廳向張瑛爭相獻媚。當時有影評說「好像『貓王』一樣受到很多女子的追逐和崇拜」，[8]但更令人想到美高梅電影《風流寡婦》（*The Merry Widow*， 1952）裡面丹尼露伯爵（Count Danilo）盛裝走進歌場，在眾艷婦蜂擁包圍下高唱情歌的景象。既然要重現當年的薛氏戲寶，電影裡面的主題曲唱段，大部份襲用覺先聲班的唱曲版本，但也經過李願聞和潘焯的刪訂。張瑛和羅艷卿在電影裡面的曲藝唱腔，少不了是電影的宣傳重點。「張瑛從影十餘年，初開金口大唱『薛腔』」成為主要賣點。另外，又強調「羅艷卿飾演女國王，唱功腔圓韻潤。尤其是卿姐天賦的美麗身段，充分流露了她的嫵媚撩人」。[9]最後兩句，應該是指羅艷卿在電影裡面的性感出浴場面。在這裡，女性身體已經物化成為電影場面景觀的一個部份。所受荷里活電影的影響，是十分清楚的。

《璇宮艷史》極為賣座，掀起一片仿拍荷里活宮闈片的熱潮。電懋連續開拍《璇宮艷史續集》（1958）、《月宮寶盒》（1958）和《歷盡滄桑一美人》（1958）（印象中是改編自《Scaramouche》，中譯《美人如玉劍如虹》，1952）。演員同樣都是張瑛、羅艷卿和梁醒波。此外，金門影業公司又攝製《駙馬艷史》（1958），出資拍攝的梅綺自演公主珍娜、張瑛演裁縫駙馬莫理臣。同年，國華公司相繼推出《賊王子》（何非凡、梅綺）和《賊王子續集》。1959年，邵氏公司開拍《玻璃鞋》，由當時的新星張英才和林鳳主演，多了一重青春氣息。

criticized. On the other hand, after 1949, the pursuit of western taste and visual spectacle as exemplified by *Romance of the Jade Hall* was preserved in Cantonese opera films of the orphan island of southern Chinese culture – Hong Kong, the colony.[5] MP & GI making *My Kingdom for a Husband* in 1957 was indeed the continuation of this pursuit. We can understand the historical position of the film from this perspective of Cantonese opera history.

My Kingdom for a Husband was a major production of MP & GI's Cantonese arm. Director Tso Kea paid a lot of attention to the film's spectacle effects like sets, decorations and composition. Even the promotion campaign stressed that "the film's story, sets, costumes and even the composition of its images and the choice of songs are informed by a romantic and exaggerated approach, recreating the qualities of Sit's production."[6] The very first scene takes place in a westernized club, with Cheung Ying singing a song while wearing a suit and playing a white violin. (The song is "Couple in Harmony", a rather traditional number.) He is swamped by fashionably dressed women in the audience. One review comments: "Like Elvis, he is admired by many women."[7] But the scene is even closer to the moment in the MGM film *The Merry Widow* (1952), when Count Danilo enters and sings while flanked by women. Most of the songs are samplings of numbers in Sit's production, though not without revisions. The singing of the stars was heavily hyped, touting "Cheung's singing debut in Sit's tone after a decade in film" and "Law Yim-hing's luscious voice" as well as her "beautiful body,"[8] the last point a reference to the bathing scene. The objectification of the female body becoming a part of the spectacle is another sign of the film's Hollywood influence.

The film was a big hit, spawning a trend of Hollywood-style palatial drama. MP & GI followed with a sequel, *My Kingdom for a Honeymoon* (aka *The Romance of Jade Hall, Sequel*, 1958), as well as *The Magic Box* (1958) and *True Love* (1958, probably adapted from MGM's *Sacramouche*, 1952), also starring Cheung Ying, Law Yim-hing, and Leung Sing-po. In 1958, Jinmen also produced *The Prince's Romantic Affairs*, starring Mui Yee (Mei Yi), who financed it, and Cheung

餘話：從《璇宮艷史》到《龍翔鳳舞》

1957 年 9 月 17 日《新晚報》的「台前幕後」專欄，簡單介紹過新片《璇宮艷史》後，又報導兩部國際／電懋公司的製作情況：國際公司近期開拍兩部戲軏相近的影片，一部是《封面女郎》，七彩國語歌舞片，由李湄、張仲文合演。另一部是粵語片《廣告女郎》，由文蘭主演。當年電懋國語組所籌拍的《封面女郎》，即今天已經公認是國語歌舞片經典的《龍翔鳳舞》（1959）。上面專欄說《龍翔鳳舞》和《廣告女郎》戲軏相近，應該是就劇情內容來說。如果就刻意突出電影的景觀性、積極發揮電影視覺效果，成為吸引觀眾的重要手段和原則來說，則《璇宮艷史》和《龍翔鳳舞》兩片是相似的、相通的。

《龍翔鳳舞》是電懋繼《曼波女郎》（1957）之後製作的另一部國語青春歌舞片。李湄、張仲文分飾歌舞團的一

《璇宮艷史》
My Kingdom for a Husband

《龍翔鳳舞》中的兩場歌舞——
《妹妹我愛你》（上）和《春之歌》（右）。
Two musical numbers in *Calendar Girl*.

雙姊妹，孫金柳和孫銀箏。歌舞團姊妹故事是荷里活歌舞片的常見題材。這個故事的原型，可以追溯到美高梅最初期的第一部歌舞片《百老滙之歌》(*The Broadway Melody*，1929)。邵氏1967年攝製的《香江花月夜》，也是這個故事原型的變奏。

《龍翔鳳舞》的製片宋淇和導演陶秦，是有意識的要仿效荷里活，製作一部中國式的歌舞片(film musical)。電影裡面的豐富景觀效果，集中表現於十多場的歌舞場面。電影裡面，歌舞團的第一個正式演出項目便是〈毛毛雨〉，可能是姚敏藉此向上海流行曲傳統和黎錦暉致敬。接下的〈妹妹我愛你〉，原本亦是黎錦暉的三十年代作品。這一場的背景設置在一個現代城市(香港？上海？模糊不清？)的大廈天台，中間是閃亮的巨型廣告霓虹光管。李湄反串男裝和張仲文調情，兩人又唱又跳，有頗重的東洋（寶塚歌舞團）味道。另一場〈玫瑰玫瑰我愛你〉則純粹是百老匯的舞台景象。在滿佈紅玫瑰花瓣後幕的舞台，李湄和陳厚表演「查爾斯頓舞」(Charleston)，色彩的配搭十分仔細、和諧。〈娘子軍進行曲〉的視像處理更加刻意。李湄和張仲文穿上軍裝在鏡子前舞動，二人的影像在多面鏡子之間互相反射，做成眾女兵向前邁進的視覺效果。最後一場〈春之歌〉，運用俯鏡呈現由多位舞者(穿羅傘裙、戴闊邊帽)併砌而成的花形圖案，令人想起美高梅另一部名片《歌舞大王齊格菲》(*The Great Ziegfeld*，1936)裡面的經典歌舞場面。同場李湄、張仲文和陳厚三人在桃紅柳綠的春天花園大跳恰恰。這一場的主要插曲〈三輪車上的小姐〉本來是陳歌辛的名曲，原唱者是屈雲雲。有趣的是，1958年的《璇宮艷史續集》裡面也出現了這支樂曲，填上新詞後由張瑛和羅艷卿對唱。

Ying; and Guohua released *Prince of Thieves* and a sequel. The next year, Shaw Brothers released *Glass Slippers*, an adaptation of *Cinderella*, introducing youth appeal by starring rising stars Cheung Ying-choy (Zhang Yingcai) and Lam Fung (Lin Feng).

Concluding Remarks: From *My Kingdom for a Husband* to *Calendar Girl*

On September 17, 1957, The New Evening Post, after offering a brief introduction to the new release *My Kingdom for a Husband*, reports on the progress of two MP & GI films: "Two films of similar stories are being made, one is the colour Mandarin film *Cover Girl*, starring Li Mei and Diana Chang Chung-wen (Zhang Zhongwen), and the other is the Cantonese film *The Girl of the Year*." *Cover Girl* is actually *Calendar Girl* (1958), recognized today as a classic of Mandarin musicals. The report mentions "similar stories". Indeed, in terms of highlighting spectacle and realizing visual effects to attract audiences, *Calendar Girl* and *My Kingdom for a Husband* are more similar.

Calendar Girl is MP & GI's follow-up to the youthful musical *Mambo Girl*. Li and Chang play a pair of sisters in a song-and-dance company, a familiar Hollywood premise that can be dated back to MGM's first musical, *The Broadway Melody* (1929). The same story is also used in Shaw's 1967 film *Hong Kong Nocturne*.

The film's producer Stephen Soong (Song Qi) and director Tao Qin were obviously trying to imitate Hollywood to create a Chinese film musical. Sumptuous spectacle effects are presented in over a dozen musical numbers. The first performance by the troupe is "Drizzles", likely a tribute to Shanghai pop. This is followed by "I Love You My Sweet Little Sister", sampling a 1930s song. The number is set on the rooftop in a modern city (Hong Kong? Shanghai? Or without identity?), with a huge neon sign in the middle. Li is in drag, romancing Chang as they sing and dance in a style reminiscent of the Japanese song-and-dance troupe Takarazuka. Another is "Rose, Rose I Love You", a purely Broadway number, with Li and

《龍翔鳳舞》憑藉着重新編寫的三十年代上海流行曲、各式各樣的西方流行舞蹈、華麗悅目的服飾裝扮、精心設計的場景畫面，為電影院的觀眾帶來五彩繽紛的景觀效果和視聽娛樂。其實上面的幾項描述，也適用於電懋粵語組的《璇宮艷史》，不過將第一項換成「三十年代省港粵劇」而已。《龍翔鳳舞》屬國語歌舞片，根源上溯《百老匯之歌》；《璇宮艷史》是粵語戲曲片，間接受到西片《璇宮艷史》的影響。（巧合的是，兩部荷里活電影都是在 1929 年推出。）如果説電懋的《璇宮艷史》繼承了三十年代的省港商業粵劇文化，那麼，《龍翔鳳舞》就是 1949 年以前的上海流行曲在香港的延續和拓展。這兩套別具意義的香港電影，都是電懋公司的產品。它們既反映了五十年代廣東文化和上海文化在香港的相遇（南北和），也説明了電懋公司當年的文化生產角色。

歌舞台上的娘子軍
"Women Soldiers" in *Calendar Girl.*

Peter Chen Ho (Chen Hou) dancing the Charleston on a stage covered in petals of red roses. The visual effects of "The Women Soldier March" are even more elaborate. Li and Chang, in para-military uniforms, dance in front of a series of mirrors, creating the effect of a multitude of soldiers marching forward. The last scene, "Song of Spring", offers an overhead shot of the dancers, creating a flower pattern reminiscent of the musical numbers of MGM's *The Great Ziegfeld* (1936). A number in the scene, adapted from another Shanghai pop "Girl on a Tricycle", features Li, Chang and Chen doing the cha-cha in a blooming garden. Interestingly, the same number also appears in the sequel *My Kingdom for a Honeymoon*, a duet with different lyrics sung by Cheung and Law.

With new interpretations of 1930s Shanghai pop, a variety of western dance steps, magnificent costumes and carefully designed sets, *Calendar Girl* provides audiences with colourful spectacles and entertainment. Interestingly, the same principles also applied to *My Kingdom for a Husband*. While the former is a Mandarin film that traces back to *The Broadway Melody*, the latter is a Cantonese film whose lineage goes back to *The Love Parade*. If *My Kingdom for a Husband* inherits the commercial Cantonese opera culture of the 1930s, *Calendar Girl* is a continuation of pre-1949 Shanghai pop. Both culturally significant works and both MP & GI products, the films illustrate not only the meeting of Cantonese and Shanghai cultures in Hong Kong but also the cultural role played by MP & GI during the 1950s.

Translated by Sam Ho

註

1. 見 John Kobal: *Gotta Sing Gotta Dance: A Pictorial History of Film Muscials*, London: Hamlyn Publishing Group,1971, pp. 54-57 及網頁 *http://www.dandugan.com/maytime/f-lovepa.html.*
2. 見麥嘯霞，〈廣東戲劇史略〉，中國文化協進會編：《廣東文物》，香港：中國文化協進會， 1941 ，頁 824；及〈曲譜〉，錢廣仁編：《新月曲集》，第 3 期， 1931 ，頁 30-33 。
3. 見余慕雲，〈薛覺先和電影〉，《粵劇研究》（薛覺先紀念專號），第 4 期， 1987 年 12 月，頁 62 。
4. 除了出任宣傳部主任外，麥嘯霞本身既是一名「開戲師爺」（粵劇編劇），也是一名電影導演。他撰寫的〈廣東戲劇史略〉，是第一篇從嚴肅的學術眼光討論粵劇歷史的文章，見註 2 。
5. 見粵曲研究社：《璇宮艷史》，廣州：五桂堂， 1930 年代。
6. 見羅卡，〈後記：時代的開始與終結〉，第十七屆香港國際電影節回顧特刊，香港：市政局， 1993 ，頁 77 。
7. 見《國際電影》，第 23 期， 1957 年 9 月，頁 37 。
8. 見〈璇宮艷史〉，《新晚報》， 1957 年 9 月 15 日。
9. 見《璇宮艷史》宣傳小冊， 1957 年 9 月。

容世誠，新加坡國立大學中文系副教授。研究興趣包括明朝戲劇、粵劇、以及新加坡中國戲曲的社會歷史。

Yung Sai-shing, associate professor of Chinese Studies at National University of Singapore. His research interest includes Ming drama, Cantonese opera, and social history of Chinese opera in Singapore.

Notes

1. See John Kobal: *Gotta Sing Gotta Dance:A Pictorial History of Film Musicals*, London: Hamlyn Publishing Group, 1971, pp. 54-57 and website: *http://www.dandugan.com/maytime/f-lovepa.html.*
2. See Mai Xiao-xia, "Brief History of Cantonese Theatre" in Chinese Culture Promotion Association, ed., *Guangzhou Artefacts* (in Chinese), Hong Kong: Chinese Culture Promotion Association, 1941, p. 824 and Qian Guangren, ed., *Collection of New Moon Songs* (in Chinese), vol. 3, 1931, pp. 30-33.
3. In addition to publicity, Mai also wrote plays and directed films. His "Brief History of Cantonese Theatre" is the first article to approach Cantonese opera history from a serious academic angle. See Chinese Culture Promotion Association, ed., op. cit.
4. See Cantonese Opera Research Soceity: *My Kingdom for a Husband* (in Chinese), Guangzhou: Wu Gui tang, 1930s.
5. See Law Kar, "Epilogue: The Beginning and End of an Era" in *Mandarin Films and Popular Songs: 40's – 60's*, the 17th Hong Kong International Film Festival Catalogue, Hong Kong: Urban Council, 1993, p. 77.
6. See *Screen International* (in Chinese), no. 23, September 1957, p. 37.
7. See "My Kingdom for a Husband" in *New Evening Post* (in Chinese), September 15, 1957.
8. See promotional pamphlet for *My Kingdom for a Husband* (in Chinese), September 1957.

天堂的異鄉人

- 邁克 -

黃金屋抑或顏如玉？

這是一個好地方
大家叫它人間天堂
它白天是繁華市場
到晚上變成了溫柔鄉
溫柔鄉溫柔鄉溫柔鄉
究竟哪裡是溫柔鄉？
燦爛的燈光教人眼花繚亂
哪裡去尋找那溫柔鄉？

故事尚未展開，聲帶上混雜的男女異口同聲率先唱出了憧憬和隱憂。在人生路不熟的城市碰運氣，的確不比遠足旅行，探險帶來的新鮮刺激縱使令人興奮，總蓋不過生計沒有着落引起的惶恐。這是《温柔鄉》（1960）的主題曲，歌裡形容的忐忑芳心，屬於即將在香港着陸的

Strangers in Paradise

- Michael Lam -

House of Gold or Beauties of Tenderness?

This is a nice place
They call it paradise on earth
By day it's a glorious market
By night an abode of tenderness
Tenderness, tenderness, tenderness abode
Where indeed is the abode of tenderness
Eyes blinded by lustrous neon
Where indeed to find the abode of tenderness?

Even before the story starts, the men and women on the soundtrack have voiced in song the longing and the worries. Trying one's luck in a strange city is no picnic, for no excitement of any adventure can overcome the fear of joblessness. This is the theme song of *Bachelors Beware* (1960) and the worrisome heart belongs to Ding (Linda Lin Dai). On the ship bound for Hong Kong, it's natural that she's anxious about her future. But if she's worried about being lonely in a strange place, that's totally unnecessary – not because two of her cousins had

女主角丁小圓（林黛）。在駛向目的地的輪船上，如果她曾經為自己不明朗的前途憂慮，那是完全可以理解的，然而假如她擔心的是陌生環境裡舉目無親的孤立，那就大可不必——不是因為早有兩個先上岸的表哥作為十拿九穩的投靠對象，而是因為五六十年代電懋電影中，與她處境相若的外來人多如過江之鯽，絕對不會找不到聆聽吐苦水的耳朵。

最接近的是《六月新娘》(1960)裡的汪丹林(葛蘭)——也是經海路登陸，也是以結婚為訪港大前提，甚至飾演準新郎的同樣是張揚。丁小圓這位表妹顯然是初次離鄉，奉姑母之命千里迢迢移船就磡和表哥親上加親，汪丹林卻是見多識廣的當代遊牧民族，跟隨招搖撞騙的父親由上海跑到香港，從香港又移到日本，兜了個大圈終於再回歸香港。一個沒有正職的「女結婚員」[1]，東奔西跑為的當然是歸宿問題。劇本雖然沒有提，她在日本的搜索行動可想沒有達到合乎理想的成績，否則不會悻悻然吃回頭草——當初與董少爺（張揚）訂婚，是權宜的騎牛搵馬，找得到條件更佳的快婿肯定蟬過別枝，反正訂婚沒經過法律手續，而且山高皇帝遠，董家就算在當地有點勢力也鞭長莫及。

她一面正氣向半路殺出的追求者林亞芒（田青）解釋，説的倒是真心話：「你生長在外國，不明白中國女子要的是穩定可靠的愛情。」林亞芒是來自菲律賓的樂師，自然不能提供「穩定可靠」的基本要求——所謂愛情，是生活的代名詞。他聽了大受刺激，反唇相譏：「你是指金錢、地位、生活的保障。」可是這有甚麼不對？不是為了追求更自由的空氣，更舒適的生活，更容易掌握的未來，才毅然離鄉背井嗎？這點連初來埗到的丁小圓也非常清楚，遑論見過世面的汪丹林。天堂之為天堂，還不是因為它有可以委託終生的黃金屋？

「女結婚員」在想甚麼?
The "marriage professional" pondering her professional ethics?

landed before her but because in the MP & GI films of the 1950s and 1960s, newcomers like her are only too plentiful.

The closest is Wang Danlin (Grace Chang / Ge Lan) in *June Bride* (1960), who also comes by boat to marry – her groom also played by Chang Yang (Zhang Yang). While Ding is leaving home for the first time to marry her cousin, Wang is a modern day nomad, following her swindler of a father from Shanghai to Hong Kong, then Japan, and back to Hong Kong. A "marriage professional"[1], she travels looking for professional fulfillment. It goes without saying that her job search in Japan has not been fruitful, or she wouldn't have come crawling back to Tung (Chang), whom she has engaged as Plan B.

She explains with total conviction to a new suitor, Lin Yamang (Tian Qing): "You grew up overseas, you don't understand that Chinese girls want a steady and dependable love." Lin, a musician from the Philippines who obviously cannot satisfy her "steady and dependable" requirement, retorts: "You mean money, position and a protected life." But what's wrong with that? Isn't the pursuit of freedom, comfortable life and a better future the very reason so many leave home? Isn't Hong Kong a paradise because of its houses of gold?

Lin and Wang meet on the ship. Both coming to Hong Kong for a better life, they're literally "on the same boat". There are indeed many outsiders in *June Bride*, coming from different backgrounds. There is also the sailor Mai, played by Roy Chiao (Qiao Hong), an actor who seems to be going through a "foreigner phase" in his career. In *June Bride*, he is a Chinese American with the address "329 Lincoln Street, San Francisco"; in *Ladies First* (1962), he looks like an authentic Hong Kong person, but casually discloses that "my family hasn't come out," revealing that he's a new immigrant, not yet ready to bring his parents out from the Mainland. Of course, the last example is a

林亞芒和汪丹林在船上結識，到香港為了討生活——兩人名副其實「搭同一條船」。《六月新娘》特多來自不同背景的外地人，除了汪與林，還有由喬宏飾演的水手麥勤。這時期的喬宏有成為「老外專家」的傾向，接二連三替影片添增異國情調：在《六月新娘》是住址「舊金山林肯街329號」的美國華僑；在《玉樓三鳳》（1960）是興沖沖訪筆友的星洲華僑；在《好事成雙》（1962）看似地道香港人，無意間卻透露「家人沒有出來」——大陸新移民，還沒有完全安頓，所以父母仍然住在內地。當然，最末的例子舉得有點荒謬，那時電懋的國語影片中，熙來攘往有哪一個不是廣東人所謂的「外省人」？那似乎是心照不宣的設定，毋須明言大家也共識的——也因為如此，喬宏在《好事成雙》無關宏旨的一句對白帶來意想不到的震動，像突然亮出的鏡子，照出沒有人分心留意過的真實。

麥勤應該是少小離家渡海到美洲謀生的金山阿叔，省吃儉用十四年，一心一意回到東方準備娶個賢能淑德的老婆——1949年以前就離開中國了，和當時香港一般移民不一樣。他是張愛玲小說裡常見的那種在外國吃過虧的男性——吃過生活的虧，也吃過女人的虧——到頭來思念着故鄉，遙不可及的一切都有說不出的好，包括恭順的、穿旗袍的、善於低頭的舊式中國女子。帶着封了塵的記憶來到一切在迅速改變的香港，難怪他驚惶失措，一天到晚借酒逃避現實了。

從男性角度看，這爿人間天堂供應的是實惠的顏如玉。不嚮往家庭生活的男人，在這裡找得到傳統婚姻以外的許多可能性，尤其如果手裡有幾個錢。直率坦白的麥勤揚着白花花的鈔票到處尋女伴，絲毫不覺得自己在變相召妓，女性尊嚴還不曾在曙光初露的新風氣裡覓得微妙的平衡位置。再樂觀的旁觀者，也不敢認為《六月新

little absurd, for in MP & GI films, who isn't an immigrant? This goes without saying, which is exactly why Chiao's casual disclosure has such impact, like a suddenly produced mirror, reflecting a neglected truth.

Mai must be one of those "American uncles" who left young. After 14 years of frugal life, he comes back to the East for a good wife. Unlike most immigrants of the time, he has left China before 1949. He's one of those men who has tasted defeat overseas – in life and with women – and looks at the old homeland with rosy fondness, especially women who wears *qi pao* and who knows how to lower their heads. Arriving with dusty memories, he is shocked by the rapidly changing Hong Kong. No wonder he takes to the bottle.

In male eyes, this is a shopping paradise for beauties. Mai goes about his shopping flashing bank notes, unaware that it's glorified prostitution, for it's a time when female dignity has yet to find a balance in the emerging modernity. Even optimists won't look at the happy endings in these two films as victories for women – the heart of the groom in *June Bride* still belongs to a former lover and Ding's defeat of her love rivals in *Bachelors Beware* doesn't guarantee love. Wang is too smart to not realize that Lin is right, that her marriage to Tung is but a deal of mutual consent, long-term prostitution with legal protection. Even the innocent Ding should know that the abode of tenderness she longs for is occupied – it's men's turf and women can only be the "tenderness" in that "abode".

Peaches or Pears?

Coming to this new and wonderful land,

Seeing only strangers,

Hi, Hi, Hi… and Hi,

Acquainted in one day, friends in two,

Bosom buddies by the third…

You sir, a child's heart underneath the silver hair,

You mad'm, forever young,

娘》和《溫柔鄉》的大團圓結局代表女主角的勝利：前者的新郎，一顆心始終繫於相好多年的歌女（丁好）身上，後者縱使智退風流表哥的三個女友（包括粵語片熟面孔于素秋），並不表示奪得麵包的同時攫取了玫瑰。聰明的汪丹林，不會不知道林亞芒沒有說錯，她和董少爺的結合只是一宗你情我願的交易，有法律保障的長期賣淫。而天真的丁小圓也不會不明白，她盼望的溫柔鄉，老早已經被她表哥霸佔了——那是一個由男性主導的地盤，女性爭得頭崩額裂，也只能委身當「鄉」裡的「溫柔」。

桃抑或李？

來到呀這新鮮好呀好地方
見到的都是陌呀陌生的人
你好我好大家介紹一聲
一天生疏兩天熟
三天交情生呀生了根
誠心誠意相知深

這一位某先生白髮童心
這一位某太太永遠年輕
每一位 gentleman 個個都天真
所有的 ladies 個個是美人

歌名〈好地方〉，唱歌的是葉楓。不不，唱歌的是《桃李爭春》（1962）裡葉楓飾演的夜總會歌女李愛蓮——拍馬屁拍得接近肉麻的歌詞，描寫了劇中人無奈的處境，絕對和飾演者的品格無關。乍聽它和〈溫柔鄉〉大同小異，細想才悟出其中的分別。同樣天花亂墜把香港譽為天上有地下無的樂園，〈溫柔鄉〉以第三人稱描繪丁小圓初到貴境的患得患失，〈好地方〉卻單刀直入，由李愛蓮以第一人稱向顧曲周郎拋媚眼。本來，娛樂場

Every gentleman a child at heart,
Every lady a great beauty

The song is "Wonderful Land", sung by Julie Yeh Feng (Ye Feng). No, it's sung by the nightclub songstress Li, played by Yeh in *It's Always Spring* (1962). The flattery in the lyrics betrays the hardships of the character, not the actress. Though also describing Hong Kong as a paradise, this song is different from that in *Bachelors Beware*. The praise it sings is the kind of seduction routinely offered in nightclubs, and behind Li's honeyed words are actually sorrow and despair.

Li is a newcomer who has come too late. All the good jobs are taken, by those who have landed earlier. Worse, she not only has to seek love but also a living. Ding and Wang have to make a living too, but they make things easier by coupling it with their search for love. Not only is Li without a love target on which to sink her claws, she has in tow a sister, one who begs suspicions of an illegitimate child. It doesn't help that Li's from Singapore. Immigrants from up north always have an arrogance against the proverbial south, and those coming from near the equator have no choice but to accept their second-class status. Working hard to overcome this handicap, they may end up trying too hard. Arriving at the beginning of *It's Always Spring*, Li is asked by reporters to compare the men of Singapore and Hong Kong. She smiles: "Singapore men are steady; ideal husbands. Hong Kong men are energetic; ideal lovers." Many an energetic ego must have been massaged.

She may be the Singing Queen of Singapore, but in a strange land, she has to start from scratch. Invited to sing at the nightclub, she willingly obliges, ignoring the insult that it's actually an audition. She laces her flattery with extra sugar, determined to take the plunge. But as she sings about the "gentleman" and the "lady", the film shows us a host of foolish clowns, making the "wonderful land" in the lyrics all the more ironic. Yet she soldiers on. "Acquainted in one day,

所就是甜言蜜語滿天飛的地方，嘻嘻哈哈的場面話，誰拿它當真誰自討苦吃。可是這宗個案非比尋常，剖開來盡是酸楚和淒涼。

李愛蓮不但是個從外地來到香港發展的異鄉人，而且來得太晚了一點。所有優質的崗位，都被搶灘的幸運兒佔據了，防守得嚴之又嚴，遲到的倒霉鬼休想越俎代庖鵲巢鳩佔。更窘的是，除了謀愛之外她還要謀生——當然丁小圓、汪丹林她們也謀生，但那是與謀愛以一箭雙鵰的方式平行進行的，省氣力得多。論天賦條件，李愛蓮比她們更勝一籌，可際遇卻遠遠不及，既沒有老早瞄準的獵物恭候她施展擒拿功，還拖着一個少不更事的妹妹——說是妹妹，然而很容易令人懷疑是私生女。

來自新加坡，顯然也使她自覺矮了半截。北方的同胞一般帶着傲氣，鼻孔朝天瞧不起華南一帶的「南蠻」。南洋比南蠻的領土更靠近赤道，地位與地理形勢成正比例，來自該地的華僑，在移民群中只好忍氣吞聲屈居二等居民的位置。為了力爭上游，不得不時時打醒十二分精神，一有機會，做甚麼都特別賣力。可惜往往事倍功半，客套過了火變成奉承，讚美加了班淪為擦鞋。《桃李爭春》才開場，我們已經知道她有備而至了。接機的記者提問刁鑽的難題，要她比較港新兩地的男性，她不慌不忙笑着答：「新加坡男人老實，是理想的丈夫；香港男人活潑，是理想的情人。」被讚活潑的一群，可想靈魂立即坐上了沙發椅。

冠着星洲歌后的名銜跑碼頭，聽起來威風，實際不得不從最基本做起，拜客送禮吃飯應酬樣樣親力親為。在夜總會臨時被邀上台獻唱，雖然明知是變相的試唱，對成了名的歌手是侮辱，在別人的屋簷下惟有欣然接受。難得的派名片良機，當然不可錯失，心思縝密選一碗加重蜜糖的迷湯向台下灌，越甜越好——她是下定決心賭一

「新加坡男人老實，是理想的丈夫」——《桃李爭春》

Yeh Feng on stage, delivering her ego massage in *It's Always Spring*.

鋪大的，把自己整個全押上了。單看歌詞，還不能完全明瞭她的城府：唱到「每一位gentleman個個都天真，所有的 ladies 個個是美人」，鏡頭看見的是醜態百出的小丑。這種戲劇性的諷刺，等於暗暗否定了「好地方」的意義。

「一天生疏兩天熟，三天交情生了根」，還有第二段的「南北同是一家春，一心一意不離分」，顯然是李愛蓮一廂情願的幻想。又不是手持仙棒的吃飯神仙，幾句諂媚和巴結怎能打通長期閉塞的經脈？幸好她並不天真，隨時處於戒備狀態，應付無所不在的排擠。正式登台演唱，以一身熱帶風情裝扮亮相，不惜把自己物件化，迎合捧場客貪新鮮喜獵奇的心理。停不了顧盼生姿更是必然的，眉目傳情頻密到一個程度，簡直有如有求必應全天候的發電廠。甚至動妹妹李小蓮（張慧嫻）的腦筋，找個適當的時機將她當作一種招徠手段——這片綠葉一直扮演《白蛇傳》小青的角色，這時忽然搖身一變，有點成了慘被販賣的童妓的況味，掉進了《海上花列傳》的世界裡。

《桃李爭春》選角非常有趣，[2]構成了文本之外驚心動魄的張力：李愛蓮的對頭陶海音，由慣走風騷路線的李湄飾演，兩位艷星邪鬥邪，一反傳統正邪對立的作風——試想想葉楓碰上的假如是林黛或者尤敏，局面會多麼不同。劇本顯然偏袒掛頭牌的陶海音，尤其在下半場，李愛蓮潰不成軍，連表演舞蹈的機會也沒有，完全被剝削還擊餘地。然而鏡頭迷戀的是風華正茂的葉楓，一舉手一投足閃爍無可抗拒的艷光，無聲無息與劇本展開了波濤洶湧的暗鬥。最後雖然以和解作收場，無可置疑李愛蓮是陶海音的手下敗將，任憑表現再出色，也要靠較早佔領山頭的師姐高抬貴手，才可以在彈丸之地討得立足之點。意外的最後微笑，卻偏偏出現在她臉上：謝幕的

失敗乃成功之母——
做不成空中小姐，結婚也是一個好出路。

From one profession to another: Soo Fung quits air hostessing to become a wife.

肩並肩載歌載舞，身材高䠷的葉楓以男裝上陣，輕而易舉搶去了所有的鋒頭。

這裡或者還有另一個性別政治的教訓：女人要戰勝爬頭的同性，最快捷妥善的辦法是把雙腳插進異性的鞋裡。

雲吞抑或餛飩？

賣餛飩呀賣呀賣餛飩，賣餛飩

要是你吃了我的熱餛飩

肚子吃飽混身熱呀熱騰騰

要是你不吃我的熱餛飩呀

怎麼知道餛飩味道香呀香噴噴？

一疊連聲以叫賣家鄉小食作綽頭，是陶海音在《桃李爭春》使出的終極撒手鐧。俗語說得好：胃是通往心的捷徑，何況這一客滾熱辣的餛飩還有治療思鄉愁緒的功能。來自南洋的李愛蓮這回凶多吉少了──就算使出混身解數捧上味道更香濃的咖喱雞和燒沙爹，食客嘴裡的味蕾也喚不起記憶熟悉的溫柔。

這一招編劇安排得不動聲息，老早埋下了伏線：開場不久，陶海音由夜總會下班回家，等待女兒的母親準備了餃子作宵夜。不經意的細節暗寫他們是北方人，[3]帶着原有的飲食習慣移居香港，沒有染上當地人的「壞習慣」──廣東人一般以粥作上床前的點心。劇情發展到緊張關頭，越鬥越勇的李愛蓮把她逼到牆角，事業的前景和愛情的信心同時動搖得厲害，苦惱之際愛女心切的母親又來喊她吃餃子。這倒令她靈機一觸，編了首〈賣餛飩〉對付意氣風發的敵人。兩個在機會主義掛帥的小島爭飯碗的異鄉人，始終是代表大中原的一位佔優勢。

陶海音餛飩的叫賣迴蕩起似曾相識的市音，教曾經於另一個城市聽過沉寂黑夜裡一聲聲街頭呼喚的人，掉進渾渾噩噩的舊夢去。廣東人也有類似以蔬菜或肉碎作餡的

「要是你不吃我的熱餛飩呀，
怎麼知道餛飩味道香呀香噴噴？」
"If you try not my hot dumplings,
You won't know how great they taste."

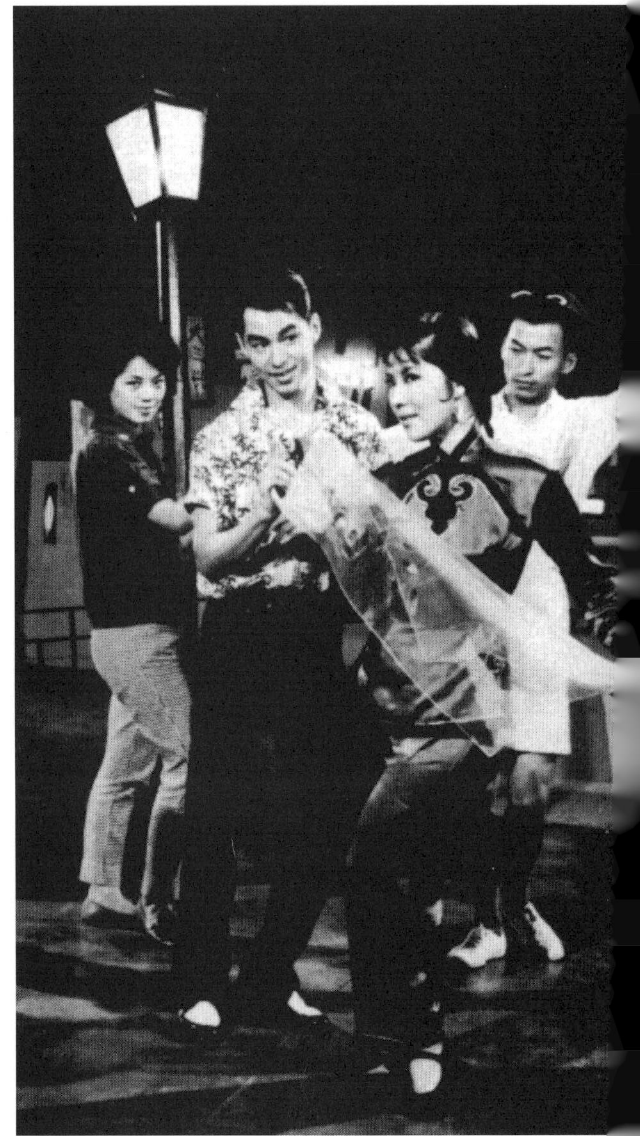

friends in two, bosom buddies by the third," followed by "North and south the same family in spring, the same heart and mind doesn't part…." What wishful thinking!

The casting of the film is very interesting, creating an extra-textual tension. Li's rival is Tao, played by a Li Mei known for sultry roles. Two seductresses going against each other, wreaking havoc on the good girl vs. bad tradition – imagine Yeh Feng going against Linda Lin Dai or Lucilla You Min and one can readily imagine a different film. It's also worth noting that the names Tao and Li are plays on the Chinese title of the film, "Taoli Zhenchun", an idiom that means "peaches and pears vying for spring". And the "spring" that the peach and the pear fights for can be either the billing glory at the Nightclub Spring Breeze or the heart of the hunk Xu (Roy Chiao).

The script obviously favours the pear, Tao. This is especially true in the second half, when the peach, Li, is totally defeated, denied even of a chance to

麵食，俗名雲吞，想是餛飩南下後的變種。北方人吃餛飩總是專心一致，不像南方人的雲吞，許多時候夾着麵條一起吃，「雲吞麵」久而久之成了連體嬰，如果不願意受到麵條的干擾，點菜時必需聲明要「淨雲吞」。

這種輕視簡潔主義的性格也延續到吃麵的習慣，廣東人擅長的炒麵一向大鑼大鼓，嘴刁的食客把品評的着眼點放在佐料上，很少關注麵條本身的優劣。北方人下麵，配料往往只有點到即止的油鹽蔥，麵條不但是主角，演的還是獨角戲。在《野玫瑰之戀》（1960），有一場過場戲歐陽莎菲飾演的慈母給深宵歸家的梁漢華（張揚）下肉絲麵。看似完全出於無心的芝麻綠豆，卻特別教人感到她對寶貝兒子沉溺式的關愛——生活那麼艱辛，竟然奢侈地將昂貴的肉絲充當可有可無的佐料！梁漢華後來的人格墮落，這種周到得令人感到窒息的母愛恐怕多少要負點責任。

同期電懋製作中，以食大作文章的首推《南北和》（1961）。它也是香港影壇少見的、以社會上不同族群的衝突為主題的影片，編劇巧妙利用飲食習慣的差異作例子，管窺同住難的深層文化因素，可以說深入淺出舉一反三，使觀眾發出會心微笑。裁縫張三波（梁醒波）極端痛恨由北方南下的「侵略者」，最看不過眼外江佬的滑頭充闊，偏偏操國語的死對頭老李（劉恩甲）不但把西裝店開在隔壁與他短兵相接，還搬進了同一間寓所跟他朝對口晚見面。他女兒麗珍（白露明）也不爭氣，這麼多人不喜歡，就愛上不諳粵語的北佬文安（雷震）。老李雖然不像張三波明目張膽仇視非我族類，骨子裡卻蔑視廣東人的保守老舊，認為他們窩囊沒出息。當然，他的女兒翠華（丁皓）的戀愛對象永輝（張清），正是他瞧不起的南方同胞。

翠華和永輝私下談婚論嫁，自然而然把話題扯到食的頭

dance. But a peach is a peach, and all that script biases are not going to dull the delicious luster of Yeh Feng. Although Li's final conciliation with Tao depends on the latter's helping hand, Yeh's radiant beauty and ravishing allure easily monopolises the camera's focus. Indeed, it is on her face that the last smile lingers – when they take their bow in the final song-and-dance, the taller Yeh, in men's garb, easily outshines Li Mei's Tao.

Perhaps there is another lesson in sexual politics here: For a woman to pass another woman in front, the best way is to slip into a pair of men's shoes.

Wanton or Dumpling?

Dumplings, dumplings, great dumplings,

Eat my steaming hot dumplings,

Your stomach full, your body warm.

But if you try not my hot dumplings,

You won't know how great they taste.

Selling hometown snacks in song is Tao's secret weapon in *It's Always Spring*. Not only is the way to the heart through the stomach, this bowl of steaming hot dumplings brings the heart all the way back to the old hometown. For Li, this is a connection all the saucy curry and fragrant satay from Singapore cannot make.

The script sets this up early and quietly. When Tao goes home after work, her mom is waiting with a bowl of dumplings, casually establishing their northern origin,[2] for dumplings are not the designated midnight snack of the Cantonese, who prefer congee. When Tao is troubled by Li's professional and romantic threats, the mother beckons again with more dumplings. Instantly inspired, she composes this *Dumpling Song*. When two newcomers fight for a living in this opportunistic island, it is the Mainland representative who has the upper hand. The Cantonese have a similar concoction, but their wantons always go with noodles, unlike the northerners' undivided faithfulness to dumplings. They apply the same devotion to their noodles.

上。也不知道是發自真心，還是覺得有向男朋友派定心丸的必要，她開門見山宣稱：「北方菜又鹹又多油，我們當然餐餐吃廣東菜。」還怕誠意被懷疑，進一步表示效忠，揚言最愛霉香鹹魚——這一切父親都偷聽了，氣得直跳腳。張三波和麗珍的爭持更正面，固執的前者深以「食在廣州」為榮，叛逆的後者大言不慚公佈：「我情願吃臭豆腐！」誰都知道，霉香鹹魚和臭豆腐分別是南北民間食物中的「極品」，嗜愛者寵幸有嘉，厭惡者走避不及。如此工整的對仗，以最極端的實例嘲諷南北的水火不容，實在是電影飲食笑料中的高筆。

因《南北和》而衍生的《南北一家親》(1962），依然由梁醒波和劉恩甲飾演狹路相逢的冤家，這回兩人且經營飯店，可是建築在食品上的笑料居然幾乎欠奉。北地胭脂李曼珍(丁皓)為了討好男友的粵籍父親沈敬炳(梁醒波)，初次上門拜訪特地獻上一底蘿蔔糕。沈喜出望外，連忙要她即席表演，教授沈伯母（馬笑英）蒸製地道廣東點心的秘訣。橋段蜻蜓點水一掠而過，既沒有進一步伸展，也沒有對調位置的呼應，遠不及《南北和》南腔北調唱對台戲一浪接一浪的精采。

倒是承接了在灰色地帶設立兩不管地頭的啟示——《南北和》結局雙方言和的場所是日本餐館，而決意排除上一代地域偏見的年輕人，約會的地點是西式咖啡座。《南北一家親》的兩對南北鴛鴦也愛在西餐廳碰頭，那似乎是一片安樂的淨土，不受老古董們煩絮爭執波及的安全地帶。在外國人管轄的區域覓得暫時的寧靜，鴕鳥似地避開了黨派間權力的鬥爭，這種描寫極像影射上海租界，可能是編劇張愛玲潛意識的「自傳色彩」。我們這位對飲食素有研究的作家，雖然沒有透過廚藝整色整水，卻在食肆的安排上流露了沒有經過大腦批核的心事。

Unlike the Cantonese way of smothering noodles with ingredients, northerners take theirs with minimal condiments. In *The Wild, Wild Rose* (1960), when the pianist comes home at night, his doting mother is waiting with a bowl of noodles with shredded pork. This small detail reveals the mother's indulgence and raises questions about its effect on the son's eventual down fall. For when times are tough, how can she throw pork into noodles that would've been fine by themselves?

Food also plays a big role in *The Greatest Civil War on Earth* (1961). It's also a rare Hong Kong film that portrays the conflict between different communities. The script skilfully uses eating habits to examine deep structure issues, creating comedy out of cultural differences. Tailor Cheung (Leung Sing-po / Liang Xingbo) hates northerners, but Li (Liu Enjia), who dislikes the Cantonese, opens a tailor shop next to Cheung's and moves in the same building. Making things worse, Cheung's daughter Lai (Christine Pai Lu-ming / Bai Luming) is in love with a northerner, Wen (Kelly Lai Chen / Lei Zhen), and Li's daughter Hwa (Kitty Ting Hao / Ding Hao) also falls for a southern lad, Fai (Cheung Ching / Zhang Qing).

When Hwa and Fai talk about marriage, food naturally becomes a topic. As if to appease her future husband, she declares: "Northern dishes are salty and greasy; we will have Cantonese food every meal." And if that's not enough, she declares that salted fish to be her favourite. Not to be outdone, Lai announces on her end: "I'd rather eat stinky bean curd!" Salted fish and stinky bean curd are the "extreme" delicacies of, respectively, Cantonese and northern cuisines. The symmetry in the film's use of food to parody cultural intolerance is a highpoint in the history of "food cinema".

The Greatest Wedding on Earth (1962), something of a sequel, again stars Leung and Liu. This time out, they're running rival restaurants, but – surprise! – food jokes are few

另一部由她編寫的《小兒女》(1963),則從最具外省風味的食物螃蟹着手,趣妙地帶觀眾入戲。擁擠的公共汽車上,王景慧(尤敏)突然覺得臀部被捏了一把,回頭一望,形跡可疑的孫川(雷震)正面露笑容,準備向她搭訕。「色狼來了」的警報馬上扯起,不甘受辱的她連忙顯露都市新女性抗暴本色,伸出玉手狠狠送給他一記準而響的耳光。一切當然是場誤會,孫川原來是個多年不見的老同學,光天化日向她施祿山之爪的,是他提着的新鮮螃蟹。生動的引子除了有立即抓緊觀眾注意力的效能,也微妙交代了兩個角色的家庭背景——都是由蘇浙一帶移居香港的外地人。

這個附會乍聽非常牽強——廣東人難道不吃蟹?吃,當然吃,然而和上面提過的麵條情況一樣,廣東人炮製螃蟹的手法通常很大陣仗,陪襯的配料霸道地與主角爭妍鬥麗,妹仔絲毫不給主人婆面子。就算是清蒸,吃的方式也和外省人不一樣,總是許多菜式中的一款——《小兒女》兩次吃螃蟹,桌上都單單只有一道菜,是典型外省人的「獨食」。

近年吃大閘蟹於香港是普遍的秋季口部運動,四十年前卻是收保在「北極圈」的秘密——《南北一家親》的北方館子門口招牌畫着一隻蟹,兩個老廣看見後不屑地説了一句:「我地唔食京菜」,掉頭就往對面的粵菜館走。然而大閘蟹不都包紮得結結實實麼,怎麼《小兒女》的橫行公子可以張牙舞爪,達成權充媒人的使命?會不會其實另有曲折的隱筆——洋澄湖特產市場上找不到,就地取材買了普通的螃蟹聊慰思鄉情切的胃?[1]

擠在小島上的異鄉人,誰吃得最不亦樂乎?答案非常出人意表,不是眾多北地來客的任何一位,而是《桃李爭春》甫由新加坡抵埗的李小蓮。冷眼旁觀姐姐李愛蓮施展媚功在陌生的環境打天下的同時,她不停地把各式各

《小兒女》中的螃蟹故事
The crab story in *Father Takes a Bride.*

and far between. Northern lass Jan (Ting), in an effort to please her lover's Cantonese father, Shum (Leung), brings with her turnip cakes (bought from Shum's restaurant) in her virgin visit. Shum is beside himself in joy but requests an instant cooking demonstration. *The Greatest Wedding*, however, pulls its punches in food jokes, never offering a corresponding gag to the turnip-cake bit and failing to reach the intensity of parody in *The Greatest Civil War*.

It does inherit the practice of establishing neutral zones. In *The Greatest Civil War*, the final peace negotiation takes place at a Japanese restaurant and the young people determined to erase ethnic biases meet always in coffee shops. The young lovers in *The Greatest Wedding* also meet at western restaurants, safety zones sheltered from the crossfire of the stubborn parents. Finding temporary retreat in foreign turf to hide head from party warfare seems like a reference to the concessions of Shanghai, possibly an autobiographical touch from scriptwriter Eileen Chang (Zhang Ailing), known for her understanding of culinary matters.

Another Chang script, *Father Takes a Bride* (1963), hooks up with the audience through a crab, a northern food item. In a crowded bus, the maiden Wang (You Min) suddenly feels a pinch on her buttocks. She turns around and finds Sun (Lai Chen) smiling at her, ready to strike up a conversation. Instincts of a city woman take over and she gives him a slap on the face, loud and clear. All is of course a big misunderstanding. Sun is a long ago friend and the pincher is actually a pair of pincers, belonging to a crab in the basket he's carrying. This prologue not only grabs a quick hold of the audience, but also introduces the characters' family background, that both came from the Suzhou-Zhejiang area.

But don't Cantonese eat crabs too? Of course they do, but, similar to their way with noodles, the Cantonese cook crabs with a wide variety of other

樣的零食往嘴裡送，口腔一刻沒有空閒過。那大概是性心理的側寫，朦朧的渴望找不到正規的出路，惟有寄情於吃。

飛上青天抑或畫地為牢？

我要飛上青天，上青天

我要飛上青天，上青天

我上七重天

逍遙自在像神仙

不是夢話連篇是信念

我要飛上青天

飛上青天

歌名六個字，唱歌的一位不厭其煩唱完又唱，反反覆覆加加減減，令人疑心其實她對展翅騰雲沒有太大把握，揚聲唸唸有辭，不外企圖製造事在必行的氣勢替自己壯膽。《空中小姐》(1959) 插曲多首，〈我要飛上青天〉負責打頭陣——其實是如假包換的主題曲，未畫龍先點睛，像個金碧輝煌的雕花畫框，一早穩穩妥妥掛在牆上，情節聽候時機乖乖在它劃定的範圍內就位。一曲終了，呆滯的鏡頭眼定定盯着幾個七彩繽紛的氫氣球，酷得簡直接近冷酷，目擊它們緩緩升空——逍遙自在飛上青天的，原來不是力竭聲嘶指天誓日那一位。

五六十年代，當空中服務員蔚為香港女性一項時髦的職業選擇，明明是與時差捉迷藏的侍應生，卻被扣上無限浪漫的幻想。有幸被選中的從業員身價百倍，誰也不認為她們和茶樓的企枱或菜館的女招待是同行，彷彿跟地心吸力的距離一拉遠，整個人便形而上地高貴起來，就算淑女加入行列也不失身份。《南北和》的張三波看見新搬來的鄰居李翠華穿着整潔漂亮的航空公司制服，一個箭步就跳到酸溜溜的結論：「行李摩登，唱時代曲，

現代遊牧民族的愛情故事
Grace Chang wants to "fly to the blue skies" but is grounded on land with Roy Chiao.

food stuff. Even with simple steaming, crab is only one among many dishes on the table. But in both crab dinner scenes of *Father Takes a Bride*, the crustacean is the only course. [1]

Among the strangers cramped in the island, who has the most fun eating? No, it's not one of the many northerners but a newcomer from the south, the teenage sister in *It's Always Spring*. Watching her sister Li making her seductive way through the new land, the girl never stops putting snacks in her mouth. Is such oral fixation an expression of hazy but unfulfilled sexual desire?

Fly to the Skies or Grounded on Land?

I want to fly to the blue skies,

The blue skies.

I want to scale the seven heavens,

To be merry like fairies.

Not murmurs in a dream,

But a belief firmly held.

I want to fly to the blue skies,

The blue skies.

The first line of the song is sung over and over again, as if the singer actually has no confidence spreading her wings and is repeating the words to convince herself. There are several songs in *Air Hostess* (1959) and "I Want to Fly to the Blue Skies" is the first, establishing the film like an ornate frame, hung on the wall from day one and waiting for the rest of the story to fill up the picture. At the end of the song, the camera fixes on a few colourful balloons, rising slowly to the blue skies, but witnessing their ascend is not the person who sings so determinedly about flying.

In the 1950s and 1960s, flight attendants were trendy professionals. Waitresses who play hide-and-seek with time zones, they were romanticized by virtue of their freedom from gravity. In *The Greatest Civil War on Earth*, Cheung leaps to a conclusion when he sees Hwa in her uniform:

當空中小姐—— 一定是外江女！」真是一言驚醒夢中人，空中小姐追上潮流、獨立、華麗的形象，正是廣東老鄉心目中外省人的縮影。北方佳麗傾巢而出不翼而飛，當然完全順理成章。

電懋國語片裡女性從事各行各業的都有，若論最具津津樂道價值，吸引到最多人投身的，則非空中服務員莫屬。李翠華的同行姐妹包括《四千金》（1957）的四妹（蘇鳳），和《空中小姐》所有四十歲以下的女主角、女配角和女閒角——可憐的蘇鳳成為罕見的「成功乃失敗之母」的實例，這次居然考試不及格，只能當地勤人員。奮不顧身向高空發展，如果她們有後顧之憂，使她們和大地保持聯絡的錨也並不坐落於香港。南中國海沿岸的小島只是一塊方便的跳板，一顆生逢其時的踏腳石。正因為如此，三天兩頭從啟德機場飛往外地，從來沒有牽腸掛肚之苦，只有瞻望機會之樂。

縱觀這個時期的電懋國語片，我們找不到一個腰是腰背是背的「香港人」，新的人類品種仍在加工製造中，住在島上的異鄉人還沒有堂正的身份可以認同。《南北和》與《南北一家親》這兩部國粵語夾雜的不是冤家不聚頭喜劇，[4] 在着力描寫族群間碰撞的過程中，變相突出了「國語人」與環境的格格不入——當然廣東人不是土生土長的當時也不少，然而就算剛剛由廣州南下的新客，操的卻是與本土人相同的一種方言，打成一片沒有隔膜，遭排斥的可能較低。缺乏強烈的對比，還可以得過且過裝聾作啞，兜口兜面展示文化背景生活習慣的差距，教人不得不正視一直秘而不宣的浪人無根感。這批影片提供的，其實是過渡期被孤立的心境寫照，情節再匪夷所思光怪陸離，原則上也是有特殊歷史意義的寫實片。

"Fancy luggage, sings Mandarin pop, air hostess – must be a northern girl!" Indeed, flight attendants are chic, independent and elegant, exactly the northerner image the Cantonese have in mind.

The women in MP & GI films have their share of jobs, but the most cherished profession that likely attracted many viewers to join ranks must be flight attending. Every actress under 40 in the film is, well, an air hostess. With their eyes on the skies, their land connection is not Hong Kong, the island that's little more than a stepping stone to something bigger. That's why when they march towards Kai Tak Airport in their smart uniforms, there's not a trace of parting sorrow but the pure joy of catching dreams.

In the MP & GI films of the period, there is not one truly Hong Kong person. The people that will come to define the island are still in the making and the new immigrants have no model with which to identify. The comedy of feuding rivals in *The Greatest Civil War* and *The Greatest Wedding* [3] calls attention to the Mandarin speakers' problems with integration – there were also lots of Cantonese immigrants, but they spoke the same dialect and were less likely to be rejected. When the differences in culture are displayed on plain sight, we're forced to look squarely at the once buried sense of rootlessness. What these films provide is a portrait of loneliness during that period of transition; the plots may be outrageous, but there is realism in their historical significance.

It's interesting that this rootless bunch never has any anxiety about identity. This problem doesn't exist because they don't consider Hong Kong home. Even with no future plans, they always feel they would move away. With an arrogance about their background and a contempt for the ground under their feet, they develop a special way of life. But as they assimilate, that distinguished quality is lost. Authentic Hong Kong characters began to appear

最有趣的一點，是這些沒有歸屬感的男女老幼，從來都沒有身份認同的煩惱——問題並不存在，因為他們不把香港當家，縱使沒有明確的計劃，下意識覺得有一天終會遷往別處。興興頭頭過一日算一日，積極謀取更佳出路，加上對自己背景的驕傲和對居住地的輕蔑，凝聚成別具一格的生活方式，一種由脾氣演變成的空氣。漸漸被當地人同化後，這種外省人特質跟着消逝，銀幕上熱熱鬧鬧湧現了地道的香港人：陳寶珠的工廠妹，許冠傑的打工仔，一個個龍精虎猛在上了軌道的大都會吐氣揚眉。電懋的國語時裝片，彷彿一夜之間遭淘汰，後期的《太太萬歲》（1968）、《三朵玫瑰花》（1965）和《家有賢妻》（1970）等等，統統是強顏歡笑的苟喘殘延，當年的風姿綽約和抖擻精神蕩然無存。國語片時代在端端正正劃上句號前，其實早就暗暗結束了。許多人把明星質素的直線下跌歸咎為電懋停產的原因，那當然很大程度上可以成立，但更致命的癥結，是最省招牌的時裝片，已經不再與觀眾息息相關，失去了存在理由。

非常意外，早被影壇淡忘的這股鬱香的空氣，三十多年後竟然在王家衛的《花樣年華》（2000）漾起一絲餘韻。它雖然是粵語片，牽動的卻是似曾相識的國語片情懷。精心重塑的舊時景象，罩着久違的不安於室的氛圍，儘管瑰艷的彩色取代了純樸的黑白，過來人敏感的鼻子一下就嗅了出來。蘇麗珍（張曼玉）和周慕雲（梁朝偉）藕斷絲連的情慾探戈，不但是《情場如戰場》（1957）、《六月新娘》這類求偶喜劇文藝腔的變奏，而且是南北對對碰溫和的回應。在寫字樓任打字員的蘇麗珍，飾演她老闆的雷震是當時電懋的當家小生，進一步加強了致敬的色彩。而採用時代曲歌名作片名，也是喚起塵封記憶的手勢——可惜周璇徹底是另一個時代的聲音，不能供應電懋影片插曲慣

on screen: Chan Po-chu (Chen Baozhu)'s factory girl, Sam Hui (Xu Guanjie)'s working man. The modern-era Mandarin films of MP & GI seemed to have vanished overnight, with later films like *Darling Stay at Home* (1968) and *The Homemaker* (1970) not retaining the former glory of the studio's works. Many had maintained that the drop in star quality was a major reason for MP & GI's production halt. While this is not an invalid argument, the key is in the loss of relevance of the modern-era films that is MP & GI's trademark.

Over 30 years later, this long-forgotten quality makes a surprise appearance in Wong Kar-wai (Wang Jiawei)'s *In the Mood for Love* (2000). Although it's a Cantonese film, the sentiments it evokes are those of the Mandarin cinema. Although the black and white images are tinted by glorious colours, the restless atmosphere cloaked in the carefully reconstructed images of the past does not escape sensitive eyes. The tango of desire between Su Li-zhen (Maggie Cheung / Zhang Manyu) and Chow Mo-wan (Tony Leung Chiu-wai / Liang Chaowei) is not only a continuation of romantic comedies like *The Battle of Love* (1957) and *June Bride*, but also a gentle response to the confrontations between north and south. Playing Su's boss is none other than Lai Chen, a top star of MP & GI underscoring the sense of tribute. The Chinese title, that of a Mandarin pop song from yesteryear, is also a gesture to arouse dusted memories – too bad Zhou Xuan's voice belongs to another era, not quite evocative of the MP & GI times. Su's husband takes frequent trips to Japan and Chow later moves to Singapore and Burma, their footprints all over Asia matching that of the nomadic MP & GI bunch. And Chow's wife, her face never revealed, may well be a flight attendant.[4]

有的卜卜脆。蘇的丈夫常常去日本公幹，周後來於新加坡和緬甸落腳，足跡在亞洲地圖印來印去，具備了電懋人物遊牧成性的風範——周那位從不露面的太太，甚至很有可能是空中小姐。[5]

葛蘭爽朗的歌聲又響起來了：「……逍遙自在像神仙，不是夢話連篇是信念……」不論是如願飛了上青天，還是陰差陽錯終於畫地為牢，異鄉人的故事依然活在天堂的集體記憶裡。

註

1. 張愛玲獨創的名詞，泛指把婚姻當作終身事業的女子——《六月新娘》的編劇正是張愛玲。
2. 所謂桃李爭春，指的是「李」愛蓮和「陶」海音爭奪「春」風殿夜總會台期。不過令桃李你爭我奪的春，也可以是夾在她們之間的許兆豐(喬宏)。這方面李愛蓮也是輸家，最終只分配到第二男主角陶正聲(雷震)。
3. 香港人口中的「北方人」歷來籠統，凡是華南以北的都被歸為同類。基本上是種歧視，連面目方言也不願意辨別，不把對方當作有性格有靈魂的個體。
4. 這兩部影片再加《南北喜相逢》(1964)，通常被統稱「南北系列」。但是其實《南北喜相逢》完全不做南轅北轍的文章，嚴格來說不應該歸入同一類。見宋淇，〈文學與電影中間的補白〉，《聯合文學》，第30期，1987年4月。當中他指出張愛玲寫的《南北喜相逢》「原暫名為《香園爭霸戰》，後來電懋公司大概認為既然《南北和》與《南北一家親》賣座，索性改名為《南北喜相逢》」。
5. 《花樣年華》關於吃的段落也非常有趣：蘇麗珍家裡現放着眾人羨慕的電飯煲，卻提不起勁落手落腳下廚煮住家飯，情願提着一隻鑊買外賣——呼之欲出是性生活的隱喻。難怪醒目的旁觀者看不順眼，在背後批評：「哎唷，外出買碗麵，都着得乍漂亮！」

編按

[1] 在螃蟹的問題上，參見羅卡在本書〈管窺電懋的創作/製作局面：一些推測、一些疑問〉一文。

邁克，自由寫作人。近作為《狐狸尾巴》(牛津大學出版社，2001)。
Michael Lam, free-lance writer. Recent publication: *Oops! Here We Go Again* (OUP, 2001).

Grace Chang's pleasant singing rises yet again: "…To be merry like fairies. Not murmurs in a dream, but a belief firmly held…." For these exiled strangers, their dream to fly up to the blue skies may have been fulfilled, or, instead, they have been grounded on land forever. Regardless, their stories live on, in the collective memories of the paradise.

Translated by Sam Ho

Notes

1. A term invented by novelist Eileen Chang, referring to women who treats marriage as a life-time job. *June Bride* is written by none other than Chang.
2. For the people of Hong Kong, "northerners" is a generalised term as anyone coming from north of South China is considered one. It's essentially prejudice, never looking at these strangers as individuals.
3. Together with *The Greatest Love Affair on Earth* (1964), these films are called the "north-south films". But *Love Affair* has nothing to do with north-south conflicts. See Stephen Soong (Song Qi), "The space between Literature and Film" in *Lianhe Wanxue*, (In Chinese) no. 30, April 1987. He points out that when Eileen Chang wrote the script, it was "called *Battle at Fragrant Garden*, but MP & GI probably saw the popularity of *The Greatest Civil War on Earth* and *The Greatest Wedding on Earth*" and decided to give the film a "north-south" spin in its Chinese title and its corresponding "greatest... on earth" English title.
4. Food scenes in *In the Mood for Love* is also interesting. Su has a fancy rice cooker in her home, yet she prefers to go for take-out. The sexual innuendoes can be readily read between the lines. No wonder an observer criticizes her for getting so dressed up for a bowl of noodles.

Editor's note

[1] The "crab scene" is also discussed in Law Kar's "A Glimpse of MP & GI's Creative / Production Situation: Some Speculations, Some Doubts" in this volume.

Close-ups

特寫

羽毛留下的秀麗筆跡：秦羽劇本初探

- 梁秉鈞 -

張愛玲編的喜劇《情場如戰場》（1957）裡，林黛扮演刁蠻小姐葉緯芳，把三個男的戲弄於股掌之上，成為全場觀眾焦點；但扮演賢淑姊姊葉緯苓的那位演員，站在她身旁也毫不失色。姊姊穿着精心設計的旗袍，舉止大方，待人得體，不突出自己，卻教人不由得不多看幾眼。到了片末，愛情成熟，又會流露出女性的温柔與頑皮來，叫人相信是個有潛質的演員。奇怪的是，後來電懋電影裡她露面不多，倒是《國際電影》雜誌仍有很多關於她的介紹。她就是以編劇見重於電懋的秦羽了！

電懋的一項特色，是有不少文人參與編劇工作。張愛玲就是其中一個著名例子。但張愛玲實際留港日子不長，編劇也只是副業。秦羽又名秦亦孚，卻是專業編劇，在五六十年代電懋的階段，據説寫了差不多二十部劇本。秦羽與張愛玲有相似的地方，都是出身書香門第，她的外祖老爺是朱啟鈐老先生，自少中英文修養都很好。她

《情場如戰場》中的姊（秦羽）與妹（林黛）
Sibling rivalry in *The Battle of Love*: Chin Yu (right) and Lin Dai.

Elegant Trails of the Quill: A Preliminary Study of Scripts by Nellie Chin Yu

- Leung Ping-kwan -

In Eileen Chang (Zhang Ailing)'s comedy *The Battle of Love* (1957), Linda Lin Dai played a spoiled young lady Ye Weifang who had three men wrapped around her finger. She was the focus of attention, yet the actress beside her playing the good and dutiful sister Ye Weiling, was not at all eclipsed by her glamour. Elegant, well-mannered, wearing an exquisitely designed *qi pao*, she was eye-catching without trying to be. Towards the end of the film, when romance was in bloom, she exuded feminine charm and playfulness, showing every promise of a good actress. Yet strangely, she rarely appeared in MP & GI's subsequent films, though the studio magazine *International Screen* carried many articles about her. She is none other than Nellie Chin Yu (Qin Yu), MP & GI's prized scriptwriter!

A characteristic of MP & GI was the literati's involvement in scripts. Eileen Chang is a well-known example. But Chang did not spend that much time in Hong Kong, nor was script-writing her main job. Chin Yu ("Yu" is the Chinese word for "feather"), on the other hand, was a professional scriptwriter. She was

是香港大學文學士，還慕名在經學大師射陵外史老先生帳下深造，選讀《左傳》、《戰國策》、駢文及詩賦。我們翻閱舊雜誌，看見學生時代的秦羽在姚克導的話劇《清宮怨》裡飾演珍妃，在《雷雨》的英文舞台劇飾演繁漪（能夠同時飾演珍妃、繁漪，又演善良的葉緯苓，可不是這麼簡單的一回事哩！），在港大莎劇《第十二夜》朗誦序幕，在電懋紅星響應麗的呼聲電台義唱節目裡朗誦莎士比亞詩作，穿着自己設計的衣裳，與林黛、尤敏、林翠諸位談笑風生，我們彷彿可以回想香港電影一個年輕多姿的階段：一個文人參與電影事業的年代。留意五六十年代文壇的人對秦羽這名字並不陌生：她寫散文，又曾在馬朗主編的《文藝新潮》第一期翻譯劇本《藍色深淵》（英國劇作者雷荻根Terence Rattigan作，改編成電影名為《孽海情潮》（*The Deep Blue Sea*，慧雲李主演），亦在今日世界出版社譯出亨利詹姆士（Henry James）的小說《碧廬冤孽》（*The Turn of the Screw*）（亦曾改編成電影《The Innocents》，1961，狄波拉嘉主演）。如果今日大家覺得這作者陌生，要再從舊雜誌、從不齊全的影帶膠片中去重新併合這名字所代表的東西，那只不過是因為這個城市沒有很好的記性罷了。

從《紅娃》開始

秦羽在港大畢業後入電懋當編劇，第一齣戲就是電懋不惜工本的野心大製作《紅娃》（1958），該片是電懋第一齣彩色片，由岳楓導演，在日本富士山下的御殿場實地拍攝，歷時七個月，耗資百萬。拍成後電影打破賣座紀錄，後來還參與亞洲影展，電影得到好評，也包括秦羽的編劇在內。

我們今天看不到《紅娃》的拷貝，但根據資料看來，這劇本也不容易寫。這不是秦羽日後擅長的時裝喜劇、青春愛情劇，而是以東北為背景的江湖遊俠傳

said to have written almost 20 scripts for MP & GI between the 1950s and 1960s. The two women in fact share the background of coming from a scholarly family. Since a child Chin had sound knowledge of English and Chinese. Flipping through old magazines, we see the student Chin Yu appearing in Yao Ke's play *Sorrows of the Forbidden City* and an English staging of *Thunderstorm*, reading the opening act of Shakespeare's *Twelfth Night* in a university performance and reciting the bard's sonnets when MP & GI stars went on charity programmes on radio. She dressed in clothes she designed herself, sharing jokes with Lin Dai, Lucilla You Min, and Jeanette Lin Cui. She seems to bring us back to a young and colourful period in Hong Kong cinema, when the literati was involved in film. Chin is no stranger to those familiar with the literary circles of the 50s and 60s: she wrote essays and published translations of dramatist Terence Rattigan's play *The Deep Blue Sea* (which has been made into a film in 1955 directed by Anatole Litvak

奇。在文學的角度來說，這大概近乎三四十年代東北作家端木蕻良或是從大陸移居台灣的作家如司馬中原和朱西甯等人的作品，風格以粗獷為主。據說秦羽為了編《紅娃》，特別浸淫在舊小說中，盡量想寫好人物的口語，看來秦羽一開始就是對語言和風格很敏感的編劇。我們今天看《紅娃》的本事和電影小說，劇中既有豪邁遊俠的龍家，貪婪陰險的刁三爺一家，也還有不同個性的婦人薄荷油和守寡的二楞子娘，脂粉氣的花吉玉和死心塌地為主盡忠的長發，加上天真又硬朗的紅娃，以及她與小伙子龍哥的一段熱戀。看來在人物造型上也下了不少工夫。

據說寫《紅娃》時，秦羽為了細寫男女主角的感情進展，特別設計了這麼一場戲：紅娃先在手裡抱着一頭小羊，然後小羊從她懷中跑到地上，再又投入男主角的懷抱中。這微妙的傳情，可見秦羽深諳含蓄之道。

《紅娃》
Scarlet Doll

and starring Vivien Leigh) and Henry James' *The Turn of the Screw* (also made into a film, *The Innocents*, directed by Jack Clayton and starring Deborah Kerr, 1961). If you are unfamiliar with this writer today, if you have to reconstruct the things her name represents from old magazines and incomplete video prints, it's only because this city doesn't have a good memory.

Starting from *Scarlet Doll*

After graduating from university, Chin joined MP & GI as a scriptwriter. Her first film was the ambitious and big budget *Scarlet Doll* (1958), the company's first colour feature. Directed by Yue Feng and filmed on location at the royal court under Mount Fuji, it took seven months to complete and cost a million. The film broke box office records and received favourable critical comments, including praises for Chin's script.

We are unable to watch *Scarlet Doll* today. But judging from material on the film, it was not an easy script to write. It was not the modern comedies or romantic dramas Chin came to be known for. It was a wandering swordsman legend set in the north-east. From a literary point of view, its raw and primitive style was reminiscent of the style of northeastern writer Duanmu Hongliang, or Mainland writers who emigrated to Taiwan, such as Sima Zhongyuan and Zhu Xinling. To write *Scarlet Doll*, Chin was said to have steeped herself in old novels to capture her characters' speech. From the start, it seems, she was a scriptwriter with a keen sensitivity to language and style. Today, in the film's synopsis and novel, one finds the Long family of high-minded swordsmen, the greedy and sinister Diao family, women of different types, the heavily powdered Hua Jiyu, the fiercely loyal Chang Fa, plus the innocent but tough Scarlet Doll with her passionate love affair with the young man, Brother Long. Chin must have worked hard on her characters.

Chin was said to have specially written a scene to show the romantic development of the leads: Scarlet Doll was holding a goat, which then ran from her arms and jumped right into the arms of the male lead. This

《紅娃》雖是北方豪邁的遊俠傳奇，主角卻是紅娃，惹起觀眾注目的也是善良嬌嗔的林黛。電懋一個特色，是旗下有不少年輕貌美獨當一面的女演員，秦羽又是擅寫女性心理的編劇，自然如魚得水了。

電懋電影與五六十年代香港文化同步發展，一方面繼承四九年以前國內的文化，又同時受外國荷里活影響，逐漸過渡，拍出更多中產背景的都市喜劇及言情劇來。秦羽跟着下來在1959年完成的三個劇本，便分別是為三個女演員而寫的：林黛的《三星伴月》（陶秦導演）、尤敏的《玉女私情》（唐煌導演）和林翠的《二八佳人》（易文導演）。

玉女的形象與私情

《玉女私情》裡秦羽成功塑造了尤敏的玉女形象，正如《二八佳人》裡塑造了一個佻皮爽朗的林翠一樣。兩片都是寫成長中的少女，《二八佳人》是寫下一代不理父母反對談戀愛的輕鬆喜劇，《玉女私情》卻要複雜點，不光寫年輕人愛情，也寫到兩代之間的複雜感情。秦羽寫得最好的是少女心事。在《玉女私情》開頭，寫尤敏這女兒放學回家，幫父親王引買回煙草、稿紙，要父親吃東西，這一連串自然而又親暱的動作設計，立即令我們明白了他們兩人親密又相依為命的關係，也令在旁邊離去多年現在冒充姨母回來的生母王萊心裡不是味兒！

電影改編自杜寧小説，曲折傳奇的橋段或許與此有關：當年拋棄丈夫女兒離家出走的生母，現在與丈夫回來，想把喜愛音樂的女兒帶到義大利深造。期間又加入父親為女兒買生日蛋糕被車撞倒，結果要割掉一條腿的悲劇。最後甚至揭示出來：父親原來也不是生父，母親現在的丈夫才是生父。父親為了令女兒去外國去得放心，甚至一改常態向她喝罵，不要她留在身邊！在這種種突變之中，女兒無奈地接受現實打算離

delicate romantic exchange shows that Chin Yu deeply understood the art of subtlety.

Although the film was a northern story of the sword, the protagonist was Scarlet Doll and the audience's focus was also the kind and bashfully pretty Lin Dai. MP & GI was known for its young, beautiful, and talented actresses, and as Chin was a scriptwriter adept at writing about the feminine psyche, they took to each other like fish to water.

MP & GI developed in synchronicity with Hong Kong culture in the 1950s and 1960s. Not only had it inherited the pre-1949 culture of the Mainland, but it also came under the influence of Hollywood, and gradually began filming more urban comedies and melodramas about the bourgeoisie. In 1959, Chin completed three scripts, which she wrote for three actresses: *The More the Merrier* for Lin Dai, *Her Tender Heart* for You Min and *Too Young to Love* for Lin Cui.

The Image of the Innocent Maiden and Illicit Love

In *Her Tender Heart*, Chin successfully created the image of the innocent maiden for You Min, just as she did for a playful and candid Lin Cui in *Too Young to Love*. The subject of both is a young girl growing up. But whereas *Too Young to Love* is a light-hearted comedy about how the younger generation disregarded parental objections to their romance, *Her Tender Heart* deals additionally with the complex relationship between generations. Chin was best at writing about the delicate feelings of young girls. In the opening of *Her Tender Heart*, You Min was seen buying cigarettes and writing paper for her father Wang Yin on her way home from school, and then persuading him to eat. This sequence of natural and intimate gestures painted a clear picture of their close and mutually dependent relationship. That also makes her mother Wang Lai, who has left them years ago and returns posing as an aunt, feel good bitter.

The film was adapted from Du Ning's novel, which

perhaps explains its devious and intriguing plot. The mother who had abandoned her husband and daughter years ago returns with her new husband in the hope of bringing the musically talented daughter to study music in Italy. Then tragedy strikes – the father, on his way to buy a birthday cake for the daughter, was hit by a car, and had to have his leg amputated. What's more, it's revealed in the end that the mother's new husband is the girl's biological father. And the father, hoping to make his daughter leave with peace, begins mistreating her on purpose. Exasperated by such dramatic changes, the daughter prepares to leave but changes her mind.

The daughter's decision is moving of course. But I feel it would've been even more so if the story is less melodramatic. For example, the father not only loses a leg in an accident, but goes limping to see his daughter off at the airport, and, as a final flourish, falls to the ground! Another example is the mother. In the first half, she shows the complex and conflicting emotions of the runaway mother, but after her husband's arrival, becomes nothing more than an accomplice in persuading the daughter to leave. As such, the daughter's choice is less difficult. If the film had been less melodramatic and focuses instead on the daughter's choice, the story would've been more heart-warming and its impact more meaningful.

The other innocent maiden Chin created was Kitty Ting Hao (Ding Hao), for *Devotion* (1960), an adaptation of Chi Ren's original novel. In the film, Ting Hao plays both the mother and the daughter. The former is a servant-girl who falls in love with the young master, gets pregnant, and dies a miserable death – a clichéd plot, which, nonetheless, differentiates itself from Cantonese dramas as it unravels. The daughter goes to school, and despite dropping out later to work as a songstress to support her family, wins the true love of a man (Roy Chiao / Qiao Hong). Unlike the mother's master, Chiao's character is ready to sacrifice everything for love. Playing the mother as a young girl, Ting is every bit the cute and innocent maiden. As the daughter, she is a flamboyant songstress and flamenco

去，但最後在登機前一刻還是捨不得，決定留下來。

女兒重人情的選擇固然感人，但我以為有些情節若不那麼煽情，説不定感人更深！比方王引飾演的父親，既因車禍斷腿，最後一跛一跛走往機場看女兒離去，還要摔倒地上。又如王萊飾演的母親，在前半來得有戲，能演出離家母親那種既親又疏的複雜心理，後半場丈夫來後，就單向地變成只是慫恿女兒離去的「幫兇」，人物一下子變片面了，選擇的複雜性也減低了。我以為若果減低這些煽情戲份，純看女兒在生父母與養父之間選擇，人情味會更濃厚、意義也更深呢！

秦羽筆下塑造的另一個玉女是改編自癡人原著的《母與女》（唐煌，1960）中的丁皓，丁皓分飾母女兩人。母親是婢女，愛上少爺，懷了孩子，坎坷而逝，故事的橋段並不新鮮；比較不同粵語殘片的發展是後來女兒受教育，雖因家貧棄學披上歌衫，卻得到喬宏飾演的志堂的真愛。而且與當年的少爺受父母所擺佈不同，今日的志堂願為愛情犧牲一切。丁皓演母親年輕時的玉女形象不出羞嗔嬌俏，演新一代的女兒卻又唱歌又大跳西班牙舞。電懋的電影正發展於香港社會邁向都市化的年代，秦羽也是較敏感地寫出都市少女形象的編劇。當然若以少女心情而言，還是《玉女私情》寫得最好。

看《玉女私情》的時候我也想到後來王天林的《小兒女》（1963），這是另一位對現代女性心理極有體會的作家張愛玲編劇的。相像是因為尤敏、王引與王萊吧。我立即又想到：電影其實是許多人合作的成果。這時期的電懋電影，可説有一個健全片廠制的雛型，每齣電影有監製的策劃、製片的執行、有一群有文化素養的導演與編劇、有美術與音樂的專才，有一群出色的男女主角如林黛、尤敏、葛蘭、葉楓、林翠、張揚、雷震、陳厚，又有一群出色的甘草演員如王萊、歐陽莎菲、王引、田

《三星伴月》中的三角喜劇
It's never too much because it's *The More the Merrier.*

dancer. MP & GI's films were made in an era when Hong Kong was moving towards urbanization and Chin was able to create a refreshing image of a young city girl. But as far as young girls' feelings are concerned, *Her Tender Heart* is a better script.

Her Tender Heart reminds me of a later film, Wang Tianlin's *Father Takes a Bride* (1963), written by a writer with tremendous insight into modern women's psyche, Eileen Chang. I suppose it's because You Min, Wang Yin, and Wang Lai are in both films. I then thought of something else: a film is a collaborative effort. At the time, MP & GI already had a developed studio system. There were producers, executive producers, directors and scriptwriters with strong cultural backgrounds, experts in art and music, distinguished stars – Lin Dai, You Min, Grace Chang, Chang Yang (Zhang Yang), Peter Chen Ho (Chen Hou) etc. – and a staple of brilliant character actors, like Wang Lai, Wang Yin and Liu Enjia. Each production was the combination of these elements. Discussing filmmakers, we tend to concentrate on the style and contribution of the individual, but we should also take into account the influence of all the other elements. Eileen Chang's emotional depiction in *Father Takes a Bride* is more refined but the film has less local colour. Details such as crabs, outlying islands, and stepmothers are not necessarily unique to Hong Kong. By comparison, Chin's young Hong Kong student is a more vivid image.

The Gender Wars

The Lin Dai of *The More the Merrier* is merely an extension of the mischievous and wilful Lin Dai of *The Battle of Love*, the only difference being she's married this time. After her husband had presumably died when his boat sank, she marries his good friend. And when her husband returns unexpectedly after four years, she's already in love with a third lover. Like in *The Battle of Love*, she shuttles back and forth among three men. Eileen Chang's treatment of the female lead in *Battle* is more bold and direct and she also accentuates male repression. This, however, is diluted by the more conservative approach of the director who

青、劉恩甲等。每齣電影是這些不同元素的組合配搭。我們討論個別導演、編劇、演員的時候，當然想追溯每人的特色和貢獻，但也不能忽略整體的合作和互相的影響呢！編劇來說，張愛玲的心理刻劃在《小兒女》中更細緻，但香港色彩淡點，如螃蟹、離島、後母等細節不一定要具體寫香港。相比之下秦羽塑造的尤敏這香港女學生形象更見鮮明。

性別的戰爭

《三星伴月》裡的林黛，基本上是《情場如戰場》那個淘氣任性的林黛的延續。只不過這次她結了婚，又因丈夫覆舟而歿，再嫁他的好友，不料四年後丈夫突然歸來，她又愛上新情人，結果同樣是周旋在三位男性之間。張愛玲在《情場如戰場》中對女主角的處理比較直率大膽，又突出男主角的自我壓抑，只是導演處理比較保守，又加入張揚教訓女主角不要一味貪玩之類的話。秦羽的編劇似乎以輕鬆為主，沒有甚麼批判，還加入梁醒波的烏龍律師胡鬧一番。但在荷里活式橋段下，也有些貌似顛覆的玩笑，如女主角在僕人辭工後，把家務平均分配給新舊兩丈夫，要他們以工作表現來讓她決定下嫁誰。當然那個年代和那時的觀眾不容顛覆去得太遠，到最後這女主角愛上第三者還是以替他做家務收場！在荷里活的公式內可以開開玩笑、樂趣卻正在貌似顛覆而又實在遵循之間。

《同床異夢》(1960)女主角李湄也是這類型女角，卻比林黛更成熟。電影由夢境開始，未幾就夢境成真，女主角真在影展獲獎。她跟着就和所愛的雷震結婚，但婚後又開始鬧別扭，不肯與丈夫同房，喜歡揮霍。影片中她丈夫的兄弟張揚要伸張正義，執着過往的醜聞要她讓步，做回賢妻良母。這就展開一場性別戰爭。

電影裡的張揚也有幾分像《情場如戰場》裡的張揚，是

throws in scenes like Chang Yang lecturing Lin Dai about fooling around. Chin Yu seems to have opted for light-heartedness in her script, which is not very judgmental and is sprinkled with slapstick humour generated by Leung Sing-po (Liang Xingbo), the slipshod lawyer. But having said that, there are a few seemingly subversive jokes in the Hollywoodesque plot. After her servant resigns, for example, the lady of the house assigns domestic chores equally to her old and new husbands, announcing her intention to let their performance decide whom she will marry. Of course the audience and society of that era would not have allowed such subversion to go too far. In the end, she falls in love with a third party and ends up cleaning the house for him! Jokes are allowed within the Hollywood formula, and the pleasure lies between the looks of subversion and the deed of compliance.

The female lead in *The Bedside Story* (1960), Li Mei, is the same type of character, only more mature. The film starts with a dream, which soon comes true – the female lead wins an award at a film festival. She then marries Kelly Lai Chen (Lei Zhen) her love, but after marriage, undergoes a change of temperament. She refuses to sleep with him and spends lavishly. Her husband's brother Chang Yang, out to restore justice to his brother, tries to blackmail her into becoming a gentle and dutiful wife, kicking off a gender war.

Chang Yang's role is slightly similar to the one he played in *The Battle of Love* – a good upright man nonetheless blind to the subtleties of romance and seduction, one who's afraid of love. Although he shows signs of liking his secretary Wang Lai, he doesn't give vent to his sentiments. He's so intent on disciplining his sister-in-law that he moves in with the couple to keep an eye on her. The film seems to have inherited the war of the genders in *Battle*. In the end, Li Mei brings Chang and Wang Lai together, leaving herself and Lai Chen to live happily ever after.

The sympathies of these films always lie with the female protagonists. Even the stereotypical "bad woman" shows an endearing face in Chin Yu's script. She is also treated more civilly, unlike in Cantonese

個一本正經的好男子，就是不解風情，「無膽入情關」，對他女秘書王萊似有好感，又沒有表達出來。他一心只想管着弟婦，甚至搬去與他們同住好看牢她。本片好似繼承《情場如戰場》的性別之戰，最後還是李湄靈機一觸，想出妙計，既撮合了張揚和王萊，而李湄和雷震一對小夫妻也可以好好生活下去了。

這些電影同情的角度，往往是放在女主角那一邊，即使是傳統印象中的所謂「壞女人」，在秦羽的劇本中，總也有她本性善良可愛的一面，在處理上也比較文明，不像五十年代的粵語片那樣訴諸家族宗法、妯娌閒言的批判。到後來的《野玫瑰之戀》（王天林，1960）更可作為代表。

《野玫瑰之戀》一開頭是張揚飾演的音樂教師與女朋友站在夜總會門前，為自己由音樂教師貶為洋琴鬼感到委屈。剛進去沒多久就聽到葛蘭這「野玫瑰」唱歌，唱的是：愛情不過是一種普通的小玩意，一點也不希奇；男人不過是消遣的東西，有甚麼了不起？唱歌的女人有時還會發出野獸般的吼叫！完全是一個「攞命女人」的形象，好似是正經男人最反對的壞女人！這很可以發展成一個知識份子對抗通俗文化、好男人批判壞女人的作品。但電影編導的角度卻完全不是這樣。

電影裡的好男人一下子就被吸引過去了！上述葛蘭開頭的那場歌舞，導演用不少鏡頭，插入觀眾的反應，尤其是張揚凝視的特寫。有不少鏡頭，是從張揚的角度看出去的。而嘲弄「愛情不過是種普通小玩意」這支曲子，還是從歌劇《卡門》的音樂改編過來。不光如此，後面葛蘭一場又一場載歌載舞，又跳西班牙舞、又穿和服扮蝴蝶夫人，唱的都是歌劇藝術歌曲改編成帶戲謔意味的國語時代曲。若果說高雅對抗通俗、男性貶低女性，編導顯然沒有選擇前一種位置。

dramas of the 1950s, which would have her harshly condemned by family and clan. This angle is exemplified by the film *The Wild, Wild Rose* (Wang Tianlin, 1960).

The film opens with a music teacher, played by Chang Yang, standing at the entrance to a nightclub with his girlfriend, grieving over his new job as a lowly club pianist. Once inside, Grace Chang, the Wild Rose, could be heard singing, "Love is nothing more than a common play thing. Men are only an amusement to kill time. What's so great about them?" The songstress, who would even make growling noises from time to time, fits thoroughly into the image of the *femme fatale* – the kind of women upright men love to hate! This could have turned into a work about the intelligentsia resisting popular culture, the good man condemning the bad woman. Yet the script steers clear of these perspectives.

Instead the good man is seduced almost instantly! In the opening song and dance sequence with Grace Chang, the director inserts shots of the audience's response, especially close-ups of the gazing Chang Yang. The song about love as a plaything is adapted from the music of *Carmen*. In fact, all the numbers in Grace Chang's musical scenes – as a flamenco dancer, a kimono-clad Madame Butterfly – are operatic pieces adapted into Mandarin pop. Among the positions of high versus popular culture and men disparages women, the script has clearly not chosen the first position.

The film has its share of melodrama, such as a two-women catfight, bullies, imprisonment, suspicion and jealousy. In the end, the film takes Carmenesque turn as a man kills a woman out of jealousy, then discovers she truly loves him. The most seemingly promiscuous woman is actually the most innocent. In this war of the genders, the man realises, only after destroying his opponent, that he's the greatest loser.

Sun, Moon and Star and Others: The Feminine Perspective of Adapting Classics

It is not easy to adapt Xu Su's 300,000-word novel *Sun, Moon and Star* into film. Xu's original intention

電影用了不少通俗劇的橋段，包括兩女打架、惡棍凌人、鋃鐺入獄、愛情的懷疑與妒忌。電影發展到最後，原來真是一個卡門式的故事：男的因為妒忌而殺死了女子，才發覺她是真心愛自己的。以為最水性楊花的女人，原來是最純真的女人。在這場性別戰爭中男人毀滅了對方，才發覺輸得最慘的是自己。

《星星．月亮．太陽》及其他——名著改編的女性角度

要把徐速先生三十萬字的長篇《星星．月亮．太陽》改編成電影，不是一件容易事。徐速本是寫一篇散文，寫了四千字，連星星也沒寫成，只好連載，每期四千到六千字，寫成十多萬字初稿，後來加以修改在 1953 年出版。1962 年新版附記裡，作者告訴我們：十年共印過十一版，總銷數達十萬冊以上。作者謙虛說他有所不滿，並且趁舊紙型壞了重排新版的機會，清理詞句和段

was to write an essay. But after 4,000 words and Star wasn't even covered, he turned it into a serial novel of 4,000 to 5,000 words per episode. He wrote a first draft of over 100,000 words, then made amendments and published the piece in 1953. In the appendix to the new 1962 edition, he told us, "Eleven editions have been printed in 10 years, with sales of over 100,000 volumes." In modesty, the author explained that he was dissatisfied with the novel and took the chance to polish wordings and paragraphing, fine-tune the plot, and work on the characters. The last, he said, was due to the film's influence.

In an article published in *Sing Tao Evening News* in 1970, entitled "The Writing of the Novel and Its 'Disasters'", he mentioned the two difficulties he encountered writing the serial novel. The first was the form: the physical limitations of turning a prose into a novel. The pace of the latter was slower, but such is the way of novels. The problem was that characters appear without prior planning. He tried to make up for that in the new edition, like explaining Ah Lan's fiancé, Qiuming's family background, Ah Nan's abrupt entrance appearance and the coincidental meeting up north. The second difficulty was the theme. He felt a straightforward account was not enough. There had to be a central theme. He considered having the three women represent "truth", "kindness", and "beauty", but felt it awkward. He also wanted to integrate tragedy into the novel. He believed there were three kinds of tragedies: those meant by Providence, those man-made, and the inevitable caused by circumstances. The last, to his understanding, is the highest level of tragedy. Hence the male lead Xu Jianbai could not reunite with any of the three women in the end.

The adaptation of *Sun, Moon and Star* was an interesting case, a colourful testimony to the complexity of high and popular culture in Hong Kong. Novels are usually considered serious and refined, while film adaptations are said to be lowbrow and entertaining. *Sun, Moon and Star* (1961) held various kinds of attraction for the audience of course. It was a

落、增刪情節、在人物描繪上加工。他並說最後一點是受了電影的影響。

作者後來1970年發表在《星島晚報》的一篇〈本書寫作經過及其「災難」〉，更具體談到寫作這長篇時的兩項困難：第一是形式問題：由散文發展成長篇，先天上不免有限制，節奏較緩慢，但作者説長篇小説一般如此，只可惜人物出現往往沒安排伏線，後來在新版中設法彌補，如交代阿蘭未婚夫、秋明的家世、以及修訂阿南出場的生硬以及北上相遇的巧合。第二是主題思想問題：作者覺得光講故事不夠，要建立一個主題思想，所以想用三位女主角代表真、善、美，但自己也覺得牽強；他又想將悲劇意境糅合在小説裡，他覺得悲劇有三類：天意的、人為的，以及形勢發展而不得不如此，依他個人了解是後者才是悲劇最高境界，所以一定要安排男主角徐堅白到頭來與三個女性都不能復合。

《星星・月亮・太陽》的改編是個有趣的例子，為香港雅、俗文化的複雜多元提供多一個豐富例證。一般都説文藝小説高雅嚴肅，電影改編往往通俗娛人，但以《星星・月亮・太陽》（1961）來説，電影出動了電懋當家花旦尤敏、葛蘭、葉楓來飾演三位不同性格的女性，加上張揚、田青、劉恩甲、吳家驤、歐陽莎菲、王萊數十位演員，姚敏的音樂，斥重資大場面拍攝一年半才完成這上下兩集鉅片，當然未嘗沒有種種吸引觀眾的條件，但製片宋淇、導演易文和編劇秦羽的功力又不是媚俗可以概括的。即以秦羽的改編為例，也補充了原著，發揮了新的魅力。

秦羽的改編，最成功是把三個女角寫得更完整更豐滿。如果説徐速的追求是藝術的言談、悲劇的觀念，秦羽的故事版本則更有具體現代生活人情，調動增刪了的情節更令人感覺到人物感情的收發與去向。徐速曾説長篇本

mega movie in two parts that took a year and a half to complete, starring MP & GI's divas You Min, Grace Chang, Julie Yeh Feng (Ye Feng) as three different women, tens of actors – including Chang Yang, Tian Qing, Liu Enjia, Wu Jiaxiang, Ouyang Shafei, Wang Lai – Yao Min's music, and expensive grand scenes. Yet the work of producer Stephen Soong (Song Qi), director Evan Yang (Yi Wen), and scriptwriter Chin Yu cannot adequately be summed up as popular. Chin's adaptation, for instance, not only complements the original, but exudes a flair of its own.

The most successful part of Chin's script is that she made the three female characters more complete. If Xu Su was after artistry of speech and concepts of tragedy, Chin Yu's version is richer in the actual sensibilities of modern life. The changes she made to the plot help to elucidate the characters' emotional development. Xu Su once said that a novel should not be narrated from a first person point of view. Actually the problem lies elsewhere. As we follow the male protagonist's narration, we fail to detect any reflection and detachment on the writer's part. We can only hear the character's self-explanations, judgments, and general remarks. Chin's narration makes good use of the film medium to create three-dimensional characters, and portray their interrelationships. After the opening clip, she abandons the amorous man's soliloquy for a sensitive depiction of female sensibilities using a feminine perspective.

The overall structure of Chin Yu's adaptation is bold but matters of the heart are handled delicately. In the opening, Du Mu's poem is represented visually by a painting-like background, accompanied by music Yao Min wrote for the poem. Later in another scene, Jianbai and Ah Lan are seen talking about the legend of the cowherd and the weaver under a canopy of stars. The fusion of scene and feelings is just right. Although these ingredients can be found in the original too, it's a bit too loose and confused to do them credit. The adaptation is focused and concise, silencing reasoning to feel with the heart.

不宜以第一身敘述，其實問題不在那裡。只是我們跟隨男主角的敘述，卻感覺不到作者對第一身男角的反省與距離，多聽到這角色的自辯與自解，議論與概論。秦羽的敘述卻善用了電影媒介立體地點畫角色造型、體現人物往來關係，更在開頭的楔子以後，離開了男性多情者的自白，從女性的角度細膩體會女性的感情。

秦羽的改編，整體的結構方面大刀闊斧，寫情方面卻補回不少細緻筆墨。電影開場，把杜牧「銀燭秋光冷畫屏，輕羅小扇撲流螢」的七夕化為畫景，配以姚敏為詩譜的音樂，發展到堅白與阿蘭分手前看星説牽牛織女的神話，情景交融恰到好處。材料原著也有，但原著略散漫蕪雜，改編濃縮集中，不説理而動以情。

這還是小節而已，重要的是上集主要劇情的從新調動。在原著的第三至二十六章裡，堅白離開了鄉下到縣裡讀中學，因兩家阻隔而與初戀情人阿蘭失去聯繫。他對表妹秋明漸生感情，但收到阿蘭的信，又惹起舊情，沒多久又還對第三個女子阿南有了傾慕之心。到他回鄉奔喪，重逢阿蘭，要與她私奔，跟自己有婚約的表妹也回來了，而他又同時約了阿南一起去北方。讀來不但情節互相排擠抵消，最大問題是我們沒法感受男主角的感情線索，有時甚至產生荒謬的感覺。

秦羽的改編卻令人物關係發展比較合情合理：堅白離開了阿蘭去縣裡讀書，碰到家裡替他訂親的表妹，先是抗拒，然後在病中得她照顧而漸生好感，但又同時做夢夢見阿蘭怪他，內心掙扎之餘收到阿蘭的信説已有對象，他失意之餘與表妹發展了愛情。為祖母奔喪回家，重逢阿蘭，才從弟弟口中知悉對方為了令他死心而騙他，乃愛火重燃，決意私奔。秋明表妹卻在這時也來奔喪，遇見阿蘭，阿蘭終黯然退出，叫表妹告訴堅白。堅白聽了消息，萬念俱灰，覺得負了阿蘭又騙了表妹，終於自己

These are only minor changes. The most significant change is the rearrangement of the plot in the first part. In Chapters 3 to 26 of the original, Jianbai, who has left his village to go to school in the county, loses touch with his first love Ah Lan due to their families' intervention. Gradually he develops feelings for his cousin Qiuming, but feels his old flame rekindled when he receives Ah Lan's letter. Soon after, he falls for a third woman Ah Nan. When he sees Ah Lan again on returning home for his grandmother's funeral, he wants to elope with her. But his cousin has come too, and he has also made a date with Ah Nan to go to the north. The elements of the convoluted plot rejects and cancels each other out. The biggest problem is we could not understand the thread of the man's feelings, which, at times, border on the absurd.

Chin's adaptation renders a more reasonable of the development of the characters' relationships. Jianbai leaves Ah Lan to study in the county, where he bumps into Qiuming, the cousin, whom his family has picked out as his wife. He resents her at first, then develops more positive feelings when she nurses him during his illness. At the same time, however, he sees Ah Lan reproaching him in his dream. While this emotional struggle is going on, he receives a letter from Ah Lan telling him she has already found someone. Daunted, he began a relationship with his cousin. On returning home for the funeral, he hears that Ah Lan had made up that story to make him forget her. His love for her rekindled, he decides to elope with her. However cousin Qiuming has also come home for the funeral and the two women meet. Ah Lan sadly decides to withdraw, asking Qiuming to relay her decision to Jianbai. The crestfallen Jianbai feels he had let Ah Lan down and deceived his cousin. He decides to leave home and travel north and on the train, sees the brave and noble Ah Nan, telling her classmates to come out of their ivory towers as war is just around the corner.

Chin's adaptation consists basically of rearrangements, additions and deletions. Yet it makes the emotional development much more plausible. More importantly, it makes the portrayal of the three women more

離家北上。然後在北上的火車中才第一次遇見豪邁的阿南，正對同學説國家已到了最緊張的時刻，戰爭爆發在即，叫大家從象牙塔中走出來。

秦羽的改編，基本上好像只是調動了一些情節，作了一些增刪，但情感發展的線索卻合乎人情多了。而且最重要的是，三個女性角色的刻劃都變得更清晰豐滿了。先説阿南：阿南的出場比原著中平平無奇的敘述更有效果，一下子把她堅強爽朗的性格突出出來，又刪去了原著中傳奇又巧合的家庭背景，減低了她的文藝背景，突出她對國家大事的關注，給予她與前面兩個女性不同的性格，在這新的處境中也更合理地發展了堅白對阿南的仰慕。

最成功的可能還是對葛蘭飾的秋明的刻劃，在原著中，幾乎沒甚麼空間發展堅白與秋明的感情，有時她夾在兩個女人之間，不見堅白對她有深感情，她有時甚至還顯得酸澀、憤慨，令我們看不見作者希望描畫的良好教養、宗教薰陶、溫柔文雅、謙讓仁慈的風度，倒是在電影中，在秦羽的編寫、葛蘭的演繹、易文的導演之下，這角色具體可愛得多：從最初家庭洋化的佈置、鋼琴和小狗的襯托、燒菜的逞強、服侍病人倦極睡倒在床上、從鏡中窺見堅白湊近的臉孔、聽到堅白夢囈時陰影蓋過了臉孔，還有朦朧表示感情的〈月朦朧〉一曲（姚敏選曲，周之原詞：「這是你的秘密還是我的心事，同樣的都朦朧……」），也比原著中引用的古詩「怨望啼相候，愁眠夢不成」現代、含蓄，自然得多。

尤敏飾演的阿蘭，原著中也寫出完整的性格，尤敏的演技，前後不同的髮型打扮都更好地演繹出她的變化。但最成功地寫出幾個女性、尤其是阿蘭與秋明關係的，還主要靠秦羽的彩筆，這我們可以集中從兩場對白中看出來：

情敵變知己：《星星・月亮・太陽》中的尤敏（右）與葛蘭

The feminine perspective: Grace Chang and You Min (right) in *Sun, Moon and Star.*

complete and vivid. Ah Nan is given a far more effective appearance than the original lacklustre narration. It highlights her strong and gallant personality while leaving out her intriguing coincidence-filled family background, lightens her cultural background while bringing out her concern for her country. She is given a personality different from the previous two women, which makes Jianbai's admiration all the more credible.

The most successful is probably the portrayal of Qiuming by Grace Chang. In the original, there is almost no space for her relationship with Jianbai to develop. She is caught between the two other women, and Jianbai's feelings for her seem shallow. At times she even comes across as bitter and angry, which veils the qualities the author attributes to her – well-bred, nurtured by religion, gentle, graceful, kind, and modest. It is in the film, with Chin's script, Chang's acting and Evan Yang's direction that this character comes alive. We see her home with its westernized décor, complete with piano and puppy, and her demonstrations of cooking skills. We see her falling asleep, exhausted from nursing her patient, catching a glimpse of Jianbai's approaching face in the mirror, and her overcast face as Jianbai sleep-talks. Besides, the choice of the song "Hazy Moon" which gives obscure expression to love (chosen by Yao Min with lyrics by Zhou Zhiliang: "This is your secret or my heart's longings, both obscure they are…"), is more modern, subtle, and natural than the original classical poetry.

Ah Lan, You Min's character, is given a round portrayal in the original. You Min's acting, her differing hairdos and dress styles express better of her evolvement. But the best portrayal of the women, especially Ah Lan and Qiuming's relationship, is given by Chin. This can be seen from the dialogues of two scenes.

The first scene is when Qiuming comes to visit Ah Lan as the latter is packing up before her elopement with Jianbai. At first Qiuming chides her from a moralistic standpoint, "He is engaged to me and now wants to elope with you. His father will be very angry and his relatives will look down on him!" Then Ah Lan reveals

一場是阿蘭收拾東西準備與堅白私奔，秋明來看她。起先是秋明站在倫理道德的立場説對方：他跟我訂婚，又跟你私奔，他父親一定會發脾氣，親戚朋友會看不起他！然後阿蘭剖白孤兒的背景、目前的病況：還有一兩年的命，走就走吧！難道受了這麼多年的折磨，臨死也不能快活一天嗎？品性善良的秋明到此也感動了，就倒過來勸對方走，覺得自己錯怪了她。但到這時，阿蘭反而內疚，決意不走，叫對方去見堅白了。整場對話見到兩個人不同的背景與想法，但又不失善良為人着想的性格。原著由男角第一身敘述，交代對話就沒有這樣細緻的心理轉折。

至於另一場，是秋明走後，阿蘭病了一場。後來小説第三十節，堅白從朋友的來信知道：秋明求阿蘭不要死。秋明離家前到醫院看阿蘭。「只知道阿蘭打算病好後，決定回上海去投考護士學校，至於她們還談些甚麼，別人就不得而知了。」

編劇秦羽就在這「別人不得而知」的空白上，創造了一場動人的對白。秋明先是勸阿蘭跟她回家，阿蘭執意不肯。秋明鼓勵阿蘭去當護士，改變自己的命運。秋明見阿蘭不願意到她家去，是覺得不想成為他人負擔，就進一步説自己也需要對方，現在只有對阿蘭才能説自己心裡話。這樣談着，兩人拉着手，秋明叫阿蘭答應她，阿蘭終於點頭。這裡我們看到編劇很好地從原著的空白發揮，把秋明善良聰明的性格寫得更具體，而阿蘭下面的轉變，也就預先帶出來了。編劇從兩人對話層層開展，寫出女性心理，刻劃逐步建立起來的女性友誼。這種女性的角度，補充了原著中男性浪漫話語，給星星、月亮、太陽這三個比喻填充了栩栩的形象。寫到這裡已經

her orphan's background and the seriousness of her illness. "You have only one or two years of life left. Go, go! You've endured so much all these years. Don't you deserve a little happiness before you die?" Deeply moved, the compassionate Qiuming persuades her to go, feeling she had accused her unjustly. But it is now Ah Lan's turn to feel guilty. She decides not to go and asks Qiuming to see Jianbai. The different backgrounds and ways of thinking of the two women, who are nonetheless both thoughtful and sympathetic, are evident in the scene's dialogue. Such delicate twists and turns of emotions are absent from the man's first person narration of the original.

In the other scene, Qiuming has left and Ah Lan is ill. In Chapter 30 of the novel, Jianbai finds out from a friend's letter that Qiuming had begged Ah Lan to hang on. Before leaving home, she goes to see Ah Lan at the hospital. "It's only known that Ah Lan decided to return to Shanghai after her recovery and apply to nursing school. As to what else they talked about, nobody knew."

Qiu wrote a very moving dialogue to fill in the blank that "nobody knew". Qiuming tries to persuade Ah Lan to go home with her but the latter refuses. She persuades Ah Lan to change her fate to become a nurse. Realizing that Ah Lan refuses because she doesn't want to be a burden, she adds that she too needs Ah Lan, the only person with whom she can exchange confidences. As they talk, they begin holding hands. Qiuming asks Ah Lan to say yes, and the latter finally nods. Chin makes use of the novel's blank space to highlight Qiuming's kindness and intelligence, setting the stage for the changes in Ah Lan's life. Through the conversation, Chin scripts the feminine psychology and the growing friendship between the women. This feminine perspective fills the void left by the romantic monologue in the original, giving the metaphors of the sun, moon and star more life-like images. I have written too much. I was going to analyse another adaptation, *A Story of Three Loves* (1964, in which Lin Cui and Grace Chang's roles are largely faithful to the original but instilled with a modern spirit), but it will just have to wait.

太長，本來還想分析另一本名著《啼笑姻緣》的改編（林翠與葛蘭的角色基本上忠於原著但也加進了現代的精神），只好期諸異日了。

但最後不能不提的是國泰時期的彩色古裝闊銀幕黃梅調歌唱片《蘇小妹》（1967），取材自馮夢龍《今古小説》、通俗小説《今古奇觀》裡《蘇小妹三難新郎》及宋人筆記裡的故事改編而成，但秦羽的改編也搞搞新意思。一開始，我們見到閨房中的蘇小妹與秦少游。秦對着觀眾説：「你們就知道我們的韻事和佳話，可不知道娶個才女，那罪過可不好受！」然後蘇小妹又對觀眾説：「説哪裡話，你們不知道，嫁給才子，那個滋味，也夠你瞧的！」於是你一段我一段的開始了回憶。結尾秦少游又收到女子的詩帖，蘇小妹追着要來看，蘇東坡面對觀眾説：「又吵起來了！」然後偷偷地説：「其實詩是我寫的！」就此喜劇收場。編劇以這種現代影劇中角色直接對觀眾説話的手法，輕鬆地把有關蘇小妹秦少游的軼事串連成篇。

除了把古人軼事弄得趣味盎然，用現代手法表達以外，另一特色當然還是強調女性的角度了。不同京劇《賺文娟》之強調詩妓文娟，把秦少游寫成風流倜儻的文士，秦羽的改編並不認同傳統的文士風流，電影中有一段出現了真假三個秦少游，甚至包括了草包子劉恩甲在內，把男性的性幻想像泡泡那樣戳穿了。改編強調了蘇小妹的聰明機智，在男女性別的世界中易服喬裝，輾轉周旋，以文采和人情在性別的戰爭中勝了一仗，又給對方留有餘地，保存了面子。秦羽也以此片獲得了亞洲電影節的最佳編劇獎。

梁秉鈞，嶺南大學教授，人文學科研究中心主任，近著有《東西》（牛津大學出版社，2000）。
Professor Leung Ping-kwan, Director of Centre for Humanities Research, Lingnan University. Recently published: *East-West Matters* (OUP, 2000).

Finally I have to mention *Wife of a Romantic Scholar* (1967), the wide-screen *Huangmei Diao* (Yellow Plum Opera) musical of the Cathay era. The story is adapted from Feng Menglong's popular novel *How Su Xiaomei Thrice Tested Her Bride*, and stories from notes of the Song dynasty. But Chin manages to throw in a few new ideas. The film opens with Su Xiaomei and Qin Shaoyou in Su's boudoir. Facing the audience, Chin says, "You only know about our quaint anecdotes and romantic rumours. What you don't know is the hardship of marrying a talented woman!" Then it's Su Xiaomei's turn to address the audience: "That's not true. What you don't know is the troubles of having a talented husband!'

They begin reminiscing, one after the other. At the end, Master Qin receives another poem from a woman. Su Xiaomei tries to grab it from him as he runs from her. Su Dongbo the poet says to the audience, "They're at it again!" Then, as an aside: "Actually it was I who wrote it!" The film ends on this comic note. Using the modern cinematic technique of addressing the audience directly, Chin lightheartedly links up the anecdotes of Su Xiaomei and Qin Shaoyou. Besides jazzing up ancient stories, which she tells with a modern twist, Chin's other feature is her emphasis on the feminine angle. Unlike the Peking opera *Zhuan Wenjuan*, which focuses on the poet-courtesan Wen Juan and portrays Qin Shaoyou as a dandy, Chin's adaptation does not identify with the traditional figure of the playboy-scholar. In one episode, three Qin Shaoyous appear, both real and fake, including the uncultured Liu Enjia. Such arrangements put a needle to the bubble of male sexual fantasy. Su Xiaomei's quick-wittedness is stressed. Cross-dressed as a man, she interacts with different folks and wins the gender war with her literary talents and connections. Yet she leaves adequate face-saving space for the other party. It was also with this film that Chin Yu won the Best Screenplay Award at the Asian Film Festival.

Translated by Piera Chen

片場如戰場：當張愛玲遇上林黛

- 林奕華 -

對於有志從事「電影編劇」的人，有個說法不知道是恭維抑或揶揄挖苦：他可以不會寫字，不懂戲劇，但不能不知道何謂「妥協」——由對老闆言聽計從，到迎合市場口味，遷就導演水平，以至貼身服侍幕前演出的阿哥阿姐——小則修改被他們認為不合形象的情節，工程大了，隨時要重新度身，把原來的劇本撕了，由頭做起。

「度身訂造」本來也不是甚麼mission impossible，只是明星就是明星，他們絕對有辦法讓個人魅力膨脹到旁人沒有立足的空間。所以，假若編劇就是裁縫，他手工要好之餘，更重要的，是懂得如何在明星的表現跟影片的整體取得比例上的平衡，不然的話，便會弄巧反拙，頭重腳輕。其中一個可以被引用為反面教材的例子，是在一部名叫《情場如戰場》（岳楓，1957）的電影的開場裡。

劇本明白而又簡潔寫着：

The Film Set Battle: When Eileen Chang Meets Lin Dai

- *Edward Lam* -

Most screenwriters in Hong Kong understand that "compromise" is part of their job. They have to cater to investors, market trends, directors' demands and the whims of stars, who may ask for revisions that range from minor alterations to complete overhauls.

To produce a custom-made script is not really mission impossible. Stars are stars. They are certainly capable of dominating films with their presence. If the screenwriter is a tailor, not only must he be good at his craft, he also has to find a balance between the stars and the film itself. Otherwise, it will result in the kind of paradigmatic scene in the beginning of the film *The Battle of Love* (Yue Feng, 1957).

The script states succinctly:

Night. A close-up of mistletoe. Dance music in the background.

(Zoom out, a steamed up window comes into focus; light rays beam from the window, and on it, the silhouette of a X'mas tree.

A family party is being held.

夜。特寫：門燈下，大門上掛着耶誕節常有葉圈。跳舞的音樂聲。

鏡頭拉開，對着蒸氣迷濛的玻璃窗，窗內透出燈光，映着一棵耶誕樹的剪影。樹上的燈泡成為一小團一小團的光暈。

室內正舉行一個家庭舞會。

（L.S.：年輕的女主人帶着陶文炳走到葉緯芳跟前，替他們介紹……文向芳鞠躬，請她跳舞。）

（M.S.：文與芳舞。）

以上都是啞劇。

當該段文字變成影像，首先被放大的，乃導演最想讓觀眾「眼前一亮」的女明星林黛，而不是女主角緯芳。為了有此效果，他加入了編劇在劇本中並未詳加描述的視覺元素——林黛頭上帶着閃亮的皇冠，綁住馬尾上的絲帶也是閃的，耳環在耳畔晃來晃去是閃的，身上那襲佔去了四分一個舞池的大傘裙，也是從胸前閃閃閃到裙裾。當觀眾（如我）被她閃得幾乎睜不開眼，隨着其他賓客陸續在慢搖鏡中出現，才發現為了不讓茄哩啡搶去女明星的光芒，他們（當然）只能一律「粗衣麻布」（causal wear）！而她才是那株掛滿燈泡的耶誕樹。

對我來説，那便是《情場如戰場》第一個令我忍俊不禁之處。但我不認為它的滑稽可笑是來自編劇的神來之筆，「功勞」，相反，我在自己的笑聲中聽見了對編劇的一點同情：儘管一開場「緯芳」的身份已被「林黛」的明星氣質蓋過，但為了「顧全大局」（叫觀眾繼續目不轉睛的把戲看完），編劇對導演在處理上的失衡也只能感到無可厚非。

尤其當他或她所參與的不是一齣獨立製作，而是由片廠制度催生出來的（其中）一件電影製成品。我的意思

(L.S. : The young hostess is introducing Tao Wenbing to Ye Weifang…Tao asks her to dance.)

(M.S. : Tao and Ye dance.)

Scenes above are silent.

When turning text into visuals, the director would most desire to have the persona of the big star Linda Lin Dai magnified on screen, not the character Ye Weifang. To this end, detailed visual elements are injected into the script: Lin wears a dazzling crown, an equally glittering ribbon on her pigtail, twinkling earrings on her ears and a radiant ball gown that fills almost a quarter of the dance floor. While viewers (like me) are nearly blinded by her glitter, other guests gradually appear in the slow pan, all dressed in casual wear so they won't steal the limelight. Turns out that Lin is herself the Christmas tree.

That was the first thing in the movie that made me laugh. It is certainly not the screenwriter's stroke of genius. In my laughter was pity for the screenwriter.

是，在《情場如戰場》面世的五十年代香港，片廠是主要生產電影的地方（定期為院線提供影片），「電影」的功能因而離不開消費和娛樂，是以明星成了片廠制度的「經濟支柱」，其他崗位的人們，則鮮會分享到同等份量的光芒（glamour）。那時的香港式片廠製作，愈是標榜豪華瑰麗，愈是鞏固了只有演員才是明星，而不會有明星製片、明星導演（換個時尚的稱呼，便是「作者導演」，例子：晚上也墨鏡照戴的王家衛），更不曾出現過明星編劇——除非，這個人帶着明星身份來寫劇本，像《情場如戰場》的作者：張愛玲。

張愛玲當然是明星，不止，還是明星中的明星——她的家世，作品受歡迎和擁戴的程度，還有烘托着她的成就的城市——上海，足以使她「在星群裡也放光」。只不過屬於張愛玲的光（鋒）芒，隨着她離開原居地而來到中途站似的香港，似乎已在減弱之中。

今非昔比的原因，可以是「電影媒體所能給她的發揮空間，到底不似散文和小説」。又若這理由有流於表面之嫌，很多人都會願意相信，她在電影創作上並未能得心應手純是受到際遇不佳而導致的心境變化所影響。《情場如戰場》是張愛玲以香港為背景的第一個電影劇本，但它並非完成在她人生中第二次住在香港的三年間，卻是在赴美定居之後。當時的她，面對着前景的許多未知之數和身份的不確定，「生活問題」必然是她想得最多的一件事，但是為了謀生，她卻不得不把現實給她的壓力轉化成像《情場如戰場》裡的脱離現實：俊男美女在豪華大別墅裡談情説愛，優哉悠哉。縱然他們的話語仍是帶着「張愛玲式」的機智、俏皮，但論其戲（喜）劇力量，《情場如戰場》明顯遠遠追不上同是出自她手筆的《太太萬歲》（桑弧，1947）。

《太太萬歲》的女主角由蔣天流飾演，但當這部片走進

For the sake of "larger interest" (so that the enchanted audience will be all eyes from the very beginning), the screenwriter has to make sacrifices, such as having his character overwhelmed by a star.

This is especially true when the film concerned is hastened by the studio system. When *The Battle of Love* was made in the 1950s, most films were produced in studios (to ensure regular supply for theatre circuits). Movies simply served as entertainment. Thus, stars became the "economic mainstay" of the studio system, while other workers seldom shared the same glamour. The more the studio productions in Hong Kong stressed spectacle and grandeur, the more the actors emerged as real stars. There were no star producers, no star directors (now called auteurs, like Wong Kar-wai with his trademark shades) and certainly no star scriptwriters – unless they brought their own fame into scriptwriting, like Eileen Chang (Zhang Ailing), the writer of *The Battle of Love*. Chang was an exception. Her illustrious background, the popularity of her works and the city that orbits around her – Shanghai – were sufficient to make her shine even among stars. However, Eileen Chang's glamour seemed to be diminishing after she left Shanghai to come to Hong Kong.

A simple reason may be that she could not write as freely in film as in essays or novels. But many would like to believe that her scripts suffered because of the changes in her life. *The Battle of Love* is the first Chang script set in Hong Kong. The work started during her second three-year stay in Hong Kong, but was not completed until after she had settled in the U.S. Faced with an uncertain future and an uncertain status, "livelihood" must have been the question uppermost in her mind. For the sake of livelihood, she had to transform the pressure of reality into the unreality of *The Battle of Love* – where handsome men and beautiful women play the game of love in a splendid villa. Though their dialogues are still filled with Chang's usual wit and humour, the drama or comedy of *The Battle of Love* is far inferior to her earlier work *Long Live the Wife* (Sang Hu, 1947).

了「名氣殿堂」，毫無疑問，它所造就的明星是張愛玲。到了《情場如戰場》，「張愛玲」儘管仍舊享受着「掛頭牌」式的待遇，然而唯有通過真正雪亮的眼睛——歷史，我們才會清楚看見表象和事實有着相當大的出入。

翻開1956年11月號的《國際電影》（國際電懋的官方畫報），有篇標題為「張愛玲編劇，林黛主演《情場如戰場》」的宣傳稿，內文如下：

著名女作家張愛玲，以寫《傳奇》、《傾城之戀》等小說名馳文壇……她的寫作才能是多方面的，所寫的舞台及電影劇本，另有她的獨特風格。去年國際公司成立劇本編審委員會，她被邀擔任編審委員之一。

介紹張的這段文字，看似只是開場白，後面，應該還有更多她與電懋淵源的交代，不料筆鋒一轉，她卻成了舖排林黛出場的台階：

林黛的演技，她是非常欣賞的，本來她預定專誠給她寫一劇本，恰巧美國某出版公司聘她擔任編輯，立即要她赴美就任，於是編劇的事，因她匆遽離港而耽擱了下來。

直至前月，張愛玲自美國寄給國際公司一個劇本，她說是在百忙中寫好的，並且一再叮囑，這個戲無論如何要由林黛主演，因為女主角的個性與外型，她是以林黛作對象來創作的。國際對於這一劇本，非常重視，除了決定由林黛任女主角之外，導演一職，已選定由岳楓擔任，岳楓接受這任務後，常約林黛共同研讀劇本，他們覺得張愛玲的故事劇本、人物創造，果然不同凡響……

編劇向導演建議由誰來扮演筆下角色的情況誠屬普遍，但是建議本身不會令一般編劇成為一篇宣傳稿的主角。若從這角度來看，不論《情場如戰場》到底是先有演員，還是先有編劇，電影公司都已盡足本份

前後景的故事——林黛與張揚、秦羽與陳厚

Foreground and background: Lin Dai and Chang Yang, Chin Yu and Peter Chen Ho.

——給予張愛玲一定的面子。但是在這禮待的背後，不能說是完全沒有委屈張愛玲的地方，甚至可以說，門面上是肯定了張愛玲的影響力，實際是把她當綠葉，而林黛才是牡丹。

這當然也可以被視為互相輝映。只不過當事情有了時間的距離，歷史自會把真義告訴我們——以張愛玲和林黛在彼時彼地的名氣（如今叫「人氣」）來較量，前者多少有點落難才女的況味，她所擁有的只能算是虛名，後者卻是實實在在的「前途無可限量」。而張愛玲的處境之所以使人感喟，乃在於她愈是被擺上神枱，愈似是明升暗降。而這一切又跟她的不在狀態是那麼的不謀而合。

皆因連「寫作」這拿手好戲，她都忽然生手起來——起碼在片廠制度下作業的電影人眼中是這樣。單以《情場如戰場》的戲名為例，初時是叫《情戰》。為此，戲未開拍，在一份被電影公司內部傳閱的審稿意見書上，戲名首先受到某位不署名行家（可能是製片人）的彈劾[1]：

片名《情戰》發音不亮，末字不屬平（最好陽平），難於響亮有勁。而且本片為流線型輕鬆喜劇，應改一流線型新型片名，庶幾一見即知內容大概，較可吸引觀眾。

片名之外，尚有對編劇技巧的貶多褒少。在表現形式方面，不署名人士的批評是：

最大毛病在於各劇中人之性格、心理刻劃均欠明朗。葉緯芳（林黛）既愛史榕生（張揚），劇中毫無線索交代。描寫陶文炳（陳厚）……何啟華（劉恩甲）二人實無甚分別；緯芳玩弄之方法毫無差異，二人之反應亦似出一轍，即其相互對白亦無甚不同，本劇既以此兩人與緯芳之談情說愛為主要之穿插，如無變化差異，必難有戲劇性之效果。緯苓（秦羽）爽快明朗有點男性化但不及緯芳有吸引力，但劇中除做到不及緯芳有吸引力外，其餘

照片中的姐姐有口難言
Peter Chen Ho, caught in the crossfire in *The Battle of Love*.

The lead actress in *Love Live the Wife* is Jiang Tian-liu. But if it is to enter the hall of fame, its star would be Chang. She is also given top billing in *The Battle of Love*, but only through history would we see the discrepancies between image and reality.

An issue of *International Screen* published in November 1956 contains the article "*The Battle of Love*, screenplay by Eileen Chang, starring Lin Dai". It says "celebrated author Eileen Chang gained fame in the literary circle with her works *Wonderful Stories* (Zhuan Qi) and *Love in a Fallen City* (Qing Cheng Zhi Lian)… A versatile writer, she produces stage and screen plays with a distinctive style. When MP & GI set up a script committee last year, she was invited to join." Yet, this tribute to Chang suddenly becomes a prelude for Lin's entry: "Due to Chang's high regard for Lin Dai's acting, a plan was installed to write a script for her. But when she left Hong Kong to take up an editing post in the United States, the plan was shelved… Last month, Chang sent a script to MP & GI from the States, which she said she wrote amid a busy schedule. She insisted that Lin star in the film, since the persona of the main character is based on her. MP & GI decided to cast Lin as the lead, and assigned Yue Feng as director. Yue has discussed the script with Lin several times. Both find Chang's plot and characterisations extraordinary…"

It is not unusual for scriptwriters to offer casting suggestions. But such suggestions don't usually become the subject of a publicity article. Regardless of who came first – the writer or the actress – the company had made an effort to show Chang some respect. But that doesn't mean that it'd be fair to her. One might even say that while it apparently affirmed Chang's importance, she was used as a foil to Lin, the real star.

Of course, they could also be seen as complementing each other. But through the distance of time, we have come to see the matter in its true light. If we weigh the

毫無表現，男性化隻字未提，爽直明朗跡近老實木訥，史榕生自稱可愛之型，恰與緯苓相似。又緯苓對文炳應有主動爭取之輕微描述，否則過於平淡，不能在本片佔一席之地。

場面設計，他乾脆越俎代庖：

陶文炳何啟華之開打，史榕生勸架之遭殃，均宜以別出心裁之形式出之（例如柔道、拳擊之相互出現）。……本片季節為自聖誕至夏季，游泳服裝出現機會不少。開首之跌入游泳池，拍攝上借景困難，譬如誤（筆者註：原文作「誤」字，可能是「改」）拍溜冰鞋仰天跌交等亦可應付過去（當然溜冰鞋要有一伏線）。

還有：

……化裝舞會一場（如服裝不便可改為普通舞會）中何啟華之壽相、陶文炳之多情……葉緯苓之情場失意，均可藉此表現，穿插新式舞蹈（例如轉身跳錯人、壽頭不能跳舞之狼狽等均可增加戲劇效果），目下電影之歌唱俗例，亦可乘機加入。

而對於全片的結局，他認為「緯芳盛裝候接王壽南之子必須改去，否則緯芳對榕生之愛情無法交代，而緯芳必不能得到觀眾的同情。」

僅供內部參考的這份「備忘錄」，除反映出行內人士對技術配合的考量，還包含了對劇本如何不足的分析和評價。我在前面說的「張愛玲不在狀態」，一部份是基於知道她在當時的處境，但《情場如戰場》從故事大綱到人物性格、對白，以至細節上的粗糙（也就是欠缺細節），確是與張愛玲之前的作品大有出入。而對於備忘錄所列出的「毛病」，我也同意有對症下藥的必要。

於是，當我把張愛玲全集中的《情場如戰場》文字劇本拿來跟電影一對照，連隨發現頗有一些不同之處。不致影響大局的不去說它（陳厚從原著中的在黑暗中跌落室

fame of Chang's against Lin's, the former was a writer in exile, while the latter was an up-and-coming star. The higher they put Chang on a pedestal, the more we feel she had been downgraded. She was equally let down by her own writing, which was hardly in form.

The truth is, Chang seemed to have lost her flair for writing, at least to the eyes of studio-groomed filmmakers. The first clue was in the original film title, *Love Battles* (*Qing Zhan*). Before shooting began, the title was criticised anonymously (possibly by a producer) in a script appraisal report[1]: "The title 'Qing Zhan' sounds rather flat. A sleek light comedy like this deserves a sleek and fashionable title. It should be self-explanatory and be able to attract the audience at once."

The writer was also critical of the writer's skills: "The greatest problem is with characterisation. The psychological states of the characters are unclear. The script offers no hints as to the love of Ye Weifang (Lin Dai) for Shi Rongsheng (Chang Yang / Zhang Yang). The two characters Tao Wenbing (Peter Chen Ho / Chen Hou) and He Qihua (Liu Enjia) are almost inextinguishable. Weifang flirts with them the same way, eliciting almost identical responses and monotonous dialogues. The flirtations among the trio threading the story plot and designed to heighten the drama of the film have defeated their own purpose. Weiling (Nellie Chin Yu / Qin Yu) is supposed to be candid, more outgoing and less attractive than Weifang. But apart from being less attractive, she is neither outgoing nor candid, only dull. Shi Rongsheng is supposed to be a likeable character, but he comes across the same way as Weiling. Also, one should touch lightly on Weiling's overtures to Wenbing or else this subplot would be too insignificant."

He even boldly suggested scene designs: "The duel between Tao Wenbing and He Qihua, and the mediator Shi Rongsheng being afflicted with injury should be spiced up (such as employing judo against fistfight)… The film, set in the time between Christmas and summer, allows plenty of opportunities for exhibiting swimming costumes… Since it is difficult to borrow

內泳池，妙想天開的設計！）變了因替林黛拍照而失足墮入室外泳池（雖合情理但平庸得多）。改動最大的有兩點，一是刪掉了林黛與秦羽兩姊妹的兩場對手戲，二是把原著中林黛對張揚的暗戀從不動聲色改成三番四次的「賊喊捉賊」——不斷對他高呼：我恨你！我恨你！

從哪些情節需要改動，或哪些場面被刪掉的落實，不難看見「明星制度」是怎樣支配大片廠制度所生產的電影。而當編劇也不外是生產線上的其中一對手，不管他或她的來頭多大，最終還是要以演員擅長的戲路作為創作的依歸。以《情場如戰場》為例，秦羽和林黛被刪掉的對手戲中，有一場是林黛飾演的妹妹拿着針，為姊姊秦羽身上的衣裙縫補（不排除是林黛故意把秦羽的舞衣扯破），二人繼而開展一場近似爭男友的談判。一向沒有妹妹那般直接的秦羽，在這裡忽然單刀直入得很，毫不諱言的表示對陳厚有意；而一直還在吊住陳厚胃口的林黛，便在此刻不小心的把針戮入了秦羽的腰部。「噯呀，針戮了你一下，是不是？疼不疼？」劇本裡的妹妹說。電影版本把這一幕整個抽起，我懷疑是導演擔心無法說服觀眾那一針只是「意外」，如果照拍不誤，便會令人覺得妹妹的角色太過工於心計，又或那份不好惹已超出了「淘氣」、「俏皮」的範圍而進入了「狠辣」、「狡詐」的禁區，那麼公司便是把對林黛的投資押在極其冒險的一注。屆時若因角色不討好而引起觀眾反感，不單會招致公司蒙受損失，更會令「林黛」從 hot property 降級為負資產。

吊詭的是，正如製片先生所言「劇中人之性格，心理刻劃均欠明朗……」偏偏在電影中被刪去的那一場，卻是對女主角有着最立體的描寫。除了有意無意傷害姊姊的身體來向她示威，之後她更義無反顧地對她承認（宣言！）說：「（文炳／何教授）我兩個都要。」「王壽南

眼神的故事
The story is

location to film the opening scene featuring a fall into the swimming pool, it can be conveniently replaced by a fall while skating (which should of course foreshadow a bigger event)… The costume party scene (which can be scaled down to a normal ball depending on the availability of costumes) can serve as the arena to display He Qihua's banal and dull appearance, Tao Wenbing's ardour as well as Ye Weiling's blunders in love, blended with the most original dances (such as turning to dance with a wrong partner, the blockhead's clumsiness in dancing etc.) and popular song numbers."

As for the ending, he commented that "the episode in which the beautifully dressed Weifang expects the arrival of Wang Shounan's son must be cut. Otherwise, Weifang's love for Rongsheng would be unaccounted for and Weifang would certainly not get the audience's sympathy."

Apart from technical considerations, this internal memo also includes the writer's analysis and evaluation of the script's flaws. I had said that Chang's writing had suffered because of the changes in her life, but it fails to justify the crudeness of the script. It is indeed a far cry from Chang's previous works. I also agree that the "shortcomings" listed in the memo need to be addressed.

When I compared the script of *The Battle of Love* in *Complete Works of Eileen Chang* with the movie, I found quite a number of differences. Apart from minor changes, like Chen falling into an indoor pool in the dark (an ingenious idea!) was changed to his falling into an outdoor pool while taking Lin's picture (logical but mundane), there are two major differences: first, two scenes between the Lin and her sister Chin were cut; second, Lin's secret crush on Chang was made

的兒子明天就來了，一個文炳，一個何教授，你還不夠嗎？」「不行，我喜歡熱鬧，愈多愈好。」

張愛玲在寫女主角分頭玩弄一肥一瘦的兩個男人時，的確只是把同一番台詞說了兩遍，在新意的角度上，無疑是交了白卷。但是如果上述那場兩姊妹的對手戲沒被抽走，觀眾便有機會知道她不光是為了好玩，而是出於內心有着莫大的空虛！

只是這樣一來，緯芳的性格很容易便會墮入「文藝片」的窠臼而不適合在「流線型輕鬆喜劇」中興波作浪，達到與眾同樂的目的了。

難怪從現在的電影版本看來，林黛所演的，並不是張愛玲筆下那個以為暗戀對象故意跟自已鬥氣，實則是自己和自己過不去的緯芳；而是打一開場便旗幟鮮明，並以一聲聲「我恨你！」來向「表哥」求愛的「表妹」。「緯芳」與「表妹」之間的落差，正好表現在文字劇本與電影的另一個不同之處：那是當表哥榕生站在樓梯腳下，當着文炳與何教授質問站在樓梯上的緯芳到底愛誰。文字的版本是：

榕生：「你得先回答這問題。」

芳回答：「不回答，就不讓我走？」

「噯。」

芳：「好，你們問我愛誰，那我就告訴你們。（向榕）我愛你。」

電影則改成：

「我愛我表哥。」

原作中的「我愛你」是緯芳在沒有事先張揚之下亮出她的愛情底牌，既令讀者吃了一驚，又不禁將信將疑。而在這個有點像捉迷藏的關係裡，「緯芳」的性格便多了複雜性。然而電影中把緯芳眼覷眼地 confront 表哥榕生

explicit, with her yelling repeatedly, "I hate you! I hate you!".

From these changes, it's not hard to see how the "star system" dominated the films produced under the studio system. Writers, no matter how famous, were only one pair of hands in the assembly line. Ultimately, they could only make products that fit the actors. In one of the cut scenes, Lin, the younger sister, mends her sister's dress (not ruling out the possibility that Lin had damaged it). The sisters then enter into a negotiation on boyfriends. The usually reserved Chin suddenly declares openly her love for Chen. At that moment, Lin, who has been stringing Chen on, accidentally jabs Chin with her needle. "Oops, were you pricked? Does it hurt?" To cut this from the film makes me wonder if the director feared that the audience would not believe it was an accident. The "mischievous" or "lively" younger sister would be seen as "sly" and "crafty". Not only would an unsympathetic character cause damage to the studio, it would also turn Lin from hot property to negative asset.

While the studio manager criticises the unclear "psychological states of the characters", it's in the cut scene that Lin's character is portrayed most graphically. Apart from the needle attack, she declares unrepentantly, "I want both of them." "Wang's son is coming tomorrow. With both Wenbing and He, aren't you satisfied already?" "No, the more, the merrier."

Portraying Lin's flirts with the men, Chang merely made Lin say the same line twice. But if the cut scenes were retained, the audience would know that she does that to fill a void in her heart. But then, Weifang would become a melodramatic characters, unfit for "light comedy" entertainment.

改為將他放在他者的位置，緯芳便成了傳統模式中的傳統角色——表妹當然是愛表哥的，管她是怎樣的「表妹」，更不用問她是怎樣的一個人。

因此，林黛在詮釋緯芳時，再沒有需要作出任何冒險或沒有把握的探索，所以《情場如戰場》於 1965 年面世至今，最為人津津樂道的仍是片中那停不了地嬌嗔、瞪眼、瞇眼和皺鼻子的「可愛」的林黛，而不是張愛玲所創造的葉緯芳。寫到這兒，我忽然想到荷里活的《亂世佳人》——為甚麼我們懷念的都是郝思嘉，而並不是扮演她的慧雲李呢？

這個例子容或舉得一點也不恰當，甚至離題了。只是它多少讓我想到張愛玲作為編劇與作家所得到的不同待遇。作為作家的她，筆下每個人物都有充足的篇幅去發展自己的生命，而她的文字亦永遠主宰着讀者的想像，是以每次當她的小說搬上銀幕，飾演者都面臨挑戰（誰不怕被張迷擲石？）。這時候，你可以說她是一個神。但當她作為電影編劇，特別是要為某特定的演員（或題材）來創作時，她的身份和地位便有了很大的逆轉——且不論在一干的宣傳稿上，她是被怎樣的吹捧和抬舉。

《情場如戰場》之後，張還替電懋陸續編了《六月新娘》（1960）、《南北一家親》（1962）、《小兒女》（1963）、《南北喜相逢》（1964）、《一曲難忘》（1964）和沒有拍成電影的《魂歸離恨天》。[2] 每次有新片開拍，官方宣傳刊物上仍會把她的名字加以突出，如「電懋掌握了今日最佳劇作者之一的張愛玲……」、「由名女作家張愛玲執筆寫成劇本，內容質素的豐富，不失為此時此地一幅世紀風情畫……」、「出自張愛玲手筆……其成就的驚人，非庸俗者所可望其項背。」

光看文字，她的「明星」地位仍是相當牢固。不過，宣傳稿不比一般文章，寫它要懂得竅門，讀它更是一次解

No wonder that in the film, Lin's role is not the Weifang in the script, who believes that the man she secretly loves is picking quarrels with her, while in fact she is fighting herself. Instead, she is the girl who expresses her love by telling her cousin "I hate you!". When the cousin, at the foot of the stairs in front of Wenbing and He, questions Weifang, who is standing on top of the stairs, the script goes: "You have to answer this question first." "If I don't, you won't let me go, will you?", Weifang replies. "That's right." Weifang: "OK, I'll tell you whom I love. (To the cousin) I love you." In the film, this line becomes "I love my cousin."

In the original script, Weifang's sudden declaration surprises and puzzles the readers. Weifang thus takes on a complexity in this cat-and-mouse relationship. But in the film, she doesn't confront her love directly. She becomes an archetypal character – a girl naturally falls for her cousin, no matter what kind of girl she is.

Playing Weifang, Lin doesn't need to take risks or venture into the unknown. That is why *The Battle of Love* has been remembered for the coquettish and charming Lin, rather than for the character Weifang created by Chang. Yet *Gone with the Wind* (1949) is best remembered for Scarlett O'Hara, rather than the Vivien Leigh who played her.

The comparison may be far-fetched. Yet, I am reminded of the radically different treatment Chang received as an author and as a screenwriter. As an author, she has ample space to develop her characters. Her writing always dominate the readers' imagination. That is why every time her work is adapted into film, the actors face a great challenge (who is not afraid of being booed by Eileen Chang's fans?). But when she wrote for films, especially when she had to write for certain stars (or certain themes), her status suffered, regardless of how she was praised in publicity articles.

After *The Battle of Love*, Chang also wrote *The Greatest Wedding on Earth* (1962), *Father Takes a Bride* (1963), *The Greatest Love Affair on Earth* (1964), *June Bride* (1960) and *Please Remember Me* (1964) for MP & GI, as well as *Yungui Lihengtian* which was not filmed.[2] When those films were

碼，讀者必須有着不被文字牽着鼻子走的決心，才能從中發掘到較為接近事實的一鱗半爪。在本文的尾聲，讓我們分享刊登在1962年9月號《娛樂畫報》中有關《南北一家親》的一段報道：「故事大綱由秦亦孚〔泰羽〕執筆，編劇由名女作家張愛玲執筆。這是電懋當局早與張愛玲取得默契者，但張愛玲僑居美國多年，對香港現實環境有了生疏，所以遲遲未能下筆。電懋當局俯候再三，張愛玲決定來港編撰，抵港之後，張愛玲即深入各階層實地觀察，搜集素材，準備充份，才開始動筆⋯⋯」洋洋灑灑的背後，其實藏有多少隱衷？若要把它拍成電影，劇本該由誰來寫？哪一位演員可以勝任出演張愛玲？抑或時移世易，張愛玲編劇一角，今天誰敢問津？

編按

[1] 這份意見書現存於香港電影資料館內。

[2] 左几在電懋粵語片組曾拍過一部《魂歸離恨天》(1957)，編劇署名何愉，其實是左几的化名，與張愛玲無關。

林奕華，舞台工作者。近作為《張愛玲，請留言》，憑《紅玫瑰白玫瑰》(1994)獲金馬獎最佳改編劇本獎，《半生緣》音樂劇是他下一個演出計劃。

Edward Lam, choreographer and stage director. Recent work: *Who's Calling Eileen Chang?*

launched, the official magazine would praise Chang, publishing such sensational headlines as: "MP & GI has one of the best screenwriters today, Eileen Chang", "written by famous writer Eileen Chang, the rich story is no less than a slice of life of this time and this place", "written by Eileen Chang…the outstanding script is not your run-of-the-mill screenplays."

From these articles, it might seem that Chang remained a "star". But one must take such articles with a pinch of salt. One quote from a report on *The Greatest Wedding on Earth* published in *The Screen and Stage Pictorial* in September, 1962: "The story outline was drafted by Qin Yifu (Chin Yu), while the script was written by renowned writer Eileen Chang. This was a deal between MP & GI and Chang. But since Chang had lived in the States for years, she had gotten out of touch with Hong Kong society and had put off writing it. After repeated requests by MP & GI, Chang decided to come to Hong Kong to accomplish the task. Upon arrival, she immediately set out to research different sectors of society and make observations on the spot before she started writing…" What is behind all these? If this episode in Chang's life were to be made into a film, who should write the script? Who could play Eileen Chang? Or, in this day and time, who would dare tackle the role of Eileen Chang, the screenwriter?

Translated by Christine Chan

Editor's notes

[1] A copy of the report is catalogued and kept at the HKFA.

[2] Tso Kea directed a Cantonese film in 1957 of the same title for MP & GI; he also wrote the script in his pseudonym, Ho Yu.

淺談多產奇人王天林

- 石琪 -

王天林是香港影視界資深奇人，我對他的從影經歷很感興趣，但談論他的作品很困難。因為他拍片非常多產，除了數以百計的粵語片、國語片之外，還有很多香港沒有放映的潮語片、廈語片，甚至泰國片、菲律賓片，而且古裝和時裝、喜劇和悲劇、武俠和文藝、歌舞和神怪，甚麼品種都有，我卻看得極少。實際上他的影片多數現已失傳，想找來看也找不到。坦白說，我看王天林兒子王晶的電影就齊全得多。

王天林近年在一些港片做演員，如《暗花》(1998) 和《瘦身男女》(2001)，他自成一格的演出亦給我深刻印象。但對他過去執導的影片實在認識不足，今次「應召」寫稿，才通過香港電影資料館，看到他在電懋／國泰時期拍攝的一批作品，然而也欠缺他在「亞洲電影節」得獎的《家有喜事》(1959)，和他在國泰後期較有名的武俠笑片《神經刀》(1969)。

Prolific Oddball: Wang Tianlin

- Sek Kei -

Wang Tianlin is an oddball of Hong Kong cinema. I am interested in his life in film but find writing about his work difficult. He was so prolific that on top of making over 100 Cantonese and Mandarin films, he also directed films in the Chaozhou and Amoy dialects, and even Thai and Filipino films. He made contemporary and costume pictures and dabbled in genres that include comedies, tragedies, martial arts, dramas, musicals and fantastic movies. He also started acting in recent years and his unique style impresses me. Most of his films are lost and I had seen only a fraction of his surviving output. In fact, I have a more complete knowledge of the works of his son, Wong Jing (Wang Jing).

Drafted to write this article, I managed to see some of his MP&GI / Cathay films, though his Asian Film Festival winner *All in the Family* (1959) and the later *A Mad, Mad, Mad Sword* (1969) were unavailable.

Wang was born in Shanghai in 1928 and joined the film industry after coming to Hong Kong in his teens, quickly earning the nickname "king of assistant

其實資料館為王天林做的口述歷史訪問特別豐富有趣，他暢談自己經歷與影壇掌故，十分生動。[1]

王天林1928年生於上海，少年時代來香港，很年輕便加入影壇，成為「副導演王」，1950年正式執導的首作是《峨嵋飛劍俠》，正式揚名是1956年鍾情主演的《桃花江》。他聲稱從廿歲至四十歲（約1950年代至1970年代），拍過三四百部電影，還曾經一年拍廿四部片，實在多產得驚人。不過據他說：有些影片不用王天林的名字，又有不少影片只在外埠放映。

1973年起他加入無線電視台，憑他豐富的拍片經驗，對早期電視劇集如《啼笑姻緣》、《書劍恩仇錄》，以至《陸小鳳》等作出不少貢獻。

在五六十年代香港影壇，尤其是粵語片，像王天林那樣多產多樣化的影人相當普遍。他受學校教育不多，屬於在片場從低做起的成功典型，顯然全憑自己吸收學習和掌握機會，有片就拍，條件極差亦要設法完成。他在口述歷史訪問中有一段說得妙，原來他兒子王晶讀完中大，要去英國讀電影，但王天林說：「我話電影唔使讀，要睇，睇就得。去片場睇多幾個月，當年就乜都識。最緊要係有心。佢而家仲心心不忿，話我當年唔畀佢去讀電影。」

由於看得太少，了解有限，這裏無法談論王天林電影作品的個人特色，以及他在五六十年代港片的具體成就，這方面必須深入研究才行。但似乎可以說，橫跨國粵語片，是王天林一大特色。當年香港國粵語片楚河漢界，觀眾對象大有不同，雖有影人兩邊走，但像王天林那樣真正「腳踏兩條船」的，顯然很例外。他做到南北跨界，亦可稱為七十年代以來港片從分化變為合流的前奏先聲。

directors". He debuted as a director with *The Flying-sword Hero from Emei Mountain* (1950) but didn't become known until *Songs of Peach Blossom River* (1956). He claimed to have made over 300 films, sometimes as high as 24 in a year, though some are made with pseudonyms. In 1973, he joined TVB and contributed significantly to shaping early TV dramas.

Prolific filmmakers like Wang were common in 1950s and 1960s Hong Kong cinema, especially on the Cantonese side. He was not well educated and, typical of his time, rose through the ranks to success. He learned on the job, persisting through unfavourable conditions. In his Oral History interview for the Film Archive, he talked about Wong Jing's desire to study film in England: "No need to study film. Just watch. Watch on the set for a few months and you'll learn everything. He's still upset about it today that I didn't let him go." [1]

Having watched only a small fraction of his output, it's impossible to talk about the characteristics of his films or his accomplishments during the 1950s and 1960s. But it is safe to say that Wang is marked by his ability to straddle both the Mandarin and Cantonese cinemas, which were largely exclusive territories. Though there were some who did switch from one to another, a filmmaker who truly worked on both cinemas at the same time was exceptional. Wang's crossing between the northern and the southern was also a prelude to the Hong Kong cinema's integration of these sensibilities in the 1970s.

It was thus natural that the popular MP&GI comedy *The Greatest Civil War on Earth* (1961) directed by Wang would break the barrier between Mandarin and Cantonese films, portraying the conflicts between northerners and southerners while addressing the very realistic need to look at fellow citizens as travellers on the same boat.

According to Wang, scriptwriter Stephen Soong (Song Qi) originally wrote *The Greatest Civil War on Earth* as a play for charity fundraising, inspired by a Mainland film which used two different dialects. There was not enough material for a film when Wang was

因此，電懋1961年大受歡迎的喜劇片《南北和》由王天林執導，順理成章地打破國粵語片界限，反映了當時香港社會外省移民（北）與本土廣東人（南）的現實矛盾，亦迎合了同舟共濟的現實需求。《南北和》由宋淇編劇，據王天林說，宋淇寫的原是為慈善籌款演出的單幕話劇，靈感其實來自大陸一套用兩種不同方言拍的戲，交到王天林之手，本來素材不夠。大概他在電影劇本上作了補充，最重要是他處理國語演員和粵語演員都熟練，尤其讓南北兩諧星梁醒波和劉恩甲都有生動發揮。因此《南北和》在香港很賣座，帶起一個潮流，還導致台灣也曾大拍類似題材。

現在重看《南北和》仍然很有趣，亦很有意義，因為今日香港人要重新面對大陸同胞，而粵語文化和國語（普通話）文化亦再度發生相拒又相吸，像冤家又是親家的關係。王天林接着拍了《南北一家親》（1962）和《南北喜相逢》（1964），由上海才女張愛玲編劇，但都是她從俗的「行貨」，成績不及《南北和》。

1963年王天林導演的國語愛情、家庭倫理片《小兒女》，亦由張愛玲編劇，編與導都較用心。片中大女兒（尤敏）懷念亡母、愛護兩個年幼弟弟（鄧小宇、鄧小宙），很擔心教書爸爸（王引）娶後母，但她弄巧反拙，好心做壞事，幾乎釀成悲劇。今日看來，三兒女的「後母恐懼症」太過份，片中的戲劇性炮製亦很牽強，不過在數十年前，類似情況常在現實發生，我知道當年有些單親家長（尤其是寡母），就由於子女反對而放棄再婚機會。

《小兒女》其實善意地指出兒女的錯，不應對家長再婚抱有偏見和誤會。妙在四十年代張愛玲參與編劇的上海名片《哀樂中年》（桑弧，1949），老父親特別開明，爭取自由，衝破子女們世俗的保守的拘束。至於王天林

assigned the film and he probably had to add to the script. The film also owed much to his familiarity with both Mandarin and Cantonese actors, especially his success in eliciting lively performances from the comedians Leung Sing-po (Liang Xingbo) and Liu Enjia. The film became a big hit in Hong Kong, creating a trend and spawning imitators in Taiwan.

The film remains interesting to watch today, because once again, the people of Hong Kong have to face Mainlanders and the paradoxical relationship of mutual attraction and resentment that exists between the Cantonese and Mandarin (Putonghua) cultures. Wang went on to direct *The Greatest Wedding on Earth* (1962) and *The Greatest Love Affair on Earth* (1964), both written by Eileen Chang (Zhang Ailing) in what are the writer's compromise with the mainstream and both are not as good as the original.

The melodrama *Father Takes a Bride* (1963), also written by Chang, is more accomplished. It is the story of a daughter who, because of her love for her dead mother and her younger brothers, is troubled by her father's desire to remarry. Looking at it today, the children's "stepmother fear" seems overwrought and the film's drama too forced, but such situation did occur during those times. Interestingly, *Sorrows and Joys of a Middle-aged Man* (Sang Hu, 1949), which Chang also wrote, is about a widowed father who overcomes his children's conservative views with his open-minded pursuit of freedom. The plot of *Father Takes a Bride* is not very convincing and the film's strength lies in its daily details such as washing hair, eating dinner and especially scenes in buses and ferry boats.

Dealing with generation conflicts, Wang's *Lily of the Valley* (written by Wang Liuzhao, 1962) is more intense. The fault lies with the parent, the widowed mother (Wang Lai) who listens too much to her lover (Zhu Mu), resulting in the pains repeatedly inflicted on the daughter (Lucilla You Min). The mother eventually kills her lover before killing herself.

Lily of the Valley and *Father Takes a Bride* are the two sides of the same coin, illustrating Wang's

處理《小兒女》，劇情本身不大自然，好在加添了日常生活小節，例如洗頭、吃飯，我較喜歡擠巴士和搭船到離島的情景。

王天林拍兩代恩怨，更強烈是1962年汪榴照編劇的《火中蓮》。此片錯在家長——寡居媽媽（王萊）太遷就壞情夫（朱牧），累到女兒（尤敏）屢受傷害，結果媽媽殺情夫後自殺，作為補償。

《火中蓮》和《小兒女》可說是一體兩面，顯出王天林作為導演沒有成見，不會只拍某方好、某方壞。《南北和》也是家庭片，拍上海人家與廣東人家兩對父女，互相諷刺鬥法又合作愉快，這種絕不偏於一面的喜劇關係最可愛。

在我看到數目有限的王天林導演影片中，最出色無疑是1960年黑白國語片《野玫瑰之戀》，編劇是另一才女秦亦孚（即秦羽）。此片把西方著名的吉卜賽女郎卡門改為香港夜總會歌女，還把比才歌劇《卡門》名曲改為國語時代曲，由葛蘭載歌載舞，唱得很流行。

如果說王天林很多影片只是接單交貨，按章工作的話，《野玫瑰之戀》就肯定是他一件工整優異的好作品，時隔四十年觀看，仍然傑出。有趣的是，王天林自稱沒有看過歌劇《卡門》，但可能看過改編的外國電影，例如美國岳圖柏林明嘉1954年導演的現代黑人版《卡門瓊絲》。王天林版本由日本資深的服部良一改編歌曲，說起來，五十年代初木下惠介的《卡門還鄉》，也在日本掀起東洋版《卡門》熱。

無論如何，《野玫瑰之戀》在當年港片大概自成一格，亦與電懋公司其他歌舞片不同，音樂與劇情人物合為一體，演唱場面拍得奔放強勁，鏡頭和剪接精確，而且全片有着相當嚴謹的黑色電影風格。

(左)《南北一家親》
(右)《小兒女》
(left) *The Greatest Wedding on Earth*
(right) *Father Takes a Bride*

impartial stance. *The Greatest Civil War on Earth* is also a family drama, portraying two families whose parents and children at once clash and collaborate together. Such an approach to comedy is indeed charming.

In the limited number of Wang Tianlin films I had watched, the best is undoubtedly *The Wild, Wild Rose* (1960), written by another talented female writer, Nellie Chin Yu (Qin Yu). The film portrays Carmen, the gypsy character from Bizet's opera, as a Hong Kong nightclub singer, changing some of the arias into Mandarin pop, sung by star Grace Chang (Ge Lan) to her own dancing.

If many of Wang's films are works rushed to meet deadlines, *The Wild, Wild Rose* is definitely a film of even accomplishment that remains appealing forty years later. It is interesting that Wang claimed never having watched *Carmen* but might have watched an adapted film, like Otto Preminger's *Carmen Jones* (1954). Regardless, the film is unique among Hong Kong films of its time and is also different from other MP&GI musicals. With music, story and characters that perfectly complement each other, the film's music scenes are shot energetically, its editing precise and its *noir*-style photography outstanding.

Chang, who usually doesn't play "the bad woman", exudes a wild, seductive charisma. Although this Hong Kong Carmen later becomes Camille and Madame Butterfly, sacrificing for her lover in the film's adherence to Eastern morality, her independence from patriarchal control and societal restraints is powerful. Women's films of the 1950s and 1960s often feature rich female characters, such as the rebellious Hung Sin-nui (Hong Xiannü) in the Cantonese film *The Rouge Tigress* (1955). By contrast, the women in today's Hong Kong are much weaker.

Also made in 1960, Wang's *Death Traps* is also a *noir*-ish film about a bad woman. Li Mei plays an alcoholic dance hall girl who, while drunk, arranges to have her love rival killed, resulting in a series of thrilling but funny situations. The film is obviously influenced by Hollywood and is not as accomplished

本來不演「壞女人」的葛蘭，在此片強烈發揮了煙視媚行、狂野誘惑的魅力，非常突出。雖然，這個香港卡門後來又成為茶花女和蝴蝶夫人，終於為愛郎犧牲，迎合「東方情義」，但片中葛蘭不受男權控制、不受世俗約束的獨立性格，實在逼人。其實五六十年代香港女性片豐富多采，紅線女在秦劍粵語片《胭脂虎》（1955）中也非常反叛，相比之下，今日香港片的女性反而脆弱了、輕浮了。

同在1960年，王天林另一部《殺機重重》，也是黑色風格的壞女人奇情片。李湄扮演酗酒舞女，大醉時買兇殺情敵，此後誤會重重，構成驚險喜劇。這一部明顯受西片影響，不及《野玫瑰之戀》，但李湄亦演得妙，片中拍澳門實景則有西洋風味，黑夜的石卵街巷追逃，就特別注重異鄉氣氛。

王天林1959年執導《樑上佳人》，林黛演女賊也妙趣，但受姚克原著話劇所限，這女賊太天真純情，非常不夠壞，而且太少動作，王天林就缺乏發揮機會。1964年他拍張恨水名著《啼笑姻緣》，由於全部在片場拍攝，技法拘束了，不過處理女角也不錯，片中葛蘭街頭唱鼓書，就有中國傳統風味。後來她屈就於軍閥的淫威，「變壞」和變瘋了，那種性格轉變和悲劇命運是有劇力的。

王天林擅長拍女性，憑《桃花江》（1956）捧紅小野貓鍾情就是例子，與他的「麻甩佬」外型不同。單以這批電懋片來說，他拍女星丁皓、白露明、尤敏、葛蘭、林翠、林黛等，都比小生有吸引力，男星則以梁醒波、劉恩甲這對諧星最生動，這情況當然因為那是女星時代，尤其在電懋。其實他拍性格男星如王引和喬宏，也好過拍白臉小生雷震、張揚和趙雷，特別是喬宏做忠做奸都很爽朗。

左右為難 一
《樑上佳人》
Between a
and a soft p
Lady on the

as *The Wild, Wild Rose*. Li, however, turned in a fine performance and the film's Macau scenes are rich in location atmosphere.

In *Lady on the Roof* (1959), Linda Lin Dai is also appealing as a female thief, though, limited by the script adapted by Yao Ke from a play, the character doesn't go far enough as a bad woman. Also, without much action, Wang seemed handcuffed. The 1964 film *A Story of Three Loves*, based on a Zhang Henshui novel, is also rather restrained, probably because it was shot in a studio. Again, the female protagonist (Grace Chang) stands out. Her street performance scenes succeed in capturing a sense of Chinese tradition and when she is later forced by the warlord to turn "bad", the transformation and the sense of tragic fate are dramatically powerful.

That Wang is good at portraying women can be seen in his making a star out of Chung Ching (Zhong Qing) in *Songs of Peach Blossom River*. In his MP&GI films, actresses like Kitty Ting Hao (Ding Hao), Christine Pai Lu-ming (Bai Luming), You Min, Grace Chang, Jeanette Lin Cui and Linda Lin Dai are always more attractive than their male costars. That was of course an era of actresses, especially at MP&GI, yet the men who have left the best impressions in Wang's films are Leung Sing-po and Liu Enjia, both comedians characterised for their heft. In fact, he is also better with character actors like Wang Yin and Roy Chiao (Qiao Hong) than romantic leads like Chang Yang (Zhang Yang) and Chao Lei (Zhao Lei), especially Chiao, who is good both as heroes and villains.

Wang's handling of male actors is a subject that calls for more study. He made many male-oriented Cantonese films in the 1950s, but I had not seen most of them. Certainly the so-called "new era of masculine films" was not ushered in until the late 1960s at Shaw Brothers by Chang Cheh (Zhang Che), who, together

但他處理男性有何特色則有待研究。五十年代他拍過很多以男角為主的粵語武俠片和粵劇歌唱片，我都沒有看過。可以肯定的是，香港電影的「新派男性陽剛時代」，到六十年代中後期才由張徹在邵氏掀起，並由他與胡金銓加強和革新了港片的武打動作感。妙在王天林有些電懋影片由張徹編劇，主要是當時流行的女性片，較趣怪一部是1961年時裝喜劇《遊戲人間》，愛好運動的丁皓故意女扮男裝，與白露明「同性」戀，丁皓同時又「男扮女裝」，愛上舉重大隻佬喬宏。性別錯體得很誇張。

奇怪的是，常拍歌唱片與武俠片的王天林，在電懋／國泰後期導演的古裝黃梅調或「變種越劇調」片，以及古裝武俠片，多數無精打采。或許因為這兩類片是邵氏強項，加上電懋因大老闆陸運濤空難喪生而元氣大傷，欠缺當時得令的能唱能打明星吧？事實上，六十年代末的國泰公司停留在舊派片場方式，與邵氏的旺盛新氣象對比強烈。不過，國泰在內外困境中也曾變招變新，尤其在武俠片方面——1969年王天林的怪雞喜劇《神經刀》大受歡迎，片名亦成為流行俗語。隨後來自台灣的王星磊和張曾澤，分別拍出創新風格的《虎山行》(1969)和《路客與刀客》(1970)，都很獨特；來自粵語影壇的楚原拍出《龍沐香》(1970)，則首先建立了此後十多年大受歡迎的楚原（加古龍）式武俠風格。然而對這公司來説卻為時已晚，挽不回結束的命運了。

後來王天林在電視之外也偶有拍片，但限於「散工」。至於他歷年來的代表作，則需要搜尋整理，亦需更有資格的研究者來評述。

編按

[1] 香港電影資料館為王天林先後做了兩次口述歷史訪問，分別為1997年4月11日及2001年10月23日。

石琪，資深影評人，著有《石琪影話集》(1-8冊，次文化堂，1999)。

Sek Kei, renowned film critic; author of *Sek Kei Film Reviews* (vol. 1-8, Subculture, 1999).

《神經刀》

A plate goes flying in *A Mad, Mad, Mad Sword.*

with King Hu (Hu Jinquan), revolutionised Hong Kong cinema with their action aesthetics. It is interesting to note that Chang Cheh scripted some of Wang's MP&GI films, most of them women-oriented dramas. One is the comedy *You were Meant for Me* (1961), in which Ting masquerades as a man to strike up a "lesbian" romance with Pai, while the male character she assumes romances the muscle-bound Chiao by assuming the role of a woman. A high-flying case of gender bending.

Wang had made lots of musicals and action films, but the regional opera films and martial arts films he made at MP&GI/Cathay are mostly mundane. Perhaps it is because both genres were dominated by Shaws and that Cathay was unable to attract top stars in the genres after Loke Wan Tho's death. In fact, Cathay was stuck in an outdated mode of filmmaking during that period, a sharp contrast to the energetic vigour of Shaws. Cathay did try to keep up with the times, especially in martial arts films. Wang's action comedy *A Mad, Mad, Mad Sword* was very popular and its Chinese title, *shen jing dao*, became a popular vernacular phrase, its usage lasting to this day. Other Cathay martial arts films such as Wang Xinglei's *Escort over Tiger Hills* (1969) and Zhang Zengze's *From the Highway* (1970) are also original entries to the genre. On the Cantonese side, Chor Yuen (Chu Yuan)'s *Cold Blade* (1970) also established the Chor-cum-Gu Long style of martial arts films that would became very popular and remained so for over a decade. However, such innovative efforts were unable to save the company from its inevitable demise.

Translated by Sam Ho

Editor's Note

[1] Interview with Wang Tianlin, Hong Kong Film Archive, on April 11, 1997 and October 23, 2001.

從左几看
電懋粵語片的特色

- *李焯桃* -

左几六十年代導演的電影（尤其是改編張恨水原著那五部），我們會比較熟悉。他拍於五十年代的作品也不少，其中當以電懋（前身為國際）的出品最有睇頭，票房和評論屢創佳績。這回得睹他拍於1957及1958年的四部文藝片——《魂歸離恨天》（1957）、《琵琶怨》（1957）、《黛綠年華》（1957）及《美人春夢》（1958）——儘管成績頗見參差，卻起碼證實了他作為導演的早熟和水準穩定，電懋較佳的製作條件使他如虎添翼。此外，不論取材、改編方法、人物刻劃（包括選角）或拍攝風格，在粵語影壇可謂頗有作者風範。

儘管早於1955年電懋甫成立時，左几已為其粵語片組拍出《余之妻》（原著徐枕亞）及《愛情三部曲》，翌年再拍出同是巴金原著的《火》，但他同時仍有替其他電影公司效力。其後兩年他才只拍電懋出品，成績也較可

A Look at MP & GI Cantonese Films Through the Work of Tso Kea

- *Li Cheuk-to* -

We are more familiar with Tso Kea's (Zuo Ji) work of the 1960s, especially the five films adapted from Zhang Henshui novels. He also made a lot of films in the 1950s and the most noteworthy should be those made at MP & GI (formerly International Films). I had a chance to watch four of his *wen yi* films[1] made in 1957 and 1958 for this occasion. Although the works are uneven, they at least verify his early maturity and steadiness of his directorial skills, which are allowed to develop under the superior production environment of MP & GI. In terms of subject matters, adaptation approach, character development (including casting) and photographic style, he can be considered an auteur of the Cantonese cinema.

Although Tso had directed *My Wife, My Wife* (1955), *Three Stages of Love* (1955) and *Fire* (1956) for the MP & GI in its early Hong Kong years, he was also making films for other companies. He worked for MP & GI exclusively the

觀。1959年他脫離電懋，接着的不論戲曲片如《王寶釧》(1959)和《帝女花》(1959，片上字幕導演龍圖，實為左几)，或喜劇片《金山大少》(1959)，皆頭頭是道。或可反映出他的電懋時期，也是穩定環境下磨練自己而進入的成熟階段。

期間八部作品，[1] 除四部左几自承「比較適合自己發揮」的文藝片外，[2] 還穿插了大鑼大鼓古裝歌唱片《半世老婆奴》(1957)、奇裝異服加歌唱噱頭的宮闈鬧劇《璇宮艷史》(1957)、《璇宮艷史續集》(1958)及添食之作《月宮寶盒》(1958)。其中自以《璇宮艷史》最為轟動，首映一周收入逾二十萬，據説打破當年粵語片的票房紀錄。[3] 影片能夠哄動一時，主要由於改編自戰前薛覺先的首本舞台劇，[4] 加上張瑛首開金口唱歌，而且唱的又是薛腔。[5] 此外場面豪華，佈景宏偉，與服裝、道具一樣充滿古靈精怪的仿西洋趣味，把電懋的「電影製片廠」較優厚的片場設施盡情利用，的確不乏視聽之娛。

與《璇宮艷史》的流行小曲不同，《半世老婆奴》的大鑼大鼓粵劇歌唱較能配合古裝的民間故事題材。但影片較同類粵語片突出的，是利用了當時仍屬罕見的電影特技手法，把原著《聊齋誌異》中一節〈馬介甫〉裡的法術形象化呈現出來，觀眾大感新奇。例如狐仙輕吹一口氣把悍婦推到連退十數步栽倒地上，便是利用倒拍技巧；縫衣一幕則用動畫慣見的 Stop Motion；天兵巨人懲戒悍婦一場大量運用疊印，效果雖不如理想，但想來在當年已算大膽的嘗試。[6]

這些粵語歌唱片或多或少都是商業計算的噱頭之作，反映了電懋管理層靈活的市場觸覺。但左几一樣全力以

next two years and the result was more impressive. After he left in 1959, works produced that year like the opera films *The Story of Wang Baochuan* and *Tragedy of the Emperor's Daughter*, or the comedy *The Chair* are all quite accomplished, indicating that he had matured through his MP & GI experience.

In 1957 and 1958, he made eight films at MP & GI.[2] In addition to the four *wen yi* films that he felt he "was best at making,"[3] he also made the opera film *Hen-pecked Husband* (1957), the exotic musical *My Kingdom for a Husband* (aka *The Romance of Jade Hall*, 1957), its sequel *My Kingdom for a Honeymoon* (aka *The Romance of Jade Hall [Sequel]*, 1958) and its spin-off *The Magic Box* (1958). Among them, *My Kingdom for a Husband* was most successful, reportedly breaking box-office records.[4] Its popularity is due largely to the famous Sit Kok-sin (Xue Juexian) opera on which it's based,[5] star Cheung Ying's (Zhang Ying) singing debut[6] as well as the exotic, faux western costumes and props allowed for by the MP & GI studio system.

Different from the light pop of *My Kingdom for a Husband*, the music in *Hen-pecked Husband* is the full orchestra opera more suitable for its folksy plot. Different from similar Cantonese films is the special effects, like the use of reverse photography to realise the fox incarnate's[7] breath that blows a shrew back a dozen paces, plus the use of stop motion and double exposure. Though some of the effects are flawed, they were bold attempts for its time.[8]

These market-driven, gimmicky sing-song films are shaped by MP & GI's commercial savvy, yet Tso put his heart into them just the same. Their success in turn allowed him to make his preferred *wen yi* films. During those years, directors of Cantonese films usually had to work in every genre and Tso was no exception.

赴，在選角和拍攝上一絲不茍；影片賣座又可令他拍回愛拍的文藝片。當年的粵語片導演大都拍遍各種不同類型，左几自然也不例外。

他喜歡改編名著或西片的傾向，在電懋的四年已表現得十分明顯。《魂歸離恨天》(1957) 取材自英國愛蜜莉．勃朗蒂名著《咆哮山莊》，卻把故事簡化成一則有情人不能終成眷屬的愛情悲劇。原著女主角與他人結合有其階級提升的考慮，梅綺嫁給張清卻是為了報恩，而且發生在張瑛離家兩年多又杳無音訊後，再過半年他衣錦還鄉卻已來得太遲。原著對兩主角的狂戀不至全盤肯定，對其破壞性以及男主角的復仇心理有深刻的描寫；影片卻把青梅竹馬的關係變成至死不渝的愛情而盡情謳歌，二人不能結合的障礙先是兄妹名份（儘管無血緣關係），繼而是梅綺成了有夫之婦——倫理不可違，是非常粵語片又非常左几的。三年後左几改編易卜生《群鬼》的《慈母心》(1960)，對亂倫主題的處理更為直接，卻同樣保守。

歌頌浪漫愛情與反封建其實一體兩面，是五十年代粵語片常見的主題，這方面《魂歸離恨天》可說上承《愛情三部曲》及《火》的餘緒。左几其後三部文藝作品，便從改編文學名著轉為改編荷里活片及流行小說，感性上較為現代，題材也更加大膽。

初睹《琵琶怨》最使人意外的，是它竟然是左几八年後的《珍珠淚》(1965) 的前身。不但情節幾乎一模一樣，吳楚帆在兩片中更飾演同一個娛樂捐主任／花捐局長的角色，叫趙七或跛三都沒分別，瘸腿特徵一以貫之，鋒芒畢露的演出風格亦如出一轍。當然，兩片細節也有差異，主要是因應兩位女主角演員不同的形象和氣質。《琵琶怨》中飾唐小玲的芳艷芬是花旦王，性格一向柔中帶剛，因此她為趙七所乘乃由於醉心粵劇，急於成

（左起）《魂歸離恨天》，《琵琶怨》，《珍珠淚》
(From left) *Love Lingers On, The Sorrowful Lute, Tears of Pearl*

His fondness for adapting classics or Western films was already evident in his MP & GI years. *Love Lingers On* (1957) was based on the English novel *Wuthering Heights*, but while class consideration is involved in the female protagonist's marriage in the original, Mui Yee's (Mei Yi) in the film is driven by gratitude and Cheung Ying's long loss of contact after leaving home. In the novel, the romance is portrayed with reservation and the male protagonist is later marked by vengefulness. But the romance in the film is undying purity, initially hampered by the lovers' brother-sister relationship (in name but not in blood ties) and later by Mui's marriage – typical of both Cantonese films and Tso. Three years later, Tso adapted Ibsen's *Ghosts* as *Salvation* (1960), dealing with the "incest" issue even more directly but with the same conservative slant.

Common themes of 1950s Cantonese films, praising love and opposing feudalism are two sides of the same coin. *Love Lingers On* is in fact a continuation of *Three Stages of Love* and *Fire*. In his next three *wen yi* films, Tso switched from adapting classics to adapting Hollywood, taking on bolder subject matters and more modern sensibilities.

The biggest surprise of watching *The Sorrowful Lute* (1957) was that it's a precursor of *Tears of Pearl* (1965). Not only are the plots almost identical, Ng Cho-fan (Wu Chufan) actually plays much the same character – a corrupt KMT official who regulates "entertainment", i.e. opium, gambling and prostitution – his gait equally limping and his performance equally brilliant. There are minor differences, mostly to adjust to the personalities of the lead actresses. In *Lute*, the lead, played by Fong Yim-fun (Fang Yanfen), is an opera devotee whose gentle disposition is laced

名，趙雖以金屋為餌，仍要用強污辱了她。《珍珠淚》中飾方珍珠的苗金鳳卻嬌柔得多，因此她的動機便更多是貪慕虛榮，跛三向她施暴前替她戴上珍珠項鍊，便把她完全征服了。此外，由於是芳艷芬，自然安排唐小玲「紅透南洋」，並加插多場粵劇歌唱（從〈昭君出塞〉到〈鳳儀亭〉）；苗金鳳在《珍珠淚》往星洲發展一段，卻寫成沉迷煙酒，演出失準備受劣評。

有趣的是《琵琶怨》掛名的編劇是陳雲，《珍珠淚》卻標明左几編導。從左几多數兼任編劇的作風看來（有時並不具名），[7]《琵琶怨》劇本可能部份出自他的手筆。無論如何，這部改編自占士・格尼、桃麗絲・黛主演的《琵琶怨》（*Love Me or Leave Me*，查理士・維多，1955）的同名電影，「僅僅借了那部片子的骨架，[8] 而充實骨架的血肉，卻是舊時廣州的老倌生活。如此一改，便使它適合國情……使觀眾覺得親切好睇。」[9] 事實上，影片拍得充滿地方風味（如大新天台新派歌舞劇場與粵劇場毗鄰的佈景），高潮一幕台上演出〈鳳儀亭〉與台下趙七的心情相呼應，亦可謂匠心獨運。左几的場面調度不但井井有條，更不乏運用道具的神來之筆，如二人在南洋關係決裂一場，吊扇扇葉的影子投在唐小玲身上轉動的設計，便一直延續至《珍珠淚》。

翌年的《美人春夢》（1958）則改編自另一美國片《紅顏恨史》（*The Girl in the Red Velvet Swing*，李察・費利沙，1955）。「吳楚帆即是雷・米蘭的角色，不過易工程師為畫家；張瑛即是花利・格蘭加的角色，白露明即是鍾・歌蓮絲。」[10] 這回由於欠缺《琵琶怨》的地方風味而變成橫的移植，人物劇情難免顯得較為蒼白，猶如空中樓閣。不過從作者論的角度考慮，左几選擇改編這個故事卻別有深意存焉。

跟《琵琶怨》一樣，《美人春夢》的中心也是一段二男

with toughness. Her violation by the Ng character results from her desire for fame and Ng has to force himself on her. But the lead in *Tears* is played by a more passive Miu Kam-fung (Miao Jinfeng), whose downfall is caused by greed and vanity – Ng puts a necklace around her neck and she is conquered. Capitalising on Fong's star power, the former film features several opera numbers as Fong's character strikes it big in Southeast Asia. But in *Tears*, the lead's Singapore tour is a huge failure due to her indulgence in vices.

While *Lute*'s script is credited to Chan Wan (Chen Yun), *Tears* is written by Tso himself. Tso often doubled as writer in his films (though not always credited),[9] and likely contributed to *Lute*'s script also. Regardless, the film is adapted from the Hollywood film *Love Me or Leave Me* (1955), which bears the same Chinese title, *Pipa Yuan*, "borrowing only the structure[10] and fleshing it out with the lifestyle of Guangzhou opera stars so that it's more suitable for Chinese audiences."[11] The film indeed is spiced with regional flavours, the climax's correspondence between opera performance and the Ng character's feelings is particularly memorable. Tso's mise-en-scene is smooth and his use of props is often brilliant (like the fan's shadow rotating on the female lead, a design repeated in *Tears*).

Memories of Love (aka *A Lovely Girl's Lovely Dreams*, 1958) is again adapted from a Hollywood film, *The Girl in the Red Velvet Swing* (1955). "Ng is the Ray Milland character… Cheung Ying is Farley Granger and Christine Pai Lu-ming (Bai Luming) is Joan Collins."[12] Lacking the regional colours of *Lute*, the film is somewhat thin and pretentious, but in *auteurist* terms, this adaptation is significant.

爭一女的三角關係，卻有着微妙變奏。最有趣是吳楚帆幾乎扮演了相反的角色，從壓榨者變成受害人。他飾演的中年成名畫家韋狄楓，愛上夜總會歌女梅依華（白露明）（與《琵》中芳艷芬飾粵劇女伶相呼應），卻受困於一段痛苦的婚姻——他當年為事業有成而娶富妻，就像《琵》中唐小玲急於出頭而屈服於趙七淫威之下（因而兩片皆有離婚情節）。窮藝術家成名須依附權貴，是兩片一貫主題。《琵》中吳楚帆的霸道氣燄，在《美》中則由飾演揮霍無道、恃勢凌人的富家子張瑛承繼下來。另一方面，吳又保持栽培愛人／藝人的角色，送她入學寄宿並負擔一切費用。

但作為女主角真愛這一點上，吳楚帆站的其實是《琵》中黃千歲的位置，然而性格立體得多（突出了他的軟弱）。他在二片的演法更是一百八十度的轉變，從七情上面、咄咄逼人到談吐溫柔、百忍成金，簡直是一次演技幅度的示範。當然，他始終欠缺畫家氣質又是另一回事了。張瑛飾演富家子囂張跋扈一面固然手到拿來，後段一改常態憑細心體貼贏得梅依華芳心，亦演出了疑幻疑真的曖昧，兩男主角不再像《琵琶怨》那樣忠奸分明。可惜白露明演技有限，梅依華一角只一味天真幼稚，追求浪漫愛情時一直陷於被動而不自知（如不知畫家是有婦之夫），既演不出禍水紅顏的殺傷力，亦缺乏《琵》的唐小玲失足後再回頭的滄桑感。

若非如此，梅依華與韋狄楓的一段忘年戀，當可有更微妙的發揮。如她自小與母親（李月清）相依為命，戀父情意結呼之欲出。中年有婦之夫與懷春少女發生不倫之戀，題材在當年粵語片可謂大膽。《琵琶怨》女主角亦有貪慕虛榮而自甘墮落之嫌，由芳艷芬演出更是罕見。雖說改編自荷里活片，相信亦只有電懋這類大公司才有這種魄力，而不用畏首畏尾。

(左頁上)《琵琶怨》
(左頁下)《黛綠年華》
(左)《美人春夢》

(Top, opposing page) *The Sorrowful Lute*
(Bottom, opposing page) *The Tender Age*
(Left) *Memories of Love*

As in *Lute*, *Memories* is also centred on a love triangle, but with subtle variations. The most interesting is Ng, his character the victim instead of the oppressor. He is a famous painter who falls in love with a nightclub singer (echoing the opera singer in *Lute*) but is handcuffed by a loveless marriage – he had married a rich girl to help his career, just like the opera singer in *Lute* (and both films involve a divorce). The theme of poor artists reaching fame by bowing to the powerful runs through both films. While the bullying oppressor role is assumed by Cheung, Ng's character continues the gesture of nurturing his lover, sending her to school.

As the true love of the female protagonist, Ng assumes the role played in *Lute* by Wong Chin-sui (Huang Qiansui), though with a more three-dimensional character. Embodying opposites, Ng's performances in the films are demonstrations of his range as an actor, though his lack of a painterly quality is another matter. Cheung's turn as an obnoxious rich boy is not only proficient, his switch in the second half also delivers an ambiguity not found in *Lute*. But Pai's skills as an actress is limited, unable to convey her character's capacity to cause harm and lacking the dejectedness of Fong in *Lute*.

As such, the May-December romance could have been better developed. The singer grew up with her mother, a situation crying out for the Electra complex. Such subject matter is rare for Cantonese films of the time, as is the suggestion of vanity in *Lute*, the character in question being played by Fong even more unusual. Though both films are Hollywood adaptations, such boldness could only be allowed by such established studios as MP & GI.

《黛綠年華》(1957)在取材大膽方面更進一步。紫羅蓮飾演女學生韓湘瑩，投靠范家後耳濡目染上流社會的豪奢，兼敵不住小白臉譚尊尼（張瑛）的愛情攻勢，失身給薛行長（劉克宣）後險墮風塵，便有如《琵》的唐小玲與《美》的梅依華的綜合版。影片通過她這外來者的角度，逐步揭露那座港島半山區的別墅華麗外表下的污垢腐朽，格局嚴謹戲味盎然，又與另一部同是改編鄭慧小說的《紫薇園的秋天》(秦劍，1958)的開場（白燕受聘來到紫薇園任家庭教師）和佈局，有異曲同工之妙。由此可見，鄭慧頗受英國十九世紀哥德式小說的影響，左几改編她的《黛綠年華》，正好與同年取材《咆哮山莊》拍成《魂歸離恨天》相呼應。

不管劇中人怎樣輕描淡寫(「做不名譽的事」)，《黛》的題材其實聳人聽聞——交際花出身的范太太（黎灼灼）在丈夫破產自殺後，把僅有一座別墅變成夜夜笙歌的銷金窩，操縱三個仍在上學的女兒，叫她們陪有錢人消遣兼賣淫。長女黛妮（梅綺）懷孕後被迫打胎，小產流血過多身亡，三女黛瑜患上梅毒致雙目失明，次女黛敏見勢不妙，竟把母親財物席捲私逃。范太太受刺激過度，神經失常，殺人後束手就捕。這樣一個家庭倫理社會大悲劇，左几導來不慍不火，雙生雙旦及一眾性格演員亦恰如其份，避免了《琵琶怨》中黃千歲或《美人春夢》中白露明演技不逮的缺陷。

有趣是當年的評論，大多對影片題材不以為意，甚至為它敢於暴露上流社會陰暗面喝采。更有甚者，不約而同拿它與同期另一鄭慧原著的電懋國語片《四千金》(陶秦，1957)相比，結論是《黛綠年華》更勝一籌——「因為本片有較強烈的現實生活氣味，它揭露了一些所謂上

The Tender Age (aka *The Splendour of Youth*, 1958) is even more daring. Tsi Lo-lin (Zhi Luolian) plays a young student who seeks shelter from a rich family and is corrupted by its decadence and the handsome rogue she falls for – in short, a blend of the leads in *Lute* and *Memories*. Through her outsider's gaze, the film slowly but carefully reveals the decay beneath the elegant façade of the rich family's mansion, similar to the opening of another film also adapted from a Zheng Hui novel – *Autumn Comes to Purple Rose Garden* (1958). It can be seen that Zheng is greatly influenced by 19th century gothic literature and Tso's adapting her is in line with *Love Lingers On*, which is based on *Wuthering Heights*.

Tender is actually quite sensational. Mrs. Fan (Li Zhuozhuo), a former "society girl", turns her mansion into a house of questionable repute, forcing her school-age daughters into prostitutes. One daughter dies after having an abortion, one is blinded by syphilis and the third runs off with everything. Fan becomes insane, commits murder and is arrested. Tso handles this family tragedy with the right touch and he is aided by uniformly good performances by his stars and supporting actors, avoiding the acting inadequacies with Wong in *Lute* or Pai in *Memories*.

It is interesting to note that reviews of the time praise the film's exposé of high society's dark side. Almost unanimously, they compare it with another MP & GI Mandarin film *Our Sister Hedy* (1957), also based on a Zheng novel, and find the Cantonese film better, "because it has a stronger touch of real life, revealing the hypocrisy and evil of high society… and pointing out that 'one needs courage to live' and asking us to abandon vanity.... Such a healthy theme is a far cry from *Our Sister Hedy*'s portrayal of pampered girls easily getting husbands while enjoying the comfort of luxurious life."[13]

Although such left-wing criticism has its ideological bend, they unwittingly reveal a major difference between 1950s Mandarin films and Cantonese films. The former are more middle-class, creating

流人物的偽善與邪惡，公開了交際花的痛苦和委屈，同時也指出，『生活在這個世界上就必須有勇氣』，教人拋掉虛榮心和慎於交友。這一主題無疑是健康有益的，與《四千金》寫幾個淘氣、野性、好鬧事的少女輕易地嫁得個好丈夫，讚揚奢華生活的舒服、寫意，自不可同日而語了。」[11]

這種左派評論固然有其意識形態的偏頗，卻無意中點出了五十年代國語片與粵語片一大差異。那就是國語片一般比較中產趣味，傾向美化現實和編織觀眾陶醉的白日夢；粵語片則一般較迎合草根，趣味近街坊小市民，暴露社會陰暗面也較為直接。這些分歧，即使同是電懋公司出品亦不例外。

另一方面，電懋出品的粵語片又自有其特色。除製作質素較高，取材較大膽外，也有不少受國語片模式或感性的影響。左几較能站穩粵語片傳統本位，像《璇宮艷史》雖走西化豪華的逃避主義娛樂路線，仍不失其駁雜胡鬧那一派傳統粵劇基礎。他的文藝片改編原著或西片的方法，亦與傳統粵語片或他為其他公司拍的電影無異，加上重用粵語片資深演員（張瑛、梅綺、吳楚帆、紫羅蓮等合作最多），拍成的優質作品，足可與中聯膾炙人口的出品相提並論。

反觀另一位資深粵語片導演莫康時，同是電懋粵語片組骨幹，作品成績便不如理想。一個主要原因，是莫康時在電懋拍的多是喜劇，卻偏偏放棄了粵語喜劇的市井背景、民間題材等特色；[12] 企圖貼近電懋自成一派的國語喜劇風格（幽默雋永，構思巧妙，人物突出）之餘，卻無法做到劇本上起碼的嚴謹。無論《太太緝私團》（1961）、《傻偵探》（1962）或《錦繡年華》（1963），

daydreams that beautify reality; the latter cater more to the grass root, and are more direct in exposing society's darker side. This difference is no exception to even MP & GI.

Yet the studio's Cantonese films have its own characteristics. Other than better production quality and more daring subject matters, they're also influenced by Mandarin films. Tso was able to stand firm on Cantonese film traditions. *My Kingdom for a Husband*, for example, never loses the loose, farcical nature of Cantonese films despite its westernised escapism approach. His mode of adapting classics and western movies for *wen yi* films is also very Cantonese while his use of veteran stars like Ng and Cheung results in films that measure up to the classics of The Union Film Enterprise Ltd..

The work of another Cantonese director of MP & GI, Mok Hong-si (Mo Kangshi), is not as outstanding. One reason is that Mok made mostly comedies; instead of retaining the folksy flavours of Cantonese film, he tried to emulate the wit, clever plotting and distinct characterisations of MP & GI's Mandarin comedies but failed to achieve the craftsmanship of the scripts. *Inspectress General* (1961), *False Alarm* (1962) and *Make It Mine* (1963) are marked by forceful plots and uneven tempo, their sense of comedy nothing like Mok's cherished 1950 film *Broker Lai and the Smart Fei-tin Nam* or *Factory Queen* (1963), made around the same period.

This can be traced back to the different approaches adopted by Mandarin and Cantonese comedies. The above comedies are all films with westernised, middle-class sensibilities, which Cantonese filmmakers often lacked. *False Alarm* stars Leung Sing-po (Liang Xingbo) and Liu Enjia and is a take-off of *The Greatest Civil War on Earth* (1961), while *Make It Mine* features four daughters, like a Cantonese version of *Our Sister Hedy*. In situations common to Cantonese films, Cheng Kwun-min (Zheng Junmian) masquerades as a

皆充滿巧合和牽強的情節，節奏拖沓，喜劇感比莫康時當年名作如《經紀拉與飛天南》（1950）或同期佳作如《工廠皇后》（1963），實在相差太遠了。

那完全可追溯至國、粵語喜劇不同的路數。上述三片皆為中產背景及西化趣味，《傻偵探》由梁醒波和劉恩甲主演，固有明顯的仿《南北和》（1961）味道，《錦繡年華》有梅蘭菊竹四個女兒，亦有如粵語版的《四千金》。然而粵語片的編、導、演皆欠缺那份中產情趣和優悠感性，執行起來遂進退失據。《傻》中鄭君綿扮起女傭，《錦》中張英才也扮女人，皆粵語喜劇慣見的招數，放在中產背景裡卻格格不入。國語喜劇一向演員為劇本服務，受此原則牽制的梁醒波與譚蘭卿（《太太緝私團》），或鄧寄塵（《錦繡年華》），雖是一代笑匠，都難再有「人物凌駕於情節，演員凌駕於角色」的即興神采。[13]

此外，莫康時又毫不避重就輕，《傻偵探》的種種偵探術及擒匪的動作追逐場面，以至《錦繡年華》的實驗室爆炸，皆把粵語片導演處理這方面場面的弱點暴露無遺。他又不像左几般大量沿用老戲骨，起用的年輕主角演員（如白露明、林家聲、胡楓和張英才）又難勝大任。

事實上，演員往往是影響一部粵語片成敗的關鍵，像莫康時的《苦命鴛鴦》（1963）與左几的《美人春夢》，主線都是白露明戀上有婦之夫，但後者有吳楚帆和張瑛支撐大局，前者的羅劍郎演技卻相差太遠了，莫康時導技再好，也無法力挽狂瀾。

maid in *Alarm* and Cheung Ying-choi (Zhang Yingcai) also appears in drag in *Make It Mine*, but they seem incongruous in middle-class settings. Within the Mandarin comedy environment of actors servicing scripts, even such comic veterans as Leung and Tam Lan-hing (Tan Lanqing) (in *Inspectress General*) are unable to deliver their usual sparks of spontaneity.[14]

Mok is also unable to avoid the genre's usual pratfall, exposing the flaws of Cantonese directors in such situations as the detective's sleuthing techniques and chase scenes in *False Alarm* and the explosion in *Make It Mine*. Unlike Tso's practice of casting veterans, he also uses young actors (Pai, Wu Fung [Hu Feng] and Cheung Ying-choi) who can't rise to the occasion.

In fact, actors are the key in the success of Cantonese films. Both Mok's *Bitter Romance* (1963) and Tso's *Memories* feature Pai's affair with a married man, but while the latter has Ng and Cheung to carry the show, the former's Law Kim-long (Luo Jianlang) is a much less actor, whose problems even a director as accomplished as Mok cannot fix.

Translated by Sam Ho

註

1. 八部影片的公映次序如下：《魂歸離恨天》1957年5月2日，《半世老婆奴》1957年5月17日，《璇宮艷史》1957年9月12日，《琵琶怨》1957年10月16日，《黛綠年華》1957年12月11日，《璇宮艷史續集》1958年5月21日，《月宮寶盒》1958年7月16日，及《美人春夢》1958年10月22日。
2. 見李焯桃，〈左几訪問〉，於舒琪編：《六十年代粵語電影回顧》，第六屆香港國際電影節回顧特刊，香港：市政局，1982，頁47。
3. 見《國際電影》，第24期，1957年10月。
4. 故事來自梅禮士・司花利亞和珍納・麥唐娜主演的美國片《璇宮艷史》(*The Love Parade*, 劉別謙，1929)。另見本書容世誠，〈從《璇宮艷史》到《璇宮艷史》：荷里活電影與五十年代粵語戲曲片〉。
5. 見李慕長，〈璇宮艷史〉，《大公報》，1957年9月19日。
6. 同年的粵語神怪戲曲片《無頭東宮生太子》，特技便更加粗糙。
7. 同註2，頁46。
8. 該片背景是美國20年代禁酒時期的爵士樂壇。
9. 見林江，〈琵琶怨〉，《新晚報》，1957年10月19日。
10. 見何觀(即張徹)，〈從《美人春夢》談粵片語言〉，《新生晚報》，1958年10月23日。
11. 見李慕長，〈黛錄年華〉，《大公報》，1957年12月14日。此外，林江，〈「粵片述評」專欄〉，《新晚報》，1957年12月13日內的說法亦大同小異。
12. 有關粵語喜劇片的特色，可參閱羅卡，〈香港國、粵語喜劇片對比的一些觀察〉，於李焯桃編：《香港喜劇電影的傳統》，第九屆香港國際電影節回顧特刊，香港：市政局，1985，頁10-12。
13. 同上，頁11。

李焯桃，影評人，現任香港國際電影節總經理。大衛・博維爾：《香港電影王國——娛樂的藝術》(香港電影評論學會，2001)中文版編輯。

Li Cheuk-to, film critic. Now General Manager of the Hong Kong International Film Festival. Editor of the Chinese version of David Bordwell's *Planet Hong Kong – Popular Cinema and the Art of Entertainment* (Hong Kong Film Critics Society, 2001).

Notes

1. Literally "literary art films", *wen yi* film is a designation for non-action drama, usually with modern settings and romance plots.
2. The eight films and their release dates are: *Love Lingers On*, May 2, 1957; *Hen-pecked Husband*, May 17, 1957; *My Kingdom for a Husband* (aka *The Romance of Jade Hall*), September 12, 1957; *The Sorrowful Lute*, October 16, 1957; *The Tender Age* (aka *The Splendour of Youth*), December 11, 1957; *My Kingdom for a Honeymoon* (aka *The Romance of Jade Hall [Sequel]*), May 21, 1958; *The Magic Box*, July 16, 1958; and *Memories of Love*, October 22, 1958.
3. See Li Cheuk-to, "An Interview with Zuo Ji" in Shu Kei, ed., *Cantonese Cinema Retrospective (1960-69)*, the 6th Hong Kong International Film Festival, Hong Kong: Urban Council, 1982, p. 52.
4. See *International Screen* (in Chinese), no. 24, October 1957.
5. The opera is inspired by the Hollywood film *The Love Parade* (1929). See also Yung Sai-shing, "From *The Love Paradise* to *My Kingdom for a Husband*: Hollywood Musicals and Cantonese Opera Films of the 1950s" in this volume.
6. See Li Muchang, "*My Kingdom for a Husband*" in *Ta Kung Pao* (in Chinese), September 19, 1957.
7. "Fox incarnate" (*hu xian*) is one of those spirits in Chinese mythology in which animals, after attaining supernatural powers, can turn into human form. They are just as likely evil or virtuous, the best known among the latter being the title character in the folktale *White Snake*.
8. The Cantonese opera film, *The Headless Queen Bears a Son*, released the same year, features much cruder special effects.
9. See Li Cheuk-to, "An Interview with Zuo Ji", op. cit., p. 51.
10. Background of the film is the jazz music scene during the 20s Prohibition in the US.
11. See Lin Jiang, "*The Sorrowful Lute*" in *The New Evening Post* (in Chinese), October 19, 1957.
12. See He Guan (alias for future director Chang Cheh / Zhang Che), "A Look at Cantonese film language through *Memories of Love*" in *New Life Evening Post* (in Chinese), October 23, 1958.
13. See Li Muchang, "*The Tender Age*" in *Ta Kung Pao* (in Chinese), December 14, 1957; also Lin Jiang's review of the film in *New Evening Post* (in Chinese), December 13, 1957, has similar views.
14. For more on the characteristics of Cantonese comedies, see Law Kar, "A Comparative Analysis of Cantonese and Mandarin Comedies" in Li Cheuk-to, ed., *The Traditions of Hong Kong Comedy*, the 9th Hong Kong International Film Festival, Hong Kong: Urban Council, 1985, p. 15.

姚敏的「電懋風格」

- 黃奇智 -

說姚敏的作品有「電懋風」也許會有點標新立異之嫌。五十年代中期至六十年代初期的香港國語電影，不管是「兩大」(電懋和邵氏)的，或是其他獨立製片公司出品的電影裡的配樂，來來去去都不外出自有限的三四個人的手。「兩大」的配樂，多由綦湘棠和姚敏兩位擔任，但那風格的分別主要還是作曲家本人的獨特個性，而不是所謂的「電懋風」或「邵氏風」。

然而說姚敏的電影音樂有「電懋風」亦無不可：這主要是在他的電影插曲方面。要是細心留意他為新華影業公司及一些獨立公司，甚至是一些邵氏電影寫的插曲，那純粹的海派流行曲，亦即所謂時代曲的味道是十分明顯的。特別是為新華寫的插曲，這家公司一度以拍攝歌唱電影為主，而觀眾——尤其是南洋方面的觀眾——看電影很大程度也為聽歌，那時代曲風味濃厚是理所當然的。但「電懋風」又是甚麼一回事呢?

The "MP & GI Style" in Yao Min's Film Music

- *Wong Kee-chee* -

To say that Yao Min's film music displayed a MP & GI Style may sound a bit farfetched. Between the mid-1950s and the early 1960s, the music in Hong Kong Mandarin films was written by only a small handful of composers, with Kei Shang-tong (Qi Xiangtang) and Yao Min taking up most of the writing for the productions of the "Two Majors" – MP & GI and Shaw Brothers. If style is what one is considering, it is logical that the composer's individual style, rather than the production styles of the studios that one should be discussing.

But it is possible, if one so inclines, to speak of Yao Min's MP & GI Style. In this respect, it would be his film songs rather than his film music that will be the crux of the matter. On close examination, the songs Yao Min wrote for the productions of Hsin Hwa, most of Shaws and various independent companies conformed closely to the stylistic characteristics of standard Shanghainese Pops (or if one prefers, *shi dai qu*, the Song of the Times). This is especially so with the songs he wrote for the Hsin Hwa films, since this

姚敏的歌曲風格，除了秉承海派歌曲的婉約溫柔外，最突出的還是他的吸收及融會多種樂曲風格的才能。他曾經當過歌星，所以在寫曲時也對個別歌手的長處和短處，以至於個人特色特別敏感。同樣地，在寫作電影插曲時，他的這份敏鋭觸覺也使他對電影氣氛情節有更深的體會，因而作出適當的遷就。

電懋出品的電影，大多是現代題材，而且在一定程度上顯得很「摩登」。而所謂的「摩登」傾向，不免亦涉及西洋化。姚敏為電懋寫的插曲，惹人注目的大部份都以這些西化歌曲為主。同樣都是以美國三四十年代的著名跳舞樂隊領班Glenn Miller的編曲風格為基調，同樣由女主角葛蘭演唱的插曲，在兩部影片裏，風格上就有着明顯分別。為獨立製作出品的《酒色財氣》(1957) 寫的〈你在想甚麼〉，也許因為是當年國語電影不成文地規定了必須「為要有歌所以唱歌」的關係，到時候便非得要唱一首歌不可，寫出來便只能是徹徹底底的正宗時代曲。而在電懋出品的《心心相印》(1960) 裡的那首〈不管你是誰〉，由於電影是探討現代社會裡的愛情及夫妻關係的「摩登」題材，而且歌還是在夜總會的舞池裡邊跳邊唱，也就順理成章地比較完全西化，更接近 Glenn Miller 的味道了。

電懋的一些明星歌手的個人風格，還有她們給觀眾的印象，也可能是造成姚敏的「電懋風格」的另一些重要原因。他為電懋的《桃花運》(1959) 寫的三首歌曲（主題曲〈桃花運〉、〈家家有本難唸的經〉和〈家花哪有野花香〉），由歌星潘秀瓊為女主角葉楓幕後代唱，歌曲風格就跟大約同期出品，由姚敏自資拍攝，潘秀瓊主演的《哪個不多情續集》(1962) 裡的插曲風格相距不遠。反之，寫給能演能唱的電懋當家花旦葛蘭演唱的電影插曲，就予人電懋風十足的感覺了。葛蘭在《曼波女

姚敏指導葉楓練歌
Yao Min rehearsing with Julie Yeh Feng.

company once specialised in the so-called "singing movies". The Mandarin movie audience at that time, especially those in Singapore and Malaysia, often went to the movies expecting to listen to an abundance of songs, since they were looking for an all enveloping form of entertainment that pleases dramatically as well as musically. As such, the inclusion of standard Shanghainese style songs, which were the mainstream at the time, was in many ways a matter of course. But then, what about this business of MP & GI Style?

As a talented songwriter well versed in the elegant and sophisticated Shanghai style, Yao Min was also adept in adopting various musical styles, both Chinese and Western, and integrated them into his works. He used to be a singer back in Shanghai, which brought about his sensitivity in recognizing the longs and shorts and the special qualities in the styles of different singers when he was writing. Such sensitivity was translated into the attention he paid to mould his film songs around the tone and feel of the music of the films he worked on.

MP & GI productions were usually contemporary subjects, involving quite a certain degree of trendiness, and trendiness in those days, often meant westernization. Yao's better noted MP & GI film songs were in most cases trendy, western styled songs. During the late 1950s, he wrote two songs – both arranged in the 1930s and 1940s Big Band style of Glenn Miller, and both were sung by the leading actress Grace Chang (Ge Lan). Owing to the acknowledged stipulation in Mandarin films in those days that there must be a song to every film (the more the better), the song "What Are You Thinking?", from the independently produced film *Booze, Boobs & Bucks* (aka *Wine, Women and Money*, 1957) was written in the manner of a standard *shi dai qu*, so as to conform to the regulation. The song "I Don't Care Who You Are" from the MP & GI film *The Loving Couple* (1960) was a different matter altogether.

The Loving Couple was a trendy film on the questions related to love and married life in modern societies, and the song was sung by the leading lady while

郎》（1957）裡唱的〈我愛恰恰〉，還有《空中小姐》（1959）裡的〈我要飛上青天〉和〈廟院鐘聲〉等歌曲，不獨是她的招牌歌，還是姚敏眾多具代表性的電影歌曲裡的重要作品。也因為葛蘭的重要電影作品都是在她隸屬電懋期間拍攝，觀眾便很自然地把她跟電懋連繫在一起，反倒忽略了她給別的公司拍的戲，甚至把那些其他公司的出品都一概算在電懋名下。其他一些被公認為電懋當家花旦的女明星如尤敏、葉楓、林翠等，都有給別的電影公司拍片，也同樣地在這些公司的電影裡或是在唱片上唱過姚敏寫的歌，觀眾自由聯想，不免也給姚敏沾上一點「電懋風」了。

事實上，電懋的一些重要出品，都跟姚敏的音樂拉上關係。當年被視為香港國語歌舞電影里程碑的《龍翔鳳舞》（1959），就由姚敏負責配樂和編寫插曲。六十年

獲最佳電影音樂獎的姚敏
Yao Min and his Best Film Score trophy.

（後排右起）姚敏、易文、王天林與葛蘭宴請服部良一夫婦
(From left, standing) Yao Min, Yi Wen, Wang Tianlin and (sitting) Grace Chang during a dinner with Hattori Ryoichi and his wife.

dancing to a flirtatious number in a nightclub. This gave the license for the song to be more western, and hence, closer to the Glenn Miller style.

The charismatic appeal of the major MP & GI stars and their individual personalities too contributed to the impression that Yao Min had a MP & GI Style. The songs he wrote for the MP & GI film *The Wayward Husband* (1959) , sung by the singer Poon Sow-keng (Pan Xiuqiong) in place of the leading actress Julie Yeh Feng (Ye Feng), were very similar in style to the songs from *Who Is Not Romantic! (Part 2)* (1962), starring Poon Sow-keng and released shortly before the MP & GI film. But the songs Yao wrote for Grace Chang, one of the major MP & GI actresses reputed for her singing and acting, had a definite MP & GI feel about them. The songs Chang sang in the films *Mambo Girl* (1957) – such as "I Love Cha-Cha" – and *Air Hostess* (1959) became her representational hits and ranked among Yao Min's more important film songs. As Chang made her best films while under contract with MP & GI, she became identified with the studio to such an extent that the audience forgot that she made films for other companies as well. The same applied to other major MP & GI stars such as Lucilla You Min, Yeh Feng and Jeanette Lin Cui, who also sang Yao Min's compositions in their films and on records. Such associations by the audience gave rise to the impression that Yao Min was closely related to MP & GI.

代中期黃梅調電影大行其道，電懋這類製作的樂曲，大部份都由姚敏編寫。在利用民間戲曲和曲藝，以至民歌風格元素方面，姚敏較矚目的作品也大都是在電懋這時期的電影插曲裡。這包括了《花好月圓》（1962）裡的〈俏冤家〉（採用評劇旋律）、《啼笑姻緣》（1964）裡的改良京韻大鼓、《空谷蘭》（1966）裡的〈九個郎〉（東北民歌改編），還有《落馬湖》（1969）裡的幾首插曲（其中包括整理和改編廣西民歌〈知道不知道〉）。這原因說穿了不外是這期間「兩大」競爭日益熾烈，電懋方面跟姚敏簽了約，將他變成「御用樂師」。同樣都是利用民歌元素，姚敏的另一首重要作品，1961 年的〈待嫁女兒〉（採用東北民歌風格），卻是邵氏電影《燕子盜》（1961）裡的插曲。

所以，說姚敏的作品有「電懋風」，說到底其實是不成風的。若說真有「電懋風」，那便是片廠制度下的統一風格，就如公司的註冊商標一樣，代表着那家公司的特色。作曲家為某家電影公司寫音樂，不過是整體裡的一個組成部份，難免被整體氣氛籠罩。但創作者是一個獨立個體，有一己的思想和特性。細想姚敏給「兩大」寫的其他著名電影插曲如〈三年〉、〈神秘女郎〉等，誰又能清楚分辨哪首是「邵氏風」，哪首是「電懋風」呢？

黃奇智，現從事藝術創作，並任翻譯及文字編輯工作，亦曾主持電台音樂節目。曾舉辦多次個人畫展，近作有《時代曲的流光歲月，1930-1970》（三聯書店，2001）。

Wong Kee-chee, artist, translator and book editor. Hosted radio music programmes. Recent publication: *The Age of Shanghainese Pops, 1930-1970* (Joint Publishing, 2001).

As a matter of fact, Yao Min was linked to some of MP & GI's biggest productions. One of which was the 1959 Hollywood style musical *Calendar Girl* (1959), considered a landmark in Mandarin musical film in the 1950s. Yao Min wrote the music and arranged all the songs (taken from *shi dai qu* hits from the 1930s up to the 1950s) in that film. When the *huangmei diao* (Yellow Plum Opera)films became the dominating trend in the mid-1960s, the music in the MP & GI productions of such films was all written by Yao Min. In Yao Min's own explorations of the Chinese operatic and folk song styles, his more important works in this direction were almost exclusively 1960s MP & GI film songs. These included "The Irresistible Tease" in *Love in Bloom* (1962) – making use of the Northern Chinese *Ping Ju* melodies – the modified Pekinese Drum Songs in *A Story of Three Loves* (1964), the folk song influenced "Nine Young Men" in *Forget Me Not* (1966) and the songs from *Gunfight at Lo Ma Lake* (1969, including the very popular arrangement of the Guangxi folk song "Do You Know?"). It is interesting to note that, during this period the competitions between the "Two Majors" became increasingly fierce, and MP & GI signed Yao Min as its "exclusive composer" to guarantee the appeal of its film music. Another notable work in Yao Min's exploration of the folk song style, the 1961 "On the Eve of My Wedding" however, was in fact a Shaws film song, taken from the film *The Swallow* (1961).

As such, one might say that there in fact, is no such thing as the MP & GI Style in Yao Min's film music. If there is a MP & GI Style at all, it will be the general production style under a film studio, which, like the trademark of a merchandise, is representative of the company which produced it. The film music composer is an independent individual with his own thoughts and personality. As a component part in the entity which is the film studio, his "film studio style" is just the reflection of the studio's overall aesthetics. Considering Yao Min's repertoire of film songs, and his well known film songs such as "Three Years" and "Mysterious Girl", can one really pinpoint the "MP & GI-ness" or "Shaws-ness" of these songs?

電懋男星的定格印象

- 左桂芳 -

五十年代的台灣，樸實安謐。周遭認識的人大多過着幾乎完全相同克勤儉樸的日子，豪華奢富是個遙遙而陌生的名詞。不表示沒有享受養尊處優生活的特權階級存在，只是鳳毛麟角，很少遇見罷了。電氣化時代尚未普及，觀賞電影算是最平民化的娛樂，或在戲院、或在露天，男女老少專注盯看銀幕，隨着劇中情節起伏，喜怒哀樂細微流注心田腦海，也算是一種集體文化記憶。

那是一段國語電影稱霸的黃金時代，絕大多數影片來自香港出品，以上海影人為主，就某種政治社會意涵而言，滿足了許多避難外省籍人士那份鄉愁，和暫時逃離現實的幻想。

在 1956 年以前所看到的香港國語電影，片頭出現製片公司的標幟，有一座古典寶塔似的永華、海中燈塔狀的新華、中間二條蛇形樣式「SS」字母的邵氏父子公司，

Freeze-frame Impressions of MP & GI's Male Stars

- Tso Kuei-fang -

Taiwan in the 1950s. Unpretentious, tranquil. Most people carried on almost the same industrious and frugal existence. Luxury and grandeur were alien concepts. That does not mean a privileged class with an affluent lifestyle did not exist; they were just rare. As electricity was not popular yet, watching movies was the favourite mass entertainment. Audiences of all ages would sit in cinemas or outdoor screenings, eyes glued to the screen, letting the plot fill their hearts and minds with joy, anger, sadness, or ecstasy. This was a kind of collective cultural memory.

That was the heyday of Mandarin films. Most of them were produced in Hong Kong, mainly by Shanghai filmmakers. From a socio-political perspective, these films provided temporary relief with nostalgia and escape from reality for the many Mainlanders who had fled their homeland.

In pre-1956 Hong Kong Mandarin films, the film company's logo would appear in the opening. There was Yung Hwa's pagoda, Hsin Hwa's lighthouse, and

都是中國傳統圖徽，激不起太多聯想，直到國際電懋公司出現，以一座巍峨壯麗大廈由遠而近倏然聳立，伴隨而來的是澎湃磅礴的襯底音樂，一新觀眾耳目，感覺是：摩登、洋派、有氣勢。

1956年起，由國際、電懋到國泰，歷經三次易名改組，至1971年結束拍片業務為止，總計十五年歷史，嚴格説來，自崛起後的七八年間，也就是陸運濤主政期間，是電懋公司如日中天極盛時期，不僅影片產量多而精緻，各類人才也集一時之選，其中演員更是直接面對觀眾最為人知曉且受崇拜的對象。

不可諱言，電懋女星的鋒芒聲勢凌駕於男星之上，一方面中國傳統電影向以女性為主，影片內容題材對女性着墨關注較多，另方面電懋女星的確燦爛耀眼：林黛、尤敏、葛蘭、林翠、李湄、葉楓，都是票房號召力極強的赫赫巨星。從電懋影片中，諸多以女性角色作為片名十分普遍的情形看來，可見電懋女星受倚重偏愛之深。相形之下，男星的光亮度稍弱，然而他們之中仍有為數頗多才華出眾、魅力可觀者，不容忽視，應予以肯定。

在電懋芸芸男星中，每人表演場域不同，風格不一，各擅所長。以最受矚目的小生演員來説，陳厚瀟灑優雅、張揚英挺俊朗、雷震温文清逸、趙雷雍容貴氣、喬宏則雄偉豪邁，各有其獨特氣質。另外以性格戲路見長的如王引、羅維、唐菁，甘草人物劉恩甲、吳家驤等，都是演技洗練各擅勝場，為電懋影片增添無數光彩的重要功臣。

陳厚

陳厚最初參加邵氏，卻在新華拍攝第一部作品《秋瑾》（1953），為張善琨賞識，視為可造之才，開始拍片，

舞步瀟灑的陳厚教林黛跳恰恰

Peter Chen Hou, the best dancing man in Mandarin film, puts his moves on Linda Lin Dai.

Shaws' snake-like double "s" – all traditional Chinese emblems that left little space for imaginations. Then MP & GI appeared and, with it, a stately high-rise, first distant then close, accompanied by majestic, stirring music. Modern, westernized, and grand, it was refreshing.

Since 1956, the company was restructured and renamed three times, from International to MP & GI to Cathay. The heyday of this 15-year establishment whose business ended in 1971, took place during the seven or eight years after its inception, that is, when Loke Wan Tho was in charge. Not only did it produce a large number of excellent films, it had under its umbrella the cream of experts in different areas. Among them, its actors, given their direct relationship with the audience, were the best known and most worshipped.

One cannot deny that MP & GI's actresses outshone their male counterparts. Partly due to the tendency of traditional films to focus on women. And MP & GI's

當時新華主要小生演員是黃河和羅維，他只能屈居配角。但是他年青外型佳且又力求上進，同時為良友、榮華等小型獨立影片公司拍戲，不斷累積表演經驗。不久時來運轉，他與李麗華合演《黑妞》（1956），和鍾情主演《湘西趕屍記》（1957）、《特別快車》（1957）後，開始獨當一面，成為各方看好的新紮男主角。繼已轉入亞洲公司，在《金縷衣》（1956）和《滿庭芳》（1957）二片中，終於找對戲路，展現獨樹一格的喜劇才華。電懋成立，他加入，成為公司首屈一指的喜劇小生，從此演藝事業更上層樓，聲譽更隆。

陳厚在電懋期間佳作連連，如《人財兩得》（岳楓，1957），他飾演周旋於前任、現任妻子間的丈夫，既要討好懷孕中的妻子丁皓，又不能得罪滿懷心機前來攪局的離婚妻子李湄，整日疲於奔命，最後皆大歡喜。《提防小手》（陶秦，1958），陳厚與林翠兩個妙手空空的男女扒手，闖入富豪梁醒波家中行竊，鬧得雞犬不寧，惹出一連串笑話，是一部荷里活式的諧趣喜劇。《雲裳艷后》（唐煌，1959），在這部以展現女主角林黛曼妙身材為主的歌唱片中，陳厚飾演服裝店小店員，經常到孤兒院交送待縫製的衣服，迷上麗質天生的孤女林黛。一番巧妙安排下，林黛變成轟動一時的服裝表演皇后，結果既造福於孤兒院，也成就了好姻緣。諸如此類型喜劇片尚有《情場如戰場》（岳楓，1957）和《三星伴月》（陶秦，1959）等，陳厚的表演屬於機靈幽默、渾然天成，絲毫不見輕浮流氣，是上乘的喜劇魅力演員。

除此之外，他尚具備中國男演員一向缺乏的舞蹈才華。在《曼波女郎》（易文，1957）和《龍翔鳳舞》（陶秦，1959）二片中，他舞步優雅、舉止帥氣，分別搭配女主

風度翩翩的張揚（《情天長恨》）

A leading man to remember:
Chang Yang in *An Affair to Remember.*

divas were indeed glamorous: Linda Lin Dai, Lucilla You Min, Grace Chang (Ge Lan), Jeanette Lin Cui, Li Mei, and Julie Yeh Fung (Ye Feng) were superstars. From MP & GI's frequent use of female characters' names as film titles, one can tell how important its actresses were. By comparison, the actors received less attention. Yet many of them showed outstanding talent and charisma that equally deserve recognition.

MP & GI's actors had different appeals and styles. Among the popular ones, Peter Chen Ho (Chen Hou) was charming and smooth; Chang Yang (Zhang Yang), upright and handsome; Kelly Lai Chen (Lei Zhen), mannered and graceful; Chao Lei (Zhao Lei), stately and elegant, and Roy Chiao (Qiao Hong), masculine and straightforward. They all exuded their own brand of charm. Besides, character actors such as Wang Yin, Lo Wei (Luo Wei), Tang Qing, Liu Enjia and Wu Jiaxiang were all accomplished actors. Together they added glorious colour to MP & GI's films.

Peter Chen Ho

Peter Chen Ho began his career at Shaws but made his debut at Hsin Hwa with *Qiu Jin, the Revolutionary Heroine* (1953). Zhang Shankun felt he had potential. At the time Hsin Hwa's male leads were Huang He and Lo Wei and Chen could only play supporting roles. But as he was young, good-looking and diligent, small, independent film companies such as Liangyou and Ronghua hired him as well, enabling him to stock up on experience. Soon he had his break. After doing *Black Tulip of Inkabough* (1956) with Li Lihua, and *Holiday Express* (1957) with Chung Ching (Zhong Qing), he came to be recognized as a rising star. He joined Asia Pictures and came into his own as a comedian in *The Story of a Fur Coat* (1956) and *Life with Grandma* (1957). He joined MP & GI, becoming a top comedy actor. There, his career skyrocketed.

Chen played many impressive roles at MP & GI. In *A Tale of Two Wives* (1958), he plays of a husband caught between his former and current wives. He has

角葛蘭、李湄和張仲文作精彩演出，十分賞心悅目。

陳厚也擅拍文藝戲，如《天長地久》（陶秦，1959）、《四千金》（陶秦，1957）和《蘭閨風雲》（1959）都令人懷念。唯一遺憾的是他的樣貌太富現代感，不能作古裝打扮，看似受到限制，其實專注於時裝劇中揮灑自如，開創更耀眼佳績，反倒是一項收穫。

張揚

同樣不適宜拍古裝戲的電懋男星是張揚。張揚原屬邵氏父子公司，第一部戲《少奶奶的秘密》（陶秦，1956）即登男主角之位，飾演李麗華的情人備受矚目，與趙雷同為當家小生。1956年加盟電懋後，表演格局開闊，個人風格呈現明朗，加上其高帥外型稱勝於儕輩演員，巨星氣勢自不同凡響。在電懋影片中，張揚幸運地得到許多充份發揮機會，他可以溫文儒雅，也可以風流倜儻，甚至出格演些豪邁俠義或陰險狡詐的角色，雖然稱不上全才，至少不算狹隘。

《春色惱人》（易文，1956），一部探討年華蹉跎都會女性愛情觀的精彩之作，張揚飾演圍繞在女主角李湄身邊眾男性之一的新聞記者，他熱情豪邁、戀愛至上，卻無意受婚姻束縛，是自私的享樂主義者。《無頭案》（陶秦，1957），張揚初試反派戲路，演一個面善心惡謀財害命之徒，是他所有演出作品中，唯一僅見突兀的角色。銀幕上的他，絕大多數仍以正面君子形象建立觀眾好感與信心。許多輕鬆喜劇如《香車美人》（易文，1959）、《溫柔鄉》（易文，1960）、《同床異夢》（卜萬蒼，1960）、《太太萬歲》（王天林，1968）等，都顯示他風度翩翩瀟灑自在的印跡，另外他演出多疑善妒、優柔寡斷等性格缺失角色也處處可見，如《雨過天

his hands full on the one hand pleasing his pregnant wife Kitty Ting Hao (Ding Hao), and, on the other, appeasing the scheming and malicious ex Li Mei. It all ends on a happy note however. In the Hollywoodesque comedy *Beware of Pickpockets* (1958), Chen and Lin Cui are two nimble-fingered burglars who break into the home of tycoon Leung Sing-po (Liang Xingbo), causing a string of humorous situations. In the musical *Cinderella and Her Little Angels* (1959), centred around the alluring Lin Dai, Chen is a boutique salesman who makes deliveries to an orphanage. There he falls under the spell of the gorgeous orphan Lin. After a series of coincidences, Lin becomes a celebrated fashion model, a turn of fate which not only benefits the orphanage but concludes in a happy marriage for her. Similar comedies include *The Battle of Love* (1957) and *The More the Merrier* (1959). Chen was a natural – humorous and quick-witted without being flippant, a comedian of the first-rate.

Chen also had an asset most Chinese actors did not – he could dance. In *Mambo Girl* (1957) and *Calendar Girl* (1959), he is every bit the expert dancer, displaying elegant dexterity in every move. Partnering with Grace Chang in one film and Li Mei, and Diana Chang Chung-wen (Zhang Zhongwen) in the other, he is a delight to watch. Chen was also good at dramas, with memorable performances in films such as *Our Sister Heidy* (1957) and *Tragedy of Love* (1959). His only setback is an overly modern face, making him unsuitable for period roles, a limitation that turned out to be a blessing, allowing him to refine his skills in modern dramas.

Chang Yang

Chang Yang is another MP & GI actor not suited for period films. Affiliated originally with Shaws, he made his debut as the male lead in *The Secret of a Married Woman* (1956), drawing much attention as Li Lihua's lover. He and Chao Lei were the two male leads of the

青》（岳楓，1958），敘述他喪偶後帶着兒子與另有一女的寡婦李湄合組家庭，遭逢失業打擊，復聽信夙有成見的姐姐挑撥離間，引致夫妻失和。《野玫瑰之戀》（王天林，1961），他原是一位正直的青年樂師，迷戀上歌女葛蘭，又因妒生恨失手將之殺死，釀成悲劇。《星星·月亮·太陽》（易文，1961），一部史詩式戰爭愛情片，故事中心人物是出身優裕家庭的青年張揚，在抗戰前後分別與三位不平凡的堅強女性尤敏、葛蘭和葉楓發生戀愛，然而因個性游移不定，終與幸福無緣而抱憾終生。這部獲得極高評價的優秀影片，也是張揚表演生涯最精彩的代表作品。

張揚於電懋期間拍片數量極多，然而他與陳厚都不宜古裝扮相，無論是武俠片《女俠文婷玉》（王天林，1960）、鬼怪神奇片或是黃梅調的《鎖麟囊》（王天林，1966）、《聊齋誌異續集》（唐煌，1967），都非他所長。其實在既有表演領域裡，能適當突顯個人風格，予以深刻印象者，都是彌足珍貴的。

趙雷

以古裝戲路獨步影壇的趙雷，也出自邵氏，初上銀幕與歐陽莎菲合演《小夫妻》（王引，1953）開始嶄露頭角，1954年與尤敏搭檔演出《人鬼戀》，1958年再與樂蒂合演《倩女幽魂》（1960），都是扮演儒雅書生角色而備受好評。此後趙雷在李翰祥導演一系列歷史宮闈片中數次飾演各朝皇帝，氣度威儀頗受肯定，得到「皇帝小生」的美譽。

1963年趙雷加盟電懋，仍以拍攝古裝片為主，一方面其個人形象戲路早已深入人心。另方面當時古裝片正值熱潮。予人印象深刻的有《深宮怨》（王天林，1964）中飾演為愛情看破紅塵出家為僧的清世祖、《嫦娥奔月》

窈窕淑女，君子好逑——《鎖麟囊》中的趙雷與樂蒂
Chao Lei, in one of his many period roles, romancing Loh Ti in *A Beggar's Daughter.*

（袁秋楓，1966）中天怒人怨的昏君后羿、《蘇小妹》（王天林，1966）中文采風流的詩人秦少游，趙雷演來駕輕就熟，自有獨到之處。

以民初為背景的《啼笑姻緣》，王天林，1964），他飾演封建社會及軍閥惡勢力下的知識青年，演技固佳，但是比起早期他在邵氏拍過的《亂世妖姬》（王引，1956）和《黃花閨女》（李翰祥，1957）來，則有逾齡成熟及時不我予之感。《女人·女人》（吳家驤，1967），故事衝擊力強，他也試圖勾勒複雜的心理空間，表演張力令人動容。可惜此時武俠動作片大興，為順應潮流，他轉型接演俠客和007占士邦英雄片，在銀幕上大施拳腳。不久國泰結束，他便退隱從商。總結趙雷在電懋近十年歲月，雖然已入夕陽之境，然也留下燦爛晚霞，值得細細品味。

雷震

外形神清骨秀的雷震，流露着江南世家子弟高雅氣質，在眾男星中別具一格，與眾不同。從1955年考入國際公司到1968年離開國泰的十三年裡，雷震始終不離電懋，正如他銀幕上的形象：長情而執着。

大多數時候，我們看到他演出溫厚情深的男性：《金蓮花》（岳楓，1956），敘述書香門第少爺戀上賣唱歌女，兩人突破樊籠尋求婚姻自由。《珍珠淚》（王天林，1962），敘述被貶至人間的海中鮫奴與凡世書生的一段纏綿戀情，最後鮫奴返回龍宮不歸，多情書生殉情而死。《情深似海》（易文，1960），一對相親相愛的患難夫妻，丈夫罹患絕症奇跡治癒後，不幸因車禍意外死亡，留下綿綿遺恨。在這些影片中，雷震以他特具的氣質神韻和演技，恰如其份的表達出劇中人物應有的哀惋深情，十分深刻動人。

雷震與尤敏共舞
Lai Chen sharing a dance with Yon Min in *All in the Family.*

company at the time. Joining MP & GI in 1956, his repertoire widened and he gradually developed a distinctive personal style. Tall and handsome, he easily stood out from the other actors. He had unmistakable star quality.

MP & GI's productions offered Chang vast opportunities to hone his skills. He could play a gentle scholar, a Casanova, even a dauntless swordsman or a villain. He may not be an all round actor, but his repertoire was far from narrow. In *Gloomy Sunday* (1956), an excellent study of a city woman whose time has passed, Chang is a journalist and one of many men surrounding Li Mei. Passionate and free-spirited, he is a selfish hedonist who resists marriage. In *Murder in the Night* (1957), Zhang tries his hand at playing a murderer, a villainous role he seemed unfit to play. He is much better being positive and heart-winning – chivalrous and effortlessly elegant in comedies such as *Our Dream Car* (1959), *Bachelors Beware* (1960), *The Bedside Story* (1960) and *Darling Stay at Home* (1968), though at times marked by character flaws, like suspicion, jealousy, and indecision. In *For Better, For Worse* (1959), for example, he is a widower who marries a widow but almost ruins the marriage by succumbing to his sister's prejudices against widows. In *The Wild, Wild Rose* (1960) he plays an uptight musician who is seduced by songstress Grace Chang. The film ends in tragedy when, in a fit of jealousy, he killed her by accident. In *Sun, Moon and Star* (1961), an epic war romance, Chang is convincing as a young man from a rich family who falls in love with three extraordinary women before and after the war. But his own indecisiveness ruins his chances for happiness, and he is left with regrets for the rest of his life. This highly acclaimed film is the finest in Chang's career.

Chang Yang was an extremely prolific actor during his time at MP & GI. Yet, like Peter Chen Ho, he was not convincing in period costumes. Whether in swordplay romances like *Lady Musketeer* (1960), period horror like *The Haunted* (1967), or *huangmei diao* (Yellow Plum Opera) musicals like *The Lucky Purse* (1967) he was less than impressive.

唐菁為之着迷的，是人，是鬼，還是仙？

Tang Qing with a fairy, a ghost or a vixen?

Chao Lei

Also from Shaw Brothers but unlike Chang Yang, Chao Lei specialized in period dramas. He first caught the public's eye in his debut as Ouyang Shafei's husband in *Little Couple* (1953). In 1954, he was paired with You Min in *Beyond the Grave* and in 1958, with Betty Loh Ti (Le Di) in *The Enchanting Shadow*. In both, his part as a scholar won wide acclaim. Subsequently he was cast as the part of emperor of different dynasties in a series of historical films by director Li Hanxiang. His regal bearing and awe-inspiring air earned him the reputation of the "emperor actor".

Chao joined MP & GI in 1963, and continued to specialize in period films. It was because his image had already left a deep impression. Besides, period films were the rage. His more memorable roles include the Qing Emperor who becomes a monk because of love in *Romance of the Forbidden City* (1964), the wicked and loathsome tyrant in *Lady on the Moon* (1966), the poet Casanova in *Wife of a Romantic Scholar* (1967). Chao's seamless and effortless acting made him unique in all his roles.

In *A Story of Three Loves* (1964), a film set in the early days of the Republic, he plays an educated young man living under the authoritarianism of warlords and traditional society. His acting is good, but, compared to his earlier works at Shaws, he seems too mature for his part. There is a sense that time had passed him by. In *Passion* (1967), his attempts to portray the complex psychology of his character sustains a tension that is very moving. Unfortunately, swordplay action had become the trend and he had to switch to martial artists and 007 James Bond-type roles, doing his share of fist-fights and high kicks. Soon Cathay went out of business and he withdrew from the limelight to become a businessman. Though Chao had past his time in the almost ten years at MP & GI, he nevertheless left beautiful and cherished memories with his roles.

除了擅演癡情角色，獲得觀眾共鳴與肯定外，雷震演出喜劇也迭有佳績：《睡美人》（唐煌，1961），他飾演一個愛作白日夢的小窮職員，在夢境中發生許多奇遇，劇情諷刺幽默。另外王天林導演的「南北和系列」影片，以香港為背景因地域觀念差異產生的方言趣事為題材，深受歡迎，也引起強烈迴響，其中就雷震個人表現來説，《南北喜相逢》（王天林，1964）成績最佳。

在電懋影片中，雷震也曾詮釋特殊角色，如《小情人》（陶秦，1958）中個性陰鬱的跛足賣藝人、《古屋疑雲》（易文，1960）中蓄意謀財的歹惡司機、《人之初》（吳家驤，1963）中誤入歧途的竊賊等，但在影迷心目中，他仍是不帶邪氣一派斯文的中國傳統書生典型，處處顯露真切優雅有致。

喬宏

喬宏魁偉壯碩充滿陽剛氣息的身型，是他與電懋其他小生截然有別的典型。1949年他在台灣第一部國語影片《阿里山風雲》，演一個毫不起眼的小角色，1955年在白光提攜下以新人之姿在香港影壇出現，1957年加入電懋，1970年離職，前後十三年，大約拍了三十部影片。

喬宏在電懋初期，被定位在純粹表現體魄氣概的刻板戲路上，如《青春兒女》(易文，1959)、《三星伴月》（陶秦，1959）、《鐵臂金剛》（王天林，1960）等。一方面展露壯實修偉的體格，另方面也和女主角談情説愛，十分接近荷里活英雄救美肌肉男生路線。中期以後，他的演技日臻成熟，戲路漸廣，終於有了令人印象深刻的不同面貌。

笑意盈盈的葉楓安慰型男喬宏

The hulking Roy Chiao comforted by a smiling Yeh Feng.

Kelly Lai Chen

The elegant Lai Chen, with his air of a young man of high birth from the south of Yangtze area, stood out from other male stars. From 1955, when he was signed by International Films, to 1968, when his tenure at Cathay ceased, he stayed with the same company for the entire thirteen years. This is consistent with his on-screen persona: steadfast in love and persevering.

Most of the time he plays the gentle and romantic male. *Golden Lotus* (1957) is the story of a young man from an intellectual family who breaks from societal shackles to marry a songstress. In *Her Pearly Tears* (1962), a maid of the dragon-emperor is banished to the human world and falls passionately in love with a scholar. In the end the creature returns to the palace under the sea and the scholar commits suicide. *Forever Yours* (1960) is about a married couple who has been through thick and thin. The husband falls fatally ill, but miraculously recovers, only to die in a car accident, leaving in his wake a string of regrets and love unfulfilled. In all these productions, Lai never fails to deliver moving performances as a passionate lover.

Besides gaining audience recognition for his love-sick roles, Lai also gave outstanding performances in comedies. In *Sleeping Beauty* (1960), he plays a wage slave who loves to daydream, filling his dreams with strange encounters at once funny and satirical. He also appeared in director Wang Tianlin's North vs South series (his best performance being in the inaugural film, *The Greatest Civil War on Earth*, 1961), which is marked by dialect-related jokes arising from the cultural-geographical differences in the Hong Kong population. The films were enthusiastically received and elicited strong response from the public.

《深宮怨》(王天林，1963)敘述清朝順治皇帝與秦淮名妓董小宛之間的一段異族戀愛故事，喬宏飾演投降滿清的明臣洪承疇，是個性格複雜的爭議人物。《啼笑姻緣》中飾演粗魯橫暴的軍閥柳大帥。歌舞片《教我如何不想她》(易文、王天林，1963)中飾演一位氣度恢宏溫厚情摯的歌舞團班主。武俠片《虎山行》(王星磊，1969)飾演掙扎於民族大義與夫妻愛恨糾葛中的空門和尚，都是內心戲極重的佳作。

離開國泰後，喬宏依然活躍影壇，拍片無數，電懋公司成為他奠下日後輝煌演藝事業最初的基石。

唐菁

唐菁原是有「台灣第一小生」之稱的演員，戲路廣闊，亦正亦邪能文能武，擅演性格突出硬派角色。1962年於《颱風》(中影出品，潘壘導演)飾演粗獷貪焚的逃犯普獲好評，1963年以《黑夜前黎明》獲第二屆金馬獎影帝，接着電懋邀他加盟到港拍片。

在小生林立的電懋公司，唐菁星運發展未如預期順遂，首先拍攝的《聊齋誌異》(唐煌，1965)，他飾演耽溺女色見異思遷的書生，雖然有三位女主角張慧嫻、白冰、陳方以眾星托明月方式陪襯搭配，發揮空間依然有限。反倒不如《亂世兒女》(袁秋楓，1966)飾演違叛國家出賣手足的反派人物來得精彩生動。在電懋與中影合作攝製的《雷堡風雲》(李嘉，1965)中，他演智勇雙全的國軍參謀長也亮眼出色。之後再拍過一、二部片子後即離開電懋轉到邵氏等公司發展。算起來他只能算是電懋的過客，有過短暫光芒惜未能光芝四射。

Lai played atypical roles too, such as the dark and gloomy crippled street artist in *A Little Darling* (1958), the cunning driver in *Corpses at Large* (1960), the thief who makes a wrong turn in life in *Father and Son* (1963). Yet, to his fans, he remained the virtuous and gentle classic scholar-type, graceful and personable in every way.

Roy Chiao

Roy Chiao's towering and robust physique was what set him apart from MP & GI's other male stars. In 1949, he played a minor and inconspicuous role in Taiwan's first Mandarin feature *Wind and Storm over Alishan*. Then in 1955, he reappeared with the support of Bai Guang. Joining MP & GI in 1957, he left in 1970, starring in about 30 films in his thirteen years with the company.

In his early days at MP & GI, Roy Chiao was cast only in stereotypical muscle-flexing roles, such as *Spring Song* (1959), *The More the Merrier* (1959) and *The Iron Fist* (1960). He would flaunt his brawn while wooing the female lead. His roles are very similar to the Hollywood hero who saves damsels in distress. From his mid-MP & GI period onwards, his acting matured and his repertoire broadened. He began to make an impression with his diverse personas.

In *Romance of the Forbidden City* (1964), a story about the inter-ethnic love story between the Qing Emperor and a famous courtesan, Chiao plays a Ming dynasty minister who has surrendered to Qing. It's a complex and controversial character. In *A Story of Three Loves*, he is a vulgar and despotic warlord; in the musical *Because of Her* (1963), he is the magnanimous leader of a dance troupe. In the swordplay romance *Escort over Tiger Hills* (1969), he plays a Buddhist monk torn between nationalist sentiments and a love-hate marital relationship. These are all quality films requiring portrayal of complex emotions.

既導且演的男演員

電懋也有幾位既是導演又具演員雙重身份的優秀男星，王引、羅維和吳家驤，他們均是從影歷史悠久，生活歷練豐富，執導電影固有成就者，然而做演員能直接與觀眾溝通，充份達到表演慾望的滿足感，因此都留下可觀的演出成績，值得在此討論。

王引在銀幕上向以演技洗練沉穩著稱，在電懋的影片數量不多但質感極佳。他在《紅娃》（岳楓，1958）中飾演義薄雲天的北方硬漢，《玉女私情》（唐煌，1959）中飾演忍辱負重宅心寬厚的慈父，《愛的教育》（鍾啟文，1961）和《小兒女》（王天林，1963）中飾演謙和仁愛的教師等，都是佳作。

羅維在電懋演出作品數量較多，《家有喜事》（王天林，1959）和《早生貴子》（唐煌，1962）都是飾演一心想納妾的中年富商，演來頗為討喜，不過多數仍以飾演個性強烈鮮明的負面角色居多，如《無語問蒼天》（羅維，1961）中強暴啞女的偽善小人及《深宮怨》中權傾天下的多爾袞等，都是舉足輕重且突出的角色。

吳家驤擅長詮釋各類市井小人物，正反悲喜均能勝任，屬於典型甘草演員。他在電懋演出作品不少，難得的是能在平凡中見其深度，他在《金玉奴》（王天林，1965）中飾演乞丐幫主金松，曾獲第四屆金馬獎最佳男配角。

電懋男星各具特色，細數不盡，在聚光燈下爭妍鬥麗的女星群外，他們仍能獲得響亮喝采與肯定，是值得欣慰之事。

左桂芳，台北國家電影資料館特約研究員，最近與姚立群合編了《童月娟》（台北電影資料館，2001）。
Tso Kuei-fang, project researcher at the Chinese Taipei Film Archive. Recently co-edited *Tong Yuejuan* (Chinese Taipei Film Archive, 2001).

After leaving Cathay, Chiao went on to act in many films. But it was MP & GI that laid the cornerstone of his brilliant acting career.

Tang Qing

Originally exalted as "Taiwan's number one actor", Tang Qing had a wide repertoire. He is equally good as the hero or the villain, in drama as in action. His specialty is strong characters with striking personalities. He first won acclaim for his role as a boorish and greedy fugitive in *Typhoon* (1962). After he won Best Actor at the 2nd Golden Horse Awards for *Dawn Before Night* (1963), he was recruited by MP & GI.

At MP & GI, where leading men abound, Tang's career did not develop as smoothly as expected. He first played the part of a fickle and licentious scholar in *Fairy, Ghost, Vixen* (1965). Although surrounded by three leading ladies, there is little room for development. In comparison, his portrayal of a traitor who betrays country and comrades is far more inspired. Leaving MP & GI after a few years to continue his career at Shaws, Tang can only be counted as a passing stranger at the company, creating sporadic sparks that never consistently shined.

MP & GI's male stars are all unique in their own ways and too numerous to list in their entirety. As the paparazzi clamoured for a smile or a word from MP & GI's dazzling prima donnas, their male counterparts too received their share of applause and recognition. And for this they should be pleased.

Translated by Piera Chen

Flashbacks

倒敘

歐德爾：草創時期的得與失

英人，歐德爾

我在香港出生和受教育，上過 Central British School，即今天的英皇佐治五世中學。家父歐德禮是當年香港有名的演藝經理人，進口不少大片和明星。[1] 他是猶太裔白俄羅斯人，原來姓 Obadovsky，不是 Odell，他父親的家鄉在俄羅斯的 Odessa〔編按：位於現時的烏克蘭〕，後來他被共產黨趕了出來，去了天津，再偷渡去了美國。第一次世界大戰期間，他已成為美國公民，為美軍打仗。因常被美國朋友說成是蘇聯間諜，他索性把姓改為 Odell。戰後，他在一家名為 Getz Brothers的美國貿易公司找到工作，以公司代表的身份被派到香港。在香港獃了一段時間後，他拿到英國的證件，所以我在香港出生，成為英國人。

家母來自法國的 Alsace Lorraine，她父母以前是 Sennett Frères 珠寶公司的老闆。外婆在港島的薄扶林道建有一

From Distribution to Production: Albert Odell on a Key Cathay Moment

Born Odell, British

I was born and educated in Hong Kong. I went to Central British School (CBS), now called King George V. My father is Harry Odell, the leading impresario in Hong Kong.[1] He imported big films to Hong Kong, and all the famous artists too. He was Jewish of white Russian origin. His original surname was not Odell, but Obadovsky. His father came from Odessa, Russia (now Ukraine). Kicked out by the communist, he went to Tianjin and later to the United States as a stowaway. During WWI, he fought for the American army as an American citizen. He changed his name to Odell because his American friends always accused him of being a Russian spy. After the war, he got a job for Getz Brothers, an American trading company and was sent to Hong Kong. He took up British papers after a period of stay in Hong Kong, so I was born in Hong Kong as British.[2]

My mother was from Alsace Lorraine. Her parents used to own this jewellery company, Sennett Frères. My grandmother built her home on Pokfulam Road and after she passed away, my mother sold it to the

間大宅，她過身後，家母把房子賣給香港大學，那裡現在大概已成為港大的宿舍。我們一直住在香港，直到日本人來到，我才輟學，離開香港。在大陸留了一年後，我又回到香港。[2]

接管永華片場

打仗期間，我為美國 Frieder電影公司工作，他們擁有全東南亞區共和影片公司的放映特權。他們的主公司在菲律賓，在其他地區並沒有人，所以在 1948 年的時候，我被薦到新加坡為他們開辦事處。我們需要找院線放映我們的電影，那時候只有邵氏和國泰兩個陣營，邵氏既然對我們無甚興趣，很自然我便與國泰合作起來。我在社交場合認識陸運濤，我們都打高爾夫球，更在 1951 年一起贏過高球的獎杯。國泰有他們的院線，卻沒有發行部，我於是促成國泰的人，主要是陸運濤其中一個拍檔何亞祿，組成國際電影發行公司，我是股東之一，隨後我也在 1951 年離開 Frieder。我、陸運濤、何亞祿各擁有新公司百分之三十的股權，餘下的百分之十則是陸運濤劍橋時期的好友，曾是歷史科教授的約翰・伊特名下；提起這事便令人傷心，下面再談吧。

1954 年，我為了與日本松竹株式會社的發行生意，往日本途經香港的時候，接到陸運濤的電話，他説他與李祖永和他的永華片場有些瓜葛，當時已有傳言指李祖永陷入財政困難。李從上海帶了一千萬元來港，當年的一千萬可不是今天的一千萬啊！但大部份的錢卻倒進了鹹水海。他搞製片，不過因為某些政治原因拒絕發行，他甚至寧願把底片燒掉都不把它們發行。[3]後來陸運濤發覺他的錢有去無回，他投資了錢，卻一分錢也沒有回頭。陸運濤很想拍一套叫《玫瑰玫瑰我愛你》的電影，當時有一首同名的歌曲非常流行，我猜李祖永和張善琨便慫恿他投資拍這部片，但後來一拖再拖，他們又諸多

歐德爾(左)、費魯伊及李祖永
(From left) Albert Odell, Louis Fei and Li Zuyong.

University, which has now probably been turned into Hong Kong University's dormitory. We had always lived in Hong Kong. I stopped schooling and left Hong Kong only because of our Japanese friends, haha.... After a year in China, I came back to Hong Kong.

Taking Over Yung Hwa Studios

During the war years, I worked for an American film company called Frieder Films. They had franchise business for Republic Pictures for the whole of Southeast Asia. They operated mainly from the Philippines and had nobody to look after their business elsewhere, so I came to Singapore in 1948 to open up their offices. We needed theatrical release for our films. There were only two camps at that time, Shaws and Cathay. Shaws was not interested, so I naturally became associated with Cathay. I met Loke Wan Tho socially. We both played golf and even won a golf cup together in 1951. Cathay had their own theatres, but they had no distribution at all. So I induced the Cathay people, basically Ho Ah Loke, the junior partner of Loke Wan Tho, to form International Film Distribution Agency, of which I was a partner. That's when I left Frieder in 1951. I had 30% share, Loke had 30%, Ho had 30% share. And John Ede, who used to be a history professor and a good friend of Loke from his Cambridge school days, had 10%. But that was a sore point for me. We'll come back to it later.

In 1954, I was going through Hong Kong on my way to Japan. We had a distribution deal with Shochiku Co. Ltd. I received a call from Loke. He said he was having problems with Li Zuyong and his Yung Hwa Studios. There had been rumours that Li was having serious financial difficulties. The guy brought in a fortune from Shanghai, about HK$10 million. HK$10 million at that time was not today's 10 million. Most of it went down the drain. He produced films, but refused to release them because of political reasons. He even burned the negatives rather than distributed them.[3] Eventually Loke saw that his money situation was getting a little caught up because he was not getting any profit for the money he advanced. There was this film *Rose, Rose, I Love You* that Loke had wanted so much to make. The song was very popular those days and I guess Li Zuyong and Zhang Shankun induced him into

藉口，陸便發覺有點問題。[4]片廠以債權作為他投資的抵押，所以他便採取法律行動。他叫我找香港其中一間最大的律師行——孖士打律師樓。1955年，我接管了永華片場，當時 Peat Marwick 會計師行和我一起去接收。當時我們看到的情況很慘，每個員工都拿着一疊疊當票。李祖永飛去台灣告狀，説陸運濤由左派支持，共產黨撐着陸，要搞垮他的片場。台灣政府便派戴安國過來，而他們在香港的代表是徐亨。我認識徐亨，是因為我戰後不久曾效力香港足球會，印象中那時他在東方。徐亨肯定知道陸運濤是東南亞數一數二的資本家，他怎麼會是共產黨？

我們經營了那片場有十八個月之久。李祖永整天都説片場是他的，其實片場建在一塊政府出租土地上，我們接手後不久，政府便要收回那塊地，另撥新地給我們，即現時的嘉禾片場所在。於是由陸運濤出資，由國際電影發行公司建立新的永華片廠。

參與電影製片

當我在國際電影發行公司的時候，我們國、粵語片都發行。當時邵逸夫仍未到香港創立邵氏兄弟公司，香港的邵氏片廠由邵邨人打理，主要拍些由歐陽莎菲、周曼華等明星演出的低成本製作，一個星期拍完一部電影，供給新加坡的邵氏院線。我們另起爐灶，找來大牌明星助陣。我們資助龍馬和長城公司拍片，把他們的電影發行到東南亞，因為這樣，我認識了費穆的弟弟費魯伊，並成為好朋友。

我參與製片全因國泰和永華的關係，為了抵償金錢上的損失，陸運濤接手永華片廠，他對製作產生了興趣，自然而然，我們就搞起製作來。但他的投資有出無入，直

《娘惹與峇峇》
Nonya and Baba, produced by Albert Odell.

spending money on the film.[4] But it was delay after delay. He found something wrong as he was always given excuses. He held the studio under some kind of debenture and was able to take action. He asked me to contact Johnson Stokes & Master, one of the biggest Hong Kong law firms. In 1955, I took over the studio. (The accounting firm) Peat Marvick went in with me and actually controlled the studio physically. The situation then was pathetic. Most of the employees had pawn shop tickets about this thick. Li flew to Taiwan and said that Loke was supported by the left-wings, that the communists were promoting him and that they wanted to kill his studio. The Taiwanese government then sent Dai Anguo, and their Hong Kong representative was Xu Heng. I knew Xu because I used to play football for the Hong Kong Football Club soon after the war and I think he was with Eastern Football Club. Xu knew that Loke was probably the biggest capitalist in Southeast Asia, so how could he be a communist as well?

We ran the studio for 18 months. Li always said that the studio was his, but in fact it was built on land only lent to him by the government. Soon after we took over, it was taken back by the government, who gave us a new place on Hammer Hill Road, which is where Golden Harvest is situated later on. We had to build a new studio, all financed by International Film(Singapore), by Loke Wan Tho.

Getting into Film Production

When I was with International Film (Singapore), we distributed both Mandarin and Cantonese films. That was before Run Run Shaw came to Hong Kong to form Shaw Brothers. At that time, the Shaws studio in Hong Kong was managed by Rundes Shaws. He used to make mostly very cheap films with stars like Ouyang Shafei, Zhou Manhua... and supply them to the Singapore market. He could finish almost one film every week. We, on the other hand, were able to cast the major stars in our films. We financed Dragon Horse (Loon-Ma) and Great Wall, distributing their films in Southeast Asia.

至後來我才曉得情況有多糟。開始的時候，主要為了片場有戲開，不致閒下來。但片廠的開支非同小可，荷里活一些大公司，為了維持片廠，以至劣作也拍，就是這樣破產的。總言之，陸運濤當時很信任我們，對我們言聽計從，我們只需要他不斷匯錢過來給我們，讓我們可繼續製作。

我們某程度上改變了拍粵語片的做法，戒拍七日鮮，透過與中聯合作，找來吳楚帆、張瑛等大演員。我們通常要墊支一兩萬港幣，以獲取新加坡、馬來西亞的發行權。國泰從不過問香港的版權，亦從不參與劇本創作，或他們的內部組織。

至於國語片的製作，我從來沒有真正參與過。我幫助國泰撮合了嚴俊和陸運濤組成國泰影片公司（按：這間公司與後來的「國泰」不同），嚴俊和國泰公司各佔電影製作的百分之五十。我對製作方面一無所知，嚴俊和朱旭華幫了我一大把，他們替我打通關係，招攬人才，幫我們跟別人討價還價。有陸運濤的錢、嚴俊和朱旭華的協助，我要誰便找到誰替我們拍戲，例如從日本回來發展的白光，也在我們支持下成立了國光公司。

嚴俊是少數靠得住的華人導演和製片之一，他視財如命，就算是別人的錢，他都會好好看管。但李翰祥才是功臣，他出點子，包辦大小事務。並不是嚴俊不懂得或力有不逮，而是李翰祥確有辦法，他最後亦自立門戶。直至我離開香港之前，嚴俊都是我的左右手。朱旭華也幫了我不少。他是一個很好的主管，在永華的時候，我是廠長，朱是副廠長，他把片場打理得很不錯，我不用理製作的事，只管新加坡那邊的財源；我對執導事宜一竅不通，從來不去拍攝現場，拍國語片的實際事務，都交由朱旭華和屠梅卿處理。

《風雨牛車水》
Rainstorm in Chinatown,
produced by Albert Odell.

That's how I became good friends with Louis Fei (Fei Luyi), Fei Mu's brother.

I got into production because of Cathay's past association with Yung Hwa. In trying to recover his money, Loke had to take over the studio, and automatically, he became interested in production and we all got involved. But I believe he sank his fortune. I didn't know how bad it was until later. Initially, it was a matter of keeping the studio busy. The studio is a killer from the overhead. That's how Hollywood major companies went under. They had to produce so much crap to keep the studio going. Anyway, Loke trusted us and accepted what we told him at the time. All we needed of him was keep sending money, which he did, to let us continue production.

We sort of changed the approach to Cantonese filmmaking. We did away with *chuk yat sin*(literally "seven-day catch", meaning films finished in seven days), through collaboration with Union Film Enterprises, for example. We cooperated with Ng Cho-Fan (Wu Chufan) and Cheung Ying (Zhang Ying). It was a big deal. We used to advance them something like HK$10,000 or $20,000 to get distribution rights for Singapore and Malaysia. As far as Cathay was concerned, it was strictly Singapore and Malaysia, never Hong Kong. But we were neither involved in script development nor in their organisation.

I was never really involved in Mandarin film production. For Cathay, I was instrumental on getting Yan Jun together with Loke to form Guotai Film Productions, which was mainly Yan Jun and Cathay Organisation, 50% each for film production. I knew nothing about production. Yan and Zhu Xuhua helped me a lot; they helped negotiating and getting people for me. With the financial backing of Loke and the assistance of Yan and Zhu, I was able to get whoever we could and induce them to make pictures. Bai Guang, for example, formed Guoguang after she came back from Japan.

Yan was one of the few Chinese directors and producers who were reliable. To him, money was very big; even if it was your money, he looked after it well.

離港返星

我於 1956 年返回新加坡，其實香港的生意與我無關，那不是我的事業，我在那裡只不過是因為陸運濤與李祖永的官司。那些是是非非和無謂的權術，令我決定返回新加坡，打理那屬於我的百分之三十的生意。我推薦鍾啟文給陸運濤。陸運濤見過幾個人，鍾啟文似乎是最好的人選。其實是李祖永介紹鍾啟文給我認識的，他在美國讀書，英文很好。他原來負責永華的沖片室和技術方面的工作，但跟永華大部份的員工一樣屢被欠薪，最後便離開永華，加入柯達公司工作了幾年。[5]陸運濤對他的印象不錯，請他來管理片場。鍾啟文來了後，永華變成一筆糊塗帳，後來國泰派了俞普慶和楊曼怡過來，兩人都在香港去世。自從我 1957 年離開國泰後，我對他們所知已不多。

返回新加坡，我繼續替國際電影發行公司工作，直至邵氏兄弟來找我。年青的我有點衝動，又覺得受到不公平的待遇，陸運濤對生意不太知情，公司內又有很多是非，令我覺得無甚前途。邵仁枚以不錯的條件聘用我，給我一份三年的合約，我便轉投邵氏，從 1957 年到 1960 年在那裡工作。

與國泰的官司

與此同時，我與國泰有些瓜葛。話説最初的時候，國際電影發行公司香港分公司的製作資金是經由新加坡國際總公司匯過來，全屬陸運濤的貸款。但事情的發展來得太快，香港公司蝕了很多錢，本來跟我沒關係，但作為合夥人，陸運濤堅持要我付公司所虧蝕三十萬坡幣的百分之三十，八萬元左右，時為1957年。[6]我跟當時國泰的副總裁連福明説，我沒有八萬元還給他，如果他們硬要我還，我只有破產！他説不好，又不是大數目。可

But Li Hanxiang was his brain. Li did everything. Not that Yan didn't know or couldn't, but Li was the mastermind and eventually he went out on his own. Yan was my right hand man as long as I was in Hong Kong.

Zhu too was of great assistance to me. He was a very good controller. At that time, I was president of Yung Hwa studios and Zhu Xuhua was vice-president. He did a very good job looking after the studio. I was the one who arranged with Singapore for the financing but I was never actually involved in production as such. I didn't know anything about directing. I was never on the set. With Mandarin films, everything was run by Zhu Xuhua and Tu Meiqing.

Going Back to Singapore

I came back to Singapore in 1956 because the Hong Kong part of business had nothing to do with me. It was not my business. I was there because of Loke's decision to take action against Li Zuyong. Because of all the back-stabbing and politics, I decided to come back to look after the business of which I had 30% share. I recommended Robert Chung (Zhong Qiwen) to Loke, who interviewed a few persons, and Chung seemed the best prospect. Actually it was Li Zuyong who introduced him to me. Chung was educated in the States and his English was excellent. He originally worked for Yung Hwa taking care of the laboratory and technical aspects. Later he quit Yung Hwa as he was not paid regularly, like everyone else, and joined Kodak for a few years.[5] Loke Wan Tho was very impressed with him and decided to invite him to manage the studio. After Robert Chung got involved, it became a lot of monkey business, and Cathay sent Paul Yui (Yu Puqing) and Yeo Ban Yee (Yang Manyi) over. They both passed away in Hong Kong. Since I left Cathay in 1957, I didn't know much about them. I was with Shaws from 1957 to 1960.

When I moved back to Singapore, I continued to work for International Films until Shaw Brothers got me interested. I was at the time young and hot-headed and was upset with the treatment I received. Loke didn't know too much of the business, and there was a

是，在邵氏的慫恿下，我向陸運濤採取法律行動。我或許做錯了。自此之後他再沒有和我說過半句話。

打官司期間，我仍舊是國際電影發行有限公司的合夥人，但已不再替陸運濤工作，所謂合夥亦差不多名存實亡。陸運濤將公司改組，等於是清盤，當時受理我的案件的，是位名叫李光耀的年青律師，由邵仁枚介紹。邵仁枚看過我的文件後說我的勝數很高，在 1957 年期間替我約了在李光耀的辦公室見面。他們說李光耀打官司不為錢，是為面子，如果你要告那些有頭有面的人如陸運濤，他一定會替你打。我去過他的辦公室幾次，他當時正忙於學國語。那辦公司裡陳設很普通，常有些工會的人等着他，出出入入，川流不息。最後他跟我說，「對不起，我為工會和政界的事忙不過來，我可以把你轉介給 Barker。」事情就這樣拖延下去，最後還打輸了官司。

李光耀 李金耀 柯玉芝

LEE & LEE
ADVOCATES & SOLICITORS

LEE KUAN YEW (27666)
LEE KIM YEW (27667)
KWA GEOK CHOO
E. W. BARKER

10-B, Malacca Street, (2nd Floor)
Singapore, 1
TELEPHONES: 27667, 27668
CABLE ADDRESS: "KYLEGAL"

YOUR REFERENCE:
OUR REFERENCE: EWB/WKL/63/57

15th October, 1957.

Albert Odell, Esq.,
No. 84 Robinson Road,
Singapore.

Dear Sir,

Dissolution of Partnership
International Films
Distributing Agency.

With reference to the writer's telephone conversation this morning, we confirm that it has been arranged that a meeting to take place at the office of Messrs. Drew & Napier at 2.30 p.m. on Monday next the 21st instant. The purpose of the meeting is to endeavour to reach some satisfactory solution to the difficulties which have arisen in this matter and the discussions are to be without prejudice.

Yours faithfully,

Lee & Lee

李光耀簽發的律師信

A letter from the office of Lee Kuan Yew, which represented Odell in his case against Cathay.

Courtesy of A. Odell

lot of back stabbing in his organisation. I could see that we couldn't go too far. I got an offer from Runme Shaw to work with him. He gave me a good deal. It was a three-year contract.

Dispute with Cathay

I had a dispute with Cathay. In the early stage, production money for International Films Hong Kong branch was sent through International Film Singapore branch, which was all loan money from Loke himself. Everything was so quick. A lot of money was lost in the Hong Kong operation. Basically this shouldn't concern me. But as a partner, he insisted I had to pay $80,000 out of the $300,000 the company had lost. That was about 1957.[6] At that time, the vice president and account at Cathay Organisation was Heah Hock Meng (Lian Fuming). I told him I didn't have $80,000; he could put me at bankruptcy if he wanted to go ahead. He said no as it was not a big amount. But with the encouragement from Shaws, I took legal action against Loke, which was probably a mistake. He never spoke to me again.

During the legal dispute, I was still a partner of International Films but no longer working with Loke. The partnership was sort of dormant. Loke formed a new company, which was actually kind of in liquidation. My lawyer for that particular case was a young lawyer by the name of Lee Kuan Yew. Runme Shaw talked me into it. He looked at my documents and said that I stood a good chance. He set up an appointment for me in 1957 in this quite crappy office of Lee. They said that Lee was not looking for money, he wanted face. If you want to take action against big shots like Loke, he would definitely handle your case, which he did. I went to his office several times. At that time, he was very busy studying Mandarin and always in and out of his office with tens of union people waiting for him outside. Eventually he told me, "Do you mind, I'm really too busy in politics and union business. I'll pass you on to Barker." And this dragged on and I eventually lost my case.

By then, I was already working for Shaws. At that time, Shaws and Cathay had a private arrangement

這個時候，我已經開始替邵氏工作。國泰與邵氏有個私下協定，不會挖角，所以頭六個月，我躲在羅敏申律邵氏的一間小小的子公司工作，買賣中文片。六個月後，事情被揭發，我就乾脆去邵氏負責電影發行部。

脫離邵氏

替邵氏工作了幾年後，我知道不會有很大的發展。國泰與邵氏的分別是，在國泰工作，是非多問題多，你不知自己能幹甚麼；而在邵氏工作，你會很清楚——你甚麼都幹不了。在邵氏工作過的人都知道，如果你不是邵氏家族的人而自以為有甚麼了不起，你只是在自己騙自己罷了。最後我悄然離開。

我於 1960 年離開邵氏後，陸運濤反過來控告我，他惱極我了，企圖阻止我再在電影行裡工作。我轉而從事木材業，在沙勞越獃了兩年，跟着又去了美高梅在越南的公司做了幾個月代表。陸運濤 1964 年空難去世後，1965年我得以在和路迪士尼公司找到工作，由1965到 1971 年，當了他們新加坡公司六年的代表。說出來可能不好聽，我算因陸運濤的去世而受惠，他的妹夫朱國良接手公司後，覺得以前他們對我太苛刻，連福明決定我可以幹回電影本行，但必定要經國泰發行，而所賺的錢便用來扣數。我就是這樣扣掉了三萬元，最後朱國良決定放棄追討餘下的五萬元，我於是恢復自由身。朱國良是個好人，他只是因妻子的關係才在陸運濤死後加入電影業，他其實對這門生意無甚興趣。

1971年後，我做自己的生意，搞錄影帶發行，開了間影帶出租店。我還未退休，工作可以讓腦筋活動活動嘛。

訪問：何思穎、雷競璇（2001年12月11日於新加坡）；整理：黃愛玲；翻譯：周淑賢

not to steal each other's companies and senior staff. So for the first six months, I was in the Robinson Road office. Shaws had this small company handling Chinese films and I managed it. After six months, the situation was disclosed and I went on to head film distribution in Shaws.

Leaving Shaws

After working for Shaws for several years, I figured I couldn't go too far with them. The difference between Cathay and Shaws is: when you were with Cathay, you didn't know where you were, with so much biting and politics; but with Shaws, you knew exactly where you were – you were nowhere. Whoever worked for Shaws knew that if they thought they were big shots outside the Shaw family, they were kidding themselves. I went off on my own a little.

Loke took action back against me when I left Shaws in 1960. He was very angry with me. In fact, he tried hard to prevent me from coming back to the motion picture business. So I went into the timber business in Sarawak for two years. Then I worked as MGM's representative in Vietnam for some months. Loke died in a plane crash in 1964 and I was able to get a job with Walt Disney in 1965. I was their representative in Singapore for six years, from 1965 to 1971. In a way, it may not be a nice thing to say, though, (it) went to my benefit because his estate was taken over by his brother-in-law Choo Kok Leong (Zhu Guoliang), who figured that it was too harsh on me and Heah Hock Meng decided that I could do my own film business, but the films had to be distributed by them and the money would be deducted. SG$30,000 was deducted that way. In the end, Choo waived the SG$50,000 balance and I became a free man again. Choo was a very nice chap. He just got involved when Loke died. He wasn't really interested in the business.

Since 1971, I have been on my own, distributing videotapes and running this video store. Yes, I'm still working. It keeps the brain working.

Interviewed by Sam Ho and K.S. Louie on December 11, 2001 in Singapore; collated by Wong Ain-ling.

註

1. 歐德爾的父親歐德禮曾是香港璇宮戲院的總經理。
2. 根據1957年3月2日新加坡《南方晚報》記者戴長夫的報道，歐德爾於抗戰年間走遍了中國內地，跟中國電影界與戲劇界先進關係熟絡；和平後返回香港，由於他的兄弟（應指其父歐德禮）也是香港西片公司主事，被薦去新加坡主持共和公司業務。
3. 歐德爾說的可能是1950年左右李萍倩執導的《落難公子》底片被燒一事。關於這件事，曾於永華公司工作的陸元亮說：「導演李萍倩拍了一場戲，還沒把劇本全交出來，李祖永認為沒劇本就中止拍攝。」（見黃愛玲編：《理想年代——長城、鳳凰的日子》，香港：香港電影資料館，2001年，頁11。）資深影人黃卓漢則有以下的說法：「影片已將殺青，左派影人企圖以影片作要脅，李祖永乾脆將花了好幾十萬元拍成的底片，當着李萍倩面前一把火燒掉，無形中要左派人士離開永華片廠，左派員工乃發動罷工，最後李祖永竟宣佈停止拍片，他說『老子不拍總可以了吧！』」（見黃卓漢：《電影人生——黃卓漢回憶錄》，台灣：萬象圖書，1994，頁46。）
4. 據林繼堂的說法，1952年永華工友罷工，陸運濤答應預支十五萬港元給李祖永以解燃眉之急。此外，他又以九厘息分五期再借五萬元給永華，並以六部新作之星馬等地的獨家發行權作為交換條件，而第一部影片《玫瑰玫瑰我愛你》一定要李麗華出任主角。詳見Lim Kay Tong & Yiu Tiong Chai: *Cathay 55 Years of Cinema*, Singapore: Cathay Organisation, 1991, 頁145。
5. 「永華廠長鍾啟文於1952年5月15日辭職；他已不能再容忍永華的管理不善，跟片場員工也無法溝通……他寄了一封信去國泰求職，卻要等到四年後才成事。」同上。
6. 關於歐德爾與國泰機構的這段恩怨，可參考當年新加坡報章。據1957年3月7日新加坡《南方晚報》的報道，歐德爾於1957年3月1日辭去國泰機構屬下國際電影發行公司總經理之職，雙方並於3月6日各在報章刊登啟事。何亞祿接受訪問時說陸（運濤）和他曾極力挽留歐德爾，但他去意已決，自己請求結算賬項，脫離國泰機構，自己創立位於羅敏申律（即Robinson Road）84號的自由影業公司。〔編按：不是黃卓漢的自由影業公司。〕

Notes

1. Harry Odell, Albert Odell's father, was general manager of the Empire Theatre in Hong Kong at that time.
2. According to *South Evening Post* (a Singapore newspaper, in Chinese), March 2, 1957, Odell went all over China during the war, establishing ties with the film and theatre sectors. He returned to Hong Kong after the war and because his brother (note: should be his father, Harry Odell) was in the film business, he was offered a job to run things for Republic in Singapore.
3. This is probably the film *Le'nan Gongzi*, which Li Pingqian directed in around 1950. Wong Cheuk-hon (Huang Zuohan) remembers in his memoir: "Shooting for the film was almost over and left-wing filmmakers tried to intervene. In front of Li Pingqian, Li Zuyong burned all the footage, which was shot at an expense of hundreds of thousands of dollars. So the left-wing workers staged a strike and Li announced that all production activities be stopped." See Wong Cheuk-hon: *A Life in Movies: The Memoirs of Wong Cheuk-hon* (in Chinese), Taipei: Variety Publishing, 1994, p. 46.
4. According to Lim Kay Tong, Loke agreed to advance HK$150,000 to Li Zuyong when the latter turned to Loke for assistance after the workers' strike in 1952. He also gave 5 loans of HK$50,000 at 9% interest to Yung Hwa in consideration of a 6-pictures exclusive for distribution in Singapore, Malaya, North Borneo, Sarawak and Brunei. There was also a condition stating that famous stars would be cast, and Li Lihua, earmarked to star in *Rose, Rose, I Love You* (1954), would premiere the package. See Lim Kay Tong: *Cathay - 55 Years of Cinema*, Singapore: Landmark Books, 1991, p. 145.
5. "Robert Chung, Yung Hwa's Studio Manager, resigned on 15 May, 1952. He could no longer bear the mismanagement at Yung Hwa and the problems of communication he had had on the studio floor.... He had sent an application to Cathay for a job position. However, Chung's association with Cathay was not to materialise till four years later." See Lim Kay Tong, ibid.
6. According to *Southern Evening Post* (a Singapore newspaper, in Chinese), March 7, 1957, Odell resigned from his position as International's General Manager on March 1, 1957. Both sides posted announcements on newspapers on March 3. Ho Ah Loke said in an interview that both he and Loke tried to talk Odell into staying but were unsuccessful. Odell asked to settle all accounts, leaving Cathay to form his own company, with offices at 84 Robinson Road.

竇漢勳：電懋的粵語製作

蒙竇漢勳先生提供本篇照片

從中聯到國際

我 1947 年來港，因為很想入電影圈，便經劉芳先生介紹，進了中聯。那時他們正籌拍《父與子》（1954）與《秋》（1954），我像打雜一樣，做發行外，也幫忙會計，拍《大雷雨》（1954）時還做出納，帶錢進片場給員工支薪。[1] 做了一段短時間，便轉到國際影片發行公司。當時國際就在中聯隔壁，是林永泰先生找我過去的。

國際那時是國泰機構管轄的，職員就只幾個人：經理歐德爾，林永泰和我，還有秘書陸景紈，一個會計和一個外勤。公司主要工作是發行影片，以及跟新加坡聯繫。香港拍的影片，我們買了星馬版權，再送去新加坡。另外我們也買日本片，台灣和大陸的就沒有，但經南方公司把我們後來拍攝的兩部影片賣給大陸，即《愛情三部曲》（1955）和《火》（1956）。

歐德爾很能幹，我們都佩服他。後來他給邵氏羅致，

在電懋發行部工作的竇漢勳 （1957）
Tau Hon-fun in his office, 1957.

Making Cantonese Films: Tau Hon-fun Remembers

I came to Hong Kong in 1947. I wanted to join the film industry and Lau Fong (Liu Fang) helped me get into The Union Film Enterprise Ltd. They were preparing for *Father and Son* (1954) and *Autumn* (1954) and I did odd jobs, helping in distribution and accounting. When the company was shooting *Big Thunderstorm* (1954), I even worked as teller, bringing money to the studio to pay salaries.[1] After a short period, I switched to International Films Distributing Agency. It was next door to The Union, and Lam Wing-tai (Lin Yongtai) invited me to work there.

International was part of the Cathay Organisation; it only had several staff members: general manager Albert Odell, Lam, myself, a secretary, an accountant and an errand person. We worked mostly on distribution and liaised with Singapore. We bought Southeast Asian rights of Hong Kong films and sent them to Singapore. We also bought Japanese films, but not Taiwan and Mainland productions. Later, through Southern Film Corporation we sold the two films we made to Mainland China, they were *Fire* (1956) and *Three Stages of Love* (1956).

陸運濤請來永華片廠廠長鍾啟文先生接手。國際隨之擴大業務，改名為電影懋業有限公司，開始自己拍國、粵語片。[2] 鍾啟文上任後，改用金巴利道樂宮那兒新修好的大寫字樓。陸運濤有意在香港電影業投放較多資本，搞多一些東西。我猜想，他有幾十間戲院，看到香港電影業頗蓬勃，他又有的是錢，要買片的話倒不如自己投資拍片。

粵語片製作過程

歐德爾時期，國際雖然沒有拍片，但卻斥資給一些「小組公司」拍片，現在的說法，等於是「衛星公司」。他們的劇本、卡士和製作主要內容，都要經國際拍板，國際擁有影片發行香港及星馬等主要地區的版權，我們也會到片場巡巡。像《余之妻》(1955)是左几的公司拍的，《花都綺夢》(1955)便是顧文娟的公司拍的。國泰的嚴俊也給我們拍了國語片《歡樂年年》(1956)。後來，電懋也繼續這樣做，秦劍的國藝便給我們拍了《大馬戲團》(1964)，把當時從新加坡來港表演的沈常福馬戲團也拍進去。嚴俊的國泰亦拍了我們發行的《梁山伯與祝英台》(1964)，那是跟邵氏搶拍而鬧的雙胞胎。

香港粵語片當時賣到美洲，很好的也只是一千多二千元，泰國、越南也是一千多元，星馬版權大概是四千至五千元，合共二萬多元。香港票房如果還能收到兩、三萬元，便很不錯，有錢賺了。那時大製作成本是五、六萬元，有些只一萬多二萬元；我們拍的大概是五、六萬元，很少三萬元以下的。我們的粵語片《苦心蓮》(1960)收入打破歷年紀錄，比過年還要好，一天已收了三萬多元，太平戲院的黃慶華先生對林永泰說：「你和阿勳在彌敦道攤開手走路也可以了。」[3]

我們粵語片的製作費，當時來說算是高的了，而且我們

Odell was a capable man; we thought highly of him. Later Shaws snatched him away and Loke Wan Tho replaced him with Robert Chung (Zhong Qiwen). International then expanded and was reorganised as Motion Picture & General Investment Co. Ltd. (MP & GI), and started producing Mandarin and Cantonese films.[2] Loke Wan Tho wanted to increase investment in Hong Kong films. He had many theatres and money for investment. I think he thought it's better to invest in production than doing just distribution. He could promote his own films and help his theatres in Southeast Asia.

Production Process

Under Odell, although International didn't produce films, the company would invest in "subsidiaries" that are in fact "satellite companies" in modern terms. Scripts, casts and content had to be approved. International also held Hong Kong and Southeast Asian distribution rights of the films. We would also visit sets to check things out. Films like *My Wife, My Wife* (1955) was produced by Tso Kea's (Zuo Ji) company, and Yan Jun's Guotai made the Mandarin film *Merry-Go-Round* (1956) for us.[3] Later, MP & GI continued this practice, like Chun Kim's (Qin Jian) Kong Ngee making *The Big Circus* (1964) and Yan's Guotai making *Liang San Bo and Zhu Ying Tai* (1964) to compete with the Shaws' film of the same title.

Hong Kong Cantonese films, even the good ones, were sold for $2,000 or under to America, $1,000 or over to Thailand and Vietnam and $4,000 to $5,000 to Southeast Asia, with a total income of over $20,000. In Hong Kong, box office of $20,000 or $30,000 was considered good. Big productions at the time cost between $50,000 and $60,000 and smaller ones under $20,000, but our films were mostly $50,000 to $60,000 productions, rarely below $30,000. Our Cantonese film *Bitter Lotus* (1960) broke records and made over $30,000 in one day, even better than Chinese New Year. One theatre owner told Lam: "You and Ah Fun can now walk down Nathan Road with your arms wide spread."[4]

Our Cantonese film budget was high for the time and we spent 15 to 20 working days on each film,[5]

一部戲拍十五至二十個工作天，[4] 和那些「七日鮮」的製作水準有別，他們有些戲真的是七天或十天以內拍完。當然，像中聯、光藝那些製作認真的公司，都是我們那樣的製作水準。

電懋時期的粵語片

初期在國際，林永泰是製片，我是助理製片，除發行外，也做宣傳工作。後來宣傳部請了好幾個人，無論國、粵語片，報紙的那些宣傳和廣告都是他們做好，我每天簽發的。開拍《火》時，我還是助理製片。那時，找劇本，做預算，請導演、演員等工作不會讓我去做，我在劇本拿回來後，才去執行，決定往哪裡拍，一個景拍多少時間，以至後製和配音等工作。後來廠長馬叔庸退休，我便調進永華接替了他的工作，管理片場後才給我印上製片的銜頭，漸漸我也不搞宣傳了。

國際擴充為電懋後，我們也開始搞香港二輪影院發行。當時粵語片有三條首輪院線：一條金陵、國民戲院的金國線；一條太平和龍城戲院的太平線；一條紐約、大世界線。其他的便屬於二輪，戲院較小，如沙田、大埔、香港仔那些邊緣戲院，初期入不了線。國際的粵語片，一直都是在紐約、大世界線上映。

電懋開業後，粵語片組初期沒有擴充意圖。國語片那邊，鍾啟文物色人才後開始運作，全部新班底，較有規模。粵語片初時唯一基本演員就只有白露明，大成影業公司轉給我們的，接着我們還考取了張清、方華、丁櫻。我們主力捧白露明，她算是較紅，其他的都不行，主角只能靠外借。那時粵語片演員很矜貴，很難請，但（我們）就定要用張瑛、吳楚帆，還有羅劍郎；梁醒波差不多每部戲都有份；武打的便找曹達華、石堅；女主角找林鳳、黃錦娟。

其後粵語片的拍攝計劃都是我來做的，但公司主力還

different from those *chuk yat sin* (literally "seven-day catches"). Some of them were really made in seven or ten days. Of course, serious companies like The Union and Kong Ngee had production quality similar to ours.

MP & GI's Cantonese Films

In my early days at International, Lam Wing-tai was producer and I was assistant producer. I did both distribution and promotion. Later promotions hired several people to handle all the ads for both the Mandarin and Cantonese films, which I had to approve every day. As assistant producer for *Fire* (1956), I was not supposed to do tasks like deciding on scripts or budgeting. Only after script approval would I get involved, choosing locations, deciding the time needed for shooting scenes, post-production and dubbing. Then Yung Hwa studio manager Ma Shuyong retired, and I was transferred to replace him. I started getting producer credits and gradually gave up promotion work.

After becoming MP & GI, we got into second-run theatres. At the time there were three first-run Cantonese film circuits and the rest were smaller, second-run theatres in peripheral areas like Sha Tin and Tai Po that could not join any circuits. Our Cantonese films were always shown in one of the first-run circuits.

When MP & GI started operating, the Cantonese group didn't have expansion plans. On the Mandarin side, Robert Chung scouted talents and started operation with a new team. The Cantonese group had only one staff actress, Christine Pai Lu-ming (Bai Luming), whom we got from Tai Seng. Then through auditions we got Cheung Ching (Zhang Qing), Fong Wah (Fang Hua) and Ding Ying. We focused on promoting Pai, who was more popular than the others. We had to borrow lead actors from other companies. Cantonese stars were in demand, but we would only use stars like Cheung Ying (Zhang Ying), Ng Cho-fan (Wu Chufan) and Law Kim-long (Luo Jianlang); and Leung Sing-po (Liang Xingpo) was in almost every film. Action films we would cast Tso Tat-wah (Cao Dahua), Sek Kin (Shi Jian), Patricia Lam Fung (Lin Feng) and Wong Kam-kuen (Huang Jinjuan).

是拍國語片，因為國語片的市場比粵語片大，賣埠價也高一點。那時，皇后、娛樂那些國語片首輪戲院的票價，比粵語片的高，所以始終覺得國語片好像高人一等。但話説回頭，當年香港只有兩家首輪戲院，粵語片卻有七、八家，甚至到後來聯線更多至十一至十二家，因此本地的粵語片觀眾肯定比國語片多，票房收益也不會比國語片差。

我們拍戲，初期在永華，六十年代初也租了電影製片廠，即亞洲，老闆是張國興。他們不拍片了，片場便洽我們租下來改成電影懋業公司製片廠，由我來管。永華那邊我就不管了，改由新加坡派來的美國人柏力殊管理。他是技術顧問，我們用他，是因為公司開始拍攝彩色和闊銀幕製作。管理亞洲後，我的職位才正式稱做廠長，之前雖然執行廠長職務，但職銜一直都叫廠務管理處長。

亞洲地方不小，除露天地方外，還有兩個攝影棚。有時廠不夠用，便租聯合片場，老闆是兼做配音師的劉恩澤，地點好像在深水埗福榮街。這情況下，粵語片會被排擠到外面去拍，我們在聯合拍了兩部片，其中一部是《錦繡年華》(1963)，是黃錦娟第一部片。雖説粵語片給排擠到外面，其實也不真是排擠。那時國語組製片主任王植波跟我們也談得來，不會強逼我們，只是我們自己知道粵語片始終不及國語片那麼認真，該讓一讓他們。

我們粵語片拍得不多，公司很少指定拍些甚麼。我們自己去瞭解市場，人家拿來的故事，我們看過的小説，聽過的播音，有值得拍的就會去拍。例如買了三毛錢一本的環球小説版權（編按：這類廉宜的通俗作品，時稱「三毫子小説」，以煽情題材為主），拍了《福慧雙修》(1962)，也有買武俠小説版權拍的《雙劍盟》(1962)，聽過麗的呼聲的《苦命鴛鴦》(1963)後也買回來。買

Later I was responsible for planning all the Cantonese films, but MP & GI's focus was on Mandarin films, which had bigger markets and summoned higher distribution rates. Ticket prices at first-run Mandarin theatres such as Queen's were higher than Cantonese theatres. There was a feeling that Mandarin films were a cut above.[6]

We first shot at Yung Hwa studio.[7] In the early 1960s we also rented Asia Studio. The studio boss was Zhang Guoxing. His studio stopped making films, so we rented it and I was put in charge. An American was sent from Singapore to manage Yung Hwa. He was a technical consultant, hired because we started shooting in colour and scope. Managing Asia, my title was studio manager.

Asia was big. Besides outdoor areas, it also had two sound stages. When that was not enough, Cantonese productions would be pushed out of the main studio and we would rent the Lianhe Studio. We shot two films there, one was *Make It Mine* (1963), Wong Kam-kuen's first film. Perhaps we shouldn't say Cantonese films were pushed out. Wang Zhibo, production manager of Mandarin productions, was friendly and wouldn't press us, but we understood that the quality of Cantonese films was not as high and we should make room for them.

We didn't make many Cantonese films; the company seldom told us what to make. We did our own market study, considered stories people sent us, novels and radio plays. For example, *Double Date* (1962) was based on a 30-cent novel (Editor's note: a derogatory term for pulp paperbacks). We also bought the rights of a *wuxia* novel for *Crossed Swords* (1962) and a Rediffusion Radio play for *Bitter Romance* (1963). Copyright for stories was normally $300 to $500 and, in rare cases, as high as $2,000. Airwave novels are probably in this range, though *Bitter Romance* might be close to $3,000.

We didn't need Singapore approval when choosing a story. When Robert Chung was in charge, he would ask for story outlines. His main concern was the Southeast Asian market. Films projected well for Hong Kong but not for Southeast Asia would likely be rejected. We'd choose directors, writers and cast for the approved

故事版權，一般是三百至五百元，如環球小說便是三百元，一直沒有起跌。有些會高至千多二千元，但不多，天空小說的版權就好像是這個價錢，《苦命鴛鴦》版權可能接近三千元，但我不肯定。

我們選定故事後，不需新加坡通過。鍾啟文先生做總經理時，要看故事大綱。他主要考慮香港和星馬的生意，看看有沒有觀眾，會不會受歡迎，如果一部片在香港可以，但星馬不行，也許就會否決。鍾啟文同意後把大綱發還下來，我們便考慮誰做導演，誰做編劇，找哪些演員。編劇寫好分場大綱後，我們做製片的再去計劃外景地點，盤算每個景拍多久，然後根據我們構想的班底、佈景、菲林、場租等，做製作預算，做好後交給總經理，通過後便切切實實去拍戲了，拍完還要做字幕和配音。

影片賣座原因

《苦心蓮》是我正式當製片的第一部戲。那部戲幹嗎那樣賣座？首先，故事講的是日治時期婆媳倫理關係，家庭倫理題材是粵語片觀眾所喜愛和容易接受的。那是台灣寫作人投稿的故事，我們買下，交盧雨岐編劇。其次，我覺得這個題材最適合李我，該找他來講天空小說。故事原是講惡家姑、好家翁，但我卻倒過來，寫好家姑、惡家翁，與一般人想法相反。林永泰當時已是總經理，私底下和我很要好，但為了這件事大家爭拗了好幾天，他認為李我有段時間聽眾不多，但我認為李我講這些故事最出色。最後他說，既然我堅持，就讓李我去講，給我連累也算了。

於是我們便買了麗的呼聲的廣播時間，李我依修改後的故事大綱和劇本，再潤飾一下，一直講到影片上映，不知道有沒有講了六十集。他講得真的好，節目播出時，

projects. After scene treatments were written, we'd plan for locations, estimate the number of days for each location, then did the budget based on the crew, sets, film costs and studio rental etc. Shooting would start after the general manager approved the budget, after which we also had to do the subtitles and dubbing.

The Secrets Behind Hits

Bitter Lotus was my first film after I officially became a producer. It was popular because family melodramas were popular among Cantonese audiences. Also, I decided to ask the airwave novelist Li Ngaw (Li Wo) to do an "air wave novel". The original story was about a mean mother-in-law but I reversed this usual practice and changed it to a mean father-in-law. Lam Wing-tai, a good friend, was general manager and we argued over this for days. He thought Li Ngaw was losing audiences but I thought Li was perfect for this story. He finally gave in and said, go ahead, even if it'd get him in trouble.

We bought airtime from Rediffusion and Li polished the script and started broadcasting the radio play,

很多人站在路邊、士多橫門聽，我們便知道上映時票房會好，果然未上畫便提早三天滿座。

我們的戲，不是每部都適合以天空小說的形式來做宣傳，另有一些會錄下片裡一些聲帶，再加旁述，上映時給香港電台和麗的播放。《璇宮艷史》、《魂歸離恨天》便是這樣做。播幾十集天空小說的，除《苦心蓮》，還有《翠樓春曉》。《翠樓春曉》苦情戲太多了，票房不行。那時很多人用李我的天空小說拍電影，有時故事還沒講完，便有人來買；有些則是將要拍的戲，交給他講，再向電台買回來。我們還會指定麗的找某位播音員，武俠片最會來這一套，很喜歡找鍾偉明、蕭笙和雷鳴。

《苦心蓮》之後，我們還拍了幾部成績很好的影片，如《璇宮艷史》(1957)，《福慧雙修》和《錦繡年華》。《璇宮艷史》這麼成功，其實有我不想人家知道的原因。[5] 那時我用彩色菲林，做了柯式彩色劇照，全部劇照好像都是這樣，人家還以為這部片是彩色的。另外我們不是拍闊銀幕，但劇照卻造成那效果，都是騙人的。但預告片我們照樣放黑白，觀眾看後都滿意，否則也不會湧來買票。其次此片錄了聲帶，我來旁白，交香港電台和麗的播放，我不知道這是否有幫助。

可是，一定起了作用的，是張瑛和羅艷卿在大世界和紐約兩家戲院隨片登台。當時無論國語片或粵語片，每有明星隨片登台，街上都站滿了人，很哄動。很多人喜歡看登台。他們除日場外，夜場每晚登台，開映前唱曲，張瑛唱一段，羅艷卿唱一段。張瑛在粵語片首次開腔唱歌，比較新鮮。另外，我們的佈景和服裝都很新，薛覺先搞這粵劇時已很新穎，觀眾反應很好，但我們要更新的，所以我和林永泰商量，找來了一位年輕人，叫高亮——好像是演員高威廉的兒子。他設計的佈景和服裝，我們都很滿意。但續集就不行，即使彩色的也不行。[6]

《苦心蓮》中的好新抱（白露明）與惡家翁（林坤山）
Bitter Lotus generated sweet box office.

which lasted till the film opened, with about 60 episodes. Li was brilliant. When the play was on air, people would stop on the streets to listen. We then knew that the film would do well. Indeed, tickets had been sold out three days before it opened.

We would only use radio plays as promotion for certain films, like *Second Spring* (1960), though the story was too sad and it didn't have good box office. For some — like *My Kingdom for a Husband* (aka *The Romance of Jade Hall*, 1957) and *Love Lingers On* (1957) — we would record the soundtracks, add a narration and play them on radio when the films were released. Li Ngaw's radio plays were often made into films and many were hits. People would buy the rights when the story was still playing or they would give him a story and bought the rights back from the station after it became a radio play. We would ask Rediffusion for certain radio actors, especially with *wuxia* films.

We had several hits after *Bitter Lotus*, such as *My Kingdom for a Husband*, *Double Date* and *Make It Mine*. *My Kingdom for a Husband* was a big success, for reasons I don't want people to know.[8] I made stills of the film in colour and wide-screen and people thought it was a wide-screen colour film. Though the trailer was in black and white audiences flocked to buy tickets regardless.

One thing really helped. That is to have Cheung Ying and Law Yim-hing (Luo Yanqing) perform on stage before screenings. Mandarin or Cantonese films, star appearances were big events. Cheung and Law appeared in night-time shows and performed songs from the film and it was the first time Cheung sang on film. We also used new sets and new wardrobes. Sit Kok-sin introduced new elements when he did the highly successful Cantonese opera version, but we wanted something more refreshing. We hired a young man, Gao Liang, the son of actor William Ko (Gao Weilian), and we were pleased with his designs. But the sequel was a failure, even though it was in colour.[9]

The *wuxia* film *Crossed Swords* also did well, though it wasn't a huge hit. It had a gimmick. It's black and white, but I was the first person to add colour to

還有一部生意算是較好的，就是武俠片《雙盟劍》，但未至於好到呱呱叫。唯一的噱頭是，影片本身是黑白的，但放出的飛劍、掌風等卡通，卻給我率先做了彩色。後來很多人都效法，報紙還説我取得了專利，但我沒有，只是有人鼓勵我這麼做。我有這個想法，是因為我們的劇照雖然都是黑白的，卻經常找人塗上色彩，做十六乘二十吋的大相片放在照片櫃內。當時劇照有三種尺寸，十六乘二十吋是最大的，其次是十一乘十四吋和八乘十吋。我想，既然相片可以着色，幹麼菲林不可以。但如果整部片着色就不得了，而且不容易，於是只把卡通着色。一試之下，果然可行。我請林永泰先生看過，他也説好，於是我們把所有拷貝的卡通和預告片都着色。那時有一部片馬上仿效我這種做法，聽説大觀片場的星光沖印還設有小組，專門替人搞這些卡通。

有些製作票房不佳，我們很傷心。譬如我們拍得非常之好的《美人春夢》（1958），電檢處檢查官余熙年還致電鍾啟文，説從來沒有拍得這麼好的粵語片。我們首天上畫生意很好，但第二天就跌得很厲害。《碧海浮屍》（1956）和《東床佳婿》（1956）票房差是意料中事，兩部戲都是捧新人的，上畫那天還冷清得很。那時演員不夠，我們一定要用新人，簽一些基本演員。

兩種方言，兩類觀眾

記得楊天成的小説《福慧雙修》原是國語片組買回來的，他們搞來搞去搞不好，沒法開拍，最後便扔過來，只説題材不適合國語片。我們接手拍了出來，票房收入很好，楊天成也很滿意，但改動很大。

那時粵語片和國語片的觀眾是不同的，最起碼是語言不同，而很多看粵語片的，看國語片就不太明白。我認為國語片觀眾一般文化水平高一些，我們粵語片家庭觀眾較多，像阿婆那些。他們國語片拍《四千金》（1957），

（後排左起）劇務郭少泉、導演李鐵和左几、竇漢勳、場務盧慧
（前排左起）容小意、吳楚帆、白燕、梅綺

(Back Row, from left) Lee Siu-chun, directors Lee Tit and Tso Kea, Tau Hon-fun and Lo Wai.

(Front row, from left) Yung Siu-yi, Ng Cho-fan, Pak Yin, Mui Yee.

create cartoon special effects like flying swords and palm currents. We used to tint stills in colour and display them in glass cases.[10] I thought if photos could be tinted, why not films? But it was expensive to do the whole film, so I tinted the cartoon parts. This gimmick was widely copied and I heard that the lab at Grandview Studio formed a special unit for cartoon tinting. Newspapers reported that I had patented this method. In fact I hadn't.

We were upset when some of the films didn't do well. *Memories of Love* (aka *A Lovely Girl's Lovely Dreams*, 1958) was well made, so good that a censorship officer called Robert Chung to tell him he had never seen a better Cantonese film. Opening receipts were good, but dropped dramatically on the second day. We were not surprised that *The Body of a Blackmailer* (1956) and *My Eligible Son-in-Law* (1959) had poor box office, because they were made to promote new actors. We didn't have lots of actors, so we have to find new faces.

Cantonese Film Audiences

Yang Tiancheng's novel *Double Date* was bought by the Mandarin film group. They couldn't make it work and handed the novel to us, but they didn't say why. We made the film and it did well. Yang was satisfied with the film, though many changes were made.

Cantonese film audiences were very different from those of Mandarin films. I think Mandarin audiences had better cultural backgrounds and Cantonese audiences were mainly families or old women. We wouldn't make films like *Our Sister Hedy* (1957) or *Golden Lotus* (1957) and we couldn't make films like *Calendar Girl* (1959) or *Mambo Girl* (1957). Cantonese cinema couldn't make musicals.

我們不會拍這樣的故事；他們拍《金蓮花》(1957)，我們也不會講這個題材；他們拍《龍翔鳳舞》(1959)，我們是拍不到的；他們拍《曼波女郎》(1957)，我們也拍不到，粵語片不會拍歌舞。

我所以這樣說，是鑑於《美人春夢》票房不理想，那些故事跟粵語片觀眾格格不入。我們覺得，粵語片觀眾需要較通俗的題材，通俗題材接近他們的生活和思想，容易賣座。我拍過一部《廣告女郎》(1958)，粵語片觀眾覺得不合口味，虧蝕得很厲害。同樣道理，國語片題材也要接近國語片觀眾的生活，《曼波女郎》很好，國語片觀眾比較喜歡上舞廳跳舞，他們會跑去看這些國語片。

決定拍一部戲時，我們會考慮觀眾。如果自己沒有影片放映，我們也喜歡到戲院聽聽觀眾怎麼講人家的戲。完場後和觀眾一道離開，聽聽他們談些甚麼。這是我們日常可以做的事。自己的戲，更加要在上映一、兩個星期前，先聽聽觀眾看到預告片的反應，也走到劇照櫃，看有沒有人指指點點説些甚麼。拍《美人春夢》之前，我們看過一部西片——忘了是甚麼，覺得相當好，該可以拍粵語片。結果猜錯了，全沒料到觀眾不能接受少女喜歡上了年紀的人。後來真的聽到觀眾走出戲院時罵：「哪有這樣子的！」

粵語片觀眾比較保守。尤其結局，更要遷就他們，假如留下懸疑，不讓他們知道結局，是絕對不行的，而且定要大團圓結局，壞人定要死。那時必須這樣，是拍電影的規矩。如果不恪守這個原則，你那部戲也許就會完蛋。

粵語片組的導演

左几拍我們的粵語片，拍得最多。粵語製作最初都主要找他導演，他有文學修養，喜歡拍文學改編的題材。他大多自己編劇，他能寫，劇本寫得很好。左几工作又很認真，

(左起）王天林、林鳳、竇漢勳、白露明和雷震攝於永華片場大門前

At the Yung Hwa gate:
(From left) Wang Tianlin, Lam Fung, Tau Hon-fun, Pai Lu-ming and Lai Chen.

I said this because *Memories of Love* didn't do well, as it was out of tune with the audience. The same with *The Girl of the Year* (1958), which lost lots of money. Cantonese films audiences liked ordinary subjects that were close to their lives. It is the same with Mandarin films, which must relate to the lives of its audience. *Mambo Girl* worked, because Mandarin audiences liked to dance and they would see a film like that.

We always thought about the audience. We would go to theatres to listen to what audiences said about other companies' films. With new releases, we'd go to theatres and listen to responses to trailers, or stood near film stills cases and watched if people were interested. Before filming *Memories of Love*, we saw a foreign film – I forgot the title – and thought we could make it into a Cantonese film. But we were wrong. The audience couldn't accept a young girl falling in love with an older man. Leaving the theatre, we heard a person complaining "How can it be like that?"

Cantonese audiences were more conservative. We had to cater to them, especially the ending. We could never have unresolved endings. Endings had to be happy and bad guys had to die.

Directors

Tso Kea was the director who made the most Cantonese films for us. With a literary background, he liked to adapt literature. He could also write most of his scripts, and they were good. He was a serious director, always had detailed scene treatments prepared. He didn't like popular subjects, so some of his films didn't do well, though not terribly bad. He made quality films, not melodramas like *Bitter Lotus*. *Love Lingers On*, *Fire* and *Three Stages of Love* were literary adaptations. The first was also good, but audiences didn't like it; the other two didn't make much money, but weren't failures either.

The company never pressured us. We had certain understandings and didn't have to explain everything. After *The Body of a Blackmailer* and *My Eligible Son-in-Law*, we all wore a sad face and Tso knew; we didn't have to tell him not to make such films again. In

入片場前手上一定有預先寫好的分場大綱。他不愛通俗題材，所以他有些作品的票房是差了一點點，但也不會差得很離譜。有時我們拍得很好的戲，人家稱讚的，像他的《美人春夢》，反而生意比預期差。他改編自文學名著的《魂歸離恨天》也拍得很好，但得不到粵語片觀眾的共鳴。他拍的片（層次）高一些，很少像《苦心蓮》那麼婆婆媽媽，巴金名著改編的《火》、《愛情三部曲》亦是他拍的。那些作品雖然賺錢不多，但也不會虧蝕。

其實公司方面，是不會給我們壓力的。那時我們都明白很多事情大家想法一致，不用怎麼講清楚。例如拍了《碧海浮屍》和《東床佳婿》後，大家都苦着臉。左几他自己也知道，用不着我們叫他以後別再搞這些，其實大家都有責任。我們老闆陸先生也有這種性情，不大干預我們，只要我們肯做，能完成工作，賺與蝕他都不會很緊張。假如可以，一世給他打工也是值得的。因此，我們不會因一部片上映時門庭冷落便哭喪着臉，但很自然下次開戲時會避開那些東西。但左几不愛隨波逐流，跟紅頂白。《璇宮艷史》便是他拍的，拍得很好。

除左几外，替我們拍粵語片的，還有莫康時、黃岱和王天林等等，我們請的導演不多。莫康時是賣座導演，拍小市民生活拍得好，搞喜劇尤其出色。他有喜劇細胞，很容易引人發笑，能想到我們想不到的東西。但他不是臨場搞戲那種人，不會拿着一張煙紙就拍戲。他要有分場劇本，分好場才進廠拍，但也會忽然來了靈感，他的《錦繡年華》就拍得好。王天林亦擅搞喜劇，《福慧雙修》也拍得好。哈哈笑的粵語片，都會找他拍，國語片《南北和》(1961)亦是他的作品。黃岱呢，我們覺得他擅長一些婆婆媽媽的家庭倫理，很細膩的東西。

沉痛的一頁

後來，陸先生、我們的製片王植波、新加坡那邊幾位職

竇漢勳（左二）與黃也白（右二）等攝於吉隆坡

Tau Hon-fun (second from left) and Huang Yebai (third from left) in Kuala Lumpur.

fact, we were all responsible. Loke Wan Tho was similar. He rarely interfered. He didn't care much about making or losing money, as long as we worked hard and did our job. I didn't mind working for him my whole life. We wouldn't wear a sad face if a new release didn't do well, but we'd avoid that subject. Tso didn't like to go with the flow, but he made *My Kingdom for a Husband*, a very good film.

Our other Cantonese film directors included Mok Hong-si, Wong Toi (Huang Dai) and Wang Tianlin. We didn't employ many directors. Mok was a box office director, good at making films about little people, and was exceptionally good at comedies. He had a comic touch, but he couldn't improvise. He always had detailed scene treatments before starting work. Wang Tianlin was also good with comedies. He also directed the Mandarin film *The Greatest Civil War on Earth* (1961). We would give classy Mandarin films to Evan Yang (Yi Wen) or Yue Feng. And Wong Toi was good at making stodgy melodramas or films with subtle emotions.

Then Loke Wan Tho and several colleagues died in a plane crash, MP & GI's plan to expand and to build a studio in Clear Water Bay was history. If they didn't die, and we continued with our work, it wouldn't turn out like this. People were sent from Singapore to look at our work and we understood they were going to take over. Lam Wing-tai and I and several other people wanted to leave the company. I can't remember if I was the first to resign, but I left in September. I was disheartened and didn't want to work in the film industry after such a disaster. I found a job in television, and never worked in the film industry again.

My favourite MP & GI Mandarin film is *Golden Lotus*, and my favourite Cantonese film is still *Memories of Love*.

Interviewed by Wong Ain-ling and Sam Ho on December 7, 2001. Collated by Ho Wai-leng

Translated by Grace Ng

員，都一起遇難了。當時飛機在台中摔下來，全機都是電影界的人。我們電懋正準備大搞製作的計劃亦頓成泡影，清水灣建新片場的計劃也沒有了。假如他們不是遭到不幸，我們幹下去，成績不會是這樣子。新加坡其後派人來瞭解我們工作情況，名義上是瞭解，我們明白實際上可能是接收公司。因此，我、林永泰先生、會計部和發行部的幾個人都想離開。忘了自己是否第一個辭職，總之我九月就離開了。那時我的心情，對於電影，感覺很灰，覺得電影界遇上這麼大的災難，自己也不想再在這圈子幹下去。翌年我便進了電視台，再沒有接觸電影工作了。

電懋的國語片，我最喜歡《金蓮花》，粵語片我還是喜歡《美人春夢》。

訪問：黃愛玲、何思穎（2001年12月7日）
整理：何慧玲

註

1. 《父與子》這部中聯作品是1954年1月7日公映的，《秋》則是同年2月17日，據此推算，竇漢勳該是1953年下半年進入中聯。
2. 據翁靈文所述，歐德爾於1956年調返新加坡，國際擴展並改組成電影懋業公司，由曾任永華廠長的鍾啟文出任總經理，其下主要人員為：發行部經理林永泰（後接任鍾為總經理），廠長馬叔庸（後為竇漢勳）、製片部經理宋淇等（見翁靈文，〈電影懋業公司〉，於林年同編：《戰後香港電影回顧（1946-1968）》，第三屆香港國際電影節回顧特刊，香港：市政局，1979，頁148）。歐德爾本人稱，他是調返新加坡後，才給邵氏羅致。詳見本書〈歐德爾：電懋的草創時期〉一文。
3. 據翁靈文稱，電懋粵語片組一般製作費是五萬至十多萬元，票房紀錄通常淨收五萬至六萬元，加上二輪戲院及外埠版權收入，多數影片可達一本一利的利潤（見翁靈文，〈電懋影業公司粵語片組〉，於林年同編：《五十年代粵語電影回顧展》，第二屆香港國際電影節回顧特刊，香港：市政局，1978，頁50-51）。竇漢勳則澄清，他們的粵語製作費一般都是五至六萬元，偶然有高達七、八萬的，但都不會超過十萬元。
4. 竇漢勳亦表示電懋的國語片，一般拍三十個工作天，所以比粵語片更認真。
5. 據翁靈文稱，電懋生產粵語片共計七十餘部，其中以《璇宮艷史》收入最高，達四十八萬多元（見翁靈文，〈電懋影業公司粵語片組〉，同註3）。竇漢勳也提到，《璇宮艷史》和《苦心蓮》是電懋最賣座的兩部作品，兩部票房收入其實不相伯仲。
6. 電懋只製作過兩部彩色粵語片，除《璇宮艷史》續集外，還有左几導演、張瑛和羅艷卿主演的《歷盡滄桑一美人》（1958）。據竇漢勳說《歷》片也算是賣座，但西洋劍那些題材，也許不適合粵語片觀眾，所以成績還是比預期差。

Notes

1. *Father and Son*, a Union film, was released on January 7, 1954, and *Autumn* was released on February 17 of the same year. Judging from these dates, Tau must have entered Union Film Enterprise near the end of 1953.
2. According to Weng Lingwen, Odell moved back to Singapore in 1956. The Cathay Organisation expanded operations and was renamed MP & GI, with Robert Chung (Zhong Qiwen) as general manager. Key members of his staff were Lam Wing-tai (Lin Yongtai), distribution manager; Ma Shuyong (later Tau Hon-fun), studio manager; Stephen Soong (Song Qi), chief production manager. (See Weng Lingwen, "Motion Picture & General Investment Company" in Lin Nien-tung, ed., *Hong Kong Cinema Survey: 1946-1968*, the 3rd Hong Kong International Film Festival catalogue, Hong Kong: Urban Council, 1979, p. 148). According to Odell, Shaws employed him after he went back to Singapore. For details please refer to "From Distribution to Production: Albert Odell on a Key Cathay Moment" in this volume.
3. *My Wife, My Wife* was the first Cantonese film International made in Hong Kong, Lam Wing-tai was producer and Tau Hon-fun was assistant producer and responsible for distribution. The second film is *Sweet Dreams*, a joint production with Gu Wenjuan, the wife of Leung Sing-po (Liang Xingpo). See Weng Lingwen, "The Dianmou Film Company: Cantonese Film Group" in Lin Nien-tung, ed., *Cantonese Cinema Retrospective (1950-1959)*, the 2nd Hong Kong International Film Festival catalogue, Hong Kong: Urban Council, 1978, pp. 58-59.
4. According to Weng Lingwen, the production budget of MP & GI Cantonese films were $50,000 to $100,000 per film; usually the net income was $50,000 to $60,000, plus the income from 2nd-run cinemas and overseas rights, profits from most films could equal production costs. (See Weng Lingwen, "The Dianmou Film Company: Cantonese Film Group," op. cit.). Tau Hon-fun makes a correction here: their Cantonese film production budget was $50,000 to $60,000, occasionally the budget would go up to $70,000 or $80,000, but never exceeding $100,000.
5. Tau Hon-fun also points out, the shooting period of MP & GI Mandarin films was 30 working days, so the quality standard was much rigorous than Cantonese films.
6. In the interview Tau Hon-fun also admits that there were only two first-run cinemas for Mandarin films, but there were 7 or 8 for Cantonese films. The number was increased to 11 or 12 when the cinema circuits joined together later. Therefore the audience of Cantonese films should be more than those of Mandarin films, and the box office income would not be less than Mandarin films.
7. International also distributed Yung Hwa's films in the early days. Yung Hwa fell into financial difficulties in 1954, aggravated by a fire, which destroyed its film storage. The company had to borrow money from Cathay, and was not able to repay the debt. As a result, it was agreed in 1955 that the Cathay Organisation would take over the management of Yung Hwa. See Weng Lingwen, "Motion Picture & General Investment Company," op. cit.
8. According to Weng Lingwen, MP & GI had produced 70 Cantonese films. Of these films *My Kingdom for a Husband* had the highest box office gross and took in $480,000. (See Weng Lingwen, "The Dianmou Film Company: Cantonese Film Group," op. cit.). Tau Hon-fun also mentions the film and *Bitter Lotus* were the top two grossers of MP & GI; the income of these films were very close.
9. MP & GI had made only two colour Cantonese films, one was *My Kingdom for a Husband* and *The Beauty Who Lived through Great Changes* (1958). According to Tau, the latter was a box office success, but it was a western fencing film, which the Cantonese audience might not like, so the box office was lower than expected.
10. Tau remembers the film stills had 3 sizes at the time: the largest was 16" x 12", the smaller one was 11" x 14", and the smallest was 8" x 10".

我在電懋工作的回顧

- 綦湘棠 -

一切從《翠翠》開始

我以前在香港從事電影配樂十多年（1950-1966），配電懋的片最多，今天來寫這篇「回顧」，正是前塵往事，歷歷在目，如今故人何在？舊物仍存，再一番低迴，也再一次惆悵！

就先從我如何進電影圈說起吧！

嚴俊又導又演的《翠翠》（1953，永華），是林黛初出道即成名之作，配樂是葉純之；片中共有八首插曲，葉要我寫〈你真美〉與〈不講理的姑娘〉兩首。結果影片和八首歌大受歡迎，林黛也藉此一炮而紅。我的兩首歌，在劇中都是嚴逗林而唱的，也許這就讓嚴對我留有印象。1952年他緊接下來拍《金鳳》（1956），葉純之離港回滬走了，嚴便找我接替配樂工作。我坦白對他說配樂我不懂，他就說：「有關電影的我教你，我相信你

My MP & GI Days

- *Kei Shang-tong* -

The Story Begins

I had been a film composer in Hong Kong for almost two decades (1950 – 1966). Most of my works were created for MP & GI films. Memories of those days evoke a feeling of nostalgia.

Let's start from the very beginning.

Singing under the Moon (1953, a Yung Hwa production), a film directed by and starring Yan Jun, was also Linda Lin Dai's debut film. Composer of the film was Ye Chunzhi. The film had eight songs, Ye asked me to write two of them. It turned out the film and all the eight songs were very well received, Lin Dai became a shinning star overnight. Maybe this left an impression on Yan. Ye returned to Shanghai when Yan made *Golden Phoenix* (1956); so he asked me to compose. I told him I didn't know how to compose film score; he said, "I can teach you about films, I am sure you'll do a good job…" I accepted the offer. Technically I found a solution - I used a stopwatch and metronome to calculate the time of segments that needed music.

會幹得好……」沒辦法，我只好硬着頭皮答應下來。在技術上卻自己想出來用秒錶和節拍機來計算需要配樂片段的時間，解決了大難題。

後來，嚴俊告訴我，他邀我配樂的事，事前曾和李祖永、張善琨開過會，李不置可否，張反對，他則保證我「行」。隔了很久，我曾猜想過——張是名製片家，以前是上海的影壇大亨，來港後，境況大不如前，他的新華公司，稍後才靠鍾情拍的歌唱片來支撐，所以他拍片必須穩紮穩打，不作冒險投資，片子的好壞，配樂是重要因素，搞不好的話，二三十萬成本便泡湯；而我是個籍籍無名的新丁，又非來自上海，他反對是大有道理的。我再想，那嚴又憑甚麼對我有信心？我猜他又導又演，會覺得我那首〈你真美〉上路！（「上路」是北方話，大意是在行、對路——行是行業的行，並非行路的行）。

關於〈你真美〉這首歌，詞是李雋青先生大作，原先兩段，今摘抄一段如下：——

搖船的姑娘你真美，

茶峒裡找不到第二位；

大大的眼睛長長的眉，

白白的牙紅紅的嘴，

多少人想做媒，

茶峒裡小子哪一個配？！

不知將來便宜誰。

（按：茶峒是湖南西部一小村鎮名）

當日寫作此詞，我的處理是：一、將第四句的「牙」字「兒化」，因為京話如「門兒」、「鞋兒」的「兒」字，通常是語音尾帶過的，唱起來便成了「白白的牙兒哪紅紅的嘴」；二、第五句中間加一襯字「呀」，即成為「多

Later Yan told me he had a meeting with Li Zuyong and Zhang Shankun. Li didn't have an opinion about me composing, but Zhang objected. Zhang was a famous film tycoon in Shanghai, but his golden days ended when he came to Hong Kong. His Hsin Hwa Company wasn't doing well and he couldn't afford risks. I guess he didn't trust a newcomer. Yan vouched for me. I guess he found my songs right for the film.

After my initiation to the industry, I worked on all the films with Yan and Lin. After *Golden Phoenix,* I worked on *The Orphan Girl* (1956). Other directors or companies started hiring me, such as for *Lady from the Moon* (1954), directed by Dan Duyu; *Life and Love of a Horse-cart Driver* (1956), produced by Wong Cheuk-hon (Huang Zuohan) in Taiwan, *The Fisherman's Daughter* (1956), directed by Bu Wancang etc.

The most memorable film in this period was *Red Bloom in the Snow* (1956), Li Hanxiang's first film as director. He had been unemployed for some time when an investor asked him to direct this. He asked me to write the score, but he could only pay two-thirds of my fee. He paid $300 in advance, and the remaining $700 was a post-dated cheque, but eventually it bounced. It was a good film; it was sold to Shaw Brothers. Li's talent was discovered and he signed a long-term contract with the company.

Composing for MP & GI

The predecessor of MP and GI was International Films Distributing Agency; Albert Odell was its general manager. He is Jewish, and his wife Chinese. Its first investment in film production was probably *Merry-Go-Round* (1956, produced by Yan Jun's Guotai Co.), starring Yan Jun and Lin Dai, directed by Yue Feng. The film was a musical and had several songs; Yao Min and I wrote the music part and Chen Dieyi wrote the lyrics.

One night, we were shooting a song-and-dance number in Palace Theatre. I visited the set, watching Lin rehearse with dancers. Yue was busy doing something. Yan took me aside and told me he had a new girlfriend, also an actress. He didn't tell me who and it wasn't until later that I found out she was Li Lihua.

少人呀想做媒」（中國傳統戲曲唱詞，以至流行曲中加襯字是常見的）；三、緊接下來兩小節的音樂「過門」5-5 55 |6-6 66|，這裡我特別指定歌者加上笑聲「哈哈……」；因為劇情中嚴俊在撩逗林黛時唱的，猜想嚴演出時一定是嬉皮笑臉，動作多多，七情上面地做戲的，加笑聲，便切合戲的要求了。自此，也許因此嚴便認為我懂戲，上路，才會找我配《金鳳》吧。

《金鳳》讓我入行之後，嚴林的片都是我的工作，接下來好像是《梅姑》(1956)，大概是1953、54年左右，配樂主題用〈梅花三弄〉貫串全片，這是嚴指定的。這時候，漸漸也有別的導演和公司找我，如但杜宇導的《嫦娥》(1954) 指定以四句〈擊壤歌〉古謠作歌，我又為夏厚蘭、丁聰主演的《鑽石花》(1955) 作主題曲，黃卓漢在台監製的《馬車夫之戀》(1956) 作配樂，卜萬蒼的《漁歌》(1956) 作合唱曲等。

這時期中，最記得是李翰祥首回當導演的《雪裡紅》(1956)。他原在《翠翠》做嚴俊的副手，已露才華，不知為甚麼拍《金鳳》副導不是他，而換了是何夢華；所以翰祥自己説「孵豆芽」(意謂失業在家無事做) 已頗有時日，得一據説是前雲南省主席龍雲的秘書某某 (名字我忘了) 找他拍《雪裡紅》，他便來找我，並央我幫忙少收三分一價錢替他配樂，先付了我三百元，尾數七百是期票，但後來卻不能兑現。《雪》片的戲不錯，賣給邵氏，李並被賞識而簽了長約。

為電懋做電影音樂

電懋的前身叫國際影片發行公司，總經理是歐德爾 (Albert Odell)，人説是個猶太裔，他太太是華人；這之前，他營商，也做娛樂經紀。我不知國際何時開業的，最先 (投資) 開拍的大概是《歡樂年年》(1956，嚴俊的國泰公司出品)，也由嚴俊、林黛主演，導演是人稱

Merry-Go-Round was the last collaboration between Yan and his ex-girlfriend Lin. He then went to Singapore to make *Rainstorm in Chinatown* (1956) and *Nonya and Baba* (1956), both with Li. Yan and Li later founded Golden Dragon; its productions were distributed by International. Its first film was *The Story of Yuan Yuan Hong* (1958). Li was professional and had a long career. She was thrifty, and was known as one of the rich ladies in the industry. Yan was even thriftier, frugal to both himself and others. He went to lunch with his staff and would yell out, "Waiter, BBQ pork with rice," then turned around and said, "order whatever you like." Who would order anything fancy when the boss was having BBQ pork with rice?

No Time for Love (1957), Golden Dragon's third film, had two songs, both sung by Li. After they were done, I sent in an invoice. My fee had increased, but the cheque I received was the amount when I was starting out. I asked my assistant to return the cheque, but Golden Dragon never gave me another one and Yan never asked me to work for him again.

The offices of Golden Dragon and International Films (later renamed as MP & GI) were both on Kimberley Road. The general manager of MP & GI was Robert Chung (Zhong Qiwen), head of production was Stephen Soong (Song Qi), head of both distribution and the Cantonese Film Section was Lam Wing-tai (Lin Yongtai), head of promotion was Huang Yebai.

After *Merry-Go-Round*, MP & GI produced *Surprise* (1956), directed by Tao Qin and starring Grace Chang (Ge Lan). I composed music for it. I had worked with Tao before, in *A Lonely Heart* (1956), which Tao directed for Shaws. The film starred Lucilla You Min as a nun. Tao wrote the lyrics to the songs and I composed the music. There was a song "A Night without Moonlight" in *Surprise*; Tao's lyrics were so beautiful that it instantly inspired me to write the first part with great ease. The mood of the second part was different, so I changed the key. The third part was the same as the first; so I switched back to the original E Flat Major. For musical reasons, I had to add a few characters to make it sound better. I brought the score

岳老爺的岳楓。《歡》片是部歌舞片，有多首插曲，分由姚敏和我作曲，作詞是陳蝶衣，配樂是我。

記得有天深夜裡，他們在北角璇宮戲院拍〈雪人不見了〉的一場歌舞。我跑去探班，見林黛正和一班舞蹈員在舞台上綵排，岳老爺也在忙着甚麼，嚴俊拉我到戲院後座處坐下——那時，外傳嚴林鬧分手，嚴已搬離林寓——他悄悄地說：「我已經有了新的女朋友，是圈子裡的，你也認識她的，不過，將來再告訴你吧。」其時我在猜那是誰，後來方明白是李麗華！

《歡樂年年》可說是嚴林最後合作的一部影片，之後嚴赴星馬為國際拍《風雨牛車水》（1956）和《娘惹與峇峇》（1956）兩片，便都是由李麗華任主角。嚴俊精打細算，一次外景，原班人馬，拍成兩片。支出一，收入二也。其後，嚴李合作另立一家金龍公司，出品交國際發行，創業作叫《元元紅》(1958)。李很敬業，後成影壇長春樹，她個性節儉，很早已是圈中富婆之一。嚴比李更省儉，省人也省自己。

嚴做了金龍老闆，往往領着一群下屬到鄰近的香檳酒樓午飯，才剛坐下，他便揚手高叫「伙計，給我來碗叉燒飯」。接着向大伙說：「大家喜歡吃甚麼，自己叫啊！」有人後來跟我說：「老闆吃叉飯，誰還敢叫其他？」

金龍的第三部片《遊龍戲鳳》（1957）有兩首歌，李麗華本人唱，錄好之後，我把帳單交了過去。那時我的曲酬費已提高了，金龍管錢的是李麗華表哥賈圭復先生，開來給我的支票還是我出道的老價錢，我叫助手將支票退回去，而金龍卻未有另開支票付我，嚴俊也從此再沒有找我工作了。

金龍和國際（即後來的電懋）的寫字樓都同在金巴利道，電懋在彌敦道那邊的街口，即當年的樂宮戲院後面

to Tao Qin's home for a trial performance, and explained that the extra words were in fact the climax of the song. Tao was experienced with lyrics and understood my point. He remained silent for a while and said, "Alright, let's have it your way!" In those days, the practice was to write the lyrics first before the score was completed. Only when Pathé was adapting western pop songs into Chinese songs would the lyrics be written after the music. Composers and lyricists would have discussions before a song was finalized.

MP & GI did not have a permanent recording studio those days. "A Night without Moonlight" was recorded in Grandview Studio in Diamond Hill. The band and the singer would rehearse in the studio. If mistakes occurred during recording, they had to start all over until the director or composer (or conductor) accepted it. Grace Chang sang well that night. While we were packing up, a middle-aged man approached. He was Lu Yuanliang, a renowned recording technician from Shanghai. He shook my hands and said, "I haven't heard a nice song like that for a long time." This was the first time someone praised my work to my face. I was all in a fluster and didn't know how to respond.

Recording for Pathé

Pathé would buy copyright of the film songs after recording was completed. We would rearrange the master score for the band and shorten it to around three minutes, then schedule for another slot to record for Pathé. Ye Chunzhi did the recording for all the eight songs in *Singing under the Moon*. We had coffee at Peninsula, and he introduced me to Wang Shuwei, producer of Mandarin records at Pathé. She gave me a cheque, and said, "This is your advance payment for the royalties." I never imagined I could write songs and make that much money. I'd been in Hong Kong for two years and was still a poor teacher. That additional income was more than two months of my salary.

I wrote two songs for *Golden Phoenix*; the others were written by Yao Min. The recording of *Golden*

京菜館樂宮樓的樓上。那時電懋的總經理是鍾啟文、製片部宋淇、發行部兼粵語組（稍後兼永華片廠管理）是林永泰、宣傳部是黃也白。

想起來，在《歡樂年年》之前，嚴俊還拍了部《亡魂谷》（1957）；在《歡》片之後，電懋拍攝了陶秦導、葛蘭主演的《驚魂記》（1956），兩部都是我做音樂的。陶秦未進電懋前，曾替邵氏（那時仍是邵氏父子公司）拍《零雁》（1956），尤敏飾演修女，片中有歌，陶詞我曲並配樂，故陶與我早有《零》片之緣。

《驚魂記》中一曲〈沒有月亮的晚上〉，陶的詞寫得很好，是三段體（請參看附歌譜）。我拿到歌詞，唸開頭一句即已引發靈感，很輕易地便寫了首段，第二段直覺上覺得情緒轉變，所以音樂也轉了調，到了第三段歌詞和首段相同，音樂應該再轉回原先的降E大調，但就在轉回原調之前四小節，唱的詞是：「啊——可是……」——這是陶的原作沒有的，是我硬加上去的；因為在第二段尾，就音樂的氣勢上，需要作預備轉，若僅以音樂作四小節過門，則唱的部份，似乎缺了點甚麼，跟下一段接不上，所以我加上「啊——可是」這幾個字。當日，我作好歌，到陶府試唱，並解釋「啊——」是全歌的高潮所在，刪不得的；而「可是」就像作文處理，是一種轉語調詞吧！其實陶何嘗不明白，還用我說嗎？但他也確實沉默不語有好一會，才終於決定說：「好吧，就依你的吧！」那時候作歌，都是先有詞後有曲，只有「百代」錄歐西流行曲改為中文歌詞唱的才用填詞的。故此在當日作曲的和作詞的如有問題，要商量斟酌過才定稿的。

電懋初期沒有固定片場使用，錄音也一樣臨時租用，〈沒有月亮的晚上〉是在鑽石山大觀片場內的星光錄音室錄的。那時的錄音樂隊與唱者同時一起錄音，先排練

岳楓（右）指導林黛、王萊演出《金蓮花》

Yue Feng (right) directing Wang Lai (left) and Lin Dai on the set of *Golden Lotus*

（左起）姚敏、葉楓、百代負責人汪淑衛、丁皓和綦湘棠合照

(From left) Yao Min, Yeh Feng, a Pathé representative, Ting Hao and Kei Shang-tong.

多次，練好了才正式錄音，若當中出錯，便需從頭再來，不好的叫NG，又再重來，直到導演OK才行，如導演不在場便由作曲者或錄音指揮決定。那回錄音葛蘭唱得很好，順利完成。大家在收拾東西的時候，一位斯斯文文的中年人向我走過來，先作自我介紹——原來他是以前上海電影界名錄音師陸元亮先生，他和我握手致意，還說：「長遠唔勿（沒有）聽到這麼好聽的歌了。」這是我頭一回被人當面稱讚。當時，真有點手足無措，不知如何應付。

替百代錄電影歌曲

當時電影歌曲，錄妥之後，百代多半要買版權，那就要把原樂隊伴奏的總譜另改編過，把樂隊減縮，時間長度必須在三分鐘上下（那時唱片還是七十八轉的），然後擇期再為百代錄音。當年百代自置的錄音室在銅鑼灣利舞台附近新寧招待所背後的一個地窖裡，面積不大，大約只能容納十來二十人的樂隊，而且隔音並不太好，實在不太理想。

《翠翠》的八首歌，錄音均由葉純之包辦，大概在他已替百代錄音之後的某日，約我在半島酒店喝咖啡，要介紹百代國語唱片製作人汪淑衛小姐和我見面。我去了，在版權合約上簽了字，汪小姐給我支票，並說：「這數目是版稅預支的。」老實說，作歌可以這樣輕易賣錢，那是我考進音樂院唸書時，想都沒想過的。來了香港兩年左右，還是個窮教書匠，這筆意外錢，已多過我兩個多月薪水了。

至於《金鳳》，我也有兩首歌，其他都是姚敏的。百代錄《金鳳》的歌同《翠翠》一樣，由嚴、林自己唱的，電影中聲帶是代唱的，《金鳳》各首歌錄唱片的工作，當然是姚去做了。《驚魂記》中的〈沒有月亮的晚上〉也不是我親自主持唱片錄音的，香港現在仍有此歌之百代

沒有月亮的晚上（《驚魂記》插曲）
陶秦詞　綦湘棠曲

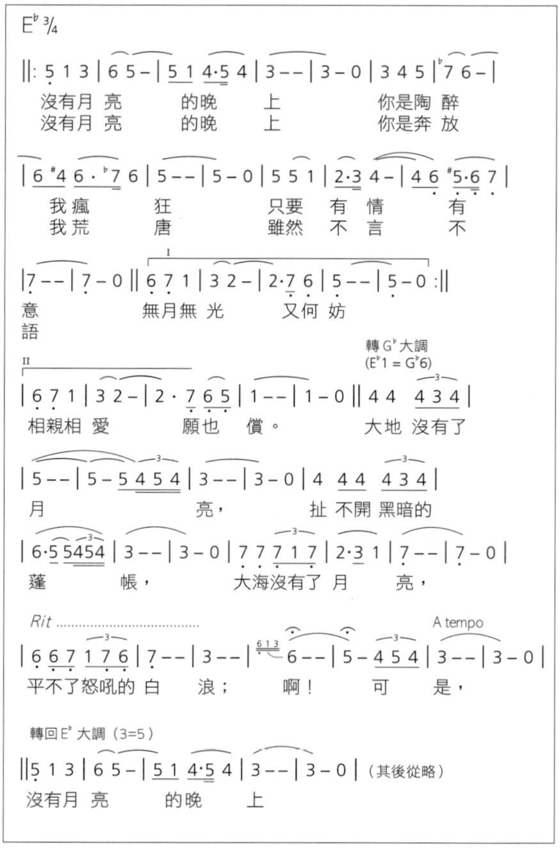

E♭ 3/4

||: 5 1 3 | 6 5 – | 5 1 4·5 4 | 3 – – | 3 – 0 | 3 4 5 | ♭7 6 – |
沒有月 亮 的晚 上 你是陶 醉
沒有月 亮 的晚 上 你是奔 放

| 6 ♯4 6· ♭7 6 | 5 – – | 5 – 0 | 5 5 1 | 2·3 4 – | 4 6 ♯5·6 7 |
我瘋 狂 只要 有 情 有
我荒 唐 雖然 不 言 不

| 7 – – | 7 – 0 || 6 7 1 | 3 2 – | 2·7 6 | 5 – – | 5 – 0 :||
意
語
無月無 光 又何 妨

轉G♭大調
(E♭1 = G♭6)

| 6 7 1 | 3 2 – | 2 · 7 6 5 | 1 – – | 1 – 0 || 4 4 4 3 4 |
相親相 愛 願也 償。 大地 沒有了

| 5 – – | 5 – 5 4 5 4 | 3 – – | 3 – 0 | 4 4 4 4 3 4 |
月 亮， 扯 不開 黑暗的

| 6·5 5454 | 3 – – | 3 – 0 | 7 7 7 1 7 | 2·3 1 | 7 – – | 7 – 0 |
蓬 帳， 大海沒有了 月 亮，

Rit .... A tempo

| 6 6 7 1 7 6 | 7 – – | 3 – – | 6 1 3 6 – – | 5 – 4 5 4 | 3 – – | 3 – 0 |
平不了怒吼的 白 浪； 啊！ 可 是，

轉回E♭大調 (3=5)

||5 1 3 | 6 5 – | 5 1 4·5 4 | 3 – – | 3 – 0 | （其後從略）
沒有月 亮 的晚 上

Phoenix for Pathé was the same as *Singing under the Moon* – the songs were sung by Yan and Lin, but on the film soundtrack, they were sung by somebody else. Yao was responsible for the recording of all songs in *Golden Phoenix*. I didn't supervise the recording of "Night without Moonlight" in *Surprise* for Pathé either. The Pathé CD of this song can still be found in Hong Kong today.

New Stars

Soon after MP & GI was founded, the company recruited eight new actors; they were Kelly Lai Chen (Lei Zhen), Yeung Kwan (Yang Qun), Tian Qing, Ling Chong (Lin Cang), Kitty Ting Hao (Ding Hao), Dolly Soo Fung (Su Feng)… *et al.* At the Chinese New Year banquet, shortly before the evening actually started, a handsome young man appeared, in an impeccably

CD流通。不過CD上葛蘭唱第一句「沒有月亮……」的「有」字唱兩個音，而在電影上則照我原譜寫的「有」唱一個音，而「亮」字唱兩個音的（請參看前附譜）。這雖説是一音之差的改動，似乎沒甚麼大不了，不過，我的原作「沒有月亮的晚上，你是陶醉我瘋狂」兩句是均衡的。「均衡」是美學要素之一，為甚麼要改動呢？要改，是不是應該先通知我，和我討論一下的呢？以前我沒有把這事向汪小姐提，因為估計提也沒有用。

電懋的新人

電懋開始了沒多久，便招考了八個新人，那就是雷震、楊群、田青、林蒼、丁皓、蘇鳳……等。這批新人剛來的那年，公司農曆新春聯歡宴在彌敦道山東街口瓊華酒樓舉行。這之前我是完全未見過他們的。那夜，快開席了，人人都就座了，突然樓梯口跑上來一位漂亮英俊的年青人，西裝筆挺，左手拿着雨衣，在梯口一停，一個亮相架式地舉目四望，看到了便瀟瀟灑灑地向那席走去，我好奇地打聽，問人：「那人是誰？」原來是雷震！

不久，公司為新人開戲——《青山翠谷》（1956），岳老爺除了導，還兼訓。片中有歌，我寫好了就進大觀片場向岳交卷，岳叫劇務把他們八個召來，一字地排立在我和岳的面前，岳叮囑每人看着手上拿的歌譜，跟我一句一句地學唱。

在教他們唱歌的過程中，我注意到丁皓發問最多，新人中她最活躍，比較突出。後來，她要求我教她唱歌，其後還要叫我作「契爺」。《青山翠谷》公映成績平平，八新人之中，其後雷震派演機會較多，而丁皓也嶄露頭角，兩人曾合演過陶秦導的《小情人》（1958）。而楊

tailored suit. He glanced around and walked gracefully towards one of the tables. I was curious and asked who he was. He was none one other than Lai Chen!

The company had a new project for the newcomers, *Green Hills and Jade Valleys* (1956). Yue was actually both director and instructor. Yue lined up the eight youngsters and told them to learn how to sing with me. Among them, Ting Hao was the most inquisitive and active. She even asked me to be her teacher. The result of the film was not exciting. But Ting and Lai later had lots of opportunities to act. The two of them later starred in *Little Darling* (1958).

Rigorous and Serious: Yue Feng

Yue was always well prepared. He would have meetings with screenwriters, actors and the crew. He would see to important issues personally, cautious but never stubborn. In a mother-daughter conflict scene in *Golden Lotus* (1957), he shot 400 ft of film in one take. For the pauses between dialogues, I thought music might help to enliven up the atmosphere, but it might also spoil the tension. We had four thorough discussions and eventually decided that no music should be added.

I admired Yue Feng's rigorous attitude. He later left MP & GI to join Shaw Brothers and made *The Deformed* (1960), with King Hu and Betty Loh Ti (Le Di). Besides writing music for the film, I also volunteered to be his second assistant director to learn more from him (he already had an assistant director Wang Xinglu, who later directed *Escort over Tiger Hills* (1969).

Golden Days

There are many factors affecting the quality of a film, among them, scripts were the most important. Stephen Soong, head of production at MP & GI, came from a theatre family. He was a close friend of the renowned writer Eileen Chang (Zhang Ailing), and he also recruited famous writer Nellie Chin Yu (Qing Yu), along with Tao Qin, Evan Yang (Yi Wen) and famous calligrapher Wang Zhibo. Later Tang Huang, Wang Liuzhao and Yuan Qiufeng also joined the rank. MP & GI had the strongest team of screenwriters in town.

群在《青》片中似無甚發揮的機會，但在《驚魂記》中曾演歹角，已開始惹人注意；到後來在林黛主演岳導的《紅娃》(1958)中，他演個不男不女的角色，聲音和表情動作都陰陽怪氣，演來精彩萬分，人皆讚好，也説岳老爺慧眼識人，挑他來演也是一絕！

嚴謹的岳老爺

岳老爺拍片，籌備工夫做足，必先開劇本會議、演員會議及工作人員會議；小事交副導去辦，大事必躬親。考慮比好多人來得周詳，卻並非固執。

記得在《金蓮花》(1957)(是林黛首次也是香港首次在東南亞影展〔後易名亞洲影展〕獲最佳女星獎的)片中有一場母女對話的戲，是主場戲也是林與王萊的對手戲。林演來非常用心，因王是圈內出名好戲之人，疏忽不得，而由於劇情需要——劇中兩母女感情衝突，情緒上連綿不斷，岳老爺也少見那麼狠勁，一個鏡頭拍這場戲，拍了400呎。由於兩人的對白，時有停頓空檔，稍有冷場，似應該用音樂襯托一下，但音樂一出，便難免破壞了劇中二人感情上僵持的氣氛，為了這場配樂問題，我和岳導演反反覆覆的討論過四次之多，終於決定不加配樂。

我很欽佩岳老爺拍片的嚴謹態度，所以，後來他離電懋過邵氏後，開拍胡金銓與樂蒂演的《畸人艷婦》(1960)，我除了配樂，還請求他讓我當第二副導(他原有的副導是王星磊)，給我個學習機會。

全盛時期的電懋

一部電影的好壞，因素甚多，除了導演和演員是顯著因素之外，劇本是起決定作用的先天性原因。電懋製片部主任宋淇是戲劇世家子弟，語、文、樂、藝，樣樣精

The office of MP & GI was different from other companies. It was always crowded. Actors and actresses would gather and chat in the production, promotion and distribution departments. It was like a big family. Laughter was always heard. Soong and Lam Wing-tai were always busy talking to people. Lam, in particular, with his correct Cantonese or clumsy Mandarin, was often arguing with someone speaking perfect Mandarin, Beijing style or with Shanghai accent. He was a funny gentleman, the source of fun and laughter in the office. In 1958, *Our Sister Hedy* won Best Picture Award at the Southeast Asian (later changed to Asian) Film Festival, and in the same year, the company hosted the charity show "Spring of a Million Flowers" in support of a fund raising campaign for the poor. Those were the golden days of MP & GI.

Every year before Chinese New Year, *Sing Tao,* the morning and evening posts, would organize a charity even. Winter clothes, foods and red pocket money would be distributed to the needy and homeless. Robert Chung decided to support the campaign, and invested all the manpower and resources in the charity show. There was one performance in Princess and one in King's theatre. Ticket prices were between $50 and $500. I was not a contract staff with MP & GI yet, but after collaborating on films like *Golden Lotus* and *Our Sister Hedy*, I was treated as part of the family. Yue Feng was director of the show and he asked me to attend production meetings.

The show was a grand musical with chorus, short skits, dances and solos. I was assigned to compose the music for the chorus of the opening and closing scenes; I even directed those scenes. Tao Qin wrote the lyrics for the songs. They were pre-recorded, and synchronized during the performance. The recording session was impressive. The band had more than 60 musicians. I didn't want that many, but when the Filipino musicians knew this was charity, they volunteered to play for nothing. In addition to MP & GI actors and actresses, I also invited over ten singers to join the chorus. The

通，他與名小説家張愛玲早屬摯交，而當時香港著名才女秦羽，宋亦早已羅致；加上陶秦、易文當導演前已是編劇名家，而名書法家王植波也加入助陣（後期尚有唐煌、汪榴照、袁秋楓等，後均兼任導演），電懋這個編劇陣容，當日在港，可謂一時無兩。

那時電懋與其他公司真的很不一樣，寫字樓中人來人往，川流不息。每天都見各大小明星在製片部、發行部、宣傳部嘻哈談笑，宋淇和林永泰大都應接不暇，尤其是泰哥，以他一口正宗廣府話或走腔國語，來跟道地京片子、上海話對陣。在吱吱喳喳聲中，這位風趣健談的好好先生，成為辦公室中開心的「擂台躉」。天天如此，公司裡上上下下，大家宛似一家人。在《四千金》獲 1958 年度東南亞影展的最佳影片獎，及同年響應「濟貧運動」，義演《萬花迎春》，那一段時期，正是電懋的全盛時代。

每逢農曆年歲晚時候，星島日晚報推行「濟貧運動」（又稱「發財運動」），向社會募集善款，派棉衣、分發糧食，或分派紅封包給貧弱露宿者，鍾啟文決定響應，動員全公司人力物力，在樂宮與娛樂兩大影院各演出一場《萬花迎春》。票價從 50 到 500 元，最高的榮譽券則多多益善，任憑捐助。那時我尚非簽了約的公司職員，但經過在《金蓮花》、《四千金》等多片合作，早已把我看成「自家人」，《萬花迎春》一開始籌備，公司指派岳楓任總導演，即着我參加編導組的會議。

《萬花迎春》是個以大型歌舞為主，並包括有大合唱、趣劇、舞蹈及歌唱等的節目，我被派負開場和最後兩大合唱的音樂和導演之責。開場的叫〈散花歌〉，另一首叫〈發財歌〉。詞是陶秦大作，這兩首大合唱也作事前錄音，演出時播帶。那回錄音可謂盛況空前，單是樂隊人數便略超六十人。我原不預備要用那麼多樂師的，誰

Yung Hwa Studio was too small for this event, so we used Studio C. I will never forget the enthusiasm and team spirit of those people.

The two performances became talk of the town. MP & GI donated all expanses. Looking back, MP & GI's concern for the underprivileged and enthusiasm in charity work was extraordinary. I think this deserves a page in the history of Hong Kong cinema!

Mambo Girl and *Our Sister Hedy*

I had many memories about *Mambo Girl* (1957). There were eight songs, all sung by Grace Chang. The lyrics were written by Evan Yang. His lyrics were always elegant, graceful and magical. They were not only entertaining, but also inspiring and uplifting. "Forgetting Your Troubles" was an example. Here is an excerpt:

Your wishes might not come true

Things might not be smooth

But your family cares about you

And your friends too

Goodwill can be found everywhere

With love and loyalty in the air

There's warmth and tenderness in your heart

And good fortune in your grasp

Only a silly fool

Will make so many complaints

Do Re Mi Fa Sol La Si, Hey!

Forget your troubles today

(Note: This was written before *The Sound of Music* released in 1965, so the use of "Do Re Mi …" was not an imitation!)

I love the lyrics and wrote the music quickly. The melody was simple and easy to sing. The style was very different from the popular songs of the time, probably the reason why it never became popular. If only composers and lyricists nowadays would pay more attention to the educational side of popular

知菲律賓樂師們聞説是做慈善的，雖然無酬，卻自動要求參加工作。合唱方面除了全體男女明星，我尚邀到十多位歌手助陣，全體加起來恐怕超過一百人了，永華的錄音室容不下，改去C棚錄。那天各人工作熱情的情景，在我腦中永難忘記。

結果兩場演出哄動全港。全部濟貧演出的一切開支，電懋全數負擔。今天回首看來，電懋全人這番關懷社會、勇於行善的精神，在當時影界中非常突出，香港電影史上似應為它記下一筆！

電懋從開始到全盛，都由鍾啟文統領，林永泰日常口中稱之為鍾波士。其實電懋波士非鍾，是星馬名人陸運濤，國泰機構的董事長。他很少來香港，我在電懋那麼多年，僅見過他一次，大概是1959年吧，他剛再婚，和新太太來。公司在美麗華酒店設宴歡迎他，介紹所有明星及高級員工和大老闆見面。當日，我在忙於寫配樂，因翌日要進廠開工，所以那宴會只能見過他一面便走。當我到達酒店，宋淇領我見他，他頗瘦削、高䠷，但斯文親切，宋連忙解釋我在趕工，不能留下陪宴，他頻頻點首回應，偕夫人和我握手，我隨即告辭了。

《曼波女郎》與《四千金》

那次我趕工是配哪一部片的，確實想不起了，但那段時期的《曼波女郎》（1957）這部歌唱文藝片，我卻擁有不少回憶。《曼波女郎》共有八首歌，葛蘭主演主唱。八首歌詞均易文作的，他的詞從來都優美、瀟灑，常有神來之筆，不僅娛樂性強，他還重視詞中涵義，寫下不少益世勉人之句，八首歌中的〈忘憂歌〉就是一例，僅摘抄一段如下：

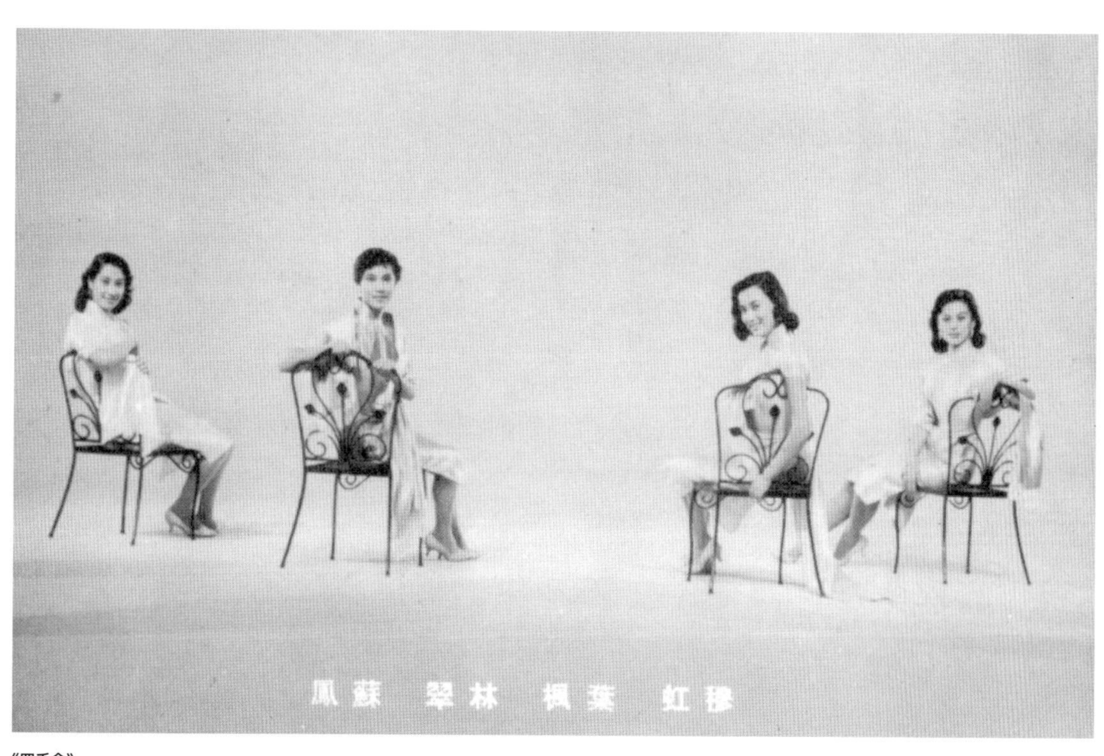

《四千金》
Our Sister Hedy

你有甚麼不如意
你有甚麼不順利
親友關心你
朋友愛護你
到處有好意
到處有情義
溫暖甜蜜在心底
幸福好運在手裡
只有大傻瓜
才會怨自己！
Do Re Mi Fa Sol La Si, 嗨！
快把憂愁都忘記

（按：此歌寫在西片《仙樂飄飄處處聞》（*The Sound of Music*, 1965）之前，這樣用「Do Re Mi ......」並非東施效顰！）

這首詞我一看就喜愛到跳起來，譜曲也很快完成，曲調簡單易記、易唱，和當時的流行曲，大異其趣，或許就因此而不流行。

我想在這裡乘機談談，那時的電影和插曲、時代曲關係上一些問題。其大前提是市場上的電影和唱片是商業性的，當日的國語電影和唱片主要市場在星馬，星馬華人非常愛好唱歌，只要是歌唱片都去看，看後有喜歡的歌便搜購唱片。如此蔚然成風，成了積習，這正是那時電影和唱片生存和發展的主因。

電影中所用的歌，非盡是時代曲，也有其他不同風格的，不過時代曲最受歡迎、賣錢。所以國語電影便有些

music.... The major markets of Mandarin films and records were Singapore and Malaysia. The Chinese in those areas loved singing; they would see every film with songs and would buy the records. That was the trend at the time.

Not all film songs were popular music; there were many different styles. But the popular ones were pop songs, generating lots of income. As such, some films would use pop songs excessively, like country girls and farmers singing popular tunes instead of traditional folk songs. Film songs should support the story. Used appropriately, they would enliven the film; otherwise, they might affect box office. Pop songs are enchanting in many ways, but I was not smart enough and never learned how to write them.

濫拍，就有了鄉下姑娘不是唱山歌，下田勞動也唱時代曲那樣有違常理的事，無以名之，只能說是硬插硬唱而已。電影歌曲原則上應配合劇情來決定的，處理和運用恰當便為片增色，否則就會影響票房，那是疏忽不得的。時代曲有其迷人本領，我自問愚拙，學也學不來，只好寫寫電影歌曲。

話得扯回來說《曼波女郎》，那時荷里活推出《Rock 'n' Roll Revue》(1955)不久，Rock得世界團團轉，《曼》片中有兩首這樣「跟風」歌曲，老實說，是宋淇先生硬逼非要我嘗試不可而寫的，錄音之後，我對宋說：「宋先生，下不為例。」另一首我印象深刻的是〈燕子舞曲〉，原因是錄音進行中，此歌內有變速度，和當中插一段朗誦式對白，而其襯底的樂音頻密而迅速，要配合得好，實非易事，幸好葛蘭小姐和樂隊通力合作，才有滿意效果。

陶秦導演的《四千金》得1958年東南亞影展最佳影片獎，劇中大姐穆虹、二姐葉楓、三姐林翠、四妹蘇鳳，戲多在林翠三姐角色身上。片中林教小孩子西洋劍，唱〈劍舞〉一曲；其時我在嶺英中學任教小學的四、五、六三級，就從中挑選了十來個小朋友幫錄此歌，歌中有「左一劍，右一劍，挑一挑呀點一點」之句。當在百代錄此唱片時，當日粵語片名導演秦劍正向林翠熱烈追求，隨侍林之左右，唱片錄妥後，我向林說：「你真是如假包換的左一劍，右一劍。」她當然明白我是甚麼意思，嫣然一笑而別。

《四千金》獲獎後，在酒樓慶功，公司把各人名下的獎座，分發各人，皆大歡喜。但我在1960年為李翰祥導的《後門》(邵氏出品)一片，也獲該年度最佳影片獎，邵氏的邵仁枚先生特從星來港，與參加該片工作人員慶

Let's go back to *Mambo Girl*. That was the time when Hollywood made *Rock 'n' Roll Revue* (Joseph Kohn, 1955). Soon the whole world was rocked by the music, and even *Mambo Girl* had two songs imitating it. Stephen Soong made me write those songs. After the recording, I told him this was the first and the last time. The other song I remembered well was "Swallow Dance". The tempo changed in the middle, and there was a monologue inserted; it's not an easy song to sing. Fortunately Grace Chang and the band worked well together and the result was good. In *Our Sister Hedy*, there was a scene where Jeanette Lin Cui taught the children to play swords, and sang the song "Sword Dance". I was teaching in a primary school then, and chose a dozen children for the song. We had a celebration party after *Our Sister Hedy* won the Asian Film Festival award. The company

功，但各部門之獎牌都未分發，而保存在公司中。從獎座分發回員工與否，可分別到兩家公司的作風及其員工對公司之歸屬感如何。

時代曲輸了給黃梅調

姚敏當年在電懋的電影中擔當重要的角色。在陶秦導演的彩色歌舞片《龍翔鳳舞》(1959)中，他用中國時代曲開山祖黎錦暉的〈桃花江〉，和三十年代上海聯華公司名片的〈漁光曲〉，把它們舊曲新編，老歌新唱(姚敏妹妹姚莉擔任此片一些幕後代唱)。結果，歌舞和影片本身都成績斐然，是電懋那時期成功的一部製作。後來的《野玫瑰之戀》(1960)也是他負責音樂，還請了日本的服部良一來作曲，大概是姚提議的吧。服部良一的編樂很精彩，只是免不了東洋味。

在我剪存的資料上，1959年港產國語片首輪賣座的幾部片中，《龍翔鳳舞》只佔第二位，《江山美人》收四十萬六千多名列第一；《龍》片收入僅是它的一半。票房數字絕對影響日後製片人的製作方針。《江》片的黃梅調勝過時代曲式的〈桃花江〉和風靡一時的電影歌曲〈漁光曲〉。在歌詞方面「桃花江是美人窩……」和「雲兒飄在海上」就不及李雋青的「做皇帝我在行」(道理在於配合劇情，非插進去的插曲)。換句話説，趣味性的劇情勝過奪目的歌舞，而從音樂趣味來看，土產黃梅調比帶洋味的老歌更合觀眾胃口，從兩片賣座數字來看，説明了當年電懋和邵氏在製片策略上的勝負，也成了各公司其後一窩蜂拍黃梅調的主因。黃梅調曲盛行，卻窒息了電影歌曲，甚至加速了流行曲的衰亡。回頭來説電懋，製片策略上吃虧，也伏下日後不振之憂。

岳楓導演、林黛主演的《紅娃》(1958)是部氣派磅礡，以大漠風沙為背景的戲，和當日流行的歌唱、言情、家庭倫理的影片不同，風格別具，但拍好了，遲遲未公

《鶯歌燕舞》中的夷光與葉楓
Maria Ye Kwong (left) and Julie Yeh Feng are *Mad about Music*.

映，原因不明。此事是否令岳老爺介懷也不得而知。但後來在1959至1960年間，岳與陶秦和公司談新約不攏，而邵氏銀彈奏效，就將岳陶兩位挖走了。

那時我仍是自由身，他們兩位初過邵氏拍的片，還由我配樂；直到邵氏將在清水灣建廠，並定下了將來要用現成的音樂唱片配樂的政策，由邵維鍈和我談合約未成。那時陶正要開拍《不了情》（1961），我也只好放棄，而專注於電懋的工作了。

鍾啟文個性比較固執，北方話說是個「軟硬都不吃」的人。為了片酬每部大概相差不過千來兩千塊，便放走了兩員大將，電懋便顯得導演人手欠缺了。稍後，不知為何他竟要親兼導演，拍了《愛的教育》（1961）、《一段情》（1962）、《一曲難忘》（1964）等片。開初和他一起工作，彼此還不太熟，漸漸因他捧丁皓的關係，才多些接觸。到拍《一段情》時，我隨他赴台拍外景戲，因我在片中飾一閒角——一名騎馬藏人，故必須同行，在台四十天，大家同住台中的鐵路飯店，吃飯也多數同在一起，加上美術主任費伯夷和鍾啟文很談得來，我們在台的生活大多是三人行（這也是我和費後來隨鍾在麗的電視工作的原因）。

從《一段情》到《諜海四壯士》

《一段情》中有兩歌，一名〈道心不堅〉，另一是〈珍貴的腰刀〉，兩詞均易文佳作，後來我才知道〈道心不堅〉內容乃根據距今約二百年西藏達賴六世的情歌改寫的。片中由朱牧領唱眾和，在永華錄此歌時我兼代唱，所以這首歌我是身兼作曲、指揮、代唱三職。但在我來說，三重身份已非首次，以前曾在陶秦導、雷震、丁皓主演的《小情人》，片中一段丁與木偶同唱的戲，代唱木偶豬八戒一角。

distributed the trophies to those involved, and everyone was happy. In 1960, Li Hanxiang's *Rear Entrance* (a Shaw Brothers production), which I composed for, also won Best Picture of the year. Runme Shaw came to Hong Kong from Singapore to join the celebration. But the trophies were kept in the company and never distributed to relevant departments. From these two incidents, one can see the difference between the two companies.

Pop vs *huangmei*

Yao Min played an important role in the films of MP & GI. He had many original ideas about music. For example, in the colour musical *Calendar Girl* (Tao Qin, 1959), he rearranged two golden oldies of the 1930s at the suggestion of Tao Qin and Soong and added new flavours to them. It turned out both the songs and the film were very successful. Yao was also responsible for the music of *The Wild, Wild Rose* (1960). He invited Japanese composer Hattori Ryoichi to rearrange the songs. Hattori's arrangement was fabulous, but there was also a certain Japanese flavour.

According to box office records, among the Hong Kong produced Mandarin films in 1959, *Calendar Girl* was only second on the top 10 list. *The Kingdom and the Beauty*, with a total of $406,000, topped the list. *Calendar Girl* generated only half of that. The traditional *huangmei diao* (Yellow Plum Opera) defeated the pop songs. In other words, an interesting story worked better than spectacular musical scenes. In terms of music, audiences preferred traditional *huangmei diao* over westernized pop songs. The box office figures of these two films indicated that the production strategy of Shaw Brothers was a success while MP & GI's was not. This also explained why other companies rushed to make *huangmei diao* films. The popularity of *huangmei diao* accelerated the decline of pop songs, and the wrong production strategy of MP & GI was one of the causes for its eventual decline.

至於〈珍貴的腰刀〉是既歌且舞西藏風味的歌曲，此歌乃是在台灣拍外景時，夜間休息時抽空寫的，事前我看過不少西藏民歌和舞曲，但我未到過西藏，怎能憑空亂寫？所以此歌之後半舞曲完全是一模一樣的藏曲，而歌的部份，因詞的國語音之高低關係，無法全盤藏化，唯有大致接近來應付了，但易文這首詞寫得好美好美，像以下四句：

這裡是我們的家鄉，

這裡是美麗的地方，

冬天裡的雪山像白色的波浪，

春天裡的草原就像毛毯一樣。

易文把西藏形容得像個世外桃源，真叫人心醉啊！可惜《一段情》這戲未能造成哄動，成績平平。

在《一段情》之後，易文開拍過一部清宮片《西太后與珍妃》（1964），西太后是李湄，光緒是雷震，珍妃則是台灣玉女明星張美瑤，喬宏演肅順，……大概那時我的其他配片工作不像從前那麼忙，向易文請纓當《西》片副導，記得這是部彩色片，我為了保險不出漏子，便把每場的佈景、服裝、演員的化裝和所用的道具等一律拍下彩色硬照，以存紀錄。清裝的頭飾又比較繁瑣，記錄不清，「連戲」就會出問題。雖說場記有責任記下來，但副導卻需負更大責任。這片雖也有兩首歌，但沒有甚麼突出的地方，我在實際拍攝工作的知識上，卻因而大有收穫。

易文又拍過一部歌舞片《鶯歌燕舞》（1963）。主演者我僅記得有葉楓，這位長腿美麗紅星，在拍《一段情》時，張揚對她朝思夜想（我記不起那時他倆是熱戀還是新婚），拍外景時，簡直大半在夢遊狀態。難怪古人

Between 1959 and 1960, Yue and Tao were negotiating their contracts. Both were not happy. Shaw Brothers offered them a better deal so they left MP & GI. I was still freelancing, so they asked me to compose music for their films. I worked for both directors until Shaw Brothers built a new studio in Clear Water Bay and set up a new policy of using only ready-made music in their films. The studio wanted to sign a contract with me, but it didn't work out. Tao was about to start shooting *Love Without End* (1961), but I had to give up the opportunity to concentrate on MP & GI productions.

Come to think of it, Robert Chung was rather stubborn. MP & GI lost its two major directors over a small amount of $2000 a film. Later, for unknown reasons, he even took up directing and made several films, including *Education of Love* (1961), *A Fine Romance* (1962), *Please Remember Me* (1964). I went to Taiwan with him for the location shooting of *A Fine Romance*. We stayed in the same hotel for 40 days and ate together. It was then I started to know him better, and this was the reason why I joined Rediffusion TV to work with him later.

From *A Fine Romance* to *Four Brave Ones*

There are two songs in *A Fine Romance*. Evan Yang wrote the lyrics for both. It was not until much later that I found out the lyric of one of the songs was based on love poems written by the 6th Dalai Lama 200 years ago. In the film, the song was sung by Zhu Mu, but I sang his part at recording, so I was composer, conductor and vocalist. This was not the first time I played a triple role. In *Little Darling*, there was a scene when Ting Hao was singing in a puppet show, and I sang for one of the puppets.

Another song in *A Fine Romance* was written in Tibetan folk music style. It was written at night while location shooting in Taiwan. I watched Tibetan folk dances and listened to their music, but I had never been to Tibet. I used Tibetan folk dance music for the

說，美人如玉，不錯，英雄氣短，也是真的。葉的聲音得天獨厚，是個次女高音，暗些、厚些，低些便更像白光。在《鶯》片中，葉大展歌喉，成績不弱，可惜我自問非寫這類音樂的材料，把全片歌曲弄得不倫不類。《鶯》片失敗，我難辭其咎！而此片是否亦影響及易文後來離開電懋，去台灣另求發展，但終於回港入邵氏當邵老闆秘書？則難於肯定。

《人之初》(1963) 為吳家驤首任導演的片，他真是隆而重之，抖擻精神上陣，對我說：「我想把〈天倫歌〉分三節來用，頭一段襯片頭字幕，一開場是個瓦簷，雨水在滴瀝滴瀝地下，然後字幕出來，第二節和末段，我會分開用在戲裡分段的地方（意即過場式插用）。」

〈天倫歌〉原是三十年代上海聯華影片《天倫》之主題歌，好像是女高音郎毓秀獨唱，僅鋼琴伴奏，詞是鍾石根，作曲的是我老師的老師黃自教授。這首電影歌早已編入《中國藝術歌曲全集》中，全中國中學生都唱過，至少也聽過的。

我再翻看黃作〈天倫歌〉原譜，在適當的地方分斷，分成三段，這一點不難，但原則上不能再以一具鋼琴來伴奏。在氣氛、氣派上，頭四句「人皆有父，翳我獨無，人皆有母，翳我獨無」保存女高獨唱，之後改為合唱，大合唱結束。

但片頭的瓦簷雨聲滴瀝怎辦？經過構思後，我跑去紅磡瓷器店買回大大小小百多隻瓷碗，用竹條兒串上一粒小珠，用以敲碗；便把那碗聲（是樂音）代替平常電影中的雨聲效果。碗聲經過頗費時的選擇，挑選好了便用墨筆在碗心寫下音名，以便錄音時，樂師（菲籍的）按譜敲打，還得示範如何輕擊，要平均，要漸強等等。這個片頭吳家驤特別設計，而我也配合他的要求來個特別設計。

三部綦湘棠參予作曲或配樂的電影：《雨過天青》、《溫柔鄉》、《情天長恨》。
Three films on which Kei Shang-tong worked: *For Better, For Worse; Bachelors Beware*; and *An Affair to Remember.*

順便提提唐煌的《諜海四壯士》(1963)，唐也指定用黃自寫的〈旗正飄飄〉合唱曲（韋瀚章詞），也要我分節來用。〈旗正飄飄〉原有合唱譜人聲部份不改動，原為鋼琴伴奏改編成大樂隊，並加Side Drum(小鼓，軍樂隊用的)，樂隊中注重用銅管樂，尤以Trumpet(長號)部份，應予突出使用。結果真是聲威大振，轟轟烈烈，豪氣干雲地表達了我師公原曲之曲情曲意！

很可惜，我改編黃自師公那兩首名曲，百代不會用(大概以為市場不需要)，未有把它們錄成唱片，這實在是很遺憾的事。

電懋營運走下坡

電懋營運狀況走下坡，公司中少了嘻哈笑聲，士氣當然不振，大家都悶在心裡，像受了委屈，有氣難伸。尤其是在女星群中，蘊釀風暴了，有指丁皓受捧在前，「電懋三小」之一的張慧嫻得寵於後，皆鍾波士之大過。於是平地生波，聯同起來向新加坡告狀，在這一發不可收拾之情勢下，鍾啟文逼得辭職引退。後來雖有泰哥(林永泰)接任掌舵，但電懋的局面，正合一句「將軍一去，大樹飄零」，寫到這兒，不禁唏噓歎息！

鍾的被逼引退，雖說是人事傾軋所致，我從另一角度看，卻認為以他大半個洋人似的性格，和為人誠信厚道(這和他家庭背景、學養、出身大有關係)，實在與當日電影圈的流風格格不入。

一件往事可佐證他的率真誠信。

那是在他離電懋後，當了麗的電視中文台總監的事。那天晚上大約十時左右，他興高采烈地拉我去新寧招待所酒吧坐坐，一坐下，便一臉愉快還急於要說甚麼似的樣子——老實說，鍾從來予人印象是嚴肅，不苟言笑，難

second half of the song, which was a dance number; but because the lyrics were in Mandarin, I had to modify the Tibetan music and wrote something similar. But Evan Yang's (Yi Wen) lyrics were very, very beautiful. He described Tibet as Shangri-la, an enchanting place. Unfortunately, the film didn't attract much attention. The box office was not exciting.

After *A Fine Romance*, Yang made *The Imperial Lady* (1964), a film about the imperial court of the Qing Dynasty. I volunteered to be assistant director. It was a colour film. To ensure nothing went wrong, I took colour photos of the set, costume, make up and props for record. The headdresses in Qing dynasty were quite complicated. Without a complete record, the continuity of the film would be affected. This film also had two songs, but both were unimpressive, but I did learn a lot about production from shooting the film.

The next film Yang made was *Mad about Music* (1963). It was a musical with Julie Yeh Feng (Ye Feng) in one of the leading roles. She had a beautiful voice, the voice of a mezzo-soprano. If her voice were more low-pitched and a bit tougher, she would sound like Bai Guang. Yeh revealed her singing talent in this film, and the result was promising. Unfortunately I was not good at that kind of music, and the songs were nondescript. I should be responsible for the failure of the film. But I was not sure whether this was the reason Yang left MP & GI for Taiwan and eventually ended up at Shaws.

Father and Son (1963) was Wu Jiaxiang's first film as director. He treated it with full vigour. He told me, "I want to divide 'The Song of Family' into three parts. The first is for the opening credits. When the film starts, there is a tile roof, with raindrops dripping on the ground, then roll the credits. The second and the last parts will be used as a transition between different sections of the film." "The Song of Family" was a well-known piece composed by my teacher's teacher Professor Huang Zi for *Song of China* (aka *Filial Piety*, a classic film of the 1930s. Almost every secondary school student knew it.

得露齒的；眼前的他，實在少有。他等侍者走開，才輕聲告我：「我剛跟（無線電視經理）Mr. 王吃過飯，大家談好君子協定，他們再不會向我們挖人了。」

好消息，真該慶祝慶祝！……但後來如何呢？那晚上，我見他那麼滿懷高興，實在不敢澆他冷水，當時我的感覺是：他和人家頭一次交手，頭一回見面，一頓飯，也許幾句話便敲定一樁大事。在我，就會是個問號了。

真是福無重至，禍不單行，就在鍾啟文辭職之後，大約一年多，陸運濤和夫人在台中墜機，那是 1964 年 6 月震驚星港台的大事。那日，鍾波士正在我家閒聊，一聽到電台播出噩耗，便頻頻電詢台北國際公司（電懋在台的發行總代理，其總經理夏維堂，亦因陪陸同機遇難）；如是焦急等候消息，屢說若仍在職的話，「我不讓他坐普通班機的，以他的身份，一定要用包機！」言下之意，乃怪罪於接待陸運濤的人，辦事輕忽、安排不善，以致造成這叫人婉惜、哀傷的慘劇。

數日後，電懋在亞洲片廠（在永華大門左旁山邊）設靈舉行追悼會。鍾啟文單獨親來弔唁，神情肅穆，行禮如儀；我見緊隨鍾後行禮的，竟然是岳楓和陶秦，兩位都是已離電懋的舊臣，相信他們當日仍會對故主情深，但已空留遺恨吧！我在人叢中，目睹此情此景，暗自悲嗟，真是欲語無言。

新加坡國泰機構在陸死後開董事會，要商討新決策，因電懋屬陸個人辦的，非機構之直屬公司，為今之計是否由機構接辦下去？傳聞有把電懋停辦之議，陸母陸老太以董事身份反對停辦，聲言電懋乃其子生前創辦的唯一事業，為了紀念他，不許將電懋結束。

I read the original score, and divided it into three parts. This was not difficult. But I could not only use a piano for accompaniment. For the right mood, I kept the first four verses sung by a soprano, and end the song with a chorus. To create the sound of raindrops on the tile roof, I brought back over a hundred bowls of different sizes from a ceramic shop in Hung Hom. I tied a small bead to a bamboo stick, and used it to tap on the bowl. The sound would be used as the effect of raining. It took some time to choose the bowls. When a bowl was chosen, I would mark the name of the note on the bowl for the musicians. The opening credits sequence was custom-tailored by Wu Jiaxiang, and I specially designed the music for him.

I also want to talk about *Four Brave Ones* (1963), directed by Tang Huang. He asked me to use another Huang Zi song and divide it into parts. The vocal part of the original chorus remained unchanged, but the piano accompaniment was rearranged into big band, with a side drum added. I emphasized the brasses, especially the trumpet. The result was a grand marching song with no distortion on the spirit and mood of the original song.

MP & GI's Decline

As business operations declined, there was less laughter in the office. Morale was low, but there was no outlet for complaints. There was jealousy among the actresses and Robert Chung was to blame. A formal complaint was sent to Singapore and Chung had to resign. Lam Wing-tai took over as the company's leader, but things were never quite the same again.

It was said that Chung's resignation was due to office politics. But viewing it from another angle, I would say it was because of Chung's personality. Being a sincere and honest gentleman, well educated and westernized, he was not a match for the film industry. The following incident is rather telling. During his Rediffusion days, he was director of the Chinese Channel. He invited me to a pub. It was about 10 p.m. He was excited and had something urgent to say. This was rare because he

跟着機構之副董事長連福明，派俞普慶來港任（過渡性）總經理，主持製片大計。其時導演陣容尚有易文、唐煌、王天林、袁秋楓、吳家驤（其後有孫家雯）等。這段時期頗為混亂，踏入寫字樓便有人事滄桑，今非昔比之感。

電懋改招牌稱國泰，最後一任的總經理是楊曼怡，他何時接任已不復憶，依稀記得他初來時，只稽核帳目，大概也在監察公司行政吧，那時電懋已呈頹勢了。其實，在林永泰任內，已呈敗象，最大問題是製片計劃外泄！弄到戲未開便讓邵氏搶先拍了。那時製片部仍是由宋淇領導。因為接連發生雙胞，公司中真弄得天下大亂。電懋像啞子吃黃蓮，有苦自己知，終於忍無可忍，和對手正面交鋒是黃梅調的《寶蓮燈》（1964），那時電懋總動員上下一心，全力以赴。

永華廠ABC三個影棚，燈光通明二十四小時拍攝，各導、各星均各有指派任務。總之，大家日夜均留在廠中，片一拍好，即沖即印，馬上看試片，剪好毛片，我即看，預備配樂前工夫（配樂由我負全責），看罷，分好要配樂的分段，部份給姚敏和李厚襄兩位分擔。三人合作配樂，恐是史無前例！到錄音當天，通宵開工，若樂譜尚未完成，樂隊依然坐在錄音室中等候，姚、李、我三人輪流各自指揮自己所寫的配樂，我也記不起第二天早上是何時收工的，只記得趕急回家睡一覺，醒來又入廠開工「混音」（把音樂和B copy之聲帶混合好，再印C copy發行）。那一戰，誰勝誰敗，已無意義；但那番拼搏精神，令總經理和片場小工一同捱到天亮。我覺得上下一心是電懋本色，電懋有凝聚力，應該大有前途，但內奸葬送了這麼一家好公司，奈何！

was a serious person and seldom smiled. After we ordered drinks, he whispered, "I just had dinner with Wang, the manager of TVB (Television Broadcast Limited). We had a gentleman's agreement. He promised not to raid our staff." I didn't want to discourage him, so I kept silent. He met a person for the first time, and made an important agreement on the dinner table. If I were him, I definitely would not trust that person.

About a year after Robert Chung resigned, Loke Wan Tho and his wife died in a plane crash in Taichung. It was a great shock in Singapore, Hong Kong and Taiwan. Chung was at my home when we heard the news on the radio. He called International in Taipei many times. "If I were still there, I would only fly him in chartered flights," he said. A few days later, MP & GI held a memorial service in Asia Studio. Chung went to pay his respects, all by himself, followed by Yue Feng and Tao Qin. They had left the company for some time, but had not forgotten their old boss.

After Loke's death, there were rumours that MP & GI would be closed. But Loke's mother objected. MP & GI was the only career his son established and she wouldn't allow them to close it down.

Later MP & GI was restructured into Cathay Organisation (Hong Kong). MP & GI was already on the decline. In fact, it started when Lam Wing-tai was still manager. Its project plans kept leaking. Shaws would make the film before we even started. Soong was still producer. It was not long after that it declared war on its competitor and made the *huangmei diao* film *The Magic Lamp* (1964). MP & GI pooled the efforts of all their staff in their struggle for survival.

We shot around the clock at the three Yung Hwa studios. Films were developed immediately, rushes edited, and I would add the music. Yao Min and Li Houxiang would help too. That was probably the first time we three composers worked for one film. We would work overnight, the band waiting for the unfinished pieces to come. Yao, Li and I conducted our

末了，我個人在電懋最後兩片的工作，也許是易文的《最長的一夜》(1965)，特別向日本借來紅星寶田明來任男主角；另一是抗日戰爭片《草莽喋血記》(1966)，兩片均有歌，算是不過不失之作，那時我在國泰已是意興闌珊，只等約滿，因鍾啟文已在1963年為麗的開辦了香港首創的中文電視，早已邀我過去再度合作了。

附記

〔一〕我與電懋約滿為1963年6月，但1966年還再為李翰祥之《冬暖》配樂，（此片交國泰發行）。時李已在台開辦國聯公司，債務纏身，亟待《冬暖》配妥，發行可還些債。李央我配合，儘快配成，但我在麗的日間要上班，只能夜間寫作，其時，我又戒了吸香煙惡習，故這次寫作過程苦不堪言，終於用了四十多夜才寫成。《冬暖》乃我配樂的最後一部電影了。

回味個人的配樂生涯，苦雖苦，其中卻樂趣無窮。寫作時整個人投入劇中，簡直不知現實的人間何在。一部配完，翌日即出海釣魚「洗腦」；兩三天後，又再迎接新的，不同風格的，不同故事、背景的……，部部都是新挑戰。可惜戰了十多年，配過多少部電影我記不清了。但全部都是「劣貨」，那是肯定的。終於，我疲倦了，提早解甲改行了。

〔二〕今年(2001)看過李安的《臥虎藏龍》，非常非常欣賞譚盾的配樂。個人孤陋寡聞，在記憶中，國語片的配樂（大陸的除外，因少看到），以《臥》片最佳，譚盾真行！片中一場屋頂躍奔，導、演、攝、剪、樂……均一流的，其妙處在乎節奏，而樂配得真好絕啊！

綦湘棠，電懋主要電影配樂與作曲家。
Kei Shang-tong, major composer for MP & GI film music.

own pieces. I don't remember when we finished recording, only that I rushed home to get some sleep before going back for the mixing. Who won the war? It really doesn't matter anymore, but the fighting spirit of the staff was impressive. With such morale, MP & GI should have a bright future if it was not for the traitors.

My last MP & GI films were *The Longest Night* (1965) and *The Fugitive* (1966). The songs I wrote for them were OK but not exceptional. No longer enthusiastic, I accepted Chung's invitation to join Rediffusion once my contract expired. We had another chance to work together again.

Postscript

1. My contract with MP & GI expired in June 1963, but I composed for Li Hanxiang's *The Winter* in 1966 (the film was distributed by Cathay). Li urged me to finish the score quickly so he could generate income from distribution. I was working full time at Rediffusion and could only work at night. That was also the period I quit smoking, so the process was painful. It took me over 40 nights to finish the job. *The Winter* was the last film I scored.

2. I am very impressed by Tan Dun's film music in *Crouching Tiger, Hidden Dragon* (2000). In my memory, this is the best score among Mandarin films (apart from Mainland Chinese films, which I seldom watch). The direction, acting, cinematography, editing, music… etc. in the chase sequence on the rooftop was great, creating a wonderful rhythm. And the music? Simply impeccable!

Translated by Grace Ng

朱美蓮：國泰與我

生於電影之家

我在 1950 年 10 月 27 日生於馬來西亞的吉隆坡。對於電影，最早的記憶大概是跟着爸爸到電影院。那時候，爸爸協助他的大舅陸運濤打理在馬來西亞的戲院。我們在吉隆坡有三家戲院，一家中文，兩家英文，而爸爸通常在晚飯後，會帶着我到戲院視察。

另外就是電影節、影展。那時我很迷電影，特別是電懋的電影，基本上那時只看電懋作品。還記得 1959 年在吉隆坡舉行的亞洲影展，九歲的我負責向步下飛機的明星獻花，看見他們走出來，我很是興奮，特別是看到我的偶像尤敏。

我媽媽（陸婉婷）是陸運濤的妹妹，爸爸（朱國良）就是他妹夫。外祖父陸佑十四歲時乘船到了星洲，再到馬來西亞當錫場礦工，所以子女都在大馬出生。陸運濤生

Portrait by Willie Tang

Last Person Carrying the Torch: Meileen Choo on Cathay's Family Legacy

Born into the Film Industry

I was born on 27th October 1950, Kuala Lumpur, Malaysia. My first memories of film were probably things like going to the cinemas with my father, who was at that time helping his brother-in-law, Loke Wan Tho, to look after the operation in Malaysia. My dad used to go to the cinemas after dinner to make spot checks. We had three cinemas in Kuala Lumpur, one Chinese and two English halls.

Another kind of memory was film festivals. I remember the Asian Film Festival held in Kuala Lumpur in 1959. In those days, I was very much into movies, especially the Cathay movies. Actually, those were about the only films that I watched. I was crazy about Lucilla You Min. I was nine years old and used to be the flower girl presenting bouquets to the stars when they arrived at the airport. When the stars came, I was very excited. I finally got the chance to see my idol You Min!

My mother (Choo Yuen Theng / Lu Wanling) is Loke's sister, so my father (Choo Kok Leong / Zhu Guoliang)

於吉隆坡，他留學回來才到新加坡定居。我父母、舅舅都是馬來西亞籍，直至新加坡獨立。

外祖父很早便去世，那時媽媽只有一歲，舅舅兩歲。有關他的事跡，都是從外婆口中得知。外婆（林淑佳）是外祖父第四任太太，她比外祖父年青很多。外祖父死後，業務便由她打理，後來再由陸運濤繼承。外婆是個了不起的商人，她在1937年策建國泰大廈，成為當時新加坡最高的建築物。〔1〕她更是開創國泰電影事業的人；她購入了第一家電影院，〔2〕原作為地產的投資，當時舅舅仍在劍橋唸書，後來學成歸來，對電影大感興趣，致力發展。陸運濤和外祖母的關係很好，他們常常一起談生意經，而負責決策的還是陸運濤。

至於我父親那邊，我們已是第四代華僑，曾祖父由中國大陸移居馬來西亞，祖父在大馬出生。

電懋的黃金時代

陸運濤時代的電懋可說是最光輝的黃金時代，就像文藝復興。電懋備受注目，亦因他的緣故——陸運濤有他的魅力，他興趣廣泛，熱愛觀鳥、人文、藝術，博覽群書。他喜愛成為眾人注目的中心，樂於參加各種影展活動。電懋與旗下的明星一樣光芒四射。他人緣好，圈中不少演員、導演，甚至外國名人如希治閣，都跟他相熟。

在他領導之下，電懋的聲名日隆，電影屢獲獎項，更捧紅了不少明星，如尤敏、葛蘭、葉楓等。當時的演員制度與今天有別，比較像荷里活，明星都簽到我們旗下。他們注重形象，不會隨便在普通地方吃飯，彷彿高不可攀。舅舅最喜歡尤敏和葛蘭，葛蘭聰慧，尤敏個性獨特，甜美可人。

五十年代的陸運濤夫婦與希治閣、占士史超域及金露華合照

Loke Wan Tho and wife Christine with James Stewart, Alfred Hitchcock and Kim Novak.

is his brother-in-law. My grandfather on my mother's side, Loke Yew, landed in Singapore and went to work in Malaysia. He was only fourteen then. So his children were all born in Malaysia. Loke Wan Tho was born in Kuala Lumpur. After his studies, he came back and settled in Singapore. My uncle, my father and my mother were Malaysian, until Singapore became independent.

Loke Yew passed away very early, when my mother was one and my uncle two. It was grandmother (Lim Cheng Kim / Lin Shujia) who told us his stories. She was his fourth wife, much younger. When he passed away, she took up the business before Loke Wan Tho came in.

Grandmother was a great businesswoman. She built Cathay Building, the tallest building in Singapore in 1937. [1] In fact, she was the the founder of Cathay Organisation. She bought the first cinema as a property play, when my uncle was still in Cambridge. [2] He liked it when he came back and expanded the business.

The relationship between Loke and his mother was very close. He talked a lot to her about business. But it was always his decision.

Loke Wan Tho and MP & GI's Glamour Days

Cathay under Loke Wan Tho had its glamorous days, somewhat like the Renaissance . It was very much in focus, because of Loke. My uncle had a certain charisma. He was well known for lots of things. He was interested in anthropology, ornithology, and in art. He was well-read. He took part in film festivals and enjoyed the limelight. In those days, MP & GI and our stars were very glamorous. He knew people personally and he was friendly. He knew people like Alfred Hitchcock.

In terms of creating an image for Cathay, he was very successful. A lot of films were awarded and he created many stars such as You Min, Grace Chang (Ge Lan), Julie Yeh Feng (Ye Feng). The system was very much like Hollywood. The stars were contracted to us. They couldn't go out to eat ordinary food, like the stars today. They were

陸運濤與荷里活、香港和大馬的影人、商人都有合作，例如馬來西亞商人何亞祿，他在大馬有些小院線，陸運濤便與他合作院線和合拍馬來語電影。高峰時期，我們擁有的戲院達八十家。電懋的電影主要在星、馬上映，亦賣埠至緬甸、越南、泰國等地，林黛還到過曼谷參加首影禮。所以在東南亞地區，電懋的中文片都為人熟悉。

在我眼中，舅父是紳士一名，在商場上，特別是競爭激烈的電影行業，有時會吃虧。在商言商，電懋經營不易，真正賺錢的電影寥寥可數，電懋外表風光，但實際上卻刻苦經營。

家父是公司董事，對電影方面的日常參與並不多，雖然出埠時也會視察業務。他協助舅父打理在馬來西亞的業務，包括橡膠園和其他的生意，也兼顧電影業務。他是一個很好的副手，協助打理，管理財政，例如當舅父説香港那邊的財政有甚麼需要，他會馬上想法子，把事情弄妥。他從不是決策者，但默默支持。事實上，在家族裡，陸運濤被視為一家之主，各人對他都很支持，他突然離世，對外婆、媽媽的打擊很大。

六四年空難

1964 年，我十四歲，記得那晚父母和我正在家裡看電視，快要吃宵夜之際，吉隆坡一個職員來電話，告訴我們台灣空難的消息，陸運濤夫婦和一班高層人員從台灣回來的飛機墜毀。那是半夜一、兩點，父母第一時間駕車到新加坡，守在外婆身邊。然後由父親去台灣辨認遺體，處理後事，安排把骨灰運回馬來西亞，在吉隆坡舉行大型的葬禮。那兩個禮拜我們就在震驚、傷痛中度過。

陸運濤和一班高層遇難去世，國泰公司一片黑暗，正如所有電影公司都與其創辦人緊緊相連，如梅鐸和霍士、邵逸夫和邵氏、陸運濤和電懋，陸去世後，電懋一片混

unattainable. He created all that. You Min, Grace Chang were my uncle's favourites. My uncle thought that Chang was intelligent and You had a fantastic character; her nature was very sweet.

MP & GI films mainly travelled in Malaysia, Singapore. He also sold films to Burma, Vietnam, and Thailand. So people in Southeast Asia got to know Cathay mainly through Chinese films.

My uncle had connections with Hollywood, Hong Kong and had partnerships with people like Ho Ah Loke, a Malaysian businessman who had a small chain of cinemas and was making Malay films. At its peak, we had about 80 cinemas.

My uncle is a gentleman. He used both his own funds and also that of some of his Malaysian and Singapore companies to finance MP & GI. In the film business, he was too gentlemanly. It's quite a cut-throat business and too many people took advantage of him because of his character. In terms of business, it was very difficult. Not many of the films were profitable. I think it's a paradox. The image of MP & GI was very successful, but in real terms, it was struggling. Business was tough.

My father was a Director in the company, but he was not actively involved in day-to-day operation of the film business. He would keep an eye on it and he would check whenever he travelled through. He looked after all my uncle's interests in Malaysia, like rubber plantations and other businesses, not only cinema. He was a very good second person, to do run around and to manage finance. For example, if my uncle needed to send money to Hong Kong, my father would come up to see how to get things organised. He was never on the forefront, not a decision maker, but rather a supporter. In my family, every body was supportive for my uncle. He was regarded as head of the family. So when he died, her mother and her sister were devastated.

The 1964 Accident

I was 14 at the time. I remember that my parents and I were watching Roger Moore on TV and the programme had just finished. We were going to have supper. Then

亂。當時我們可以做的是，馬上找人填補高層人員的位置，另外又要向合作夥伴、發行商保證公司不會倒下去。爸爸親自去了美國一趟，會見主要電影公司、國際發行商的負責人，介紹自己，並保證國泰運作如常。

電懋結業的傳聞到處流傳，在最困難的時期，我們還是熬了過來。

璀璨轉趨平淡

家父與舅父很不同，他修讀農科，對種植橡膠的熱衷多於搞電影，接下電影這個攤子，他其實老大不願意。舅父喜歡宣傳，是風頭人物，家父的為人則比較低調，對他來說，參加影展這種東西更是可免則免。國泰變得不一樣，家父集中基本的工作，搞好管理，而不是搞宣傳、形象。昔日的光芒，像片場、明星，最後都通通黯淡下來，國泰變得低調，更像一盤生意，我們不再走在前線，慢慢的靜下來。

1971年國泰結束片場，轉為專注電影的發行。作出這樣的決定，可謂情非得已。舅父去世後，我們從新加坡派了兩人過去（香港），包括製作經理俞普慶，另一位是會計出身的楊曼怡，卻不是電影業的材料，最後都沒搞好，公司決定停產。決定結束製片部和片廠的時候，剛好鄒文懷脫離邵氏，自立門戶（嘉禾），我們遂把片廠轉讓給他，而鄒的影片亦透過我們作國際發行，李小龍的電影，就是由我們發行到星馬。

到八十年代，在新的經濟政策下，華人公司需出售百份之三十的股份給馬來人，加上盜版猖獗，國泰終於結束在馬來西亞的業務。1983年重返大馬的時候，今非昔比，我們在策略上亦作出改變，以前國泰的戲院遍佈馬來西亞大城小鎮，而現在只有在大城市才有我們的院線。我們對電影的熱情亦不如陸運濤的時代，生意轉向多方面發展。

朱國良與《The Bonanza》男主角米高蘭頓攝於派拉蒙片廠（1966）

Choo Kok Leong with Michael Landon on the *Bonanza* set in 1966.

the phone call came. One of our staff at Kuala Lumpur who had connection with the press said there had been a plane crash in Taiwan and my uncle and his wife plus a lot of our senior executives were on the flight. It was one or two a.m. The first thing my parents did was to drive down to Singapore, to be with my grandmother. My father then went to Taiwan, to identify my uncle and aunt's bodies and to make arrangements for the ashes to be brought back. There was a huge funeral in Kuala Lumpur, and the two weeks were traumatic for us.

It was quite a dark period, after Loke and the executives died in the accident. I think every film company is closely tied to the person at the top, like Murdoch and Fox, Run Run Shaw and Shaws, Loke and Cathay. When Loke passed away, nobody knew where we would go. We lost many executives and we had to find replacements. We had to assure our partners and film distributors that the company must go on. My father made a very long trip to the US, met with all the major studios and international distribution heads, to introduce himself and to assure that Cathay was still in the business.

Rumours were flying around, saying that we were going to close. We went through tough time, but we survived.

Back to the Bottom Line

My father, also a gentleman, was very different from Loke. He had his training in agriculture and was basically a rubber planter. He was more interested in it than in films. It was with great reluctance that he went into the business. My uncle enjoyed publicity; my father did not. He tried to avoid it. He was quite a shy man. For him, attending film festivals would be a big burden. Cathay under him was very different. My father concentrated on bottom work, cleaning up messes, streamlining things, rather than on image building. Cathay became very subdued. We sold out all the glamorous things, stars, studios. It was more a business than an image, or studio. We were no longer propelled to the forefront. We did enjoy being quieter and more "bottom-lined".

把家族生意上市

家父退休後，我在1985年接手國泰機構的業務，家父直至去世前兩年，仍不時到公司來。他在1996年辭世，享年八十六歲。我們父女關係很好，就如朋友一樣。我跟父親很相似，同樣害羞，怕成為眾人注目的對象，我想，我不是繼承國泰的適當人選，只是命運使然。如果舅父不是這樣突然去世，我可能會以記者為業。

到我接手的時候，國泰的形勢已不甚好，買片方面，中西電影，國泰仍具競爭力，但我們已負債纍纍，環境、情勢亦已不一樣。舅父曾害怕電視的出現會影響電影，但電視來了，人們仍看電影，我們還是生存下來，但後來競爭的形式已不一樣，不同的娛樂相繼出現，盜版的問題更是失控。

這樣的形勢下，我的策略是盡量不與競爭者硬碰，例如，現在我們與邵氏之間，存着的是良性競爭，這在舅父那競爭白熱化的年代是不可能的。我們重新定位，多元發展，國泰仍保留電影業的一個角色，但電影不再是核心業務，我們發展新的業務，例如地產及向海外投資。國泰現在是上市公司，而我是大股東，家族其他成員好像已沒再擁有國泰的股份，最後這關，由我一人守着。

國泰兩年前在新加坡股票交易所上市。把它上市一直是舅父的心願，只是他在生的時候形勢不許可，後來他又不幸去世。我從來沒把國泰看作是自己的，它屬於舅父陸運濤，上市可以保證在我離開後，公司仍可延續，因為最重要的，是延續他這份事業。

We sent two Singaporeans there: Paul Yui (Yu Puqing), as head of production; the other person Yeo Ban Yee (Yang Manyi) was accountant by profession. They were not cut out to manage all that and it was a mess. It was better if we stopped production. In 1971 we closed down our studios and Cathay concentrated on distribution. When we wanted to close the studio, Raymond Chow was parting with Shaws and he needed an outlet. Cathay opened its door to him. He took over our studio and we distributed his films. We have all the international distributions, all the Bruce Lee films.

In the 1980s, Cathay terminated its business in Malaysia because of the new economic policy. We had to sell 30% of the shares to the Malay people. Piracy was rampart. Business was going down. We had to divert our business out of Malaysia.

We came back in 1983. Our strategy had changed. In the old days, we had cinemas everywhere. Now we only have them in the major cities. Our interest in the film business is not as keen as my uncle and his original business became fragmented.

From Family Business to Public Company

After my father retired in 1985, I took over the business. He still came to the office, until two years before he passed away. He passed away in 1996 at the age of 86. We had a very good father-daughter relationship, just like friends. I am the continuation of my father. I, too, shy away from the limelight. I don't think I was meant to be the person taking over Cathay. It is just fate and circumstances.

Cathay at that time was not in terribly good shape. It was still competitive in terms of buying films, both English and Chinese. We were also in debt. Times were different. My uncle was afraid of the expansion of TV. But when TV came, we survived as cinema was still an entertainment that people would go to. But now, competition comes in different forms. Piracy is something beyond our control. There are a lot more other forms of entertainment.

My strategy now is, first of all, to try not to fight as much with my competitors. We can say that our competition with Shaws is more friendly now. And we

在我看來，家族事業不一定由子女繼承，由家族建立起來的國泰，最好以上市公司的形式延續，後人可以股東的身份擁有股權，而公司則應由專業人才經營管理。雖然身為國泰的主席，我現在已是半退休，我只負責訂立一些公司的政策和方向，管理的職責落在總裁黃顯輝身上，他是專業人士，與我們家族毫無關係。

重投電影製作

1995年，經過多時的沉寂，新加坡的本地電影製作開始復蘇。我受邀去看一齣名為《新新兵小傳》(1996）的本地劇作，看後感到它很有潛質。不少新加坡人曾服兵役，當中不乏有趣之處，定能搔中觀眾的笑穴。這影片我們需要得到國防部的協助拍攝，製作期間牽涉不少麻煩，他們起初十分謹慎，因為政府當局恐怕有損形象；不過，亦由於是與新加坡空軍合作，我們等於有一班包括正規和後備軍人等的「現成」觀眾，宣傳也乘勢鋪天蓋地展開。另外，導演和編劇都是星洲演藝界中的知名人物，電視訪問和宣傳等都很容易安排。電影作小規模公映後得到很好的口碑，成為最好的宣傳。《新新兵小傳》的成本約八十萬坡幣，票房收入達一百五十萬，是當時的一個紀錄。

第二套是與徐克的電影工作室的聯合製作。施南生和我是多年好友，我本人亦很欣賞徐克的作品。我當時到了香港，施南生給我看了幾段動畫電影《小倩》(1997)的片段，動畫的質素很高，給我很深的印象。我想：日本動畫在香港大行其道，但本地已很久沒有拍攝過中文動畫，加上年前《倩女幽魂》(1987）電影的成功……於是我決定投資這部電影。我們投資了七十五萬美金作為製作成本，結果影片在新加坡收了六十萬坡幣，我們並包辦日本以外的國際發行權。

refocused and diversified our business. Cathay is always part of the film industry, but cinema is not our main business. We develop new businesses, like property development. We also have investments overseas. Cathay is now a public company. I'm the major shareholder, but I don't think any other members of the family have shares anymore. So I'm the last person carrying the torch.

Cathay is listed on the Singapore stock exchange starting two years ago. It was my uncle's wish, but because of other circumstances during his time, and his unfortunate death, we couldn't go public then. For some strange reasons, I never consider Cathay as mine. It belongs to my uncle. The public issue came to ensure its continuity when I am gone. It is important to keep his legacy.

I do not believe that children should inherit all the assets. The Cathay built by a family should continue as a public company. People can own it by being shareholders, but it should be managed by professionals. I'm now semi-retired. Being the Chairman of Cathay, I am only involved in policy-making and direction of the company. We have a CEO, Wong Heang Fine, who manages the company now. He is a professional, not related to us in any way.

New Ventures

In 1995, local film production was starting to come alive again. I was invited to watch a local play entitled *Army Daze* (1996). I felt there was potential. So many Singaporeans had been through National Service and a comedy on the funnier aspects of it might hit the right target. The production was fraught with many problems because I needed the assistance of the Ministry of Defense. They were very wary in the beginning because Singapore authorities do not like to be portrayed with the wrong image. The marketing was extensive as we tied up with the Singapore Armed Forces, a ready made audience of full-time and reservist personnel. Both director and scriptwriter are well known personalities in the entertainment industry in Singapore, so interviews and TV appearances were arranged easily. After the initial sneaks, word of mouth

《哪個不夠》(梁智強自導自演，1999)是另一齣由我們製作的電影。話說我被檳州政府邀請作檳城影展的嘉賓，在往檳城的機上，梁智強就坐在我的鄰座。梁智強是新加坡的喜劇演員，正籌備一齣本地製作。他主持的綜合節目很成功，又寫了不少劇本。我當時問他有沒有興趣自編自導一齣電影，因為我覺得他很有潛質，他初執導筒亦會成為傳媒和我們做電影宣傳的一個話題。不久，他自己編劇及主演的《錢不夠用》(T.L.Tay 導演，1998)一片面世，獲得空前的成功，更是到目前為止最成功的本地製作。後來，我們拍的《哪個不夠》成本是八十萬坡幣，票房收了一百二十萬，《哪個不夠》在馬來西亞和台灣都有上映，可惜成績不如理想。

構思基金，放眼將來

不過，我們的目標不只是新加坡市場。新加坡近年來一直嘗試搞好電影業，可是，我們並沒有特別的外景場地，要拍城市景，不必來新加坡；拍戰爭片的話，不如選菲律賓、泰國、馬來西亞。其次，這裡沒有一個創意的環境。藝術、創意是最主要的問題，而這些東西需時間培養發展，不可一蹴即就。劇本就更是新加坡電影的一個大問題。這裡的人又不願意當技術員，總之，前路遙遙。

再加上國際市場對星洲電影的興趣不大，這裡市場太小，要打入外國市場，非得要和外面合資製作。對於未來的計劃，我希望能製作一些打進國際(西方)市場的電影，我在構思一個電影基金，新加坡是集資的好地

少年朱美蓮與父母親參觀片廠

The teenage Meileen Choo visiting the studio with her father, Choo Kok Leong.

helped to sell the film on its own. *Army Daze* was made at a cost of SG$ 800,000 and the box office collection was SG$ 1.5M, a record at the time.

Our second film was a co-production with Tsui Hark's Film Workshop. Nansun Shi has been a friend of mine for a very long time and I have always had great admiration for Tsui Hark's work. I was in Hong Kong on a trip and Nansun showed me a few scenes of *A Chinese Ghost Story – The Tsui Hark Animation* (1997) and I was very impressed by the quality of the animation. Again I thought of the odds that were in favour of this project – the popularity of Japanese animation in Hong Kong, the first Chinese animation film in a very long time, a story that had proved successful as a feature film *A Chinese Ghost Story* (1987) some years earlier – and decided to invest in it. Our share of the production cost was US$ 750,000 and the box office takings in Singapore were SG$ 600,000. We cover all international rights except Japan.

Another film we produced was *That One No Enough* (1999). I was invited as a guest of the Penang State Government to a film festival there. On the flight I sat next to Jack Neo, a local comedian. He was in the midst of making a local film. I knew of the success of his television variety show and knew that he had written many of the scripts himself. I asked if he's interested in writing a script and directing it himself. I felt he had the potential and his directorial debut would give the film another aspect for the press to write about and for us to market the film. Shortly after, his film (*Money No Enough*, 1998) was released to tremendous success – it is the most successful local production to date. The cost of *That One No Enough*, which Neo directed, was SG$ 800,000 and the box office collection was SG$ 1.2M. The film was also released in Malaysia and Taiwan but unfortunately did not do well there.

History Will Judge

Singapore is trying to create a local film industry in the last couple of years. However, we don't have locations, we don't have an environment of creativity, though it's changing, we don't have technicians. Singapore films

方。我期望將來國泰能推動一個拍攝高質素亞洲電影的基金；此外，我亦希望找到資金重拍國泰的經典電影，如《星星‧月亮‧太陽》(1961)。亞洲電影在國際很有潛力，《臥虎藏龍》(2000)便是一個例子。如果這個基金可以實現，我會計劃到中國，或韓國拍攝影片。

我們在影業、星馬電影的角色，就由歷史來評價吧，一般人都當局者迷，我希望放遠目光，我關心的不只是國泰的未來，而是整個電影行業的去向。

訪問：何思穎(2001年12月12日於新加坡及其後電郵通訊)；整理及翻譯：周淑賢

編按

[1] 國泰大樓位於Dhoby Ghaut，地盤於1937年落實，建築設計包括電影院。國泰戲院於1939年10月3日開始啟用。詳見Lim Kay Tong: *Cathay ——55 Years of Cinema*, Singapore: Landmark Books, 1991, p. 97.

[2] 陸佑夫人於1936年創辦吉隆坡光藝戲院(Pavilion Theatre)。

don't have overseas appeal. The market is too small. You need to go to co-productions for overseas market. Singapore is not a market that we are targeting for. We hope to make films that will travel to the West. I hope I can create a film fund. Singapore's strength is its financial strength. I hope Cathay will one day develop a fund to make Asian films, good quality films. There is a lot of potential for Asian films. *Crouching Tiger, Hidden Dragon* (2000) is an example. We are also looking into remaking of Cathay classics, like *Sun, Moon and Star* (1961).

History will judge what my role is, or my role in Singapore film history. A lot of people just care what is important in their own context, but for me, I look at a bigger picture – not only Cathay, but the entire film industry.

Based on interview by Sam Ho on December 12, 2001 in Singapore and further e-mail communications. Collated by Sarah Chau.

Editor's notes

[1] The Cathay Building, with a theatre in it, started construction in 1937. The building opened officially on 3 October, 1939. Lim Kay Tong: *Cathay – 55 Years of Cinema*, Singapore: Landmark Books, 1991, p. 97.

[2] Mrs Loke Yew established the Pavilion Theatre in 1936 in Kuala Lumpur.

國泰片場最後歲月：一個小工的回憶

- 石琪 -

我在國泰片場工作過，直至 1971 年停業遣散，雖然只是美工部一個小工，但也算親身經歷過香港國泰製片廠的最後一段歲月。

進入國泰，大概是 1968 年末吧？那時唐書璇剛在這片場拍完《董夫人》（1970）（是她獨立製作，不是國泰出品）。還記得初上班時，聽到片場中人嘲笑唐書璇，說她過了鐘無錢補水，就哀求工作人員延遲下班，拍完預定鏡頭才走，他們當然不理睬。又說她請來的印度攝影師自大兼亂搞，不知拍甚麼！

那時我已經在《中國學生周報》電影版投稿，認識了主編羅卡、一些青年文友和電影發燒友，還拍短片了，想入片場體驗和學習一下。介紹我入國泰的就是周報文友亦舒，她在國泰編劇部工作。當年亦舒和蔡浩泉住在彌敦道，我就跟她在彌敦道搭巴士到彩虹邨，再上斧山道

永華片場大門
The front gate of Yung Hwa.

The Last Days of Cathay Studio: Memories of a Young Assistant

- Sek Kei -

I was working at the Cathay Studio when it closed in 1971. Though I was just a young assistant in the art department, I did have some personal experiences of the Cathay Studio in its last days.

I started at Cathay probably in 1968. Shu Shuen (Tang Shuxuan) had just finished shooting there *The Arch* (1970) (it was independently produced by Shu). I remembered hearing people laughing at her back, that she couldn't afford overtime pay, so she urged the crew to stay until all the shots were finished. Of course no one listened. And they said her Indian cinematographer was pompous and didn't know what he was doing!

I was writing for *The Chinese Student Weekly* and met editor Law Kar, other young writers and assorted film buffs there. I was making short films and wanted to work at a studio to gain some experience. Isabel Ni (Yi Shu), a fellow writer at the *Weekly* who was working at the Cathay's script department, introduced me. She and Cai Haoquan were living on Nathan Road, so I took the bus with her from Nathan Road to Choi

片場，去見編劇部主任董千里。（多年後提起，亦舒好像不記得這回事，我也不知道她在國泰有沒有編過劇，總之她在國泰時間不長。）

接着見到總經理楊曼怡和從義大利讀電影回來的孫家雯。我本來想做場記，但他們說場記要女不要男，知道我會畫公仔，就叫我到美工部，幫年輕佈景師趙德克的手。從來才發現「上當」，因為隨後也陸續進入國泰的周報朋友吳宇森、林年同和金炳興，都做了場記，然後做副導演。還有小克，也跑來做場記，他們都是男的，不是女的。或者後來制度有變吧？

說起孫家雯，我們當時都讀過他在《新晚報》寫義大利留學經歷，知道他是貝托魯奇的同學，劉芳剛和白景瑞亦和他同時在義大利讀電影。孫家雯在國泰很活躍，不久劉芳剛也做了國泰導演。到國泰結束後，林年同、金炳興輾轉跑到義大利讀電影，連周報編輯羅卡也去了。

那時，我們崇拜義大利電影大師如維斯康堤、安東尼奧尼，而意大利西部片、性喜劇、神偷妙賊片亦在香港叫座。但國泰始終沒有「義大利化」，反而七八十年代麥嘉、洪金寶的影片走紅，顯然受到不少義大利舊片的影響。

入了美工部，就發現和實際拍片是兩個世界。我們準備好佈景，他們才來打燈擺機拍攝。我們工作完畢他們才開工，一開工便關廠門亮紅燈，想看也難。當然可以抽空混進去看看，但打燈擺機一弄便幾小時，悶死人，所以我後來寧願一心做觀眾，因為實際拍片很悶。

坦白說，進國泰之前，我很少看國泰電影，連國泰前身電懋的影片也看得不多，不喜歡那種舊式片場拍法。當然，電懋曾經很光彩，星光熠熠，載歌載舞，不過我入

Hung, then went to the studio on Hammer Hill Road to see Dong Qianli, head of the script department. (Years later, Ni had no recollection of the incident. I'm not sure if she had written any scripts at Cathay, only that she worked there briefly.)

Then I met general manager Yeo Ban Yee (Yang Manyi) and Sun Jiawen, who just finished studying film in Italy. I wanted to be a continuity person, but they wanted a woman. They knew I could draw, so they sent me to the art department, to assist the young set designer Chiu Tak-hak. Later I found I was "cheated", because other male *Weekly* writers like John Woo, Lin Nien-tung and Kam Ping-hing managed to work in continuity and later became assistant directors. Perhaps the system had later changed.

Talking about Sun Jiawen, we had read about his Italian experiences on *The New Evening Post* and knew he studied with Bernado Bertolucci. Liu Fanggang and Bai Jingrui were also there. Sun was very active in Cathay and soon Liu Fanggang also became a director there. After Cathay closed, Lin, Kam and editor Law Kar eventually left for Italy to study film.

We admired Italian masters like Visconti and Antonioni. Spaghetti westerns, Italian sex comedies and heist films were also popular in Hong Kong. However, Cathay never "Italianized", yet traits of Italian classics can be found in 1970s and 1980s made popular by Karl Maka and Sammo Hung.

Working in the art department, I found it totally different from actual filmmaking. The crew only came to set the lights after we were done with the sets. Studio doors were locked and the red light turned on when shooting started. Of course we could sneak in, but setting lights took hours, and I was bored. Since then, I have chosen to watch films instead, because filmmaking is so dull.

To be honest, I seldom saw Cathay movies, even those by MP & GI. I didn't because I didn't like those traditional studio productions. Certainly, MP & GI had

陳曼玲
Melinda Chen Man-ling

its golden days, with many big stars, and those wonderful musicals. But by the time I was there, those glory days were over. Big stars like Grace Chang (Ge Lan), Lucilla You Min, Julie Yeh Fung (Ye Feng), Kitty Ting Hao (Ding Hao), Li Mei, and even Christine Pai Lu-ming (Bai Luming) were gone. It was a time of transition. The remaining stars were no longer popular and newcomers like Maggie Li Linlin, Hilda Chou Hsuan (Zhou Xuan) and Charles Chin (Qin Xianglin) were not quite stars yet. Now only few people still remember Melinda Chen Man-ling, the most popular Cathay star at that time.

The art department was headed by Bao Tianming, a veteran set designer from Shanghai. He looked a little like SAR Chief Excecutive Tung Chee-hwa. He came to work wearing a suit and tie, carrying his own lunch thermos. Many film veterans would come visit him and talked about old times in Shanghainese. (They were usually not scriptwriters, directors or actors, but belonging to the variety of studio roles that were beyond outsiders' understanding.) Bao's story about shooting the classic *Sorrows of the Forbidden City* (1948) was impressive. The film was made in the former Yung Hwa studio, and Bao was responsible for the sets. He went to the Imperial Palace in Beijing, took photos, made drawings and measured the palace, then built a replica in the studio with great details. In the emperor's scene at the ancestral temple, the lighting should go through the window frame, but the effect couldn't be obtained. So a piece of glass was placed in front of the camera, with lines of sunlight delicately hand-painted on it to create the effect.

At the time *Sorrows of the Forbidden City* was criticized in China and someone seized the opportunity to re-release the film in Hong Kong. Bao was sad because he found the quality of production declining and, of course, Cathay couldn't measure up to Yung Hwa. Bao was a former Yung Hwa staff, and the Cathay studio was in fact the former Yung Hwa studio. When I was in Cathay, Yung Hwa's sign was still on the studio

國泰時已是末落期，沒有葛蘭、尤敏、葉楓、丁皓、李湄，以至白露明等明星，那時青黃不接，留下的舊星過氣了，新進的李琳琳、周萱、秦祥林等還未成名，當家花旦陳曼玲現在也很少人記得了。

美工部主任是來自舊上海的老牌佈景師包天鳴，樣子和髮型都有點像現在香港特首董建華，天天穿西裝打領帶，提着私家保温飯壺上班，中午自己吃。片場中常有講上海話的資深行家來找他談天述舊（但通常不是編導演，片場內有各行各業，並非外界所知）。印象最深是聽包天鳴談昔日在永華公司拍攝名片《清宮秘史》（1948），他負責佈景，專誠跑到北京故宮繪圖拍照度尺寸，然後在香港的片場搭宮殿佈景，一絲不苟。拍光緒皇在祖宗廟堂一場，光線要從大窗框格透射進來，燈光打不出這種效果，就在攝影機前放透明玻璃，細心用人手繪出一排排光線。

包天鳴提到這往事，因為大陸文革批判《清宮秘史》，香港乘機重映這舊片，令他感歎今非昔比，新製作再無昔日的水準，國泰與永華更不能相比。包天鳴是永華舊人，其實國泰片場就是永華片場，我工作時期，片場大門口仍有永華招牌。但拍《清宮秘史》的大概是舊永華片場，後來才遷到斧山道，被電懋接收，還加建亞洲片場，再變國泰。

聽説李翰祥青年時代，在永華美工部工作過，他做導演後作品中的佈景就很出色。我在國泰做小工的時期，李翰祥從台灣回港，租借國泰片場拍《騙術奇譚》（1971），大受歡迎，開創了騙術財色喜劇路線，一直影響到後來整蠱作怪的許冠文喜劇，以及王晶、周星馳的賭片。

可以説，國泰後期的影片，似乎多數不及其他小公

gate, though *Sorrows* should be made at the old Yung Hwa studio before it was later moved to Hammer Hill Road and before it was taken over by MP & GI, to which was added Asia studio to become Cathay studio.

It is said that Li Hanxiang had worked at Yung Hwa's art department. The films he directed had some really outstanding set designs. When I was at Cathay, Li came back to Hong Kong from Taiwan and rented Cathay studio to make *Legends of Cheating* (1971). The film was a hit and a new comedy genre of cheating was born, its influence found later in Michael Hui's satiric comedies and the gamblers films of Wong Jing and Stephen Chiau.

One might say that most of the films produced by Cathay during its later days were not as popular as those made in its studio by smaller companies. Sometimes Connie Chan Po-chu would shoot films there and we were excited to see her. After Cathay closed, this studio became the Golden Harvest studio and another golden era started. It was where the internationally renowned Bruce Lee films and the Hui Brothers hits were made and it later became Jackie Chan's base, bringing more glory days to Hammer Hill Road. But the Golden Harvest studio was demolished several years ago when the government withdrew the land.

My days at the art department were quite happy. The best thing was that we were away from the centre of power. Cathay was built on a hill; senior management offices were near the main entrance, but the art department was on the top of the slope and we had to climb to our office. So the top belonged to the "low men", the carpenters, clay workers, painters and electricians as well as props and wardrobe people.

The art department may be tiny, but there was office politics, with different generations of set designers competing with each other. But as production numbers dropped, there was nothing left to compete.

司租用該片場的製作受歡迎。有時陳寶珠片也在國泰片場拍戲，我們很高興見到她。國泰結束後，這片場變為嘉禾片場，這才威風，拍出國際矚目的李小龍片，大賣座的許氏兄弟片，然後是成龍片大本營，為斧山道吐氣揚眉。不過，嘉禾片場數年前亦被政府收地清拆了。

其實在美工部工作的日子相當愉快，妙在「山高皇帝遠」。因為國泰建在山坡，公司大人物都在門口附近的寫字樓，美工部則「高高在上」，要行斜路攀登，辛苦得多。所以高處其實是「下層」，屬於勞工階級，木工組泥工組漆工組電工組都在那裡，還有道具組和服裝間。

小小美工部，本來也有「辦公室政治」，老中青佈景師明爭暗鬥。不過，國泰拍片愈來愈少，無利可圖，於是無權可爭，同事們反而在清清閒閒中變成和和好好的難兄難弟，而且美工部助手們主要是年輕人，愈清閒愈好玩。於是小子們談天說地，下棋、睡覺、看書、畫畫，爬山探險，中午結伴跑到鑽石山、彩虹邨吃飯，甚至到啟德遊樂場玩耍或看電影。我們經常遲到早退，輪流代同事在大門口打鐘卡，累到國泰老臣子屠梅卿常在上下班時把守門口，查問犯規的小鬼們。其實屠梅卿很好人，大家都不怕他，但都佩服他對片場十分忠心，從天未光到天黑都在巡來巡去。

美工部人人來歷不同，趙德克原是越南華僑，後來和國泰女同事香希嬋結婚，雙雙跑到法國去了。丘詩銘來自武漢美術學院，後來到了新加坡電視台。至今仍然不時見面的文錫彬則擅長繪畫花布。還有幾個從大陸游水來港的，亦有在台灣讀建築系回來的，也有一兩個原是畫戲院廣告的學徒。有些專門寫書法，有些專門畫片場大幅背景（坦白說，當年佈景很假，背景畫得更失真）。

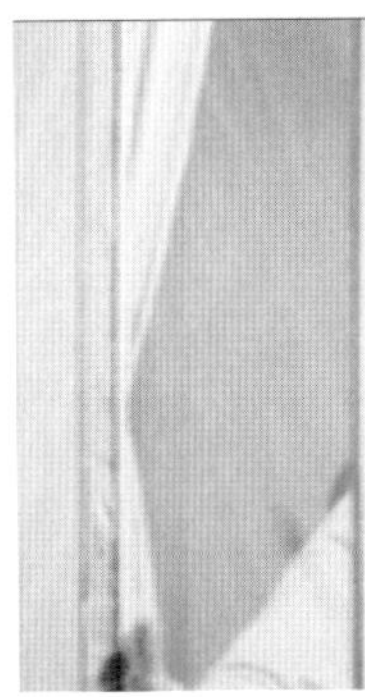

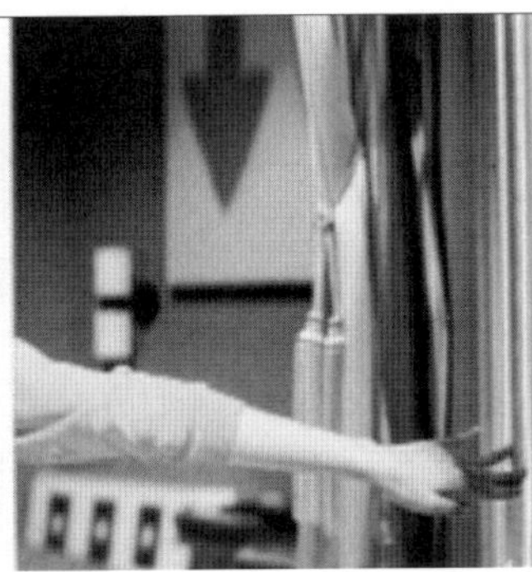

Maggie Li Linlin and Leung Sing-po in *The Homemaker.*

We became brothers. Since most of the assistants were young men, the less work, the more fun. We had long chats, played chess, took naps, read books, drew pictures, hiked and went in groups to lunch at Diamond Hill or Choi Hung, sometimes even going to Kai Tak Amusement Park or movies. We arrived late and left early and took turns to punch cards for each other. This prompted Tu Meiqin, a long-time Cathay staff, to guard the front door to check on our mischief. Tu was actually very kind and we were not afraid of him. Instead, we admired his loyalty to the studio, because he was always patrolling the place, from dawn till dusk.

Colleagues of the art deaprtment had different backgrounds. Chiu Tak-hak was from Vietnam. He later married another Cathay colleague and went off to France together. Qiu Shiming graduated from art college in Wu Han and later worked for television in Singapore. Wen Xibin, whom I still see from time to time, was good in painting fabric. There were several who swam to Hong Kong from the Mainland, an architecture graduate from Taiwan, and two who were billboard painting apprentices. Some of these people specialized in calligraphy, some in painting large backgrounds (to be honest, film sets in those days looked far from real and background sets were even worse). The most interesting person was a young assistant, who was a member of the Hong Kong Soccer Youth Team and took regular leaves for overseas matches. Another assistant was mischievous and absent-minded. He didn't know much about art but was definitely a chess prodigy, beating everyone at the studio.

We were friendly with the carpenters, clay workers, painters and props workers. Some of them were very old (I remembered there was a woodcraft worker who looked like a hermit) while some were child workers who probably came from families whose parents and grandparents worked for years at the studio. Props workers had particularly complicated backgrounds. There was a father and a son; the father had a scar on his face, and he claimed he was once a gangster, but

最妙是畫背景的一個小助手是小球王，入選香港青年足球代表隊，到時到候便請假到外埠比賽，名叫温耀球。另一個小助手天真好玩，烏龍頑皮，又不大懂美術，卻是小棋王，在片場戰無不勝。

我們和木工泥工漆工和道具工人混得很熟，他們有的很老（記得一個很老的雕花工人活像大隱士），有的只是童工，大概祖孫三代同在片場謀生。道具工人似乎特別龍蛇混雜，記得有一對父子，父親疤面，他自稱入過幫會，卻被幫會「揾笨」，五十年代叫他們向左派機構放火打人，他不但受傷，還被警方拘捕，幫會卻不理會。

美工部旁邊是飯堂，一對上海夫婦打理，由於片場拍片不多，所以生意不旺，食品不佳。但飯堂一個小女兒漂亮活潑，時時跑過來玩，有時拍片她亦去做做戲，常被上海媽媽叫她「練功」。多年後聽舊同事説，她長大入了電視台做藝員，就是經常表演危險雜技的楊盼盼。

包天鳴先生天天對着這群懶鬼嘩鬼，自然有代溝，更感片場愈來愈不像樣，但無可奈何。其實他偶然談起永華時代是很艱苦的，當初高薪從上海請他和其他一流人才來港，不惜工本，後來嚴重虧蝕，他們經常無糧出。

陸運濤的電懋時代最有錢，雄心萬丈，美工部除了佈景師包天鳴，還有名家費伯夷負責美術（他的助手羅文後來亦是佈景師，不是歌星那位），但到國泰時代便低落了，被邵氏佔盡上風。包天鳴當然只能按章工作，他始終把守崗位，對我們很和氣，天天幫我們接電話（因為美工部電話就在他的桌上），我們亦靠他的收音機聽講波，尤其是温耀球。

那段日子，我對電影製作完全學不到甚麼，只是略為增加了一些美工常識，並且做了包天鳴最後一個助手。現

《家有賢妻》中的李琳琳與梁醒波

was betrayed by the mob. He was ordered in the 1950s to set fire to leftist organisations and beat up people; he was injured and arrested, but the gang abandoned him.

Next to the art department was the canteen, managed by a Shanghai couple. The studio wasn't making many films so business was slow and food was bad. But they had a lovely daughter who came over often. Sometimes she played minor roles in films. Her Shanghai mom always asked her to "practice her skills." Years later, I was told she grew up to become the television actress Sharon Yeung Pan-pan, who is known for performing dangerous acrobatic stunts.

Working with lazy, boisterous lads like us, Bao naturally felt the gap, making one feel even worse about the studio. But he couldn't do anything about it. Occasionally, he would tell us about the difficult times at Yung Hwa. The studio hired him and other first-rate talents from Shanghai with high salaries when money wasn't a problem, but soon the studio was in debt, and they often didn't get paid.

MP & GI during Loke Wan Tho's time was its most prosperous. The studio was ambitious. Besides Bao, the art department also had the famous artist Rex Fay (Fei Boyi); his assistant Luo Wen, later also became a set designer. After MP & GI became Cathay, the studio went downhill and Shaw Brothers studio became industry leader. Bao, of course, could only work according to rules. But he kept at his post and was kind to us, answering phone calls for us because the department's phone was on his desk. And we listened to soccer matches on his radio, expecially the soccer player.

I didn't learn anything about film production, only gaining a little knowledge in art and becoming Bao's last assistant. Now, watching the credits of MP & GI or Cathay films and seeing Bao's name, I'd be hit with memories about him.

As an assistant, I had little chance to work with directors. I remember that Wang Liuzhao (who had written film reviews for the *Weekly*) was quiet and skinny, Evan Yang (Yi Wen) and Tu Guangqi were

在看到電懋、國泰電影片頭名單上包天鳴的名字，便會引起回憶。

做小工，不大和導演接觸，印象中汪榴照（他曾在《中國學生周報》電影版寫影評專欄）很瘦削很沉默，易文和屠光啟都客客氣氣，王星磊則有時跑上美工部找資料看畫冊，和我們聊天，王天林不大見到。楚原入國泰後，見得較多。

做場記的吳宇森上美工部最多，那時趙德克拍短片也上了癮，有時下班便和我、吳宇森、小克等去拍短片。《死結》(1969)的女主角曹仲蘭便是國泰廣告部同事。聽說敬海林當年也在廣告部做過(後來他做導演，拍過《家在香港》，1983）。

當年我和林年同先後在九龍城太子道、聯合道一起租房住，直至我和陸離結婚。那是上班自由散漫、下班看戲拍短片又拍拖的窮快活日子。但林年同在國泰比我忙得多，因為他很快做了副導演和編劇，後來還有機會做導演，叫蔡浩泉入國泰幫手（那時亦舒和蔡浩泉分手了）。印象中林年同的影片剛剛開拍，公司便要結束，拍不成。林年同隨後到了義大利再回來，研究電影理論和中國電影美學，有重要論著，亦是「香港國際電影節」港片回顧專題的首位主持人，並於浸會學院(現名浸會大學)任教，創辦電影系，可惜壯年逝世，終於與導演拍片無緣。

金炳興亦是著名影評人，後來在影視編劇方面很有貢獻，也做過導演，但只拍了一部《我為你狂》(1984)。這群入過國泰的《中國學生周報》朋友中，始終留在影壇工作，成為名導演的，就是吳宇森。

説起來，國泰小職工待遇低微(至於有職員乘機發財，就不是小工所能知道)，勝在放足假期，好像也有醫療保險。最妙的是結業遣散，大眾搵工轉業後，忽然政府

polite and Wang Xinglei often came to our department to look at picture books and chatted with us. We seldom saw Wang Tianlin, but saw Chor Yuen often.

John Woo, working in continuity, frequently visited. Chiu Tak-hak was by then deeply involved in short films and would work with me and Woo on films after work. Tso Chung-lan, the actress of *Dead Knot* (1969), a film I made with Woo, was a colleague from the advertising department. I heard that Jing Hailin, who became a director and made *Home at Hong Kong* (1983), also worked at the advertising department once.

Lin Nien-tung was my roommate and we rented rooms at Prince Edward Road and Junction Road until before I married Ada Loke. Those were poor but happy days, when we could work without discipline, go to movies, make short films and date after work. But Lin had a busier schedule because he soon became assistant director and scriptwriter. He even became director, and recruited Cai Haoquan to join Cathay to help him (Cai and Isabel Ni had broken up already). His film just started shooting when the company was closed, and the film was never made. Later Lin went to Italy to study film theories and published important works on Chinese cinema aesthetics after he returned. He was also the first programme coordinator of the Hong Kong International Film Festival's Hong Kong Retrospective section and taught at Baptist College (now University), setting up the film department there. Unfortunately he died young and never got the chance to direct.

Kam Ping-hing, also a renowned critic, has made important contributions to television screenwriting and also became a director, though *Pale Passion* (1984) is his only work. Among this group of *The Chinese Student Weekly* writers who had worked at Cathay, only one person stayed in the film industry. He eventually became a renowned director and he is John Woo.

The pay of a young assistant was meagre (some people were said to have taken advantage of the company and got rich, but that was far beyond my knowledge), but there were plenty of holidays. I think we had medical

通知還可補領一筆錢，據說因為某些工人不滿遣散費太少，向勞工署投訴得值，於是其他員工也可分享。

片場解散後，美工部各散東西，有入電視台的，有做廣告的，亦有做建築或室內設計的，有做水警的，有做新界村長的，温耀球則做了甲組球員，有段時期在報章體育版不時見到他的名字。幾次農曆新年，年輕舊同事們相約到包天鳴家中拜年，他都很高興。幾年後包天鳴逝世，電影界似乎沒有甚麼表示。

石琪，資深影評人，著有《石琪影話集》（1-8冊，次文化堂，1999）。
Sek Kei, renowned film critic; author of *Sek Kei Film Reviews* (vol. 1-8, Subculture, 1999).

insurance too. An interesting interlude: after the company closed and we had gone on to new jobs, I received government notice that there was additional compensation. Apparently some staff members were not satisfied with the severance pay and their complaint was accepted by the Labour Department, which granted all of us extra money.

After the studio closed, the art department went everywhere. Some entered television, some advertising; some worked in architecture or interior design; one became a marine police and one a village elder in the New Territories. Wan Yiu-kau the soccer player became a professional player and we read his name in the sports page from time to time. For several years, the young assistants got together and visited Bao during Chinese New Year. He was delighted. Then he died several years later, but the film industry didn't seem to have done anything to commemorate him.

Translated by Grace Ng

Biographies

Editor's note

These are biographies of some of the key MP & GI and Cathay personnel, though many important contributors on both the Hong Kong and Singapore sides are missing due to lack of available information. We only hope that their biographies will be compiled later. We would like to thank Mary Wong, who helped us gather information in Japan for Hattori Ryoichi.

Written by:
Yu Mo-wan, Angel Shing, emily lo, Sam Ho, Mary Wong and Wong Ain-ling

Edited by:
Wong Ain-ling, Angel Shing, Lee Chun-wai

人物小傳

編按

這輯人物小傳基本上包括了國泰及電懋最核心的工作人員，當然遺漏還是不少的，譬如長期在國泰電懋工作的佈景包天鳴、美術費伯夷、剪接王朝曦、化裝方圓、劇務主任屠梅卿等，都苦於找不到足夠的資料而只能從缺。至於國泰機構（香港）有限公司時期的台前幕後工作人員，包括新加坡副總裁連福明、後期接替俞普慶出掌國泰總經理之職的楊曼怡等，我們也只能指望將來有機會才作整理了。於此，我們特別感謝身在日本的黃淑嫻，專誠為我們去尋找有關服部良一的生平資料，並撰寫成小傳。

撰寫：余慕雲、盛安琪、羅潔顏、何思穎、黃淑嫻、黃愛玲
整理、校閱：黃愛玲、盛安琪、李俊慧

製片／管理 Producer/ Management Personnel

何亞祿（1901 - 1982）

南美洲英屬新畿內亞人，香港大學機械工程科畢業生。1926年開始經營電影院和從事電影發行業務。1948年，他連同自己經營的多間電影院，一併加盟新加坡國泰機構屬下的國際戲院有限公司，然後擴充為陸氏戲院有限公司，負責主持新公司。同年，履任國泰機構排片部主任和董事經理。1951年，他又創立克里斯製片廠，1953年陸運濤加入合辦國泰克里斯製片廠，專門出產巫語片，拍攝了星馬第一部彩色片《真假王子》（1953）、非常賣座的《吸血人妖》（1957）和第一部寬銀幕影片《人妖之誓》（1958）等。他使到國泰機構不獨專注電影發行，更進而為一家製片機構。他從事電影放映、發行和製作工作超過三十年，被譽為卓越的製片家和影壇怪傑，是國泰機構首腦人之一。1959年離開國泰後，自組「獨立影業公司」和印尼合作拍片，曾編導過《苦盡甘來》。1982年9月16日病逝，享年81歲。

製片／管理 Producer/ Management Personnel

黃也白（1917.1.16 - 1998.9.4）

上海人，上海新華藝術專科學校畢業生，畢業後進入新聞界工作，當過上海《華美晚報》編輯、香港《上海日報》主編，在上海創辦過《誠報》。1952年開始從事電影工作，出任香港永華影業公司宣傳主任。永華被國際（電懋前身）接管後，他成為國際的宣傳主任。繼後國際改為電懋，再改為國泰，都是他當宣傳主任。他在國泰機構當宣傳主任長達十六年，1969年離開國泰，進入邵氏工作過一段短時期。1970年他創辦新世紀電影公司，出品過《吾愛吾妻》（1970）等四部影片。1974年又創辦萬星影業公司，出品過《霹靂小子》（1974）等三部影片。1966年到1973年，他是港九自由影劇總會的主席，由於工作出色（包括創辦「國語電影欣賞週」），先後獲得台灣政府獎狀、台灣教育部及文化局頒發金馬獎兩座。

HE Yalu / Ho Ah Loke (1901 - 1982)

Native of British New Guinea (now Papua New Guinea), Ho Ah Loke graduated with a degree in Mechanical Engineering from the University of Hong Kong. First involved in exhibition and film distribution in 1926. In 1948, his theatre chains were incorporated into the newly formed International Theatres Ltd under the banner of Cathay Organisation of Singapore, later expanded to be known as Loke's Theatres Ltd. He was appointed head of the new group. Became section head of film scheduling department and board director-manager of Cathay in the same year. Had his own production company Keris Studio and teamed up with Loke Wan Tho in 1953 to form Cathay Keris Studio. Produced a series of Malay films including Singapore and Malaysia's first ever colour film, *Bamboo of Yearning* (*Buloh Perindu*, 1953), the box office hit *The Vampire* (*Pontianak*, 1957), and the first Cinemascope feature *Curse of the Vampire* (*Sumpah Pontianak*, 1958). An excellent producer and filmmaker, Ho holds the key to Cathay's success in film production, injecting into Cathay his over thirty-year experience in film exhibition, distribution, and production. In 1959, he left Cathay to establish Independent Film Company and co-produce films with Indonesian companies. Also credited as scriptwriter-director of *Every Cloud Has a Silver Lining*. He passed away on September 16, 1982 at the age of 81.

HUANG Yebai (1917.1.16 - 1998.9.4)

A Shanghai native who graduated from Xinhua Art Academy, Huang had been editor for Shanghai newspapers and founded his own paper *Cheng Post* in his early years. His first venture in the film industry was as publicity officer at Yung Hwa Motion Picture Company in Hong Kong in 1952, a post that he resumed at International Films Distributing Agency (later restructured as MP & GI) after its takeover of Yung Hwa. Left Cathay in 1969 and worked briefly for Shaws. Founded New Century Film Company in 1970, producing a total of four films including *My Love, My Wife* (1970), and Wanxing Film Company in 1974, producing another three films. As chairman of the Hong Kong and Kowloon Cinema & Theatrical Enterprise Free General Association Limited from 1966 to 1973, Huang's contributions in this capacity earned him recognition and several awards presented by the Taiwan government. Passed away at the age of 81.

製片／管理 Producer/ Management Personnel

陸運濤（1915.6.14 - 1964.6.20）

廣東人，生於吉隆坡。英國劍橋大學文學士和歷史系碩士。他是富甲星馬的國泰機構總裁，又是馬來亞銀行和馬來亞航空公司等大機構的董事長。他亦是大慈善家，對提倡、贊助和推動星馬等地的教育、藝術事業作了不少貢獻。他是「拿督」(華人在馬得到的最高榮譽之一），又曾獲英國、日本等國家頒發勳銜。1955年，他接管了永華片場，將國際電影發行公司改組為電影懋業公司（簡稱電懋），集製作、發行、院線於一身，有規劃地全面發展電影事業，直接引發了邵逸夫於1957年從新加坡登陸香港，興建影城，成立邵氏（兄弟）公司。電懋的經營方式現代化，在其片廠制度下，星光熠熠，佳作連篇，其中包括獲得亞洲影展最佳影片獎的《四千金》(1957)、獲得金馬獎最佳影片的《星星・月亮・太陽》(1961)等；至於電影發行業務，也在東南亞做得極為成功。他曾是英國蘭克電影公司董事、美國霍士電影公司董事。在台灣一次空難中喪生，享年只有49歲。

LU Yuntao / Loke Wan Tho (1915.6.14 -1964.6.20)

A Cantonese native born in Kuala Lumpur, Malaysia, Loke received a BA in Literature and an MA in History from the University of Cambridge. President of the eminent Cathay Organisation and Board Chairman of Malayan Banking Berhad and Malayan Airways. Particularly noted for his philanthropy and contributions to education and the arts in Singapore and Malaysia and had been conferred knighthood by his native country, Malaysia, as well as Britain and Japan. Took over the Yung Hwa studios in 1955 and later restructured the International Films Distributing Agency into MP & GI, marking his venture into the film industry. Under his leadership, Cathay had developed into a modern movie empire with its own distribution, exhibition and production. Many MP & GI classics are still being savoured today. Among them are Best Film awardees at the Asian Film Festival and the Golden Horse Film Festival, *Our Sister Hedy* (1957), and *Sun, Moon and Star* (1961). Cathay's distributing business did equally well in Southeast Asia. Loke served also as board member at Rank and Fox film companies. He died at the age of 49 in an air disaster in Taiwan.

製片／管理 Producer/ Management Personnel

歐德爾（1924 - ）

英籍猶太人，在香港出生，曾就讀於香港大學。抗戰期間，先後在重慶的美國雷電華公司發行電影和在當地的英國大使館工作，與不少影人結交。抗戰勝利後，加入新加坡的共和公司。1951年進入新加坡國泰機構，主持國際電影發行有限公司，以代理和發行香港影片為主。1954年被派到香港創立國際影片發行公司（電懋前身），並出任總經理。1954年，他在國際設立了粵語片製作組，出品了不少傑出的粵語片，又支持嚴俊和白光等組織國泰和國光等公司，出品了多部優秀的國語影片。1955年助陸運濤接收了永華片廠，監督興建成新永華片場，並出任廠長，使國際／電懋的電影質素提高及保持穩定，對邵氏做成了極大的威脅，可說是國際／電懋草創時期的大功臣。1957年他向國際請辭，表面是說自組「自由影業公司」拍片，實際是被邵氏挖角，在邵氏工作了三年。七十年代開始在新加坡從事錄影帶發行及經營影音店。

ODELL, Albert (b. 1924)

British of Russian and Jewish origins, born and raised in Hong Kong. During the anti-Japanese war, Odell worked briefly at Radio-Keith-Orphem and the British Embassy in Chongqing, and joined the Singapore branch of Republic Pictures after the war. Joined Singapore's Cathay Organisation in 1951 and headed International Film Distribution Agency. Posted to Hong Kong in 1954 to establish International Films Distributing Agency and became its general manager. Between 1954 and 1956, International Films produced a number of acclaimed Cantonese films. The establishment of Yan Jun's Guotai and Bai Guang's Guoguang were both financed by International Films under Odell. The results are a harvest of fine independent features. He personally oversaw the takeover of Yung Hwa Studios and the building of the new studio at Hammer Hill Road while managing operations at the same time. In a brief period of time, Cathay caught up with Shaws, and even surpassed its arch-rival with some exceptionally fine-quality movies. Odell handed in his resignation in 1957 to set up his own film company, only to join Shaws shortly on favourable terms. He is now running a video rental store in Singapore.

製片／管理 Producer/ Management Personnel

宋淇（1919 - 1996）

浙江吳縣人。燕京大學西洋文學畢業生。畢業後在母校任教多年。1930至1940年代，他曾在上海從事話劇工作，編寫過《皆大歡喜》等名劇，領導過有名的金都劇團。1948年他出任香港「美國新聞處」出版編譯部主任。他曾用林以亮的筆名，發表過不少文章，其後輯成《林以亮佚文集》。1955年他受聘為國際影片發行公司（後改組為電懋）劇本編審委員會四個編審人之一，張愛玲就是由他介紹為電懋寫劇本的。他在電懋亦編過《南北和》（1961）、《有口難言》（1962）等劇本。約於1957年他轉任電懋製片部主任，由他負責製作的名片，有《空中小姐》（1959）、《野玫瑰之戀》（1960）等。1965年，他加盟邵氏，出任編審委員會主任。1968年開始，他受聘於中文大學，任校長特別助理，兼任該校的翻譯研究主任。1996年12月3日病逝香港，享年77歲。

製片／管理 Producer/ Management Personnel

王植波（1924 - 1964）

上海人，上海聖約翰大學文學士和東吳大學法學士。他是著名的書法家，著有《中國各種書法》、《毛筆筆觸鋼筆字》、《鋼筆字帖》等有關書法的專著。1952年他開始編寫電影劇本，第一部是《王魁與桂英》。從1952年到1964年，他替永華、新華、邵氏等公司編寫過十二個電影劇本，其中名作有《春天不是讀書天》（1954）、《碧血黃花》（合編，1954）、《楊貴妃》（1962）等。1955年開始，他替國泰機構屬下的電影公司（包括嚴俊主持的國泰公司和電懋）編寫過七個電影劇本，其中名作有《風雨牛車水》（1956）、《娘惹與峇峇》（1956）、《寶蓮燈》（合編，1964）、《聊齋誌異》（合編，1965）等。《女人．女人》（1967）是他編寫的最後一個劇本，也是遺作。他從50年代起參與電懋的製片工作，曾是電懋的製片主任。他又曾參與影片《兒女英雄傳》（1959）、話劇《清宮怨》的演出。1964年與陸運濤等電影界名人，在台灣一宗飛機失事中身亡，享年只有40歲。他的夫人是有名的畫家和演員翁木蘭。

SONG Qi / Stephen Soong (1919 - 1996)

A native of Zhejiang. Studied Western Literature at the University of Yanjing and taught there after graduation. Soong's involvement in stage drama began in the 1930s and 1940s in Shanghai, having scripted acclaimed works such as *Everyone's Happy* and led the renowned Jindu Drama Troupe. Came to Hong Kong in 1948 to take up the post of publication and translation officer at the US Information Service (USIS). Soong has published many articles under the pseudonym Lin Yiliang. Hired by International Films Distributing Agency (later renamed MP & GI) in 1955 as one of its four core script committee members. The illustrious writer Eileen Chang (Zhang Ailing) was introduced into MP & GI by Soong. Became MP & GI's production supervisor around 1957 and is best remembered for the success of *Air Hostess* (1959) and, *The Wild, Wild Rose* (1960) etc. Joined Shaw Bros in 1965 as head of the script department. Employed by the Chinese University of Hong Kong in 1968, serving as special assistant to the Vice-Chancellor and head of Department of Translation Studies. Passed away in Hong Kong on December 3, 1996 at the age of 77.

WANG Zhibo (1924 - 1964)

A Shanghai native, Wang graduated with a BA from St John's University and obtained a law degree from Soochow University. A famed Chinese calligrapher, having written several books on calligraphy. Debuted as scriptwriter in 1952, with a script for *A Scholar's Adventures* (1952). Between 1952 and 1964, he has scripted a dozen films for companies such as Yung Hwa, Hsin Hwa, and Shaws including *Spring is in the Air* (1954), *The 72 Martyrs of Canton* (co-written, 1954), *Yang Kwei-fei, the Magnificent Concubine* (1962). Also scripted for Cathay's subsidiaries such as Yan Jun's Guotai and MP & GI. Among his seven works from this period are *Rainstorm in Chinatown* (1956), *Nonya and Baba* (1956), *The Magic Lamp* (co-written, 1964), and *Fairy, Ghost, Vixen* (co-written, 1965). *Passion* (1967) is his posthumous work. Wang joined MP & GI's production department in 1950s and had been its production supervisor. Died in an air disaster with several MP & GI executives including Loke Wan Tho in 1964. Famous painter and actress Weng Mulan is his wife.

製片／管理 Producer/ Management Personnel

俞普慶（1904 - 1970）

生於上海，畢業於上海東吳大學，獲文學士學位。1940年他出任美國派拉蒙影片公司天津分公司經理，1949年升為該公司上海總公司總經理，1950年調任新加坡分公司經理，主管全馬來西亞發行業務。1957年應星洲國泰機構聘任國際影片發行有限公司（後改名國泰影片發行公司）經理，主管國泰機構經營的電影發行業務。1964年派任香港電懋公司（後改組為國泰）經理，負責製片業務。1964至1970年，電懋和國泰在他的領導下，出產過一百部影片，其中名作有尤敏和李麗華主演的《梁山伯與祝英台》（1964）、《聊齋誌異》（1965）、《虎山行》（1969）、《家有賢妻》（1970）、《路客與刀客》（1970）等。1970年6月25日病逝香港，享年66歲。

製片／管理 Producer/ Management Personnel

鍾啟文（1919 - 1993）

廣東人，生於1919年10月31日。香港大學畢業生。1948年應李祖永之聘出任香港永華電影製片廠廠長。繼後，廠方保送他到美國學習彩色攝影和沖印技術，學成後升任永華影業公司總經理。1955年星洲國泰機構接管永華，其後歐德爾辭離國際，1957年國際改組為電懋，聘請鍾啟文擔任總經理。在職七年期間，電懋出品的影片豐富多姿，建立了獨特的片廠風格。六十年代初，初次執導的作品是《愛的教育》（1961），隨後還執導過《一段情》（1962）和《一曲難忘》（1964）。1962年電懋人事紛亂，鍾辭職離開。其後進入麗的電視中文台當台長。1979年辭去中文台的職務，移民定居美國，改為從事彩色沖印。1993年9月逝世。

YU Puqing / Paul Yui (1904 - 1970)

Born in Shanghai. Graduated with a BA from Soochow University. Appointed manager of Paramount Picture's Tianjin branch in 1940 and soon promoted to become general manager of its Shanghai headquarters. Posted to Singapore to oversee the company's distribution business in Malaysia. Employed as manager of International Film Distribution Agency by Singapore's Cathay Organisation in 1957. Appointed manager of MP & GI in 1964, mainly responsible for its production operation. Over one hundred films were produced during his tenure at both MP & GI and Cathay, among them Lucilla You Min and Li Lihua's *Liang San Bo and Zhu Ying Tai* (1964), *Fairy, Ghost, Vixen* (1965), *Escort over Tiger Hills* (1969), *The Homemaker* (1970), and *From the Highway* (1970). Passed away in Hong Kong on June 25, 1970 at the age of 66.

ZHONG Qiwen / Robert Chung (1919 - 1993)

A Cantonese native who graduated from the University of Hong Kong, Chung was recruited by film magnate Li Zuyong to head Yung Hwa Film Studios. Subsequently sponsored by Yung Hwa to study colour photography and film processing in the States. Appointed general manager when Loke Wan Tho restructured International Films into MP & GI in 1957. His seven-year tenure coincided with the most fruitful period of MP & GI. Made his directorial debut with *Education of Love* (1961), followed by *A Fine Romance* (1962), and *Please Remember Me* (1964). Resigned in 1962 following changes of personnel at MP & GI. Joined Rediffusion Television as director of the Chinese channel shortly afterwards. Resigned from his work at RTV and migrated to the States in 1979 where he continued to pursue a career in colour film processing. Passed away in September 1993.

朱國良（1910 - 1996）

馬來西亞華僑，生於吉隆坡，英國牛津大學華德漢學院學士，曾在牛津杜維治學院攻讀。大學畢業後，曾在馬來西亞政府和雷登農學院任職，是多間馬來西亞銀行、橡膠公司、錫礦公司的董事。1959年，出任新加坡國泰機構的董事，是董事長陸運濤的左右手。同年被委任為馬來西亞上議會議員。1964年陸運濤墮機罹難，他接任新加坡國泰機構董事長，1965年把電懋改組為國泰機構（香港）有限公司，擔任董事長。國泰在他領導下，繼續進行製片和影片發行工作，直至1971年結束製片部。他主管香港國泰六年間，出品超過九十部電影，其中傑出的作品有《亂世兒女》（1966）、《虎山行》（1969）、《家有賢妻》（1970）、《路客與刀客》（1970）等。1985年他因年事已高，宣佈退休。退休後，國泰機構的工作，由他的女兒朱美蓮接手管理。1996年病逝，享年86歲。

朱旭華（1906 - 1988）

浙江寧波人，上海大廈大學畢業。十九歲開始寫第一個電影劇本《哥哥的艷福》（1927），筆名朱血花。抗戰期間曾出任《廣西日報》經理，和成都區戲院代表。1945年他和蔣伯英在香港創辦了大中華電影公司，任經理和轄下製片廠的廠長。1948年與李祖永創辦「永華電影公司」，並擔任廠長一職，負責一切製片事宜。直至李祖永病逝，「永華」的業務便結束了。及後，他便協助歐德爾成立國際影片發行公司。國際改組為電懋後，仍主管宣傳和製片工作。1956年他在電懋支持下，創辦了國風影片公司，出品過叫好又叫座的電影，如林黛、嚴俊、胡金銓、張翠英等主演的《金鳳》（1956）；及蕭芳芳成名作《苦兒流浪記》（1960）等。1966年他離開電懋，替邵氏創辦電影雜誌《香港影畫》，任主編和兼任邵氏演員訓練班主任。退休後，於1980年移民定居美國。1988年病逝，享年82歲。

ZHU Guoliang / Choo Kok Leong (1910 - 1996)

A Malaysian Chinese born in Kuala Lumpur, Malaysia. Studied at University of Oxford and upon graduation, returned to work for the Malaysian Government and Serdang Agricultural College. Joined Singapore's Cathay Organisation as a board director in 1959 to assist President Loke Wan Tho. Appointed Member of the Parliament in the House of Lords Malaysia the same year. When Loke died in an air disaster in 1964, Choo took over as managing director of Cathay (Singapore) and restructured MP & GI to become Cathay Organisation (Hong Kong) the year after. Cathay, under Choo's six-year leadership, continued its distribution business and produced more than 90 films, including *A Debt of Blood* (1966), *Escort over Tiger Hills* (1969), *The Homemaker* (1970), and *From the Highway* (1970). Choo announced his retirement in 1985 and Cathay's business was succeeded by his daughter Meileen Choo. Passed away at the age of 86.

ZHU Xuhua (1906 - 1988)

A native of Ningbo, Zhejiang province. A graduate from Shanghai's Daxia University. Debuted at 19 with his first script *Brother's Romantic Fortune* (1927). During WWII, Zhu was manager of the *Guangxi Daily* and a representative of cinemas in the Chengdu area. Co-founded Great China Film Company with Jiang Boying in Hong Kong, and worked as both general manager and head of studios. Co-founded Yung Hwa Motion Picture with Li Zuyong, and became publicity manager and head of studios, carrying on the two roles after MP & GI took over Yung Hwa. Financed by MP & GI, Zhu established his own company Guofeng, producing such memorable works such as *Golden Phoenix* (1956), starring Lin Dai, Yan Jun, and King Hu; and *Nobody's Child* (1960), starring Josephine Siao. Joined Shaws to become founder and publisher of the magazine *Hong Kong Movie News* while supervising its actor training class. Retired in 1980 and migrated to the US. Passed away at the age of 82.

導演 Director

莫康時（1908.12.25 - 1969.4.15）

廣西籐縣人。上海滬江大學法律系畢業生。因喜愛電影藝術，畢業後進入上海蘇城電影公司學習編劇。1932年他和李應源等合編了電影劇本《里影》。1935年應香港鳳凰影片公司邀請，來港執導默片《日落》。1939年在香港開始編劇工作，編寫的《銀燈照玉人》（1940）備受好評。其他名作還有《姑緣嫂劫》（1939）、《拜金的人》（1952）、《女兒心》（1954）等。1940年他開始執導，第一部是《大地回春》，戰後香港出產的第一部影片《情燄》（1946）也是他執導的。從1939年到1969年，他一共執導過一百三十多部影片。他執導的喜劇片最獲好評，其中名作有《經紀拉》（1950）、《十字街頭》（1955）等，以客席身份為電懋執導的《太太緝私團》（1961）、《傻偵探》（1962）等，也屬這種類型。其他作品還有《大富之家》（1963）、《巴士銀巧破豪門計》（1965）、《女殺手》（1966）等。《多情高竇貓》（1969）是他執導的最後一部影片。十個粵語片名導演（包括李鐵、吳回等）結為異姓兄弟，稱為「十大導」，他是大阿哥。病逝香港，享壽61歲。

導演 Director

唐煌（1916 - 1976）

上海人，南京國立政治大學畢業。1939年開始加入中央電影製片廠，從事新聞電影工作。八年間編導了不少新聞紀錄片，如《一切為了人民》、《一切為了勝利》等。1947年他執導了第一部故事片《尋夢記》。1953年他來香港後執導的第一部故事片是《丈夫日記》，其後在香港執導過亞洲出品的《傳統》（1955）、邵氏出品的《蓬萊春暖》（1957）等影片。1958年加盟電懋，在電懋執導的第一部影片《玉女私情》（1959）是他的代表作。從1958年到1971年，他在電懋一共執導過三十餘部影片，其中有《雲裳艷后》（1959）、《六月新娘》（1960）、《長腿姐姐》（1960）、《諜海四壯士》（合導，1963）、《聊齋誌異》（1965）等。《蛇王與閻王》（1972）是他執導的最後一部影片。1972年，國泰停止了影片生產後，他轉入麗的電視當編導。1975年轉到佳藝電視，仍任編導。病逝香港，享年60歲。

MO Kangshi/Mok Hong-si (1908.12.25 - 1969.4.15)

A Guangxi native and a Law graduate from Shanghai's Hujiang University. A keen lover of film arts, Mok entered Sucheng Film Company in Shanghai to study scriptwriting. Invited by Fenghuang Film Company to direct his Hong Kong debut, the silent feature *Sunset,* in 1935. Officially launched his scriptwriting career in 1939, receiving rave reviews for *The Spotlight* (1940). Other acclaimed works include *Marriage Made in Heaven* (1939), *Gold Diggers* (1952), and *Sweet Seventeen* (1954). Debuted as a director in 1940 with *Spring Returns to the Good Earth* and credited as director of the first post-war film, *Flames of Lust* (1946). A prolific director who has directed over 130 films between 1939 and 1969, among them his signature comedies *Broker Lai* (1950) and *Crossroads* (1955). Other noted works include *A Sorrowful Millionaire* (1963), *The Girl in the Bus* (1965), and *Lady Bond* (1966). His last film is *The Romantic Girl Who Plays Hard-to-Get* (1969). Passed away at the age of 61.

TANG Huang (1916 - 1976)

Native of Shanghai. Graduated from the National University of Politics in Nanjing. Entered the Zhongyang Film Studio in 1939, working on newsreels and during his stay of eight years, produced and wrote a number of documentary newsreels. Directed his first feature *The Story of Dream-chasing* in 1947. Made his Hong Kong debut with *Diary of a Husband* in 1953, followed by *Tradition* (1955) for Asia Pictures and *Springtime in Paradise* (1957) for Shaws. Joined MP & GI in 1958 and is best remembered for *Her Tender Heart* (1959). Directed some 30 films between 1958 and 1971, including *Cinderella and Her Little Angels* (1959), *Sister Long Legs* (1960), *Four Brave Ones* (co-directed, 1963), and *Fairy, Ghost, Vixen* (1965). *A Resort Called Hell* (1972) was his last work at MP & GI. Switched to Rediffusion Television to work as a director-scriptwriter after Cathay ceased production in 1972 and in 1975 to CTV. Passed away at the age of 60.

導演 Director

陶秦（1915 - 1969）

原名秦復基，浙江省慈谿縣人，畢業於上海聖約翰大學文學系。畢業後曾任電影説明書翻譯。1942年開始從事電影編劇，第一部是《人海慈航》，這期間也寫了《萬紫千紅》、《桃花潭水》等電影劇本。四十年代末期至五十年代初期，他在上海和香港編寫的劇本，拍成名片的有《花街》（1950）、《説謊世界》（1950）、《禁婚記》（1951）等。1952年他首次執導，作品是長城的《一家春》。從1952年到1967年，他執導了近五十部電影。陶秦在電懋的時間雖然不算長，卻以其敏鋭的現代觸覺，樹立了某種典型的電懋風格，如《四千金》（1957，獲亞洲影展最佳影片獎）、《小情人》（1958）、《龍翔鳳舞》（1959，獲亞展最佳音樂獎）等。其後他轉投邵氏，也成績斐然，計有獲第九屆亞展五項金禾獎的《不了情》（1961）、第一屆金馬獎最佳導演獎的《千嬌百媚》（1961）、第十屆最佳喜劇片的《花團錦簇》（1963）、第十一屆最佳歌曲特別獎的《萬花迎春》（1964）和第十三屆最佳影片獎的《藍與黑》（1966）。1969年公映的《陰陽刀》，是他執導的最後一部影片。1969年5月16日，因胃癌病逝香港，享年54歲。

TAO Qin (1915 - 1969)

Original name Qin Fuji. A native of Zhejiang province and a Literature graduate from Shanghai's St John's University. Kicked off his film career as a translator of film handbills and began his scriptwriting career in 1942 with *Sail of Kindness Through the Sea of Human*. The film scripts he wrote in Hong Kong and Shanghai during the late 1940s and early 50s were made into classics such as *The Flower Street* (1950), *Awful Truth* (1950), and *A Night-time Wife* (1951). Debuted as director with Great Wall's *Father Marries Again* (1952). Among the some 50 films he made, Tao is best remembered for his MP & GI works *Our Sister Hedy* (1957, Best Film Award at the 4th Asian Film Festival), *Calendar Girl* (1959, Best Music Award at the 6th), Shaw's *Love Without End* (1961, five Golden Hay Awards at the 9th), *Love Parade* (1963, Best Comedy Award at the 10th), *The Dancing Millionairess* (1964, Best Song Award at the 11th), *The Blue and the Black* (1966, Best Film Award at the 13th), and winner of the Best Director Award at the 1st Golden Horse Film Festival, *Les Belles* (1961). Died of stomach cancer in Hong Kong on May 16, 1969 at the age of 54.

導演 Director

王天林（1928.9.11 - ）

浙江紹興人，上海出生，曾在香港培正中學就讀。1947年開始從事電影工作，當過場記、助導、副導演，亦做過電影沖印、錄音、剪輯等工作。1950年開始執導，第一部是粵語片《峨嵋飛劍俠》，成名作是國語片《桃花江》（1956）（掀起了歌唱片的潮流）。拍攝《地下火花》（1958）時，王天林在泰國相遇電懋的宋淇，回港後即受推薦加入電懋，並一直留至七十年代初國泰時期。在電懋的日子可説是其電影生涯的黃金期，拍了不少出色的作品，包括獲得第七屆亞洲影展最佳導演獎的《家有喜事》（1959）、《樑上佳人》（1959，金泉出品，電懋班底）、《野玫瑰之戀》（1960）、《南北和》（1961）、《小兒女》（1963）、《啼笑姻緣》（1964）等。他亦替粵語片組拍過不少影片，其中有《翠樓春曉》（1960）、《福慧雙修》（1962）等。王天林是一名多產導演，作品近二百部，而且幾乎甚麼類型都拍過，五十年代還執導過不少潮語片和廈語片。他執導的最後一部影片是《大鬥大》（1979）。1973年他轉當電視劇監製，監製過電視名劇《書劍恩仇錄》、《楚留香》、《萬水千山總是情》等，對本地電視劇發展影響至深。其後偶有在電影和電視劇中客串演出，1989年開始又常在杜琪峰的作品中客串演出。編導王晶是他的兒子。

WANG Tianlin (b. 1928.9.11)

A native of Shaoxing, Zhejiang province. Born in Shanghai and studied in Hong Kong's Pui Ching Middle School. Entered the film industry in 1947, working as script continuity, assistant director, deputy director, and had taken up technical posts such as processing, sound recording and editing. His directorial debut was *The Flying-sword Hero from Emei Mountain* (1950). *Songs of the Peach Blossom River* (1956), a Mandarin musical, established his stature and raised the curtain on the musical hit trend. Met Stephen Soong (Song Qi) while shooting *Underground Sparks* (1958) in Thailand. Soong introduced him to MP & GI where he stayed until the early 1970s. The MP & GI days marked the peak of his film career with works like *All in the Family* (1959, Best Director Award at the 7th Asian Film Festival), *The Wild, Wild Rose* (1960), *The Greatest Civil War on Earth* (1961), and *A Story of Three Loves* (1964). In his thirty-year career, Wang has directed innumerable films, from Chaozhou to Amoy dialect films, from slapslick comedies to swordplays and musicals. *The Utmost Greatness* (1979) is his last directorial effort. Entered TVB as television producer in 1973, yielding some of the most popular TV series of the time. Has made guest appearances in a number of Johnny To films in recent years. Father of director-scriptwriter Wong Jing.

導演 Director

嚴俊（1917 - 1980）

本名嚴宗琦，南京人。曾在北京輔仁大學和上海大廈大學攻讀。早年是著名的話劇演員。1938年開始當電影演員，參演的第一部影片是《新地獄》(1939)，當主角的第一部影片是《浮雲掩月》(1943)。從1938年到1970年，主演過近百部電影，其中名作有《一代妖姬》(1950)、《新紅樓夢》(1952)、《楊貴妃》(1962)、《武則天》(1963)等。由於戲路廣闊，有「千面小生」之稱。1952年開始執導，第一部是《巫山盟》(1953)，共執導過五十多部電影，其中名作有《翠翠》(1953，林黛成名作)、《梁山伯與祝英台》(1964，電懋)，和獲得亞洲影展最佳影片獎的《萬古流芳》(1965)等。1971年公映的《玉面俠》是他執導的最後一部影片。他創辦過國泰、金龍、和合等電影公司，其中國泰得到國際（電懋前身）的支持，出品影片皆由他們發行，較出色的作品有《歡樂年年》(1956)、《風雨牛車水》(1956)、《亡魂谷》(1957)等。1972年他因患心臟病息影。翌年和有「影壇長青樹」之稱的妻子李麗華移居紐約。他在美國從事過銀行、飲食業等。1980年8月18日病逝美國，享年63歲。

導演 Director

易文（1920.12.26 - 1978.3.29）

原名楊彥岐，江蘇吳縣人，上海聖約翰大學文學系畢業生。畢業後在新聞界工作，做過記者和香港《星島日報》的編輯。1948年開始從事電影編劇工作，編寫的第一部電影劇本是《風月恩仇》。他一共編寫過六十多個電影劇本，其中名片有《閨怨》(1952)、《楊娥》(1955)等。他首次執導的作品是《名女人別傳》(1953)。從1953年到1970年，他執導了四十多部電影，從1957年開始成為電懋的中堅導演，拍了不少極富都市味的佳作，包括《春色惱人》(1956)、《曼波女郎》(1957)、《姊妹花》(1959)、《空中小姐》(1959)、《香車美人》(1959)、《情深似海》(1960)和《星星・月亮・太陽》(1961，獲第一屆金馬獎最佳影片獎)等。《精忠報國》(1972年在台上映)是他執導的最後一部影片。1970年出任邵氏宣傳經理，自此一直從事電影行政工作。他出版過八部小說和散文集，並曾翻譯《好萊塢工作臨場錄》一書。病逝於香港，享年57歲。

YAN Jun (1917 - 1980)

Original name Yan Zongqi. Native of Nanjing. Studied at Beijing's Furen University and Shanghai's Daxia University, and was a famed stage actor before debuting on the silver screen with *New Hell* (1939). Dubbed "leading man with a thousand faces", Yan had acted in nearly 100 films, including classics such as *A Strange Woman* (1950), *Modern Red Chamber Dream* (1952), *Yang Kwei-fei, the Magnificent Concubine* (1962), and *Empress Wu Tse-tien* (1963). Yan's directorial debut was *Love Eternal* (1953). He went on to direct over 50 features throughout the years, producing hit films like *Singing under the Moon* (1953, Linda Lin Dai's first claim of fame), *Liang Sanbo and Zhu Yingtai* (1964), and the winner at the Asian Film Festival, *The Grand Substitution* (1965). Yan was the mastermind behind Guotai, Golden Dragon Films and Hehe Films. Guotai was financially supported by International Films producing such films as *Merry-Go-Round* (1956) and *The Valley of the Lost Soul* (1957). Announced his retirement from the screen in 1972 and migrated to New York with his actress-wife Li Lihua. Passed away on August 18, 1980 at the age of 63.

YI Wen / Evan Yang (1920.12.26 - 1978.3.29)

Original name Yang Yanqi, a native of Jiangsu province. A Literature graduate from St John's University. Worked as journalist and editor of a Hong Kong newspaper *Sing Tao Yat Po* before entering the film industry as scriptwriter in 1948. His first script is *The Story of Wind and Moon*. *Always in My Heart* (1952) and *The Heroine* (1955) are two outstanding works among the sixty scripts he has written. His directorial debut *Notorious Woman* (1953) lifts the curtains on some forty subsequent films including the highly rated *Mambo Girl* (1957), *Sun, Moon and Star* (1961), *My Darling Sister* (1959), and *Air Hostess* (1959). *The Patriots* (released in Taiwan in 1972) was his last film. In 1970, he took up the role of publicity manager at Shaws and since then was involved in administrative work. Yang has published eight novels and short stories collections, and translated a book on Hollywood filmmaking. Passed away in Hong Kong at the age of 57.

導演 Director

袁秋楓（1924.7.15 - ）

安徽廬江人，在哈爾濱出生。北京中國大學政經系畢業，後進入新聞界，當過戰地記者。1950年開始從事電影工作，初時是名導演馬徐維邦的副導演。1954年升任導演，首作是廈語片《荒江女俠》，繼後導演過一些廈語片和潮語片。1959年開始執導粵語片，第一部是《風雲奇女子》（1960），他執導的粵語片名作有《血灑黑龍街》（1960）等。1961年他轉導國語片，首作是《夜半歌聲》（1962）。1965年加盟電懋，為電懋／國泰執導的第一部電影是《嫦娥奔月》（1966）。他在電懋和其後的國泰，一共執導過七部電影，如《亂世兒女》（1966）、《鐵馬銀鈴》（1967）等，《青春的旋律》（1968）是他在國泰執導的最後一部影片。1968年，他和雷震、樂蒂等創辦了金鷹影片公司，創業作《風塵客》（1968）就是他導演的。1970年邵氏聘請他接替鄒文懷出任製片經理。三年後他辭職及退出影壇，投資出版事業。

YUAN Qiufeng (b. 1924.7.15)

A native of Anhui. Born in Ha'erbin. A graduate of Economics and Politics from Beijing's China University. After a brief tenure as a war journalist, Yuan launched his filmmaking career in 1950 studying under the famed director Ma Xu Weibang. Debuted as director in 1954 with the Amoy-dialect feature *Heroine of the Lone River*. His Mandarin debut was *Mid-nightmare* (1962). Joined MP & GI in 1965 and made his first film for the company, *Lady on the Moon* (1966). Directed seven features for MP & GI and later Cathay, including the acclaimed *A Debt of Blood* (1966). *Teenager's Holidays* (1968) is his last work at Cathay. Established Golden Eagle Film Company with Kelly Lai Chen (Lei Zhen) and Betty Loh Ti (Le Di) and directed their inaugural film, *The Vagabond Swordsman* (1968). Shaw Brothers recruited Yuan to succeed Raymond Chow as production manager in 1970. Resigned three years later and retired from the industry to invest in the publishing industry.

導演 Director

岳楓（1910.7.29 - 1999.7.3）

原名笪子春，江蘇丹陽人，上海出生。1929年進入電影界。1933年執導第一部影片《中國海的怒潮》，一舉成名。於1935年執導《逃亡》，好評如潮，奠定了大導演地位。1942年，岳楓加入了張善琨組織的偽中聯／華影，迫於形勢與日本人稻垣浩合導過《春江遺恨》（1944）。勝利後，始終難逃「漢奸」之嫌，被迫停影，直至1947年脱罪，執導《玫瑰多刺》。1949年受張善琨之邀來港加入長城公司，拍了《蕩婦心》（1949）、《血染海棠紅》（1949）等。1953年，岳創辦大方影片公司，拍了《小樓春曉》（1954）。接著，經歐德爾引薦執導《歡樂年年》（1956），對日後電懋的歌舞片有深遠影響。正式加入國際後，拍過《青山翠谷》（1956）、《金蓮花》（1957）、《情場如戰場》（1957）、《紅娃》（1958）、《雨過天青》（1959）等八部電影。1959年加入積極拓展的邵氏，直至1974年退休，最後一作是《惡虎村》（1974）。岳楓多產而專業，四十多年導演生涯共拍了近百部電影，均有一定水準。岳亦能編劇，以葛瑞芬為筆名編寫的《畸人艷婦》（1960）及《為誰辛苦為誰忙》（1963）分別獲1961年亞洲影展及1963年金馬獎最佳編劇獎；據説用此名發表的，均為他與太太（名演員羅蘭）合作的劇本。岳楓退休後，一直留在香港至病逝。

YUE Feng (1910.7.29 - 1999.7.3)

Real name Da Zichun. A native of Jiangsu province. Born in Shanghai. Entered the film industry as apprentice after graduating from secondary school in 1929. Promoted to assistant director in 1931, and directed his first film *Tide of China's Seas* in 1933, followed by *Taking Flight* in 1935, both to critical success. During WWII Yue Feng joined Zhang Shankun's Japanese controlled China United Film Company in 1942. Considered a collaborator after the war because of this sensitive issue, he was not allowed to make films until 1947 with *Roses with Thorns*, when the label was taken away. Came to Hong Kong in 1949 and joined Zhang's Great Wall Company, making great films such as *A Forgotten Woman* (1949) and *Blood Will Tell* (1949). Made *Merry-Go-Round* (1956) upon the recommendation of Albert Odell for Guotai. The film had great influence upon the later MP & GI musicals. Soon joined International Films (later renamed MP & GI) and made 8 films in total, including *Green Hills and Jade Valleys* (1956), *Golden Lotus* (1957), *The Battle of Love* (1957), *Scarlet Doll* (1958), and *For Better, For Worse* (1959). Joined Shaw Brothers in 1959 and stayed there until his retirement in 1974. Prolific and professional, Yue Feng made nearly 100 films in 40 years, all with high quality. Also wrote screenplays, using the pen name Ge Ruifen. It is said that the work of Ge Ruifen was a collaboration of Yue Feng and his wife (famous actress Luo Lan). Yue Feng retired in 1974 and lived in Hong Kong until he passed away in 1999.

導演 Director

左几（1916 - 1997）

原名黃左基，廣東南海人，廣州大學社會系畢業生。1937年開始從事電影工作，初當編劇，第一個劇本是《賣花女》（1938）。他又當過場記，和做過電影沖印及剪接等工作。1947年他和望雲合導了《小夫妻》，獨立執導的第一部影片是《遊鳳戲龍》（1948）。從1947年到1969年，他一共執導了七十多部電影，除了一部是潮語片，其餘都是粵語片。國際（電懋的前身）的創業作《余之妻》（1955）便是由他執導的。他在電懋執導了十七部粵語片，其中有《愛情三部曲》（1955）、《璇宮艷史》（1957）、《魂歸離恨天》（1957）、《黛綠年華》（1957）、《琵琶怨》（1957）、《美人春夢》（1958）等。他執導的粵語片經典作，有粵劇戲曲電影《帝女花》（1959）、改編自張恨水原著的《落霞孤鶩》（1961）、《夜深沉》（1962）、《秦淮世家》（1963）及《一水隔天涯》（1966，兼任作詞，該片主題曲流行了很長時間）等。他執導的最後一部影片是《追求妙遇》（1969）。他執導的影片多數是他自己編劇（筆名何愉）的。1968年他加盟麗的電視，曾監製《華龍探案》等電視劇集，並曾主理麗的編劇組、麗的藝員訓練班。1981年升任創作組經理。八十年代初退休，移居加拿大後創辦了影視協會，並繼續從事劇藝工作。1997年1月17日病逝温哥華。

ZUO Ji / Tso Kea (1916 - 1997)

Original name Wong Cho-kei. A native of Nanhai, Guangdong province. Graduated from the University of Guangzhou with a degree in Sociology. Debuted as a scriptwriter in *The Flower Girl* (1938), and as director with *The Dragon is Teased by the Beautiful Pheonix* (1948). Between 1947 and 1969, Tso directed over 70 Cantonese features, including *My Wife, My Wife* (1955), the inaugural film of International Films, and 16 other Cantonese films for MP & GI, most of them immensely popular hits such as *My Kingdom for a Husband* (aka *The Romance of Jade Hall*, 1957), *Love Lingers On* (1957), *Three Stages of Love* (1955), and *The Tender Age* (aka *The Splendour of Youth*, 1957). Outside of MP & GI, his best remembered works are *Princess Cheung Ping* (1959), screen adaptations of Butterfly novelist Zhang Henshui's *Many Aspects of Love* (1961), *Sombre Night* (1962), and *The Songstresses* (1963). *Beyond the Horizon* (aka *A Story Between Hong Kong and Macau*, 1966) is perhaps his best known. Tso Kea is also a prolific scriptwriter, scripting for most of his films under the pseudonym Ho Yu. Joined Rediffusion TV in 1968, producing *Detective Warren's Files* and other series while also heading the script unit and its actor training class. Promoted to manager of the creative unit in 1981 and stayed with the station until migrating to Canada in the early 1980s. There he established the Film & TV Association. Passed away on January 17, 1997.

編劇 Scriptwriter

秦羽（1929 - ）

本名朱蕿，浙江紹興人，在北京出生。香港大學文學系畢業生，有「才女」之稱。在港大攻讀時，曾演出過《清宮怨》和英語的《雷雨》等話劇。1956年進入電懋當編劇主任，共編寫過十一個電影劇本，第一個電影劇本是《紅娃》（1958）。其他名作有《玉女私情》（1959）、《野玫瑰之戀》（1960）、《星星・月亮・太陽》（1961，獲第一屆金馬獎最佳影片獎）、《啼笑姻緣》（1964）和《蘇小妹》（1967，獲第五屆金馬獎最佳編劇獎）。《蘇小妹》是她編寫的最後一個劇本。她也曾參與過電影演出，第一部是《碧血黃花》（1954）；電懋出品名片《情場如戰場》（1957），她亦是主要演員之一。1962年和一位醫生結婚，婚後仍在電懋工作。她和姚克等領導的劇本審查委員會，是電懋能夠出品不少傑出影片的大功臣。1967年退出影壇，移居加拿大。

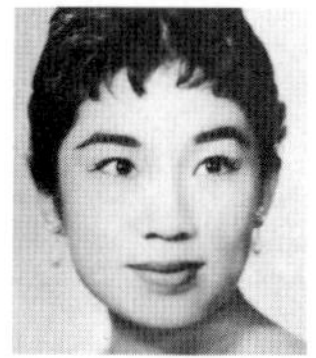

QIN Yu / Nellie Chin Yu (b. 1929)

Chin is a native of Shaoxing, Zhejiang province, and born in Beijing. A Literature graduate from the University of Hong Kong. Had performed on stage in her university days. Entered MP & GI as screenplay supervisor in 1956, producing her first film script for *Scarlet Doll* (1958). Among her eleven film scripts are *Her Tender Heart* (1959), *The Wild, Wild Rose* (1960), *Sun, Moon and Star* (1961, Best Film Award at the 1st Golden Horse Film Festival), *A Story of Three Loves* (1964), and her last script, *Wife of a Romantic Scholar* (1967, Best Screenplay at the 5th Golden Horse). Her screen debut was in *The 72 Martyrs of Canton* (1954), and subsequently in MP & GI's acclaimed work *The Battle of Love* (1957). Following her marriage with a doctor in 1962, Chin continued to work at MP & GI, chairing with Yao Ke its script committee and often credited as one of the masterminds behind the company's success. Chin announced her retirement in 1967 and emigrated to Canada.

編劇 Scriptwriter

孫晉三（1914 - 1962）

清華大學畢業生，他是第一個考取「庚款」（庚子賠款）的留學生，以公費進入美國哈佛大學攻讀戲劇。哈佛畢業後，曾往歐美考察戲劇，回國後出任南京中央大學戲劇和外國文學教授。1955年，他應國際電影發行公司（電懋前身）之聘，出任該公司劇本編審委員會主持。在此期間他編寫過一個電影劇本《紅顏青燈未了情》（1961），由名導易文拍成電影，頗獲好評。另他又主編過一份純文藝雜誌，名為《時與潮文藝》。1962年8月3日病逝香港，享年只有48歲。

編劇 Scriptwriter

汪榴照（1926.5.30 - 1970.8.6）

原名汪兆炎，江蘇武進人，台灣國立政治大學專修科畢業。畢業後為台灣《新生報》寫影評，後來成為該報影劇版主編。在此期間，著有《電影叢談》，翻譯過《好萊塢外史》和《最新電影技術》二書。1954年他進入台灣中央電影公司當編審組長，1957年執導《路遙知馬力》等兩部台語片。1958年他應香港電懋聘請，來港做編導，第一部影片是《風流寃家》（1958）。從1958年到1970年，他在電懋編過超過二十個劇本，其中有獲得第七屆亞洲影展最佳編劇獎的《家有喜事》（1959）、獲得第三屆金馬獎最佳編劇獎的《諜海四壯士》（1963，他並為該片的導演之一）、《神經刀》（1969）等佳作。他在電懋共執導過五部影片，包括《夏日初戀》（1968）和《狼與狼》（1969）等，《洪福齊天》（1970）是他在電懋執導的最後一部影片。1967年轉入邵氏當編導，編作有《觀世音》（1967），執導作品有《大丈夫能屈能伸》（1970）等。後因神經衰弱等原因，仰藥自殺，死時年僅44歲。《蛇王與閻王》（1972）是他的劇本遺作。

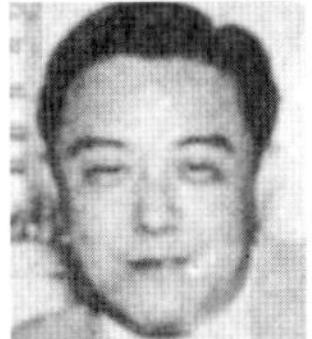

SUN Jinsan (1914 - 1962)

Graduate of Qinghua University, Sun was the first scholar on the Gengzi Compensation to undertake Drama Studies at Harvard University. Sun went on a study tour in the US and Europe before returning to China to teach drama and comparative literature in Nanjing Central University. In 1955, International Films (later renamed MP & GI) extended to him an invitation to join the company as a script committee member working along with Yao Ke and Stephen Soong (Song Qi). *Till the End of Time* (1961) directed by Evan Yang (Yi Wen) was his only script. Sun has also published a fine-art magazine *Time and Tide*. Died from an illness on August 3, 1962 at the age of 48.

WANG Liuzhao (1926.5.30 - 1970.8.6)

Original name Wang Zhaoyan. Native of Jiangsu province. After graduating from Taiwan's National Changchi University, he worked for *Xinsheng Daily* as a film critic and later edited the film and drama section of the paper. Employed by Taiwan's Central Motion Picture Company in 1954 as head of its scriptwriting unit. Directed two Taiwan films in its local dialect in 1957 before debuting as scriptwriter-director at MP & GI in 1958 with *Pretty Tease*. Produced more than twenty scripts for the company, including *All in the Family* (1959, Best Screenplay Award at the 7th Asian Film Festival), *Four Brave Ones* (1963, co-directed, Best Screenplay Award at the 3rd Golden Horse Film Festival), and *A Mad, Mad, Mad Sword* (1969) etc. *The Lucky Ones* (1970) is his last MP & GI film. Switched to Shaws in 1967 and continued working as scriptwriter-director, scripting *The Goddess of Mercy* (1967) and directing *What's Good for a Goose* (1970). Committed suicide at age 44. *A Resort Called Hell* (1972) is his last screenplay.

編劇 Scriptwriter

姚克（1905 - 1991）

原名姚成龍，又名莘農，安徽人。蘇州東吳大學畢業生，曾在美國耶魯大學攻讀戲劇，有洋狀元之稱。大學畢業後在文化界工作。和友人合辦過電影文學創作所、苦幹劇社，著有《怎樣演出戲劇》等著作。他是劇作家，寫過廿多個劇本，其中最有名是《清宮怨》，還有《西施》、《楚霸王》等歷史劇。1936年他編寫了第一個電影劇本《清明時節》，繼後他還編寫過《清宮秘史》(1948)、《一代妖姬》(1950)、《豪門孽債》(1950)等名片的劇本。1955年，他應國際影片公司（電懋前身）聘請，出任劇本編審委員會四個主要成員之一（其他三個成員是孫晉三、張愛玲和宋淇），電懋在他們的領導和指導下，出品了不少經典作和傑作，不過他本人倒似乎沒有為電懋寫過劇本。六十年代他曾任教於中文大學。1969年初移居美國，一度執教於夏威夷大學和加州大學。1976年曾一度短期回港，出任麗的電視戲劇顧問和編劇訓練班導師。1991年12月18日病逝美國，享年86歲。

YAO Ke (1905 - 1991)

Original name Yao Chenglong, alias Shen Nong. Native of Anhui. Graduated from Soochow University and furthered his studies in Drama at Yale University. Entered the cultural circle upon graduation and was a core member of Kugan Theatre Troupe. A renowned playwright, Yao has over twenty scripts to his credits, among them famed historical dramas such as *Sorrows of the Qing Palace* and *Xi Shi* (*Beauty of Beauties*). His film debut came in 1936, with script for *The Qing Ming Season* and went on to write scripts for classics including *Sorrows of the Forbidden City* (1948), *A Strange Woman* (1950), and *The Insulted and Injured* (1950). Invited by International Films Distributing Agency (later renamed MP & GI) in 1955 to join their script committee. Together with the other three members – Sun Jinsan, Eileen Chang (Zhang Ailing) and Stephen Soong (Song Qi), these intellectuals marked the style of MP & GI productions. Taught at the Chinese University of Hong Kong in the 1960s. Migrated to the US in early 1969, where he continued teaching at the University of Hawaii and the University of California. He came back to Hong Kong for a brief stay in 1976, appointed drama advisor to Rediffusion Television and instructor of its acting class. Passed away on December 18, 1991 at the age of 86.

編劇 Scriptwriter

張愛玲（1920.9.19 - 1995.9.8）

原籍河北豐潤，上海市出生，本名張煐，1930年改名張愛玲。祖父是當年清廷要員張佩綸，祖母是李鴻章的女兒。1939年考入香港大學，從滬來港，其後因日軍進攻香港而中斷了大學生活，1942年5月返回上海。1943年發表〈沉香屑・第一爐香〉、〈沉香屑・第二爐香〉、〈金鎖記〉、〈傾城之戀〉、〈封鎖〉等十多篇小說，在文壇上聲名大噪。1946年寫了《不了情》(1947)和《太太萬歲》(1947)兩個電影劇本，很受歡迎，1948年將〈金鎖記〉改編成電影劇本，但沒有開拍。1952年7月重返香港，入美國新聞處工作，期間認識了宋淇、鄺文美夫婦，成終生摯友。1955年被邀加入國際（後易名電懋）劇本編審委員會。1956年2月赴美。1957至1964年間，為電懋寫了多個電影劇本，包括《情場如戰場》(1957)、《人財兩得》(1958)、《桃花運》(1959)、《六月新娘》(1960)、《南北一家親》(1962)、《小兒女》(1963)、《南北喜相逢》(1964)和《一曲難忘》(1964)，期間亦曾計劃編寫《紅樓夢》，惟最終擱置，其後寫了改編自西片的《魂歸離恨天》，亦沒有開拍。宋淇於陸運濤空難後不久離開電懋，張愛玲也從此沒再編寫電影劇本，並一直客居美國，1995年9月8日被發現猝斃於其洛杉磯公寓內。

ZHANG Ailing /Eileen Chang (1920.9.19 - 1995.9.8)

A native of Hebei province. Original name was Zhang Ying, but was changed to Zhang Ailing; Eileen was her English name. Her grandfather Zhang Peilun was an important official of the imperial court of the Qing Dynasty, her grandmother was the daughter of Li Hongzhang, an important figure in Chinese history. Educated in Shanghai and admitted to University of Hong Kong in 1939. Returned to Shanghai in May 1942 when Hong Kong was under Japanese occupation. Started publishing a series of short stories which won her instant fame in the literary world. Wrote the screenplays of *Love Without End* (1947) and *Long Live the Wife* (1947) in 1946. Made an adaptation of her short fiction *The Golden Cangue* in 1948, but it was never made into a film. Came back to Hong Kong in July 1952 and met Stephen Soong (Song Qi) and his wife. Soong invited her to join the script committee of International Films (later renamed MP & GI) in 1955. Went to USA in February 1956. Wrote many screenplays for MP & GI from 1957 to 1964, including *The Battle of Love* (1957), *A Tale of Two Wives* (1958), *June Bride* (1960), *The Greatest Wedding on Earth* (1962), *Father Takes a Bride* (1963), and *Please Remember Me* (1964). Stephen Soong left MP & GI soon after Loke Wan Tho's plane crash, and Eileen Chang has never written any screenplays since. She lived in the US and passed away in her Los Angeles apartment.

編劇 Scriptwriter

張徹（1924.1.17 - ）

原名張易揚，浙江青田人，1924年在杭州出生，成長在上海。父親是割據浙江的「省長」夏越的副手，掌管軍隊，其後戰敗兵潰，全家逃去上海。少年時到四川做流亡學生，中學畢業後入重慶的中央大學法學院政治系，其後輟學加入一個社教工作隊。抗戰勝利，受到張道藩的識拔，被任為文化運動委員會的專員，派駐上海。1949年隨國民黨政府撤退去台灣，並導演了他的第一部影片《阿里山風雲》（1950）。1957年應李湄之邀往香港編導《野火》（1958），其後一度專業寫稿，筆名沈思，並以何觀之名撰寫影評。1960年簽約電懋，先後編寫了《無語問蒼天》（1961）、《賊美人》（1961）、《遊戲人間》（1961）、《桃李爭春》（1962）等劇本，風格細緻輕快，與後來的陽剛味大異其趣。一年後加盟邵氏，初任編劇，從《蝴蝶盃》（1966）開始執導，《獨臂刀》（1967）票房百萬，奠定了他作為導演的基礎，其後的《大刺客》（1967）、《獨臂刀王》（1969）、《死角》（1969）、《遊俠兒》（1970）、《馬永貞》（1972）、《刺馬》（1973）、《洪拳小子》（1975）等影片，皆突顯陽剛之氣，扭轉了六十年代以女性為中心的電影主流，對後來的香港電影影響深遠。

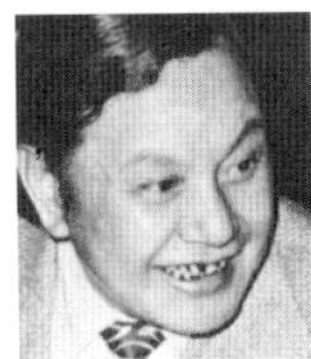

ZHANG Che / Chang Cheh (b. 1924.1.17)

Real name Zhang Yiyang. A native of Qingtian county, Zhejiang province, brought up in Shanghai. Went to Sichuan when he was a teenager, and entered university in Chongqing but left not long afterwards. Appointed special cultural commissioner after WWII, and sent to work in Shanghai. Then went to Taiwan with the KMT Party in 1949, and directed his debut *Happenings in Ah Li Shan* (1950). Came to Hong Kong upon the request of actress Li Mei to write and direct *Wild Fire* in 1958. Became professional writer for a short period, then signed a contract with MP & GI in 1960 and wrote several screenplays for the studio, including *Song without Words* (1961), *The Girl with the Golden Arm* (1961), *You were Meant for Me* (1961), and *It's Always Spring* (1962). Light and subtle, these works seem miles away from the masculinity in his later works. Joined Shaw Brothers a year later and became director from *The Butterfly Chalice* (1966) onwards. Made the box office hit *One-armed Swordsman* (1967), which proved his talent as a director. This success was followed by films like *The Assassin* (1967), *Dead End* (1969), *The Wandering Swordsman* (1970), *Boxer from Shantung* (1972), *The Blood Brothers* (1973), *Disciples of Shaolin* (1975) etc, and created a new trend. The mainstream of 1960s' cinema, in which woman was the center of focus, was forever gone.

音樂 Music

服部良一（1907.10.1 - 1993.1.30）

服部良一是大阪一泥公仔匠之子，有兩姊兩妹，家境清貧。六歲時，參加了教會的合唱團，開始認識管風琴等西洋樂器。十六歲的時候，加入了為一所鰻魚店做宣傳的「出雲屋少年音樂隊」。三年後，服部加入了大阪交響樂團吹雙簧管，他的音樂才能得到樂團的指揮家Emmanuel Metter的賞識，私人教授他西洋音樂的理論，服部一生視他為恩師。廿四歲時第一次被聘為唱片公司的作曲家，五年後轉到當時執西洋音樂界牛耳的哥倫比亞公司就職。1938年開始為東寶的電影作曲，第一部是《鐵腕都市》，其後有《支那之夜》（1940）、《我的鶯》（滿映／東寶， 1943）等等。1938年他以慰問團的身份赴上海時，認識了音樂家陳歌辛、梁樂音、黎錦光及姚敏。戰後他曾為白光主演的日本電影《蘭燈之戀》（1951）作曲，白光以日語主唱。其後服部和香港再結緣，主要是因為亦徒亦友的姚敏的關係，服部曾參與《女秘書艷史》（1960）、《野玫瑰之戀》（1960）、《香港之夜》（1961）、《小兒女》（1963）及《教我如何不想她》（1963）等電懋電影的音樂工作，當中與姚敏合作的《野玫瑰之戀》可算是代表作品了。1968年，服部參與了井上梅次為邵氏拍攝的首四齣電影的音樂工作。當姚敏在1967年去世後，服部感到香港電影的取向改變了，他亦無意再到香港。

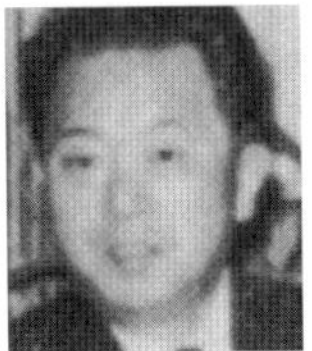

HATTORI Ryoichi (1907.10.1 - 1993.1.30)

Son of a poor clay doll maker in Osaka. Joined a church choir at the age of 6, and started to learn about western instruments. Joined the Izumoya Young People's Band which did promotion for an eel shop at the age of 16. Three years later, joined the Osaka Symphony Orchestra to play the oboe. Emmanuel Metter, conductor of the orchestra at that time, appreciated Hattori's talents and offered him private lessons in western music theories. At age 24, a record company employed him as composer. Joined the Columbia Company five years later. Started composing music for Toho in 1938, the first film being *Iron Wrist City*, followed by *China Night* (1940), *My Nightingale* (Manchuria Movie Association / Toho, 1943), etc. He met Yao Min and other musicians when he visited Shanghai in 1938, forming a friend / mentor relationship with Yao. After the war, Hattori composed songs for the Japanese film *Koi no rantan* (1951), starring Bai Guang, who sang the songs in Japanese. Later, his ties with Yao brought him to Hong Kong, composing music for such MP & GI films as *Miss Secretary* (1960), *The Wild, Wild Rose* (1960), *A Night in Hong Kong* (1961), *Father Takes a Bride* (1963), and *Because of Her* (1963). *The Wild, Wild Rose,* a collaboration with Yao Min, was considered a classic. Composed music for the first four films Inoue Umetsugu made for Shaw Brothers in 1968. After Yao Min died in 1967, Hattori didn't want to work for the changed Hong Kong industry anymore. Passed away in 1993, at the age of 85.

綦湘棠（1919.11.11- ）

原名綦湘鍱，出生於廣東南海佛山鎮，原籍為湖南衡山縣人。國立音樂院畢業，曾在中華交響樂團工作，任演奏部幹事。抗戰期間，先參加香港青年會之隨軍服務團，後加入演劇四隊工作。1948年返港，在嶺英中學任小學音樂教員七年。1950年開始為電影作曲，首作為《翠翠》（1953），這亦為林黛的成名作。《翠翠》中之第一及第二兩首插曲〈你真美〉和〈不講理的姑娘〉就是他的作品。他為國語電影寫過不少歌曲，如《四千金》（1957）的〈劍舞歌〉、《曼波女郎》（1957）的〈忘憂歌〉、〈我的天堂〉，和《温柔鄉》（1960）與《香車美人》（1959）的主題歌等均屬他的佳作。他為電影配樂，始於1956年之《金鳳》。從1955年起，他已為電懋的影片作曲與配樂，但直至1962年8月才正式簽約加盟。在電懋他的配樂名作頗多，如《四千金》、《蘭閨風雲》（1959）、《天長地久》（1959）、《無語問蒼天》（1961）等。其他配樂作品尚有邵氏的《後門》（1966）、國聯的《冬戀》（1969）等。1973年7月他移民定居加拿大。

QI Xiangtang / Kei Shang-tong (b. 1919.11.11)

A native of Hunan and born in Foshan Township, Guangdong. Graduated from the National Music Academy, Qi's first tenure was at the Chinese Symphony Orchestra. During WWII, he joined a service unit of the Hong Kong Youth Association and later its drama troupe. 1950 saw his launch into the film music world of Hong Kong, producing the hits "You Are So Pretty" and "Unreasonable Girl" for Linda Lin Dai's classic *Singing under the Moon* (1953) and subsequently the popular song numbers "Sweet Dance" for the award-winning feature *Our Sister Hedy* (1957), "Forget Your Sorrows" and "My Heaven" for *Mambo Girl* (1957), as well as the theme songs of *Bachelors Beware* (1960) and *Our Dream Car* (1959). In 1956, Qi started composing film scores with *Golden Phoenix* (1956). Though Qi's collaboration with MP & GI began in 1955, it was only in August 1962 that he officially signed a contract to join their rank. Among his well-received scores are for such classics as *Our Sister Hedy, Wedding Bells for Hedy* (1959), *Tragedy of Love* (1959), and *Song without Words* (1961). Other film scores include *Rear Entrance* (1966) for Shaws and *The Winter* (1969) for Guolian. Migrated to Canada in July 1973 and has been residing there since.

姚敏（1917.11.13 - 1967.3.30）

原名姚振民，生於上海，童年家境小康，喜愛流連大世界遊藝場，鑽研地方戲曲。父親去世後，當了數年海員，對西方流行音樂產生興趣。三十年代末返上海，與妹妹姚英、姚莉組成大同社，在多家電台承辦自演的歌唱節目，很受歡迎。又曾在張善琨大世界的齊天舞台任小型樂隊領班，負責部份「連台京戲」。除自學多種樂器彈奏及作曲，日後更拜服部良一為師。1938年加盟上海百代唱片公司。1939年進入國華公司，負責影片作曲，第一部是周璇主演的《解語花》（1941）。抗戰時期中斷了音樂事業，戰後作曲極多，唱片風行全國及東南亞。1950年來港，在麗的呼聲從事播音工作。1952年香港百代成立，獲聘主持作曲部門。1954年為王龍的《十九層地獄》首次同時負責電影作曲及配樂。1955年為邵氏出品，李香蘭主演的《金瓶梅》作插曲。其為《戀之火》（1956）所作的插曲，更被荷里活電影《蘇絲黃的世界》改編成街知巷聞的〈叮噹歌〉。他為電懋寫過不少好歌，如《曼波女郎》（1957）、《龍翔鳳舞》（1959，獲亞洲影展最佳音樂獎）、《野玫瑰之戀》（1960）、《桃李爭春》（1962）等片中的插曲。其邵氏作品《神秘美人》（1957）奪得亞展最佳歌曲獎、《千嬌百媚》（1961）獲得亞展和金馬獎的最佳音樂榮譽。1967年因急病撒手塵寰。

YAO Min (1917.11.13 - 1967.3.30)

Real name Yao Zhenmin. Developed a special interest in Chinese operas since childhood. His father died after he finished primary school. Became a sailor for several years during which he got interested in western pop music. Returned to Shanghai in the end of the 1930s and formed Datong Troupe with his two sisters Yao Ying and Yao Li. The trio performed live song and music programmes in radio stations in Shanghai, and became very popular. Basically self-taught, he later learned music composition from renowned Japanese composer Hattori Ryoichi. Joined Pathé Records in 1938. Started composing film songs in *The Flower that Understands* (1941), starring Zhou Xuan. His music career was interrupted by WWII, but became a prolific and popular songwriter after the war. Came to Hong Kong in 1950 and joined Rediffusion. Headed the department of composition in Hong Kong Pathé Records, which was founded in 1952. Since the songs he wrote for the Shaw film *Chin Ping Mei* (1955, starring Li Xianglan), he had written music for many films. Among his memorable works at MP & GI included *Mambo Girl* (1957), *Calendar Girl* (1959), *The Wild, Wild Rose* (1960), and *It's Always Spring* (1962). The song he wrote for *Flesh and Flame* (1956), a Shaw Brothers production, later rearranged by the Hollywood production *The World of Suzie Wong,* became the world famous "Ding Dong Song". The music he composed for another Shaw Brothers production *Les belles* (1961) won Best Film Score in both Asian Film Festival and the Golden Horse Award. Yao Min died unexpectedly in 1967.

女星 Actress

白露明（1937.1.6 - ）

原名許麗琼，廣東人，生於香港。自小愛好粵劇，曾追隨名伶夫婦薛覺先唐雪卿，以本名及藝名筱綠川客串小角。就讀德貞女子中學期間，約於1955年，受粵劇老師林紹游及誼母任劍輝鼓勵，到大成投考電影演員，獲蔣偉光賞識，加入影壇，改名白露明。主演首作《有女萬事足》(1955)，開始被冠以「銀壇靚女」稱號。接著參演《詐癲納福》(1956)、《兒心碎母心》(1958)等約十部作品。1958年得林永泰邀入電懋，首先於粵語片組與巨星吳楚帆合演《美人春夢》(1958)。兩年後，藉極為賣座的《苦心蓮》(上、下集，1960)奠定台柱地位。《南北和》(1961)成績美滿，開始「國粵雙棲」。首齣國語主演作品為《遊戲人間》(1961)，其他國語片有《好事成雙》(1962)、《諜海四壯士》(1963)、《人之初》(1963)等。及至1964年底粵語片組解散，並於翌年不再合作為止，共為電懋機構演出約廿五部電影，其中約十五部為粵語片，最末上映的一部是《自作多情》(1966)。1965年初與大律師沈澄結婚，此後息影。

女星 Actress

丁皓（1939.10.9 - 1967.5.23）

原名丁寶儀，原籍廣東東莞，生於澳門，為家中長女，嬰幼時居廣東韶關。官宦世家，父親丁紀謝曾任參謀長。幼隨父征戰，旅居西南省區多處，以至越南，二次大戰後棲上海數年，遊蹤遍至京滬蘇杭，自小有語言及仿演天份。1950年遷居香港，十四五歲投考國際(電懋前身)演員班，獲岳楓和鍾啟文提拔，主力國語片。在電懋八年，作品約二十齣，首作《青山翠谷》(1956)，成名作《小情人》(1958)，另有《母與女》(1960)、《南北和》(1961)、《遊戲人間》(1961)、《荷花》(1963)等作品。擅演俏皮妞兒，有「小情人」、「小丁皓」之稱，與白露明、蘇鳳同為電懋力捧的第二代玉女。1963年底與電懋關係破裂，旋即結婚，並以自由身進軍粵語影壇，以《鬼兇手》(1964)打頭陣，最後一部是《四姊妹》(1966)。1965年與夫分居，1966年赴洛杉磯圖發展，翌年手執兒子照片仰藥自殺。一生參演電影三十餘齣，享年廿七。

BAI Luming / Christine Pai Lu-ming (b. 1937.1.6)

Real name Xu Liqiong. A native of Guangzhou, born in Hong Kong. She was interested in Cantonese opera at an early age, and had been trained under the famous actor Sit Kok-sin (Xue Juexian) and his wife Tong Suet-hing (Tang Xueqing). While attending Tack Ching Girls' Middle School, she was encouraged by the celebrated opera actress Yam Kim-fai (Ren Jianhui), and joined Tai Seng Film Company in 1955. Her debut film was *Now That I've Got a Daugher, Everything's O.K.* (1955). Also starred in *The Wise Guys Who Fool Around* (1956), *Mother's Broken Heart* (1958) and a dozen other films. In 1958, Lam Wing-tai (Lin Yongtai) invited her to join the MP & GI Cantonese Film Unit, and she had her first collaboration there with superstar Ng Cho-fan (Wu Chufan) in *Memories of Love* (aka *A Lovely Girl's Lovely Dreams*, 1958). *Bitter Lotus* (1960, Parts I & II) was a huge box office hit. *The Greatest Civil War on Earth* (1961) was well received and she started appearing in Mandarin films. Her Mandarin film credits include *You were Meant for Me* (1961), *Four Brave Ones* (1963), *Father and Son* (1963) etc. Until the end of 1964 when the Cantonese Film Unit was dissolved, she had made approximately 25 films for MP & GI, around 15 of them Cantonese features. She got married and retired from screen life in 1965.

DING Hao/Kitty Ting Hao (1939.10.9 - 1967.5.23)

Real name Ding Baoyi. A native of Dongguan county, Guangdong province. Born in Macau. Followed her father, a senior officer of the army, to the south-western provinces, and even to Vietnam during her childhood. Lived in Shanghai after WWII for several years, and had travelled to cities such as Beijing, Suzhou and Hangzhou. Came to Hong Kong in 1950 with her family, and joined the actor's training class of International Films (the predecessor of MP & GI) in her teens. Her talent was soon discovered by director Yue Feng and producer Robert Chung (Zhong Qiwen), and started making Mandarin films. She stayed in MP & GI for 8 years and made about 20 films. Her debut film was *Green Hills and Jade Valleys* (1956), and reached stardom with *Little Darling* (1958). Her other memorable films included *The Greatest Civil War on Earth* (1961), *You were Meant for Me* (1961), and *Little Lotus* (1963). Her relationship with MP & GI coming to an end in 1963, she got married and started to work in Cantonese films. Her Cantonese film debut was *The Murderer is a Ghost* (1964) and her last film was *Four Sisters* (1966). Went to Los Angeles in 1966 and committed suicide the next year at the age of 27. She had made a total of about 30 films.

女星 Actress

葛蘭（1934 - ）

原名張玉瑛，浙江海寧人，在上海讀中學，1949年隨家人移居香港，並繼續中學教育，其間經常參與戲劇表演。1952年唸高三時瞞着父母投考卜萬蒼主持的泰山演員訓練班，在《七姊妹》（1953）中初登銀幕，即嶄露頭角，其後繼續為其他電影公司拍片，包括《碧血黃花》（1954）、中泰合作的《玉鳳》（1955）及《酒色財氣》（1957）。1955年簽約電懋的前身「國際」，首作為《驚魂記》（1956）。其後電懋特為她開拍《曼波女郎》（1957），她亦憑此片聲名大噪，以健康、活潑、能歌擅舞的形象成為電懋台柱之一。名作有《空中小姐》（1959）、《香車美人》（1959）、《星星・月亮・太陽》（1961）及國語歌舞片經典作《野玫瑰之戀》（1960）等。1961年與望族之後高福全結婚，停影十個月後復出主演《教我如何不想她》（1963），直至《啼笑姻緣》（1964）才正式退出影壇，共拍過三十多部戲。葛蘭以多才多藝見稱，從小接受音樂訓練，包括鋼琴、正統聲樂及京劇唱功，曾在電影中演唱京劇、崑曲，並在京劇名伶章遏雲的戲曲片《王寶釧》中客串。此外，她亦於1954年在美國片《江湖客》中客串。她也是歌唱紅星，為百代灌過不少唱片，並在美國紅歌星丹娜・蕭的電視節目中演出，其後更灌錄美國唱片《葛蘭之歌》。九十年代初期，百代公司重新發行她的唱片，曾引起一陣轟動。

GE Lan / Grace Chang (b. 1934)

Real name Zhang Yuying. A native of Zhejiang province. Born in Nanjing and grew up in Shanghai. Came to Hong Kong in 1949 with her family and joined Taishan Film Company's actor's training class in 1952. Her film debut *Seven Sisters* (1953) attracted much attention. Meanwhile, she made films with other companies, works include *The 72 Martyrs of Canton* (1954), *Booze, Boobs and Bucks* (aka *Wine, Women and Money*, 1957). She signed a contract with International Films (the predecessor of MP & GI) in 1955 and debuted there with *Surprise* (1956). *Mambo Girl* (1957), a film tailor made for her, was an instant success. With a healthy, lively image and her talent in singing and dancing, Chang soon became one of the major female stars of MP & GI. Among her most memorable films were *Air Hostess* (1959), *Our Dream Car* (1959), *Sun, Moon and Star* (1961), and the Mandarin musical classic *The Wild, Wild Rose* (1960). She got married in 1961 and made *Because of Her* (1963) after a 10-month break. *Story of Three Loves* (1964) is her last film before she retired from the screen. She had made over 30 films in total. Chang is a versatile actress who had received music training since childhood, including piano, formal vocal training and in Peking opera. She was also a popular singer, having made many records with Pathé, and performed in US singer Diana Shaw's TV programme. She also recorded an album in the United States. Pathé re-distributed her records in early 1990s.

女星 Actress

樂蒂（1937.8.29 - 1968.12.27）

原名奚重儀，浦東人，上海出生，為演員雷震胞妹，在家排行第六，故有小名「六弟」。父母早逝，自幼隨外婆生活，由於外公顧竹軒在上海經營天蟾大舞台，自小鍾愛演戲。1949年，她隨外婆來到香港，先入讀伊維英文學校，後於1953年考入長城公司當基本演員，並取「六弟」諧音「樂蒂」為藝名，在處女作《絕代佳人》（1953）中飾侯可堅一角。1958年，樂蒂因感在長城的發展不大，轉投邵氏，憑《倩女幽魂》（1960）一片走紅，有「古典美人」之譽。這時期的其他佳作還有《畸人艷婦》（1960）、《梁山伯與祝英台》（1963）和《大地兒女》（1965）等。1962年，她跟演員陳厚結婚，成為銀壇一時佳話，惜五年後二人宣告仳離。1964年，樂蒂約滿邵氏，改投電懋，並分別於《金玉奴》（1965）、《最長的一夜》（1965）、《鎖麟囊》（1966）、《亂世兒女》（1966）、《扇中人》（1967）、《太太萬歲》（1968）等多部影片中參與演出。1967年間，她與雷震和袁秋楓合組金鷹公司拍武俠片如《太極門》（1968）、《風塵客》（1968）等，並交由電懋發行，惟票房成績欠佳。1968年底，樂蒂因服過量安眠藥身亡。

LE Di / Betty Loh Ti (1937.8.29 - 1968.12.27)

Real name Xi Zhongyi. A native of Pudong. Born in Shanghai. She was the younger sister of actor Kelly Lai Chen (Lei Zhen). Her parents died when she was still a child and was brought up by her maternal grandmother. Since her grandfather Gu Zhuxuan was owner of an opera house in Shanghai, she developed a passion in acting at a young age. Came to Hong Kong with her grandmother and brother in 1949, joined Great Wall in 1953 and made her debut in *The Peerless Beauty* (1953). Moved to Shaw Brothers in 1958, and reached stardom with *The Enchanting Shadows* (1960). She married Peter Chen Ho (Chen Hou) in 1962 but divorced in 1967. Joining MP & GI (later restructured into Cathay) after her contract with Shaw Brothers expired in 1964, she had appeared in many Cathay films, including *The Beggar's Daughter* (1965), *The Longest Night* (1965), *The Lucky Purse* (1966), *A Debt of Blood* (1966), *The Magic Fan* (1967), and *Darling Stay at Home* (1968). She formed Gold Eagle Film Company with her brother Kelly Lai Chen and director Yuan Qiufeng in 1967. The company made a number of *wuxia* films, such as *Duel at the Supreme Gate* (1968) and *The Vagabond Swordsman* (1968). Distributed by MP & GI, they are far from box office successes. With an unsuccessful marriage and an unsuccessful career, Loh Ti died of an overdose of sleeping pills at the age of 31.

女星 Actress

李湄（1929.9.1 - 1994.5.12）

原名李景芳，學名李桂芳。父任職政府經濟部，母受過高等教育，幼時環境優裕。原籍吉林，家在河北，戰時遷居上海、南京，中小學時在重慶，和平後返北京，入讀華北大學政治系。1949年到香港，當過打字員、服裝設計、新月唱片公司作詞人。1950年改名李倩，任民生公司編劇，第一個劇本是《黃金世界》。1952年競選香港小姐後易名李湄，於《流鶯曲》(1954)中首任主角。其早年作品以《名女人別傳》(1953)較受注意，兩三年內作品十多齣，以獨立製片為主。1955年12月簽約國際(電懋前身），加盟首作《春色惱人》(1956）參賽亞洲影展，後以《雨過天青》(1959)再證演技，更藉《龍翔鳳舞》(1959）、《桃李爭春》(1962)等歌舞片大放異彩，獲禮聘到日本主演「寶塚劇場」歌舞劇《香港》，也為百代公司錄過唱片。在電懋最後一作是《西太后與珍妃》(1964)。李形象冶艷而豪邁，兼具文才，演過多種角色，共曾演出近五十部影片。其中有與韓國演員合作的《雨不灑花花不紅》(1959）和與菲律賓演員合作的《蛇女思凡》(1958）。後期名片有《大馬戲團》(1964）。曾於1956年創辦北斗公司，自任製片及女主角等，出品包括張徹在香港導演的首作《野火》(1958）。1967年與美國前中央情報局官員結婚，定居美國並息影經商，晚年患癌病逝。

LI Mei, Helen (1929.9.1 - 1994.5.12)

Real name Li Jingfang. A native of Jilin province. Her father was a civil servant of the Economics Department, her mother a well-educated woman. Spent her childhood in Hebei, later the whole family moved to Shanghai and Nanjing because of the war. Went back to Beijing after the war and enrolled at the University of North China. Came to Hong Kong in 1949 and joined Minsheng Co. as a scriptwriter in 1950. Her first screenplay was *The Golden World* (1953). Participated in the Miss Hong Kong pageant in 1952 and changed her name to Li Mei. Her film debut was *Strayed Beauty* (1954). She attracted much attention in the film *Notorious Woman* (1953) and made over 10 films in the next couple of years. Signed a contract with International Films (the predecessor of MP & GI) in December 1955 and debuted with *Gloomy Sunday* (1956). Her talent was further proven in *For Better, For Worse* (1959), and her singing and dancing talents fully fulfilled in *Calendar Girl* (1959) and *It's Always Spring* (1962). She even recorded for Pathé. Her last film with MP & GI was *The Imperial Lady* (1964). Li Mei is a versatile actress and also a writer. Made almost 50 films in her career. Her later works include *The Big Circus* (1964), and her last film was *International Secret Agent* (1967). Founded Beidou Film Company in 1956, produced and appeared in *Wild Fire* (1958), the first film director Chang Cheh (Zhang Che) made in Hong Kong. She retired from the screen after her marriage to an ex-officer of CIA in 1967 and moved to the United States. Died of cancer in 1994.

女星 Actress

林翠（1936 - 1995）

原名曾懿貞，廣東中山人，生於上海，1949年隨家人南遷香港，在聖士提反女子中學讀書，1953年考入自由影業公司，年僅十七歲，憑處女作《女兒心》(1954)一炮而紅，成為了自由的台柱，有「學生情人」之譽。在自由公司的三年合約期內，拍了《終身大事》(1955）、《馬車伕之戀》(1956）、《薔薇處處開》(1956）等影片，期間也外借給其他公司，如為藝華拍了《化身姑娘》(1956）。1957年11月1日加入電懋，當時尚同時為邵氏拍戲，像《夜來香》(1957）、《移花接木》(1957)等，不久就專隸電懋，作品包括《四千金》(1957）、《青春兒女》(1959）、《愛的教育》(1961）、《啼笑姻緣》(1964）、《情天長恨》(1964）、《空谷蘭》(1966）、《蘇小妹》(1967)等，《游龍戲鳳》(1968)是她主演的最後一部影片。1959年與秦劍結婚，1967年離婚，不久下嫁王羽，1975年離異。同年創辦真納影片公司，出品有《十三不搭》(1975)和《香港式離婚》(1976）。1977年移居美國，轉而經商。1995年2月22日哮喘病發，歿於台灣家中。

LIN Cui, Jeanette (1936 -1995)

Real name Zheng Yizhen. A native of Zhongshan county, Guangdong province. Born in Shanghai. Came to Hong Kong with her family in 1949 and studied in St. Stephen's College. Joined Liberty Film at the age of 17 and reached stardom with her debut film *Sweet Seventeen* (1954). Became a major star in Liberty and made several films during her 3-year contract with the company, including *Life and Love of a Horse-cart Driver* (1956) and *Season of Budding Roses* (1956). During this period she had also been on loan to other companies and made films like *Girl in Disguise* (1956) for Yihua Co. Joined MP & GI on November 1, 1957, while still making films for Shaw Brothers like *He Has Taken Him for Another* (1957). Soon she worked exclusively for MP & GI, and made films such as *Our Sister Hedy* (1957), *Spring Song* (1959), *Education of Love* (1961), *An Affair to Remember* (1964), and *Wife of a Romantic Scholar* (1967). *No Time for Love* (1968) was her last film. Lin married film director Qin Jian in 1959 and divorced in 1967. Re-married actor Wang Yu, but divorced again in 1975. In the same year she set up Jeanette Film Company and produced *Sup Sap Bup Dup* (1975) and *Divorce Hong Kong Style* (1976). She migrated to the United States in 1977 and opened a restaurant. Died of asthma at home in Taiwan on February 22, 1995.

女星 Actress

林黛（1934.12.26 - 1964.7.17）

原名程月如，藝名來自她的英文名字「Linda」讀音。廣西人，生於廣西賓陽縣，幼年在桂林、重慶、南京，曾就讀廣西省立藝術專門學校音樂系，父親是政界名人程思遠。1948年移居香港，1950年被袁仰安羅致長城旗下，卻因其父的政治背景，未能在左派公司有所發揮。1952年轉投永華，憑《翠翠》(1953)一舉成名，展開十一年璀璨銀壇事業，為永華、國泰、邵氏、電懋等公司主演了五十多齣電影。1957年憑電懋《金蓮花》首度獲亞洲影展最佳女主角，其他電懋名作有《情場如戰場》(1957)、《亡魂谷》(1957)、《紅娃》(1958)、《雲裳艷后》(1959)、《樑上佳人》(1959，電懋班底，外借金泉公司)、《温柔鄉》(1960)，皆為時裝片，其美麗慧黠的形象甚有觀眾緣。後以邵氏《貂蟬》(1958)、《千嬌百媚》(1961)、《不了情》(1961)一再登上亞展影后寶座。此外，邵氏時期的《江山美人》(1959)、《花團錦簇》(1963)也膾炙人口。廿六歲時與名門之後龍繩勳結婚，育有一子，未滿三十歲自殺身亡，彼時《寶蓮燈》(1965)及《藍與黑》(上、下集，1966)仍在拍攝中。

LIN Dai, Linda (1934.12.26 - 1964. 7. 17)

Real name Cheng Yueru. Born in Binyang county, Guangxi province. Spent her childhood in Guilin, Chongqing and Nanjing. Her father Cheng Siyuan was a famous politician. Came to Hong Kong in 1948 and joined Great Wall in 1950. Rejected by the leftist Great Wall because of her father's political background, she joined Yung Hwa Film Company in 1952. Her debut *Singing under the Moon* (1953) shot her to stardom overnight. This was the beginning of a brilliant 11-year career, totalling some 50 films for Yung Hwa, Guotai, Shaw Brothers and MP & GI. Lin Dai won her first Best Actress award in the Asian Film Festival in 1957 with *Golden Lotus*, a MP & GI production. Other MP & GI films include *The Battle of Love* (1957), *The Valley of the Lost Soul* (1957), *Scarlet Doll* (1958), *Cinderella and Her Little Angels* (1959), *Lady on the Roof* (1959), and *Bachelors Beware* (1960), most of them romantic comedies. Subsequently, with *Diau Darling* (1958), *Les Belles* (1961), and *Love Without End* (1961), all Shaw productions, she won three more Best Actress awards in the Asian Film Festival. Married tycoon Long Shengxun at the age of 26. Committed suicide before her 30th birthday, leaving behind a son and two unfinished films: *The Lotus Lamp* (1965) and *The Blue and The Black* (1966, Parts I & II).

女星 Actress

蘇鳳（1939 - ）

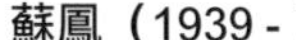

原名李紹娟，原籍廣東番禺，生於上海，父親經營西藥業，在上海協進中學求學時已參加學校話劇團演出。十三歲那年隨家人南下香港，在培道女子中學讀書。1956年考入電懋，同期還有丁皓、雷震、田青、林蒼等人，處女作是《青山翠谷》(1956)，其後一直留在電懋。蘇鳳多演第二女主角或配角，卻以斯文嫻靜的氣質，令人留下深刻的印象。曾參與演出十多部影片，包括《四千金》(1957)、《蘭閨風雲》(1959)、《六月新娘》(1960)、《野玫瑰之戀》(1960)、《星星・月亮・太陽》(1961)等，1962年結婚後息影。

SU Feng / Dolly Soo Fung (b. 1939)

Real name Li Shaojuan. A native of Panyu, Guangdong province. Born in Shanghai. Her father ran a pharmaceutical business. She received her secondary education in Shanghai, and had participated in the drama group in school. Came to Hong Kong with her family when she was 13. Joined MP & GI in 1956, her contemporaries included Kitty Ting Hao (Ding Hao), Kelly Lai Chen (Lei Zhen), Tian Qing, Ling Chong (Lin Cang). Her debut film was *Green Hills and Jade Valleys* (1956). Never a big star, Soo Fung remains special with her simplicity and modesty. Stayed in MP & GI throughout her career and made a dozen films, including *Our Sister Hedy* (1957), *Wedding Bells for Hedy* (1959), *June Bride* (1960), *The Wild, Wild Rose* (1960), and *Sun, Moon and Star* (1961). She retired from acting after her marriage in 1962.

女星 Actress

王萊（1927.2.12 - ）

原名王德蘭，原籍山東，落籍東北，生於官宦家庭，在北京出生及長大。1944年於北平師範大學女子附屬中學高中畢業，與上海影人劇團團長賀賓結婚。1949年跟夫婿合組華光劇團，正式開始演戲並改藝名王萊，其中飾演西太后的《清宮外史》大受歡迎。1951 年從影，首部作品是上海大同出品的《神龕記》，但遭禁映，1952年8月來港發展及定居，成功向羅維推薦所攜《美男子》話劇劇本改編為電影，並參演一角。此後半個世紀，演出了約二百部電影，有「千面女星」之譽。在港先後效力四維、永華、亞洲、新華、邵氏等公司，佳作有《春天不是讀書天》（1954）、《傳統》（1955）、《長巷》（1956）、《滿庭芳》（1957）等。在日本拍攝《紅娃》（1958）期間，鍾啟文邀請加入電懋為基本演員，1957 至 1969 年間為電懋及其後的國泰演出超過五十部電影，參演名片如《金蓮花》（1957）、《玉女私情》（1959）、《同床異夢》（1960）、《野玫瑰之戀》（1960）、《小兒女》（1963），憑《人之初》（1963）首次獲金馬獎最佳女配角獎。七十年代回復自由身，分別為香港邵氏、台灣中影等演出超過五十部電影，如《應召女郎》（1973）、《金玉良緣紅樓夢》（1978）等。八十至九十年代，演出約二十部電影，其中憑《小葫蘆》（1981）、《海峽兩岸》（1988）、《推手》（1991）再獲金馬獎最佳女配角獎。

WANG Lai (b. 1927.2.12)

Real name Wang Delan. A native of Shandong province. Born in Beijing, graduated from the Subsidiary Girls Middle School of the Peking Teachers College. Joined the Film Workers Drama Troupe led by actor He Bin in 1943 and married him the next year. Founded Huaguang Troupe with her husband in 1949 and started to act in films in 1951. Came to Hong Kong in August 1952, and starred in *The Handsome Man*. Since then, Wang Lai had appeared in more than 200 films. A versatile actress, she was crowned "actress with a thousand faces". Worked for many major studios in Hong Kong, including Yung Hwa, Asia, Hsin Hwa, Shaw Brothers, etc. While shooting *Scarlet Doll* (1958) in Japan, Robert Chung (Zhong Qiwen) invited her to join MP & GI. Between 1957 and 1969, she had starred in over 50 films in MP & GI, and later Cathay. Some of her selected roles in this period: *Golden Lotus* (1957), *Her Tender Heart* (1959), *The Bedside Story* (1960), *The Wild, Wild Rose* (1960), *Father Takes a Bride* (1963) etc. Won her first Best Supporting Actress in the Golden Horse Award for her performance in *Father and Son* (1963). Became a freelance actress in the 1970s, and worked for different studios henceforth, such as Shaw Bothers in Hong Kong and Central Motion Picture in Taiwan. Won three more Best Supporting Actress in the Golden Horse Awards including Ang Lee's *Pushing Hands* (1991). Her most recent film is Ann Hui's *My American Grandson* (1991). She now splits time between Hong Kong and Canada.

女星 Actress

葉楓（1937.10.19 - ）

原名王玖玲，湖北漢口人，11歲與家人移居台灣，於當地讀中學。1954 年被美國環球公司錄取為演員，惜最後拍片計劃告吹。同年來港後經李翰祥及李祖永引介，加入永華，但公司旋即倒閉。其後新天及國風兩公司亦曾與她洽商拍戲，皆不成事，直至1957年受宋淇之邀進入電懋才正式開始加入影壇，第一部作品《四千金》（1957）。她個子高挑、身材豐滿、聲音低沉，在電懋女星中以浪漫及冶艷形象見稱，在《桃花運》（1959）、《長腿姐姐》（1960）、《睡美人》（1960）、《女秘書艷史》（1960）、《星星・月亮・太陽》（1961）及《桃李爭春》（1962）等片有頗突出的表演。葉雖未受過正式音樂訓練，在影片中表演歌舞也頗出色，並與百代公司簽約，灌錄唱片。1962 年與電懋約滿後轉投邵氏，主演《山歌戀》（1964）、《血濺牡丹紅》（1964）、《癡情淚》（1965）及《碧海青天夜夜心》（1969）等片。拍罷《春蠶》（1969）後息影，1975 年在唐書璇的《十三不搭》中客串演出，前後共拍戲二十多部。葉楓與電懋影星張揚於1961年結婚，1965年離婚，同年與邵氏影星凌雲結婚，其後仳離，後來再婚。息影後從商，經常來往香港、內地、美國。

YE Feng / Julie Yeh Feng (b. 1937.10.19)

Real name Wang Jiuling. A native of Hankou, Hubei province. Moved to Taiwan with her family at the age of 11. In 1954, she won a part for a Universal Studio production to be shot in Taiwan but the film never got off the ground. Recommended by Li Hanxiang and Li Zuyong, Yeh Feng came to Hong Kong and signed a contract with Yung Hwa, but the company soon closed down. Stephen Soong (Song Qi) invited her to join MP & GI in 1957 and she made her first film *Our Sister Hedy* (1957). Tall, slender and sexy with a husky voice, Yeh had built up a unique image of the romantic but cool beauty in such films as *Sister Long Legs* (1960), *Sleeping Beauty* (1960), *Miss Secretary* (1960), *Sun, Moon and Star* (1961), and *It's Always Spring* (1962). Though she never had formal music training, she had talent and even signed a contract with Pathé as a singer. After her contract with MP & GI expired in 1962, she joined Shaw Brothers and made many films, including *The Shepherd Girl* (1964), *Pink Tear* (1965), *The Warlord and the Actress* (1964), and *Unfinished Melody* (1969). Before her retirement she made *Farewell My Love* in 1969, and a guest appearance in Shu Shuen's *Sup Sap Bup Dup* in 1975. Now she is a businesswoman and often travels between Hong Kong, Mainland China and the US. 2002 marked her comeback, when she announced plans to appear in several concerts.

女星 Actress

尤敏（1935.5.7 - 1996.12.29）

原名畢玉儀，廣東花縣人，香港出生，父為粵劇名伶白玉堂。自小因父母忙於工作，而被送往澳門，由外婆照料。1952年，就讀於澳門聖心學校的她，獲邵邨人發掘，力邀加盟。尤敏加入邵氏，主演了她入行的首作《玉女懷春》（1952），但這片最終未嘗上映。之後，她再替邵氏拍了《殘生》（1953）、《同林鳥》（1955）、《龍鳳配》（1957）、《紅粉干戈》（1959）等二十多部電影，並因其清麗脱俗的氣質，贏得影壇「玉女」稱號。1958年，尤敏約滿邵氏，轉投電懋，先憑《玉女私情》（1959）和《家有喜事》（1959）兩片接連獲第六和第七屆亞洲影展最佳女主角獎，其後以《星星・月亮・太陽》（1961）榮獲第一屆金馬獎最佳女主角獎。其他佳作還有《無語問蒼天》（1961）、《火中蓮》（1962）及《小兒女》（1963）等。尤敏亦獲電懋力捧，成為跨國女星，《香港之夜》（1961）、《香港之星》（1963）及《香港・東京・夏威夷》（1963）等片令她瘋靡日本。1964年，當尤敏拍罷其最後一部片《深宮怨》後，即下嫁富商高福球，自此退出影壇。雖然尤敏也曾為邵氏拍了不少影片，但觀眾總是將她和電懋聯繫在一起。1996年底，尤敏因心臟病病逝於香港。

男星 Actor

陳厚（1929.7.1 - 1970.4.16）

原名陳尚厚，上海人，畢業於上海聖芳濟學校，1950年隨家人赴港，先在洋行工作。1953年，應徵邵氏公司獲取錄，但最終嫌薪酬太少，沒有簽約。後因獲監考之一的導演屠光啟賞識，推薦他入新華公司，從而進入電影界，參演《秋瑾》（1953）。1957年，陳厚在《特別快車》中初挑大樑。同年，轉入電懋，並憑《曼波女郎》（1957）一片聲名大噪。有「喜劇聖手」之稱的他，接著先後替電懋、邵氏和國泰這三家公司拍片，代表作包括有電懋的《情場如戰場》（1957）、《天作之合》（1957）、《龍翔鳳舞》（1959）和邵氏的《千嬌百媚》（1961）、《花團錦簇》（1963）、《小雲雀》（1965）等。經歷過一次的婚姻失敗，陳厚於1962年與女星樂蒂再婚，惟這段姻緣在1967年結束。1970年，陳厚因腸癌病逝美國，終年40歲。

YOU Min, Lucilla (1935.5.7 - 1996.12.29)

Real name Bi Yuyi. A native of Guangdong province. Born in Hong Kong, but brought up by her grandmother in Macau. Her father was famous Cantonese opera singer Pak Yuk-tong (Bai Yutang). While still in school, she was discovered by Runde Shaw, who signed her up in 1952 to appear in *Anything Can Happen* (never released). She then starred in over 20 films for the Shaw studio, including *A Thread of Life* (1953), *Tragedy of Vendetta* (1955), *Love and War* (1959) etc. When her contract with Shaw Brothers expired in 1958, she joined MP & GI and made *Her Tender Heart* (1959) and *All in the Family* (1959). She won Best Actress in the 6th and 7th Asian Film Festival respectively with the two films, followed by the great box office success of *A Night in Hong Kong* (1961) in Japan. Lucilla You Min became the only star in MP & GI who really made it to the non Chinese-speaking market. With *Sun, Moon and Star* (1961), she won Best Actress in the 1st Golden Horse Award. After finishing her last film *Romance of the Forbidden City* in 1964, she married Hong Kong business tycoon Gao Fuqiu and retired. Died of a heart attack in Hong Kong in 1996.

CHEN Hou/Peter Chen Ho (1929.7.1 - 1970.4.16)

Real name Chen Shanghou. A native of Shanghai. Came to Hong Kong with his family in 1950. Started working with Shaw Brothers as actor in 1953, but did not sign a contract with the studio because the salary was too low. Director Tu Guangqi recommended him to join Hsin Hwa Company. His film debut was *Qiu Jin, the Revolutionary Heroine* (1953) and his first leading role was in *Holiday Express* (1957). Joined MP & GI and became popular after *Mambo Girl* (1957). Regarded as "Holy Hand of Comedy", Chen had appeared in films produced by MP & GI, Shaw Brothers and Cathay. Among his most memorable films were MP & GI films *The Battle of Love* (1957), *Happy Union* (1957), *Calendar Girl* (1959); and Shaw Brothers productions *Les belles* (1961), *Love Parade* (1963), and *The Lark* (1965). After an unsuccessful marriage, he married a second time, to actress Betty Loh Ti (Le Di). Their marriage ended with a divorce in 1967. Chen died of colon cancer in the United States in 1970, at the age of 40.

男星 Actor

鄧小宇（1951.10.31 - ）

電懋童星。貴州人，香港出生。父親鄧廷琮本為貴州富戶，1949年逃難來港，苦學負笈美國唸航空管理，將年幼的鄧小宇交託女傭照料。受該女傭的影響，鄧小宇愛上演戲；其父於是在他七歲那年，代他寫信報考電懋小演員。試鏡當日天份畢露，獲岳楓選中參演《我們的子女》（1959）。之後，又為電懋演出過《雨過天青》（1959）、《愛的教育》（1961）、《人之初》（1963）、《小兒女》（1963）等多部電影。直至升上中學，才停止拍片。鄧小宇修業於美國喬治亞州大學新聞系和譚普大學傳理系，1976年與胡君毅、丘世文和陳冠中創辦《號外》雜誌；自1983年起，改而協助父親打理家族生意。

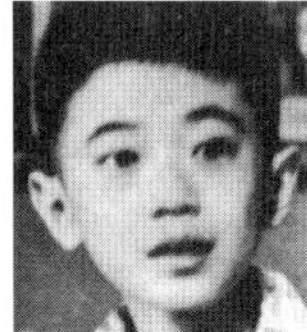

DENG Xiaoyu / Peter Dunn (b. 1951.10.31)

Child actor of MP & GI. A native of Guizhou province. Born in Hong Kong. Young Peter Dunn fell in love with acting at a young age. His father, noticing his interest in acting, sent him to an MP & GI audition at the age of 7. His talent impressed director Yue Feng who cast him in *Our Beloved Son* (1959). His screen debut was followed by a series of other MP & GI films, including *For Better, For Worse* (1959), *Education of Love* (1961), *Father and Son* (1963), and *Father Takes a Bride* (1963). Dunn's acting career ended when he entered secondary school. Graduated from the University of Georgia and Temple University, Dunn founded *City Magazine* with Joseph Yau (Qiu Shiwen), John Chan Koon-chung and others in 1976. The magazine became a local cultural icon of the 1970s and 1980s. He left *City Magazine* in 1983, and has since been helping his father to manage the family business.

男星 Actor

雷震（1933.9.3 - ）

原名奚重儉，祖籍浦東，上海出生，四歲喪父，十四歲喪母，由外婆照料長大。1949年隨外婆來港，曾入讀遠東航空學校。1955年底，成功考入電懋的前身「國際」，改藝名雷震，並於《青山翠谷》（1956）中首度演出。其後主演《金蓮花》（1957）及《小情人》（1958）等，憑其文弱優雅的書生氣質贏得「憂鬱小生」的稱號。之後，他在電懋參演了《四千金》（1957）、《我們的子女》（1959）、《家有喜事》（1959）、《樑上佳人》（1959，金泉出品）、《情深似海》（1960）、《無語問蒼天》（1961）、《花好月圓》（1962）、《小兒女》（1963）、《教我如何不想她》（1963）、《七重天》（1966）、《青春夢》（1967）等多部電影。1968年，他與胞妹樂蒂和袁秋楓創辦金鷹公司，出品過《風塵客》（1968）等七部武俠片。雷震自1971年退居幕後，專心經營合股的天工電影沖印公司業務達廿一年。近年，偶爾亦會在電影中客串演出，包括王家衛執導的《花樣年華》（2000）。

LEI Zhen /Kelly Lai Chen (b. 1933.9.3)

Real name Xi Zhongjian. A native of Pudong. Born in Shanghai. Brought up by his maternal grandmother when both his parents died. Joined MP & GI at the end of 1955, and debuted with *Green Hills and Jade Valleys* (1956). Then he appeared in *Golden Lotus* (1957) and *Little Darling* (1958) and started gaining fame among the audience. Lai was basically a MP & GI star. His gentle manners created a vulnerable and sensitive image for him, quite unusual in Hong Kong actors. Other films include *Our Sister Hedy* (1957), *Our Beloved Son* (1959), *All in the Family* (1959), *Tragic Melody* (1960), *Song without Words* (1961), *Father Takes a Bride* (1963), *Seventh Heaven* (1966), and *Young Love* (1967). He founded the Golden Eagle Film Company with his sister Betty Loh Ti and director Yuan Qiufeng. The company had produced 7 *wuxia* films, including *The Vagabond Swordsman* (1968). Retired from acting in 1971 and had been managing his own film laboratory for 21 years. He made occasional guest appearances in local films in recent years such as in Wong Kar-wai's *In the Mood for Love* (2000).

男星 Actor

劉恩甲（1916 - 1968）

河北省鹽山縣人，幼年曾在吉林、天津等地生活，後肄業於哈爾濱商業專科學校。1937年，考入滿洲映畫協會，正式開展其影藝事業，期間拍過《蜜月快車》、《田園春光》等片。1947年，轉投北京「中電三廠」，但未幾即應張駿祥導演的邀請，於1949年來港參演永華公司出品的《火葬》（1949）。此後，繼續留港拍戲，並憑《拜金的人》（1952）一片漸為香港觀眾認識。1956年，他正式加盟電懋（後改名國泰），擅演喜劇諧角，曾參演《金蓮花》（1957）、《情場如戰場》（1957）、《兩傻大鬧太空》（1959）、《星星．月亮．太陽》（1961）等多部影片，尤以《南北和》（1961）的演出最為成功。他最後演出的一部電影為國泰出品的《大丐俠》（1968）。1968年4月25日心臟病發逝於香港，終年52歲。

LIU Enjia (1916 - 1968)

A native of Yanshan county, Hebei province. Spent his childhood in Jilin, Tianjin, attended School of Commerce in Ha'erbin. Recruited by the Manchuria Movie Association in 1937 and started his career as an actor. Joined the Zhongdian Studio 3 in Beijing but soon left the studio. Came to Hong Kong in 1949 upon the request of director Zhang Junxiang to play in his *Hearts Aflame* (1949), a Yung Hwa production. After completion of the film, Liu stayed in Hong Kong. He joined MP & GI in 1956. Liu was a talented comic actor and had appeared in many MP & GI films, among them: *Golden Lotus* (1957), *The Battle of Love* (1957), *Riots in Outer Space* (1959), and *Sun, Moon and Star* (1961). His most popular performance was in *The Greatest Civil War on Earth* (1961). Died of a heart attack in Hong Kong on April 25, 1968, aged 52. His last film was *To Kill a Rover* (1968), a Cathay production.

男星 Actor

喬宏（1927 - 1999）

山西臨汾人，曾先後於重慶廣益中學和上海美童公學唸書。韓戰期間到了台灣，當過電台播音員和美軍翻譯。1955年，他輾轉到了日本，並結識在當地經營餐廳的著名女星白光。時白光正欲回港自資拍片，喬宏遂在她的帶領下來港拍戲，首作為白光名下國光公司出品的《鮮牡丹》（1956）。1957年，白光息影，把他推薦給電懋為基本演員。自此，因身型魁梧而有「影壇雄獅」之稱的喬宏即備受重用，除接連主演了《青春兒女》（1959）、《空中小姐》（1959）、《鐵臂金剛》（1960）、《遊戲人間》（1961）、《好事成雙》（1962）、《亂世兒女》（1966）和《虎山行》（1969）等多部電影外，又因其通曉英語、日語、韓語、國語、粵語、滬語和廈門語，而獲蘭克公司邀請參演西片《港澳輪渡》（1959）。1970年，喬宏脫離國泰，成自由身，轉走性格演員及喜劇演員路線，參演了唐書璇導演的《董夫人》（1970）。1980年後，他又嘗試參與電視劇的演出。身為虔誠基督徒的喬宏，自1994年與愛妻金彥平（前「麗的呼聲」播音員）移居美國西雅圖後，一直致力傳道工作，偶爾才回港參演電影。1996年，喬宏憑《女人，四十。》（1995）贏得香港電影金像獎和金紫荊獎最佳男主角。1999年4月16日心臟病發於西雅圖去逝，享年72歲，其遺作為福音電影《天使之城》（1999）。

QIAO Hong / Roy Chiao (1927 - 1999)

A native of Linfen county, Shanxi province. Attended schools in Chongqing and Shanghai. Went to Taiwan during the Korean War. Before becoming an actor, he was a radio broadcaster and an interpreter for the US Army. Went to Japan in 1955, and met the famous Mandarin actress Bai Guang who had plans of coming back to Hong Kong. She asked Chiao to come along and cast him in *Fresh Peony* (1956), a debut for both Bai's Guoguang Company (financed by MP & GI) and Chiao. Before her retirement in 1957, Bai recommended Chiao to MP & GI. With his athletic physique, Chiao soon became one of the important actors of the company and starred in many well-received features: *Spring Song* (1959), *Air Hostess* (1959), *The Iron Fist* (1960), *Ladies First* (1962), *A Debt of Blood* (1966), and *Escort over Tiger Hills* (1969). Chiao left Cathay in 1970 and starred in Shu Shuen's *The Arch* (1970). He became actively involved in TV after 1980. A devoted Christian, Chiao has been actively involved in missionary work after emigrating to Seattle in 1994 with his wife. Made occasional appearances in Hong Kong cinema since then. Won Best Actor of the Hong Kong Film Awards with Ann Hui's *Summer Snow* (1995). Died of a heart attack in Seattle on April 16, 1999 at the age of 72. His last work *Sometimes, Miracles Do Happen* (1999) is made for the church.

男星 Actor

田青（1935 - 1993）

原名田春生，上海出生的河南人，1949年來港，以半工讀方式就讀教會學校三育中學，畢業後初作傳教工作，決定轉行後考入國際公司為演員，與雷震、丁皓、蘇鳳等同期，第一部影片為《青山翠谷》（1956）。國語片時期曾在《春潮》（1960）中擔任男主角。田青戲路廣闊，在《四千金》（1957）、《家有喜事》（1959）、《雲裳艷后》（1959）、《野玫瑰之戀》（1960）、《星星・月亮・太陽》（1961）等多部電懋重頭戲中有頗重的戲份。因為能操流利廣東話，1964年在電懋傾力發展粵語片組時，調派為公司的粵語片當家小生，拍過《舊愛新歡》（1964）及《自作多情》（1966）等，可惜粵語片組在陸運濤空難後不久即結束，他也回到性格演員的行列，重拍國語片。1970年轉投邵氏公司，然後在八十年代以自由身份活躍於港台兩地，演出以配角、諧角或反派居多，例如《天字第一號》（1981）、《上海之夜》（1984）等。1993年6月2日病逝香港，享年58歲。

TIAN Qing (1935 - 1993)

Real name Tian Chunsheng. A native of Henan province. Born in Shanghai. Came to Hong Kong in 1949, and completed his secondary education as part time student. Joined International Films and made his first full-length feature *Green Hills and Jade Valleys* (1956) along with his contemporaries Kelly Lai Chen (Lei Zhen), Kitty Ting Hao (Ding Hao) and Dolly Soo Fung (Su Feng). He was frequently assigned supporting roles, and became a multi-functional character actor. Works include *Our Sister Hedy* (1957), *All in the Family* (1959), *Cinderella and Her Little Angels* (1959), *The Wild, Wild Rose* (1960), and *Sun, Moon and Star* (1961). *Torrents of Spring* (1960) is one of the rare Mandarin films in which he played the leading role. Transferred to the Cantonese Film Unit in 1964 and became its major actor, starring in *I Love Them Both* (1964) and *I'll Make My Own Choice* (1966) among others. The Cantonese Film Unit was closed down after Loke Wan Tho died in a plane crash and Tian Qing rejoined the team of character actors for Mandarin films. Joined Shaw Brothers in the 1970s, then became a freelance actor in the 1980s, actively involved in both Hong Kong and Taiwan cinema. Passed away in Hong Kong on June 2, 1993 at the age of 58.

男星 Actor

吳家驤（1919.7.7 - 1993.3.20）

原籍安徽省歙縣，因祖父宦遊湖北漢口，而寄籍當地。出生於北京，幼年時在江西九江外祖母家住了五年，後在漢口市立高級職業學校修讀紡織科。抗戰初期，曾參與漢口「抗敵後援會」以及上海業餘劇人協會的舞台演出，其後加入陸軍政工隊，未幾在重慶加入中國電影製片廠當實習演員，這期間只參演過三部影片，話劇卻演過很多。1945年底來香港，第一部參演的影片為《蘆花翻白燕子飛》（1946），接著先後參加了永華及五十年代公司，1953年開始擔任副導演工作，第一部影片是屠光啟導演的《玫瑰玫瑰我愛你》（1954）。吳家驤為不可多得的性格演員，1957年9月受聘於電懋公司，演出作品包括《無頭案》（1957）、《桃花運》（1959）、《同床異夢》（1960）、《無語問蒼天》（1961）等，期間也兼任副導演，追隨屠光啟、易文等導演。第一部獨立導演的影片是《人之初》（1963），其他作品包括《都市狂想曲》（1964）和《女人・女人》（1967）等。1965年約滿電懋，轉投邵氏旗下，任基本演員及導演。脫離邵氏之後，只導演了一部《春滿芭提雅》（1976）。1980年在台加入中國電視公司為基本演員。1993年在港病逝，享年74歲。

WU Jiaxiang (1919.7.7 - 1993.3.20)

Actor, director. A native of Anhui province. Born in Beijing. Acted in over a hundred plays on stage during wartime. Came to Hong Kong at the end of 1945, and acted in *Gone are the Swallows When the Willow Flowers Wilt* (1946), his first film made in Hong Kong. Later worked for Yung Hwa and 50th Year Motion Pictures, Inc. and started working as assistant director in 1953 for Tu Guangqi's *Rose, Rose, I Love You* (1954). Joined MP & GI in September 1957 as a character actor and had since appeared in films such as *Murder in the Night* (1957), *The Wayward Husband* (1959), *Song without Words* (1961). Also worked as assistant director during this period, collaborating with Tu Guangqi, Evan Yang (Yi Wen) etc. His directorial debut was *Father and Son* (1963), other directorial works included *Cosmopolitan Fantasy* (1964), *Passion* (1967). Joined Shaw Brothers as actor and director in 1965. Directed only one film, *Springtime in Pattaya* (1976) after leaving Shaw Brothers. Joined China Television Company as actor in Taiwan in 1980. Passed away in Hong Kong at the age of 74.

張揚（1930 - ）

原名招華昌，廣東南海人，幼年隨家人從廣東到北方，在天津讀初中，後來又到北京讀高中，其後考入輔仁大學政治經濟系，但只讀了一年就於1951年來港定居。來港後曾任出入口會計。1953年考入邵氏公司為基本演員，第一部影片是與尤敏合演的《黑手套》（1953）。1956年轉投電懋公司，第一部戲是《春色惱人》（1956），其後的《紅娃》（1958），奠定了當家小生的地位。張揚的外型俊偉，適合演時裝片，其他電懋時期的佳作還有《情場如戰場》（1957）、《雨過天青》（1959）、《同床異夢》（1960）、《野玫瑰之戀》（1960）、《温柔鄉》（1960）、《星星・月亮・太陽》（1961）、《情天長恨》（1964）等。他於1961年與葉楓結婚，1965年離異，翌年初與圈外人沈貝蒂結婚，然後赴台灣拍片。曾當導演，作品包括與羅維合導的《糊塗福星》（1974年在台上映）、《阿牛出獄記》（1975年在台上映）等。1975年離開影壇，移民赴美國經商。

ZHANG Yang / Chang Yang (b. 1930)

Real name Zhao Huachang. A native of Nanhai county, Guangdong province. He went to the north with his family when he was a young boy, received his education in Tianjin and Beijing, later enrolled in the Economics Department of Furen University. After the first year at the university, he came to Hong Kong in 1951. Worked as accountant of a trading company before joining Shaw Brothers in 1953. His debut film was *Black Gloves* (1953), co-starring Lucilla You Min. Joined MP & GI in 1956. The first film he made there was *Gloomy Sunday* (1956). Later, *Scarlet Doll* (1958) made him a major star of the company. His other MP & GI works included *The Battle of Love* (1957), *For Better, For Worse* (1959), *The Bedside Story* (1960), *The Wild, Wild Rose* (1960), *Bachelors Beware* (1960), *Sun, Moon and Star* (1961), and *An Affair to Remember* (1964). He married Julie Yeh Feng (Ye Feng) in 1961 but divorced in 1965. He remarried the next year and went to Taiwan to continue his career in acting. He had also directed several films, but achieved no major successes. Retired from the film industry in 1975, emigrated to the US and became a businessman.

Filmographies

Filmography of Mandarin and Cantonese Films
Filmography of Cathay Keris Films

Editor's note:

The filmography of Mandarin and Cantonese films contains not only films produced by International Films, MP & GI and the reorganised Cathay but also those by Cathay's satellite companies or companies that received Cathay's financial backing. As for the Taiwan films financed by Cathay, either directly or indirectly, further study and collection of data is needed.

片目

國粵語片總目
國泰克里斯片目

編按

後附國粵片總目除了國際、電懋和1965年電懋重組後的國泰機構所出品的影片外，亦包括了其「子」公司以及其他受其資助的電影公司的作品在內。至於其他直接或間接受電懋資助的台灣電影，則有待進一步的研究與整理。

國粵語片總目 Filmography of Mandarin and Cantonese Films

整理：余慕雲、盛安琪、李俊慧　編校：黃愛玲
Compiled by : Yu Mo-wan, Angel Shing, Lee Chun-wai　Edited by : Wong Ain-ling

	影片名稱	片名漢語拼音	香港首映日期	語別	出品公司	監製 / 製片	編劇 / 原著	導演	主要演員	音樂 / 附註
1	余之妻 My Wife, My Wife	Yu Zhi Qi	1955/05/05	粵語	國際	歐德爾	何愉（即左几）/ 徐枕亞	左几	吳楚帆、紫羅蓮、 梅綺、周坤玲	
2	花都綺夢 Sweet Dreams	Huadu Qimeng	1955/08/26	粵語	國際	歐德爾 / 顧文娟	唐滌生 / 唐滌生， 改編自多寶劇團舞台劇	唐滌生	任劍輝、白雪仙、 梁醒波、鳳凰女	音樂領導：羅寶生
3	愛情三部曲 Three Stages of Love	Aiqing Sanbuqu	1955/10/26	粵語	國際	歐德爾 / 林永泰	江揚、何愉 / 巴金	左几	吳楚帆、白燕、 梅綺、黃曼梨	
4	斷鴻零雁記 The Lone Swan	Duanhong Lingyan Ji	1955/12/22	粵語	國際	歐德爾 / 吳楚帆	李晨風 / 蘇曼殊	李晨風	吳楚帆、紫羅蓮、 李月清、黃曼梨	音樂：李元
5	菊子姑娘 Miss Kikuko	Juzi Guniang	1956/02/16	國語	國泰 （嚴俊）	歐德爾 / 王龍	嚴俊	嚴俊	嚴俊、林黛、 劉恩甲、羅維	音樂：姚敏，作詞：狄薏、司徒明； 〈雪山盟〉作曲：姚敏，作詞：狄薏（即陳蝶衣）
6	火 Fire	Huo	1956/03/29	粵語	國際	歐德爾 / 林永泰	何愉、江揚 / 巴金	左几	張瑛、紅線女、 梅綺、李月清	音樂：居仁，作曲：李願聞、盧家熾
7	驚魂記 Surprise	Jing Hun Ji	1956/07/27	國語	國際	歐德爾	陶秦	陶秦	王豪、葛蘭、 羅維、王萊	音樂：綦湘棠
8	歡樂年年 Merry-Go-Round	Huanle Niannian	1956/08/04	國語	國泰 （嚴俊）	歐德爾 / 屠梅卿	羅臻	岳楓	嚴俊、林黛、 劉恩甲、陳又新	音樂：綦湘棠、姚敏， 作曲：綦湘棠、姚敏，作詞：狄薏（即陳蝶衣）
9	碧海浮屍 The Body of a Blackmailer	Bihai Fushi	1956/09/06	粵語	電懋	鍾啟文 / 林永泰	何愉	左几	張清、丁櫻、 黃楚山、李鐵	
10	風雨牛車水 Rainstorm in Chinatown	Fengyu Niucheshui	1956/09/17	國語	國泰 （嚴俊）	歐德爾 / 屠梅卿	王植波	嚴俊	嚴俊、李麗華、 劉恩甲、高寶樹	音樂：綦湘棠，作曲：姚敏；〈琵琶怨〉、 〈春風秋雨〉作曲：姚敏，作詞：王植波
11	春色惱人 Gloomy Sunday	Chunse Naoren	1956/10/19	國語	電懋	鍾啟文 / 屠梅卿	易文 / 徐訏	易文	王豪、李湄、 張揚、王元龍	作曲配樂：綦湘棠； 〈春色惱人〉作曲：綦湘棠，作詞：易文 原名《流水落花春去也》 台灣上映時名《春去也》 1967 年重映易名《春風一度空遺恨》
12	青山翠谷 * Green Hills and Jade Valleys	Qingshan Cuigu	1956/11/16	國語	電懋	鍾啟文 / 屠梅卿	岳楓	岳楓	雷震、蘇鳳、 丁皓、田青	作曲：綦湘棠，作詞：李雋青
13	星洲艷跡 Romance in Singapore	Xingzhou Yanji	1956/11/16	粵語	國際	歐德爾 / 顧文娟	林川	林川	梁醒波、張清、 周坤玲、鳳凰女	音樂：林兆鎏，撰曲：羅寶生
14	鮮牡丹 Fresh Peony	Xian Mudan	1956/11/28	國語	國光	白光	白光	白光、 羅臻	羅維、白光、 楊志卿、喬宏	〈春光曲〉作曲：司徒容，作詞：羅臻； 〈四季歌〉作詞：李雋青，編曲：江風； 〈勸酒歌〉作曲：司徒容，作詞：李雋青
15	娘惹與峇峇 Nonya and Baba	Niangre Yu Baba	1956/12/29	國語	國泰 （嚴俊）	歐德爾 / 屠梅卿	王植波	嚴俊	嚴俊、李麗華、 劉恩甲、姜南	音樂：綦湘棠； 〈雨後虹光〉作曲：姚敏，作詞：王植波
16	金蓮花 Golden Lotus	Jin Lianhua	1957/02/14	國語	電懋	鍾啟文 / 屠梅卿	岳楓	岳楓	雷震、林黛、 劉恩甲、王萊	音樂：綦湘棠；〈相思苦〉作曲：姚敏、綦湘棠， 填詞：李雋青、綦湘棠；〈媽媽要我嫁〉、 〈早生貴子〉作曲：綦湘棠、姚敏，填詞： 李雋青；〈小兩口吵嘴〉作曲：姚敏， 作詞：李雋青

17	曼波女郎 Mambo Girl	Manpo Nülang	1957/03/06	國語	電懋	鍾啟文 / 宋淇	易文	易文	陳厚、葛蘭、 丁皓、劉恩甲	音樂：綦湘棠；〈曼波女郎〉、〈回來了〉、〈我的天堂〉、〈天皇皇〉、〈忘憂歌〉、〈青春女兒〉作曲：綦湘棠；〈我愛恰恰〉、〈今宵樂〉作曲：姚敏；〈曼波女郎〉、〈回來了〉、〈我的天堂〉作詞：李雋青；〈我愛恰恰〉、〈今宵樂〉、〈天皇皇〉、〈忘憂歌〉、〈青春女兒〉作詞：易文
18	新華春夢	Xinhua Chunmeng	1957/03/27	國語	電懋				黃河、李湄、 王元龍、洪波	1964/12/26 改名《燕京春夢》於台灣重映
19	無頭案 Murder in the Night	Wu Tou An	1957/04/11	國語	電懋	鍾啟文	陶秦	陶秦	張揚、葛蘭、 王萊、張翠英	
20	魂歸離恨天 Love Lingers On	Hungui Lihentian	1957/05/02	粵語	電懋	鍾啟文 / 林永泰	何愉 / 白朗恩； 原著《咆哮山莊》	左几	張瑛、梅綺、 周坤玲、張清	音樂：盧家熾； 〈青山綠水好春暉〉作曲：盧家熾，作詞：李願聞
21	半世老婆奴 Hen-pecked Husband	Banshi Lauponü	1957/05/17	粵語	電懋	林永泰 / 鍾啟文	左几 / 蒲松齡	左几	梁醒波、紫羅蓮、 鳳凰女、黃千歲	音樂領導：盧家熾，作曲：李願聞、潘焯 改編自《聊齋誌異》之〈馬介甫〉
22	情場如戰場 The Battle of Love	Qingchang Ru Zhanchang	1957/05/29	國語	電懋	鍾啟文 / 吳楚帆	張愛玲	岳楓	陳厚、林黛、 張揚、秦羽	音樂：李厚襄
23	兩傻大鬧攝影場 Riots at the Studio	Liangsha Danao Sheyingchang	1957/08/08	國語	電懋	鍾啟文	易文	易文	金銓、劉恩甲、 丁皓、王萊	
24	香港東京蜜月旅行 Hong Kong-Tokyo Honeymoon	Xianggang Dongjing Miyue Lüxing	1957/08/29	國語	電懋、 國際		野村芳太郎	野村芳太郎	嚴俊、林黛、 岸惠子、有馬稻子	
25	璇宮艷史 My Kingdom for a Husband (aka *The Romance of Jade Hall*)	Xuangong Yanshi	1957/09/12	粵語	電懋	鍾啟文 / 林永泰	左几 / 薛覺先 同名舞台粵劇	左几	張瑛、羅艷卿、 梁醒波、譚蘭卿	作曲：李願聞、潘焯
26	亡魂谷 The Valley of the Lost Soul	Wanghun Gu	1957/10/10	國語	國泰 （嚴俊）	鍾啟文、 歐德爾 / 王龍	狄薏（即陳蝶衣）	嚴俊	嚴俊、林黛、 劉恩甲、沈雲	音樂：綦湘棠；〈悲歌〉、〈愛花要愛最嬌媚〉 作曲：姚敏，作詞：狄薏
27	琵琶怨 The Sorrowful Lute	Pipa Yuan	1957/10/16	粵語	電懋	鍾啟文 / 吳楚帆	陳雲 / 改編自西片《琵琶怨》 (Love Me or Leave Me, 1955)	左几	吳楚帆、芳艷芬、 黃千歲、吳桐	音樂：盧家熾；粵曲：盧家熾，作曲：李願聞， 作詞：李願聞、潘焯 折子戲：〈樊梨花〉、〈穆桂英〉、〈鳳儀亭〉、〈四美人〉
28	四千金 Our Sister Hedy	Si Qianjin	1957/11/14	國語	電懋	鍾啟文 / 宋淇	陶秦 / 鄭慧原著	陶秦	林翠、葉楓、 蘇鳳、穆紅	音樂：綦湘棠；〈劍舞歌〉作曲：綦湘棠，
29	天作之合 Happy Union	Tianzuo Zhihe	1957/12/04	國語	電懋	鍾啟文 / 宋淇	易文	易文	嚴俊、李麗華、 丁皓、陳厚	作曲：綦湘棠，作詞：周之原
30	黛綠年華 The Tender Age (aka *The Splendour of Youth*)	Dailü Nianhua	1957/12/11	粵語	電懋	鍾啟文	左几 / 鄭慧原著《黛綠年華》	左几	吳楚帆、紫羅蓮、 梅綺、張瑛	音樂：蘇民
31	人財兩得 A Tale of Two Wives	Rencai Liangde	1958/01/01	國語	電懋	鍾啟文 / 宋淇	張愛玲	岳楓	陳厚、李湄、 劉恩甲、丁皓	音樂：綦湘棠 1957 年先在台灣上映
32	殺妻案 Over My Dead Body	Sha Qi An	1958/01/08	粵語	電懋	鍾啟文 / 林永泰	左几	左几	張瑛、梅綺、 胡楓、李鵬飛	配樂：蘇民

國粵語片總目 Filmography of Mandarin and Cantonese Films

	影片名稱	片名漢語拼音	香港首映日期	語別	出品公司	監製 / 製片	編劇 / 原著	導演	主要演員	音樂 / 附註
33	南洋亞伯 Kuala Lumpur Nights (aka *The Old Man of Southeast Asia*)	Nanyang Yabo	1958/02/05	粵語	電懋 顧文娟	歐德爾 /	林川	林川	梁醒波、張清、周坤玲、鳳凰女	音樂：林兆鎏、李蘇、梁漁舫，撰曲：羅寶生 又名《吉隆坡之夜》
34	紅娃 Scarlet Doll	Hong Wa	1958/03/20	國語	電懋	鍾啟文 / 宋淇、馬叔庸	秦亦孚（即秦羽）	岳楓	王引、林黛、張揚、劉恩甲	音樂：綦湘棠，作曲：綦湘棠、姚敏
35	黑俠擒兇 The Black Mask	Heixia Qinxiong	1958/03/26	粵語	電懋	鍾啟文 / 林永泰	左几 / 望雲	左几	吳楚帆、白燕、丁櫻、方華	配樂：蘇民
36	提防小手 Beware of Pickpockets	Tifang Xiaoshou	1958/04/17	國語	電懋	鍾啟文		陶秦	陳厚、林翠、文蘭、梁醒波	
37	廣告女郎 The Girl of the Year	Guanggao Nülang	1958/04/18	粵語	電懋			左几	梁醒波、羅艷卿、張清、丁櫻	
38	璇宮艷史續集 My Kingdom for a Honeymoon (aka *The Romance of Jade Hall, Sequel*)	Xuangong Yanshi Xuji	1958/05/21	粵語	電懋	鍾啟文 / 林永泰	左几	左几	張瑛、羅艷卿、梁醒波、譚蘭卿	音樂：盧家熾，撰曲：李願聞、潘焯； 〈香池蜜月〉撰曲：李願聞、潘焯
39	小情人 Little Darling	Xiao Qingren	1958/06/19	國語	電懋	鍾啟文 / 宋淇	萬方	陶秦	雷震、丁皓、羅維、胡金銓	音樂：綦湘棠
40	月宮寶盒 The Magic Box	Yuegong Baohe	1958/07/16	粵語	電懋	鍾啟文 / 林永泰	譚新風	左几	張瑛、梅綺、羅艷卿、方華	配樂：蘇民
41	美人春夢 Memories of Love (aka *A Lovely Girl's Lovely Dreams*)	Meiren Chunmeng	1958/10/22	粵語	電懋	鍾啟文 / 林永泰	左几 / 改編自西片《紅顏禍水》(The Girl in the Red Velvet Swing, 1955)	左几	吳楚帆、白露明、張瑛、莫蘊霞	音樂：盧家熾、顧嘉輝；作曲：盧家熾； 〈紅鞦韆美人〉作曲：盧家熾，作詞：靳夢萍
42	歷盡滄桑一美人 The Beauty Who Lived through Great Changes	Lijin Cangsang Yi Meiren	1958/12/24	粵語	電懋	鍾啟文 / 林永泰	左几	左几	張瑛、羅艷卿、馮毅、梁醒波	音樂：盧家熾，配樂：蘇民， 填詞：李願聞、潘焯
43	東床佳婿 My Eligible Son-in-Law	Dongchuang Jiaxu	1959/01/28	粵語	電懋	歐德爾 / 林永泰	左几	左几、歐德爾	張清、田青、黎灼灼、楊業宏、方華、丁櫻、李鐵、李亨	
44	青春兒女 Spring Song	Qingchun Ernü	1959/02/14	國語	電懋	鍾啟文 / 宋淇	易文、王植波	易文	陳厚、林翠、葛蘭、喬宏	音樂：綦湘棠；〈青春兒女〉作曲：綦湘棠， 作詞：周之原；〈姐姐的話〉作曲：綦湘棠， 作詞：易文
45	龍翔鳳舞 Calendar Girl	Longxiang Fengwu	1959/03/04	國語	電懋	鍾啟文 / 宋淇	陶秦	陶秦	李湄、張仲文、陳厚、羅維	音樂：姚敏；〈妹妹我愛你〉作曲：姚敏， 作詞：沈華；〈何日君再來〉作詞：沈華， 改編曲：姚敏 別名《日曆女郎》
46	桃花運 The Wayward Husband	Taohua Yun	1959/04/09	國語	電懋	鍾啟文 / 宋淇	張愛玲	岳楓	陳厚、葉楓、劉恩甲、王萊	音樂：綦湘棠；〈桃花運〉、〈野花香〉、 〈家家有本難念的經〉作曲：姚敏， 作詞：李雋青 1958 年已於台灣上映

47	三星伴月 The More the Merrier	Sanxing Banyue	1959/04/23	國語	電懋	鍾啟文 / 宋淇	秦亦孚	陶秦	陳厚、林黛、 雷震、喬宏	
48	我們的子女 Our Beloved Son	Women De Zinü	1959/05/02	國語	電懋	鍾啟文 / 宋淇	岳楓	岳楓	雷震、李湄、 劉恩甲、陳芸	作曲：綦湘棠
49	玉女私情 Her Tender Heart	Yunü Siqing	1959/05/21	國語	電懋	鍾啟文 / 宋淇、馬叔庸	秦亦孚 / 杜寧原著《女兒心》	唐煌	王引、尤敏、 張揚、藍天虹	音樂：綦湘棠
50	空中小姐 Air Hostess	Kongzhong Xiaojie	1959/06/04	國語	電懋	鍾啟文 / 宗淇	易文	易文	雷震、葛蘭、 喬宏、葉楓	音樂：姚敏；〈我要飛上天〉作曲：姚敏、 作詞：李雋青、易文；〈廟院鐘聲〉、 〈我愛卡力蘇〉作曲：姚敏，作詞：易文 1958 年已於台灣上映
51	貴妃風流 A Romantic Lady	Guifei Fengliu	1959/06/18	國語	金龍	嚴俊		嚴俊	李麗華、嚴俊、 王引	電懋發行
52	香車美人 Our Dream Car	Xiangju Meiren	1959/07/09	國語	電懋	鍾啟文 / 宗淇	易文	易文	張揚、葛蘭、 雷震、劉恩甲	
53	天長地久 Tragedy of Love	Tianchang Dijiu	1959/08/06	國語	電懋	鍾啟文 / 宋淇	陶秦	陶秦	陳厚、葉楓、 喬宏、王萊	音樂：綦湘棠；〈天長地久〉、〈笑哈哈〉 作曲：綦湘棠，作詞：沈華
54	兩傻大鬧太空 Riots in Outer Space	Liangsha Danao Taikong	1959/08/13	國語	電懋	鍾啟文 / 宋淇	王天林	王天林	蔣光超、劉恩甲、 丁皓、李英	音樂：綦湘棠；〈火星上的愛情〉 作曲：姚敏、綦湘棠，作詞：李雋青
55	雨過天青 For Better, For Worse	Yuguo Tianqing	1959/08/20	國語	電懋	鍾啟文 / 宋淇	岳楓	岳楓	張揚、李湄、 蘇鳳、陳寶珠	音樂：綦湘棠
56	二八佳人 Too Young to Love	Erba Jiaren	1959/09/17	國語	電懋	鍾啟文 / 宋淇、馬叔庸	秦亦孚（即秦羽）	易文	張揚、林翠、 葉楓、雷震	音樂：姚敏； 〈初戀滋味〉作曲：姚敏，作詞：易文
57	姊妹花 My Darling Sister	Zimei Hua	1959/09/30	國語	電懋	鍾啟文 / 宋淇、馬叔庸	易文	易文	雷震、葛蘭、 張小燕、蘇鳳	音樂：姚敏；〈燕子舞曲〉作曲：綦湘棠， 作詞：周之原，〈瘋狂的週末〉、 〈猜不出是甚麼情意〉作曲：姚敏，作詞：易文
58	風雨歸舟 The Long Voyage Home	Fengyu Guizhou	1959/10/22	國語	國泰	鍾啟文	王植波	嚴俊	嚴俊、李麗華、 吳家驤、李英	
59	家有喜事 All in the Family	Jiayou Xishi	1959/11/12	國語	電懋	鍾啟文 / 宋淇、馬叔庸	汪榴照	王天林	雷震、尤敏、 羅維、丁皓	音樂：劉宏遠，作曲：姚敏
60	童軍教練 The Scout Master	Tongjun Jiaolian	1959/11/20	國語	電懋	鍾啟文 / 宋淇	陶秦	陶秦	梁醒波、陳寶珠、 蔣光超、翁木蘭	音樂：綦湘棠； 〈童子軍進行曲〉作曲：綦湘棠，作詞：韋瀚章
61	逃亡四十八小時 48 Hours in Escape	Taowang Sishiba Xiaoshi	1959/12/09	國語	電懋、 國際	歐德爾 / 屠梅卿	易文 / 改編自易文 原著短篇小說〈強盜〉	易文	王引、林翠、 羅維、王萊	
62	蘭閨風雲 Wedding Bells for Hedy	Langui Fengyun	1959/12/17	國語	電懋	鍾啟文 / 宋淇、馬叔庸	陶秦 / 鄭慧	陶秦	葉楓、林翠、 穆虹、蘇鳳	音樂：綦湘棠；〈跳繩歌〉 作曲：綦湘棠，作詞：沈華 別名《四千金續集》
63	雲裳艷后 Cinderella and Her Little Angels	Yunchang Yanhou	1959/12/31	國語	電懋	製片：宋淇、 馬叔庸	王月汀	唐煌	陳厚、林黛、 蘇鳳、王萊	音樂、作曲：姚敏，作詞：李雋青
64	野姑娘 The Wild Girl	Ye Guniang	1960/01/14	國語	電懋、 國泰	鍾啟文	何夢華	何夢華， 導演顧問： 嚴俊	嚴俊、丁皓、 梁醒波、吳家驤	音樂：綦湘棠，作曲：姚敏、綦湘棠

國粵語片總目 Filmography of Mandarin and Cantonese Films

	影片名稱	片名漢語拼音	香港首映日期	語別	出品公司	監製 / 製片	編劇 / 原著	導演	主要演員	音樂 / 附註
65	春潮 Torrents of Spring	Chun Chao	1960/01/21	國語	電懋	鍾啟文 / 屠梅卿	陶秦 / 屠格涅夫	陶秦	田青、李湄、 林翠、林靜	音樂：綦湘棠，作曲：綦湘棠， 作詞：沈華 1957 年已於台灣上映
66	六月新娘 June Bride	Liuyue Xinniang	1960/01/27	國語	電懋	鍾啟文 / 宋淇、馬叔庸	張愛玲	唐煌	張揚、葛蘭、 喬宏、蘇鳳	音樂：姚敏；〈六月新娘〉、〈海上良宵〉、 〈迷離世界〉作曲：姚敏，作詞：易文
67	三鳳求凰 They All Say I Do	Sanfeng Qiu Huang	1960/02/04	粵語	電懋	鍾啟文 / 林永泰		吳回	張瑛、白露明、 莫蘊霞、鳳凰女	
68	長腿姐姐 Sister Long Legs	Changtui Jiejie	1960/02/06	國語	電懋	鍾啟文 / 宋淇、馬叔庸	汪榴照	唐煌	葉楓、林翠、 喬宏、王萊	音樂：李厚襄
69	七喜臨門 Seven Lucky Ones	Qixi Linmen	1960/02/10	粵語	電懋	鍾啟文 / 林永泰		王天林	張瑛、梅綺、 梁醒波、張清	音樂：林兆鎏
70	苦兒流浪記 Nobody's Child	Ku'er Liulang Ji	1960/02/17	國語	國風	製片：朱旭華	吳鐵翼	卜萬蒼	王引、蕭芳芳、 陳燕燕、羅維	作曲：劉宏遠，作詞：李雋青
71	女秘書艷史 Miss Secretary	Nü Mishu Yanshi	1960/03/10	國語	電懋	鍾啟文	易文	易文	雷震、葉楓、 李湄、喬宏	
72	古屋疑雲 Corpses at Large	Guwu Yiyun	1960/03/24	國語	電懋	鍾啟文 / 宋淇、馬叔庸	宋曉筌	易文	張揚、丁皓、 雷震、蘇鳳	音樂：綦湘棠 原名《鬼屋殭屍》
73	情深似海 Forever Yours	Qingshen Sihai	1960/04/07	國語	電懋	鍾啟文 / 宋淇、馬叔庸	易文	易文	雷震、葛蘭、 王萊、劉恩甲	
74	母與女 Devotion	Mu Yu Nü	1960/04/21	國語	電懋	鍾啟文 / 宋淇、馬叔庸	秦亦孚 / 癡人	唐煌	張揚、丁皓、 喬宏、王萊	音樂：綦湘棠；作曲：綦湘棠， 填詞：易文，撰詞：易文
75	喋血販馬場 Time is Running Short	Diexue Fanma Chang	1960/05/19	國語	金鳳	製片：姚健明 策劃：王龍	蕭銅 / 上官牧	王引	王引、葉楓、 井淼、王豪	音樂：姚敏，作曲：姚敏，作詞：司徒明 電懋發行
76	心心相印 The Loving Couple	Xinxin Xiangyin	1960/05/26	國語	電懋	鍾啟文 / 宋淇、馬叔庸	易文	易文	陳厚、葛蘭、 林翠、雷震	音樂：姚敏， 〈不管你是誰〉作曲：姚敏，作詞：易文
77	快樂天使 Happily Ever After	Kuaile Tianshi	1960/06/16	國語	電懋	鍾啟文 / 宋淇、馬叔庸	汪榴照	易文	喬宏、尤敏、 謝家驊、王萊	音樂：服部良一
78	同床異夢 The Bedside Story	Tongchuang Yimeng	1960/06/23	國語	電懋	鍾啟文	秦亦孚	卜萬蒼	李湄、張揚、 雷震、王萊	
79	鐵臂金剛 The Iron Fist	Tiebi Jingang	1960/07/07	國語	電懋	鍾啟文	謝文	王天林	喬宏、葉楓、 王萊、吳家驤	作曲：姚敏
80	桃花淚 Tragic Melody	Taohua Lei	1960/07/28	國語	電懋、 金城	鄭天仕 / 茅蘆	鄭天仕、何觀 （即張徹）	羅維	雷震、尤敏、 歐陽莎菲、羅維	音樂：李義之
81	苦心蓮上集 Bitter Lotus (Part 1)	Kuxin Lian (Shangji)	1960/08/03	粵語	電懋	鍾啟文 / 林永泰	盧雨岐 / 李我 、高永輝	黃岱	羅劍郎、白露明、 鳳凰女、馮寶寶	音樂：居仁
82	苦心蓮大結局 Bitter Lotus (Part 2)	Kuxin Lian (Dajieju)	1960/08/10	粵語	電懋	鍾啟文 / 林永泰	盧雨岐 / 李我 、高永輝	黃岱	羅劍郎、白露明、 鳳凰女、馮寶寶	音樂：居仁
83	辮子姑娘 Miss Pony Tail	Bianzi Guniang	1960/08/17	國語	電懋	鍾啟文	汪榴照	唐煌	雷震、葛蘭、 李香君、張清	
84	喜相逢 Dreams Come True	Xi Xiangfeng	1960/08/27	國語	電懋	鍾啟文 / 宋淇、馬叔庸	易文	卜萬蒼	雷震、丁皓、 劉恩甲、吳家驤	音樂：服部良一，作曲：姚敏，作詞：李雋青

85	女俠文婷玉 Lady Musketeer	Nüxia Wen Tingyu	1960/09/08	國語	電懋	鍾啟文	吳鐵翼 / 秦亦孚	王天林	張揚、李湄、 王萊、田青	
86	紅男綠女 Swindler's Delight	Hongnan Lünü	1960/09/15	國語	電懋	鍾啟文 / 宋淇、馬叔庸	汪榴照	卜萬蒼	喬宏、葉楓、 蘇鳳、劉恩甲	音樂：劉宏遠
87	野玫瑰之戀 The Wild, Wild Rose	Ye Meigui Zhi Lian	1960/10/04	國語	電懋	鍾啟文 / 宋淇、馬叔庸	秦亦孚	王天林	張揚、葛蘭、 王萊、蘇鳳	音樂：姚敏，作曲：服部良一，歌詞：李雋青
88	玉樓三鳳 Between Tears and Laughter	Yulou Sanfeng	1960/11/10	國語	電懋	鍾啟文 / 宋淇、馬叔庸	汪榴照 / 王潔心	唐煌	李湄、丁皓、 喬宏、王萊	音樂：綦湘棠
89	温柔鄉 Bachelors Beware	Wenrou Xiang	1960/11/17	國語	電懋	鍾啟文 / 宋淇、馬叔庸	易文	易文	張揚、林黛、 雷震、于素秋	音樂：綦湘棠；〈温柔鄉〉(序曲、主題曲、泳衣展覽會插曲) 作曲：綦湘棠，作詞：易文
90	樑上佳人 Lady on the Roof	Liangshang Jiaren	1959/11/26	國語	金泉	歐陽天 (即鄺蔭泉)	易文 / 熊式一舞台劇改編	王天林	雷震、林黛、 蔣光超、吳家驤	音樂：李厚襄 電懋發行
91	翠樓春曉 Second Spring	Cuilou Chunxiao	1960/11/30	粵語	電懋	鍾啟文 / 林永泰	盧雨岐 / 李我	王天林	羅劍郎、白露明、 梁醒波、陳好逑	音樂：居仁
92	殺機重重 Death Traps	Shaji Chongchong	1960/12/08	國語	電懋	鍾啟文 / 宋淇、馬叔庸	文安	王天林	喬宏、李湄、 田青、歐陽莎菲	音樂：劉宏遠；作曲：姚敏，作詞：李雋青 又名《危機重重》
93	睡美人 Sleeping Beauty	Shui Meiren	1960/12/14	國語	電懋	鍾啟文 / 宋淇、馬叔庸	汪榴照	唐煌	雷震、葉楓、 丁好、劉恩甲	
94	天倫淚 Debt of Love	Tianlun Lei	1961/01/26	國語	電懋		蕭銅	易文	王引、張小燕、 唐菁、盧碧雲	
95	南北和 The Greatest Civil War on Earth	Nanbei He	1961/02/14	國語 粵語	電懋	鍾啟文 / 宋淇	宋淇	王天林	雷震、白露明、 張清、梁醒波	音樂：劉宏遠
96	殺人王大戰扭計深 Man Killer against the Tricky Man	Sharenwang Dazhan Niujishen	1961/03/22	粵語	電懋	鍾啟文 / 林永泰	王風 / 周白蘋	王天林	曹達華、白露明、 陳錦棠、李蘭	
97	體育皇后 Beauty Parade	Tiyu Huanghou	1961/03/30	國語	電懋	鍾啟文 / 宋淇	汪榴照	唐煌	雷震、丁皓、 羅維、張清	音樂作曲：姚敏，作詞：李雋青、周之原
98	夜夜杜鵑啼 Song of a Nightingale	Yeye Dujuan Ti	1961/05/24	粵語	電懋	鍾啟文 / 林永泰	藍菲 / 李我 (天空小説)	黃岱	胡楓、白露明、 馮寶寶、李香琴	
99	無語問蒼天 Song without Words	Wuyu Wen Cangtian	1961/06/15	國語	電懋	鍾啟文 / 宋淇	張徹	羅維	雷震、尤敏、 羅維、洪洋	
100	文婷玉火海殲仇 Venture of Lady Musketeer	Wen Tingyu Huohai Qianchou	1961/06/28	國語	電懋	鍾啟文 / 宋淇	吳鐵翼	王天林	張揚、李湄、 蘇鳳、王萊	音樂：劉宏遠
101	賊美人 The Girl with the Golden Arm	Zei Meiren	1961/07/27	國語	電懋	鍾啟文 / 宋淇	張徹 / 趙筠	唐煌	喬宏、葉楓、 羅維、麥玲	
102	愛的教育 Education of Love	Ai De Jiaoyu	1961/08/03	國語	電懋	鍾啟文 / 宋淇	陳鳴琴	鍾啟文	王引、林翠、 雷震、王萊	音樂：綦湘棠，作曲：綦湘棠，作詞：周之原
103	遊戲人間 You were Meant for Me	Youxi Renjian	1961/08/31	國語	電懋	鍾啟文 / 宋淇	張徹	王天林	雷震、丁皓、 白露明、喬宏	音樂：姚敏
104	香港之夜 A Night in Hong Kong	Xianggang Zhi Ye	1961/09/21	國語	電懋、 東寶	鍾啟文 / 宋淇	井手俊郎	千葉泰樹	寶田明、尤敏、 王引、馬力	音樂：松井八郎；作曲：松井八郎、服部良一，填詞：李雋青

國粵語片總目 Filmography of Mandarin and Cantonese Films

影片名稱	片名漢語拼音	香港首映日期	語別	出品公司	監製 / 製片	編劇 / 原著	導演	主要演員	音樂 / 附註
105 太太緝私團 Inspectress General	Taitai Jisi Tuan	1961/11/01	粵語	電懋	鍾啟文 / 林永泰	莫康時	莫康時	林家聲、白露明、 梁醒波、譚蘭卿	音樂：劉宏遠
106 紅顏青燈未了情 Till the End of Time	Hongyan Qingdeng Weiliao Qing	1961/11/02	國語	電懋	鍾啟文 / 宋淇、籐本真澄	孫晉三	易文	張揚、林翠、	音樂：綦湘棠 李湄、田青
107 懸崖 The Cliff	Xuan Ya	1961/11/18	國語	電懋		趙之城	宗由	唐菁、丁皓、 柯玉霞、崔小萍	
108 星星・月亮・太陽（上集） Sun, Moon and Star (Part 1)	Xingxing Yueliang Taiyang (Shangji)	1961/12/08	國語	電懋	鍾啟文 / 宋淇	秦亦孚 / 徐速	易文	張揚、尤敏、 葛蘭、葉楓	音樂：姚敏；作曲：姚敏， 作詞：周之原、易文、周之敏
109 星星・月亮・太陽（下集） Sun, Moon and Star (Part 2)	Xingxing Yueliang Taiyang (Xiaji)	1961/12/30	國語	電懋	鍾啟文 / 宋淇	秦亦孚 / 徐速	易文	張揚、尤敏、 葛蘭、葉楓	音樂：姚敏；作曲：姚敏， 作詞：周之原、易文、周之敏
110 早生貴子 Crusade against Daddy	Zaosheng Guizi	1962/02/03	國語	電懋	鍾啟文 / 宋淇	文望	唐煌	羅維、王萊、 林翠、洪洋	音樂：劉宏遠
111 有口難言 Golden Silence	Youkou Nanyan	1962/02/15	國語	軒轅		林以亮（即宋淇）	婁貽哲	嚴俊、林黛、 王萊、蔣光超	電懋發行 軒轅創業作
112 桃李爭春 It's Always Spring	Taoli Zhengchun	1962/02/21	國語	電懋	鍾啟文 / 宋淇、馬叔庸	張徹、易文	易文	葉楓、李湄、 喬宏、雷震	音樂：姚敏；〈賣餛飩〉、〈不唱睡不着〉、 〈好地方〉、〈多情世界〉作曲：姚敏， 作詞：易文；〈桃花江〉、〈我愛你〉、 〈海上彩虹〉作曲：姚敏，作詞：張徹
113 火中蓮 Lily of the Valley	Huo Zhong Lian	1962/03/29	國語	電懋	鍾啟文 / 宋淇	汪榴照	王天林	張揚、尤敏、 喬宏、王萊	音樂：綦湘棠
114 傻偵探 False Alarm	Sha Zhen Tan	1962/05/02	粵語	電懋	鍾啟文 / 林永泰、 竇漢勳	潘蕃	莫康時	胡楓、白露明、 梁醒波、劉恩甲	音樂：綦湘棠
115 野花戀 Come Rain, Come Shine	Yehua Lian	1962/05/17	國語	電懋	鍾啟文 / 宋淇	張徹	唐煌	張揚、葉楓、 蘇鳳、王萊	音樂：劉宏遠
116 萍水奇緣 The Male Bride	Pingshui Qiyuan	1962/06/02	國語	電懋	鍾啟文 / 宋淇	易文	易文	雷震、丁皓、 于素秋、王萊	
117 珍珠淚 Her Pearly Tears	Zhenzhu Lei	1962/06/29	國語	電懋	鍾啟文 / 宋淇	張徹	王天林	雷震、尤敏、 賀賓、王萊	音樂：姚敏，作曲：姚敏，作詞：易文、張徹
118 好事成雙 Ladies First	Haoshi Chengshuang	1962/08/02	國語	電懋	鍾啟文 / 宋淇	汪榴照	易文	喬宏、林翠、 田青、王萊	音樂：綦湘棠
119 雙劍盟 Crossed Swords (Part 1)	Shuang Jian Meng	1962/08/15	粵語	電懋	鍾啟文 / 林永泰	潘蕃 / 蹄風， 新報連載小說改編	龍圖	曹達華、于素秋、 白露明、梁醒波	音樂：劉宏遠
120 雙劍盟大結局 Crossed Swords (Part 2)	Shuang Jian Meng (Dajieju)	1962/08/22	粵語	電懋	鍾啟文 / 林永泰	潘蕃 / 蹄風， 新報連載小說改編	龍圖	曹達華、于素秋、 白露明、梁醒波	音樂：劉宏遠
121 花好月圓 Love in Bloom	Hua Hao Yue Yuan	1962/08/30	國語	電懋	鍾啟文 / 宋淇	汪榴照	唐煌	雷震、葉楓、 田青、王萊	音樂：姚敏，作曲：姚敏，作詞：易文 台名《新玉堂春》
122 一段情 A Fine Romance	Yi Duan Qing	1962/09/13	國語	電懋	鍾啟文 / 宋淇	蕭銅 / 皮述民	鍾啟文	張揚、丁皓、 羅維、王引	音樂：綦湘棠；作曲：綦湘棠，作詞：易文； 〈贈別〉作曲：綦湘棠，作詞：易文
123 南北一家親 The Greatest Wedding on Earth	Nanbei Yijiaqin	1962/10/11	國語	電懋	鍾啟文 / 宋淇	張愛玲 / 秦羽	王天林	雷震、白露明、 丁皓、張清	音樂：劉宏遠

124 福慧雙修 Double Date	Fu Hui Shuang Xiu	1962/12/25	粵語	電懋	林永泰 / 竇漢勳	潘藩 / 楊天成	王天林	張清、林鳳、白露明、張英才	音樂：劉宏遠
125 香港之星 Star of Hong Kong	Xianggang Zhi Xing	1963/03/21	國語	電懋、東寶	鍾啟文 / 鍾啟文、藤本真澄	笠原良三	千葉泰樹	尤敏、寶田明、王引、團令子	音樂：松井八郎
126 苦命鴛鴦 Bitter Romance	Kuming Yuanyang	1963/03/27	粵語	電懋	林永泰	潘藩 / 盧寶華（麗的呼聲天空小說改編）	莫康時	羅劍郎、白露明、李香琴、金雷	
127 金箭盟 Golden Arrow	Jinjian Meng	1963/04/25	國語	電懋	鍾啟文 / 宋淇	蕭銅	羅維	田青、林翠、洪洋、羅維	音樂：劉宏遠
128 鶯歌燕舞 Mad About Music	Yingge Yanwu	1963/06/25	國語	電懋	鍾啟文 / 宋淇	易文	易文	夷光、葉楓、田青、洪洋	音樂：姚敏，作曲：姚敏、綦湘棠，作詞：周之原
129 三紳士艷遇 Three Gentlemen from Tokyo	San Shenshi Yanyu	1963/07/10	國語	電懋、東寶	鍾啟文、藤本真澄	笠原良三	杉江敏男	三船敏郎、尤敏、森繁久彌、小林桂樹	
130 荷花 Little Lotus	He Hua	1963/07/26	國語	電懋	鍾啟文	汪榴照	唐煌	張揚、丁皓、羅維、王萊	
131 教我如何不想她 Because of Her	Jiao Wo Ruhe Bu Xiang Ta	1963/07/31	國語	電懋	林永泰 / 黃也白	易文	易文、王天林	雷震、葛蘭、喬宏、王萊	音樂：服部良一；作詞：易文
132 人之初 Father and Son	Ren Zhi Chu	1963/08/15	國語	電懋	林永泰 / 黃也白	吳家驤 / 連龢	吳家驤	王引、白露明、雷震、王萊	音樂：綦湘棠
133 錦繡年華 Make it Mine	Jinxiu Nianhua	1963/09/18	粵語	電懋	林永泰 / 竇漢勳	潘藩	莫康時	林鳳、白露明、黃錦娟、李紅	音樂：劉宏遠
134 小兒女 Father Takes a Bride	Xiao Ernü	1963/10/02	國語	電懋	鍾啟文 / 宋淇	張愛玲	王天林	王引、尤敏、雷震、王萊	音樂：服部良一；作曲：綦湘棠；作詞：周之原
135 諜海四壯士 Four Brave Ones	Diehai Si Zhuangshi	1963/10/18	國語	電懋	林永泰 / 黃也白	汪榴照	唐煌、汪榴照	張揚、白露明、夷光、張美瑤	
136 香港・東京・夏威夷 Hong Kong, Tokyo, Honolulu	Xianggang Dongjing Xiaweiyi	1963/11/01	國語	電懋、東寶	藤本真澄、林永泰	松山善三	千葉泰樹	寶田明、尤敏、林冲、加山雄三	音樂：松井八郎
137 孟麗君 Meng Li Jun	Meng Lijun	1963	國語	電懋	鍾啟文		嚴俊	嚴俊、李麗華、楊群、錢蓉蓉	
138 西太后與珍妃 The Imperial Lady	Xi Taihou Yu Zhenfei	1964/01/08	國語	電懋	林永泰 / 王植波	汪榴照	易文	雷震、李湄、張美瑤、喬宏	
139 寶蓮燈 The Magic Lamp	Bao Lian Deng	1964/01/23	國語	電懋	林永泰 / 王植波	王植波、易文、汪榴照、曾直夫、董千里	王天林、易文、唐煌、吳家驤、羅維	電懋全體演員	十周年紀念作
140 啼笑姻緣 A Story of Three Loves	Ti Xiao Enyuan	1964/02/12	國語	電懋	林永泰 / 王植波	秦亦孚 / 張恨水	王天林	趙雷、林翠、葛蘭、王引	音樂：綦湘棠；作曲：姚敏，作詞：李雋青 1964/08/08 改名《京華春夢》於台灣上映
141 啼笑姻緣大結局 A Story of Three Loves (Sequel)	Ti Xiao Enyuan (Dajieju)	1964/02/26	國語	電懋	林永泰 / 王植波	秦亦孚 / 張恨水	王天林	趙雷、林翠、葛蘭、王引	音樂：綦湘棠，作曲：姚敏，作詞：李雋青
142 一家之主 Head of the Family	Yijia Zhi Zhu	1964/03/11	粵語	電懋	林永泰 / 竇漢勳	潘藩 / 楊天成	莫康時	張英才、白露明、李紅、司馬華龍	

國粵語片總目 Filmography of Mandarin and Cantonese Films

	影片名稱	片名漢語拼音	香港首映日期	語別	出品公司	監製 / 製片	編劇 / 原著	導演	主要演員	音樂 / 附註
143	大馬戲團 The Big Circus	Da Maxituan	1964/03/26	國語	國藝	秦劍 / 朱旭華	秦劍	秦劍	張揚、曾江、 李湄、藍娣	音樂：綦湘棠 國藝影業公司乃秦劍創辦， 此作是秦劍執導的首部國語片
144	鸞鳳和鳴 The Better Halves	Luanfeng Heming	1964/04/17	國語	電懋	林永泰 / 王植波	狄薏（即陳蝶衣）	羅維	田青、鍾情、 張慧嫻、劉恩甲	音樂：姚敏，作曲：姚敏，作詞：曾直夫
145	情天長恨 An Affair to Remember	Qingtian Changhen	1964/06/06	國語	電懋	林永泰 / 黃也白	羅維 / 伊達	羅維、 王天林	張揚、林翠、 白冰、李芝安	音樂：姚敏
146	秦香蓮 The Story of Qin Xianglian	Qin Xianglian	1964/07/19	國語	電懋		陳一新	陳一新、 嚴俊	李麗華、嚴俊、 楊群、梁醒波	
147	一曲難忘 Please Remember Me	Yiqu Nanwang	1964/07/24	國語	電懋	鍾啟文	張愛玲	鍾啟文	張揚、葉楓、 田青、李芝安	
148	舊愛新歡 I Love Them Both	Jiuai Xinhuan	1964/08/26	粵語	電懋	林永泰 / 竇漢勳	盧雨岐 / 艾雯 （改編自商業電台廣播劇）	蔣偉光	田青、林鳳、 白露明、金雷	
149	都市狂想曲 Cosmopolitan Fantasy	Dushi Kuangxiangqu	1964/08/28	國語	電懋	林永泰 / 王植波	汪榴照	吳家驤	張揚、夷光、 雷震、李芝安	音樂：李厚襄
150	南北喜相逢 The Greatest Love Affair on Earth	Nanbei Xixiangfeng	1964/09/09	國語	電懋	林永泰 / 王植波	張愛玲	王天林	雷震、白露明、 鍾情、劉恩甲	音樂：劉宏遠
151	深宮怨 Romance of the Forbidden City	Shengong Yuan	1964/10/08	國語	電懋	林永泰 / 王植波	董千里	王天林	趙雷、尤敏、 喬宏、羅維	音樂：綦湘棠，作曲：姚敏，作詞：李雋青
152	生死關頭 The Crisis	Shengsi Guantou	1964/10/29	國語	電懋	林永泰 / 王植波	易文	易文	王引、張美瑤、 張揚、羅維	
153	梁山伯與祝英台 Liang San Bo and Zhu Ying Tai	Liang Shanbo Yu Zhu Yingtai	1964/12/25	國語	電懋		陳一新	嚴俊	李麗華、尤敏、 嚴俊、雷震	
154	金玉奴 The Beggar's Daughter	Jin Yunu	1965/01/29	國語	電懋	林永泰	陳蝶衣、王天林	王天林	趙雷、樂蒂、 吳家驤、姜南	音樂及作曲：姚敏，作詞：李雋青
155	聊齋誌異 Fairy, Ghost, Vixen	Liaozhai Zhiyi	1965/05/27	國語	電懋	林永泰 / 王植波	王植波、易文、 汪榴照 / 蒲松齡	唐煌	唐菁、白冰、 張慧嫻、陳方	音樂及作曲：姚敏，歌詞：撰自《詩經》
156	珠聯璧合 In Fact I Love You	Zhu Lian Bi He	1965/06/23	粵語	電懋			蔣偉光	田青、白露明、 劉恩甲、梁醒波	
157	最長的一夜 The Longest Night	Zuichang De Yiye	1965/07/01	國語	電懋	林永泰	易文	易文	寶田明、樂蒂、 王萊、吳家驤	音樂：綦湘棠，作曲：姚敏
158	三朵玫瑰花 Three Smart Girls	Sanduo Meiguihua	1965/07/29	國語	電懋		姜南	唐煌	張慧嫻、劉小慧、 田青、李芝安	
159	雷堡風雲 The Gunfight at Thunder Fort	Leibao Fengyun	1965/08/12	國語	電懋、 中影、台製		汪榴照 / 楊念慈〈廢園舊夢〉	李嘉	張美瑤、唐菁、 葛香亭、魏蘇	
160	鳳凰 Phoenix	Fenghuang	1965	國語	新華	楊世慶	楊世慶		張美瑤、楊群	據童月娟說，電懋投資 三份之一 台灣製作
161	鎖麟囊 The Lucky Purse	Suolin Nang	1966/01/01	國語	明星	黃韜 / 周秀興	魯漢	王天林	張揚、樂蒂、 田青、文愛蘭	音樂及作曲：姚敏，作詞：李雋青 國泰機構發行

161	自作多情 I'll Make My Own Choice	Zi Zuo Duoqing	1966/01/15	粵語	國泰機構	林永泰 / 竇漢勳		王天林	田青、白露明、 梁醒波、曾慧	
162	嫦娥奔月 Lady on the Moon	Chang'e Benyue	1966/01/20	國語	國泰機構	朱國良	易凡	袁秋楓	趙雷、樂蒂、 李芝安、田青	
163	七重天 Seventh Heaven	Qi Chong Tian	1966/02/11	國語	國泰機構	朱國良	董千里	唐煌	雷震、白冰、 田青、李琳琳	
164	草莽喋血記 The Fugitive	Caomang Diexue Ji	1966/02/25	國語	國泰機構	朱國良	易文	易文	張揚、林翠、 雷震、孫琦	
165	亂世兒女 A Debt of Blood	Luanshi Ernü	1966/04/07	國語	國泰機構	朱國良 / 王植波	易凡	袁秋楓	喬宏、樂蒂、 范麗、田青	音樂：綦湘棠，作曲：姚敏
166	空谷蘭 Forget Me Not	Kong Gu Lan	1966/04/12	國語	國泰機構	林永泰 / 王植波	易文	易文	張揚、林翠、 夷光、劉恩甲	音樂：姚敏
167	麒麟送子 Little Matchmaker	Qilin Song Zi	1967/02/07	國語	國泰機構	朱國良	楊世慶	王天林	張揚、林翠、 梁醒波、范麗	音樂：周藍萍
168	扇中人 The Magic Fan	Shan Zhong Ren	1967/03/10	國語	國泰機構	朱國良	李愛山、魯愚 / 蒲松齡	唐煌	趙雷、樂蒂、 王萊、田青	音樂及作曲：姚敏，作詞：李雋青、李愛山 根據《聊齋誌異 • 阿繡》改編
169	曼谷之夜 Night in Bangkok	Mangu Zhi Ye	1967/03/18	國語	國泰機構		笠原良三	千葉泰樹	加山雄三、張美瑤、 星由里子、志村喬	
170	女人·女人 Passion	Nüren Nüren	1967/03/31	國語	國泰機構		王植波	吳家驤	趙雷、林翠、 范麗、王琛	
171	鐵馬銀鈴 The Iron Horse	Tiema Yinling	1967/05/11	國語	國泰機構	朱國良	方玲	袁秋楓	趙雷、江虹、 雷震、王萊	
172	香港白薔薇 The White Rose of Hong Kong	Xianggang Bai Qiangwei	1967/05/20	國語	國泰機構、東寶	藤本真澄	池田一朗	福田純	寶田明、張美瑤、 山崎努、馬驥	港日合作 1966/07/01 於台灣上映
173	黃金島 Isle of Gold	Huangjin Dao	1967/06/30	國語	國泰機構	朱國良	韋森	易文	張揚、白冰、 李芝安、蘇祥	
174	青春夢 Young Love	Qingchun Meng	1967/08/03	國語	國泰機構	朱國良	易凡	袁秋楓	張揚、江虹、 雷震、李琳琳	
175	聊齋誌異續集 The Haunted	Liaozhai Zhiyi (Xuji)	1967/08/17	國語	國泰樑構	朱國良	曾直夫、李愛山、 宋海靈 / 蒲松齡	唐煌	張揚、張慧嫻、 李芝安、容蓉	音樂：姚敏，作曲：姚敏，作詞：李愛山
176	危險人物 Woman in Danger	Weixian Renwu	1967/09/07	國語	國泰機構	朱國良	易凡	袁秋楓	趙雷、夷光、 江山、莫愁	
177	諜海蛟龍 Operation Bangkok	Diehai Jiaolong	1967/09/28	國語	國泰機構	朱國良	唐煌	唐煌	江山、白冰、 碧差拉	
178	蘇小妹 Wife of a Romantic Scholar	Su Xiaomei	1967/10/26	國語	國泰機構	朱國良	秦亦孚	王天林	趙雷、林翠、 張慧嫻、田青	音樂 / 作曲：姚敏，作詞：李雋青
179	英雄膽 Operation Macau	Yingxiong Dan	1967/11/09	國語	國泰機構	朱國良		唐煌	江山、張慧嫻、 陳曼玲、周萱	
180	原野游龍 The Wandering Knight	Yuanye Youlong	1967/12/08	國語	國泰機構	朱國良	易凡	易文	趙雷、林翠、 李芝安、田青	又名《游龍戲鳳》

國粵語片總目 Filmography of Mandarin and Cantonese Films

	影片名稱	片名漢語拼音	香港首映日期	語別	出品公司	監製 / 製片	編劇 / 原著	導演	主要演員	音樂 / 附註
181	第一劍 The First Sword	Diyi Jian	1967/12/28	國語	國泰機構	朱國良 / 楊曼怡	韋森	屠光啟	趙雷、陳曼玲、田青、王萊	音樂：周藍萍
182	血灑紅玫瑰 The Crimson Rose	Xuesa Hong Meigui	1968/01/18	國語	國泰機構	朱國良 / 楊曼怡	韋森	王天林	雷震、林翠、趙雷、白冰	
183	太太萬歲 Darling Stay at Home	Taitai Wansui	1968/01/28	國語	國泰機構	朱國良 / 楊曼怡	楊青	王天林	張揚、樂蒂、田青、李琳琳	音樂：顧嘉煇 作曲：周藍萍
184	水上人家 The Boat Girl	Shuishang Renjia	1968/02/15	國語	國泰機構	朱國良 / 楊曼怡	易文	易文	陳厚、陳曼玲、容蓉、王萊	音樂：周藍萍
185	逃 Escape	Tao	1968/03/14	國語	國泰機構	朱國良 / 楊曼怡	易凡、李溯	袁秋楓	雷震、江虹、狄娜、田青	音樂：周藍萍
186	決鬥惡虎嶺 Travel with a Sword	Juedou Ehuling	1968/04/10	國語	國泰機構	朱國良 / 楊曼怡	楊青	王天林	趙雷、樂蒂、范麗、喬宏	音樂：顧嘉煇
187	波斯貓 Persian Cat	Bosi Mao	1968/04/20	國語	國泰機構	朱國良	魯愚	唐煌	江山、張慧嫻、狄娜、王琛	
188	描金鳳 The Fortune Teller's Daughter	Miao Jinfeng	1968/06/27	國語	國泰機構	朱國良	陳蝶衣、連穌	吳家驤	雷震、李芝安、梁醒波、王萊	1966 年已於台灣上映
189	笑面俠 The Smiling Swordsman	Xiaomian Xia	1968/07/11	國語	國泰機構	朱國良 / 楊曼怡	張森	姜南	田青、陳曼玲、陳浩、譚伊俐	
190	青春的旋律 Teenager's Holidays	Qingchung De Xuanlü	1968/07/18	國語	國泰機構	朱國良 / 楊曼怡	方玲	袁秋楓	金川、李琳琳、鹿瑜、王萊	
191	蒙妮妲日記 Diary of Monita	Mengnitan Riji	1968/08/01	國語	國泰機構	朱國良 / 楊曼怡	楊青 / 依達	易文	金川、汪玲、康妮、陳浩	
192	雁翎刀 The Invisible Sabre	Yanling Dao	1968/08/08	國語	國泰機構	朱國良 / 楊曼怡	韋森	屠光啟	趙雷、陳曼玲、金川、喬宏	
193	大丐俠 To Kill a Rover	Da Gai Xia	1968/08/22	國語	國泰機構	朱國良 / 楊曼怡	張森	汪平	張冲、張慧嫻、陳浩、江山	
194	夏日初戀 Summer Love	Xiari Chulian	1968/08/31	國語	國泰機構	朱國良 / 楊曼怡	楊青 / 依達	汪榴照	金川、江虹、李琳琳、周萱	
195	千手佛 Buddha with 1000 Arms	Qianshou Fo	1968/09/26	國語	國泰機構	朱國良	陳銅民	姜南	趙雷、康妮、狄娜、金川	
196	紅梅閣 Red Plum Pavilion	Hongmei Ge	1968/10/10	國語	國泰機構	朱國良	王天林	王天林	趙雷、容蓉、樂蒂、雷震	音樂：姚敏，作詞：楊世慶、董千里
197	玉龍吟 Jade Dragon	Yulong Yin	1968/10/16	國語	國泰機構	朱國良 / 楊曼怡	張森	高立	田青、陳曼玲、江青、朱牧	
198	游龍戲鳳 No Time for Love	Youlong Xifeng	1968/11/14	國語	國泰機構	朱國良	魯愚	唐煌	陳厚、林翠、狄娜、江山	音樂：顧嘉煇
199	月夜琴挑 Spring Time Affairs	Yueye Qintiao	1968/11/28	國語	國泰機構	朱國良	董千里	易文	張揚、張慧嫻、陳青、田青	
200	七大盜 The Desperate Seven	Qi Dadao	1968/12/12	國語	國泰機構	朱國良 / 楊曼怡	張森	王天林	趙雷、江虹、田青、江山	音樂：顧嘉煇

201	春暖人間 Song of Our Family	Chunnuan Renjian	1968/12/24	國語	國泰機構	朱國良 / 楊曼怡	唐煌	唐煌	張揚、李琳琳、 張慧嫻、容蓉	
202	鐵骨傳 Iron Bones	Tiegu Zhuan	1969/01/16	國語	國泰機構	朱國良 / 楊曼怡	董千里	易文	金川、陳曼玲、 陳青、朱牧	作曲：周藍萍
203	落馬湖 Gunfight at Lo Ma Lake	Luo Ma Hu	1969/02/06	國語	國泰機構	朱國良	易文 / 陳定山	易文	張揚、白冰、 周萱、唐菁	
204	一劍情深 The Violet Mansion	Yijian Qingshen	1969/02/15	國語	國泰機構	朱國良 / 楊曼怡	屠光啟	屠光啟	金川、陳曼玲、 秦祥林、康妮	
205	孫悟空大鬧香港 Monkey in Hong Kong	Sun Wukong Danao Xianggang	1969/03/20	國語	國泰機構	朱國良 / 楊曼怡	汪榴照	唐煌	田青、張慧嫻、 江山、容蓉	
206	黑豹 The Black Panther	Hei Bao	1969/03/28	國語	國泰機構	朱國良 / 楊曼怡	爾華	汪平	張冲、江虹、 秦祥林、容蓉	
207	盜璽 The Royal Seal	Dao Xi	1969/04/17	國語	國泰機構	朱國良 / 楊曼怡	宋漢	王天林	趙雷、陳曼玲、 田青、朱牧	
208	狼與狼 Here Come the Wolves	Lang Yu Lang	1969/05/01	國語	國泰機構	朱國良 / 楊曼怡	汪榴照	汪榴照	陳浩、張慧嫻、 周萱、梁醒波	
209	亡命八傑 Eight for the Border	Wangming Bajie	1969/05/15	國語	國泰機構	朱國良 / 楊曼怡	張森	高立	趙雷、夏雯、 江山、朱牧	改名《人傑傳》於台上映
210	蓮花寨 Lotus Camp	Lianhua Zhai	1969/06/12	國語	國泰機構	朱國良 / 楊曼怡	韋森	屠光啟	秦祥林、陳曼玲、 江山、朱牧	
211	乘龍快婿 My Father-in-Law	Chenglong Kuaixu	1969/07/10	國語	國泰機構	朱國良 / 楊曼怡	汪榴照	唐煌	田青、容蓉、 梁醒波、張淇	
212	聊齋誌異三集 The Spirits	Liaozhai Zhiyi (Sanji)	1969/07/16	國語	國泰機構	朱國良 / 楊曼怡	李愛山、吳鐵翼、 余如斯	唐煌	田青、容蓉、 李琳琳、陳青	
213	嘉嘉 Affection	Jiajia	1969/08/15	國語	國泰機構	朱國良 / 楊曼怡	高立	高立	趙雷、孟莉、 田青、王萊	
214	四武士 A Pearl in Command	Si Wushi	1969/08/22	國語	國泰機構	朱國良 / 楊曼怡	田歌	文石凌	張冲、陳曼玲、 朱牧、王琛	
215	神經刀 A Mad, Mad, Mad Sword	Shenjing Dao	1969/09/10	國語	國泰機構	朱國良 / 楊曼怡	汪榴照	王天林	田青、秦芸、 朱牧、孟莉	音樂：周藍萍
216	虎山行 Escort over Tiger Hills	Hushan Xing	1969/10/15	國語	國泰機構	朱國良 / 楊曼怡	宋項如	王星磊	喬宏、周萱、 宗由、江青	音樂：顧嘉煇
217	試情記 How Love is Tested	Shiqing Ji	1969/11/27	國語	國泰機構	朱國良 / 楊曼怡	田歌	王天林	張揚、周萱、 孟莉、萬儀	音樂：顧嘉煇
218	龍吟虎嘯 The Challenge	Longyin Huxiao	1969/12/04	國語	國泰機構	朱國良 / 楊曼怡	李影	李影	秦祥林、康妮、 李影、孟莉	
219	楓林渡 Mallow Forest	Fenglin Du	1969/12/25	國語	國泰機構	朱國良 / 楊曼怡	郭嘉	汪平	張冲、陳曼玲、 秦祥林、趙雷	
220	家有賢妻 The Homemaker	Jia You Xianqi	1970/01/09	國語	國泰機構	朱國良 / 楊曼怡	劉芳剛	劉芳剛	陳浩、李琳琳、 王琛、梁醒波	
221	神槍手 Magnificent Gunfighter	Shenqiang Shou	1970/01/29	國語	國泰機構	朱國良 / 楊曼怡	江揚	易文	趙雷、李琳琳	

國粵語片總目 Filmography of Mandarin and Cantonese Films

影片名稱	片名漢語拼音	香港首映日期	語別	出品公司	監製 / 製片	編劇 / 原著	導演	主要演員	音樂 / 附註
222 恭喜發財 The Lucky Strike	Gongxi Facai	1970/02/05	國語	國泰機構	朱國良 / 楊曼怡	劉芳剛	劉芳剛	謝榮、胡茵茵、梁醒波、蘇祥	
223 路客與刀客 From the Highway	Luke Yu Daoke	1970/02/20	國語	國泰機構	朱國良 / 楊曼怡	張曾澤 / 司馬中原	張曾澤	楊群、胡茵茵、崔福生、宗由	音樂：周藍萍
224 鷹爪手 The Eagle's Claw	Yingzhao Shou	1970/03/19	國語	國泰機構	朱國良 / 楊曼怡	田歌	文石凌	張冲、譚伊俐、李影、馮毅	
225 火鳥第一號 Violet Clove and Firebird	Huoniao Diyi Hao	1970/03/26	國語	國泰機構	朱國良 / 楊曼怡	楚原	楚原	張冲、陳曼玲	
226 小蘋果 An Apple a Day	Xiao Pingguo	1970/04/04	國語	國泰機構	朱國良 / 楊曼怡	張森	張森、汪平	劉丹、宣玲玲、陳青、朱牧	
227 洪福齊天 The Lucky Ones	Hongfu Qitian	1970/04/16	國語	國泰機構	朱國良	汪榴照	汪榴照	王琛、張淇	
228 壯士血 The King's Sword	Zhuangshi Xue	1970/04/30	國語	國泰機構	朱國良 / 楊曼怡	屠光啟	屠光啟	趙雷、秦祥林、曾媚媚、唐沁	
229 翠寒谷 The Rivals	Cuihan Gu	1970/05/14	國語	國泰機構	朱國良 / 楊曼怡	章如	羅熾	趙雷、張冲	
230 千面賊美人 Night is Not Made for Stealing	Qianmian Zei Meiren	1970/05/21	國語	國泰機構		方龍驤	屠光啟	張冲、夏雯	
231 屠龍 Unconquered	Tulong	1970/06/11	國語	國泰機構		易文	易文、梁銳	朱牧、江虹、田青	改名《呂四娘》於台上映
232 我愛莎莎 The Apartment	Wo Ai Shasha	1970/07/09	國語	國泰機構		蔣芸	林福地	秦祥林、譚伊俐	
233 狠心的人 The Ruthless Heart	Henxin De Ren	1970/07/09	國語	國泰機構		張森	張森	胡茵茵、張淇、謝榮、虞慧	台灣攝製
234 錄音機情殺案 Dial for Murder	Luyinji Qingsha An	1970/07/16	國語	國泰機構	朱國良 / 楊曼怡	楚原、林年同	楚原	張冲、南紅、夏雯、喬宏	音樂：顧嘉煇
235 神龍奇俠 The Fabulous Protectress	Shenlong Qixia	1970/07/30	國語	國泰機構	朱國良 / 楊曼怡	王冲	梁銳	白宇、周萱	
236 玉樓春夢 The Lost Spring	Yulou Chunmeng	1970/08/27	國語	國泰機構	朱國良 / 楊曼怡	楚原	楚原	楊群、陳曼玲、宣玲玲、孟莉	音樂：顧嘉煇
237 鬼皮 The Devil's Skin	Gui Pi	1970/09/17	國語	國泰機構	朱國良 / 楊曼怡	張森	高立	孫濤、胡茵茵、江山、孟莉	
238 殺戒 Forbidden Killing	Sha Jie	1970/10/01	國語	國泰機構		郭嘉	汪平	張斌、陳曼玲	
239 雪路血路 Mission to Die	Xuelu Xuelu	1970/12/18	國語	國泰機構	朱國良	林福地	林福地	田野、張小燕	
240 異鄉客 Unknown Swordsman	Yixiang Ke	1970/12/22	國語	國泰機構		方龍驤	王天林	秦祥林、陳青、朱牧、江山	

241	龍沐香 Cold Blade	Long Mu Xiang	1970/12/31	國語	國泰機構		楚原	楚原	高遠、陳曼玲、 胡茵茵、張斌	音樂：吳大江
242	關不住的春光 The Extra Duty of a Governess	Guanbuzhu De Chunguang	1970	國語	國泰機構	朱國良 / 楊曼怡	張森	唐煌	陳曼玲、江山、 馬劍棠、江海、田青	音樂：顧嘉煇，作曲：周藍萍
243	嫁不嫁 My Suitors	Jia Bu Jia	1970	國語	國泰機構	朱國良 / 楊曼怡		唐煌	喬宏、張淇、 江山、李影	音樂：吳大江，作曲：顧嘉煇 1972/08/24 於台灣上映
244	孫悟空再鬧香港 Monkey Comes again	Sun Wukong Zai Nao Xianggang	1971/01/26	國語	國泰機構		李愛山	唐煌	田青、譚伊俐	
245	浪子之歌 The Lark	Langzi Zhi Ge	1971/03/04	國語	國泰機構		張森	文石淩	張冲、秦祥林	
246	藍色的夢 Blues in the Dream	Lanse De Meng	1971	國語	國泰機構		張曾澤	張曾澤	胡茵茵、江山、 王萊、秦藝	
247	雲姑 Her Vengeance	Yun Gu	1971	國語	國泰機構	朱國良 / 楊曼怡	趙玉崗、朱牧	朱牧	秦祥林、胡茵茵、 張冲、朱牧	音樂：吳大江 1971/12/22 於台灣上映
248	劍魂 The Living Sword	Jian Hun	1971	國語	國泰機構		張森、朱夜	汪平	秦祥林、陳曼玲	
249	今天不上課 Please Sir, We're Sorry!	Jintian Bu Shangke	1972/05/04	國語	國泰機構	朱國良 / 楊曼怡	張森	張森	謝榮、上官燕兒、 張斌、孫濤	音樂及作曲：顧嘉煇 台名《對不起老師》
250	黃色殺手 The Yellow Killer	Huangse Shashou	1972/12/15	國語	七海		邵峰	邵峰	白鷹、李湘、 秦沛、姜南	音樂：顧嘉煇 又名《殺手》 國泰機構發行 七海公司是李翰祥主政國聯時代的經理邵峰自己的公司
251	蛇王與閻王 A Resort Called Hell	Shewang Yu Yanwang	1972	國語	國泰機構	朱國良	汪榴照	唐煌	田青、龍君兒、 張斌、王琛	1973/01/17 於台灣上映
252	風流艷盜 Many Faces of a Diamond	Fengliu Yandao	1972	國語	國泰機構	朱國良 / 楊曼怡	張森	屠光啟	張冲、夏雯、 王琛、韓湘湘	音樂：顧嘉煇
253	馬家溝 Pursued	Majia Gou	1972	國語	國泰機構		劉維斌	文石淩	田野、張小燕、 萬儀、齊連奎	1970 年開拍
254	霸行三千里 The Captive	Bahang Sanqian Li	1972	國語	國泰機構			李影	唐沁、謝榮、 劉丹、程世英	1970 年開拍
255	伏虎榜 To Skin a Tiger	Fuhu Bang	1972	國語	國泰機構				唐沁、田青、 趙雷	1972/04/19 於台灣上映
256	浮雲朵朵 Her Tender Age	Fuyun Duoduo	1974	國語	國泰機構		張瑄	王琛	江虹、謝榮、 宣玲玲、江山	1974/04/23 於台灣上映
257	花落水流紅 The Falling Petals	Hualuo Shuiliu Hong	1974	國語	國泰		趙雷、高立	趙雷、 高立	秦祥林、陳曼玲、 江山、朱牧	1970 年開拍
258	大賊王 The Great Highway Man	Da Zei Wang	1974	國語	國泰			羅熾	譚伊俐、張斌、 趙明、徐天川	1970 年開拍

* 國際公司國語組新人（蘇鳳、丁皓、林蒼、田青、雷震、天冲、楊群等），於1956年在導演岳楓指導下，拍攝了一齣名為《互愛》(Mutual Love, Hu Ai) 的獨幕短劇，作為訓練課程一環。（該片並沒有公映）

國泰克里斯片目 Filmography of Cathay Keris Films

整理：余慕雲、李俊慧
Compiled by : Yu Mo-wan & Lee Chun-wai

	影片名稱	首映日期	導演	主要演員	附註
1	真假王子 Bamboo of Yearning (Buloh Perindu)	1953	B.S. Rajhans	Rusini、Shariff Medan	
2	浪子回頭 Insaf	1954	葛利斯南（L. Krishnan）	Rusini、Osman Gumanti、Mala Ratina	
3	誘惑 Nafsu	1954	葛利斯南	魯邁拿（S. Roomai Noor）、瑪麗亞曼多（Maria Menado）、Rusini	
4	馬來亞明日 Terang Bulan Di-Malaya	1954	B.S. Rajhans	Raden Mochtar、Rusini	又名《馬來亞的月亮》
5	慈母淚 Tangisan Ibu	1954	葛利斯南	魯邁拿、M. 亞民（M. Amin）、Mislia	
6	決鬥 Pertarohan	1954	葛利斯南	魯邁拿、瑪麗亞曼多	
7	盲女淚 Duka Nestapha	1955	B. S. Rajhans	Shariff Medan、Mislia	
8	情海戀歌 Irama Kaseh	1955	Laurie Friedman	魯邁拿、Netty Herawati、Rusini	
9	馬來亞之珠 Mutiara Dari Malaya	1955	Laurie Friedman	魯邁拿、Mislia、Sr Uniati	
10	金錢萬能 Selamat Hari Raya	1955	葛利斯南	魯邁拿、瑪麗亞曼多	
11	兄弟鬩牆 Saudaraku	1955	Laurie Friedman	魯邁拿、Mislia	
12	別矣吾愛 Selamat Tinggal Kekasehku	1955	葛利斯南	魯邁拿、Chang Lye Lye	
13	Kaseh Menumpang	1955	葛利斯南	魯邁拿、Rusini、Adek Jaffa	
14	吐氣揚眉 Adam	1956	魯邁拿	魯邁拿、烏美嘉東（Ummi Kalthoum）	
15	禱告 Azan	1956	葛利斯南	魯邁拿、Mislia	
16	偉大的愛 Dondang Sayang	1956	葛利斯南	魯邁拿	
17	不見天日 Mega Mendong	1956	葛利斯南	魯邁拿、阿德克凡胡辛（Adek Wan Hussain）、R. Suriani	片中童星阿德克凡胡辛獲亞洲電影節最佳童星獎
18	吸血人妖復仇記 Revenge of Pontianak (Dendam Pontianak)	1957	卑恩勞（B. N. Rao）	瑪麗亞曼多、莎瑪亞末（Salmah Ahmad）	
19	錯誤的疑心 Salah Sangka	1957	卑恩勞	魯邁拿、Shariff Medan	
20	吸血人妖 The Vampire (Pontianak)	1957	卑恩勞	瑪麗亞曼多、M. 亞民	
21	大傻入城 Che Mamat Parang Tajam	1958	魯邁拿	莎瑪亞末、華希得沙爹（Wahid Satay）	曾名《諧謔者》
22	婆羅洲處女 Virgin of Borneo	1958	葛利斯南		何亞祿監製
23	人妖之誓 Curse of the Vampire (Sumpah Pontianak)	1958	卑恩勞	瑪麗亞曼多、莎瑪亞末、馬洛佛（Mustapha Maarof）	
24	油鬼子復仇記 Serangan Orang Minyak	1958	葛利斯南	M. 亞民、拉蒂花奧瑪（Latiffah Omar）	曾名《油人復仇》
25	仙菓奇緣	1958	K.M. Baskar	拉蒂花奧瑪、瑪麗亞曼多、M. 亞民、阿白都拉傑克（Abdullah Chik）	
26	未婚父親 Satay	1958	K.M. Baskar	華希得沙爹、莎瑪亞末、普得拉華克（Puteh Lawak）、愛迪阿里（Aidi Ali）	曾名《沙爹》 片中童星愛迪阿里獲亞洲電影節最佳童星獎
27	神秘之屋 Slimy Man (Orang Lichin)	1958	葛利斯南	M. 亞民、瑪麗亞曼多	
28	油鬼子 Oily Man (Orang Minyak)	1958	葛利斯南	莎瑪亞末、魯邁拿、拉蒂花奧瑪、M. 亞民、諾定亞末	曾名《油人》
29	形影相隨	1958		盧斯范尼、芸海華絲	克利斯布里西斯（法國）公司出品
30	仙女下凡 Jula Juli Bintang Tiga	1959	卑恩勞	莎瑪亞末、諾定亞末、拉蒂花奧瑪、華希得沙爹	
31	啞子吃黃蓮 Victim of Slander (Korban Fitnah)	1959	P. L. Kapur	瑪麗亞曼多、Siput Sarawak	

32	瑪蘇莉 Mahsuri	1959	卑恩勞	魯邁拿、Kasmah Booty	獲亞洲電影節特獎
33	妒婦禍 Radin Mas	1959	葛利斯南	拉蒂花奧瑪、諾定亞末、M. 亞民、Siput Sarawak	參加第七屆「亞展」
34	妙人福星 Rasa Sayang Eh	1959	葛利斯南	華希得沙爹、莎瑪亞末、M. 亞民	曾名《愛的呼聲》
35	紅白雙姝 Bawang Puteh, Bawang Merah	1959	魯邁拿	拉蒂花奧瑪、烏美嘉東	參加第七屆「亞展」
36	神秘之虎 Hantu Rimau	1960	Palam Groom	魯邁拿、林瓊麗（Mary Lim）、Siput Sarawak	
37	伊斯蘭之光 Nur Islam	1960	K. N. Baskarn	莎瑪亞末、諾定亞末、Siput Sarawak、Mahmud Jun	
38	潘多伯伯 Pak Pandir Modern	1960	Kaber Yeo	魯邁拿、M. 亞民、華希得沙爹、露絲葉蒂瑪（Rose Yatimah）	參加第七屆「亞展」
39	獅子城 Lion City	1960	Yi Sui	胡姬（Wu Zi）、Fan En	國語作品
40	黑手黨 Black Hand Gang	1960			獲亞洲電影節最佳鬧劇獎
41	Che Mamat Parang Tumpol	1960	魯邁拿	拉蒂花奧瑪、華希得沙爹、M. 亞民、普得拉華克（Puteh Lawak）	
42	巫醫爭妻 Bomoh's Bride (Tunang Pak Dukun)	1960	魯邁拿	露絲葉蒂瑪、阿白都拉傑克、Mahmud Jun	
43	蘇丹瑪目遇難史 Sultan Mahmood Mangkat Dijulang	1961			
44	古城英傑 Hang Jebat	1961	哈申漢尼夫（Hussain Haniff）	諾定亞末、M. 亞民、拉蒂花奧瑪、Siput Sarawak	
45	豐盛港之花 Seri Mersing	1961	Salleh Ghani	諾定亞末、露絲葉蒂瑪、Rosnani Jamil	
46	抗暴英雄 Lela Satria	1961	魯邁拿	烏美嘉東、華希得沙爹、Salleh Melan	
47	神秘謀殺案 No Lights for Murder	1961			
48	莉丹公主 Puteri Gunong Ledang	1961	魯邁拿	華希得沙爹、花蒂瑪亞茉（Fatimah Ahmad）、Mazlan Ahmad、Mahmud Jun	
49	巾幗女傑 Siti Zubaidah	1961	卑恩勞	瑪麗亞曼多、拉蒂花奧瑪、諾定亞末、Mahmud Jun	
50	擂台選駙馬 Jalak Lenteng	1961	Salleh Ghani	烏美嘉東、拉蒂花奧瑪、Mahmud Jun、Yusoff Latiff	
51	糊塗妙人 Gado-Gado	1961			
52	Sallan Mahmood Mangkat Dijulang	1961	K.M. Baskar	M. 亞民、諾定亞末、瑪麗亞曼多、Sipur Sarawak、Rosnani	
53	Sumpitan Rachun	1961	魯邁拿	拉蒂花奧瑪、林瓊麗、魯邁拿	
54	孤兒淚 Yatim Mustapha	1961	卑恩勞	馬洛佛、拉蒂花奧瑪、Siput Sarawak、Habibah Harun	
55	獅城烈女 Dang Anom	1962	哈申漢尼夫	諾定亞末、花蒂瑪亞茉、M. 亞民、Mahmud Jun	
56	傻人趣史 Chelorong Cheloreng	1962	魯邁拿	華希得沙爹、M. 亞民、拉蒂花奧瑪、Ibrahim Jaafar	
57	俠女花蒂瑪 Tun Fatimah	1962	Salleh Ghani	瑪麗亞曼多、諾定亞末、Yusoff Latiff	
58	七仙女 Jula Juli Bintang Tujoh	1962	卑恩勞	拉蒂花奧瑪、烏美嘉東	
59	邪惡的眼睛 The Devil's Eye (Mata Shaitan)	1962	哈申漢尼夫	花蒂瑪亞茉、諾定亞末、Siput Sarawak、Yusoff Latiff	
60	黃色的船 Lanchang Kuning	1962	M. 亞民	諾定亞末、拉蒂花奧瑪	
61	馬來亞巨人 Badang	1962	魯邁拿	華希得沙爹、露絲葉蒂瑪、Zainol Gemok	
62	黎明的影子	1962	奧斯瑪伊斯蓮		代表印尼參加第十屆「亞展」 曾名《黎明之影》 克利斯貝豐尼（印尼）公司出品

國泰克里斯片目 Filmography of Cathay Keris Films

	影片名稱	首映日期	導演	主要演員	附註
63	Korban Kaseh	1962	哈申漢尼夫	烏美嘉東、諾定亞末、拉蒂花奧瑪、Habibah Harun、Abu Bakar Yem	
64	Mabok Kepayang	1962	哈申漢尼夫	華希得沙爹、蘇泣耶（Suraya Harun）	
65	Mata Shaitan	1962	噲申漢尼夫	諾定亞末、花蒂瑪亞茉、Mahmud Jun、Siput Sarawak、Yusoff Latiff	
66	蕩女癡郎	1963	M. 亞民	諾定亞末、拉蒂花奧瑪	
67	歡天喜地	1963			
68	Bayangan Diwaktu Fajar	1963	Osman Ismail	魯邁拿、拉蒂花奧瑪、Noorfani Vusoff	
69	Chempaka Biru	1963	卑恩勞	露絲葉蒂瑪、蘇泣耶、嘉沙里蘇曼特利（Ghazali Sumantri）、Haji Arshad	
70	Chuchu Datok Merah	1963	M. 亞民	諾定亞末、拉蒂花奧瑪、露絲葉蒂瑪	
71	Darah Ku	1963	Ramon Estella	瑪麗亞曼多、勒史拉密（Malek Slamet）	
72	Gila Talak	1963	哈申漢尼夫	華希得沙爹、花蒂瑪亞茉、Yusoff Latiff	
73	Gul Bakawali	1963	卑恩勞	諾定亞末、拉蒂花奧瑪	
74	Masuk Angin Keluar Asap	1963	哈申漢尼夫	烏美嘉東、華希得沙爹	
75	Pontianak Kembali	1963	Ramon Estella	瑪麗亞曼多、勒史拉密	
76	Rumah Itu Dunia Aku	1963	M. 亞民	魯邁拿、拉蒂花奧瑪、露絲葉蒂瑪	
77	Raja Bersiong	1963	Ramon Estella	瑪麗亞曼多、勒史拉密	
78	Tajul Ashikin	1963	M. 亞民	諾定亞末、露絲葉蒂瑪、華謙（A. Rahim）	
79	東京之夜 Night in Tokyo (Malam di Tokyo)	1963	哈申漢尼夫	瑪麗亞曼多	
80	Ayer Mata Duyong	1964	M. 亞民	諾定亞末、蘇拉耶、Malek Selamai	
81	兩武士 Two Warriors (Dua Pendekar)	1964	哈申漢尼夫	露絲葉蒂瑪、Salleh Melan、Yusoff Lariff	
82	手足情仇 Hutang Darah Di-bayar Darah	1964	哈申漢尼夫	諾定亞末、露絲葉蒂瑪、華謙	
83	亂世奸雄 Palace of Blood (Istana Berdarah)	1964	哈申漢尼夫	花蒂瑪亞茉、Ahmad Osman	
84	Kalong Kenangan	1964	哈申漢尼夫	拉蒂花奧瑪、Yusoff Latiff、Salleh Melan、嘉沙里蘇曼特利（Ghazali Sumantri）	
85	福至心靈 Crazy Mat (Mat Tiga Suku)	1964	哈申漢尼夫、密山多(Mat Sentol)	密山多	
86	魔女驚魂 Pontianak Gua Musang	1964	諾定亞末	蘇拉耶、勒史拉密、烏美嘉東	
87	Panglima Besi	1964	M. 亞民	諾定亞末、露絲葉蒂瑪	
88	Wan Perkasa	1964	諾定亞末	勒史拉密、拉蒂花奧瑪、Salleh Melan、Siput Sarawak	
89	Chinta Kaseh Sayang	1965	哈申漢尼夫	拉蒂花奧瑪、諾定亞末、Tony Rahman、Ahmad Osman	
90	Ikan Emas	1965	M. 亞民	拉蒂花奧瑪、嘉沙里蘇曼特利、諾定亞末、Siput Sarawak	
91	Jiran Se-Kampong	1965	哈申漢尼夫	露絲葉蒂瑪、Ahmad Osman	
92	Kaseh Ibu	1965	諾定亞末	拉蒂花奧瑪、Bat Latiff	
93	恩仇愛恨 Mata Dan Hati	1965	M. 亞民	露絲葉蒂瑪、馬洛佛、勒史拉密、華拉（M. Wari）、Fatimahwati	
94	Muda Mudi	1965	M. 亞民	馬洛佛、露絲葉蒂瑪、Fatimahwati、Siput Sarawak、Tony Kassim	
95	Patong Chendana	1965	M. 亞民	拉蒂花奧瑪、諾定亞末	

96	Tiga Botak	1965	密山多	蘇拉耶、華希得沙爹、密山多
97	Anak Dara	1966	M. 亞民	蘇拉耶、密山多、華希得沙爹、Tony Kassim
98	Dua Kali Lima	1966	M. 亞民	密山多、華希得沙爹
99	靈魂之詩 Sonnet of the Soul (Gurindam Jiwa)	1966	M. 亞民	拉蒂花奧瑪、諾定亞末
100	Naga Tasek Chini	1966	諾定亞末、拉蒂花奧瑪	諾定亞末、拉蒂花奧瑪
101	Udang Di-Sebalek Batu	1966	哈申漢尼夫	露絲葉蒂瑪、花蒂瑪亞茉、Ahmad Osman
102	Dosa Wanita	1967	M. 亞民	花蒂瑪亞茉、烏美嘉東
103	Mat Raja Kapor	1967	密山多、M. 亞民	密山多、勒史拉密、Tony Kassim
104	Mat Bond	1967	密山多、M. 亞民	密山多
105	Play Boy	1967	諾定亞末	諾定亞末、Rosnani Jamil
106	Kekaseh	1968	諾定亞末	花蒂瑪亞茉、Salim Bachik、Norma Zainal
107	Mat Lanun	1968	密山多	密山多、Ani Jaafar、Ibrahim Pendek
108	Pop Muda	1968	M. 亞民	Fatimahwati、Siput Sarawak、Tony Kassim
109	Si Murai	1968	諾定亞末	馬洛佛、密山多、勒史拉密
110	Keranda Berdarah	1969	諾定亞末	馬洛佛、Tony Kassim、S. Noni、Shariff Doi
111	Keris Emas	1969	M. 亞民	Kuswadinata、Ani Jaafar
112	Mat Toyal	1969	密山多	密山多、多拉沙拉華（Dollah Sarawak）、Mohd Latif
113	Nafsu Belia	1969	諾定亞末	勒史拉密
114	Sial Wanita	1969	M. 亞民	花蒂瑪亞茉、諾定亞末、Sa'adiah
115	Serikandi	1969	M. 亞民	諾定亞末、Tony Kassim、S. Noni、Malek Selamar
116	Aku Mahu Hidup	1970	M. 亞民	Kuswadinata、Ani Jaafar
117	Lobang Neraka	1970	諾定亞末	馬洛佛、Kuswadinata、S. Noni、Malik Selamat
118	Mat Karong Guni	1970	密山多	密山多、多拉沙拉華、Normadiah
119	Puaka	1970	M. 亞民	Aziz Jaafar、Dayang Sofiah
120	Jahanam	1971	M. 亞民	諾定亞末、Sa'adiah
121	Mat Magic	1971	密山多	密山多、John Calvert
122	Semusim Di-Neraka	1971	M. 亞民	Norma Zainal、Aziz Jaafar、Salleh Melan
123	Semangat Ular	1972	M. 亞民	馬洛佛、Emma Desita
124	Hati Batu	1973	M. 亞民	拉蒂花奧瑪、Salleh Melan、S.Azam
125	Satu Titek Di-Garisan	1973	M. 亞民	拉蒂花奧瑪、Aziz Jaafar、Dayang Sofiah

編按：國泰克里斯專門攝製巫語（馬來亞語）影片，1960 年《獅子城》是唯一例外的國語作品。

名稱對照表
Glossary

人名

編按：

1. 本對照表列出於本書英文部份提及的人物名稱，依漢語拼音序排列。
2. 本書內文採用各人本身常用的中／英文名字。本身無英文名字的，譯名依 據過往曾出版的英文書刊所載或拼音(國語片影人及來自中國大陸的人物用漢語拼音）列出；同一人有不同寫法的，表中括以「又名」，內文取較常用的一個。出版有關香港電影的英文書籍，最傷腦筋的就是人物的名字問題。誠然，統一地用漢語拼音是最方便的辦法，但又容易因而忽略了地區及時代的氣味，例如不少國泰電懋的影人均有外國名字，不但反映了時代的氛圍，更與國泰電懋比較洋化的形象非常吻合。

影片 / 電影機構名稱

編按：

1. 本對照表列出於本書英文部份提及的影片及電影機構名稱，依漢語拼音序列出。
2. 英文片名依據原始資料(正式公映時的名字)或過往曾出版的電影書刊所載列出，如無正式英文片名，始自行翻譯。
3. 表中同一部影片有多於一個中文／英文名字的，括以「又名」或「原名」。

Personalities

Editor's Notes:

1. This glossary comprises names of film personalities published in the English version of this publication, listed in the order of their *pinyin* transliterations.
2. English names as adopted by the film personalities themselves are used in this publication. Wherever such names are not available, transliterations used in previous English publications, *pinyin* transliterations of Mandarin personalities or Cantonese transliterations of Cantonese personalities are used. Aliases are accordingly listed in cases where discrepancies of names appear, while the formal name entries are used in the main text.

Film Titles/Organisations

Editor's Notes:

1. This glossary comprises film titles and names of film organisations published in the English version of this publication, listed in alphabetical order.
2. English titles listed are the official titles or names that appeared in original filmic materials and publications of the day. Literal translations or *pinyin* of titles and names are rendered where no English names are available.
3. Original or other known film titles are accordingly listed in this glossary.

人名 Personalities

漢語拼音 / Pinyin	中文名字 / Chinese Name	英文名字 / English Name
Bai Guang	白光	
Bai Jingrui	白景瑞	
Bai Luming	白露明	Christine Pai Lu-ming
Bai Ying	白鷹	
Bao Tianming	包天鳴	
Bu Wancang	卜萬蒼	
Cai Haoquan	蔡浩泉	
Cao Dahua	曹達華	Tso Tat-wah
Cha Liangyong (alias Jin Yong)	查良鏞（即金庸）	Louis Cha
Chen Baozhu	陳寶珠	Connie Chan Po-chu
Chen Dieyi	陳蝶衣	
Chen Hou	陳厚	Peter Chen Ho
Chen Manling	陳曼玲	Melinda Chen Manling
Chen Tongmin	陳銅民	
Chen Yun	陳雲	Chan Wan
Cheng Bugao	程步高	
Cheng Long	成龍	Jackie Chan
Chi Ren	癡人	
Chu Yuan	楚原	Chor Yuen
Cui Fusheng	崔福生	
Dai Anguo	戴安國	
Dan Duyu	但杜宇	
Deng Xiaoyu	鄧小宇	Peter Dunn
Di Long	狄龍	Ti Lung
Di Na	狄娜	Tina Ti
Ding Hao	丁皓	Kitty Ting Hao
Ding Ying	丁櫻	
Dong Qianli	董千里	
Dou Hanxun	竇漢勳	Tau Hon-fun
Fang Hua	方華	Fong Wah
Fang Yanfen	芳艷芬	Fong Yim-fun
Fei Boyi	費伯夷	Rex Fay
Fei Luyi	費魯伊	Louis Fei
Fei Mu	費穆	
Fu Baoshi	傅葆石	Poshek Fu
Gao Liang	高亮	
Ge Lan	葛蘭	Grace Chang
Gu Mei	顧媚	Carrie Ku
Gu Zhongyi	顧仲彝	
Han Yingjie	韓英傑	
He Guan (alias Zhang Che)	何觀 （即張徹）	
He Guanchang	何冠昌	Leonard Ho
He Qirong	何啟榮	
He Yalü	何亞祿	Ho Ah Loke
He Yu (alias Zuo Ji)	何愉（即左几）	Ho Yu (alias Tso Kea)
Hong Jinbao	洪金寶	Sammo Hung
Hong Shuyun	洪叔雲	Hung Suk-wan
Hong Xiannü	紅線女	Hung Sin-nui
Hong Yang	洪洋	
Hu Feng	胡楓	Wu Fung
Hu Jinquan	胡金銓	King Hu
Huang Dai	黃岱	
Huang He	黃河	
Huang Jinjuan	黃錦娟	Wong Jin-juan

人名 Personalities

漢語拼音 / Pinyin	中文名字 / Chinese Name	英文名字 / English Name
Huang Qiansui	黃千歲	Wong Chin-sui
Huang Qizhi	黃奇智	Wong Kee-chee
Huang Shuxian	黃淑嫻	Mary Wong
Huang Yebai	黃也白	
Huang Zhuohan	黃卓漢	Wong Cheuk-hon
Huang Zi	黃自	
Jia Ling	嘉玲	Ka Ling
Jiang Boying	蔣伯英	
Jiang Dawei	姜大衛	David Chiang
Jiang Guangchao	蔣光超	Chiang Kwong-chao
Jiang Nan	姜南	
Jiang Qing	江青	Chiang Ching
Jiang Tianliu	蔣天流	
Jiao Xiongping	焦雄屏	Peggy Chiao Hsiung-ping
Jin Yong (alias Cha Liangyong)	金庸（即查良鏞）	Louis Cha
Jin Bingxing	金炳興	Kam Ping-hing
Jing Hailin	敬海林	
Jing Ting	靜婷	
Le Di	樂蒂	Betty Loh Ti
Lei Zhen	雷震	Kelly Lai Chen
Li An	李安	Ang Lee
Li Guangyao	李光耀	Lee Kuan Yew
Li Hanxiang	李翰祥	
Li Houxiang	李厚襄	
Li Junqing	李雋青	
Li Lihua	李麗華	
Li Linlin	李琳琳	Maggie Li Linlin
Li Mei	李湄	Helen Li Mei
Li Minwei	黎民偉	Lai Man-wai
Li Oufan	李歐梵	Leo Lee Ou-fan
Li Pingqian	李萍倩	
Li Wo	李我	Li Ngaw
Li Xianglan	李香蘭（即山口淑子）	Yamaguchi Yoshiko, Shirley
Li Xiangqing	李香琴	Lee Hong-kum
Li Xiaolong	李小龍	Bruce Lee
Li Zhian	李芝安	
Li Zhuotao	李焯桃	Li Cheuk-to
Li Zuyong	李祖永	
Lian Fuming	連福明	Heah Hock Meng
Liang Bingjun	梁秉鈞	Leung Ping-kwan
Liang Chaowei	梁朝偉	Tony Leung Chiu-wai
Liang Xingbo	梁醒波	Leung Sing-po
Liang Yusheng	梁羽生	
Lin Cang	林蒼	Ling Chong
Lin Chong	林沖	
Lin Cui	林翠	Jeanette Lin Cui
Lin Dai	林黛	Linda Lin Dai
Lin Feng	林鳳	Patricia Lam Fung
Lin Niantong	林年同	Lin Nien-tung
Lin Shujia	林淑佳	Lim Cheng Kim
Lin Yihua	林奕華	Edward Lam
Lin Yongtai	林永泰	Lam Wing-tai
Ling Bo	凌波	
Liu Enjia	劉恩甲	

人名 Personalities

漢語拼音 / Pinyin	中文名字 / Chinese Name	英文名字 / English Name
Liu Fanggang	劉芳剛	
Liu Jialiang	劉家良	Lau Kar-leung
Liu Xiaohui	劉小慧	
Liu Yafo	劉亞佛	
Liu Yichang	劉以鬯	
Lu Li	陸離	Ada Loke
Lu Wanting	陸婉婷	Choo (Loke)Yuen Theng
Lu You	陸佑	Loke Yew
Lu Yuanliang	陸元亮	
Lu Yuntao	陸運濤	Loke Wan Tho
Lu Yuqi	盧雨岐	
Luo Jianlang	羅劍郎	Law Kim-long
Luo Ka	羅卡	Law Kar
Luo Lie	羅烈	Lo Lieh
Luo Mingyou	羅明佑	
Luo Wei	羅維	Lo Wei
Luo Wen	羅文	
Luo Yanqing	羅艷卿	Law Yim-hing
Ma Shizeng	馬師曾	Ma Si-tsang
Ma Shuyong	馬叔庸	
Mai Jia	麥嘉	Karl Maka
Mai Ling	麥玲	
Mai Xiaoxia	麥嘯霞	
Mai Ke	邁克	Michael Lam
Mei Qi	梅綺	Mui Yee
Miao Jinfeng	苗金鳳	Miu Kam-fung
Mo Chou	莫愁	Lily Mok Chau
Mo Kangshi	莫康時	Mok Hong-si
Mu Hong	穆虹	
Ouyang Shafei	歐陽莎菲	
Ouyang Yuqian	歐陽予倩	
Pan Xiuqiong	潘秀瓊	Poon Sow Keng
Qi Xiangtang	綦湘棠	Shang-tong Kei
Qiao Hong	喬宏	Roy Chiao
Qin Jian	秦劍	Chun Kim
Qin Xianglin	秦祥林	Charles Chin
Qin Yifu (alias Qin Yu)	秦亦孚 (即秦羽)	
Qin Yu (alias Qin Yifu)	秦羽（即秦亦孚）	Nellie Chin Yu
Rong Shicheng	容世誠	Yung Sai-shing
Ruan Lingyu	阮玲玉	
Sha Rongfeng	沙榮峰	Sha Yung-fong
Shangguan Lingfeng	上官靈鳳	
Shao Cunren	邵邨人	Runde Shaw
Shao Renmei	邵仁枚	Runme Shaw
Shao Yifu	邵逸夫	Run Run Shaw
Shi Jian	石堅	Sek Kin
Shi Nansheng	施南生	Nansun Shi
Shi Qi	石琪	Sek Kei
Shu Qi	舒琪	Shu Kei
Song Qi	宋淇	Stephen Soong
Su Feng	蘇鳳	Dolly Soo Fung
Sun Jiawen	孫家雯	
Sun Jinsan	孫晉三	
Sun Yue	孫越	

人名 Personalities

漢語拼音 / Pinyin	中文名字 / Chinese Name	英文名字 / English Name
Tan Bingwen	譚炳文	Tam Ping-man
Tan Lanqing	譚蘭卿	Tam Lan-hing
Tan Dun	譚盾	
Tang Huang	唐煌	
Tang Jia	唐佳	Tang Chia
Tang Qing	唐菁	
Tang Shuxuan	唐書璇	Shu Shuen
Tao Qin	陶秦	
Tian Han	田漢	
Tian Qing	田青	
Tong Yuejuan	童月娟	
Tu Guangqi	屠光啟	
Tu Meiqing	屠梅卿	
Wang Jiawei	王家衛	Wong Kar-wai
Wang Jing	王晶	Wong Jing
Wang Lai	王萊	
Wang Liuzhao	汪榴照	
Wang Shuwei	汪淑衛	
Wang Tianlin	王天林	
Wang Xinglü	王星磊	
Wang Yu	王羽	Jimmy Wang Yu
Wang Yuanlong	王元龍	
Wang Zhibo	王植波	
Weng Lingwen	翁靈文	
Weng Mulan	翁木蘭	On Mu-lang
Wu Chufan	吳楚帆	Ng Cho-fan
Wu Jiaxiang	吳家驤	
Wu Yusen	吳宇森	John Woo
Wu Zuguang	吳祖光	
Xia Houlan	夏厚蘭	
Xia Yan	夏衍	
Xiao Fangfang	蕭芳芳	Josephine Siao
Xiao Peipei	小珮珮	
Xiao Tong	蕭銅	
Xie Xian	謝賢	Patrick Tse Yin
Xu Guanjie	許冠傑	Sam Hui
Xu Guanwen	許冠文	Michael Hui
Xu Heng	徐亨	
Xu Ke	徐克	Tsui Hark
Xu Su	徐速	
Xu Xu	徐訏	
Xu Yan (alias Yao Ke)	許炎（即姚克）	
Xue Juexian	薛覺先	Sit Kok-sin
Yan Jun	嚴俊	
Yang Panpan	楊盼盼	Yeung Pan-pan, Sharon
Yang Hansheng	陽翰笙	
Yang Manyi	楊曼怡	Yeo Ban Yee
Yang Qun	楊群	
Yang Tiancheng	楊天成	
Yao Ke (alias Xu Yan)	姚克（即許炎）	
Yao Min	姚敏	
Ye Chunzhi	葉純之	
Ye Feng	葉楓	Julie Yeh Feng
Ye Yueyu	葉月瑜	Yeh Yueh-yu

人名 Personalities

漢語拼音 / Pinyin	中文名字 / Chinese Name	英文名字 / English Name
Yi Guang	夷光	Maria Ye Kwong
Yi Shu	亦舒	Isabel Ni
Yi Wen	易文	Yi Wen (alias Evan Yang)
You Jing	游靜	Yau Ching
You Min	尤敏	Lucilla You Min
Yu Muyun	余慕雲	Yu Mo-wan
Yu Puqing	俞普慶	Paul Yui
Yuan Qiufeng	袁秋楓	
Yue Feng	岳楓	
Yue Hua	岳華	Elliot Yueh Hua
Zhang Ailing	張愛玲	Eileen Chang
Zhang Che (alias He Guan)	張徹（即何觀）	Chang Cheh
Zhang Henshui	張恨水	
Zhang Huixian	張慧嫻	Anette Chang
Zhang Jiande	張建德	Stephen Teo
Zhang Junxiang	張駿祥	
Zhang Manyu	張曼玉	Maggie Cheung
Zhang Meiyao	張美瑤	Chang Mei-yao
Zhang Qing	張清	Cheung Ching
Zhang Shankun	張善琨	
Zhang Xiaoyan	張小燕	
Zhang Yang	張揚	Chang Yang
Zhang Ying	張瑛	Cheung Ying
Zhang Yingcai	張英才	Cheung Ying-choi
Zhang Zengze	張曾澤	
Zhang Zhongwen	張仲文	Diana Chang Chung-wen
Zhao Deke	趙德克	Chiu Tak-hak
Zhao Lei	趙雷	Chao Lei
Zheng Boqi	鄭伯奇	
Zheng Hui	鄭慧	
Zheng Junmian	鄭君綿	Cheng Kwan-min
Zheng Peipei	鄭佩佩	Cheng Pei-pei
Zhi Luolian	紫羅蓮	Zi Lo-lin
Zhong Baoxian	鍾寶賢	Stephanie Chung Po-yin
Zhong Qing	鍾情	Chung Ching
Zhong Qiwen	鍾啟文	Robert Chung
Zhou Manhua	周曼華	
Zhou Xingchi	周星馳	Stephen Chiau
Zhou Xuan	周萱	Hilda Chou Hsuan
Zhou Xuan	周璇	
Zhou Yibai	周貽白	
Zhu Guoliang	朱國良	Choo Kok Leong
Zhu Meilian	朱美蓮	Meileen Choo
Zhu Mu	朱牧	
Zhu Shilin	朱石麟	
Zhu Xuhua	朱旭華	
Zou Wenhuai	鄒文懷	Raymond Chow
Zuo Guifang	左桂芳	Tso Kuei-fang
Zuo Ji (alias He Yu)	左几（即何愉）	Tso Kea (alias Ho Yu)

外國人名 Foreign Personalities

英文名字 / English Name	中文名字 / Chinese Name
Ahmad, Fatimah	花蒂瑪亞茉
Ahmad, Salmah	莎瑪亞末
Ali, Aidi	愛迪亞里
Amin, M.	M. 亞民
Antonioni, Michelangelo	安東尼奧尼
Berlin, Irving	愛文柏林
Bertolucci, Bernado	貝托魯奇
Bizet, Georges	比才
Bordwell, David	大衛博維爾
Brecht, Bertolt	布萊希特
Callas, Maria	卡拉絲
Caruso, Enrico	卡魯索
Chandler, Raymond	陳德勒
Chevalier, Maurice	梅禮士司花利亞
Chiba Yasuki	千葉泰
Collins, Joan	鍾歌蓮絲
Cukor, George	喬治寇克
Curtiz, Michael	米高寇蒂斯
Dan Reiko	團令子
Dietrich, Marlene	瑪蓮德烈治
Ede, John	約翰依特
Faulkner, William	福克納
Fitzgerald, Scott	費茲傑羅
Ford, John	尊福
Foucault, Michel	福柯
Granger, Farley	花利格蘭加
Haniff, Hussain	哈申漢尼夫
Hasegawa Kazuo	長谷川一夫
Harun, Suraya	蘇拉耶
Hattori Ryoichi	服部良一
Hawks, Howard	侯活鶴斯
Hitchcock, Alfred	希治閣
Huston, John	尊侯斯頓
Huxley, Aldous	赫胥黎
Ibsen, Henrik	易卜生
James, Henry	亨利詹姆士
Kalthoum, Ummi	烏美嘉東
Kam Ping-hing	金炳興
Kasahara Ryozo	笠原良三
Kayama Yuzo	加山雄三

英文名字 / English Name	中文名字 / Chinese Name
Kerr, Deborah	狄波拉嘉
Krishnan, L.	葛利斯南
Kurosawa Akira	黑澤明
Kusabue Mitsuko	草笛光子
Laemmle, Jr., Carl	小卡爾拉姆耳
Lang, Fritz	費立茲朗
Lanza, Mario	馬里奧蘭沙
Lehár, Franz	萊哈
Leigh, Vivien	慧雲李
Lubitsch, Ernst	劉別謙
Maarof, Mustapha	馬洛佛
MacDonald, Jeanette	珍妮麥當奴
Mamoulian, Rouben	魯賓孟穆里安
Matsuyama Renzo	松山善三
Menado, Maria	瑪麗亞曼多
Mérimée, Prosper	梅里美
Milland, Ray	雷米蘭
Murdoch, Rupert	梅鐸
Noor, S. Roomai	魯邁拿
Odell, Albert	歐德爾
Odell, Harry	歐德禮
Offenbach, Jacques	奧芬巴哈
Omar, Latiffah	拉蒂花奧瑪
Preminger, Otto	岳圖柏林明嘉
Puccini, Giacomo	普契尼
Rao, B. N.	卑恩勞
Rattigan, Terence	雷荻根
Romberg, Sigmund	西蒙隆伯
Satay, Wahid	華希得沙爹
Sentol, Mat	密山多
Shakespeare, William	莎士比亞
Slamet, Malek	勒史拉密
Sternberg, Josef von	約瑟馮史登堡
Takarada Akira	寶田明
Verdi, Giuseppe	威爾第
Visconti, Luchino	維斯康堤
Whale, James	占士威爾
Yachigusa Kaoru	八千草薰
Yatimah, Rose	露絲葉蒂瑪

影片 Film Titles

英文片名 / English Title	中文片名 / Chinese Title	漢語拼音 / Title in Pinyin	年份 / Year	備註 / Remarks
48 Hours in Escape	逃亡四十八小時	Taowang Sishiba Xiaoshi	1959	
Affair to Remember, An	情天長恨	Qingtian Changhen	1964	
Affection	嘉嘉	Jiajia	1969	
Air Hostess	空中小姐	Kongzhong Xiaojie	1959	
All in the Family	家有喜事	Jiayou Xishi	1959	
Apartment, The	我愛莎莎	Wo Ai Shasha	1970	
Apple a Day, An	小蘋果	Xiao Pingguo	1970	
Arch, The	董夫人	Dong Furen	1970	
Army Daze	新新兵小傳	Xin Xin Bing Xiaozhuan	1996	
Autumn	秋	Qiu	1954	
Autumn Comes to Purple Rose Garden	紫薇園的秋天	Ziwei Yuan De Qiutian	1958	
Bachelors Beware	温柔鄉	Wenrou Xiang	1960	
Bamboo of Yearning (Buloh Perindu)	真假王子		1953	巫語片
Battle of Love, The	情場如戰場	Qingchang Ru Zhanchang	1957	
Beauty Parade	體育皇后	Tiyu Huanghou	1961	
Beauty Who Lived through Great Changes, The	歷盡滄桑一美人	Lijin Cangsang Yi Meiren	1958	
Because of Her	教我如何不想她	Jiao Wo Ruhe Bu Xiang Ta	1963	
Bedside Story, The	同床異夢	Tongchuang Yimeng	1960	
Beggar's Daughter, The	金玉奴	Jin Yunu	1965	
Better Halves, The	鸞鳳和鳴	Luanfeng Heming	1964	
Between Tears and Laughter	玉樓三鳳	Yulou Sanfeng	1960	
Beware of Pickpockets	提防小手	Tifang Xiaoshou	1958	
Beyond the Grave	人鬼戀	Rengui Lian	1954	
Big Boss, The	唐山大兄	Tangshan Daxiong	1971	
Big Circus, The	大馬戲團	Da Maxituan	1964	
Big Thunderstorm	大雷雨	Da Leiyu	1954	
Bitter Lotus (Part 1)	苦心蓮上集	Kuxin Lian (Shangji)	1960	
Bitter Lotus (Part 2)	苦心蓮大結局	Kuxin Lian (Dajieju)	1960	
Bitter Romance	苦命鴛鴦	Kuming Yuanyang	1963	
Black Mask, The	黑俠擒兇	Heixia Qinxiong	1958	
Black Panther, The	黑豹	Hei Bao	1969	
Black Tulip of Inkabough	黑妞	Hei Niu	1956	
Blood Stained Flowers	碧血黃花	Bixue Huanghua	1954	
Blue Angel, The	藍天使		1930	德國片
Boat Girl, The	水上人家	Shuishang Renjia	1968	
Body of a Blackmailer, The	碧海浮屍	Bihai Fushi	1956	
Booze, Boobs & Bucks	酒色財氣	Jiuse Caiqi	1957	
Bride of Frankenstein, The	科學怪人的新娘		1935	美國片
Broadway Melody, The	荷里活之歌		1929	美國片
Broker La and the Smart Feitiannan	經紀拉與飛天南	Jingji La Yu Feitian Nan	1950	
Buddha with 1000 Arms	千手佛	Qianshou Fo	1968	
Caine Mutiny, The	叛艦喋血記		1954	美國片
Calendar Girl	龍翔鳳舞	Longxiang Fengwu	1959	
Carmen	卡門		1984	法國片
Carmen Jones	卡門瓊絲		1954	美國片
Casablanca	北非諜影		1942	美國片
Chair, The	金山大少	Jinshan Dashao	1959	
Challenge, The	龍吟虎嘯	Longyin Huxiao	1969	
China Night	支那的夜		1940	日本片
Chinese Boxer, The	龍虎鬥	Long Hu Dou	1970	
Chinese Ghost Story - the Tsui Hark Animation, A	小倩	Xiaoqian	1997	
Chinese Ghost Story, A	倩女幽魂	Qiannü Youhun	1987	
Cinderella and Her Little Angels	雲裳艷后	Yunchang Yanhou	1959	
Cliff, The	懸崖	Xuanya	1961	

影片 Film Titles

英文片名 / English Title	中文片名 / Chinese Title	漢語拼音 / Title in Pinyin	年份 / Year	備註 / Remarks
Cold Blade	龍沐香	Longmu Xiang	1970	
Come Drink With Me	大醉俠	Da Zuixia	1966	
Come Rain, Come Shine	野花戀	Yehua Lian	1962	
Corpses at Large	古屋疑雲	Guwu Yiyun	1960	
Cosmopolitan Fantasy	都市狂想曲	Dushi Kuangxiangqu	1964	
Country Girl, The	蓬門淑女		1954	美國片
Crazy Mat (Mat Tiga Suku)	福至心靈		1964	巫語片
Crimson Rose, The	血灑紅玫瑰	Xuesa Hong Meigui	1968	
Crisis, The	生死關頭	Shengsi Guantou	1964	
Crossed Swords （Part 1）	雙劍盟	Shuang Jian Meng	1962	
Crossed Swords （Part 2）	雙劍盟大結局	Shuang Jian Meng（Dajieju）	1962	
Crouching Tiger, Hidden Dragon	臥虎藏龍	Wo Hu Cang Long	2000	
Crusade against Daddy	早生貴子	Zaosheng Guizi	1962	
Curse of the Oily Man (Sumpah Orang Minyak)	油人的詛咒		1958	巫語片
Curse of the Vampire (Sumpah Pontianak)	人妖之誓		1958	巫語片
Darling Stay at Home	太太萬歲	Taitai Wansui	1968	
Days of Being Wild	阿飛正傳	Afei Zhengzhuan	1990	
Dead Knot	死結	Sijie	1969	
Death Traps	殺機重重	Shaji Chongchong	1960	
Debt of Blood, A	亂世兒女	Luanshi Ernü	1966	
Debt of Love	天倫淚	Tianlun Lei	1961	
Deep Blue Sea, The	孽海情潮	Niehai Qingchao	1955	英國片
Deformed, The	畸人艷婦	Qiren Yanfu	1960	
Desperate Seven, The	七大盜	Qi Dadao	1968	
Devil's Eye, The (Mata Syaitan)	邪惡的眼睛		1962	巫語片
Devil's Skin, The	鬼皮	Gui Pi	1970	
Devotion	母與女	Mu Yu Nü	1960	
Dial for Murder	錄音機情殺案	Luyinji Qingsha An	1970	
Diary of Monita	蒙妮妲日記	Mengnitan Riji	1968	
Diau Darling	貂蟬	Diao Chan	1958	
Double Date	福慧雙修	Fuhui Shuangxiu	1962	
Dragon (Gate) Inn	龍門客棧	Longmen Kezhan	1967	
Dreams Come True	喜相逢	Xi Xiangfeng	1960	
Eagle's Claw, The	鷹爪手	Yingzhao Shou	1970	
Education of Love	愛的教育	Ai De Jiaoyu	1961	
Eight for the Border	亡命八傑	Wangming Bajie	1969	
Empress Wu Tse-tien	武則天	Wuzetian	1962	
Enchanting Shadow, The	倩女幽魂	Qiannü Youhun	1958	
Escape	逃	Tao	1968	
Escort over Tiger Hills	虎山行	Hushan Hang	1969	
Extra Duty of a Governess, The	關不住的春光	Guanbuzhu De Chunguang	1970	
Fabulous Protectress, The	神龍奇俠	Shenlong Qixia	1970	
Factory Queen	工廠皇后	Gongchang Huanghou	1963	
Fairy, Ghost, Vixen	聊齋誌異	Liaozhai Zhiyi	1965	
False Alarm	傻偵探	Sha Zhentan	1962	
Father and Son	人之初	Ren Zhi Chu	1963	
Father and Son	父與子	Fu Yu Zi	1954	
Father Takes a Bride	小兒女	Xiao Ernü	1963	
Fine Romance, A	一段情	Yi Duan Qing	1962	
Fire	火	Huo	1956	
First Sword, The	第一劍	Diyi Jian	1967	
Fisherman's Daughter, The	漁歌	Yuge	1956	
Fist of Fury, The	精武門	Jingwu Men	1972	
Flowers of Love (Bunga Percintaan)	戀之花			巫語片
Flying-sword Hero from Emei Mountain	峨嵋飛劍俠	Emei Fei Jian Xia	1950	

影片 Film Titles

英文片名 / English Title	中文片名 / Chinese Title	漢語拼音 / Title in Pinyin	年份 / Year	備註 / Remarks
For a Handful of Rice (Untuk Sesuap Nasi)	一把米			巫語片
For Better, For Worse	雨過天青	Yuguo Tianqing	1959	
Forbidden Killing	殺戒	Sha Jie	1970	
Forever Yours	情深似海	Qingshen Sihai	1960	
Forget Me Not	空谷蘭	Kong Gu Lan	1966	
Fortune Teller's Daughter, The	描金鳳	Miao Jinfeng	1968	
Four Brave Ones	諜海四壯士	Diehai Si Zhuangshi	1963	
Frankenstein	科學怪人		1931	美國片
Fresh Peony	鮮牡丹	Xian Mudan	1956	
From Here to Eternity	紅粉忠魂未了情		1953	美國片
From the Highway	路客與刀客	Luke Yu Daoke	1970	
Fugitive, The	草莽喋血記	Caomang Diexue Ji	1966	
Giant	巨人		1956	美國片
Girl in the Red Velvet Swing, The	紅顏恨史		1955	美國片
Girl of the Year, The	廣告女郎	Guanggao Nülang	1958	
Girl with the Golden Arm, The	賊美人	Zei Meiren	1961	
Glass Slippers	玻璃鞋	Boli Xie	1959	
Gloomy Sunday	春色惱人	Chunse Naoren	1956	
Golden Arrow	金箭盟	Jinjian Meng	1963	
Golden Lotus	金蓮花	Jin Lianhua	1957	
Golden Phoenix	金鳳	Jin Feng	1956	
Golden Silence	有口難言	Youkou Nanyan	1962	
Gone are the Swallows When the Willow Flowers Wilt	蘆花翻白燕子飛	Luhua Fanbai Yanzi Fei	1946	
Great Caruso, The	歌王卡羅素		1951	美國片
Great Ziegfeld, The	歌舞大王齊格菲		1936	美國片
Greatest Civil War on Earth, The	南北和	Nanbei He	1961	
Greatest Love Affair on Earth, The	南北喜相逢	Nanbei Xi Xiangfeng	1964	
Greatest Wedding on Earth, The	南北一家親	Nanbei Yijiaqin	1962	
Green Hills and Jade Valleys	青山翠谷	Qingshan Cuigu	1956	
Gunfight at Lo Ma Lake	落馬湖	Luo Ma Hu	1969	
Half Way Down	半下流社會	Ban Xialiu Shehui	1957	
Hang Jebat	古城英傑		1961	巫語片
Happily Ever After	快樂天使	Kuaile Tianshi	1960	
Happy Union	天作之合	Tianzuo Zhi He	1957	
Haunted, The	聊齋誌異續集	Liaozhai Zhiyi（Xuji）	1967	
Head of the Family	一家之主	Yijia Zhi Zhü	1964	
Headless Queen Bears a Son, The	無頭東宮生太子	Wutou Donggong Sheng Taizi	1957	
Hen-pecked Husband	半世老婆奴	Banshi Laoponü	1957	
Her Tender Heart	玉女私情	Yunü Siqing	1959	
Here Come the Wolves	狼與狼	Lang Yu Lang	1969	
Holiday Express	特別快車	Tebei Kuaiche	1957	
Home at Hong Kong	家在香港	Jia Zai Xianggang	1983	
Homemaker, The	家有賢妻	Jiayou Xianqi	1970	
Hong Kong Nocturne	香江花月夜	Xianggang Hua Yueye	1967	
Hong Kong, Tokyo, Honolulu	香港・東京・夏威夷	Xianggang Dongjing Xiaweiyi	1963	
Hong Kong-Tokyo Honeymoon	香港東京蜜月旅行	Xianggang Dongjing Miyue Lüxing	1957	
How Love is Tested	試情記	Shiqing Ji	1969	
Hsi Shih Beauty of Beauties, The	西施	Xi Shi	1965	
I Love Them Both	舊愛新歡	Jiuai Xinhuan	1964	
I'll Make My Own Choice	自作多情	Zizuo Duoqing	1966	
Imperial Lady, The	西太后與珍妃	Xitaihou Yu Zhenfei	1964	
In Fact I Love You	珠聯璧合	Zhulian Bihe	1965	
In the Mood for Love	花樣年華	Huayang Nianhua	2000	
Inn of the Goddess, The	觀音客棧	Guanyin Kezhan	1971	沒有完成的影片
Inspectress General	太太緝私團	Taitai Jisi Tuan	1961	

影片 Film Titles

英文片名 / English Title	中文片名 / Chinese Title	漢語拼音 / Title in Pinyin	年份 / Year	備註 / Remarks
Invisible Man, The	隱形人		1933	美國片
Iron Bones	鐵骨傳	Tiegu Zhuan	1969	
Iron Fist, The	鐵臂金剛	Tiebi Jingang	1960	
Iron Horse, The	鐵馬銀鈴	Tiema Yinling	1967	
Isle of Gold	黃金島	Huangjin Dao	1967	
It's Always Spring	桃李爭春	Taoli Zhengchun	1962	
Jade Bow, The	雲海玉弓緣	Yunhai Yugong Yuan	1966	
Jade Dragon	玉龍吟	Yulong Yin	1968	
June Bride	六月新娘	Liuyue Xinniang	1960	
Kingdom and the Beauty, The	江山美人	Jiangshan Meiren	1959	
King's Sword, The	壯士血	Zhuangshi Xue	1970	
Kuala Lumpur Night (aka The Old Man of Southeast Asia)	南洋亞伯	Nanyang Yabo	1958	
Ladies First	好事成雙	Haoshi Chengshuang	1962	
Lady from the Moon	嫦娥	Chang'e	1954	
Lady Musketeer	女俠文婷玉	Nüxia Wen Tingyu	1960	
Lady on the Moon	嫦娥奔月	Chang'e Benyue	1966	
Lady on the Roof	樑上佳人	Liangshang Jiaren	1959	
Lark, The	浪子之歌	Langzi Zhi Ge	1971	
Legends of Cheating	騙術奇譚	Pianshu Qitan	1971	
Liang San Bo and Zhu Ying Tai	梁山伯與祝英台	Liang Shanbo Yu Zhu Yingtai	1964	
Life With Grandma	滿庭芳	Manting Fang	1957	
Lily of the Valley	火中蓮	Huo Zhong Lian	1962	
Lion City	獅子城	Shizi Cheng	1960	
Little Couple	小夫妻	Xiao Fuqi	1953	
Little Darling	小情人	Xiao Qingren	1958	
Little Lotus	荷花	Hehua	1963	
Little Matchmaker	麒麟送子	Qilin Song Zi	1967	
Lone Swan, The	斷鴻零雁記	Duanhong Lingyan Ji	1955	
Lonely Heart, A	零雁	Ling Yan	1956	
Long Live the Wife	太太萬歲	Taitai Wansui	1947	
Long Voyage Home, The	風雨歸舟	Fengyu Guizhou	1959	
Longest Night, The	最長的一夜	Zuichang De Yiye	1965	
Lost Spring, The	玉樓春夢	Yulou Chunmeng	1970	
Lotus Camp	蓮花寨	Lianhua Zhai	1969	
Love Eterne, The	梁山伯與祝英台	Liang Shanbo Yu Zhu Yingtai	1963	
Love in Bloom	花好月圓	Huahao Yueyuan	1962	
Love Lingers On	魂歸離恨天	Hungui Lihentian	1957	
Love Me or Leave Me	琵琶怨		1955	美國片
Love of a Horse-cart Driver	馬車伕之戀	Machefu Zhi Lian	1956	
Love Parade, The	璇宮艷史		1929	美國片
Love Without End	不了情	Bu Liao Qing	1961	
Loving Couple, The	心心相印	Xinxin Xiangyin	1960	
Lucky Ones, The	洪福齊天	Hongfu Qitian	1970	
Lucky Purse, The	鎖麟囊	Suolin Nang	1966	
Lucky Strike, The	恭喜發財	Gongxi Facai	1970	
Mad About Music	鶯歌燕舞	Yingge Yanwu	1963	
Mad, Mad, Mad Sword, A	神經刀	Shenjing Dao	1969	
Magic Box, The	月宮寶盒	Yuegong Baohe	1958	
Magic Fan, The	扇中人	Shanzhong Ren	1967	
Magic Lamp, The	寶蓮燈	Baolian Deng	1964	
Magnificent Gunfighter	神槍手	Shenqiang Shou	1970	
Make it Mine	錦繡年華	Jinxiu Nianhua	1963	
Male Bride, The	萍水奇緣	Pingshui Qiyuan	1962	
Mallow Forest	楓林渡	Fenglin Du	1969	
Mambo Girl	曼波女郎	Manbo Nülang	1957	

影片 Film Titles

英文片名 / English Title	中文片名 / Chinese Title	漢語拼音 / Title in Pinyin	年份 / Year	備註 / Remarks
Man Killer against the Tricky Man	殺人王大戰扭計深	Sharenwang Dazhan Niujishen	1961	
Memories of Love (aka A Lovely Girl's Lovely Dreams)	美人春夢	Meiren Chunmeng	1958	
Merry Widow, The	風流寡婦		1952	美國片
Merry-Go-Round	歡樂年年	Huanle Niannian	1956	
Miss Kikuko	菊子姑娘	Juzi Guniang	1956	
Miss Pony Tail	辮子姑娘	Bianzi Guniang	1960	
Miss Secretary	女秘書艷史	Nü Mishu Yanshi	1960	
Mission to Die	雪路血路	Xuelu Xuelu	1970	
Money No Enough	錢不夠用	Qian Bu Gou Yong	1998	新加坡片
Monkey Comes again	孫悟空再鬧香港	Sun Wukong Zainao Xianggang	1971	
Monkey in Hong Kong	孫悟空大鬧香港	Sun Wukong Danao Xianggang	1969	
Murder in the Night	無頭案	Wu Tou An	1957	
My Darling Sister	姊妹花	Zimei Hua	1959	
My Eligible Son-in-Law	東床佳婿	Dongchuang Jiaxu	1959	
My Father-in-Law	乘龍快婿	Chenglong Kuaixu	1969	
My Kingdom for a Honeymoon (aka The Romance of Jade Hall, Sequel)	璇宮艷史續集	Xuangong Yanshi Xuji	1958	
My Kingdom for a Husband (aka The Romance of Jade Hall)	璇宮艷史	Xuangong Yanshi	1957	
My Wife, My Wife	余之妻	Yu Zhi Qi	1955	
New Women	新女性	Xin Nüxing	1934	
Night in Bangkok	曼谷之夜	Mangu Zhi Ye	1967	
Night in Hong Kong, A	香港之夜	Xianggang Zhi Ye	1961	
Night in Tokyo (Malam di Tokyo)	東京之夜		1963	巫語片
Night is Not Made for Stealing	千面賊美人	Qianmian Zei Meiren	1970	
No Time for Love	游龍戲鳳	Youlong Xifeng	1968	
Nobody's Child	苦兒流浪記	Kuer Liulang Ji	1960	
Nonya and Baba	娘惹與峇峇	Niangre Yu Baba	1956	
On the Waterfront	碼頭風雲		1954	美國片
One-armed Swordsman	獨臂刀	Du Bi Dao	1967	
Operation Bangkok	諜海蛟龍	Diehai Jiaolong	1967	
Operation Macau	英雄膽	Yingxiong Dan	1967	
Orang Minyak	油鬼子		1958	巫語片
Our Beloved Son	我們的子女	Women De Zinü	1959	
Our Dream Car	香車美人	Xiangju Meiren	1959	
Our Sister Hedy	四千金	Si Qianjin	1957	
Over My Dead Body	殺妻案	Sha Qi An	1958	
Palace of Blood (Istana Berdarah)	亂世奸雄		1964	巫語片
Pale Passion	我為你狂	Wo Wei Ni Kuang	1984	
Passion	女人·女人	Nüren Nüren	1967	
Pearl in Command, A	四武士	Si Wushi	1969	
Persian Cat	波斯貓	Bosi Mao	1968	
Phoenix	鳳凰	Fenghuang	1965	
Please Remember Me	一曲難忘	Yiqu Nanwang	1964	
Please Sir, We're Sorry!	今天不上課	Jintian Bu Shangke	1972	
Pretty Tease	風流冤家	Fengliu Yuanjia	1958	
Prince of Thieves	賊王子	Zei Wangzi	1958	
Prince's Romantic Affairs, The	駙馬艷史	Fuma Yanshi	1958	
Private Eyes, The	鬼馬雙星	Guima Shuangxing	1976	
Qiu Jin, The Revolutionary Heroine	秋瑾	Qiu Jin	1953	
Rainstorm in Chinatown	風雨牛車水	Fengyu Niucheshui	1956	
Rear Entrance	後門	Houmen	1960	
Red Bloom in the Snow	雪裡紅	Xue Li Hong	1956	
Red Plum Pavilion	紅梅閣	Hongmei Ge	1968	
Resort Called Hell, A	蛇王與閻王	Shewang Yu Yanwang	1972	

影片 Film Titles

英文片名 / English Title	中文片名 / Chinese Title	漢語拼音 / Title in Pinyin	年份 / Year	備註 / Remarks
Riots at the Studio	兩傻大鬧攝影場	Liangsha Danao Sheyingchang	1957	
Riots in Outer Space	兩傻大鬧太空	Liangsha Danao Taikong	1959	
Rivals, The	翠寒谷	Cuihan Gu	1970	
Road Back, The	西線無戰事續集		1937	美國片
Romance in Singapore	星洲艷跡	Xingzhou Yanji	1956	
Romance of the Forbidden City	深宮怨	Shengong Yuan	1964	
Rotten Bachelor Warriors (Pendekar Bujang Lapok)	墮落單身武士		1959	巫語片
Royal Seal, The	盜璽	Dao Xi	1969	
Ruthless Heart, The	狠心的人	Henxin De Ren	1970	
Salvation	慈母心	Cimu Xin	1960	
Scaramouche	美人如玉劍如虹		1952	美國片
Scarlet Doll	紅娃	Hong Wa	1958	
Scout Master, The	童軍教練	Tongjun Jiaolian	1959	
Second Spring	翠樓春曉	Cuilou Chunxiao	1960	
Secret of a Married Woman, The	少奶奶的秘密	Shaonainai De Mimi	1956	
Seven Lucky Ones	七喜臨門	Qixi Linmen	1960	
Seventh Heaven	七重天	Qichong Tian	1966	
Shaolin Temple, The	少林寺	Shaolin Si	1982	
Show Boat	畫舫璿璣宮		1936	美國片
Singing under the Moon	翠翠	Cuicui	1953	
Sister Long Legs	長腿姐姐	Changtui Jiejie	1960	
Sleeping Beauty	睡美人	Shui Meiren	1960	
Slimy Man (Orang Lichin)	神秘之屋		1958	巫語片
Smiling Swordsman, The	笑面俠	Xiaomian Xia	1968	
Some Like it Hot	熱情如火		1959	美國片
Song of a Nightingale	夜夜杜鵑啼	Yeye Dujuan Ti	1961	
Song of China (aka Filial Piety)	天倫	Tianlun	1935	
Song of Our Family	春暖人間	Chunnuan Renjian	1968	
Song without Words	無語問蒼天	Wuyu Wen Cangtian	1961	
Songs of Peach Blossom River	桃花江	Taohua Jiang	1956	
Sonnet of the Soul (Gurindam Jiwa)	靈魂之詩		1966	巫語片
Sorrowful Lute, The	琵琶怨	Pipa Yuan	1957	
Sorrows and Joys of a Middle-aged Man	哀樂中年	Aile Zhongnian	1949	
Sorrows of the Forbidden City	清宮秘史	Qinggong Mishi	1948	
Soul of China, The	國魂	Guohun	1948	
Spirits, The	聊齋誌異三集	Liaozhai Zhiyi (Sanji)	1969	
Spring River Flows East, The (Part 1)	一江春水向東流(上集)	Yijiang Chunshui Xiang Dong Liu (Shanji)	1947	
Spring Song	青春兒女	Qingchun Ernü	1959	
Spring Time Affairs	月夜琴挑	Yueye Qintiao	1968	
Star of Hong Kong	香港之星	Xianggang Zhi Xing	1963	
Story of a Fur Coat, The	金縷衣	Jinlu Yi	1956	
Story of Qin Xianglian, The	秦香蓮	Qin Xianglian	1964	
Story of Three Loves, A	啼笑姻緣	Ti Xiao Enyuan	1964	
Story of Three Loves, A (Sequel)	啼笑姻緣(大結局)	Ti Xiao Enyuan (Dajieju)	1964	
Story of Wang Baochuan, The	王寶釧	Wang Baochuan	1959	
Story of Yuan Yuan Hong, The	元元紅	Yuan Yuan Hong	1958	
Strange Woman, A	一代妖姬	Yidai Yaoji	1950	
Student Prince, The	學生王子		1954	美國片
Summer Love	夏日初戀	Xiari Chulian	1968	
Sun, Moon and Star (Part 1)	星星・月亮・太陽(上集)	Xingxing Yueliang Taiyang (Shangji)	1961	
Sun, Moon and Star (Part 2)	星星・月亮・太陽(下集)	Xingxing Yueliang Taiyang (Xiaji)	1961	
Surprise	驚魂記	Jing Hun Ji	1956	
Swallow, The	燕子盜	Yanzi Dao	1961	
Sweet Dreams	花都綺夢	Huadu Qimeng	1955	

影片 Film Titles

英文片名 / English Title	中文片名 / Chinese Title	漢語拼音 / Title in Pinyin	年份 / Year	備註 / Remarks
Swindler's Delight	紅男綠女	Hongnan Lunü	1960	
Tale of Two Wives, A	人財兩得	Rencai Liangde	1958	
Tea and Sympathy	巫山春色		1956	美國片
Tears of Pearl	珍珠淚	Zhenzhu Lei	1965	
Teenager's Holidays	青春的旋律	Qingchun De Xuanlu	1968	
Tender Age, The (aka The Splendour of Youth)	黛綠年華	Dailü Nianhua	1957	
The More the Merrier	三星伴月	Sanxing Ban Yue	1959	
They All Say I Do	三鳳求凰	Sanfeng Qiu Huang	1960	
Three Gentlemen from Tokyo	三紳士艷遇	San Shenshi Yanyu	1963	
Three Smart Girls	三朵玫瑰花	Sanduo Meiguihua	1965	
Three Stages of Love	愛情三部曲	Aiqing Sanbuqu	1955	
Throne of Blood	蜘蛛巢城		1957	日本片
Till the End of Time	紅顏青燈未了情	Hongyan Qingdeng Weiliao Qing	1961	
Time is Running Short	喋血販馬場	Diexue Fanma Chang	1960	
To Kill a Rover	大丐俠	Da Gai Xia	1968	
Too Young to Love	二八佳人	Erba Jiaren	1959	
Torrents of Spring	春潮	Chun Chao	1960	
Tragedy of Love	天長地久	Tianchang Dijiu	1959	
Tragedy of the Emperor's Daughter	帝女花	Di Nü Hua	1959	
Tragic Melody	桃花淚	Taohua Lei	1960	
Transforming Lady, The	化身姑娘	Huashen Guniang	1936	
Travel with a Sword	決鬥惡虎嶺	Juedou Ehuling	1968	
True Story of Ah Q, The	阿 Q 正傳	A Q Zhengzhuan	1958	
Two Warriors (Dua Pendekar)	兩武士		1964	巫語片
Typhoon	颱風	Taifeng	1962	
Unconquered	屠龍	Tulong	1970	
Unknown Swordsman	異鄉客	Yixiang Ke	1970	
Valley of the Lost Soul, The	亡魂谷	Wanghun Gu	1957	
Vampire, The (Pontianak)	吸血人妖		1957	巫語片
Vengeance	復仇	Fuchou	1970	
Venture of Lady Musketeer	文婷玉火海殲仇	Wen Tingyu Huohai Qianchou	1961	
Victim of Slander (Korban Fitnah)	啞子吃黃蓮		1959	巫語片
Victor/ Victoria	雌雄莫辨	Cixiong Mobian	1982	美國片
Violet Clove and Firebird	火鳥第一號	Huoniao Diyi Hao	1970	
Violet Mansion, The	一劍情深	Yijian Qingshen	1969	
Wandering Knight, The	原野游龍	Yuanye Youlong	1967	
Warrior of the Peaceful Sea (Perwira Lautan Teduh)	靜海武士			巫語片
Wayward Husband, The	桃花運	Taohua Yun	1959	
Wedding Bells for Hedy	蘭閨風雲	Langui Fengyun	1959	
Welcome, God of Wealth	接財神	Jie Caishen	1959	
White Rose of Hong Kong, The	香港白薔薇	Xianggang Bai Qiangwei	1966	
Who is not Romantic! (Part 2)	哪個不多情續集	Nage Buduo Qing (Xuji)	1962	
Wife of a Romantic Scholar	蘇小妹	Su Xiaomei	1967	
Wild Girl, The	野姑娘	Ye Guniang	1960	
Wild, Wild Rose, The	野玫瑰之戀	Ye Meigui Zhi Lian	1960	
Wind and Storm Over Alishan	阿里山風雲	Alishan Fengyun	1949	
Winners and Sinners	奇謀妙計五福星	Qimou Miaoji Wufuxing	1983	
Winter, The	冬暖	Dong Nuan	1966	
Woman in Danger	危險人物	Weixian Renwu	1967	
Written on the Wind	苦雨戀春風		1957	美國片
Yang Kwei-fei, the Magnificent Concubine	楊貴妃	Yang Guifei	1962	
You were Meant for Me	遊戲人間	Youxi Renjian	1961	
Young Love	青春夢	Qingchun Meng	1967	
Young Master, The	師弟出馬	Shidi Chuma	1980	

電影機構 Film Organisations

英文名稱 / English Name	中文名稱 / Chinese Name	漢語拼音 / Pinyin
Asia Film Production Studios	亞洲電影製片廠	Yazhou Dianying Zhipian Chang
Cathay Keris Film Productions	國泰克里斯電影製片廠	Guotai Kelisi Dianying Zhipian Chang
Cathay Organisation (Hong Kong) Ltd.	國泰機構（香港）有限公司	Guotai Jigou (Xianggang) Youxian Gongsi
Cathay Organisation (Singapore) Ltd.	國泰機構（新加坡）有限公司	Guotai Jigou (Xinjiapo) Youxian Gongsi
Cathay Studio	國泰片場	Guotai Pianchang
Central Motion Pictures Corporation	中央電影事業有限公司〔中影〕	Zhongyang Dianying Shiye Youxian Gongsi
Changgong Film Company	長弓電影公司	Changgong Dianying Gongsi
Changjiang Film Company	長江影業公司	Changjiang Yingye Gongsi
Dragon-Horse (Loon-Ma) Films	龍馬影片公司	Longma Yingpian Gongsi
Eastman Kodak (Hong Kong) Company	香港柯達公司	Xianggang Keda Gongsi
Feng Huang (Phoenix) Motion Picture Co.	鳳凰影業公司	Fenghuang Yingye Gongsi
Golden Dragon Company	金龍電影製片公司	Jinlong Dianying Zhipian Gongsi
Golden Harvest Studio	嘉禾片場	Jiahe Pianchang
Grand Motion Picture Company	國聯影片公司	Guolian Yingpian Gongsi
Grandview Studio	大觀片場	Daguan Pianchang
Great China Film Company	大中華電影企業公司	Dazhonghua Dianying Qiye Gongsi
Great Wall Pictures Corporation	長城電影製片有限公司	Changcheng Dianying Zhipian Youxian Gongsi
Great Wall Studio	長城片場	Changcheng Pianchang
Guofeng Film Company	國風影業公司	Guofeng Yingye Gongsi
Guoguang Film Company	國光影業公司	Guoguang Yingye Gongsi
Guohua Film Company	國華影業公司	Guohua Yingye Gongsi
Guotai Film Company	國泰電影製片公司	Guotai Dianying Zhipian Gongsi
Guoyi Film Company	國藝影片公司	Guoyi Yingpian Gongsi
Hong Kong and Kowloon Cinema & Theatrical Enterprise Free General Association Limited	港九電影戲劇事業自由總會	Gangjiu Dianying Xiju Shiye Ziyou Zonghui
Hsin Hwa Motion Picture Company	新華影業公司	Xinhua Yingye Gongsi
International Film Distribution Agency〔Singapore〕	國際電影發行公司〔新加坡〕	Guoji Dianying Faxing Gongsi〔Xinjiapo〕
International Films Distributing Agency〔Hong Kong〕	國際影片發行公司〔香港〕	Guoji Yingpian Faxing Gongsi〔Xianggang〕
International Theatre Ltd.	國際戲院有限公司	Guoji Xiyuan Youxian Gongsi
Jinmen Film Company	金門影業公司	Jinmen Yingye Gongsi
Jinying Film Company	金鷹影片公司	Jinying Yingpian Gongsi
Kong Ngee Co.	光藝電影公司	Guangyi Dianying Gongsi
Liangyou Film Company	良友影片公司	Liangyou Yingpian Gongsi
Lianhe Film Company	聯合影業公司	Lianhe Yingye Gongsi
Lianhua Film Company	聯華電影公司	Lianhua Dianying Gongsi
Lianhua Film Company (Shanghai)	聯華影業公司〔上海〕	Lianhua Yingye Gongsi〔Shanghai〕
Longfeng Film Company	龍鳳影業公司	Longfeng Yingye Gongsi
Mingxin Film Company, Shanghai	明星電影公司	Mingxing Dianying Gongsi
Motion Picture and General Investment Co. Ltd.〔MP & GI〕	國際電影懋業有限公司〔電懋〕	Guoji Dianying Maoye Youxian Gongsi〔Dianmao〕
Ronghua Film Company	榮華電影公司	Ronghua Dianying Gongsi
Shaw and Sons Company Ltd.	邵氏父子公司	Shaoshi Fuzi Gongsi
Shaw Brothers (Hong Kong) Ltd.	邵氏兄弟（香港）有限公司	Shaoshi Xiongdi (Xianggang) Youxian Gongsi
Shaw Studio	邵氏片廠	Shaoshi Pianchang
Tai Seng Film Company	大成影片公司	Dacheng Yingpian Gongsi
Taiwan Motion Picture Studio	台灣電影製片廠〔台製〕	Taiwan Dianying Zhipian Chang
The Union Film Enterprise Ltd.	中聯電影企業有限公司	Zhonglian Dianying Qiye Youxian Gongsi
Tianyi Film Company	天一影片公司	Tianyi Yingpian Gongsi
Union Film Company	聯邦電影公司	Lianbang Dianying Gongsi
Yihua Film Enterprises	藝華電影企業公司	Yihua Dianying Qiye Gongsi
Yung Hwa Motion Picture Industries Ltd.	永華影業公司	Yonghua Yingye Gongsi
Yung Hwa Motion Picture Studios	永華電影製片廠	Yonghua Dianying Zhipian Chang

外國電影機構 Foreign Film Organisations

英文名稱 / English Name	中文名稱 / Chinese Name
20th Century Fox Inc.	二十世紀霍士
J. Arthur Rank Organisation	蘭克公司
Maria Menado Productions	瑪麗亞製作
Metro-Goldwyn-Mayer Inc.	美高梅電影公司
Paramount Pictures	派拉蒙電影公司
Radio-Keith-Orphem (RKO)	雷電華公司
Shochiku Co. Ltd.	松竹株式會社
Toho Co. Ltd.	東寶株式會社
United Artists	聯美公司
Walt Disney Company, The	和路迪士尼
Warner Brothers	華納兄弟公司

索引一：人名（按筆劃序）

索引一：人名（按筆劃序）

索引一：人名（按筆劃序）

Index I : Personalities (in alphabetical order)

392

Index I : Personalities (in alphabetical order)

Index I : Personalities (in alphabetical order)

Index I : Personalities (in alphabetical order)

Index I : Personalities (in alphabetical order)

Index I : Personalities (in alphabetical order)

索引二：片名（按筆劃序）

索引二：片名（按筆劃序）

索引二：片名（按筆劃序）

索引二：片名（按筆劃序）

Index II : Film Titles (in alphabetical order)

Index II : Film Titles (in alphabetical order)

Index II : Film Titles (in alphabetical order)

Index II : Film Titles (in alphabetical order)

Index II : Film Titles (in alphabetical order)

Index II : Film Titles (in alphabetical order)

鳴謝
Acknowledgements

Cathay Organisation Holdings Ltd.
National Archives of Singapore
Timothy P. Barnard
Meileen Choo
Paul Fonoroff
Aigner Lau
Mrs. Odell
Albert Odell
王子儀
王天林
王萊
左桂芳
石琪
朱虹
朱家欣
朱順慈
何慧玲
余少華
余永泉
余慕雲

吳詠恩
李浩昌
李焯桃
李歐梵
周淑賢
林奕華
容世誠
翁靈文
馬山
唐嘉慧
張建德
梁秉鈞
郭燕寧
陳青
陳思祥
陳靜文
陸志勤
陸離
傅葆石

喬宏
游靜
舒琪
馮潔馨
黃奇智
黃浩權
黃淑嫻
楊莉君
葉月瑜
葛蘭
雷震
雷競璇
綦湘棠
劉欣
盧振豪
邁克
鍾寶賢
譚麗雯
竇漢勳

香港電影資料館
出版刊物
Hong Kong Film Archive Publications

1995

香港早期電影軌跡展覽（1896 - 1950）（售罄）
The Early Days of Hong Kong Cinema: An Exhibition (1896 - 1950) (out of stock)

1996

六十年代粵語片紅星展覽（售罄）
Superstars of Cantonese Movies of the Sixties Exhibition (out of stock)

1997

穿梭光影五十年——
香港電影的製片與發行業展覽（1947 - 1997）
50 Years of the Hong Kong Film Production and Distribution Industries: An Exhibition (1947 - 1997)

香港影片大全第一卷（1931 - 1941）
Hong Kong Filmography Vol 1 (1931 - 1941)

1998

香港影片大全第二卷（1942 - 1949）
Hong Kong Filmography Vol 2 (1942 - 1949)

香港電影資料館珍藏展特刊
Hong Kong Film Archive Treasures: An Exhibition

1999

電影口述歷史展覽之再現江湖
The Making of Martial Arts Films –
As Told by Filmmakers and Stars

2000

香港影片大全第三卷（1950 - 1952）
Hong Kong Filmography Vol 3 (1950 - 1952)

香港影人口述歷史叢書（1）南來香港
Monographs of Hong Kong Film Veterans (1)
Hong Kong Here I Come

2001

光影中的香港（場刊及光碟）
Hong Kong on the Silver Screen (Catalogue & VCD)

五十、六十年代的生活方式——衣食住行
Living in Hong Kong – the 50s and 60s

從手藝到科技——香港電影的技術進程
Hong Kong Cinema — From Handicraft to High Tech

世紀回眸：中華電影經典展
A Century of Chinese Cinema: Look Back in Glory

自主世代
i-GENERATIONs

香港影人口述歷史叢書（2）理想年代——
長城、鳳凰的日子
Monographs of Hong Kong Film Veterans (2)
An Age of Idealism: Great Wall & Feng Huang Days

2002

劍嘯江湖——徐克與香港電影
The Swordsman and His *Jiang Hu*: Tsui Hark and Hong Kong Film

香港電影資料館工作人員
Hong Kong Film Archive Staff List

署理館長
Head (Acting)
唐詠詩
Angela Tong

行政及館務組
Administration and Venue Management

經理
Manager
王漢華
Edward Wong

行政助理
Executive Assistant
薛文慧
Jennie Sit

副經理（場務管理）
Assistant Manager (House Management)
黎玉珊
Serene Lai

副經理（樓宇管理）
Assistant Manager (Building Management)
蘇淑玲
Rachel So

修復組
Conservation

一級助理館長
Assistant Curator I
謝建輝
Edward Tse

二級助理館長
Assistant Curator II
蔣智良
Chaing Chi-leung

搜集組
Acquisition

經理
Manager
何美寶
Mable Ho

搜集助理
Acquisition Assistant
陳彩玉
Priscilla Chan

藏品註冊助理
Collection Registration
黃敏聰
Valerie Wong

節目組
Programming

節目策劃
Programmer
羅卡
Law Kar

節目策劃（拓展）
Programmer (Development)
傅慧儀
Winnie Fu

節目助理
Programme Assistants
吳月華、鄭子宏、王少芳
Stephanie Ng, Bede Cheng, Cass Wong

研究組
Research

研究主任 **Research Officer**	黃愛玲 Wong Ain-ling
研究助理 **Research Assistant**	盛安琪 Angel Shing
特約研究員 **Project Researcher**	吳詠恩 Grace Ng
特約助理 **Project Assistant**	李俊慧 Lee Chun-wai

資源中心
Resource Centre

圖書館館長 **Librarian**	邵寶珠 Monique Shiu
圖書館助理館長 **Assistant Librarians**	曾運球、譚潔冰 Chris Tsang, Pinky Tam

編輯組
Editorial

編輯 **Editorial Coordinator**	郭靜寧 Kwok Ching-ling
特約執行編輯 **Executive Editors (Project)**	歐陽鳳琪、林慧賢 Jessica Au-yang, Agnes Lam
助理編輯 **Assistant Editor**	任艷蘭 Yam Yim-lan

資訊系統組
IT Systems

經理 **Manager**	梁海雲 Isaac Leung
資訊系統助理 **Systems Assistant**	謝昭鐳 June Tse

國泰故事

出版：香港電影資料館

策劃及編輯：黃愛玲

英文編輯：何思穎

編務統籌：羅潔顏

設計：TomSenga Design

印刷：特佳印刷有限公司

初版：2002 年 3 月

定價：港幣 130 元正

國際統一書號：962-8050-16-8

THE CATHAY STORY

Publisher : Hong Kong Film Archive

Project Co-ordinator and Editor : Wong Ain-ling

English Editor : Sam Ho

Editorial Co-ordinator : emily lo

Design : TomSenga Design

Printing : Quality Printing Ltd

First Edition : March 2002

Price : HK$130

ISBN : 962-8050-16-8

香港電影資料館 Hong Kong Film Archive
香港西灣河鯉景道 50 號
50 Lei King Road, Sai Wan Ho, Hong Kong

電話 Tel: (852) 2739 2139
傳真 Fax: (852) 2311 5229
電郵 E-mail: hkfa@lcsd.gov.hk
網址 Website: http://www.filmarchive.gov.hk